John Donne
An Annotated Bibliography of Modern Criticism
1968–1978

JOHN DONNE
An Annotated Bibliography of Modern Criticism
1968–1978

John R. Roberts

University of Missouri Press
Columbia & London
1982

Copyright © 1982 by
The Curators of the University of Missouri
Library of Congress Catalog Card Number 82–1849
University of Missouri Press, Columbia, Missouri 65211
Printed and bound in the United States of America

Library of Congress Cataloging in Publication Data

Roberts, John Richard.
John Donne, an annotated bibliography of modern
criticism, 1968–1978.

Includes index.
1. Donne, John, 1572–1631—Bibliography.
I. Title.
Z8237.R63   [PR2248]   821'.3   82–1849
ISBN 0–8262–0364–7   AACR2

To the Memory
of
Pauline Elizabeth Roberts

Contents

Preface

The primary purpose of this bibliography is to provide students, scholars, and critics of John Donne with a useful aid to research. This study is the first to collect and fully annotate the vast amount of criticism and scholarship written on Donne during the period 1968–1978. The present work is a continuation of my previously published *John Donne: An Annotated Bibliography of Modern Criticism, 1912–1967* (Columbia: University of Missouri Press, 1973) and ends at 1978 because more recent studies were not always available and because bibliographical sources were often incomplete after that date.

In 1931, the tercentenary of Donne's death, T. S. Eliot announced in his essay "Donne in Our Time," in *A Garland for John Donne, 1631–1931*, edited by Theodore Spencer (Cambridge, Mass.: Harvard University Press), that "Donne's poetry is a concern of the present and the recent past rather than of the future" (p. 5). If, by his prophetic utterance of doom, Eliot intended to predict Donne's impending demise among scholars and critics, or if he thought that critical interest in Donne had reached an apex in 1931, then history has proved him quite mistaken. For during the past fifty years no fewer than two thousand books, monographs, essays, and notes on Donne have appeared; and there are no signs of diminishing interest in his poetry and prose. Even a most cursory glance at the seventeenth-century section of recent issues of the annual Modern Language Association bibliography, which is far from comprehensive, will reveal that only Milton exceeds Donne in the number of yearly entries; that typically more items on Donne appear each year than on Herbert, Crashaw, and Vaughan combined; and that Donne entries far exceed those for Dryden and are roughly twice in number those listed in the Renaissance section for Sidney. In 1931, obviously an important year for Donne studies because of the tercentenary celebration of Donne's death, only about fifty items were published, whereas in 1972, the four-hundredth anniversary of Donne's birth, approximately three times that number appeared, excluding reviews and doctoral dissertations. Quantity alone, of course, is finally rather meaningless, and admittedly any number of books and essays that have appeared are minor efforts at best, and many are repetitive, derivative, ill-conceived, and misleading. However, as I read and annotated the nearly twenty-three hundred items included in my two bibliographical studies on Donne, I was struck again and again by the fact that Donne has engaged and continues to engage some of the best minds of the scholarly world and that many studies represent major contributions to our understanding and knowledge not only of Donne but also of the seventeenth century, of metaphysical poets as a whole, and even of the very nature of poetry itself.

Nearly all serious students of literature now agree that Donne occupies a significant and permanent position in our understanding of the development of English poetry and that he is, in his own right, a major poet of continuing and lively interest. At the beginning of this century, however, many critics were by no means willing to offer Donne a seat among the great poets of our language. In 1900, and again in 1921, *The Oxford Book of English Verse* represented Donne with only eight short pieces, two of which were not actually his and one of which was only the first twenty lines of "The Extasie." A number of critics, in fact, were not only hostile to Donne's poetry but were quite scornful of those few admirers of his art. Edward Bliss Read, for example, in *Elizabethan Lyrical Poetry from Its Origins to the Present Time* (New Haven: Yale University Press; London: Humphrey Milford and Oxford University Press, 1912) openly condemned Donne's poetry for its "unmusical moments," its "imperfect utterance," and its "morbid strain" and concluded his evaluation by remarking that "Today Donne's poems are never imitated; they are not even widely read, for though he has a circle of devoted admirers, their number is small" (p. 233). And, as late as 1917, five years after the publication of Sir Herbert Grierson's monumental two-volume edition of the poems and only four years before T. S. Eliot's endorsement of Donne and the metaphysical poets, George Jackson announced in the *Expository Times* that "It must be freely admitted that neither as poet, preacher, nor letter-writer is Donne ever likely to gain the suffrage of more than a few" and proceeded to characterize most of Donne's love poems as "fit only for the dunghill" (pp. 217, 218). Fifty-five years later, in his preface to *John Donne: Essays in Celebration* (London: Methuen & Co., 1972), A. J. Smith observed that "As far as records tell this is the first time a centenary of his [Donne's] birth has been celebrated or as much as remarked" but assures his readers that "One can't conceive now that a time will come again when the names of Shakespeare, Milton, Wordsworth, Keats are known but the name of Donne is not" (p. vii). Prophecy in literary criticism is a dangerous business at best, as we have seen, but Smith would seem to be on very solid ground in making his prediction. During the past decade or so approximately one hundred books and essays have appeared annually on Donne.

The present bibliography follows, for the most part, the principles and guidelines established for my earlier volume. The annotations in this bibliography are essentially descriptive, not evaluative, because I find that what is important and/or useful to one scholar is not equally significant to another. I have made the annotations quite detailed and often quote extensively from the item in order to convey a sense of its approach and the level of its sophistication. Therefore, the reader should be able to judge for himself whether a particular book or essay will be useful for his purposes. Likewise, I have listed each item chronologically, in part so that by glancing over the various entries the reader will be able to obtain a sense of the various shifts, directions, and developments that have occurred in Donne criticism during the eleven-year period. By means of three detailed indexes (author, subject, and works of Donne cited in the annotations), the reader can easily locate individual studies that interest him.

As in my previous volume, I have attempted to make the bibliography as complete and as comprehensive as possible, yet even from the beginning, it was necessary to impose certain limitations. The basic guiding principle has been to include all books, monographs, essays, and notes specifically on Donne written between 1968 and 1978; but, in addition, I have also tried to include discussions of Donne that appear in works not centrally concerned with him. Of course, nearly all books and many articles on metaphysical poetry or on individual metaphysical poets contain some comment on or reference to Donne, but to have included all items that mention Donne in relation to Herbert, Crashaw, Vaughan, Marvell, Traherne, et al., would have extended the present bibliography far beyond manageable bounds. Since my primary intention is to list and annotate Donne criticism, I have not included all editions of his poetry and prose nor all anthologies that contain selections from his work, although I have tried to include editions that contain critical discussions and/or notes or that, for one reason or another, seem to have some special significance, such as certain privately printed editions, limited editions, and translations into foreign languages, which indicate the popularity and availability of Donne to those who do not read English. Reprints of editions and works published before 1968 have been excluded. In referring to Donne's poems I have followed Sir Herbert Grierson's text (1929), except in those few instances when it was necessary to use titles from other editions, all of which are indicated in the annotations. By doing so, I do not intend to indicate a preference for Grierson's text but simply hope to avoid confusion. Publications are listed according to the date of publication that I used in preparing the bibliographic entry; reprints, revisions, and new editions of works first published between 1968 and 1978 have been recorded when known. Book reviews have been excluded since it is impossible to locate them all and to list only those found would be misleading and not fully representative of a given work's reception. Also, brief mentions of Donne in books and articles as well as references in literary histories, encyclopedias, and anthologies have been omitted. Unpublished doctoral dissertations have been excluded, since many of them are unavailable, especially those in languages other than English, and since a number have been published, in part or totally, in later essays and books. The reader is encouraged, however, to check *Dissertation Abstracts* and *Dissertation Abstracts International* for many American ones, most of which are more than adequately annotated by their authors. Many items in languages other than English have been included (French, German, Italian, Spanish, Japanese, Dutch, Polish, Hungarian, Russian, and so on), but I have no assurance that I located all items in these languages or in lesser-known ones.

It gives me much pleasure to acknowledge and to thank all those who have been so generous and kind in assisting me with this project. I wish to thank, first of all, Melissa Poole, my current research assistant, who greatly helped me by gathering materials, checking numerous details, and proofreading, and whose dedication to the bibliography was second only to mine. I wish also to thank Douglas Collins, my former research assistant, who was especially helpful during the preliminary stages and who continued to offer valuable help long after he was no longer directly involved in the project, and William Rossi, who checked numerous entries and helped me in sundry ways. I am indebted to Gertjan W. van der Brugge, James Curtis, John M. Foley, Jadwiga Maszewska, Izumi Matsuo, Dennis Mueller, Edward Mullen, Mary Ricciardi, Robert and Hiroko Somers, Ralf Thiede, Steve Tomka, Sister Motoko Tsuchida, and Russell Zguta, who assisted me with foreign-language items, and to Jeaneice Brewer and Marilyn Voegele, librarians, who were most helpful in locating books and articles that were unavailable at the University of Missouri Ellis Library. Many Donne scholars, critics, and friends were most kind to call my attention to lesser-known materials and/or supplied me with offprints, especially Yoshihisa Aizawa, Werner Bies, Roger Cognard, Eugene Cunnar, Heather Dubrow, Maureen Farrell, Steven H. Gale, Paul D. Green, James Harner, Shonosuki Ishii, R. K. Kaul, Tatyana N. Krasavchenko, Friedrich Krey, Edward Le Comte, F. N. Lees, Valentina Libman, Peter Milward, Wolfgang Müller, W. Ostrowski, Laurence Perrine, John J. Pollock, Silvia Ruffo-Fiore, Lynn Sadler, John T. Shawcross, Giuseppe Soldano, Gary A. Stringer, Margaret Wright, and Gilbert Youmans. I owe much to my colleagues and students at the University of Missouri–Columbia and at the University of Manchester in England (where I was a visiting professor for the 1980–1981 academic year) for their helpful suggestions, insights, and encouragement; and I wish to acknowledge the Faculty Research Council of the University of Missouri–Columbia for several small grants. I am also very much indebted to Michael Smith, chief bibliographer of the Modern Humanities Research Association, for opening his file to me, and I wish to thank members of the staffs of numerous libraries, all of whom were most gracious with their time and advice, especially the University of Missouri Ellis Library, the University of Illinois Library, the Cambridge University Library, the Bodleian Library, the John Rylands University Library, and the British Library. I should also like to express my appreciation to the National Portrait Gallery, London, for permission to use the portrait of Donne that appears on the jacket. And, to my wife, Lorraine, I owe a special note of thanks for having generously supported me with her love and advice throughout the years that this bibliography was in preparation.

J. R. R.
Columbia, Missouri
1 February 1982

Abbreviations of Titles
of Journals

ABR • *American Benedictine Review*
AEB • *Analytical and Enumerative Bibliography*
AI • *American Imago: A Psychoanalytic Journal for Culture, Science, and the Arts*
AN&Q • *American Notes and Queries*
Anglia • *Anglia: Zeitschrift für Englische Philologie*
Arcadia • *Arcadia: Zeitschrift für Vergleichende Literaturwissenschaft*
Ariel • *Ariel: A Review of International English Literature*
BC • *The Book Collector*
BI • *Books at Iowa*
BLR • *Bodleian Library Record*
BNYPL • *Bulletin of the New York Public Library*
BRMMLA • *Rocky Mountain Review of Language and Literature*
BSUF • *Ball State University Forum*
BuR • *Bucknell Review*
CahiersE • *Cahiers Elisabéthains: Etudes sur la Pré-Renaissance et la Renaissance Anglaises*
CE • *College English*
CEA • *CEA Critic: An Official Journal of the College English Association*
Centerpoint • *Centerpoint: A Journal of Interdisciplinary Studies*
CentR • *The Centennial Review* (East Lansing, MI)
Centrum • *Centrum: Working Papers of the Minnesota Center for Advanced Studies in Language, Style, and Literary Theory*
CHum • *Computers and the Humanities*
Cithara • *Cithara: Essays in the Judaeo-Christian Tradition*
CL • *Comparative Literature* (Eugene, OR)
CLAJ • *College Language Association Journal*
CLS • *Comparative Literature Studies*
CollG • *Colloquia Germanica: Internationale Zeitschrift für Germanische Sprach- und Literaturwissenschaft*
CollL • *College Literature*
Costerus • *Costerus: Essays in English and American Language and Literature*
CP • *Concerning Poetry* (Bellingham, WA)
CR • *The Critical Review* (Canberra, Australia)
Critique • *Critique: Revue Générale des Publications Françaises et Etrangères* (Paris, France)
CritQ • *Critical Quarterly*
CritS • *Critical Survey*
CSR • *Christian Scholar's Review*
DHLR • *The D. H. Lawrence Review* (Fayetteville, AK)
DR • *The Dalhousie Review*
DUJ • *Durham University Journal*
EA • *Etudes Anglaises: Grande-Bretagne, Etats-Unis*
EAS • *Essays in Arts and Sciences*
EIC • *Essays in Criticism: A Quarterly Journal of Literary Criticism* (Oxford, England)
EigoS • *Eigo Seinen* (Tokyo, Japan)
EIRC • *Explorations in Renaissance Culture*

ELH • *Journal of English Literary History*
ELN • *English Language Notes* (Boulder, CO)
ELR • *English Literary Renaissance*
ELWIU • *Essays in Literature* (Macomb, IL)
EM • *English Miscellany: A Symposium of History, Literature, and the Arts*
ES (Valladolid) • *English Studies* (Valladolid, Spain)
ES • *English Studies: A Journal of English Language and Literature*
ESA • *English Studies in Africa: A Journal of the Humanities* (Johannesburg, South Africa)
Expl • *Explicator*
FHA • *Fitzgerald-Hemingway Annual*
FI • *Forum Italicum*
FMLS • *Forum for Modern Language Studies* (St. Andrews, Scotland)
GHJ • *George Herbert Journal*
GRM • *Germanisch-Romanische Monatsschrift*
HAB • *Humanities Association Review/La Revue de l'Association des Humanités*
Hermathena • *Hermathena: A Dublin University Review*
HLB • *Harvard Library Bulletin*
HLQ • *Huntington Library Quarterly: A Journal for the History and Interpretation of English and American Civilization*
Horizontes • *Horizontes: Revista de la Universidad Católica de Puerto Rico*
HSL • *University of Hartford Studies in Literature: A Journal of Interdisciplinary Criticism*
HTR • *Harvard Theological Review*
Innisfree • *Innisfree* (Hammond, LA)
IQ • *Italian Quarterly*
JAAC • *Journal of Aesthetics and Art Criticism*
JBS • *Journal of British Studies*
JEGP • *Journal of English and Germanic Philology*
JEn • *Journal of English* (Sana'a Univ.)
JGE • *JGE: The Journal of General Education*
JHI • *Journal of the History of Ideas*
JHM • *Journal of the History of Medicine and Allied Sciences* (Univ. of Minnesota)
JRUL • *Journal of the Rutgers University Libraries*
Kañina • *Kañina: Revista de Artes y Letras de la Universidad de Costa Rica*
KR • *Kenyon Review*
L&H • *Literature and History: A New Journal for the Humanities*
Lang&L • *Language and Literature* (Copenhagen)
Lang&S • *Language and Style: An International Journal*
LangQ • *The USF Language Quarterly* (Tampa, FL)
Language • *Language: Journal of the Linguistic Society of America*
LeS • *Lingue e Stile: Trimestrale di Linguistica e Critica Letteraria* (Bologna, Italy)
Library • *The Library: A Quarterly Journal of Bibliography*
LT • *Levende Talen*
LWU • *Literatur in Wissenschaft und Unterricht* (Kiel, West Germany)
MichQR • *Michigan Quarterly Review* (Univ. of Michigan)
MiltonS • *Milton Studies*
MLQ • *Modern Language Quarterly*
MLR • *Modern Language Review*
Moreana • *Moreana: Bulletin Thomas More* (Angers, France)
Mosaic • *Mosaic: A Journal for the Interdisciplinary Study of Literature*

MP • *Modern Philology: A Journal Devoted to Research in Medieval and Modern Literature*
MQ • *Midwest Quarterly: A Journal of Contemporary Thought* (Pittsburg, KS)
MSE • *Massachusetts Studies in English*
N&Q • *Notes and Queries*
NLH • *New Literary History: A Journal of Theory and Interpretation* (Charlottesville, VA)
NM • *Neuphilologische Mitteilungen: Bulletin de la Société Néophilologique / Bulletin of the Modern Language Society*
NRF • *Nouvelle Revue Française*
NS • *Die Neueren Sprachen*
Oberon • *Oberon: Magazine for the Study of English and American Literature* (Tokyo, Japan)
PakR • *Pakistan Review*
Parergon • *Parergon: Bulletin of the Australian and New Zealand Association for Medieval and Renaissance Studies*
PBA • *Proceedings of the British Academy*
PBSA • *PBSA: Papers of the Bibliographical Society of America*
PCP • *Pacific Coast Philology*
PLL • *Papers on Language and Literature: A Journal for Scholars and Critics of Language and Literature*
PMASAL • *Papers of the Michigan Academy of Science, Arts, and Letters*
PMLA • *Publications of the Modern Language Association of America*
PMMLA • *Papers of the Midwest MLA*
PoetryR • *Poetry Review* (London, England)
PPMRC • *Proceedings of the PMR Conference: Annual Publication of the International Patristic, Mediaeval and Renaissance Conference*
PQ • *Philological Quarterly* (Iowa City, IA)
PURBA • *Punjab University Research Bulletin* (Arts)
QJS • *Quarterly Journal of Speech*
QQ • *Queen's Quarterly*
Ren&R • *Renaissance and Reformation / Renaissance et Réforme*
RenP • *Renaissance Papers*
RenQ • *Renaissance Quarterly*
RES • *Review of English Studies: A Quarterly Journal of English Literature and the English Language*
RLC • *Revue de Littérature Comparée*
RLMC • *Rivista di Letterature Moderne e Comparate* (Florence, Italy)
RLV • *Revue des Langues Vivantes* (Brussels, Belgium)
RMS • *Renaissance and Modern Studies*
RNL • *Review of National Literatures*
RSLR • *Rivista de Storia e Letteratura Religiosa*
RUS Eng • *Rajasthan University Studies in English*
SAB • *South Atlantic Bulletin: A Quarterly Journal Devoted to Research and Teaching in the Modern Languages and Literatures*
SAQ • *South Atlanta Quarterly*
SB • *Studies in Bibliography: Papers of the Bibliographical Society of the University of Virginia*
SCB • *South Central Bulletin*
SCN • *Seventeenth-Century News*
SCr • *Strumenti Critici: Rivista Quadrimestrale di Cultura e Critica Letteraria*
SECOLB • *The SECOL Bulletin: Southeastern Conference on Linguistics*
SEL • *Studies in English Literature, 1500–1900*

SELit • *Studies in English Literature* (Tokyo, Japan)
SES • *Sophia English Studies*
SHR • *Southern Humanities Review*
SNL • *Satire Newsletter* (State University College, Oneonta, NY)
SoQ • *The Southern Quarterly: A Journal of the Arts in the South* (Hattiesburg, MS)
SP • *Studies in Philology*
SPWVSRA • *Selected Papers from the West Virginia Shakespeare and Renaissance Association*
SQ • *Shakespeare Quarterly*
SR • *Sewanee Review*
SRen • *Studies in the Renaissance*
SSEng • *Sydney Studies in English*
Style • *Style* (Fayetteville, AK)
Sur • *Revista Sur*
Theoria • *Theoria: A Journal of Studies in the Arts, Humanities, and Social Sciences* (Natal, South Africa)
THY • *Thomas Hardy Yearbook*
TLS • [London] *Times Literary Supplement*
Trivium • *Trivium* (Dyfed, Wales)
TSE • *Tulane Studies in English*
TSL • *Tennessee Studies in Literature*
TSLL • *Texas Studies in Literature and Language: A Journal of the Humanities*
UDR • *University of Dayton Review*
UR • *University Review* (Kansas City, MO)
UTQ • *University of Toronto Quarterly: A Canadian Journal of the Humanities*
VLit • *Voprosy Literatury*
VQ • *Visvabharati Quarterly*
WascanaR • *Wascana Review*
WCR • *West Coast Review*
WVUPP • *West Virginia University Philological Papers*
XUS • *Xavier University Studies: A Journal of Critical and Creative Scholarship* (New Orleans, LA)
YCGL • *Yearbook of Comparative and General Literature*
YER • *Yeats Eliot Review*
YES • *Yearbook of English Studies*
YR • *The Yale Review: A National Quarterly*

1968

◄§ 1. AIZAWA, YOSHIHISA. "A Study of Donne's Conceits—In Relation to the Ten Aristotelian Categories." *Bunkei Ronsō* (Jimbun-gakubu, Hirosaki Daigaku) 4, no. 2 (December): 17–28.

Analyzes the relationship between the tenor and vehicle in Donne's conceits by relating them to the ten Aristotelian categories—substance, quantity, quality, relation, place, time, position, state, action, and affection. Gives examples of Donne's use of the categories in conceits found in "The Undertaking," "The Sunne Rising," "The Canonization," "Aire and Angels," and "A Valediction: forbidding mourning."

◄§ 2. ALLEN, JOHN D. "I. Alliteration Assonance Consonance: Spenser to Auden," in *Quantitative Studies in Prosody*, pp. 1–148. Johnson City: East Tennessee University Press.

Presents a quantitative study of the uses of alliteration, assonance, and consonance in selected poems drawn from twenty-five poets from Spenser to Auden, including Donne. See especially the comparative statistical tables (pp. 60, 88, 104–12, 116). Notes the high percentage of alliterative frequencies in Donne's poetry.

◄§ 3. BAKER-SMITH, DOMINIC. "John Donne and the Mysterium Crucis." *EM* 19: 65–82.

Argues that much of Donne's religious imagery, especially his treatment of the cross of Christ, is drawn from prescholastic sources and informed by various devotional traditions and that when Donne's references to the cross are considered in the light of the complex *mysterium crucis* tradition many of his ideas and references become much more precise. Points out that Donne may have known Justus Lipsius's *De Cruce* and Jacob Grester's *De Crucis Christi* as suggested especially by the imagery of "The Crosse." Maintains that "the strength of renaissance devotional poetry is its ability to fuse patterns of feeling and of metaphor that were traditionally distinct" and calls "Goodfriday, 1613. Riding Westward" "a rehearsal of Christian veneration of the Cross" (p. 66). Argues that in the poem Donne "deliberately sets off the contrasted treatments of the Passion that have come down to him and the consequent fusion produces the third term, a dramatic heightening that pervades the entire poem and gives to the accumulated matter a distinctly individual tone" (p. 81).

◄§ 4. BEAVER, JOSEPH C. "A Grammar of Prosody." *CE* 29: 310–21.

Reprinted in *Linguistics and Literary Style*, edited by Donald C. Freeman (New York: Holt, Rinehart and Winston, 1970), pp. 427–47.

Studies certain metrical-stylistic features (such as the distribution of stress maxima and patterns of occupancy) in the first ten of Donne's *Holy Sonnets* and compares them with ten of Shakespeare's sonnets. Concludes that the study "suggests, in Donne, a metrical structure tending to support stability at the extremities of the lines, somewhat like a suspension bridge, perhaps at the expense of medial stability" whereas Shakespeare "tends to provide anchors at half way points" (p. 320). Points out that Donne often deliberately uses unmetrical lines as attention-getting devices and that one way he achieves this is by consciously putting stress maxima in off positions.

⟨⟩ 5. BECK, ROSALIE. "A Precedent for Donne's Imagery in 'Goodfriday, 1613. Riding Westward.'" *RES*, n.s. 19: 166–69.

Points out that the moralization of the heavenly system in Lydgate's translation of Guillaume de Deguileville's *Pilgrimage in the Life of Man*, a reversal of the standard one advocated by Sacrobosco in *De Sphaera*, is somewhat analogous to Donne's imagery in "Goodfriday, 1613. Riding Westward" and shows that "a moralization of the heavenly system more compatible with accepted Christian symbolism than that of Sacrobosco was current well before the seventeenth century" (p. 169).

⟨⟩ 6. BENJAMIN, EDWIN B. "Donne and Bodin's 'Theatrum.'" *N&Q* n.s. 15: 92–94.

Suggests that Donne may have known the French translation (1597) of Jean Bodin's *Theatrum Universale* (1596) and cites several parallels between Bodin's treatise on the relationship of the corporeal and the spiritual in man and Donne's "The Extasie" and "Aire and Angels." Postulates that even the titles of the two poems may have been suggested by titles in Bodin's book.

⟨⟩ 7. BUCKLEY, VINCENT. "John Donne's Passion," in *Poetry and the Sacred*, pp. 99–116. New York: Barnes & Noble; London: Chatto & Windus.

Discusses the complex and pervasive nature of the poetic passion revealed in Donne's love poetry as well as in his religious verse—a passion that is "no mere outcry, but a revelation" combined with a poetic logic that is "no mere 'tactic' of elaboration but a straining towards revelation" (p. 106). Argues that in his highly dramatic poems Donne's immense energy and subtlety "work towards opening up the experience so that, at a certain point in the poem's logic, its dimensions may be fully revealed" (p. 115). Suggests that the chief characteristic of Donne's poetry is "its openness, an openness not only to a common world but to the range of its author's own passions" (p. 115); thus Donne "does not so much explore the self as uncover and reveal it, and then in terms of situation and relationship" (p. 116).

⟨⟩ 8. CAMERON, ALLEN BARRY. "Donne and Dryden: Their Achievement in the Verse Epistle." *Discourse* 11: 252–56.

Compares Donne's "To Sir Henry Wotton: Sir, more then kisses" and Dryden's "To My Honoured Friend, Dr. Charleton" to show the artistic range of the verse epistle and to illustrate the difference between Donne's and Dryden's concepts of the role of the poet in society. Suggests that, whereas Donne's epistle is colloquial, intimate, and private, Dryden's is more structurally unified and formal and reflects his notion of the poet as public spokesman or cultural orator.

۵۶ 9. COOPER, JOHN R. *The Art of* The Compleat Angler. Durham: Duke University Press. vii, 200p.
Comments on Donne's relationship with Izaak Walton. Calls "The Baite," which Walton included in *The Compleat Angler*, "a kind of piscatorial pastoral of Marlowe's 'Come live with me'" (p. 61). Suggests that the second section of Robert Boyle's *Occasional Reflections* (1665) is reminiscent of Donne.

۵۶ 10. DONNE, JOHN. *The Poems of John Donne*. Selected, introduced, and annotated by Frank Kermode. Wood engravings by Imre Reiner. Cambridge: Printed for the Members of The Limited Editions Club at the University Printing House. xxiv, 198p.
Reprinted: New York: The Heritage Press, 1970.
First edition limited to 1,500 copies. In the introduction (pp. xi–xxi) Kermode presents a brief biographical sketch of Donne and a critical evaluation of his poetry. Maintains that Donne created a new poetry, which was often debased by less qualified imitators; comments on certain major characteristics of Donne's poetry (blend of argument and passion; uses of paradox and analogy; wit and obscurity); and claims that it is "one of the great achievements of taste and scholarship over the past century that the power and colour of Donne's poetry have been restored, and are seen to be capable of an immediate impact on the modern mind" (p. xxi). Note on the text (pp. xxiii–xxiv) points out that the text is based primarily on John Hayward's Nonesuch edition (1929) but follows Helen Gardner's text for the *Elegies* and her ordering of the *Holy Sonnets*; occasionally varies from Hayward's edition of the *Songs and Sonnets*, preferring Grierson or Gardner; and accepts Manley's edition of *The Anniversaries*. Selections, with notes, from the *Songs and Sonnets*, *Epigrams*, *Elegies*, *Epithalamions*, *Satyres*, *Verse Letters*, *The Anniversaries*, and the *Divine Poems* (pp. 1–191). Index of titles (pp. 193–94); index of first lines (pp. 195–98).

۵۶ 11. ———. *Selected Poems* [and] *Death's Duell*. Scelta, introduzione e commento di Giorgio Melchiori. (Biblioteca italiana di testi inglesi, 2.) Terza edizione riveduta e aggiornata. Bari: Adriatica Editrice. 283p.
Biographical sketch (pp. 11–28), survey of historical background (pp. 29–39) and of the literary background (pp. 39–47), and a critical introduction to Donne's poetry and its influence (pp. 47–65). Stresses, in particular, Donne's presentation of interior conflict in highly dramatic contexts, his uses of idiomatic and colloquial language, his metrical originality

and inventiveness, and his wit. Contains a selected primary and secondary bibliography (pp. 67–82) that is especially important for Italian editions, selections, and critical studies. Presents selections from Donne's poems (pp. 85–251) and *Death's Duell* (pp. 252–80). Texts in English; notes in Italian.

৺§ 12. ESCH, ARNO. "John Donne: Hymne to God my God, in my sicknesse," in *Die englische Lyrik: Von der Renaissance bis zur Gegenwart*, edited by Karl Heinz Göller, 1: 134–45. Düsseldorf: August Bagel.
Translates "Hymne to God my God, in my sicknesse" into German and explicates it. Focuses primarily on the image of the hemispheres and compares the religious treatment of this image with its treatment in the *Songs and Sonets*.

৺§ 13. FORREST, WILLIAM CRAIG. "The Kinesthetic Feel of Literature." *BuR* 16, iii: 91–106.
Examines the kinesthetic effects in lines 79–82 of *Satyre III* (pp. 102–4) and argues that the effort required to pronounce the words "suggests the physical effort of rugged mountain climbing that Donne employs as a metaphor for truth-seeking" and also "suggests the bodily strain and tension which accompanies an emotional struggle such as Donne's truth-seeker encounters" (p. 104).

৺§ 14. GOLDKNOPF, DAVID. "The Disintegration of Symbol in a Meditative Poet." *CE* 30: 48–59.
Discusses the disintegration of symbol in the poetry of Vaughan and especially Traherne "as an access route to a consideration of how symbols in general operate" (p. 48). Briefly discusses how Donne uses similes "to make highly innovative connections" (p. 50) in "A Valediction: forbidding mourning." Suggests that the symbols of the eagle, dove, and phoenix in "The Canonization" are "messages to an ingroup" and that the intellective connotations of the symbols "have virtually engulfed the imagistic elements" (p. 50). Notes that in the poetry of Donne and Herbert "an antisensuous philosophical statement is often propounded in sensuous terminology, and tension between, one might say, ideology and physiology becomes part of the overall meaning of the poetry" whereas "only traces of this dialectical struggle are found in the poetry of Vaughan and Traherne, for the imagistic bonds with nature have dissolved almost entirely" (p. 52).

৺§ 15. GORLIER, CLAUDIO. *La poesia metafisica inglese*. (Biblioteca di studi inglesi e americani, 1.) Milan: La Goliardica. 167p.
The introduction (pp. 2–17) briefly outlines the revival of interest in metaphysical poetry in the twentieth century, especially the role played by T. S. Eliot, and comments on some of the major philosophical issues that make the poetry relevant to modern readers. Chapter 1 (pp. 19–39) traces

the development of English poetry during the sixteenth century and comments on several of the philosophical and religious changes that prepared the way for the development of metaphysical poetry. By way of example, contrasts Donne's "Lovers infinitenesse" with Shakespeare's Sonnet 40. Chapter 2 (pp. 41–48) briefly discusses the nature of metaphysical wit and contrasts it with Elizabethan wit. Chapter 3, "La poesia di John Donne" (pp. 49–79), presents a biographical sketch; an extended discussion of *The first Anniversary* as a reflection of the philosophical conflicts experienced by Donne as a result of the changing world view; and a critical commentary on several major aspects of Donne's lyrical poetry, especially its uses of paradox and irony; its often elaborate imagery; its uses of conceits and emblematic images; its variety of metrical and rhythmical effects; its intellectuality, wit, and economy; and its uses of Platonic and religious language as a vehicle for secular love. Illustrates these and other aspects of Donne's art and thought by commenting on a number of poems in the *Songs and Sonets*, especially "Twicknam garden," "The Relique," "The Canonization," "Aire and Angels," "A Valediction: forbidding mourning," and "A nocturnall upon S. Lucies day." Chapter 4 (pp. 81–105) deals with Herbert; Chapter 5 (pp. 107–23) with Crashaw and the baroque; Chapter 6 (pp. 125–40) with Henry Vaughan. Chapter 7 (pp. 141–63) discusses the evolution of wit, especially in Cowley and Marvell, and comments on the decline of the metaphysical tradition. Appendix (pp. 164–67) reproduces selections (in English) from Dryden, Dr. Johnson, and T. S. Eliot.

≈§ 16. GRAHAM, DESMOND. *Introduction to Poetry*. London: Oxford University Press. vi, 168p.
Explicates "Batter my heart" primarily by pointing out and diagramming the complex interplay between its formal elements and its sense units (pp. 63–66). Also comments briefly on the paradoxes and ambiguities in lines 13–14 of the poem (pp. 29–30, 38).

≈§ 17. GRAZIANI, RENÉ. "John Donne's 'The Extasie' and Ecstasy." *RES* n.s. 19: 121–36.
Points out resemblances between the nature of ecstasy in "The Extasie" and that in Antoine Héroët's *La Parfaict Amye* (1542) and in Jacques Gohorry's French translation and continuation of Book XI of the *Amadís de Gaula* series (1554) to show that the ecstasy in Donne's poem "conforms to a secular usage, and does not call for a close application of mystical doctrines involving a 'death of ecstasy' or 'a mystical sharing of some part of the Divine Beauty and Wisdom' to explain the poem" (p. 124). Shows how Donne both adheres to "a specialized usage of 'ecstasy' that denoted a strictly amatory set of quite definite characteristics" (p. 123) and how he significantly departs from the convention in several crucial ways. Argues that such a comparison leads to a better understanding of a number of cruxes in "The Extasie," especially the use of the hypothetical by-

stander and the often-debated conclusion of the poem. For a response, see John Arthos, entry 176.

₰ 18. GREGORY, E. R., JR. "The Balance of Parts: Imagistic Unity in Donne's 'Elegie XIX.'" *UR* 35: 51–54.

Sees "Going to Bed" as "a superb example of a metaphysical poet's ability to hold in poetic solution, if not meld and unite, extremely disparate phenomena" (p. 51). Explicates the poem to show that throughout Donne maintains a subtle and skillful balance between the physical (Ovidian) and spiritual (Platonic) elements and that the imagery, though seemingly disparate, is coherent and unified.

₰ 19. HEIST, WILLIAM W. "Donne on Divine Grace: Holy Sonnet No. XIV." *PMASAL* 53: 311–20.

Detailed explication of "Batter my heart" that challenges the interpretations of John E. Parish (1963), J. C. Levenson (1953), George Herman (1953), George Knox (1956), A. L. Clements (1961), and William Mueller (1961). Sees the poem as "a series of figures expressing in three images—material, social, and personal—the necessity of Divine Grace" and suggests that the unity of the poem "is not that of imagery, for the figures of the sonnet cannot be harmonized, but that of theme" (p. 320).

₰ 20. HONIG, EDWIN, and OSCAR WILLIAMS, eds. *The Major Metaphysical Poets of the Seventeenth Century: John Donne, George Herbert, Richard Crashaw, and Andrew Marvell.* New York: Washington Square Press, 902p.

Contains a detailed critical introduction to metaphysical poetry by Edwin Honig (pp. 1–33). "John Donne" (pp. 35–316) contains a brief biographical sketch and the English poems of Donne (based on Grierson's 1929 text). Selected bibliography prepared by Milton Miller and Beverly Goldberg (pp. 867–77).

₰ 21. HUGHES, RICHARD E. *The Progress of the Soul: The Interior Career of John Donne.* New York: William Morrow and Co.; Toronto: George J. McLeod. 316p.

Attempts to re-create the interior life of Donne, primarily through a critical examination and analysis of his poetry and prose: "What we witness in the whole of Donne's art is a mind discovering itself, and in the process standing as a dramatization of today's flight from loneliness and toward a fulfilling participatory experience" (p. 9). Claims that Donne "is a man who expended himself entirely, who in grasping the particularities of experience found himself clutching a universal" (pp. 9–10). Divided into ten sections, some briefly outlining Donne's "exterior" life and the major ones commenting on his "interior" life: (1) Prologue (pp. 7–12); (2) "John Donne's Life: 1572–1602" (pp. 13–17); (3) Chapter I: "The Beginning, 1593–1598" (pp. 18–55); (4) "John Donne's Life: 1602–1615" (pp.

56–59); (5) Chapter II: "The Initial Prose and the *Songs and Sonnets,* 1598–1605" (pp. 60–124); (6) Chapter III: "The Middle Years, 1605–1609" (pp. 125–95); (7) Chapter IV: "The *Anniversaries,* 1610–1612" (pp. 196–225); (8) "John Donne's Life: 1615–1631" (pp. 226–29); (9) Chapter V: "Aftermath, 1612–1631" (pp. 230–77); and (10) Epilogue (pp. 279–81). Sees the development of Donne's interior life as relevant to the experience of modern man: "In the beginning, he practices anonymity and experiences apartness. When the intolerability of separation touches him, he turns to love; at first that love is a denial of corrosive history and eroding time. But when he apprehends a love that has penetrated time, he comes to that fulfilling and participating experience toward which all his art has been mysteriously moving. And the whole experience is worked into the grainy texture of his writings, which pay strict attention to the hard existence of things. His poetry and his greatest sermons are *in toto* another version of his entire vision, with insight and literal detail entirely absorbed into one another" (p. 281).

◀§ 22. INA, SACHIKO. "Donne no Anniversaries—Sarani Ueno Yokogi ni Mukete" [Donne's *Anniversaries*—A Step Upward on the Ladder]. *IVY* (Nagoya Daigaku), no. 7 (February): 52–63.
Cited in *Bibliography of English and Renaissance Studies in Japan: I, 1961–1970.* (Renaissance Monographs: 6), edited by Kazuyoshi Enozawa and Miyo Takano. Tokyo: The Renaissance Institute / Aratake Shuppan. Unavailable.

◀§ 23. JACKSON, ROBERT S. "'Doubt Wisely:'—John Donne's Skepticism." *Cithara* 8, no. 1: 39–46.
Examines the nature of Donne's religious commitment and Christian skepticism during his early life, especially as reflected in *Satyre III.* Sees the speaker of the poem as Donne's spiritual, inner, invisible self and the auditor as his fleshly, external, visible self. Suggests that Donne was confronted with the dilemma of choosing an "invisible" church (Roman Catholic), made so by political events, and his desire to embrace a "visible" church, which in England of the time was the Anglican. To belong to the "visible" church would have cut him off from his medieval Catholic heritage; to adhere to Catholicism would have prevented him from embracing a "visible" church. Concludes, therefore, that Donne chose the religious life of "wise skepticism" during this period.

◀§ 24. JEROME, JUDSON. *Poetry: Premeditated Art.* Boston: Houghton Mifflin Co. xxxiv, 542p.
Shows how figurative language modifies and creates meaning in "A Valediction: forbidding mourning" (pp. 137–41). Comments on the imagery, wit, complexity of tone, uses of paradox, and the spiritual temper of "Batter my heart" (pp. 300–303). Suggests that Donne's "three-person'd God" "looms a little like a multi-headed monster of mythology and thus

undercuts credibility" and that the notion of God as a tinker (line 2) "seems somehow amusing, condescending, a tonality which works against the passion and violence the quatrain calls for" (p. 302). Contains references to and examples from Donne's poetry throughout.

⋙ 25. KILEY, FREDERICK. "A Larger Reading of Donne's 'A Lecture Upon the Shadow.'" *CEA* 30: 16–17.

Argues that the crux of the major conceit in the poem is the comparison of the progress of the lovers' love to the progress of the sun in its orbit and not the issue of which way the lovers walk or what way the shadows are cast: "The poem is really focused upon the moment of noon at which the lovers pause and the little lecture in 'Loves philosophy' is delivered" (p. 17). Comments on the structure of the poem and shows how Donne effectively combines poetic insight, dialectic, and rhetoric to create a profound poem about "the sadness which comes with insight into the rhythm of Creation" (p. 17).

⋙ 26. KLAMMER, ENNO. "Cosmography in Donne's Poetry." *Cresset* (Valparaiso U.) 32: 14–15.

Discusses Donne's use of Ptolemaic cosmography as a source for his figurative language. Stresses that in his poems he "presents a fairly complete cosmography: he names it, he compares the macrocosm and the microcosm, and he finds an influential relationship between these latter two" (p. 15).

⋙ 27. LaGUARDIA, ERIC. "Aesthetics of Analogy." *Diogenes* 62: 49–61.

Comments on the Renaissance poet's interest in the play and potential of tropes and suggests that in *The first Anniversary* Donne "is inquiring into the nature of poetic trope rather than using poetic trope for ends beyond its own domain" (p. 60). Suggests that in the poem Donne asserts and overcomes the fragmentary and eccentric nature of the world. Suggests that the hyperbolic excess of the poem is intentional and serves to draw our attention "to an aesthetic idea by defeating our expectations of seeing a great analogical structure put to some use" (p. 59). Argues that the poem, "like the entire Renaissance doctrine of analogy, is based on the concept of the figurative; its relative powers are measured against the state of the world" (p. 60).

⋙ 28. LE COMTE, EDWARD. "The Date of Donne's Marriage." *EA* 21: 168–69.

Suggests that Donne married Ann More in January 1602, not in December 1601, as is commonly held. Maintains that Donne may have predated the marriage in his well-known letter to his father-in-law because Ann More was pregnant at the time of the marriage. For a reply, see Wesley Milgate, entry 122.

◄§ 29. MacColl, Alan. "A New Manuscript of Donne's Poems." *RES* n.s. 19: 293–95.

Describes a manuscript in the Halkett of Pitfirrane papers in the National Library of Scotland (MS. 6504) that contains over forty poems by Donne and comments on the relationship it has with the Hawthornden manuscript compiled by William Drummond.

◄§ 30. McQueen, William. "Prevent the Sun: Milton, Donne, and the Book of Wisdom." *Milton Newsletter* 2: 63–64.

Suggests that No. 79 of Donne's *LXXX Sermons* provides an interesting gloss on the induction of Milton's *Nativity Ode*. Points out that Donne quotes from and elaborates on a passage from the apocryphal Book of Wisdom 16:18: "It is the counsell of the wise men, *Prevent the Sunne to give thanks to God, and at the day-spring pray unto him.*"

◄§ 31. Mahl, Mary R., ed. *Seventeenth-Century English Prose.*(The Lippincott College English Series, gen. ed. Albert J. Guerard.) Philadelphia and New York: J. B. Lippincott Co. xix, 584p.

Anthology of representative prose selections, arranged chronologically to show the development of certain genres and of prose style during the seventeenth century. Presents selections from Donne's *Biathanatos* (pp. 8–17), *Ignatius his Conclave* (pp. 17–21), *Devotions upon Emergent Occasions* (pp. 21–34), *Death's Duell* (pp. 34–52), and *Sermons* XXVII and LXVI (pp. 52–56), preceded by a brief biographical chronology (p. 7). Reprints selections from essays on Donne's prose (pp. 480–91): George Saintsbury, *English Prose* (1894), pp. 83–85; (2) Austin Warren, "The Very Reverend Dr. Donne," *KR* 16 (1954): 268–77; and (3) Evelyn Simpson, *A Study of the Prose Works of John Donne*, 2d ed. (Oxford: Clarendon Press, 1948), pp. 165–70, followed by a selected bibliography (pp. 491–92).

◄§ 32. Marotti, Arthur F. "Donne's 'Loves Progress,' ll. 37–38, and Renaissance Bawdry." *ELN* 6: 24–25.

Points out that when Donne in "Loves Progress" says "Nor is the soule more worthy, or more fit / For love than this, as infinite as it" (lines 37–38) he is alluding to the popular joke about female sexual organs—the bottomless or virtually bottomless vagina. Cites additional examples of the joke in Shakespeare's *Romeo and Juliet* and in Jonson's *Bartholomew Fair*.

◄§ 33. Merrill, Thomas F. "John Donne and the Word of God." *NM* 69: 597–616. Reprinted in *Christian Criticism: A Study of Literary God-Talk* (entry 846), pp. 159–77.

Shows that Donne's understanding of the nature of preaching as sacramental event and the role of the preacher as an instrument through which the Word of God was mediated to man distinguishes him from the Anglo-Catholic position and places him on the side of the Puritan theorists.

Since Donne views the sermon as "no mere discourse, not even a sacred preparation for some ensuing sacramental encounter with the Holy Presence" but rather as "a dynamic, corporate event involving preacher, congregation and the Holy Spirit" (p. 597), he constructs his sermons "to produce crisis, to change men's lives by bringing them into direct confrontation with their God" (p. 613). Concludes that the primary appeal of Donne's sermons is, therefore, not to the intellect but to the conscience.

◄§ 34. MILLS, JERRY LEATH. "Donne's Bracelets of Bright Hair: An Analogue." _N&Q_ n.s. 15: 368.

Suggests a close analogue between Donne's image of the amatory token of a lock of hair in "The Funerall" and "The Relique" and a similar image in John Leland's _Assertio inclylissimi Arturi_ (1544), which was translated by Richard Robinson in 1582 as _A Learned and True Assertion of the original, Life, Actes, and death of . . . Prince Arthure._ Notes that Leland, following an account found in the works of Giraldi Cambrensis, describes the exhumation of remains thought to be those of Arthur and Guinevere at Glastonbury in 1191 and notes that in the tomb a yellow lock of woman's hair was discovered.

◄§ 35. MITCHELL, CHARLES. "Donne's 'The Extasie': Love's Sublime Knot." _SEL_ 8: 91–101.

Argues that in "The Extasie" Donne demonstrates "not merely figuratively, but quite literally, that the union of man and woman in love creates the fusion of male and female elements—soul and body—within man" (p. 93). Observes that in the love ecstasy, the soul, freed from its body, is transplanted in the richer soil of the beloved's soul, thereby gaining strength and new knowledge about itself and its relationship to the body. Notes that when the soul returns to the body after the ecstasy, a fully human synthesis is effected between body and soul.

◄§ 36. [MORGAN], SISTER MARY CAROLINE. "The Existentialist Attitude of John Donne." _XUS_ 7: 37–50.

Finds traces of existential thinking in Donne's early life and works. Reads the poems as autobiographical statements and suggests that Donne's disappointment or dissatisfaction with human love, his doubts about the relationship between the body and soul, his sense of incompleteness and restlessness, his personal views on man's relation to God, and especially his subjectivity and reliance on experience can be compared with modern existential thought, especially with that of Jean-Paul Sartre. Suggests that even in later life Donne retained many of his existential concepts but discarded those elements that would have brought him to a totally materialistic view of the world.

◄§ 37. MUELLER, JANEL M. "The Exegesis of Experience: Dean Donne's _Devotions upon Emergent Occasions._" _JEGP_ 67: 1–19.

Argues that Donne's highly metaphorical treatment of Scripture in the

Devotions upon Emergent Occasions is as important as are the meditative elements identified in that work. Cites certain thematic, verbal, and imagistic parallels between Donne's method in the *Devotions* and in his sermons, especially in a series of sermons delivered in 1623 on Psalm 6. Views these sermons and the *Devotions* as "essentially two versions (one public, one private) of an attempted running translation of a segment of experience into spiritual terms" (p. 13). Argues not only that Donne adapted exegetical techniques to devotional purposes in the *Devotions* but also that his experience with the *Devotions* gave him "a greater awareness of the suggestibility of Biblical metaphor than he had previously had" (pp. 17–18), an awareness that is subsequently reflected in his sermons.

◄§ 38. MURAOKA, ISAMU. "Donne to Cusanus" [Donne and Cusanus]. *EigoS* 114: 216–17.
Discusses the possible influence of Cusanus on Donne's attitude toward knowledge, particularly his belief that one approaches truth only by realizing one's ignorance.

◄§ 39. MURRIN, MICHAEL. "Poetry as Literary Criticism." *MP* 65: 202–7.
Comments that in their elegies on Donne both Carew and Lord Herbert of Cherbury consciously imitated Donne's style and wit only to show that the uniqueness of Donne's art cannot be imitated.

◄§ 40. NAKADA, AKIHIRO. "John Donne no *Shūen*—Hart Crane e no Eikyō" [John Donne's "The Expiration" and Its Influence on Hart Crane]. *Eibungaku* (Waseda Daigaku), no. 32 (March): 67–77.
Cited in *Bibliography of English and Renaissance Studies in Japan: I, 1961–1970.* (Renaissance Monographs: 6), edited by Kazuyoshi Enozawa and Miyo Takano. Tokyo: The Renaissance Institute / Aratake Shuppan. Unavailable.

◄§ 41. ONIZUKA, KEIICHI. "The Evolution of Love and Its Limitations: On John Donne's 'Heavenly Love,'" in *Maekawa Shunichi Kyōju Kanreki Kinen-ronbunshū* [Essays and Studies in Commemoration of Professor Shunichi Maekawa's Sixty-First Birthday], pp. 65–78. Tokyo: Eihōsha.
Discusses Donne's evolving attitude toward love throughout his life. Argues that even in his secular love poems he yearns for ecstatic union between lovers and thus ultimately finds all human love disappointing and imperfect. Sees the two *Anniversaries* as transitional poems that commemorate Donne's conversion or emancipation from human and earthly love to spiritual and divine love. Maintains, however, that he never fully achieved mystical union with God because his own ego, his overly developed sense of sin, and his doubts made this kind of annihilation impossible for him. Stresses that even in the *Holy Sonnets* and in his other

religious poems Donne primarily dramatizes himself and his spiritual quest, always more fascinated by his own spiritual responses to God than by God himself. Argues that, for Donne, God was always distant, always the Other, and that in the sermons Donne presents a rather negative attitude toward mysticism, preferring reason and ecclesiastical discipline as more appropriate vehicles to faith and to God. Concludes by showing that, although Donne surrenders himself fully to God, his religion is primarily public, not private; imminent, not transcendent; and by pointing out that the ecstasy of love, so yearned for in the love poems, is absent in the religious poems, in which Donne's ego and acute self-awareness still keep him from transcending himself.

◄§ 42. PETER, HARRY WINFIELD. "Donne's 'Nocturnall' and the *Nigredo*." *Thoth* 9: 48–57.

Explicates "A nocturnall upon S. Lucies day" as a meditation on the metaphysical problem of being and nothingness that allows the poet to regain tranquillity and hope after the death of his beloved. Suggests that the poet's psychological state, his dark night of the soul, is similar to the alchemical state of *Nigredo*. Argues that through this analogy the poet is able not only to describe his black condition but also to find a solution to his metaphysical problem. Suggests that from the state of *Nigredo* the poet is transformed into a more perfect being and thus readied for a more complete and spiritual contact with his lost beloved.

◄§ 43. POMEROY, ELIZABETH. "Donne's 'The Sunne Rising.'" *Expl* 27: Item 4.

Points out that in "The Sunne Rising" Donne resolves the conflict between the external world and the internal world of the lovers by a subtle process of inversion: the microcosm of the lovers' subjective world becomes the macrocosm, and their metaphorical realm thus becomes the only truly valid world in the poem. Suggests that what began as merely playful wit is transformed by the conclusion of the poem into a serious validation of subjective reality.

◄§ 44. PRESCOTT, ANNE LAKE. "The Reception of Du Bartas in England." *SRen* 15: 144–73.

Discusses the enormous popularity and influence of the French Huguenot poet Guillaume Salluste, Sieur du Bartas, in Renaissance England and claims that he probably was "the most admired of contemporary European writers, if one excludes Erasmus and the chief figures of the Reformation" and that "his lengthy descriptions of the creation and history of the world received an adulation seldom given far better poetry" (p. 144). Notes that significantly Donne and the other metaphysical poets do not mention Du Bartas, even though his conceits and images "are sometimes so striking that it is tempting to see them as in some sense 'metaphysical'" (p. 172). Points out, however, that "the intention behind them is wholly

◄§ 52. SMITH, BARBARA HERRNSTEIN. *Poetic Closure: A Study of How Poems End*. Chicago and London: The University of Chicago Press. xvi, 289p.

Quotes Donne on the importance of poetic closure (p. 37) and points out how "Hero and Leander" (pp. 204–6) is "a virtuoso-piece of verbal symmetry, economy, and coherence" (p. 205). Comments especially on the *hyperdetermination* of the closing of the epigram, that is, when "structural completeness coincides with an unusually high degree of nonstructural order or control" (p. 204).

◄§ 53. SPACKS, PATRICIA MEYER. "In Search of Sincerity." CE 29: 591–602.

Discusses the concept of sincerity in poetry and, while recognizing the critical confusion that the term generates, concludes that it remains, nonetheless, a useful term that describes "both a quality of the poem and a quality of its effect on the reader" (p. 591). Comments on "The Flea" (pp. 593–94) in order to show that "playfulness can itself be a mode of sincerity" (p. 593). Argues that the frivolity in the poem involves serious meanings and that "the 'seriousness' of the conclusion is part of the final contemptuous joke on the woman, as the speaker for the moment accepts her system of values and turns it against her" (p. 594). Argues that Donne's main point in the poem "is not seduction but the assertion of the complexity and importance of personal experience" (p. 593). Suggests that in "A Valediction: forbidding mourning" the sense of sincerity is generated by the images and by Donne's unwillingness to simplify a complex notion. Concludes that Donne's poetic sincerity depends on his poetic technique and compares his techniques for achieving sincerity with those of Pope and Eliot.

◄§ 54. SULLIVAN, NANCY. *Perspective and the Poetic Process*. The Hague and Paris: Mouton. 56p.

Explicates the central conceit of "A Lecture upon the Shadow" (pp. 23–25), pointing out how Donne fuses "an intellectual conceit on to an emotional situation" (p. 24). Suggests that the "metrical, almost metronome-like progress of love" in the poem "gives us an almost scientific view of perspective and the poetic process" (p. 25).

◄§ 55. THOMSON, A[NDREW] K[ILPATRICK]. "The Metaphysical Poets," in *A Reader's Guide to the Poet's Pen*, pp. 26–32. Brisbane: Jacaranda Press.

Comments briefly on the metaphysical poets and certain major characteristics of their poetry (p. 26) followed by notes or glosses on individual words and phrases in "A Valediction: forbidding mourning" (p. 27) and "At the round earths imagin'd corners" (p. 28).

≈§ 56. THUMBOO, EDWIN. "Donne's 'The Bracelet (Elegie XI),' 113–114."
Expl 27: Item 14.

Shows how in the last four lines of "The Bracelet" Donne wittily plays with the medically accepted notion that gold was a cordial or restorative. Notes that Donne asks the finder of the bracelet to return it since, gold being restorative, the gold bracelet should be restored to its rightful owner. If the finder will not return the bracelet, then Donne hopes that the gold will, metaphorically speaking, be in the finder's heart and thus restore him to moral health.

≈§ 57. TRACI, PHILIP. "The Supposed New Rhetoric of Donne's Songs and Sonets." *Discourse* 11: 98–107.

Argues that Donne did not reject rhetorical ornamentation in his poetry but rather assimilated completely the existing rhetorical tradition to his own purposes. Claims that the truly revolutionary quality of Donne's poetry "is due not so much to his having discarded the chains of Elizabethan convention, but rather to his having employed the links with such colloquial, dramatic, and even comic freshness, that the chains became not binding, but both useful and decorative—fulfilling the highest demands of the poetry of any age" (p. 105).

≈§ 58. WALCUTT, CHARLES CHILD, AND J. EDWIN WHITESELL, eds. "Donne," in *The Explicator Cyclopedia*, vol. 2: *Traditional Poetry: Medieval to Late Victorian*, pp. 96–126. Chicago: Quadrangle Books.

Lists forty-three items that appeared between 1943 and 1962 in *The Explicator*, all of which are fully annotated in John R. Roberts, *John Donne: An Annotated Bibliography of Modern Criticism, 1912–1967* (entry 595).

≈§ 59. WEBBER, JOAN. *The Eloquent "I": Style and Self in Seventeenth-Century Prose*. Madison, Milwaukee, London: The University of Wisconsin Press. xii, 298p.

"Donne and Bunyan: The Style of Two Faiths" (pp. 15–52) reprinted in Stanley E. Fish, ed., *Seventeenth-Century Prose: Modern Essays in Criticism* (entry 308).

Discusses the phenomenon of seventeenth-century literary self-consciousness, which includes "consciousness of self as subject, in all the richness of the self as product and maker of his age; consciousness of self as style and thereby as a way of linking subject with object; consciousness of self in the eyes of the reader, or object, which means either opposition to or union with that reader" (p. 4). In "Donne and Bunyan: The Style of Two Faiths" (pp. 15–52) compares and contrasts Donne's *Devotions upon Emergent Occasions* and Bunyan's *Grace Abounding* to show that the former's prose is "analytical, psychological, subjective, meditative, private, self-centered, and literary" while the latter's is "reportorial, straightforward, apparently objective, taking place in public, and inviting the reader to see him as an instrument to use rather than an object of contemplation"

(p. 51). Shows how Donne turns life into art and "constructs a symbolic cosmic personality that delights in stylistic complications, and even in playful and recreative devices" (p. 252) so that in the *Devotions* Donne becomes "subject, object, and critic of his own work" (p. 252).

❧ 60. YOKOTA, NAKAZŌ. "John Donne to Schola-tetsugaku" [John Donne and Scholastic Philosophy]. *Eigobungaku Sekai* (Eichōsha, Tokyo) 2, no. 12 (March): 33–35.
Cited in *Bibliography of English and Renaissance Studies in Japan: I, 1961–1970.* (Renaissance Monographs: 6), edited by Kazuyoshi Enozawa and Miyo Takano. Tokyo: The Renaissance Institute / Aratake Shuppan. Unavailable.

❧ 61. ———. "John Donne to Shi" [John Donne and Death]. *Kiyō* (Kyōyōbu, Tōhoku Daigaku) no. 9 (December): 123–39.
Notes that Donne was obsessed with death throughout his life and explores some of the reasons for his obsession. Comments on the theme of death in Donne's poetry and prose, especially in "The Funerall," the *Anniversaries*, and several of the sermons.

❧ 62. YOSHIDA, SACHIKO. "John Donne no Shi ni okeru Parody-teki Yōso" [The Parodic Element in John Donne's Poetry]. *Kiyō* (Jimbunkagaku-hen) (Mukogawa Joshi Daigaku) no. 15 (March): 119–24.
Suggests that in his love poems Donne parodies the *Summa Theologica* of St. Thomas Aquinas. Notes, for example, that Aquinas's equation between trinity-trinitas and one becomes in Donne the union of lovers who become through their love a single entity. Points out that Donne realized that a permanent union of two into one does not exist in reality but played with these parodic variations on Aquinas in a witty manner.

1969

❧ 63. AIZAWA, YOSHIHISA. "John Donne in *The Progresse of the Soule.*" *Bunkei Ronso* (Hirosaki Daigaku) (Bungaku-hen V) 5, no. 3 (December): 19–35.
Presents a critical reading of *The Progresse of the Soule* and discusses the historical and social background of the poem. Suggests that Donne wished to point to the sin of corruption represented by the female, as well as the sin of treason.

❧ 64. AMIR, S. JAVED. "Ghalib and Donne as Love Poets." *PakR* 17, ii: 54–58.
Compares Donne and Mirza Ghalib as love poets and finds a number of similarities in their diction, imagery, style, and uses of wit. Notes that both are essentially dramatic poets, use colloquial language, are often ob-

scure, and "look at things from odd and unexpected angles, resulting in conceit" (p. 55). Suggests that Ghalib's poetry, like Donne's, "was the dialectical expression of a personal drama, where the dissonance in style, diction, imagery or thought was a dissonance inwardly felt in the soul of man" (p. 58). Briefly compares Donne's "The Sunne Rising" and "Twicknam garden" with passages from Ghalib's love poems.

⊷ 65. ARMOUR, RICHARD. *English Lit Relit: A short history of English literature from the Precursors (before swearing) to the Pre-Raphaelites and a little after, intended to help students see the thing through, or see through the thing, and omitting nothing unimportant.* Irreverently illustrated by Campbell Grant. New York: McGraw-Hill. 151p.
Humorous treatment of Donne (pp. 33–35): "He had an eye for the women, his poems being full of figures" (p. 34).

⊷ 66. BAGG, ROBERT. "The Electromagnet and the Shred of Platinum." *Arion* 8: 407–29.
Argues that Reuben Brower's *The Fields of Light: An Experiment in Creative Reading* (1951) exemplifies the serious limitations of T. S. Eliot's impersonal theory and insists that "personality is the organizing vitality of art" (p. 429). Disagrees with Brower's reading of Donne's "Show me deare Christ," presents a Freudian analysis of the sonnet, and concludes that it "enacts Freud's thesis that religious 'ideology' is a form of sexual sublimation" (p. 420). Points out instances of sexual anxiety also in Donne's secular lyrics.

⊷ 67. BAUER, ROBERT J. "The Great Prince in Donne's 'The Extasie.'" *TSL* 14: 93–102.
Argues that the many variations on the theme of separation-unto-greater-unity in "The Extasie" come to focus in the figure of the great prince imprisoned (line 68), in which "the lovers for an instant contemplate a post-ecstatic frustration, a defeat" (p. 100). Suggests that each of the lovers, however, surrenders an old self and finds a triumphant new self and that both come to realize that only through physical intercourse will their love remain permanent: "For these two, implies the poem, the need for further negotiations will never arise" (p. 100).

⊷ 68. BELL, ARTHUR H. "Donne's Atonement Conceit in the *Holy Sonnets*." *Cresset* (Valparaiso U.) 32, vii: 15–17.
Maintains that Donne "uses dramatic roles for God as a conceit which he gleaned from his theological reading; and, that Donne's 'theological conceit' consistently connotes the Atonement, the unifying motif of the Holy Sonnets" (p. 15). Suggests that Donne "expresses the 'dramatic' view of the atonement rather than the 'satisfaction' theory common to Spenser and Herrick" (p. 15) and identifies at least three sources for this view: St.

Paul, the early Fathers of the Church, and Martin Luther. Reads "Batter my heart" as "a passionate account of the work of atonement—Creation, Redemption, and Sanctification, in respective quatrains—by the 'three person'd God'" (pp. 16–17).

◆§ 69. CAVE, TERENCE C. *Devotional Poetry in France c. 1570–1613.* Cambridge: Cambridge University Press. xvi, 356p.

Surveys late sixteenth- and early seventeenth-century French devotional poetry and points out certain similarities and differences between it and Donne's religious poetry. Notes, for example, that French devotional poetry does not contain any "personal statement as forceful as Herbert's *The Collar* and Donne's *Goodfriday, 1613. Riding Westward*" (p. 307) and states that, on the whole, the French devotional poets, unlike Donne, are not major poets. Notes that an image used in the prologue of Luis de Granada's *Le Vray chemin* closely resembles that of Donne's "Batter my heart" (p. 36n) and that the opening lines of A. Favre's sonnet 40 in *Centurie premiere de sonets spirituels de l'amour divin et de la pénitence* resemble Donne's "O, my blacke soule" (p. 240n).

◆§ 70. CIRILLO, A. R. "The Fair Hermaphrodite: Love-Union in the Poetry of Donne and Spenser." *SEL* 9:81–95.

Discusses the image of the hermaphrodite as a topos of Renaissance poetry for figuring forth or symbolizing the concept of love-death and spiritual union, a union "in which the lovers are united so that they become one another, not physically but spiritually, by means of an ecstasy which annihilates those barriers separating them" (p. 85). Points out that the image of the hermaphrodite is basic to the context of "The Extasie," "whether Donne was using it seriously or cynically" (p. 90). Notes further instances of the topos implied in "Song: Sweetest love, I do not goe," "The Paradox," "The Prohibition," "A Valediction: forbidding mourning," "The Canonization," and "The Relique," as well as explicitly mentioned in "To Mr Tilman *after he had taken orders*" and in the *Epithalamion made at Lincolnes Inne.* Compares Donne's use of the image with that of Spenser in the ending of Book III of *The Faerie Queene.*

◆§ 71. COLLMER, ROBERT G. "Donne and Borges." *RLC* 43: 219–32.

Points out that, although Donne has received relatively little critical attention from Spanish-speaking critics and writers, Jorge Luis Borges, the Argentinian winner of the 1967 Nobel Prize for Literature, has been an admirer of Donne for many years. Introduced to Donne through his reading of Thomas De Quincey, Borges notes in several of his works his admiration for Donne's ability to manipulate ideas, for his imagery, and for his effective humor. Not only did Borges write a critical essay on *Biathanatos*, but it has also been suggested that Donne's treatise may have inspired "Tres Versiones de Judas." Finds little direct influence of Donne on Borges's poetry but notes some similarities between the two in certain techniques and tones.

✒ 72. CORIN, FERNAND. "A Note on Donne's 'Canonization.'" *ES* 50: 89–93.

In part a reply to W. H. Matchett's "Donne's 'Peece of Chronicle'" (*RES* n.s. 18 [1967]: 290–92). Sees the whole poem as unified by a series of contrasts "between wordliness, publicity, vanity, on the one hand, and privacy, intimacy, preciousness and sacredness, on the other" (p. 91). Analyzes in detail stanza 4 of "The Canonization" to show that all the images reinforce the contrasts set up in the poem and that "what is common to the terms (*half-acre*) *tombes, hearse, Chronicle* is the idea of a work of art whose effect relies more on display and magnificence, as opposed to *verse, sonnets* and *well wrought urne*, which are works of art of refined quality" (p. 92). Suggests, therefore, that the contrast is "one of quality, not of dimension" (p. 92). Notes that the word *peece* (line 31) should be interpreted as "a piece of work, product of work, production" and that "this fits the logical succession of words suggesting works of art and more particularly literary production, which is the meaning common to *tombes, hearse, verse, peece of Chronicle, sonnets, hymnes, half-acre tombes*" (p. 93).

✒ 73. CRUM, MARGARET, ed. *First-Line Index of English Poetry 1500–1800 in Manuscripts of the Bodleian Library Oxford.* 2 vols. New York: Index Committee of the Modern Language Association; Oxford: Clarendon Press. 1–630; 631–1257p.

First-line index of English poetry (1500–1800) in manuscripts of the Bodleian up to 1961. Five indexes: (1) Bodleian manuscripts listed by shelfmarks; (2) index of authors; (3) index of names mentioned; (4) index of authors of works translated, paraphrased, or imitated; and (5) index of references to composers of settings and tunes named or quoted. Contains 103 main entries for Donne.

✒ 74. DENIS, YVES. "Poèmes métaphysiques." *NRF* 17, no. 200: 235–46.

Presents a general introduction to metaphysical poetry and comments briefly on Donne's style. Contrasts Donne's style with that of the Edwardian poets and suggests that English poetry was reinvigorated by the discovery of metaphysical poetry in the early twentieth century: "ce fut un coup de whisky après vingt ans de tisane" (p. 235). Maintains that only personal taste can determine whether Donne is greater than Milton. Translates into French selected poems by George Herbert, Henry King, Rochester, Marvell, Fulke Greville, and Lord Herbert of Cherbury, preceded by brief biographical sketches of each.

✒ 75. DENT, R. W. "Marlowe, Spenser, Donne, Shakespeare—and Joseph Wybarne." *RenQ* 22: 360–62.

Points out that Joseph Wybarne in his *The New Age of Old Names* (1609) quotes lines 18–23 of Donne's then unpublished *Satyre IV* (with only one minor verbal variant from the accepted text). Notes that Wybarne, condemning the Brownists, writes: "But as Aslacus intends to prove this fire to bee no Element, so I thinke this fervor may be proved to be no Religion," a reference to *De natura caeli triplicis libelli tres quorum* (1597) by Cunradus Aslacus, and suggests that this work may be worth studying in connection with Donne's *The first Anniversary*.

◄§ 76. DE ROTHSCHILD, PHILIPPE, AND ANDRÉ PIEYRE DE MAND-IARGUES. *Poèmes élisabéthains* (1525–1650). Traduits et présentés par Philippe de Rothschild. Préface de André Pieyre de Mandiargues. Introduction de Stephen Spender. Notices biographiques de Christopher Ricks (translated by Philippe de Rothschild). Paris: Seghers. 415p.
Bilingual anthology of nondramatic poetry from Wyatt to Marvell and Vaughan. "John Donne (1572–1631)" (pp. 195–211) contains a brief biographical sketch and an introduction to Donne's poetry, followed by French translations (with English on the opposite page) of "The good-morrow," "The Indifferent," "The Baite," "A Lecture upon the Shadow," "Aire and Angels," "The Expiration," and "Batter my heart" (pp. 200–211). Notes (pp. 382–85) and a chronology of major literary and historical events from the death of Wyatt to the death of Marvell (pp. 401–14). Index.

◄§ 77. DONNE, JOHN. *Deaths Dvell, or, A Consolation to the Soule, against the dying Life, and liuing Death of the Body* . . . (1632). Menston, Eng.: The Scolar Press. [10],41,[3]p.
Facsimile reprint (original size) of the Bodleian Library copy of the first edition of Donne's last sermon, delivered at Whitehall on 12 February 1631. Reissued in 1633 but not reprinted separately since. (*STC* 7031).

◄§ 78. ———. *Devociones*. Versión y prólogo de Alberto Girri. (Breviarios de Información Literaria, No. 17.) Buenos Aires: Editorial Brújula. 150p.
Prologue (pp. 9–12) comments briefly on Donne's prose works and prose style and presents a general introduction to the *Devotions upon Emergent Occasions*. Suggests numerous influences on Donne's prose style and world view, such as Latin prose, the Old Testament, St. Augustine, the Vulgate, medieval and Elizabethan poets, and especially Donne's own poetry. Translates into Spanish the twenty-three Meditations (pp. 13–150) but excludes the Expostulations and Prayers. Index. No notes and no commentary.

◄§ 79. ———. *Ignatius His Conclave*. An Edition of the Latin and English texts with introduction and commentary by T[imothy] S. Healy, S. J. London: Oxford University Press. lii, 175p.

Preface (pp. v–vi); contents (p. viii); references and abbreviations (pp. ix–x); introduction: I. The Two Versions (pp. xi–xvii), II. The Historical Setting (pp. xvii–xxix), III. The Satire and the Satirist (pp. xxix–xlii); bibliographical note: I. The Latin Text (pp. xliii–xliv), II. The English Text (pp. xlv–xlviii), III. Copies Consulted (pp. xlviii–li), IV. The Text of this Edition (pp. li–lii). Latin and English texts on facing pages (pp. 1–99). Commentary (pp. 100–154). Appendix A, "Differences between the Two Texts" (pp. 155–57); Appendix B, "A Note on Sources" (pp. 158–67); Appendix C, "Donne's Collaboration with Thomas Morton" (pp. 168–73); Appendix D, "A Donne Discovery" (P. G. Stanwood's discovery of a Latin poem on Ignatius in the Hunter manuscript collection in the Library of Durham Cathedral) (pp. 174–75). The introduction traces the bibliographical history of the Latin and English versions and comments on stylistic features of both. Also outlines the historical context and comments on the satirical argument of the treatise. Extensive notes and commentary.

෴ 80. ———. *Poems, by J. D. with elegies on the authors death* (1633). Menston, Eng.: The Scolar Press. [13],406p.

Reprinted: 1970. Reprinted: Hildesheim and New York: Georg Olms Verlag, 1974.

Facsimile reprint of the first collected edition of Donne's poems (London: John Marriot, 1633) with original title page. Reproduced in original size from copy in the British Library, shelfmark G. 11415 (*STC* 7045).

෴ 81. DURAND, LAURA G. "Sponde and Donne: Lens and Prism." *CL* 21: 319–36.

Contrasts Donne and Jean de Sponde to show that, in spite of those critics who persist in seeing Sponde as a "Donne manque" (p. 319), the two poets are fundamentally unlike and that the difference "is not one of degree but one of essence" (p. 336). Comments on the religious, love, and death poetry of each to show that there is "a great dissimilarity in attitude, in range of thought and association, in the kind of poetic organization given to the matter dealt with" (pp. 329–30). Points out that Donne's poetry is highly figurative, filled with conceits, witty, and complex. It is "richer in variety of mood, tone, image, point of view" (p. 336) than Sponde's verse, which is much less complex and lacks metaphysical conceits and wit.

෴ 82. FIELDING, EDWINA. "John Donne and the New Christianity." *The Month* 42: 194–202.

Comments on Donne's conversion from Catholicism to Anglicanism and suggests that many of his writings, especially the *Anniversaries*, show that he continued to have, even after his conversion, a great respect and love for many aspects of the Roman Church.

❧ 83. FLYNN, DENNIS. "Three Unnoticed Companion Essays to Donne's 'An essay of Valour.'" *BNYPL* 73: 424–39.

Argues that three essays printed under the title "Sir Francis Walsingham's Anatomizing of Honesty, Ambition, and Fortitude" included in *Cottoni Posthuma* (1651), a collection of Sir Robert Cotton's papers published posthumously by James Howell, may have been written by Donne. Notes that Donne's "An Essay of Valour" is included in the collection, falsely ascribed to Sidney. Suggests that the false ascriptions may have been a private joke between Cotton and Donne at the expense of their patrons.

❧ 84. FRASER, RUSSELL. "On Metaphor, Mysticism, and Science." *MichQR* 8: 49–57.

Argues that the usually accepted polarity between scientist and mystic is not accurate since both share a belief in general ideas and universals. Notes that the poet, on the other hand, "moves, not from particulars to the general, but from particular to particular" (p. 57). He "is satisfied with the achieving of his limited or analogical truth" and "does not suppose that the more imperial ambition of the mystic or the codifier of general law is likely to be fruitful" (p. 52). Briefly discusses Donne's view of poetry as "an exegetical science whose mundane business is with 'such and such'" (p. 52). Suggests that his poetry "is like hermeneutics, except that the material the poet sets himself to gloss is not confined to Scripture but is drawn from the entire range of our experience" (p. 52). Sees similarities between medieval scholasticism and much of Donne's poetry since both stress that "truth must be discovered in the palpable and particular" (p. 53), and notes that for the poet, as for the nominalist, "general ideas or universals do not exist outside the mind that conceives them" (p. 57). Suggests that Shakespeare and Donne differ from their predecessors only in degree: "the kind remains what it was, still worshipful of extrinsic form" (p. 54).

❧ 85. GATCH, MILTON McC. "The Sixteenth-Century Tradition," in *Death: Meaning and Morality in Christian Thought and Contemporary Culture*, pp. 112–28. New York: The Seabury Press.

Briefly comments on Donne's views on death (pp. 125–28) as reflected primarily in the poetry. Points out Donne's images of death as sleep in two of the *Holy Sonnets* and in "Song: Sweetest love, I do not goe" and suggests that these images "dramatize the distance between the original approach to death and that of the end of the Reformation era" (p. 128). Notes that, for Donne, "only the body truly sleeps; the soul, which is the more important element of human life, is active but also loyal to the body as its lover" (p. 128).

❧ 86. GIFFORD, WILLIAM. "Donne on Candlemas at St. Paul's?" *N&Q* n.s. 16: 370–71.

Presents additional facts that challenge the assumption made by Simpson and Potter in their edition of Donne's sermons (1953–1962) that Donne customarily preached at St. Paul's on Candlemas. Points out that in a letter to George Gerrard (1629), Donne states that, because of illness, he must omit his annual Christmas sermon at St. Paul's but will make special arrangements to preach on Candlemas, which, apparently, would be unusual for him.

❧ 87. GODINO, RODOLFO. "A propósito de John Donne y sus devociones." *Sur* 321: 81–84.

Comments favorably on the first modern Spanish translation of Donne's *Devotions upon Emergent Occasions* by Alberto Girri (entry 78). Presents a brief biographical sketch of Donne and suggests that one of the main appeals of the *Devotions* is its tension between the secular and the sacred, a tension reflected in all of Donne's works. Calls the *Devotions* "la más sincera y dramática meditación sobre la muerte que exista en la literatura inglesa" (p. 83).

❧ 88. GRANSDEN, K. W. *John Donne*. Rev. ed. Hamden, Conn.: Archon Books. x, 197p.

Revision of the 1954 edition, which first appeared in the Men and Book Series (London: Longmans, Green and Co.). Takes into account certain recent work on Donne's life, his canon, the text, and his sources. Retains the discussion of the twelfth elegy even though Helen Gardner's edition rejects it; removes comments on the "Heroical l Epistle," however, in the light of Gardner's evidence. Revises and slightly expands the selected bibliography. Presents a general introduction to the study of Donne's life and works. Announces that this study is not a reassessment of Donne but rather is intended simply to serve as a "companion" for the general reader. Divided into five major parts: (1) the life (pp. 1–48), (2) the metaphysical school (pp. 49–53), (3) the secular poems (pp. 55–124), (4) the divine poems (pp. 125–47) and (5) the prose works (pp. 149–91).

❧ 89. HAEFNER, GERHARD. "John Donne: 'The Canonization'. Eine Interpretation." *NS* 18: 169–75.

Explicates "The Canonization" and stresses that the tension in the poem is, in part, created by the seeming disparity between the sacred vehicle (canonization) and the secular tenor (sexual love). Suggests that the use of paradox in Donne's poetry reflects the inner tensions of the seventeenth-century world view: "In dem Augenblick, wo das Irdische nicht mehr allein als Funktion des Religiösen verstanden wird, sondern die wechselseitige Abhängigkeit beider gesehen wird, tritt notwendigerweise die Paradoxie auf, weil sie imstande ist, beides zusammenzuzwingen" (pp. 174–75).

❧ 90. HEATH-STUBBS, JOHN. "From the Elizabethans to Milton," in *The Ode*, pp. 22–39. London: Oxford University Press.

Discusses the development of the ode and briefly contrasts the private voice of Donne's poetry with the more public voice of Jonson and the Cavaliers. Points out that, on the whole, the metaphysical poets do not apply the term *ode* to their elaborate stanzaic forms. Notes two exceptions: Marvell and Lord Herbert of Cherbury, whose "An Ode upon a Question moved, whether love should continue for ever" may owe something to Donne's "The Extasie."

⋙ 91. ⸻. "The Jacobeans," in *The Verse Satire*, pp. 22–34. London: Oxford University Press.
Surveys very briefly Donne's satires. Suggests that it was primarily the satires "which gained for Donne's poetry in general a reputation for roughness and obscurity which led to its being almost universally under-valued and neglected for nearly three centuries after his death" (p. 23). Praises Donne's *Satyres*, however, for being "vivid and dramatic in their observation of contemporary life" (p. 23).

⋙ 92. HIRABAYASHI, JIRŌ. "Ignatius His Conclave to 'New Philosophy'" [*Ignatius His Conclave* and "New Philosophy"]. *Kiyō* (Kyoto Kyōiku Daigaku) (A) no. 34 (February): 67–82.
Comments on Donne's rejection of Catholicism and his antagonism toward the Jesuits. Notes that, whereas in *Pseudo-Martyr* Donne's intention was to persuade Catholics to take the Oath of Allegiance, his purpose in *Ignatius his Conclave* is vituperation against the Jesuits. Notes that Donne knew the works of Copernicus, Galileo, and Kepler and that he uses the "new philosophy" as a skillful weapon against the ignorance of the Jesuits. Argues that *Ignatius* shows that Donne was a convinced Anglican at least four years before his ordination and obviously demonstrated to the king his ability as an Anglican controversialist.

⋙ 93. HISANO, SACHIKO. "John Donne no Paradox—Chūki no Skūkyō-shi no Baai" [Paradox in John Donne—On His Religious Poetry in the Middle Years]. *IVY* (Nagoya Daigaku) no. 8 (March): 41–55.
Cited in *Bibliography of English and Renaissance Studies in Japan: I, 1961–1970.* (Renaissance Monographs: 6), edited by Kazuyoshi Enozawa and Miyo Takano. Tokyo: The Renaissance Institute / Aratake Shuppan. Unavailable.

⋙ 94. HODGART, MATTHEW. "Forms of Satire," in *Satire*, pp. 132–87. (World University Library.) London: Weidenfeld and Nicolson.
Briefly discusses the development of formal verse satire during the late sixteenth century and calls Donne "by far the best of the Elizabethan satirists" (p. 142). Points out that, on the whole, sixteenth-century verse satire is "sadly disappointing as poetry" (p. 141) but sees Donne as an exception.

⤐ 95. HOWELL, ANTHONY. "A Question of Form." *PoetryR* 60: 41–49.

Comments on the question of form in baroque poetry and its uses of paradox and parody and points out that often Donne's poetry can be called baroque. Briefly comments on "The Flea" and suggests that the flea is a parody of Cupid.

⤐ 96. HUNTLEY, FRANK L. "Dr. Johnson and Metaphysical Wit; or, *Discordia concors* Yoked and Balanced." *PMMLA* 1: 103–12.

Attempts to view the metaphysical poets from Dr. Johnson's perspective by explaining Johnson's use of the phrase *discordia concors*. Distinguishes between "two modes of imitating world harmony," the classical and the Christian, and "describes and illustrates the difference in feeling and shape that one mode produces in Denham and Pope; and the other, in Donne and Herbert" (p. 104). Notes that "one pattern imitates the natural balance between the elements of fission and fusion; the other more daringly combines a lower into a higher value to achieve a third" and that "the balanced pattern is Pythagorean and Empedoclean and consists of two's and four's; the yoked pattern is Platonic and Christian, and often appears in three's and five's" (p. 104). Suggests that Dr. Johnson is not ridiculing the metaphysical poets but views the Augustans and the metaphysicals from a "classical" viewpoint. Concludes that "in theme and form the Augustan architectonic of wit, then, and that of Donne and Herbert both concern the poet's prime function of making artistic order out of the chaos of experience, but Augustan wit is 'classical' and Donnean wit is 'Christian' in its search for world harmony" (p. 112).

⤐ 97. INGLIS, FRED. *The Elizabethan Poets: The Making of English Poetry from Wyatt to Ben Jonson.* (Literature in Perspective.) London: Evans Brothers. 168p.

Discusses often neglected Elizabethan poets, warns against the dangers of the historical classification of poetry, and suggests that the modern enthusiasm for Donne's poetry has caused plain-style poetry to be underestimated. Compares and contrasts Donne's poetry briefly with that of Wyatt, Gascoigne, Ralegh, Sidney, Thomas Campion, Fulke Greville, Shakespeare, Jonson, and George Herbert.

⤐ 98. JEHMLICH, REIMER. *Die Bildlichkeit in der Liebeslyrik Sir Philip Sidneys, Michael Draytons und John Donnes ('Astrophel and Stella,' 'Idea,' and 'Songs and Sonets').* Kiel: Christian-Albrechts-Universität zu Kiel. 187, xv p.

Compares and contrasts the uses of metaphor and images in Sidney's *Astrophel and Stella*, Drayton's *Idea*, and Donne's *Songs and Sonets* "to assess the traditional and the non-traditional elements in the three collections to find out what they have in common and where they differ" (p. 185), and thus to obtain evidence that would allow for a reconsideration of the question of Donne's so-called modernity and his alleged revolt against the prevailing conventions of his day. Surveys the common sources and influences on all three poets—the *Greek Anthology*, Ovid, Petrarch, Ronsard, Neoplatonic love theories, Galenic philosophy, and Scholasticism and discusses by means of both historical and linguistic approaches the metaphorical structures, rhetorical strategies, and linguistic devices employed by all three poets. Shows how each uses many traditional topoi and metaphors but suggests that Donne often creates more concrete situations in his poetry and is often more sophisticated in his uses of images. Stresses that Donne, more than Sidney or Drayton, uses metaphor and images as tools for logical reasoning and points out that, although he uses a greater variety of metaphors than the other two, he creates something new only in his use of alchemical figures and images of the world. Notes, however, that Donne's use of scientific imagery is not modern in any sense. Bibliography (pp. i–xv).

⊷§ 99. KERMODE, FRANK, ed. *The Metaphysical Poets: Key Essays on Metaphysical Poetry and the Major Metaphysical Poets.* Edited with introduction and commentary by Frank Kermode. (Fawcett Premier Literature and Ideas Series, edited by Irving Howe.) New York: Fawcett Publications. 351p.

General introduction to Donne and to metaphysical poetry (pp. 11–32). Notes that Donne's "colloquial harshness, the application of his imagery, his expression, strong argument, persistent dialectical sleight-of-hand, indefatigable paradox, all add up to a new thing [in English poetry]" (pp. 20–21) but shows also that Donne used traditional themes and methods. A collection of twenty-six previously published essays and/or selections from book-length studies by diverse hands arranged under five major headings: (1) The English Background, (2) Baroque, (3) Metaphysical Poetic, (4) The Major Metaphysical Poets, and (5) Epilogue. Although most of the items in the collection make mention of Donne and are important in understanding metaphysical poetry in general, the following are especially important: (1) Frank J. Warnke, "Baroque and Metaphysical" (pp. 97–112), from *European Metaphysical Poetry* (New Haven: Yale University Press, 1961), pp. 5–21; (2) Carew, "An Elegie upon the Death of the Deane of Pauls, Dr. John Donne" (pp. 115–17), from *Carew's Poems*, edited by Rhodes Dunlap (Oxford: Clarendon Press, 1949), pp. 71–74; (3) selections from Dryden, *An Essay of Dramatic Poesy*, and from *A Discourse Concerning the Original and Progress of Satire* (p. 121), from *Essays of John Dryden*, edited by W. P. Ker (Oxford: Clarendon Press, 1900), 1:52; 2: 19, 102; (4) "Metaphysical Wit" (pp. 122–24), from Dr. Johnson, "The Life of Cowley" in *Lives of the English Poets*; (5) T. S. Eliot, "The Metaphysical Poets" (pp. 126–35), first published in 1921, from *Selected Essays*; (6) J. E. Duncan, "The Background of Eliot's [Donne] Criticism" (pp. 136–45), from *The Revival of Metaphysical Poetry* (Minneapolis: University of Minnesota Press, 1959), pp. 118–26; (7) A. D. Nuttall, "The Shocking Image" (pp. 146–57), from *Two Concepts of Allegory* (New York:

Barnes and Noble, 1967), pp. 81–91; (8) Joseph A. Mazzeo, "Modern Theories of Metaphysical Poetry" (pp. 158–71), from *MP* 50 (1952): 88–96; (9) selections from Izaak Walton, *Life of Dr. John Donne* (pp. 177–80); (10) A. J. Smith, "Donne's Invention" (pp. 181–202), from *John Donne: Songs and Sonets* (London: Edward Arnold, 1964), pp. 7–26; (11) Helen Gardner, "The Religious Poetry of John Donne" (pp. 203–21), from *Donne: The Divine Poems* (Oxford: Clarendon Press, 1952), pp. xv–xxxiii; and (12) A. Alvarez, "The Game of Wit and the Corruption of Style" (pp. 331–43), from *The School of Donne* (London: Chatto & Windus, 1961).

ᴥᔤ 100. KISHIMOTO, YOSHITAKA. "'The Autumnall' o toshite Mita Donne no Shisei" [Donne's Attitude in "The Autumnall"]. *Kiyo* (Eigo/Eibei Bungaku) (Bungakubu, Baika Joshi Daigaku) no. 6 (December): 49–62.

Argues that, although "The Autumnall" is written in the style of a courtly lyric, it does not actually belong to that genre. Suggests that the difference lies in the diction and in a certain lack of refinement, even roughness, of wit. Finds Helen Gardner's reading of the poem preferable to Grierson's interpretation.

ᴥᔤ 101. KODAMA, HISAO. "Kindai Eikoku Sekkyō Bungaku no Hassei—Latimer kara Donne e" [The Beginnings of English Sermon Literature—From Latimer to Donne]. *Kenkyū Nempō* (Bungakubu, Gakushuin Daigaku) no. 15: 1–40.

Comments on various differences among the sermons of Donne, Richard Hooker, and Lancelot Andrewes. Finds Andrewes more liturgical, Hooker more theological, and Donne more metaphysical and suggests that of the three Donne pursues his argument with greater verve. Stresses that Donne's sermons are filled with conceits, are brilliantly executed, and are argumentatively persuasive. Notes that one feels often that Donne is trying most of all to persuade himself rather than his congregation. Points out that Donne was able to develop profound metaphysical arguments out of what for others would have been mere superficial wit and discusses how Donne divides his sermons into three logically related parts rather than simply developing his sermons from key terms in the text.

ᴥᔤ 102. KOPPENFELS, WERNER von. "Donnes Liebesdichtung und die Tradition von *Tottel's Miscellany*." *Anglia* 87: 167–200.

Traces Donne's relationship to the Petrarchan tradition of earlier Renaissance poetry, especially as it is reflected in *Tottel's Miscellany*, and discusses how Donne transforms traditional themes, such as the theme of *Zefiro torna*, through the uses of irony. Comments in some detail on themes in "The Dampe," "Loves diet," and "Twicknam garden" and notes, in particular, the direct influence of Tuberville on the last two.

103. KORTE, DONALD M. "John Donne's 'Satyres' and a Matter of Rhetoric." *HAB* 20, iii: 78–81.

Contends that in *Satyre I* "the pervasive irony, the histrionics, the hyperbole, and the mock-seriousness all work towards making the satirist an ambiguous figure, one who lacks a firm moral base from which to rail *authoritatively* at folly and vice" and suggests that "because of Donne's failure to establish an authoritative *ethos* in his speaker, the satire is flawed" (p. 80). Argues that in *Satyre IV*, on the other hand, the speaker, though witty and hyperbolic, is effective because he "stands on a firm moral base" and "espouses clearly-defined values, and no heavy-handed theatrics nor anything else that would make him ambiguous undermine his position" (p. 80).

104. KRZECZKOWSKI, HENRYK, JERZY S. SITO, AND JULIUSZ ŻU-ŁAWSKI, eds. "John Donne (1573–1631)," in *Poeci języka angielskiego* [Poets of the English Language], 1:408–44. (Biblioteka poezji i prozy.) Warsaw: Państwowy Instytut Wydawniczy.

Reprinted: 1971, 1974.

Contains a general introduction to Donne's life and poetry (pp. 408–9), a selected bibliography (p. 409), and thirty poems, both secular and sacred, translated into Polish by various hands (pp. 410–44). Brief explanatory notes on individual poems (pp. 851–52).

105. KUSUNOSE, TOSHIHIKO. "The Anniversaries—Chuki ni okeru John Donne" [John Donne in His Middle Years—On the *Anniversaries*]. *Ronko* (Kanseigakuin Daigaku) no. 16 (December): 101–14.

Argues that the major theme of the *Anniversaries* is the union of the flesh and the spirit and that the main character in the poems is not Elizabeth Drury but Donne himself. Maintains that in *The first Anniversary* flesh and spirit are in conflict and are separated but that in *The second Anniversarie* they become one.

106. ———. "John Donne no Shūkyō-shi—Nikutai to Rei" [John Donne's Religious Poetry—Body and Soul]. *Bungaku Gogaku Ronshū* (Kanseigakuin Daigaku). (A special issue in honor of Prof. Akihiro Tanaka.) (April): 41–58.

Suggests that the relationship of the body and the soul is central to the artistic, moral, and religious meaning of Donne's sacred poetry and that in his religious poems he seeks to show how the body and soul are "one" and "all."

107. LAWNICZAK, DONALD A. "Donne's Sainted Lovers—Again." *Serif* 6: 12–19.

Argues for the unity of the dramatic structure and tone of "The Canonization." Maintains that Donne transforms wit into love in the poem and, through his aesthetic structure, reconciles profane and sacred love.

Suggests that the central, functional paradox in the poem, one that the reader participates in along with the "you" addressed, is the realization "that by giving up the world's identification of secular love with blasphemy is a way of discovering that love is something more than the secular world could imagine it to be" and that "profane love is more than just eros— again, as the secular world imagines" (p. 13). Suggests, however, that the final effect of the poem is somewhat unclear: "Perhaps what this means is that the reader feels that the union described in this essay is a union, a harmony, achieved only through wit and art" (p. 19).

✠ 108. LEA, KATHLEEN. *The Poetic Powers of Repetition.* (Chatterton Lecture on an English Poet, British Academy.) Oxford: Oxford University Press. 51–76 p.
Reprinted in *PBA* 55 (1971): 51–76.
Discusses the variety, delicacy, and force of the rhetorical device of repetition in English poetry. Mentions Donne's "curious mimicking of the slapping of sails" (p. 69) in his verse letter, "The Storme," and also mentions and quotes from Donne's sermon on the text "Follow me, and I will make you fishers of men" "with its fascinating exploitation of the logical, connective, and even lyrical effects of repetition" (p. 70).

✠ 109. LEAVIS, F. R. "'English'—Unrest and Continuity." *TLS*, 29 May, pp. 569–72.
The opening address at a colloquium on English studies held at the University of Wales at Gregynog. Discusses T. S. Eliot's criticism of the metaphysical poets, especially "The Metaphysical Poets" that appeared in *TLS*, 20 October 1921, pp. 669–70, and contrasts it with J. B. Leishman's "academic" criticism of Donne in *The Monarch of Wit* (1951). Maintains that the distinctive value of Eliot's Donne criticism is that it "is conditioned by its being the 'poetic practitioner's' and having the limitations of aim and scope that that description implies" (p. 571). Suggests that "what Donne, the master of the metaphysical school, did that mattered most to Eliot the poetic innovator was to bring into non-dramatic poetry the Shakespearian use of the English language" (p. 571).

✠ 110. LECOCQ, LOUIS. "John Donne," in *La Satire en Angleterre de 1588 à 1603*, pp. 358–98. (Études Anglaises, 32.) Paris: Didier.
Discusses Elizabethan satire within a historical and theoretical framework and presents a detailed explication of Donne's five satires (pp. 365–84), comments on major stylistic features of his satires, and discusses key elements in his satiric view of the world. Finds the two dominating images of *Satyre III*, the river and the mountain, as symbolic of Donne's fundamental satiric vision; the river suggests the flux, change, and corruption of life, and the mountain suggests the permanence and purity of truth from which the destruction of change can be viewed. Suggests that certain biographical facts about Donne, especially his early religious commitment

to Catholicism, help explain his inclination to hide himself in satire. Briefly compares and contrasts Donne with Thomas Lodge and with Pope.

◄§ 111. LE COMTE, EDWARD. *The Notorious Lady Essex*. New York: The Dial Press. ix, 251p.
Biography of Frances Howard, Countess of Essex, and later Countess of Somerset. Briefly comments on Donne's epithalamion written on the occasion of her second marriage (pp. 131–33) and on Donne's friendship with Robert Carr, Earl of Somerset.

◄§ 112. LEHANE, BRENDAN. *The Compleat Flea*. New York: The Viking Press. x, 126p.
Discusses the flea in history and literature and comments on Donne's "The Flea," calling it "the erotic apex of the literary flea" and noting that after it "the immoral flea is plainly pornographic" (p. 47).

◄§ 113. LEMON, LEE T. *Approaches to Literature*. New York, London, Toronto: Oxford University Press. ix, 243p.
Comments on "The Canonization," especially on the subtlety of the structure of its argument, the symbolic use of *fly* (line 20), the precise meaning of *rage* (line 39), and the skillful uses of imagery and metaphor (pp. 6–14, 50–51, 55). Discusses briefly how the stanzaic form and meter of the first quatrain of "At the round earths imagin'd corners" contribute to the tone of the poem (pp. 97–98). Comments also on the inadequacy of translation by discussing subtleties in "The Extasie" (pp. 115–16).

◄§ 114. LLOYD, CHARLES E. "The Author of Peace and Donne's Holy Sonnet XIV." *JHI* 30: 251–52.
Suggests that the second collect of Morning Prayer, the collect for peace, in the Jacobean Prayer Book may have suggested the imagery of God as enthraller-liberator and God as rapist-chastener in the closing lines of "Batter my heart."

◄§ 115. MCPEEK, JAMES A. S. "Classical Myth and the Bible in English Literature: A Selected Bibliography." *CEA* 32: 14–39.
Selected bibliography of works dealing with classical mythology and the Bible in English literature, along with a chronological listing of certain major versions or mythic reshapings of twenty representative myths and biblical stories. Cites Donne's version of the story of Noah's flood (p. 31) and his uses of the myth of the phoenix (p. 36). Primary and secondary works included.

◄§ 116. MAHONY, PATRICK. "The *Anniversaries*: Donne's Rhetorical Approach to Evil." *JEGP* 68: 407–13.
Reprinted in *Essential Articles for the Study of John Donne's Poetry*, edited by John R. Roberts (entry 786), pp. 363–67.

Sees the *Anniversaries* as "examples of deliberative-epideictic rhetoric," as "poems of process rather than fixity, of argumentation rather than exposition," and suggests that "the rhetorical treatment of evil is a key to the understanding of the sequel poems" (p. 407). Argues that to understand the poems fully one "must take into account their full rhetorical nature, including their chief cause of lament, their restricted audience, and their nuanced harmonization and mutuality as rhetorical argument based on the meditative tradition" (p. 411). Points out that "as epideictic rhetoric, the *Anniversaries* praise the heroine and what she represents, and dispraise worldliness; as deliberative rhetoric, the poetic diptychs persuade the new world to become virtuous like and through the heroine" (pp. 411–12). Concludes, therefore, that the poems possess "an ultimately indissoluable union of epideictic and deliberative rhetoric" (p. 412).

◄§ 117. MARTZ, LOUIS L. *The Wit of Love: Donne, Carew, Crashaw, Marvell.* (University of Notre Dame Ward-Phillips Lectures in English Language and Literature, vol. 3.) Notre Dame, Ind., and London: University of Notre Dame Press. xv, 216p.

Series of four lectures (revised and expanded) that were first given at the University of Notre Dame in March 1968. Chapter 1, "John Donne: Love's Philosophy" (pp. 19–58), presents a brief survey of Donne's career; comments on various portraits of him that have survived by way of illustrating his adoption of various dramatic poses in his poetry, "his way of constantly creating fictional roles out of aspects of his personality" (p. 26); and examines his philosophy of love as revealed primarily in the *Songs and Sonets.* Argues that the basic theme of all Donne's love poetry is "the problem of the place of human love in a physical world dominated by change and death" (p. 35). Attempts to show how Donne's "questing mind reveals and controls the contraries that meet within his being" (p. 58) by commenting on his love poems, especially "Aire and Angels," "Loves growth," "The Funerall," "The Relique," "The Anniversarie," "A Valediction: forbidding mourning," "The Extasie," "Lovers infinitenesse," "A Lecture upon the Shadow," and "On Himselfe." Mentions Donne throughout the remaining three chapters, primarily through comparisons and contrasts of his poetry with that of Carew, Crashaw, and Marvell. Points out the influence of Donne, especially on Carew and Marvell, and presents an analysis of Carew's elegy on Donne (pp. 97–100).

◄§ 118. MARTZ, LOUIS L., ed. *The Anchor Anthology of Seventeenth-Century Verse*, vol. 1. Edited with an introduction and notes by Louis L. Martz. (Anchor Seventeenth-Century Series, ACO-13a.) Garden City, N.Y.: Doubleday and Co. xliii, 525p.

Reprinted as *English Seventeenth-Century Verse*, vol. 1 (New York: Norton, 1973).

Parts of the introduction were originally published in *Master Poems of the English Language*, edited by Oscar Williams (New York: Trident Press,

1966), and in *The Poem of the Mind*, by Louis L. Martz (New York: Oxford University Press, 1966).

Revised edition of *The Meditative Poem: An Anthology of Seventeenth-Century Verse*, edited with introduction and notes by Louis L. Martz. (Anchor Seventeenth-Century Series, AC6.) Garden City, N.Y.: Doubleday and Co., 1963. The 1963 edition was reprinted in hardback (Stuart Editions), New York: New York University Press, 1963. Discusses in the introduction (pp. xix–xliii) general characteristics of metaphysical poetry and suggests that its use of the argued metaphor, the metaphysical conceit, is its most distinguishing feature. States that "poetry is metaphysical . . . when it seeks by complex analysis to find a central principle of being, within the bounds of a given situation" (p. xxv). Distinguishes between meditative and metaphysical poetry: "A meditative poem . . . represents the convergence of two arts upon a single object: in English poetry of the late Renaissance the art of meditation entered into and transformed its kindred art of poetry" (p. xxxii). Analyzes "Hymne to God my God, in my sicknesse" to show the convergence of the two arts of poetry and meditation (pp. xxxiii–xxxv). Maintains that "the ways in which a meditative action may be found in poetry are manifold: the meditative art is as changing, resourceful, and elusive as the mind in which the meditation is enacted" (p. xlii). Includes sixty-three poems by Donne with notes (pp. 31–132) and commentary (pp. 469–76).

◄§ 119. MAXWELL, J. C. "A Donne Echo in 'The Ring and the Book.'" *N&Q*, n.s. 16: 208.

Suggests that Browning likely had Donne's "The Bracelet" (line 112) in mind when he alluded to the restorative power of gold in *The Ring and the Book* (I, 89–90).

◄§ 120. MEADOWS, A. J. *The High Firmament: A Survey of Astronomy in English Literature*. Leicester: University of Leicester Press. x, 207p. ✓✓

Comments on how scientific discoveries and trends, especially in astronomy, are reflected in nonscientific English literature from roughly 1400 to 1900. Mentions Donne throughout by way of illustration. Shows that Donne's work reflects a keen interest in the scientific aspects of astronomy as well as in the moral and theological implications of the new discoveries and shows the influence of the work of Copernicus, Kepler, Galileo, William Gilbert, Sacrobosco, Clavius, Tycho Brahe, and others on the literary imagination of Donne.

◄§ 121. MENASCÈ, ESTHER. *Introduzione alla poesia di John Donne*. Milan: La Goliardica. 249p.

2d ed.: 1974, 217p. ("*A naked thinking heart*": *Introduzione alla poesia di John Donne*).

Historical and critical introduction to Donne's poetry, especially the *Songs and Sonets* and the *Divine Poems*, for Italian readers. Chapter 1 (pp. 1–

10) comments on Donne's reputation both in his own time and especially since World War I and argues that in his love poems and in his sacred verse Donne "si eleva al di sopra del suo tempo e trova accenti validi per ogni generazione" (p. 9). Chapter 2 (pp. 11–36) presents a biographical sketch, based heavily on Walton's account. Chapter 3 (pp. 37–45) gives an overall view of Donne's works and divides them into three major periods—those written before his marriage in 1601, those written from 1601 until his ordination in 1615, and those written from 1615 until his death in 1631—and comments on the posthumous publication of most of his work. Chapter 4 (pp. 46–84) surveys Donne's secular verse—the epigrams, the "Epithalamion made at Lincolnes Inne," the satires and elegies, the verse letters, and the *Songs and Sonets*—and concludes that Donne, more than any other poet, "ha saputo celebrare l'amore come miracolo, come sommo bene, ed esprimere l'estasi dell'unione totale con la persona amata" (p. 84). Chapter 5 (pp. 85–193) presents critical analyses of twenty-two poems from the *Songs and Sonets*. Chapter 6 (pp. 194–216) offers a general introduction to the *Divine Poems* as well as to the two *Anniversaries*. Chapter 7 (pp. 217–48) presents critical analyses of ten of the *Holy Sonnets* as well as critical commentary on "A Hymne to Christ, at the Authors last going into Germany," "Hymne to God my God, in my sicknesse," and "A Hymne to God the Father."

◄§ 122. MILGATE, W[ESLEY]. "The Date of Donne's Marriage: A Reply." *EA* 22: 66–67.

Reply to Edward Le Comte (entry 28). Disagrees with Le Comte (and Lady Mary Clive) that Donne married Ann More in January 1602 rather than in December 1601. Points out that the document upon which Le Comte based his argument "does not say that the marriage *took place* in January 1601/02, but that in that month Donne and Ann *were* free of any other marital obligations and *had* been properly married" (p. 66). A note by P. L. (Pierre Legouis ?) following the article comments on the debate and calls for a closure.

◄§ 123. MINER, EARL. *The Metaphysical Mode from Donne to Cowley.* Princeton: Princeton University Press. xix, 291p.

Pages 118–58 reprinted in *Seventeenth Century English Poetry: Modern Essays in Criticism*, edited by William R. Keast (entry 328), pp. 45–76.

Pages 99–117 reprinted in *The Metaphysical Poets: A Selection of Critical Essays*, edited by Gerald Hammond (entry 648), pp. 197–214.

The purpose of this study is "to discriminate poetic features that are particularly important to the Metaphysical style and differences possible within the style: in other words, what is lasting and what changes, what is general to the style and what is peculiar to individual writers" (p. xi). Argues (1) that metaphysical poetry is "private in mode, that it treats time and place in ways describable in terms of the 'dramatic,' the 'narrative,' the transcendent, the 'meditative,' and the 'argumentative'—and that these terms provide in their sequence something of a history of the development of Metaphysical poetry" (p. xi); (2) that "the wit of Metaphysical poetry can be characterized as definition, that is, as those logical or rhetorical processes bringing together or separating (whether in metaphor or idea) matters of similar or opposed classes; and as that dialectic, or those processes, that extend such matters by their relation in logical and rhetorical procedures" (pp. xi–xii); and (3) that "the thematic range of Metaphysical poetry can best be represented in terms of satiric denial and lyric affirmation" (p. xii). Chapter 1, "The Private Mode" (pp. 3–47), argues that the private mode is "the chief 'radical' of Metaphysical poetry, that feature differentiating it from the social and public modes of other poetry written in modern English before the late eighteenth century and the Romantic poets" (p. x). Chapter 2, "Forms of Perception: Time and Place" (pp. 48–117), explores various "forms, modes and structures of Metaphysical poems in terms of their versions of time and space" (p. x). Chapter 3, "Wit: Definition and Dialectic" (pp. 118–58), defines the "major features of Metaphysical wit in terms reflecting the poets' use of an older logic and rhetoric" (p. xi). Chapter 4, "Themes: Satire and Song" (pp. 159–213), comments on "the thematic range of Metaphysical poetry in terms of complementary elements" (p. xi), in terms of song and satire, "the former a tendency to affirmation, the latter a tendency to denial, both being capable of expression in lyricism or in satire, or in mixtures" (p. xi). Chapter 5, "Three Poems" (pp. 214–71), examines in detail Donne's "The Perfume," Herbert's "The Flower," and Marvell's "Nymph complaining for the death of her Faun." Mentions Donne throughout and frequently contrasts him with Herbert, Vaughan, Crashaw, Marvell, Traherne, Cowley, Quarles, and Dryden. Argues that "for wit, as for other central features of Metaphysical poetry, Donne is the Grand Master of the race" (p. 146). Comments on the distinguishing features of Donne's elegies, satires, love lyrics, religious poems, and occasional pieces. Considers his concept of love, time, and space; his uses of the private mode; his skillful blend of satire and lyric affirmation; his dramatic qualities; the sources of his wit and imagery; his uses of logic, rhetoric, dialectic, and definition; his uses of the emblematic and meditative modes; and his adaptation of the Roman love elegy. Comments on numerous individual poems, especially "Womans constancy," "The Canonization," "The Sunne Rising," "The Extasie," "A Valediction: forbidding mourning," "A nocturnall upon S. Lucies day," "Twicknam garden," "The Primrose," the *Elegies* and *Satyres*, and the two *Anniversaries*. Presents a very detailed reading of "The Perfume" (pp. 215–31), calling it "the finest of Donne's elegies and a presumptive proof that all of them deserve closer examination, and appreciation, than they have had" (p. 231).

∙§ 124. MINER, EARL, ed. *The Works of John Dryden: Poems 1685–1692.* H. T. Swedenberg, Jr., general editor; Earl Miner, associate general

editor; Vinton A. Dearing, textual editor. Vol. 3. Berkeley and Los
Angeles: University of California Press. xiv, 581p.

Comments on Dryden's borrowing from Donne in "Eleonora" and notes
numerous Donnean echoes and parallels in the poem (pp. 491–501).
Contains several other briefer references to Donne.

**ᴥᦒ 125. MOORE, THOMAS V. "Donne's Use of Uncertainty as a Vital Force
in *Satyre III.*" *MP* 67: 41–49.**

Argues that *Satyre III* is "not a skeptical disengagement from belief in
any given religious institution, but an urgent attempt to show what religious belief really requires of an individual" (p. 41). Suggests that Donne
maintains "that the goal is so important that every effort should be expended in order to reach it, and that success, if it is to come at all, will
come through an effort which seeks its impetus from the desperation of
the seeker's uncertainty" (p. 42). Sees the poem not as a statement of
Donne's personal quest so much as a "general plea for all men to re-
examine their religious views" (p. 42). Argues that the aim of the satire,
therefore, "is not to tell where true religion is, or what method must be
used to find it, but to describe the state of mind that is necessary if the
search is to have any chance of success" (p. 43).

**ᴥᦒ 126. MORRIS, WILLIAM E. "Donne's Use of Enallage in 'The Good-
Morrow.'" *LangQ* 8, nos. 1–2: 38.**

Reprinted with minor changes in *An&Q* 11 (1972): 19–20.

Notes that in lines 12 and 13 of "The good-morrow" Donne uses enallage, "the structural device of changing point of view (through shifts in
person, number, tense, or gender) within a sentence, shifting here from
one tense to another to indicate the progress of his thought." Suggests that
by shifting from the present to the present-perfect tense in these lines,
Donne is "attempting to express the atemporal prospect of explorers and
cartographers in their eternal (in the sense of apparently physically unend-
ing) and coextensive search for, and finding of, new physical worlds" in
contrast to the completion that the newly awakened lovers find in mutual
love.

**ᴥᦒ 127. MULDER, JOHN R. *The Temple of the Mind: Education and Lit-
erary Taste in Seventeenth-Century England.* (Pegasus Backgrounds
in English Literature.) New York: Pegasus. viii, 165p.**

Mentions Donne throughout this background study of significant aspects of seventeenth-century education and sensibility. Argues that, although education alone cannot account for the literature of the period,
an understanding of the curriculum and of the sensibility that it formed
helps the modern reader understand how Donne and other seventeenth-
century writers were read by their contemporaries and that "such knowledge is likely to bring us closer to the author's intention" (preface). Discusses (1) the training offered students in language, logic, and rhetoric; (2)

the emphasis of the curriculum on logical and dialectical argumentation; (3) seventeenth-century fondness for word play; (4) the central role that religion played in the formation of the seventeenth-century writer and reader; (5) Nowell's *Catechism* as an example and synopsis of religious ideas generally shared by writers of the period; and (6) the basic principles of biblical typology and the prevalence of typological thinking in the age. Stresses that Donne's contemporaries viewed poetry as a part of rhetoric, not as self-expression. Comments on "Loves Progress" (pp. 42–48) "because it illustrates the effect of intense training in logic and rhetoric upon literary style and taste" (p. 43). Calls the poem "an example of Donne's delight in the calculated abuse of prescribed formulae" (p. 43) and sees it, in part, as a satire on or a parody of scholasticism. Suggests that the poem has much in common with the *Praevaricatio* that was part of official academic disputations. Briefly comments on the rhetorical strategy of "A Valediction: forbidding mourning" (pp. 50–51), "The Canonization" (p. 51), and the *Anniversaries* (pp. 51, 55). Discusses "Death be not proud" (pp. 62–64) to show that Donne's contemporaries would have read the sonnet as a "cry of anguish," not as an example of Donne's confidence in eternity since "its logic is a series of false syllogisms, a hopeless argument from a helpless voice" (p. 63). Comments also briefly on Donne's uses of typology.

⋙ 128. MURPHY, JOHN. "The Young Donne and the Senecan Amble." *BRMMLA* 23: 163–67.
 Suggests that Donne's *Satyres* and verse epistles exhibit a new interest in syntactical experimentation, a "new and different sense of the ways in which English syntax, the necessary forms of complete and intelligible utterance, might be manipulated to evoke a new awareness and refocus an old awareness of the self and the world" (p. 164). Points out that Donne "exploits and controls the equivocatings of syntax to express, or better, to dramatize a genuinely metaphysical intuition under the aegis of wit" (p. 165) and demonstrates Donne's uses of syntactical ambiguity by commenting on lines from "The Calme," *Satyre I*, and *Satyre II*.

⋙ 129. MURRIN, MICHAEL. "The End of Allegory," in *The Veil of Allegory: Some Notes Toward a Theory of Allegorical Rhetoric in the English Renaissance*, pp. 167–212. Chicago: University of Chicago Press.
 Discusses how poets and theorists like Puttenham, Jonson, and Sidney "*as a group* reversed the basic axioms of allegorical rhetoric" and how "the reactions of these critics to Spenser's language manifested their practical rejection of his type of poetry" (p. 167). Suggests that Sidney and Donne represent a transitional phase of development between the poetry of the Renaissance and that of the Restoration. Sees some resemblances between Donne and Spenser, but, unlike the earlier poet, Donne "does not identify poetry with allegory" but sees it as proceeding "from wit or invention, of which allegory is a variety" (p. 190). Points out that Donne also differs

from the allegorists in that he "achieves immortality not for his vision but for himself, dreaming, thinking, and feeling" (p. 193). Compares and contrasts Donne with Sidney, Puttenham, Spenser, Jonson, and Herbert and concludes that, although he eludes classification, Donne "belongs with the craftsmen as a witty maker, but on the crucial matter of audience accommodation he sides with Spenser" (p. 194).

⋙ 130. NELLY, UNA. *The Poet Donne: A Study in His Dialectic Method.* Cork, Ire.: Cork University Press. 165p.
    Discusses the logical argumentation of Donne's poetry as well as its dialectical structure and tone and argues that Donne is a great poet "because he takes a hard look at reality: the reality of his own complex emotional and intellectual life, as well as that of the human situation in which he finds himself" (p. 4). Traces the sources of Donne's dialectical habit of mind to his own temperament, his environment and times, and to the formulative influence of his education at Oxford. Chapter 1, "The Microcosm of the Self" (pp. 7–18), discusses the dialectic in Donne's personal life, his own inward drama and conflicts, his sense of dualism and opposing loyalties, and comments on "The Blossome" as typical of Donne's subject matter and subtlety. Chapter 2, "The Macrocosm" (pp. 20–31), discusses the dialectical external events of Donne's time, especially the conflicts generated by the introduction of the "new philosophy," and comments on Donne's relationship to the poetry of his age, with an extended commentary on "Song: Goe and catche a falling starre" and "The Indifferent." Chapter 3, "The Macrocosm of the University" (pp. 33–57), explores the influence of the curriculum at Oxford with its emphasis on Aristotelianism, dialectical argumentation, and academic disputation, followed by a deemphasizing of the claims for Ramism. Chapter 4, "The Dialectic of Reality" (pp. 59–109), examines Donne's vision of reality and the resulting realism, honesty, and wit in his verse; discusses Donne's uses of conceit, paradox, and pun as tools in his dialectical method; and explains Donne's endorsement of the Aristotelian "Mean" in both his poetry and sermons. Chapter 5, "The Dialectic of Body and Soul in the Love Poems" (pp. 111–32), examines the theme of the interdependence of the body and soul in Donne's love poetry, especially as seen in "Aire and Angels" and "The Extasie," and comments on his insistence on the importance of mutual love, especially as evidenced in "The good-morrow," "The Sunne Rising," "A Lecture upon the Shadow," and "The Anniversarie." Chapter 6, "The Dialectic of Ultimate Reality in the *Divine Poems*" (pp. 134–50), discusses the *Anniversaries*, the *Holy Sonnets*, and "Hymne to God my God, in my sicknesse" and challenges Martz's argument concerning the central importance of meditation in Donne's religious verse. Maintains, in the conclusion (pp. 152–58), that what distinguishes Donne from other poets who employ a dialectical method "is the urgency of the passion pulsating through the dialectic, transforming it, even from the early days of *Satyre III*, from a dusty and coldly-correct academic exercise,

into a deeply personal search for truth; a passionate analysis of reality—
not just physical or material reality—but that metaphysical reality which
has its expression in man's own composite being, in all his conscious states
of thinking and feeling, particularly in the intimate psychosomatic relationship of human love, and which can have its dénouement only in the
ultimate, synthesizing Cause of reality, the very Ground of our Being, the
Creator Himself" (p. 154). Appendix A contains a brief passage from M. J.
Bremond's *Prayer and Poetry* (1927); Appendix B, a passage from Book X
of St. Augustine's *Confessions*. Selected bibliography.

⤜§ 131. NICHOLS, J. G. *The Poetry of Ben Jonson*. London: Routledge
& Kegan Paul. x, 177p.
Numerous references throughout to Donne. Compares and contrasts
Donne's poetry with that of Jonson, laments the past unfavorable comparisons that have been urged by modern critics, and argues that Jonson
clearly "requires a different sort of appreciation from that which Donne
requires" (p. 147). Shows that Jonson not only admired and appreciated
and even imitated Donne's poetry on occasion but that he was also fundamentally just, not envious or narrow, in his criticism of Donne's art.
Discusses, in particular, the disputed authorship of four elegies in *Under-
woods* and agrees with Helen Gardner that all four poems, including "The
Expostulation," belong to Jonson (pp. 5–7).

⤜§ 132. OGOSHI, KAZUSO. "Active and Passive Expression," in *Kotoba to
Shi* [Words and Poetry], pp. 124–31. Kyoto: Aporosha.
Presents a translation of "The Relique" with a brief critical commentary.

⤜§ 133. ORMOND, RICHARD, AND LEONEE ORMOND. *Great Poets*. London: Her Majesty's Stationery Office. 51p.
Reproduces a portrait of Donne by an unknown artist after a 1616 miniature by Isaac Oliver in the National Portrait Gallery along with "Batter
my heart," a brief biographical sketch, and a selection from Walton's *Life
of Dr. Donne* (1670) that describes Donne's appearance (pp. 14–15).

⤜§ 134. OSAWA, MINORU, ed. *Sekai Meishi Kanshō Jiten* [A Dictionary
of World Famous Poems]. Tokyo: Tokyōdo. 468p.
Several references to Donne throughout (in relation to T. S. Eliot,
Cowley, George Herbert, Marlowe, and the conceit). Major entry (pp.
173–75) presents a brief biographical sketch of Donne followed by a translation into Japanese of "A Valediction: of weeping." Offers general appreciative comments that point out Donne's blending of passion and logic,
his uses of logical argumentation, his employment of scientific and technical materials, and his uses of paradox.

⤜§ 135. PARTRIDGE, A. C. *Tudor to Augustan English: A Study in Syntax and Style from Caxton to Johnson*. (The Language Library, ed-

ited by Eric Partridge and Simeon Potter.) London: André Deutsch. 242p.

Relates the development of the English language to the literature during the period 1485 to 1785 "by analysing the effect of syntax upon style, and the importance of grammar to writing generally" (preface). Comments briefly on Donne's use of epithets (pp. 57–58) and on his placing of sonorous words at or near the end of the period in his sermons (p. 223). Presents a short stylistic analysis of Meditation 17 of *Devotions upon Emergent Occasions*: "This is reflective prose; nevertheless it preserves the usual structure of Donne's paragraphs in the Sermons, working up to an eloquent moralizing crescendo, often with resounding Latin polysyllables" (p. 74).

꿍 136. PERELLA, NICOLAS JAMES. *The Kiss Sacred and Profane: An Interpretative History of Kiss Symbolism and Related Religio-Erotic Themes.* Berkeley and Los Angeles: University of California Press. 356p.

Briefly comments on Donne's use of the kiss in "The Expiration," "To Sr Henry Wotton: Sir, more then kisses," and "A Valediction: forbidding mourning" (pp. 235, 239). Discusses also "The Extasie" and concludes that, although it does not totally repudiate Platonic love, "it does argue against the 'Platonic' idea that the body is by necessity the soul's tomb" (p. 240). Quotes from one of Donne's sermons that contains a long disquisition on the meaning of the kiss and says that "it is fascinating to see Donne quoting side by side the Platonic kiss conceit (as given by Aulus Gellius) and St. Ambrose on the divine kiss, and just as fascinating to find him making the connection between the kiss and death as ways or metaphors for the soul's spiritual migration and union with God" (p. 243). Suggests that "the most compelling idea we find here associated by Donne with the kiss—as indeed it was in the Song of Songs and in medieval writers—is that *love is as strong as death.* For it is the 'kiss' that does now what otherwise only death can do: unite the soul with God" (p. 243).

꿍 137. PEROSA, SERGIO. "La poesia metafisica," in *Storia della letteratura inglese,* 1: 116–24. (Letteratura Universale, vol. 21, ed. Luigi Santucci.) Milan: Fratelli Fabbri Editori.

Comments briefly on the spiritual crises presented in metaphysical poetry and presents a general introduction to Donne's life and to his poetry and prose (pp. 116–20), especially his religious writings. Says that Donne "fu la voce della Chiesa anglicana e, di conseguenza, il più grande predicatore di moda del suo tempo" and calls the *Holy Sonnets* "le cose più intensamente religiose che ci abbia dato la letteratura inglese" (p. 120). Briefly compares and contrasts Donne with Herbert, Crashaw, Vaughan, and Marvell. Mentions Donne throughout the volume and calls *Death's Duell* "il capolavoro del secentismo macabro" (p. 113).

✒ 138. PIPER, WILLIAM BOWMAN. *The Heroic Couplet*. Cleveland and London: The Press of Case Western Reserve University. xi, 454p.

Mentions Donne throughout this brief history of the development of the heroic couplet from Chaucer to Keats. Surveys also the varieties of its poetic uses and centers attention on the years 1585–1785, during which time "the form reveals a living and developing tradition" (p. 4). Contains twenty-five critical essays on individual poets, including one on Donne (pp. 206–9). Shows that Donne "responded to virtually every aspect of the heroic couplet which his age had discovered, using the form eclectically to embellish and enrich his own special creative intentions" (p. 209). Contrasts Donne's *Satyre II* with Marston's satires to show that Donne "made a far greater use and a far more illuminating use of the couplet's definitive and emphatic qualities than Marston did" (p. 61). Notes that Donne wrote nearly as much of his poetry in heroic couplets as in all other forms combined and suggests that "the satires reveal Donne's remarkable wit and vigor, probably, better than any other of his couplet poems" (p. 208). Discusses the similarities and differences between Donne's *Satyre II* and Pope's redaction of it to show that Donne stresses wit and drama while Pope emphasizes politeness and lucidity. Briefly mentions the influence of Ovid, Juvenal, Martial, and the medieval complaint on Donne's uses of the couplet.

✒ 139. QUINN, DENNIS. "Donne and the Wane of Wonder." *ELH* 36: 626–47.

Points out that Donne "stands at the end of the Classical-Christian tradition of wonder which prevailed in the West for centuries" (p. 626) and that "at a time when wonder was beginning to fall into disrepute, disuse, and abuse, John Donne held to the traditional view formulated by the great men of the near and distant past" (p. 647). Examines this traditional concept "by observing Donne's explicit statements about wonder, by considering the practical effect of theory on his poetic practice, and by noting, in passing, the tradition upon which Donne drew" (p. 626). Shows that Donne's view of wonder affects not only his intellectual perceptions but also his style, since wonder was closely associated with metaphor and obscurity, and also points out that Donne's view of wonder helps explain his attitudes toward mystery and miracles.

✒ 140. ———. "Donne's *Anniversaries* as Celebration." *SEL* 9: 97–105.

Reprinted in *Essential Articles for the Study of John Donne's Poetry*, edited by John R. Roberts (entry 786), pp. 368–73.

Argues that the *Anniversaries* are "commemorative, public, and joyful songs of praise" and thus "celebratory in the fullest sense of the term" (p. 97). Maintains that the poems "confront the full horror of death only to emerge into the light of Elizabeth's joy" and that the element of praise that "dominates the poems is that part of celebration which affirms the goodness of the order of things" (p. 97). Maintains, therefore, that when Donne "dispraises sin and 'the world', he does not reject God's order but rather emphasizes its restoration in the virtue of Elizabeth" (p. 97). Suggests that Donne is fully aware of the celebratory and festive nature of his poems, as reflected in *The first Anniversary*, lines 455–66.

◆§ 141. RAGO, HENRY. "The Poet in His Poem." *Poetry* 113, no. 6: 413–20.
Reprinted in *PMMLA* 1 (1969): 52–58.
Discusses the relationship of poetry to personality and distinguishes between symbol and emblem as "two kinds of sign, or two ways of using signs, each in one of two traditions that have had conspicuous relevance for the poet in our age" (p. 413). Uses several brief examples from Donne's poetry to illustrate the manner, virtues, methods of thought and art, characteristic figures, and psychology of the emblematic mode.

◆§ 142. RAUBER, D. F. "Some 'Metaphysical' Aspects of the Homeric Simile." *Classical Journal* 65: 97–103.
Suggests that Donne's use of the extended figure in stanzas 2 and 3 of "Hymne to God my God, in my sicknesse" can be viewed as "a topological distortion of the advanced Homeric simile" and "as pressing forward a process of poetic complication clearly present in Homer's use of the figure, and furthermore, carrying out the development exactly upon the lines already laid down by the epic poet" (p. 102).

◆§ 143. ROY, V. K., AND R. C. KAPOOR. *John Donne and Metaphysical Poetry*. With a foreword by Vikramaditya Rai. Delhi: Doaba House. x, 412p.
Rev. ed.: 1973. (Part I, Chapter 5 "recast to concretize the affinity between Donne's work and life and literature in our own time" [preface to the revised edition].)
Suggests that Donne's poems "reveal a synthesis of the individual, the spirit of the age and of the eternity of truth beyond his age" and attempts "to show the inseparable bond between his theme and form and to emphasize his attitude of non-commitment that forestalls any regimentation" (p. iii). Argues that "Donne's age must be considered as the beginning of the modern age" (p. 148). Divided into two major parts: (1) an introduction to the nature of metaphysical poetry and specifically to the poetry of Donne (pp. 1–150) and (2) a selection of twenty-nine poems with introductions, commentaries, and notes on each (pp. 151–412). Part I is divided into five chapters: (1) "The Two Worlds of Metaphysical Poetry" discusses the confrontation between the medieval and Renaissance world views; (2) "Metaphysical Poetry" presents a brief introduction to eight metaphysical poets—Donne, Herbert, Carew, Crashaw, Vaughan, Marvell, Cowley, and Herrick—and to the basic elements and style of metaphysical poetry, such as its baroque sensibility, its intellectuality and concentration, its "unified sensibility," its uses of wit, conceit, imagery, diction,

and versification, and its philosophical content; (3) "John Donne: An Attempt at an Interpretative Life Sketch"; (4) "John Donne the Poet" comments on the influence of the "new philosophy" on the poet's mind and sensibilities and discusses themes and techniques of his poetry, especially his attitudes toward love and religion; and (5) "Donne and Our Age" offers a sketch of the modernity of Donne's poetry and sensibility. In Part II the following poems are discussed: "The good-morrow," "Song: Goe, and catche a falling starre," "The Sunne Rising," "The Canonization," "Song: Sweetest love, I do not goe," "Aire and Angels," "The Anniversarie," "Twicknam garden," "A Valediction: of weeping," "The Flea," "A nocturnall upon S. Lucies day," "A Valediction: forbidding mourning," "The Extasie," "The Blossome," "The Relique," "This is my playes last scene," "At the round earths imagin'd corners," "Death be not proud," "Batter my heart," "Since she whom I lov'd," "Show me deare Christ," "Goodfriday, 1613. Riding Westward," "A Hymne to God the Father," "On his Mistris," "Going to Bed," *Satyre III, The Progresse of the Soule*, and the two *Anniversaries*.

•⊰ 144. RUTHVEN, K. K. *The Conceit*. (The Critical Idiom, edited by John D. Jump, vol. 4.) London: Methuen & Co. 70p.

Discusses the word *conceit*, the theoretical bases of conceits, some common types, and the decline of its use. Mentions Donne throughout and comments briefly on his uses of the numerologial conceit in "The Primrose" and his inversion of Petrarchan standards in "The Autumnall."

•⊰ 145. SAUL, GEORGE BRANDON. "The Lyric," in *Concise Introduction to Types of Literature in English*, pp. 29–41. Philadelphia: The Walton Press.

Describes Donne as "intricate, tangled, gnarled, highly subjective, speculative, analytical, intellectual, and, although basically logical, probably overrated as a poet because of the extravagant genuflections of the twentieth-century 'new criticism'" (p. 33). Advises the reader to use discrimination in seeking out the best of Donne's poems.

•⊰ 146. SAYAMA, EITARO. *John Donne: The Middle Phase—A Study Chiefly of the* Anniversaries. (Seijo English Monographs, no. 4.) Tokyo: Seijo University. ii, 137p.

Divided into two major parts: "Works in Prose and Verse Preceding the *Anniversaries*" (pp. 1–29), with a short preface (pp. i–ii); and (2) The *Anniversaries* (pp. 30–122), followed by a conclusion (pp. 123–36). Part 1 surveys for the Japanese reader *Biathanatos, Pseudo-Martyr, Ignatius his Conclave*, some of the verse epistles, *La Corona, The Litanie*, and the *Holy Sonnets*. Part 2 outlines the occasion and publication of the *Anniversaries* as well as their critical reception; presents an analysis of the structure of the two poems suggested by Louis Martz and O. B. Hardison; and paraphrases the poems, along with "A Funerall Elegie," and comments on the various themes in the poems—the "idea of a woman," the decay of the world, and the soul and death. Relies heavily on the critical positions of earlier scholars, especially Louis Martz, Richard Hughes, and Marjorie Nicolson. Agrees essentially with Martz that "considered as a whole, and especially in their structure, the *Anniversaries* are composed after the pattern of the meditation exercises" (p. 124). Suggests that the middle phase of Donne's career should be seen as a significant transition between Jack and John Donne and that, while admitting interpretations on many levels, the *Anniversaries* should be seen as Donne's "struggle in quest of a wider meaning in life" (p. 127).

◀§ 147. SCHIMMEL, ANNEMARIE, ed. *John Donne nacktes Denkendes Herz: Aus seinen poetischen Schriften und Prosawerken.* Ausgewählt, übersetzt und eingeleitet von Annemarie Schimmel. Cologne: Jakob Hegner. 195p.

Anthologizes selections from Donne's poetry and prose. Contains an introduction (pp. 11–34) with a short biographical sketch of Donne and a brief history of his critical reception through the centuries. Briefly compares Donne with Persian poetry. Presents German translations (with brief critical introductions) from the *Songs and Sonets* and the *Elegies* (pp. 35–77), *Paradoxes and Problemes* (pp. 78–83); both verse and prose letters (pp. 84–96); the *Divine Poems* (pp. 97–122); *Devotions upon Emergent Occasions* (pp. 123–78); and the sermons (pp. 179–91). Brief, unannotated bibliography (pp. 192–95).

◀§ 148. SCHOLES, ROBERT. "Word Games," in *Elements of Poetry*, pp. 33–58. New York: Oxford University Press.

Comments very briefly on Donne's ingenious, ironic, and playful uses of the conceit in "The Flea" (pp. 41–43, 53). Points out that Donne develops the conceit in a highly dramatic context and thus the images of the poem become part of the persuasive argument.

◀§ 149. SELDEN, R. "Donne's 'The Dampe', Lines 22–24." *MLR* 64: 726–27.

Argues that Donne in lines 22–24 of "The Dampe" intends "an indirect but recognizable allusion to a theme (or 'topos') descended from the Greek Anthology" (p. 727), namely the Spartan cult of an armed Aphrodite, which Donne fuses with the traditional theme of love as war that he got from Ovid, Tibullus, and Propertius. Points out that numerous Latin translations of *The Greek Anthology* were readily accessible in Donne's time; that Donne may have known T. Kendell's *Flowers of Epigrams* (1577), which contains three epigrams on the subject translated into English; and that the currency of the topic can be inferred from two epigrams of John Owen (1607) and that its continuance can be seen in two epigrams in Crashaw's *Delights of the Muses* (1646). Rejects, therefore, Helen Gardner's suggestions that Donne may have intended "in that" rather than "naked" in line 24.

ᕯ 150. SEYMOUR-SMITH, MARTIN. "John Donne (c. 1572–1631)," in
Poets Through Their Letters: From the Tudors to Coleridge, pp. 84–
122. New York: Holt, Rinehart and Winston.
Calls Donne "the first English poet whose letters have survived in significant bulk" (p. 84). Maintains that, although he infrequently mentions
his own poetry directly in his letters and although few new biographical
revelations emerge, the more than two hundred extant letters provide "an
indispensable picture of their author, which cannot be found elsewhere"
(p. 85). Presents a detailed biographical sketch of Donne, often quoting
from and referring to his letters when they illuminate some aspect of his
life or literary activity. Attempts to show that much of Donne's poetry was
shaped by his experiences and was not simply based on abstract philosophical notions. Analyzes, for example, "Loves Alchymie" (pp. 106–12) to
show how the poem faithfully reflects Donne's complex mental state during his middle years. Sees the major thematic concern of "Twicknam garden" as that of how to love sexually without being selfish and how to
perform sexually without feeling guilt and argues that in "The Extasie"
Donne describes and justifies his sexual ideals but argues neither for nor
against sex. Suggests that Donne's obsession with death was closely connected with sexual guilt and that "he was tormented by the masturbatory,
self-satisfying, purely relief-giving aspects of his sexual contact with his
wife" (p. 105).

ᕯ 151. SHAWCROSS, JOHN T., AND DAVID RONALD EMMA, eds.
Seventeenth-Century English Poetry. (Lippincott College English
Series.) Philadelphia and New York: J.B. Lippincott Co. xvii, 636p.
Contains a general introduction to seventeenth-century poetry (pp. 1–
11) and a general selected bibliography (pp. 13–14). Presents a brief introduction to Donne's life and poetry, with a selected bibliography (pp. 15–
18), and reproduces forty-five poems with explanatory notes (pp. 18–78).

ᕯ 152. SHINODA, HAJIME, AYAKO SHINODA, REIJI NAKAGAWA, YUICHI
TAKAMATSU, AND JUNNOSUKE SAWASAKI, eds. *Uta to Sonnet [Songs
and Sonets]*, in *Sekai Meishi Shū* 1, pp. 3–123. Tokyo: Heibonsha.
Translates into Japanese the *Songs and Sonets*, with no notes and no
commentary.

ᕯ 153. SICHERMAN, CAROL MARKS. "The Mocking Voices of Donne
and Marvell." *BuR* 17, ii: 32–46.
Comments on the interplay between the poet and speaker of a poem
and comments specifically on poems by Donne "in which the speaker is
a critic passing judgment on others but lacking in self-irony, a critic who,
although he may express some of the poet's ideas, is not his spokesman
and who, through some fanaticism or some exaggerated trait of personality, is himself mocked or at the very least teased by his creator" (p. 34).
Analyzes "Confined Love," a poem in which the whole argument of the

female speaker "is built on sand; and its collapse mocks her pretentions to logic and philanthropy, at the same time endorsing the ideas she opposes" (p. 35). Comments on other mocked mockers in "Breake of day," "Farewell to love," "The Indifferent," "Loves diet," "Loves Usury," "Change," "The Perfume," and *Satyre I.*

❧ 154. SIMPSON, ARTHUR L., JR. "Donne's *Holy Sonnets*, XII." *Expl* 27: Item 75.
Points out how certain biblical allusions in "Why are wee by all creatures waited on?" explain "why certain normally safe animals are pictured as dangerous" and, more importantly, give the poem "at the literal and topical level, as well as at that of figure and allusion, an additional principle of structural unity which relates basic elements of mood and tone (awe, wonder) to the central theme and paradox of the atonement."

❧ 155. STEWART, JACK F. "Image and Idea in Donne's 'The Good-Morrow.'" *Discourse* 12: 465–76.
Explicates "The good-morrow" in detail to show that it is "a poem of ecstatic self-discovery and mutuality, which gives universal reference to private emotion, by exploiting Elizabethan geography and Scholastic theology, thus mingling New World, Old World, and Other World" (p. 473). Argues that Donne's "dramatic strategy actualizes the emotion, while his intellectual strategy objectifies it, and gives it a degree of permanence" (p. 473).

❧ 156. ―――. "Irony in Donne's 'The Funerall.'" *Discourse* 12: 193–99.
Argues that in "The Funerall" the "mood of seemingly bitter frustration is controlled by irony, and refined by a metaphysical apparatus, which blends elements of theology, anatomy, and hagiolatry" (p. 193). Explicates the poem, commenting on its dramatic elements, its elaborate uses of conceit and metaphor, and its witty dialectic, to show that it can be read on two levels: "the surface level of amorous complaint and the underlying level of restrained irony" (p. 197).

❧ 157. STRONG, ROY. *The English Icon: Elizabethan & Jacobean Portraiture.* London: The Paul Mellon Foundation for British Art in association with Routledge and Kegan Paul; New Haven: Yale University Press. xvi, 388p.
Reproduces the oil portrait of Donne circa 1595 by an unknown artist and owned by the Marquess of Lothian (p. 37). Reprints (pp. 352–54) his "The Elizabethan Malady: Melancholy in Elizabethan and Jacobean Portraiture" from *Apollo* 79 (1964): 264–69, in which he describes the Lothian portrait and calls it "the most famous of all the melancholy love-portraits" (p. 353).

•◄§ 158. ———. *National Portrait Gallery: Tudor & Jacobean Portraits.*
2 vols. London: Her Majesty's Stationery Office. Vol. 1: The Text,
xiv, 390p.; Vol. 2: Plates, no pagination.
Brief biographical sketch of Donne followed by an iconographical description of an oil-on-canvas portrait of Donne (NPG 1849) by an unknown artist (plate 122), an enlarged copy of a miniature dated 1616 by
Isaac Oliver in the Royal Collection (pp. 65–66). Summarizes the iconography of Donne (p. 66) contained in Geoffrey Keynes, *Bibliography of
the Works of Dr. John Donne* (2d ed., 1932), pp. 182–84. In Volume 2
reproduces, in addition to the aforementioned oil portrait, (1) the Lothian
portrait (plate 118); (2) a portrait miniature by William Marshall (plate
119); (3) a portrait miniature by Isaac Oliver (plate 120); (4) a circular
portrait by an unknown artist, now housed in the Deanery of St. Paul's
Cathedral (plate 121), a copy of which is in the Dyce Collection in the
Victoria and Albert Museum; and (5) the stone effigy by Nicholas Stone
in St. Paul's Cathedral (plate 123).

•◄§ 159. STRONG, ROY, ed. *The Elizabethan Image: Painting in England, 1540–1620.* London: The Tate Gallery. 88p.
Reproduces the oil portrait of Donne circa 1595 by an unknown artist
and owned currently by the Marquess of Lothian (p. 66) and presents a
brief description of the portrait.

•◄§ 160. TASHIRO, TOM T. "English Poets, Egyptian Onions, and the
Protestant View of the Eucharist." *JHI* 30: 563–78.
Points out that Juvenal in his Fifteenth Satire says that Egyptians never
ate onions because they believed them to be vegetable deities but were not
reluctant to practice cannibalism. Relates how the onion became a symbol of cannibalism and was used by writers to attack the notion of the
Eucharist. Points out, for instance, that in *The second Anniversarie* (lines
423–31) Donne juxtaposes onions and corn (wheat) and wine, thus attacking "not only the Eucharist but the priesthood that administer the
Communion, since *onions* replaces *oil* from the traditional sequence, 'corn,
wine, and oil,' the last referring to Ordination through anointment and
the mystic laying-on of the hands" (p. 571). Suggests that by extension
Donne also attacks the notion of the remission of sins through Extreme
Unction and, because of the traditional association of Juvenal's onions
with cannibalism, asks "whether cannibalism is really worse than the eating of God" (p. 571). Notes that Anglicans only remembered Christ's sacrifice in the Eucharist, but Catholics *ate* their God in Holy Communion.

•◄§ 161. THOMAS, DONALD. "Censorship Before Publication: 1475–1695,"
in *A Long Time Burning: The History of Literary Censorship in England,* pp. 8–33. London: Routledge & Kegan Paul.
Briefly discusses Donne's knowledge of Aretino (p. 19). Points out a
letter of 1600 addressed to Sir Henry Wotton by Donne in which Donne

suggests that the condemnation of Aretino by the Catholic Church had only served to call attention to Aretino's books. Notes also that in *Ignatius his Conclave* Donne refers to Aretino's "licentious pictures," a reference to the pictures of Guilio Romano that accompanied Aretino's *Sonnetti Lussuriosi* (1527). For a reply, see Anthony S. G. Edwards, entry 412.

🔖 162. UNTERMEYER, LOUIS. *The Pursuit of Poetry: A Guide to Its Understanding and Appreciation with an Explanation of Its Forms and a Dictionary of Poetic Terms.* New York: Simon and Schuster. 318p.

Numerous scattered references to and brief comments on Donne. Comments on Donne's choice of an unlikely poetic subject in "The Flea" (pp. 18, 25, 66) and on his uses of the conceit in "The Flea" and in "A Valediction: forbidding mourning" (pp. 66–69). Sees many of Donne's poems as a perfect blending of sound and sense (p. 49) and suggests that his poetry is no less complex than is modern poetry (p. 73). Points out that lines in John Crowe Ransom's "Winter Remembered" have the same image-effect as do lines in Donne's "The Comparison" (p. 57) and that there are poetic resonances in the *Devotions upon Emergent Occasions* that make the division between prose and poetry often difficult (p. 121). Mentions Donne in the definition of paradox (p. 234) and of pathetic fallacy (p. 247).

🔖 163. VICKERS, BRIAN, ed. "John Donne, 1573–1631," in *Seventeenth-Century Prose: An Anthology*, pp. 93–117. (Longmans' English Series.) London and Harlow: Longmans, Green and Co.

Briefly discusses the eloquence of Donne's sermons (pp. 93–97), stressing in particular Donne's complex use of imagery and his inventive uses of syntactical symmetry. Briefly contrasts Donne with Lancelot Andrewes: "Donne is more exciting, sensational, rhetorical than Andrewes, but not so thoughtful or thought-provoking, working rather on our emotions with the twin poles of Christian exhortation, rewards and punishments, heaven and hell" (p. 93). Reproduces "The Second of my Prebend Sermons Upon My Five Psalms Preached at St. Paul's, January 29, 1626" (pp. 97–117). Notes (pp. 240–41) and brief biographical sketch (pp. 257–58). Highly selected bibliography (pp. 263–66).

🔖 164. VOSS, A[NTHONY] E[DEN]. "The Structure of Donne's *Anniversaries*." *ESA* 12: 1–30.

Argues for "the unity, integrity, and sequence of *An Anatomie of the World*, *A Funerall Elegie*, and *Of the Progresse of the Soule*, by recognizing in these poems a strong element of poetic self-consciousness, taking the 'I' figure of the poem as Donne the poet explicitly, rather than simply one extravagantly bereaved by the death of a young girl he had never seen" and shows that "the occasion and fact of the death enable Donne to dismiss the various disciplines—philosophy, aesthetics, rhetoric among them— by which man attempts to maintain an illusion of stability and wholeness in the face of the changeableness and partiality of human life, as he asserts the unique value of 'verse'" (p. 1). Sees both *An Anatomie* and *A Funerall Elegie* as Donne's defense of verse—"the first private, the second public: in the first Donne defends his medium for its creative power, its ability to embody 'she,' while in the second he defends it as a means of 'vertuous deeds'" (p. 19). Notes that *An Anatomie*, then, is concerned both with chronicling the death and with awakening the world "to the possibilities of language in Augustine's terms as a means to teach and to remind" (p. 20), but that in the second anniversary poem "verse becomes the dominant mode, and the incantatory rhythm which rises only in the eulogies and refrains of the *Anatomie* become pervasive of the whole poem" (p. 20). Describes also *An Anatomie* as Donne's *via negativa* and *Of the Progresse of the Soule* as his *via affirmativa* and shows that he "rejects the negative in so far as it negates his own medium; as either poet or preacher, he cannot reject words themselves" (p. 30). Concludes that "religious faith and poetic recognition are virtually indistinguishable in these poems" and suggests that "they combine to effect through words the transformation of the nightmare landscape of the fallen world to the vision of heaven" (p. 30).

⌐§ 165. WANNINGER, MARY TENNY. "Donne's *Holy Sonnets*, XIV." *Expl* 28: Item 37.

Points out that the essential principle of duality in "Batter my heart" extends beyond merely its paradoxical theme and two kinds of metaphor to include "duality of sonnet structure, sentence structure, and dramatic structure." Shows that, in addition to the obvious dualities of war and love, profane love and sacred love, the poem opposes "good and evil, natural and counter-natural forces, illegality and legality, reason and passion, captivity and freedom, active love and passive love, prebaptismal sin and postbaptismal sin, and the opposite boundaries of time." Argues that "this progression of antithetical concepts, metaphorically linked and culminating in violent paradox, reflects the divided nature of sinful man and serves to unify the desperate prayer of a supplicant who painfully acknowledges his weakness while calling upon a 'three person'd God' to exert a superior strength that will assure redemptive union."

⌐§ 166. WARNKE, FRANK J. "Das Spielelement in der Liebeslyrik des Barock." *Arcadia* 4: 225–37.

Reprinted, in part, and expanded as Chapter 5 of *Versions of Baroque: European Literature in the Seventeenth Century*, pp. 90–129 (entry 524). Discusses the serious playfulness in baroque lyric poetry and notes that "in solch leidenschaftlichen und tiefsinnigen Aussagan wie *The Good Morrow, Loves Infiniteness, The Anniversarie* und *The Extasie* beschwört Donne eine spielerische, fast lustige Atmosphäre, ohne dabei den Ernst seiner Aussagen im geringsten zu beeinträchtigen" (p. 227). Calls the *Songs and Sonets* a veritable compendium of baroque amorous attitudes and discusses, in particular, the playfulness of "The Canonization" as an example of baroque comic hyperbole and compares Donne to several Continental baroque poets, including Góngora, Marino, Hofmannswaldau, Quevedo, Saint-Amant, Paul Fleming, and others.

◄§ 167. WATSON, GEORGE. *The Study of Literature.* New York: Charles Scribner's Sons. 237p.

Points out that, although Donne's *Songs and Sonets* imitate the metrical forms and even the doctrines of earlier European love poetry, they do not merely imitate nor are they simply parodies of a literary past. Discusses briefly "The Relique" as an example of Donne's complex uses of his literary past and concludes that the poem clearly echoes many strands of a long tradition but that "there is only one thing, in the absolute sense, that is like this poem, and that is itself" (p. 101). Brief references throughout to Donne. Comments on Dryden's *Of Dramatick Poesie* (1668) and calls it a "subtly affectionate pastiche of a Metaphysical poem" (p. 99).

◄§ 168. WEISS, WOLFGANG. "Die Air im Stilwandel." *Anglia* 87: 201–16.

Describes the form of the seventeenth-century English lyric as a composite, specifically a blend of the *ordo naturalis* poetic vehicle with what poets were able to borrow from the available anthologies of airs. Reviews various editions of airs available to poets; comments on lyrical motifs, music, melody, and variations; and describes how the air entered the lyric tradition and remained a dynamic aspect of the genre. Refers to several of Donne's poems, by way of examples, specifically "The triple Foole" and "Lovers infinitenesse." Maintains that the inherited poetic materials remained primary but suggests that the musical aspects of the form should be more thoroughly studied.

◄§ 169. WILLIAMS, GORDON I. "The Metamorphosis of an Elizabethan Conceit." *Trivium* 4: 96–107.

Discusses various uses of the popular Renaissance theme in English love poetry of the desire of the lover to be transformed into something dear and/or near to the beloved. Mentions Donne's use of the theme in "Going to Bed," "The Flea," and a doubtful sonnet. Also suggests that when Donne "wishes to submerge his personality in love for his mistress, he envisions a two-way process: by some mystic chemistry the lovers will combine to form a single entity, so far exceeding the sum of its parts as to partake of the immortal" (pp. 102–3), a view quite different from that expressed by Anacreon: "Donne's is a positive desire, an urge to escape the grosser trammels of the human condition: the anacreontic mode means grovelling abasement" (p. 103).

◄§ 170. ———. "Ophelia's 'Show.'" *Trivium* 4: 108–11.

Discusses the foot as a primitive sexual symbol and comments on the use of the shoe (shoe-show) as a symbol for female genitals, especially by Elizabethan dramatists. Briefly suggests that lines 74–76 of Donne's "Loves Progress" may be related to the tradition: "Some Symetry the foot hath with that part / Which thou doest seek, and is thy Map for that / Lovely enough to stop, but not stay at."

◆§ 171. WILLIAMSON, GEORGE. "Donne's Satirical *Progresse of the Soule.*" *ELH* 36: 250–64.
Indicates the place and philosophical importance of Donne's *Metempsychosis* in his corpus. Argues that where Milton's *Paradise Lost* "tells how sin brought death into the world, Donne's *Progresse of the Soule* gives satirical form to the same theme, also leading from Paradise to Calvary, but obliquely ridiculing his own time" (p. 251). Shows how Donne uses Pythagorean doctrine "to justify his narrative, and adds the passage of the soul up the scale of being—vegetal, sensitive, rational—to show the evolution of original sin and to satirize its course" (p. 253).

◆§ 172. WILSON, G. R., JR. "The Interplay of Perception and Reflection: Mirror Imagery in Donne's Poetry." *SEL* 9: 107–21.
Analyzes mirror imagery in "The good-morrow," "The Extasie," "The Canonization," "Witchcraft by a picture," "The broken heart," "A Valediction: of my name, in the window," "Heroicall Epistle: Sapho to Philaenis," and "A Valediction: of weeping" and maintains that "these poems constitute a coherent entity summing up the poet's 'sexual metaphysics'" (p. 107). Suggests that these mirror images "epitomize Donne's ability to fuse intellect and emotion, reality and appearance, perception and reflection, and the physical and spiritual to create a whole greater than the sum of its parts, a creation that simultaneously defines a paradox and resolves it" (p. 107).

◆§ 173. WITHERSPOON, ALEXANDER M., AND FRANK J. WARNKE, eds. *Seventeenth-Century Prose and Poetry.* 2d ed. New York, Chicago, Burlingame: Harcourt, Brace & World. xxvi, 1094p.
Revision and expansion of the 1946 edition. Entirely revised biographical and critical introduction and updated bibliographies.
Contains selections from Donne's *Devotions upon Emergent Occasions* (pp. 60–69), Sermon XV, XXIII, and LXXII from Folio of 1640 (pp. 70–97); selections from other sermons (pp. 97–115), preceded by a short general introduction to Donne's life and prose (pp. 58–59) and a brief selected bibliography (p. 59). Contains also selections from Donne's secular and sacred poetry (pp. 735–59), preceded by a general introduction to Donne's poetry (pp. 735–36) and a short selected bibliography (p. 737). Calls Donne "a poet of major importance to our century" (p. 735) and particularly praises his ability to unite passion and intellect. The general introduction mentions Donne in several places (pp. 3–16). Reproduces in the appendix a part of Dr. Johnson's "Life of Cowley" (1779) (pp. 1053–61) and T. S.

Eliot's "The Metaphysical Poets," *TLS*, 20 October 1921, pp. 669–70 (pp. 1061–65).

◆§ 174. YOSHIDA, SACHIKO. "Futatsu no *Anniversaries* ni okeru Shi to Fukkatsu: no Theme—John Donne no Shogai no Turning Point to shite no Igi" [The Theme of Death and Rebirth in the Two *Anniversaries*—The Significance of the Turning Point in the Life of John Donne]. *Kiyō* (Mukogawa Joshi Daigaku), no. 16 (May): 117–25.

Suggests that throughout his early poetry Donne struggles with the question of the meaning of life and argues that in the *Anniversaries* he finds an answer to his search, which is to enter into the "vita activa" that leads from death to resurrection.

1970

◆§ 175. AIZAWA, YOSHIHISA. "John Donne to *Ignatius his Conclave*" [John Donne and *Ignatius his Conclave*]. *Bunkei Ronsō* (Jimbungakubu, Hirosaki Daigaku) 6: 19–38.

Presents a synopsis of *Ignatius his Conclave* and comments on its historical context. Argues that in the work Donne tried to show the foolishness of attacking the Jesuits and of the entire internecine argument among the various religious sects in general. Suggests that *Ignatius* reveals the ambiguity of Donne's feelings—for he was at once attracted to what was new and revolutionary and, at the same time, tried to protect the traditional order of things.

◆§ 176. ARTHOS, JOHN. "Correspondence." *RES* n.s. 21: 63.

Offers an addendum to René Graziani's "John Donne's 'The Extasie' and Ecstasy" (entry 17). Suggests that Donne's discussion of the relationship of the lovers in "The Extasie" may have been influenced by Giordano Bruno's discussion of love in his play, *Candelaio* (1582).

◆§ 177. ASHLEY, LEONARD R. N. "'To Touch Any Private Person Displeasantly': Satire in Elizabethan England." *SNL* 8: 57–65.

In part a review of and reaction to Louis Lecocq's *La Satire en Angleterre de 1588 à 1603* (entry 110). Argues that the roots of Elizabethan satire must be sought not only in Juvenal and Horace but also in the English society and temperament of the time: "If Elizabethan satire is to be approached with any special caveat it is probably that one must take into account the whole English tradition and not merely the literary tradition (largely classical), the entire complex relationship between satire as an art and the society that exists for satire to chide or to giggle at, to caution covertly or to excoriate blatantly" (p. 64). Suggests that, although Donne's satires are among the best of the period, he does not achieve his mark in the genre as he does in others. Points out a number of possible reasons Elizabethan satire often seems flat and dull, such as "lack of perception or lack of guts" (p. 61). Argues that Elizabethan satire was "more pretty and merry and conceited and self-conscious than bitter and taunting and scoffing and self-expressive" (p. 63).

178. BALD, R. C. "Editorial Problems—A Preliminary Survey," in *Art and Error: Modern Textual Editing*, pp. 37–61. Essays compiled and edited by Ronald Gottesman and Scott Bennett. Bloomington and London: Indiana University Press.
Briefly notes that Grierson, on the authority of the manuscripts, altered the final verb in "What if this present were the worlds last night?" from *assumes* to *assures*, a change that "alters the whole effect of the poem and brings it to the triumphant climax which Donne surely intended" (p. 38). Also notes the editorial ineptitude surrounding Donne's letters: "His contemporaries were interested in the elegance of Donne's epistolary style and the ingenuity of his compliments more than in the details of his personal relations with his friends" (p. 46).

179. ———. *John Donne: A Life*. Edited by Wesley Milgate. New York and Oxford: Oxford University Press. x, 627p.
Currently the standard and most detailed modern biography of Donne. Bald notes that Donne "must be the earliest modern major poet in English of whom an adequate biography is possible" (p. 1). Avoids subjective, autobiographical interpretations of Donne's sermons and prose works, except for anecdotes and reminiscences found in them, and also avoids using the poems as autobiography, except for the verse letters and religious poems. Surveys the development of biographical study of Donne from Walton to the present. Contains Wesley Milgate's introduction (pp. vii–viii); contents (pp. ix–x); references and abbreviations (pp. xi–xii). Divided into eighteen chapters: (1) "Introduction: On Writing the Life of Donne" (pp. 1–18); (2) "Ancestry and Parentage" (pp. 19–34); (3) "Early Life" (pp. 35–52); (4) "Lincoln's Inn" (pp. 53–79); (5) "Military Service" (pp. 80–92); (6) "Secretary to the Lord Keeper" (pp. 93–127); (7) "Marriage" (pp. 128–54); (8) "Mitcham and London" (pp. 155–99); (9) "Controversy and Conflict" (pp. 200–236); (10) "Abroad with Sir Robert Drury" (pp. 237–62); (11) "Steps to the Temple" (pp. 263–301); (12) "First Years in the Church" (pp. 302–37); (13) "In Germany with Doncaster" (pp. 338–65); (14) "Promotion" (pp. 366–88); (15) "Dean" (pp. 387–430); (16) "Preacher and Parish Priest" (pp. 431–69); (17) "Active Years" (pp. 470–507); and (18) "Last Days" (pp. 508–36). Contains four appendixes: (A) "Chronology of Donne's Life" (pp. 537–46); (B) "Donne's Children" (pp. 547–56); (C) "Donne's Library" (pp. 557–59); and (D) "Appendix on Documents" (pp. 560–83), including (1) "The Will of Donne's Father" (pp. 560–61), (2) "Donne's Will" (pp. 563–67), (3) "Donne's Complaint against Christopher Danby" (pp. 567–69), (4) "A Cipher Entrusted to Donne" (pp. 569–70), (5) "Draft of Sir Henry Martin's Judgement on Henry Seyliard's Claim to Keyston Rectory" (pp. 570–71), (6) "Minutes of a Vestry Meet-

ing at St. Dunstan's-in-the-West" (pp. 572–73), (7) "Donne's Address to Convocation, 1626" (pp. 573–75), (8) "Statement by John Donne the Younger" (pp. 575–77), (9) "Pleadings in the Suit of Sir George Grymes against John Donne the Younger" (pp. 577–83). Index (pp. 585–627). Contains eight illustrations: (1) William Marshall's engraving (? after the original by Nicholas Hilliard) prefixed to the 1635 edition of *Poems*, (2) the "Lothian" portrait of Donne at Newbattle Castle, (3) Isaac Oliver's miniature of Donne in 1616 at Windsor Castle, (4) portrait of Donne in Deanery at St. Paul's Cathedral, (5) portrait of Donne (? from the school of Cornelius Janssen) in the Dyce Collection at the Victoria and Albert Museum (presumably a copy of the portrait in the Deanery at St. Paul's), (6) Martin Droeshout's engraving of Donne used as frontispiece for the 1632 edition of *Deaths Duell*, (7) Donne's head from Nicholas Stone's effigy in St. Paul's Cathedral, and (8) reproduction of Donne's receipt to Sir Thomas Egerton, from Losely MS. 2013/31 in the Folger Shakespeare Library and of Donne's letter to Bishop John Williams, from Lincolnshire Archives, L. T. and D. 1626/II.

꿩 180. BANKS, JASON. *Notes on the Works of John Donne*. Toronto: Forum House. 117p.

Cited in *Library of Congress Catalogs. National Union Catalog. 1973–1977*, vol. 9, p. 417. Totowa, N.J.: Rowman and Littlefield, 1978. Unavailable.

꿩 181. BEWLEY, MARIUS. "The Mask of John Donne," in *Masks & Mirrors: Essays in Criticism*, pp. 3–49. New York: Atheneum.

Part of this essay appeared in "Religious Cynicism in Donne's Poetry," *KR* 14 (1952): 619–46; part was included in the introduction to *The Selected Poems of John Donne* (Signet Classics, 1967); and part is new.

Divided into three sections. Section I traces Donne's reputation and discusses the nature of metaphysical poetry. Contrasts Sir John Davies's *Nosce Teipsum* (1599) with "The Extasie" to show that the latter, although informed by philosophical concepts and technical language, is not fundamentally a philosophical poem in the Elizabethan tradition but rather explores the relationship between the two lovers. Argues that Donne's main contribution was not his subject matter but rather "in the creation of a style, the revitalization of a language that was on the point of growing tired" (p. 16), as Carew notes in his elegy on Donne's death. Section II traces Donne's religious heritage and his steps toward Anglicanism and suggests that Donne's libertine poems may have been written "not as a celebration of sexual experience, but as a subconscious strategy to assist Donne in prying himself free of Rome" (p. 24). Suggests that the *Songs and Sonets* may be seen as "a protracted exercise in how to blunt the precision of a philosophically exact language and make it unfit for its original purpose" (p. 25). Section III comments on *The Progresse of the Soule* to show that Donne's "transition to Anglicanism was not an easy one" (p. 31) and claims that the two *Anniversaries* are private jokes that celebrate his departure from Catholicism. Conjectures that Elizabeth Drury is a symbol of the Church: alive, she was the Catholic Church; dead, her ghost is the Anglican establishment. Suggests that dramatic impact is Donne's most striking characteristic and that "the conflicts in Donne's personality, reflected so perfectly in his art, his perplexities of faith and doubt, the tortured ambiguity one senses so strongly in his motives, his cynicism and his capacity for affection, the ironical quality of his self-knowledge and his psychological curiosity—all have a familiar look in our day" (p. 49).

◆§ 182. BRADBURY, MALCOLM, AND DAVID PALMER, eds. *Metaphysical Poetry*. (Stratford-Upon-Avon Studies, 11.) London: Edward Arnold; New York: St. Martin's Press. 280p.

Collection of ten essays that tries "to reflect the shifts of emphasis that have taken place since the revival of modern interest in 'metaphysical poetry'" and to show that "there is an evident desire to see these poets in new contexts, and to relate them to a more varied and extensive awareness of the different kinds of poetic activity that belong to this period" (pp. 6–7). Contains the following: (1) Patrick Cruttwell, "The Love Poetry of John Donne: Pedantique Weedes or Fresh Invention?" (pp. 11–39); (2) A. J. Smith, "The Failure of Love: Love Lyrics after Donne" (pp. 41–71); (3) D. J. Palmer, "The Verse Epistle" (pp. 73–99); (4) Louis L. Martz, "The Action of the Self: Devotional Poetry in the Seventeenth Century" (pp. 101–21); (5) M. M. Mahood, "Something Understood: The Nature of Herbert's Wit" (pp. 123–47); (6) Robert B. Hinman, "The Apotheosis of Faust: Poetry and New Philosophy in the Seventeenth Century" (pp. 149–79); (7) Joseph H. Summers, "Andrew Marvell: Private Taste and Public Judgement" (pp. 181–209); (8) Brian Morris, "Satire from Donne to Marvell" (pp. 211–35); (9) J. W. Saunders, "The Social Situation of Seventeenth-Century Poetry" (pp. 237–59); and (10) Frank J. Warnke, "Metaphysical Poetry and the European Context" (pp. 261–76). Each essay that discusses Donne has been entered separately in this bibliography.

◆§ 183. BUTLER, CHRISTOPHER. *Number Symbolism*. (Ideas and Forms in English Literature, edited by John Lawlor.) London: Routledge & Kegan Paul. xi, 186p.

Mentions Donne throughout this study of the history of numerological allegory in English poetry. Discusses *The first Anniversary* (pp. 116–20) and maintains that the second and third meditative sections of the poem (especially lines 191–246 and 247–338) "can only be understood in the light of the numerological tradition and its aesthetic" (p. 117). Shows how Donne incorporates newly discovered scientific fact and theory into his poetry while at the same time mourning the loss that the older symbolism provided. Briefly comments on Donne's notion of "tuning the soul" in "Hymne to God my God, in my sicknesse" and suggests that the source is the *Republic* (IV, 442–44) and *Phaedro* (86–94) (p. 129). Suggests that the last three stanzas of "A Valediction: forbidding mourning," which contain the famous compass image, "can in fact be interpreted as describing the completion of a circle, as they bring the poem to its full completion of 36 lines, symbolizing the 360 degrees of a circle" (p. 134).

🖙 184. CAREY, JOHN. "Part III. Seventeenth Century Prose," in *English Poetry and Prose*, 1540–1674, edited by Christopher Ricks, pp. 390–431. (History of Literature in the English Language, vol. 2.) London: Barrie & Jenkins.

Paperback ed., Sphere Books, 1970.

Outlines trends in the development of prose style during the seventeenth century. Compares and contrasts Lancelot Andrewes and Donne and comments on specific features of Donne's style, such as his uses of anaphora; his employment of interpolations and parentheses, as he "corrects, qualifies, snatches a look at the Bible, the Fathers" (p. 402); his uses of coordination rather than subordination "so that the clauses seem to fall apart, as in a baroque altarpiece the figures lean precariously to give the impression of movement momentarily arrested" (p. 402); his attempts to trap "spiritual concepts within physical analogies" (p. 403); and his uses of the macabre, the theatrical, and paradox to engage his auditors or readers.

🖙 185. CASTAGNA, ANDRÉ. *Le Siècle Élisabethain*. (Panoramas illustrés, gen. ed., Louis Forestier.) Paris: Seghers. 255p.

"Un poète moderne en 1600: John Donne" (pp. 118–20) presents a brief introduction to Donne's life and poetry. Compares Donne to Shakespeare because Donne "est un très gran écrivain, non un très bon poète mineur" (p. 118). Includes, in French, "Song: Sweetest love, I do not goe," "Song: Goe, and catche a falling starre," "Death be not proud," and two of Donne's epigrams (pp. 198–201). Short biographical note (p. 240).

🖙 186. CHINDA, YAICHIRO. "Kichi no Engi (John Donne)" [The Play of Wit (John Donne)]. *Eigo Kenkyu* (Dokkyo Daigaku), no. 4 (July): 1–21.

Discusses Ben Jonson's evaluation of Donne's poetry and finds his comments critically perceptive. Notes that Jonson especially admired "The Bracelet" and "The Calme." Discusses the two poems to illustrate the range and quality of Donne's wit.

🖙 187. COONLEY, DONALD E. "The Metaphysical Shudder: An Essay on the Unique." *LangQ* 9, nos. 1–2: 15–20.

Attempts to define more precisely what is meant by the term *metaphysical shudder* as it is applied to seventeenth-century poetry and to speculate on why the seventeenth century was so fascinated by it. Argues that the term means more than simply "that element in seventeenth-century poetry which involves a fascination with the macabre, realistic, even naturalistic details which describe the ultimate consequences of the human body" (p. 15) and concludes that it is "a unique product of the seventeenth century because the familiar vibrations of death coexisted with the equally familiar lust for the experience of life" (p. 20). Comments on "The Funerall," "The Dampe," "The Apparition," "The Relique," *The second Anniversarie,* and *Deaths Duell* to show that in Donne "the shudder has the potential of a transcendence of the realistic; it is able to amalgamate death and life, decay and faith" (p. 18).

188. COPE, JACKSON I. "Modes of Modernity in Seventeenth-Century Prose." *MLQ* 31: 92–111.
Essentially a review article of Robert Adolph, *The Rise of Modern Prose Style* (Cambridge: MIT Press, 1968), and Joan Webber, *The Eloquent "I": Style and Self in Seventeenth-Century Prose* (entry 59). Surveys developments in modern criticism of seventeenth-century prose and briefly comments on T. S. Eliot's role in the modern Donne revival.

189. CRINÒ, ANNAMARIA. *La Satira inglese.* (Problemi ed orientamenti critici di lingue e letterature germaniche. Saggi e richerche, no. 5.) Verona: Libreria Universitaria Editrice. 160p.
Brief survey of English verse satire from the Middle Ages to Byron. Presents a biographical sketch of Donne and reproduces lines 43–110 of *Satyre III,* with an Italian prose translation (pp. 68–73).

190. CROSS, JAMES, AND VINCENT NEWEY. *British and American Poetry.* Malmö, Sweden: Hermods. 212p.
Reproduces "At the round earths imagin'd corners" and "The goodmorrow" (pp. 13–14); presents a brief biographical sketch of Donne and a short general introduction to his poetry (pp. 73–74), followed by glosses on individual lines of the two poems printed (pp. 74–77).

191. CRUTTWELL, PATRICK. "The Love Poetry of John Donne: Pedantique Weedes or Fresh Invention?," in *Metaphysical Poetry,* edited by Malcolm Bradbury and David Palmer, pp. 11–39. (Stratford-Upon-Avon Studies, 11.) London: Edward Arnold; New York: St. Martin's Press.
Argues against several recent approaches that would tend to diminish Donne's stature and originality and comments on his own personal experiences of Donne's love poetry over the past forty years, from his earliest attraction to its seemingly pornographic elements to his later recognition that "to harmonize syntax with stanza is the whole secret of reading Donne's lyrics" (p. 14). Prefers the ordering of the poems in the first edition of 1633 to the more recent ordering proposed by Helen Gardner because in the former the poems "come to one as a body of verse which says in effect that *every* aspect of love is liable to be present, in reality or in imagination, at any time, on any occasion: promiscuity, misogyny, hopeless adoration,

intimate tenderness, bitter hate, Platonic adoration, frivolous cynicism, brothel-lust, monogamous devotion, all of them" (p. 17). Comments on the major features of Donne's love poems, such as their uses of setting, their uses of a dramatic speaker, their note of Ovidian libertinism as well as Platonic-Petrarchan adoration, their distinctive sense of intimacy, and their uses of natural language devoid of poetic diction. Suggests three inseparable and major ingredients in the love poems: "the analytical, the autobiographical, and the dramatic" (p. 20) and finds that their only limitations are that they deal with unmarried human love, not divine love, and that they are clearly aggressively masculine and heterosexual. Points out some possible reasons for the decline of interest in Donne among young readers of today and concludes that one thing that we can all learn from Donne's poetry is "that just because the age one lives in is blinkered, fragmented, cruel, stupid and humourless, its poetry does not have to resemble it" (p. 39).

✎§ 192. DANIELS, EDGAR F. "Donne's 'Satire III,' 52." *Expl* 28: Item 52.
Suggests that the phrase "Contemptuous, yet unhansome" in line 52 of *Satyre III* may be a Petrarchan allusion. Notes that in the conventional Petrarchan poem the lady is described as beautiful but disdainful, but "Crantz's lady is paradoxical: she is disdainful without the beauty to warrant it."

✎§ 193. DATTA, KITTY SCOULAR. "The Poetry of Contemplation: Some Continuities." *Bulletin of the Department of English, Calcutta* 6, no. 1 (1970–1971): 23–33.
Discusses the contemplative and apocalyptic strain in the thinking of Wordsworth and Coleridge and comments on their debt to the contemplative tradition in English poetry, especially to the metaphysical poets. Notes, in particular, similarities as well as differences between Donne's uses of organic images and Coleridge's use of similar images. Points out that these organic images—the stream and its source, the hill, the root—belong "to nature's process, which long ago became images of the mind's transcendence over nature in self-knowledge" and that Coleridge and Wordsworth, "standing at the beginning of the modern era, made them most characteristically their own" (p. 33).

✎§ 194. DAY, W. G. "Sterne, Josephus and Donne." *N&Q* n.s. 17: 94.
Points out that Sterne's reference to Josephus in *Tristram Shandy* (edited by James Aiken Work [New York: Odyssey Press, 1940], p. 368) is a slight misunderstanding of a passage that he borrowed from Donne's *Biathanatos*.

✎§ 195. DEFORD, SARA. *The Short Love Poems of John Donne.* Tokyo: The Hokuseido Press. 111p.
A series of lectures delivered in 1962 at Kansai Gakuin University and

intended for Japanese students. Chapter 1, "John Donne and the Nature of Metaphysical Poetry" (pp. 1–21), outlines some of the basic features of Donne's poetry, such as his interest in science, his blending of thought and emotion, his general intellectual and analytical approach to his subject, and his distinctive uses of logic and language, illustrated, in part, by analyses of "Hymne to God my God, in my sicknesse" and "The goodmorrow." Chapter 2, "The Metaphysical Conceit" (pp. 22–67), describes the nature and function of the conceit in Donne's poetry, primarily in "A Valediction: forbidding mourning," "The Flea," "Song: Goe, and catche a falling starre," "A nocturnall upon S. Lucies day," "The Sunne Rising," and "The Canonization." Chapter 3, "The Prosody of John Donne" (pp. 68–91), outlines the technical verse structure of Donne's poems, especially "The Canonization" and "The Baite," and contrasts Donne with Ralegh and Marlowe. Chapter 4, "John Donne and the Poetry of Love" (pp. 92–111) comments on the range of attitudes toward love in Donne's poetry—from cynicism to the highest spiritual conception—and on conventions that shaped his language of love. Comments on a number of poems briefly, especially "The Apparition" and "The Funerall," and concludes that, for Donne, love is "violent, catastrophic, delightful, wonderful, and necessary, by turns" (p. 111). Brief bibliography (p. 112).

⋙ 196. DELANY, PAUL. "Donne's Holy Sonnet V, Lines 13–14." *AN&Q* 9: 6–7.
Points out possible biblical allusions in the sestet of "I am a little world" to James 5:3 (Geneva version) and Revelation 17:16—passages that suggest that greed and lust will be punished at Judgment Day by fire eating the flesh. Maintains, therefore, that in lines 13–14 of the sonnet Donne says that "the fire of zeal, by driving out and consuming the desires of the flesh in this world, will 'heal' the sinner and prepare him for a glorious resurrection" (p. 7). Concludes that "the resolution of the poem comes from the union of 'fire' and 'zeal,' which are brought together by both the logical progression of the sonnet's imagery and the nexus of scriptural associations" (p. 7).

⋙ 197. DIECKMANN, LISELOTTE. "Emblematic and Mystic Hieroglyphics," in *Hieroglyphics: The History of a Literary Symbol*, pp. 48–99. St. Louis: Washington University Press.
Comments on the intimate relationship between the hieroglyphical tradition and metaphysical poetry and suggests that what Donne "brings to the hieroglyphical problem is the faith that in God and his Son, as well as in the Biblical word, the two levels of meaning [literal and metaphorical] are one and that therefore, metaphorical poetry has its roots in the essence of this mystery" (p. 93). Discusses Donne's view of the "metaphorical God" and the "metaphorical Christ," especially as expressed in his *Devotions upon Emergent Occasions* and sermons, and observes that, in Donne's works, "the intimate relationship between poetry and religion

could not be more poignantly expressed" (p. 93). Briefly compares Donne's views with those of Vaughan, Cowley, Herbert, and Quarles.

꩜ 198. DONNE, JOHN. *Five Sermons upon Special Occasions* (1626). Menston, Eng.: The Scolar Press. [288p.]
Facsimile edition reproduced in the original size from the copy in Jesus College Library, Cambridge (*STC* 7041). Contains "A Sermon preached at *Pauls* Cross," "To the Honorable the *Virginia* Company," "At the Consecration of *Lincolnes Inne* Chappel," "The first Sermon preached to K. *Charles* at St. *Iames*, 1625," and "A Sermon preached to his Maiestie at *White-hall*, 24 Febr. 1625."

꩜ 199. ———. *Juvenilia* (London, 1633). (The English Experience: Its Record in Early Printed Books Published in Facsimile, no. 239.) Amsterdam: Theatrum Orbis Terrarum; New York: Da Capo Press. n.p.
Facsimile of *Iuvenilia: or Certaine Paradoxes, and Problemes* (London, 1633) from the copy in the John Rylands Library (shelfmark: 12038 [2]). No introduction and no notes or commentary.

꩜ 200. ———. *No Man Is an Island: Selected from the Writings of John Donne,* edited by Keith Fallon. (A Stanyan Book.) Los Angeles: Stanyan Books; New York: Random House. [51p.]
Brief selections from Donne's poetry and prose, without notes or critical commentary. Reproduces often only a line or two from individual poems or prose pieces.

꩜ 201. ———. *Poems with Elegies on the Author's Death* (London, 1633). (The English Experience: Its Record in Early Printed Books Published in Facsimile, no. 240.) Amsterdam: Theatrum Orbis Terrarum; New York: Da Capo Press. viii, 406p.
Facsimile of a copy of the first edition of Donne's poems in the John Rylands Library (shelfmark: 12038). STC 7045. No introduction and no notes.

꩜ 202. DOUGHTIE, EDWARD, ed. *Lyrics from English Airs, 1596–1622.* Edited with an introduction by Edward Doughtie. Cambridge: Harvard University Press. xvii, 657p.
An edition "that brings together the verse from all those sixteenth- and seventeenth-century songbooks which contain 'airs,' with the important exception of the works of Thomas Campion" (p. vii), designed "for those scholars, students, and critics who need more than a modernized text but less than several copies in the originals, and who would be interested in details about manuscript versions, textual matters, and sources" (p. viii). Mentions Donne in several places and suggests that, although music for five of the poems in the *Songs and Sonets* has survived, "it is generally

conceded that most of Donne's poems are not suitable for singing because they are too complex," yet maintains that song lyrics may have influenced him "in his varied and intricate stanza forms and perhaps—along with dramatic blank verse—in his metrical freedom" (p. 29). Reprints, with detailed notes, the only lyrics by Donne printed in his lifetime, "The Expiration" (pp. 294–95, notes, p. 564), which first appeared in Alfonso Ferrabosco's *Ayres* (1609), and "Breake of day" (p. 389, notes, pp. 601–2), which first appeared in William Corkine's *The Second Booke of Ayres* (1612).

✒ 203. ENOMOTO, KAZUYOSHI. "George Herbert to Skinkō-shi—Donne kara Herbert e" [George Herbert and Divine Poetry—Donne to Herbert]. *Bungaku Ronsō* (Aichi Daigaku), no. 45 (December): 53–83.

Discusses Donne's influence on Herbert's poetry, especially on Herbert's use of wit, conceits, rhythm, and meter. Suggests that Donne's example encouraged Herbert to reject traditional forms of devotional poetry and to express his religious experience in a personal and individualistic style. Compares "Thou hast made me," "Batter my heart," and "Oh, to vex me, contraryes meet in one" to Herbert's poems to illustrate the point.

✒ 204. ESCH, ARNO. "Die 'metaphysische' Lyrik," in *Epochen der englischen Lyrik*, edited by Karl Heinz Göller, pp. 100–128. Düsseldorf: August Bagel Verlag.

Attributes the rebirth of interest in metaphysical poetry in the 1920s to the similarities that the poets of the time perceived between their own situation and that of Donne and his disciples. Suggests that "wit" is the distinguishing feature that sets Donne apart from his contemporary, Ben Jonson. Presents a survey of Donne's poetry based on the theory that Donne transformed, developed, and ironicized Petrarchan love poetry. Notes that, in general, Donne does not employ traditional decorative devices, above all not classical mythology, but that the dramatic tension of his poems is firmly supported by metaphor. Points out that Donne's poetry is characterized by a close union of intensive thought and passionate emotion and observes that the religious lyrics reached perfection in the three hymns of his last years, all of which originated in situations in which Donne believed he was touched by the hand of death.

✒ 205. FARMER, NORMAN K., JR. "A Theory of Genre for Seventeenth-Century Poetry." *Genre* 3: 293–317.

Argues that "a critical method that acknowledges the objective features of poetry, a method able to define genre in terms of the rhetorical motives that distinguish some poems from others" (p. 294) is more valuable in arriving at precise aesthetic distinctions than are such unsatisfactory terms as *metaphysical* and *cavalier*. Points out, for instance, that Donne's verse letters are more logically compared to Jonson's verse letters than they are to his own *Songs and Sonets* and maintains that "individual genius may often be best discovered through a comparative study of genres and the conventions which shape them" (p. 295). Presents a taxonomy of such Renaissance genres as the verse letter, funeral elegy, epithalamion, epitaph, philosophical poem, satire, ode, Ovidian elegy, allegorical poem, and sacred lyric to show that such an approach "offers an explanation for the richness of seventeenth-century poetry by showing how the lyric stood in relation to other more public genres commonly practiced at the time and how poets were able to develop the 'I' of the lyric poem with greater facility than their predecessors by virtue of cutting across generic lines and developing rhetorics of other modes as well" (p. 312). Several examples drawn from Donne.

✍§ 206. FISH, STANLEY. "Literature in the Reader: Affective Stylistics." *NLH* 2: 123–62.

Presents the case for affective criticism, a method of literary analysis that "focuses on the reader rather than on the artifact" (p. 139), and also considers some of the more obvious objections raised about the method. Illustrates how affective criticism can be applied in reading a sentence from one of Donne's sermons and argues that, although formalist analysis would show many features of the sentence, it could not bring the reader "to the point where we could see the sentence, and the mode of discourse it represents, as a deflating joke . . . to which the reader responds and of which he is a victim" (p. 134). Maintains that "to consider the utterances apart from the consciousness receiving it is to risk a great deal of what is going on" (p. 134).

✍§ 207. FOWLER, ALASTAIR. *Triumphal Forms: Structural Patterns in Elizabethan Poetry.* Cambridge: The University Press. xiii, 234p.

Discusses the numerical organization of literary works, "the composition of substantive and formal elements into spatial patterns, in an age when all art was thought of spatially" (p. ix). Comments on Donne's uses of the triumphal motif and his uses of numerology in "Ecclogue. 1613. December 26" (pp. 71–73, 107), especially the significance of the metrical center of the poem, which, like the metrical center of "The Extasie," "enthrones an image of sexual unity" (p. 73). Comments briefly also on the numerological structure in "An Epithalamion, Or mariage Song on the Lady Elizabeth," "Epithalamion made a Lincolnes Inne," and "The Primrose."

✍§ 208. FRENCH, A. L. "The Psychopathology of Donne's Holy Sonnets." *CR* 13: 111–24.

Examines a number of the *Holy Sonnets* to show that they are often marked by a complex confusion of thought and feeling and often project "feelings of fear pushed to the point of terror" (p. 111). Finds that "over and over again Donne is brought face to face with a dispensation that seems either cruel or completely incomprehensible, and that he evades the *crise de conscience* so produced by taking refuge in a quasi-logic which is either suspect or patently false" (p. 112). Suggests that the *Holy Sonnets* are interesting, however, "because they reveal not merely the particular difficulties of one uncertain man, but also some of the problems and perplexities that lie in wait for any man who is trying to write religious poetry" (p. 123), such as the unequal nature of the relationship between God and man and the inadmissibility of expressing adverse criticism of God. Finds the *Holy Sonnets* attractive because in the poems themselves there is a fundamental honesty that emerges, a transparency that "reveals irreconcilable *as* unreconciled or irreconcilable": "What for Donne the religious man may have been bluff and evasion is, for the poetry, an open admission of insolubility" (p. 124).

≈§ 209. FURBANK, P. N. "The Words Today," in *Reflections on the Word 'Image,'* pp. 49–81. London: Secker & Warburg.
Warns against some of the abuses of modern studies of imagery, especially the tendency to search out images in poems as if the images themselves were "little poems-within-a-poem" (p. 54). Indicates why comments on Donne's imagery by F. R. Leavis, especially those in "Imagery and movement: Notes in the analysis of Poetry" (*Scrutiny*, September 1945), are preferable to those by M. A. Rugoff (*Donne's Imagery: A Study in Creative Sources*, 1939) or even those by Rosemond Tuve (*Elizabethan and Metaphysical Imagery*, 1947).

≈§ 210. GLEASON, JOHN B. "Dr. Donne in the Court of Kings: A Glimpse from Marginalia." *JEGP* 69: 599–612.
Comments on Donne's marginalia (probably written in 1629) in his 1563 copy of Thomas More's *Utopia*, now in the University of San Francisco Library, and suggests that these marginalia "offer a caustic private comment on the Court of King Charles I, and—what is even more interesting—they testify to a spiritual dilemma that perplexed the Dean during his entire service as preacher to the courts of kings" (p. 599), that is, the difficulty of keeping the delicate balance between his conception of the duty of the preacher to admonish and to speak out against evil and wrongdoing and his continuing need to curry royal favor. Argues that the marginalia would suggest that Donne was not always in agreement with the king or with his policies; however, in his sermons he was obliged to support royal prerogative and to defend the wisdom of royal policies. Suggests that Donne's melancholy during his last years may have been partially the result of "his having to discharge his public duties in forms which were sometimes opposed to his own convictions" (p. 611).

≈§ 211. GRANSDEN, K. W., ed. *Tudor Verse Satire*. (Athlone Renaissance Library, edited by G. Bullough and C. A. Meyer.) London: The Athlone Press (University of London). viii, 182p.

Briefly surveys the genre of verse satire from about 1510 to 1616, tracing its development from classical satire through medieval satirical modes to the Renaissance. Mentions Donne's *Satyres* several times in the introduction (pp. 1–29). Reproduces *Satyre IV* (pp. 94–100) and suggests that lines 17–154 are based on Horace. Reproduces also Donne's "To Sr Henry Wotton: Sir, more then kisses" (pp. 100–102) and calls this satirical epistle a "reflective satire" (p. 172) and points out parallels between it and the satires of Horace and Persius. Notes on both poems (pp. 170–72).

✍§ 212. HALEWOOD, WILLIAM H. *The Poetry of Grace: Reformation Themes and Structures in English Seventeenth-Century Poetry.* New Haven and London: Yale University Press. xii, 180p.

Shows how certain Reformation ideas, interests, and attitudes shaped Donne's poetry and sermons and attempts to adjust "the 'poetics of opposites' to square with the imperatives of a historical situation in which the oppositions most certain to engage poets' imaginations were the theological oppositions which the great energies of the Reformation found waiting for revival in Augustine" (p. 17). Argues "(1) that although human nature is desperately limited in Donne's conception, that circumstance is not conclusive for human possibility; (2) that the opposites of metaphysical poetic strategy are related to a theological concept of reality which has extremely few points of contact with agnosticism or Manichaeism (certainly no more contact than can be claimed for a traditional strain of Christian dualism); (3) that the opposition of opposites in seventeenth-century poetry is not absolute as the term would be understood in metaphysics: the world and man, rather than an independent energy of evil, provide the counterweight to God, and they are of course God's own creations—evil only insofar as they withdraw from Him; (4) that the structural purpose of opposition in the poems lies not in dialectic interplay for its own rewards but, rather, in the reconciliation in which it concludes—a reconciliation which the inequality of the opposed forces makes inevitable from the outset" (pp. 23–24). Presents a critical reading of "Goodfriday, 1613. Riding Westward" to show that "while appearing to suggest that more than one kind of attitude toward the claims of the devout life is possible, in the end the poem reveals itself as a single-minded exposition of an orthodox point of view" (p. 26). Comments on the influence of revived Augustinian theology on Donne's sermons and points out that St. Augustine "is Donne's most heavily used nonscriptural source and that St. Paul is his favorite source in scripture"—a preference that is "almost a standard Reformation pattern and reflects the characteristic Reformation intensity of interest in the great Pauline and Augustinian themes of man's sin, God's mercy, and the process by which mercy acts on sin" (p. 60). Discusses how Donne's theology differs from or agrees with that of the English Calvinists. Briefly considers Donne's Augustinian meditational mode in the *Divine Poems*, especially in the *Holy Sonnets*.

◄§ 213. HANAK, MIROSLAV JOHN. "The Emergence of Baroque Mentality and its Cultural Impact on Western Europe after 1550." *JAAC* 28, no. 3: 315–26.

Considers the emergence of baroque mentality after 1550 in Italy, Spain, Germany, France, and England. Argues that baroque art and literature are "a reflection of a new and distinct world view which continues to employ Renaissance forms but loads them with an entirely different world concept" (p. 315) and suggests that the baroque is "a spiritualization of the Renaissance lust for life" (p. 316). Surveys the political and historical events of 1550–1660 to show "how this spiritualized elation replaced Renaissance *élan vital*" (p. 318). Surveys also modern scholarship on the baroque and discusses some of the major features of baroque art. Briefly comments on the baroque in English literature and mentions that Donne's *Anniversaries* may not be seen as baroque, since their "verbal acrobacy is more premeditated than truly felt existential fear" but that the *Songs and Sonets* perhaps anticipate "the terror of man's cruelty and hope for God's mercy of Gryphius's *Sonn-und-Feriertagssonnette* of 1639, which had grown out of actual experience" (p. 323).

◄§ 214. HAWKINS, SHERMAN H. "Samson's Catharsis." *MiltonS* 2: 211–30.

Discusses the catharsis of Samson and points out that in the seventeenth century the science of medicine was closely allied with ethics and theology and that in the religious writings of the period disease and its cure were taken together as a common trope. Notes that "such 'figures of speech' are grounded upon the double truth of science and religion, on the tradition of philosophical medicine anatomized by Burton, and a tradition of theological symbolism authorized by Christ himself" (p. 217). Discusses within this context Donne's *Devotions upon Emergent Occasions*, in which "sickness and recovery is made an emblem of regeneration, the dying and renewal of the Christian soul" (p. 217). Points out that both Donne and Bunyan make purgation a symbol of repentence but contrasts Donne's symbolism with that in *Pilgrim's Progress*, noting that, while "Donne's wit exalts the undignified facts of illness into metaphysical conceits," the homely allegory of Bunyan "reduces transcendental truths to almost naturalistic fictions" (p. 218).

◄§ 215. HINMAN, ROBERT B. "The Apotheosis of Faust: Poetry and New· Philosophy in the Seventeenth Century," in *Metaphysical Poetry*, edited by Malcolm Bradbury and David Palmer, pp. 149–79. (Stratford-Upon-Avon Studies, 11.) London: Edward Arnold; New York: St. Martin's Press.

Challenges the generally accepted twentieth-century view that during the seventeenth century art and science were fundamentally opposed to each other and that the new science had a generally bad effect on the

poetry of the period. Maintains that actually the artists and the new philosophers were "spiritual allies, even if they were not always aware of the
alliance, and that—despite individual and occasional antagonism—the
total effect of each group on the other was salubrious" (p. 149). Suggests
that the difference between the imaginative process of many seventeenth-
century poems and that of many earlier ones "seems to be that imaginative
creation, an inductive leap like a leap of faith, has fused sacramentalism
and empiricism" (p. 154). Comments on how Donne seemingly attempts
to break down the wall that divides nature and art. Selected bibliography
on seventeenth-century literature and scientific thought (pp. 175–79).

◀§ 216. HOEY, JOHN. "A Study of Lord Herbert of Cherbury's Poetry."
   RMS 14: 69–89.
Surveys the personal relationship between Donne and Lord Herbert of
Cherbury and compares and contrasts their poetry. Contrasts, in particular, Lord Herbert's elegy on the death of Cecilia Boulstred with Donne's
elegy in order "to reveal some of the differences in temperament and poetic technique of the two men" (p. 74).

◀§ 217. HOSHINO, TŌRU. Donne Shishu [A Collection of Donne's Poems].
   Tokyo: Shichōsha. 218p.
Translates into Japanese the Songs and Sonets and six of the Elegies:
"The Perfume," "His Picture," "The Autumnall," "The Bracelet," "On his
Mistris," and "Going to Bed."

◀§ 218. HUTCHINSON, ALEXANDER N. "Constant Company: John Donne
   and His Satiric Personae." Discourse 13: 354–63.
Discusses how Donne followed in a satiric tradition drawn from Juvenal, Horace, and Persius and considers "what the particular ethos was
which he created, and the elements in it which were not necessarily prescribed by tradition" (pp. 354–55). Discusses Donne's uses and development of personae in the Satyres and considers various aspects of his private
religious beliefs and practices, speculating on "how they provide another
dimension in the structure of the satires and the ethos of the poet" (p.
360). Points out that Donne, unlike other satirists of the time, emphasizes
the "deliberate confrontation with vice so that it could be vigorously re-
sisted and refuted" (p. 361). Notes that his personae "refuse the poisoned
meats thrust upon them and remain untainted" and that "there is none of
the subordination of philosophy and theology to the depiction of actual
vice nor of the moral ambiguity which characterizes much of the formal
verse written in the 'satyr' tradition" (pp. 361–62). Maintains that Donne's
personae have a sense of detachment that allows them to "provide an
analysis of the problems even while participating in the dramatic action—
and this detachment leads to religious comprehension" (p. 362).

ぺ♪ 219. JACKSON, ROBERT S. *John Donne's Christian Vocation.* Evanston: Northwestern University Press. viii, 192p.

Although using a variety of approaches—the historical, literary, critical, psychological, mystical, and even phenomenological—this is primarily a biographical study of "some fifteen or more years of Donne's lifetime during which he faced and resolved most of the difficulties standing between him and his vocation to the priesthood in the Anglican Church" (p. 4). Chapter 1, "The World Movement of Donne's Lifetime" (pp. 3–21), outlines various social, historical, philosophical, and theological tensions, dualities, and dichotomies that confronted his world, such as the sense of duality between the past and the present, the breakdown of an ordered and hierarchical sense of the universe, the decline of Scholasticism and the emergence of Ramism and Platonism, the changing modes of apprehension and sensibility, and the rediscovery of the Bible and ancient classics. Suggests that Donne's vocational adventure participates in and reflects this Reformation-Renaissance world of polarities. Chapter 2, "The Beginnings of Trouble: Outer and Inner" (pp. 22–38), comments on Donne's marriage, the desperate years immediately thereafter, and the resultant inner tensions that contributed to his religious development during this crucial period in his life. Presents a reading of *Satyre III*, most of which appeared earlier as "'Doubt Wisely:'—John Donne's Skepticism" (entry 23). Chapter 3, "Mannerism" (pp. 39–55), maintains that the term *mannerism* should not be exclusively confined to the aesthetic realm but is "related to religious, social, political, and literary history as well" (p. 51). Connects the term also "with depth psychology and certain aspects of existentialism and phenomenology" (p. 51) and prefers *mannerism* to *metaphysical* or *meditative* as more adequately descriptive of Donne's art and sensibility. Chapter 4, "'Resolution' Denied" (pp. 56–79), comments on the tensions, doubts, and irresolution Donne experienced when first asked by Morton to become a priest. Comments on "The Litanie" as reflecting Donne's Christian ambivalence toward worldliness. Chapter 5, "The Depth" (pp. 80–97), discusses Donne's preoccupation with death during the years immediately preceding his public acceptance of Anglicanism, especially as reflected in *Biathanatos* and *Pseudo-Martyr*. Chapter 6, "The Psychic Marriage" (pp. 98–122), comments on the sexual and marital imagery of Donne's religious poems, which, "taken all together, make up a myth of the divine-human relationship in which each of the various figures is a persona, or mask, of some aspect of Donne's own—and man's—personal existence in the world" (p. 98). Illustrates the myth through a reading of the *Holy Sonnets* and the two *Anniversaries*. Argues that in the latter Donne celebrates "the divine marriage by reconciling the most profound polarities in man's experience, symbolized chiefly in the polarities of death and birth but including also this world and the other world, heaven and earth, God and man, the eternal and temporal" (p. 118). Sees Donne as "giving up his uncommitted stance" in the *Anniversaries*: "The invisible church is not enough for man living in the visible world," and thus by means of Elizabeth Drury's "marriage to God, John Donne was reborn in the world" (p. 122). Chapter 7, "Church and State" (pp. 123–45), discusses Donne's final steps toward the Anglican priesthood and how he reconciled his inner and outer life by this act: "To use language only a bit figuratively, it is fair to say that the king of England was John Donne's pope and that he himself was an Anglicized Jesuit" (p. 144). Chapter 8, "Donne's Sonnet on Christ's Spouse" (pp. 146–75), presents a detailed reading of "Show me deare Christ" and sees it as Donne's "final resolution of the problem of national sectarianism" in which "the multiple churches and the one church are the same; so is it that in joining the fallen bride of Christ, John Donne also joined the true" (p. 174). Appendix, "A Passage from St. Thomas Aquinas's *Summa Theologica*, 'On the Mean of Virtue'" (pp. 179–80). Index.

◄§ 220. KEEN, GERALDINE. "Expert finds poem in Donne's hand." *The Times* (London), 5 June, p. 2.

Announces the discovery of Donne's autograph verse letter to Lady Carew, "A Letter to the Lady Carey, and Mrs Essex Riche, From Amyens," by Peter Croft, manuscript expert at Sotheby's, in papers of the Duke of Manchester, which from 1882 had been held in the Public Record Office. Notes that "no other autograph exists of a poem by any early poet of comparable renown." Describes the verse letter and reproduces a photocopy of the first three stanzas along with a transcription.

◄§ 221. KELLY, T. J. "Donne's 'Firme Substantiall Love.'" *CR* 13: 101–10.

Comments on a number of Donne's best-known love poems (especially "The undertaking," "The Relique," "Farewell to love," "The Autumnall," "The good-morrow," "The Sunne Rising," "Loves growth," and "Song: Sweetest love, I do not goe") in order to argue that Donne "is not a purveyor of notions about love, Ovidian, Petrarchan, Platonic, or any other, but a great dramatic poet" (p. 108). Sees the poems as dramatic in the sense that "they create a relationship of complete mutuality not mainly by talking about a woman, or so simply as using terms like 'we' and 'our,' but so far as they are love bodied forth in speech to her" (p. 109). Concludes that what the reader takes away from the poems is "not Donne as the intense and imaginative lover, but Donne as the focus of experience which is important because it is what it is" and argues that "the possibility—indeed, the reality—of that experience is imaginatively present to us only because Donne is what he is—a poet whose whole being can be informed and animated by love, whose love can be informed and animated from the quick of his being, whose wonderfully joyous alertness, whose insight, whose honesty, whose very relaxedness, even gaiety, in creative openness to intense and multifarious experience, show us so much of what being in love can mean" (pp. 109–10).

◄§ 222. KHANNA, URMILLA. "Donne's 'A Valediction: Forbidding Mourn- ✓ ✓
ing'—Some Possible Alchemical Allusions." *N&Q* n.s. 17: 404–5.
Suggests that certain alchemical notions drawn from Paracelsus concerning the technique for turning imperfect metals into pure and solid
gold may be useful in interpreting stanzas 4–6 of "A Valediction: forbidding mourning." Suggests that in these stanzas Donne describes a process
by which the two lovers' love "will *become* refined when they are parted
from each other" (p. 405). Argues that Donne is saying that "absence,
destructive of ordinary love, will in their case, prove the means of making
them realize the irrelevance of it" and that "the dull love rooted in sense
will wither whereas the refined love 'Interassured of the mind' will become even finer and be changed into 'the only good and fixed gold'" (p.
405).

◄§ 223. KISHIMOTO, YOSHITAKA. "Donne no Satyres—Sono Hyōgen ni
tsuite" [Donne's *Satyres*—On Their Expression]. *Kiyō* (Kokugo/Ko-
kubun) (Bungakubu, Baika Joshi Daigaku), no. 7 (December): 61–
72.
Discusses Donne's uses of ironic and illustrative allusions in the *Satyres*
as well as in the *Songs and Sonets*. Suggests that this line of analysis will
reveal new dimensions in the *Songs and Sonets*, which are known primarily for their wit. Notes that in both the *Satyres* and the *Songs and
Sonets* one can find a double meaning—a straightforward presentation of
a situation and a second allusive and ironic meaning.

◄§ 224. KRANZ, GISBERT. "Liebe und Vergänglichkeit: Erotische Lyrik
im England des 17. Jahrhunderts." *Antaios* 11: 512–26.
Divides English seventeenth-century poets into two groups: (1) the Puritans and the metaphysicals, who treat love philosophically and theologically, and (2) the Cavaliers, who discuss love in purely secular and sensual terms. Discusses Donne's attitude toward love and lists themes in a
number of his poems (pp. 516–20). Sees his early poems as cynical and
frivolous but notices a growing concern for the philosophical issues and
less concern for the sensual aspects of love in his later poems.

◄§ 225. KRANZ, GISBERT, ed. "John Donne," in *Englische Sonette: English und deutsche*, edited and translated by Gisbert Kranz, pp. 62–
71, 192–93. Stuttgart: Reclam.
Translates into German "Batter my heart," "I am a little world," "Oh, to
vex me, contraryes meet in one," "Thou hast made me," and "Death be
not proud" (pp. 62–71). Notes and brief comments on Donne's life and
religious sensibility (pp. 192–93).

◄§ 226. McGEE, MICHAEL C. "The Thematic Reduplication in Christian Rhetoric." *QJS* 56: 196–204.

Examines the practice and theory of Christian rhetoric "to illustrate the subtle but significant impact of Christian attitudes on evolving rhetorical theory" (p. 196) and rejects the notion that Christian rhetorics are merely "bastardizations of ancient and absolute principles" (p. 197). Comments briefly on one of Donne's sermons to show how he uses thematic reduplication that is "reminiscent of the early homilists" (p. 199), who divided the sermon into two tightly reasoned and logically redundant units: "the first is an analysis, deduction from Ultimate authority; the second is synthesis from common topics, analogies, and examples to the universal principle originally deduced from Scripture" (p. 201).

⋘§ 227. McLaughlin, Elizabeth. "'The Extasie': Deceptive or Authentic?" *BuR* 18, iii: 55–78.

Suggests that the apparently conflicting notions held by various critics about "The Extasie" may be resolved by examining "the case for deception or Sartrean self-deception, a possible psychological revision of these theories, and a detailed study of the relevance of Plotinus's philosophy to the solution of such problems" (p. 55). Comments on possible parallels between Donne's poem and the theories of such modern existentialists as Sartre and R. D. Laing and presents a detailed reading of the poem to show that it "is so replete with imagery of correspondences in the chain of being that the philosophy of Plotinus explains the total poem far more adequately than does any modern psychoanalytic approach" (p. 77). Points out, however, that "it is a curious fact that the Hellenistic mystic, the Renaissance poet, and the twentieth-century existentialists are describing closely related experiences: dissociation of part of the self as observer and evaluator, transcendence of the body, sense of union with the One" (pp. 77–78).

⋘§ 228. Mahony, Patrick J. "The Heroic Couplet in Donne's *Anniversaries.*" *Style* 4: 107–17.

Analyzes the structure of Donne's couplets in the *Anniversaries* and concludes that, in general, he often fails "to exploit the full potentialities of his medium" and has but "a restricted awareness of what can be called (to use a rhetorical term) *dispositio* in the heroic couplet, which would involve enhancing certain artistic devices by placing them in end-rhymes" (p. 114). Notes, for example, that "compared with Pope and Dryden, Donne does not favor a medial pivotality as much: he gives less emphasis to the post-fifth-syllable caesura and otherwise works with a greater caesural freedom" (p. 108). Suggests that, just as the tight, aphoristic couplets of Pope may be compared to curt baroque prose, perhaps Donne's couplets "with their looser structure and softly focused endings are indebted to the tradition of loose Baroque prose" (p. 114). Notes, however, that in *The second Anniversarie* Donne seems to achieve "an increased dramatic effect, which is partly due to his initiation of many lines with a verb—an anticipation of a Miltonic and Augustan practice to strengthen the poetic line" (p. 114).

◆§ 229. MANGELSDORF, SANDRA R. "Donne, Herbert, and Vaughan: Some Baroque Features." *Northeast Modern Language Association Newsletter* 2: 14–23.

Discusses certain baroque features in "The Canonization," as well as in Herbert's "Easter Wings" and Vaughan's "Corruption." Using terminology primarily from Heinrich Wölfflin and Wylie Sypher, finds the following baroque qualities in Donne's poem: "dynamism, derived primarily from conversational rhythms and associative thought; lack of clear-cut, observable form; a broad sweeping and slurring of sight known as relaxed vision; an affinity for the abstract as opposed to the concrete; organic unity; asymmetrical, exploratory form, as well as depth, and a sense of openness and unlimited heights and possibilities" (p. 18).

◆§ 230. MANN, LINDSAY A. "A Note on the Text of Donne's Sermon Preached at Paul's Cross, 24 March 1616/1617." *N&Q* n.s. 17: 403– 4.

Points out a possible error in the printed text of Donne's sermon preached at Paul's Cross, 24 March 1616/1617, that has escaped editors of the sermons. Finds the persistence of the error "especially odd because it occurs in an important and often-noticed passage on the right use of human faculties and makes nonsense out of the line where it occurs" (p. 403). Suggests that the phrase "not having any thing presented by the fantasie to the senses" should read "to the fantasie by the senses."

◆§ 231. MARTIN, PHILIP. "Donne in Twicknam Garden." *CritS* 4: 172– 75.

Sees "Twicknam garden" as a comic and satirical poem that "turns a clear-eyed, reducing gaze on the more foolish kinds of Petrarchan extravagance and offers instead a quite extra-conventional sense of reality" (p. 172). Argues that the poem is a critique of Petrarchan love, "an attack not so much on a way of writing as on the nature of the feeling it claimed to represent" (p. 174).

◆§ 232. MARTIN, R. D. *Notes on the Works of John Donne.* (Coles Notes.) Toronto: Coles Publishing Co. 117p.

Notes intended for undergraduate students. Biographical sketch (pp. 5– 7), outline of elements of metaphysical poetry (pp. 9–10), a brief review of Donne's poetry (pp. 10–14). Summarizes thirty-nine of Donne's poems and prose pieces and offers short critical commentaries (pp. 14–57). Reprints four critical essays (pp. 58–114): (1) a selection from Rosemond Tuve, *Elizabethan and Metaphysical Imagery* (Chicago: University of Chicago Press, 1947); (2) Joseph A. Mazzeo, "A Critique of Some Modern Theories of Metaphysical Poetry," *MP* 50 (1952): 88–96; (3) S. L. Bethell, "Gracián, Tesauro, and the Nature of Metaphysical Wit," *North-*

ern Miscellany of Literary Criticism 1 (1953): 19–40; and (4) Edgar H.
Duncan, "Donne's Alchemical Figures," *ELH* 9 (1942): 257–85. Selected
bibliography (pp. 114–17).

◄§ 233. MARTZ, LOUIS L. "The Action of the Self: Devotional Poetry in
the Seventeenth Century," in *Metaphysical Poetry*, edited by Malcolm Bradbury and David Palmer, pp. 101–21. (Stratford-Upon-Avon
Studies, 11.) London: Edward Arnold; New York: St. Martin's Press.
Claims that seventeenth-century devotion involved "an active, creative
state of mind, a 'poetical' condition . . . in which the mind works at high
intensity" and that thus the devotional poetry of the period "should not
. . . be taken to indicate verse of rather limited range, 'merely pious' pieces
without much poetic energy" (p. 103). Argues that devotional poetry is
the result of "a state of mind created by the 'powers of the soul' in an
intense dramatic action, focused upon one central issue" (p. 103). Discusses "the inimitable peculiarity of Donne's religious consciousness" (p.
105) by commenting on "If poysonous mineralls" and "Since she whom
I lov'd." Warns against overestimating the influence of Donne on the development of English devotional poetry and contrasts the instability, tension, and even querulous action of Donne's *Holy Sonnets* with the deeply
achieved sense of security and familiar confidence found in Herbert's *The
Temple*.

◄§ 234. MAZZARO, JEROME. *Transformations in the Renaissance English
Lyric*. Ithaca and London: Cornell University Press. x, 214p.
Discusses "the way forms of song become modes of vision and thought"
and shows how "the shifts undergone by the English lyric in the sixteenth
century from a musical to a rhetorical form are based on deeper changes
in modes of seeing and thinking" (p. vii). Outlines some of the shifting
views posited by modern critics concerning sixteenth- and early seventeenth-
century music, poetry, and sensibility. Chapter 5, "John Donne" (pp.
145–85), makes the case that Donne, "who wrote without music and based
his techniques upon rhetoric, established the frames for self-discovery in
the early seventeenth century" (p. 184). Comments on various features of
his technique: his ability to involve the reader immediately in the poem;
his emotionally charged language; his complex uses of the persona and
role-playing within the poems to express his own self-consciousness; his
tendency toward skepticism; and his skillful uses of colloquial diction and
metaphysical images.

◄§ 235. MEURS, J. C. VAN. "John Donne in the Twentieth Century." *LT*
270: 545–55.
Surveys briefly the development of various critical trends in Donne criticism during the twentieth century. Notes that in the 1920s and 1930s
critical evaluation of Donne not only shaped much modern criticism,
especially that of the "new critics," but also influenced practicing poets,

such as T. S. Eliot, Wallace Stevens, Allen Tate, and many others. Outlines some of the features of Donne's poetry that attracted early-twentieth-
century readers, such as his complex personality; his originality and rebellion against conventions and artificiality; his purported skepticism; his
intellectuality, wit, and sense of humor; his ability to use a speaking tone
in a highly argumentative poem; and his so-called "unified sensibility"
and skill at presenting feelings. Comments on the critical balance that
emerged from these often exaggerated claims, unfounded assumptions,
and critical positions, noting that even Eliot in time tempered his claims
for Donne. Points out that, "though Donne may no longer be seen as one
of the very greatest of English poets, he has come to occupy permanently
a higher position among English poets than he has ever had before" (p.
554).

◆§ 236. MICHENER, RICHARD L. "The Great Chain of Being: Three Approaches." *BSUF* 11: 60–71.
Explicates and contrasts three differing interpretations of the Great Chain
of Being as reflected in the works of Pico della Mirandola, Donne, and
Pope and shows how each was preoccupied in different ways with four
vital areas of existence: "the character of man, his pursuit of learning, his
search for his Creator, and the influence of such a closely built universe
upon his daily life" (p. 61). Concludes that "generalized schemes of cultural history, however informative, shed less light on a particular work
than will accrue from a careful relation of the text to the cultural, social,
and political background of the age in which it was produced" (p. 71).

◆§ 237. MILLER, PAUL W. "The Decline of the English Epithalamion."
TSLL 12: 405–16.
Traces the epithalamic tradition in England from Spenser to Crashaw
and contends that the decline of the tradition "reflects the decline of the
marriage myth that originally inspired the genre" (p. 405). The myth,
simply stated, is "that wedlock, when properly entered upon and celebrated, is a potent force to unify and bless the bridal pair and to avert evil
from them" (pp. 406–7). Comments on possible historical and religious
reasons for the decline of the myth and argues that "as the myth of marriage loses its vigor, the epithalamia increasingly find their inspiration not
in the myth itself, but in the distortion or perversion of this myth for
rhetorical or poetic effect" (p. 406). Discusses briefly Donne's "Epithalamion made at Lincolnes Inne," "An Epithalamion, Or mariage Song on
the Lady Elizabeth" and his Somerset "Epithalamion" and notes that by
1613, when Donne wrote his "whimsical Palatine and flattering Somerset
epithalamia, the decline of the form is apparent" (p. 405).

◆§ 238. MINCOFF, MARCO. "Lyrical Poetry—Elizabethan and Jacobean," in *A History of English Literature. Part I: From the Beginnings to 1700*, pp. 417–42. 2d ed. Sofia: Naouka i izkoustvo.

Surveys Donne's life and poetry (pp. 425–37) and suggests that he represents "in himself a whole new age—in his style, in his themes, in his outlook on life, his doubts and hesitations, he is in fact one of the most perfect examples of Baroque in English literature" (p. 435). Claims that his Catholic background may explain "the extremely Baroque (or Mannerist) nature of his art, his surrender to the emotional mysticism of the Counter-Reformation and flight from the Platonism of the Renaissance to scholasticism" (pp. 425–26). Mentions Donne throughout and compares him to others.

⚜§ 239. MOLHO, BLANCA Y MAURICE, eds. *Poetas ingleses metafísicos del siglo XVII.* (Preparación de textos originales, María Gomis.) Barcelona: Barral Editores. 181p.

Presents a general introduction to metaphysical poetry and poets for the Spanish reader with selections from the poetry of Donne, John Fletcher, William Drummond, William Browne, Crashaw, Lovelace, Marvell, and Vaughan. Contains an introduction, "Prólogo: John Donne y la poesía metafísica" (pp. 11–36), and nine selections from the *Songs and Sonets,* "An Epithalamion, Or mariage Song on the Lady Elizabeth," "A Hymne to Christ, at the Authors last going into Germany," four selections from the *Holy Sonnets,* and "A Hymne to God the Father" (pp. 44–89). English and Spanish on facing pages, without notes and commentary.

⚜§ 240. MORRIS, BRIAN. "Satire from Donne to Marvell," in *Metaphysical Poetry,* edited by Malcolm Bradbury and David Palmer, pp. 211–35. (Stratford-Upon-Avon Studies, 11.) London: Edward Arnold; New York: St. Martin's Press.

Broadly surveys the development and characteristics of both nondramatic and dramatic English satire from the late sixteenth century to the eighteenth century. Shows that during this time satire moved away from being a fashionable academic exercise modeled on Horace, Juvenal, Persius, and Martial to a more diversified and complex mode and became, in fact, a dialectical search for truth. Shows that satire moves away from the impersonality of the late Elizabethan era to an interest in individual character, from "the view of man as dominated by humours, or stars, or heavenly intervention, towards the realization that we are responsible for our own actions, and answerable for them" (p. 235). Comments only briefly on Donne. Points out that his satirical impulse was not confined to the *Satyres* but found expression as well in the *Elegies* and the *Songs and Sonets* and notes that, although Donne is always dramatic, "he is always dramatizing himself" and "never creates fully realized characters and subdues himself to them" (p. 214). Suggests that, in a sense, Donne's satire "is an end, not a beginning, and it is left to Marston to extend the satiric impulse into the theatre and give it a more personal context of judgement" (p. 214).

241. MURAOKA, ISAMU. "Donne no *Holy Sonnet*: 'Death, be not proud'" [Donne's Holy Sonnet: "Death be not proud"]. *EigoS* 116: 246–48.

Translates into Japanese "Death be not proud" and presents a brief explanation and analysis of the poem.

242. OKADA, HIROKO. "John Donne no Fukkatsu—Devotions no Ichi Kōsatsu" [The Revival of Donne—A Study of His *Devotions upon Emergent Occasions*]. *Kenkyū Ronsō* (Sugiyama Jogakuen Daigaku), no. 1 (March): 77–90.

Suggests that from the time of the writing of the *Devotions upon Emergent Occasions* the themes of Donne's sermons change from sin and damnation to grace and salvation. Maintains that his finest sermons were written after 1623 and examines the spiritual dynamics that prompted Donne's maturity as a sermon writer and caused the change in his choice of themes.

243. ŌKUMA, SAKAE. "Shi no Uta—'Sei Lucy no Hi ni yoseru Yoru no Uta" [The Song of Death—"A nocturnall upon S. Lucies day, Being the shortest day"]. *Metropolitan* (Tokyo Toritsu Daigaku), no. 14 (December): 64–76.

Suggests that "A nocturnall upon S. Lucies day" is unique among Donne's poems and seems quite modern. Maintains that in the poem Donne considers the hypothetical death of the speaker, which expresses both the hypothetical loss of himself and his doubts about existence itself, both quite modern themes.

244. ŌOKA, SHIN. "John Donne no Shi sono hoka" [John Donne's Poems, etc.]. *Kokobungaku* (Tokyo: Gakutosha) 15: 129–36.

Translates into Japanese "Womans constancy" and discusses in a very general way the characteristics of metaphysical poetry.

245. OSTRIKER, ALICIA. "The Lyric," in *English Poetry and Prose, 1540–1674*, edited by Christopher Ricks, pp. 119–36. (History of Literature in the English Language, vol. 2.) London: Barrie & Jenkins.

Paperback ed., Sphere Books, 1970.

Outlines the rise and decline of the lyric during the Renaissance and seventeenth century and comments on the interplay between the traditions of communal song and individual speech in the lyric. Suggests that Donne, along with Jonson, led the poetic rebellion against the "sweet line," typified by Spenser, by introducing into the lyric "greater realism, concreteness, and individual self-exploration and self-assertion" (p. 128) and by introducing "unbalanced stanza forms and rugged rhythms, learned from dramatic blank verse and following the twists of passion or dialectic, replacing mental stasis by mental process" (p. 122). Points out that Donne "kept the articulated bone of thought visible under the skin of sentence and rhythm" (p. 130), reproduced the language of prose in the lyric, injected much humor, and succeeded best when engaged in moral argument. Notes that in his poetry "the mind reveals itself in process of going about and about, in tirelessly subtle self-awareness, playing or wrestling with uncertainties, trumpeting the challenge of its wit equally in profane and sacred verse" (p. 130). Compares and contrasts Donne briefly with Jonson, Herbert, Vaughan, Traherne, Crashaw, and others.

✒ 246. P., L. "Donne's 'A Jeat Ring Sent.'" *Expl* 29: Query 2.
Asks for clarification of lines 7–8 of "A Jeat Ring sent": "Figure our loves? Except in thy name thou have bit it say, / I'am cheap, and nought but fashion, fling me'away." For a reply, see Ray L. Armstrong (entry 387).

✒ 247. PALMER, D. J. "The Verse Epistle," in *Metaphysical Poetry*, edited by Malcolm Bradbury and David Palmer, pp. 73–99. (Stratford-Upon-Avon Studies, 11.) London: Edward Arnold; New York: St. Martin's Press.
Comments on the development of the verse epistle in English poetry during the late sixteenth and early seventeenth centuries and discusses some of its major characteristics, such as its familiar style, its emphasis on the personal and on actual experience rather than on poetic fiction, its brevity, plainness, perspicuity, and its usual themes. Comments on Donne's verse epistles to show that they develop "from his compliments to friends at the Inns of Court towards a concern with virtue and the moral life, and in so doing, they become more classical in spirit" (p. 78). Points out that Donne, however, does not abandon his use of wit in these poems: "For wit in Donne's case is a way of perceiving reality, not a means of adorning it: it is a property of his mind rather than of his language" (p. 78). Sees the influence of both Horace and Seneca in Donne's epistles and notes his attraction to the stoic theme of living apart from the world, which he gives a particular Christian application. Comments on Donne's epistles to various great ladies and calls them love letters in which the major theme is the importance and nature of virtue: "Like the 'Songs and Sonets', the epistles express that heightened awareness of individuality which is for Donne the essential experience of love . . . one in which the lover finds his own identity through knowing, and being filled with the knowledge of, the lady's essential self" (p. 92). Compares Donne throughout with other writers of the period, especially Jonson, Drayton, Montaigne, Daniel, and Lodge.

✒ 248. PATTERSON, ANNABEL M. *Hermogenes and the Renaissance: Seven Ideas of Style*. Princeton: Princeton University Press. xv, 240p.
Discusses the importance and possible influence of the Seven Ideas of style contained in *Concerning Ideas* by the second-century rhetorician Hermogenes of Tarsus on Renaissance rhetoric, poetics, and aesthetics. Comments briefly on the Ideas of Reproof in Hermogenes and the style

of Donne's satires and sermons, suggesting that in the sermons he often rebels against the satiric tone and vehemence that he did so much to develop in the satirical tradition. Also briefly mentions Donne's use of the Idea of Speed, especially in "On his Mistris," "At the round earths imagin'd corners," and the *Satyres*.

◄§ 249. PHYTHIAN, B. A., ed. *Considering Poetry: An Approach to Criticism*. (The New School Series.) London: The English Universities Press. vii, 232p.
Reprints "The Sunne Rising" (pp. 53–54) with a brief critical commentary (p. 59) and stresses the dramatic elements of the poem as well as its rhetorical features and shifting tone. Reproduces "A Valediction: forbidding mourning" with study notes and questions (pp. 18–20) and "Batter my heart" (p. 136), "A Hymn to God the Father" (p. 136), and "Death be not proud" (p. 197) without notes or commentary.

◄§ 250. PITTS, ARTHUR W., JR. "Proverbs as Testimony in Donne's Style," in *Essays in Honor of Esmond Linworth Marilla*, edited by Thomas Austin Kirby and William John Olive, pp. 43–55. Baton Rouge: Louisiana State University Press.
Argues that a consideration of proverbs "is essential to any full description of Donne's style" (p. 55). Points out that Donne very often uses proverbs for a range of effects—for "allusion, amplification, paradox, and humor" (p. 43)—and examines, in particular, his use of proverbs as testimony "or as a kind of universal witness" (p. 43). Notes that proverbs were often employed by didactic writers for instruction "since they were regarded as the distilled experience of humanity expressed in a vivid, memorable fashion" (p. 44). Argues that Donne "avoids didacticism partly because of his great variety in tone and because the proverb is always a small part of a larger argument, but he frequently uses proverbs to express the 'common opinion of the multitude'" (p. 45). Observes that sometimes, however, he highlights his use of proverbs "by an introductory phrase, by its syntactic position within the poem, or by making it the conclusion of a stanza or a poem" (p. 45). Calls "The Expostulation," which is considered to be Donne's, "a cluster of proverbs unified by a central theme" (p. 49).

◄§ 251. PRAZ, MARIO. *Mnemosyne: The Parallel Between Literature and the Visual Arts*. The A. W. Mellon Lectures in Fine Arts, 1967. (Bollingen Series, 16.) Princeton and London: Princeton University Press. xv, 261p.
Reprinted, with minor revisions, 1974.
First printed as Princeton Paperback edition, 1974.
Briefly compares Donne's *Holy Sonnets* with Michelangelo's sonnets and suggests that "in his peculiar mixture of realism and Platonism, in the dramatic turn of his genius as well as in his laborious yearning for beauty and religion, in that double character of half-baffled, half-triumphant

struggle, in his power of depicting the horrors of sin and death and the terrible effects of the wrath of God, Donne is perhaps nearer to Michelangelo than to anybody else" (p. 45). Suggests that the chief characteristic of Donne's lyrics is "the nervous dialectic of his impassioned mind" (p. 97) that they present, a quality noticeable in Maurice Scève and ultimately deriving from Petrarch. Explains, however, that Donne "uses the elements of Petrarchan subject matter, but in a bizarre, unorthodox way that recalls the use of classical elements by Michelangelo in the anteroom of the Laurentian Library" (p. 97). Notices Donne's affinity with mannerist painters, especially "in the prominence given to an accessory detail, thus turning upside down what in other poets would have been the normal process" (p. 97). Compares Donne also to Pietro Bembo to show how far he "has traveled from the orthodox pattern" (p. 100) of elegant Petrarchism.

✎§ 252. RASPA, ANTHONY. "Donne as Meditator: A Note on Some Recent Oxford Publications." *Recusant History* 10: 241–43.

Argues that certain recent Oxford publications, especially *Ignatius his Conclave*, edited by Timothy Healy (entry 79), Helen Gardner's edition of the *Divine Poems* (1952), and James McDonald and Nancy Pollard Brown's edition of *The Poems of Robert Southwell, S. J.* (1967), tell us much about Donne's recusant and Catholic continental influences and suggests that Donne "re-oriented rather than tried to eradicate his Catholic formation into the mould of the English Church" and that his erudition in Catholic matter not only continued to develop after his conversion to Anglicanism, but, in fact, "represents positively the development of a very substantial part of Donne as poet, thinker and religious exercitant" (p. 242). Points out that, as a result of these more recent studies, Donne "appears standing in the flow of a Jesuit meditative tradition, able to reject and accept parts of it at will" (p. 243). Notes that, although Donne rejected and even satirized the very liberal use of the imagination stipulated in *The Spiritual Exercises* of St. Ignatius, he "harnessed the techniques for using it to create deeply felt experiences of history" (p. 243).

✎§ 253. RAUBER, D. F. "Donne's 'Farewell to Love': A Crux Revisited." *CP* 3, ii: 51–63.

Presents a stanza-by-stanza reading of "Farewell to love." Calls the poem one of Donne's "most extreme poems," maintains that there is "no other poem in the canon which matches it in bitterness or loathing," and argues that it is "one of Donne's most powerful presentations of a completely mechanistic universe in which man has no place of importance but is only the tool of alien forces" (p. 51). Comments in detail on the difficult lines 28–30, which John Hayward called "the most unintelligible in the whole canon of Donne's poetry" (as quoted on p. 51). Maintains that in the lines Donne is suggesting that nature decrees both the curse of brevity in intercourse and post-coital sadness for the purpose of promoting generation and that these degrees show that "nature performs her one task with a single-minded concentration, completely indifferent to the fate of the individual, completely indifferent to the human world" (p. 60). Suggests that Donne, like many of his contemporaries and like modern man, is filled with self-contempt because he "recognizes that he is unavoidably a part of the great machine" (p. 61).

◄§ 254. REEVES, JAMES, AND MARTIN SEYMOUR-SMITH. *Inside Poetry.* New York: Barnes & Noble; Frome and London: Butler and Tanner. vii, 178p.
Briefly explicates "A Feaver" (pp. 43–45) and calls Donne "perhaps the supreme intellectual of English love poetry" (p. 45). Stresses that the poem "has strong feeling as well as being characterized by involved thought" and notes that "the ending is lyrical and certainly rounds off the thinking with a firm and convincing emotion" (p. 45). Reproduces "His Picture" (pp. 162–63) without comment.

◄§ 255. REWA, MICHAEL. "Biography as an Imitative Art." *English Symposium Papers* (State University of New York College at Fredonia), edited by Douglas Shepard, 1: 3–28.
Briefly discusses Walton's *Life of Donne* as an example of biography "whose imitative object is a thematic action, a person's triumphing over time" (p. 8). Suggests that through carefully chosen comparisons, rhetorical devices, uses of framing, internal alliteration, and so on, Walton builds the first part of his biography upon the theme of Donne's transcending the frustrations, despair, and ravages of time that threaten to destroy him by commiting himself to a life of the spirit and that in the second half Walton simply catalogs Donne's virtues, "a catalogue that contains and defines the quality of numerous separate actions" (p. 10).

◄§ 256. RICHMOND, H. M. "Ronsard and the English Renaissance." *CLS* 7: 141–60.
Suggests that in some of his most distinctive poems (such as "The Sunne Rising," "Negative love," "Aire and Angels," "The Apparition," "The Canonization," "The Relique," "The Funerall," "Twicknam garden," "The goodmorrow," and especially "Batter my heart") Donne borrowed ideas, themes, images, tones, and even situations from Ronsard, "who offers consistently relevant precedents for Donne's idiosyncrasy, subjectivity, and verve" (p. 141). Points out, for example, that "the theological theme, the despairing sexuality, the military imagery, the alliterative verbal intensity, and the supposedly unique dramatic opening" (p. 144) of "Batter my heart" are derived from a little-known sonnet by Ronsard, beginning "Foudroye moy le corps, ainsi que Capanée" (p. 144). Argues that a detailed knowledge of Ronsard is required for an exact appreciation of Donne's poetry.

🥸 257. RØSTVIG, MAREN-SOFIE. "Ars Aeterna: Renaissance Poetics and Theories of Divine Creation." *Mosaic* 3: 40–61.

Discusses the importance of numbers and numerology in Renaissance thought and "how the tradition, dating back to Antiquity, of philosophising by means of numbers necessarily influenced the theory of artistic creation" (p. 43). Notes that since Donne mentions Pico della Mirandola and Francesco Giorgio in the same sentence in the *Essays in Divinity*, "it is likely he made their acquaintance through the one-volume French translation published in Paris in 1579" (p. 58). Maintains that if this is the case, then he would likely have read the prefaces that were contributed by the translators, Guy and Nicolas le Fevre de la Boderie, which "summarise and underline the relevance of cosmic structure to poetic theory and practice" (p. 58).

🥸 258. RUKEYSER, MURIEL. *The Traces of Thomas Hariot.* New York: Random House. 366p.

Refers throughout to Donne's relationship with persons closely associated with Thomas Hariot (1560–1621), especially the Earl of Northumberland, whom Donne asked to intercede on his behalf with George More, his father-in-law. Comments briefly on Donne's interest in the Virginia Company; his friendship with John Pory, who became secretary of the colony; his trip to Germany with Doncaster; and his connection with Essex through his relationship with Sir Thomas Egerton. Discusses briefly Spanish influences on Donne, especially Góngora.

🥸 259. SAOTOME, TADASHI. "Juso to Kaigi to Ketsui—Runessansu Jo-jōshi no Ichimen" [Curse, Doubt, and Resolution—An Aspect of Renaissance Lyric Poetry]. *SELit* 47, no. 1: 29–39.

Compares Donne to Shakespeare and suggests that Donne developed a Shakespearean dynamism within the framework of religion. Comments on the *Divine Poems*, especially the *Holy Sonnets*, and maintains that Donne's sonnets alone can equal those of Shakespeare but that, while Shakespeare continued to grope in the darkness of doubt and despair, Donne discovered a world of light in the darkness that surrounded him. Discusses Donne's attitudes toward the relationship of the body and soul, his concept of death, and his pervading Christian Platonism. Maintains that in the transition from Donne to Milton and Marvell the mystical nature of Platonism was weakened by an intellectual attitude so that it finally became merely an aesthetic and literary framework.

🥸 260. SAUNDERS, J. W. "The Social Background of Seventeenth-Century Poetry," in *Metaphysical Poetry*, edited by Malcolm Bradbury and David Palmer, pp. 237–59. (Stratford-Upon-Avon Studies, 11.) London: Edward Arnold; New York: St. Martin's Press.

Argues against the simplistic notion that the seventeenth century is only "a transition period of total conflict sandwiched between two opposed ages of relative clarity and stability, so that its social phenomena may be rationalized as developments en route between the starting-point and an end venue of a completely different kind" (p. 237) and explores some of the "particular deficiencies in the Tudor fabric which required change and which indeed began to change with the poets of 1600 to 1660" (p. 241). Suggests that the main development in the social context of poetry was "the emergence of an educated and intellectual printed-book public" (p. 257), resulting in "poetry as a national and learned art, which increasingly takes itself seriously and draws away from its roots in popular entertainment" (p. 258). Argues that, although this intellectualization produced many good effects (not the least of which was the poetry of Milton and Pope), "it lost the saving grace of the courtly age, the unity of the audiences, and through that unity, the universality of poetry" (pp. 258–59). Mentions Donne only briefly to comment on his reluctance to commit his poetry to print: "He was fundamentally the courtly satellite whose poetry was essential to his private life and thinking, but whose primary ambition was non-literary and who therefore saw no justification in making poetry public" (p. 250).

◆§ 261. SCHLEINER, WINFRIED. *The Imagery of John Donne's Sermons.* Providence: Brown University Press. x, 254p.
Attempts "to find suitable historical and linguistic contexts for the imagery of Donne's sermons" (p. 201) and thus to locate his imagery "between the co-ordinates of tradition and originality" (p. 12). Chapter 1, "Introduction" (pp. 3–12), presents the author's purpose and general approach: "I shall analyze Donne's imagery in relation to the concept of decorum, establish certain fields of imagery, then give attention to metaphors in the textual neighborhood of a trope, and finally try to place certain tropes against the background of some medieval semantic theories" (p. 12). Chapter 2, "Imagery and Decorum" (pp. 13–62), considers Donne's tropes in the light of Renaissance theories of decorum, especially the Aristotelian tradition of rhetoric as reflected in the contemporary *artes concionandi.* Analyzes a number of passages from the sermons to illustrate Donne's "awareness of decorum as a principle regulating metaphorical expression in terms of subject matter" (pp. 51–52) as well as between speaker and audience and illustrates the latter by commenting on Donne's use of learning in his preaching. Chapter 3, "Fields of Imagery" (pp. 63–162), discusses a select number of Donne's major image clusters, drawn primarily from Scripture and patristic sources—sin as sickness, life as a journey, the world as a book, the seal of the sacrament, salvation as a purchase, and the eyes of the soul—as well as less numerous ones—life as warfare, the relationship between God and man as marriage, food imagery, man as a worm, and other extended analogies. Argues that, although the list is not exhaustive, these fields "summarize to some extent the metaphorical universe of Donne as preacher" (p. 203) and suggests that his originality consists partly in his elaboration of these fields. Chapter 4, "Imagery and

Exegesis of Scripture" (pp. 163–200), examines a number of Donne's tropes "that are neither part of a conventional field of imagery nor decorous according to the Renaissance principle of hierarchy" (p. 204) to show that "there is behind his practice a traditional method based on the *vox-res* distinction, that is, the medieval theory of the special significance of the word of Scripture" (p. 200). Argues that "certain semantic theories that were the basis of conventional biblical exegesis supplied a pattern for what otherwise often appears only abstruse, overingenious, or shrewd" (p. 164). Chapter 5, "Conclusion" (pp. 201–4), succinctly summarizes the four preceding chapters. Notes, selected bibliography, and index (pp. 207–54).

ᴥᖉ 262. SCHMIDTCHEN, PAUL W. "The First Poet in the World . . . In Some Things." *Hobbies* 75 (November): 134–36.

Briefly discusses the tensions and contradictions of Donne's life; suggests that Donne would be addicted to crossword puzzles if he were alive today; and challenges Donne's statement that "No man is an island": "only suborning catastrophe can result when the island barriers of man, innately and accumulatively structured, inconsiderably are laid waste under the pseudo-concern for promoting a social good" (p. 136). Suggests that Donne "achieved an also-ran place in a second-rate galaxy, since nothing of sustained effort or major proportion ushered forth from his quill" (p. 136).

ᴥᖉ 263. SHURBANOV, ALEXANDER. "A Study of John Donne's Reform of Elizabethan Imagery." *Annuaire de l'Université de Sofia. Faculté des Lettres* 64, no 1: 229–92.

Examines Donne's reform of figurative language, especially as reflected in the *Songs and Sonets*, to show that, although his imagery has its roots in contemporary Elizabethan poetic theory and practice, he was "the most radical innovator of the short reflective lyric" (p. 229). Section 1, "The «Elizabethanness» of Donne's Imagery" (pp. 231–37), discusses similarities between Elizabethan and metaphysical imagery and argues that, since most of Donne's imagery is conventional, even in its disparagement of stock figures, he should be seen not as a rebel against but as a reformer of Renaissance tradition. Section 2, "The Imagery of the Elizabethan Sonnets" (pp. 238–60), comments on types and patterns of imagery used by the Elizabethans and stresses the abstract, compressed, nonsensuous, emblematic quality of much of the figurative language. Section 3, "Conventional Imagery Reshaped" (pp. 261–87), discusses Donne's innovations in the tradition and comments on the repercussions of these changes. Maintains that Donne primarily emphasizes tendencies that were already evident in Elizabethan imagery: he deepened the process of compression and concentration of conventional imagery, preferred abstract and unsensuous images (especially technical and scientific ones), and developed the conceit as a functional vehicle for argumentation and as the basis of the whole poem, thereby demolishing the allegorical poem based on emblematic stock imagery. Presents a summary in Russian (pp. 287–91). For a continuation, see entry 601.

≈§ 264. SICHERMAN, CAROL M. "Donne's Timeless *Anniversaries.*" UTQ 39: 127–43.
Reprinted in *Essential Articles for the Study of John Donne's Poetry,* edited by John R. Roberts (entry 786), pp. 374–86.
Calls the two *Anniversaries* "the most extended version of Donne's battle with himself" (p. 128). Presents a reading of the two poems to show that in *The first Anniversary* Donne searches "not so much for an answer as for a question; confusion and inconsistency increase until at last he emerges into the realization upon which the second poem is founded, that this world 'is not worth a thought'" (p. 128). Sees the first poem, then, "simply as an eloquent expression of the anguished discovery of failure" that "enables its sequel to attain a better balance of intellect and emotion, to attain the ultimate insights which unify the entire bipartite poem" (p. 129). Maintains that *The second Anniversarie* "shows Donne by an act of will refusing to think about the world he still occupies and, at least for the moment, finally succeeding in achieving that certainty expressed in the paradox of Holy Sonnet XIV" (p. 129). Argues that the "she" of the poem becomes identified and defined as a symbol for spiritual perfection.

≈§ 265. SMITH, A. J. "The Failure of Love: Love Lyrics after Donne," in *Metaphysical Poetry,* edited by Malcolm Bradbury and David Palmer, pp. 41–71. (Stratford-Upon-Avon Studies, 11.) London: Edward Arnold; New York: St. Martin's Press.
Surveys the love lyric after Donne to show that a change in societal attitudes toward love and sex is reflected in the poetry of the period and notes that by the end of the seventeenth century love "is no longer the figure of a relationship between our nature and a higher order" but becomes "whatever we can personally make of the human attraction between men and women" and "is mutual erotic passion and the search for sexual satisfaction" (p. 66). Examines the love poetry of Godolphin, Stanley, Townshend, Carew, Rochester, Lovelace, Suckling, Waller, and others to show that, although these poets exhibit formal virtuosity, ironic wit, intellectual control, and a dialectic manner, they also reflect that, after Donne, "the gulf between writing of love and writing of final things seems absolute" and that "sexual love no longer offered a paradigm of the issues that then confronted men" (p. 52). Notes that the only dynamic impulse left was "the lonely effort to bring home our fallen condition so as to remake oneself nearer the first state" and that, "after Donne, sexual love offered no way to that" (p. 71).

≈§ 266. ———. "The Poetry of John Donne," in *English Poetry and Prose, 1540–1674,* edited by Christopher Ricks, pp. 137–72. (History of Literature in the English Language, vol. 2.) London: Barrie & Jenkins.

Paperback ed., Sphere Books, 1970.

Comments on the distinguishing characteristics of Donne's mind and art as reflected in his secular and sacred poetry, such as the pervasive and constant play of wit; the complex uses of the conceited argument; the continual play of intelligence in highly dramatic situations; the elements of theatricality, figurative ingenuity, and realism; and the pervading comic vision that reflects a mind always determined to view human life and human relativity as they really are. Points out that essentially Donne's wit "becomes a matter of seizing what is really there; of showing in the order of our human condition the moral and metaphysical order it truly holds, and approximating to the structure of reality as every order of existence displays it" (p. 168). Maintains that the most distinguishing feature of his poetry is "its radical play of intelligence" (p. 169) and suggests that "it is the steady concern to get at the actuality of our human circumstances, and the search for ways of coming to terms with it, that holds all his poetry together in a coherent vision" (p. 170).

◄§ 267. STAMPFER, JUDAH. *John Donne and the Metaphysical Gesture.* New York: Funk & Wagnalls. xx, 298p.

Presents a critical reading of Donne's secular and religious poems in order to show that "their development, their lyric plots, their modes of fulfillment . . . show a considerable unity, and even shadow forth the poet who was their author" (p. xviii). The introduction (pp. ix–xx) comments on the peculiarly private, immediate, and personal nature of Donne's poetry and stresses his use of a lyric plot. Argues that, although he projects various personae or uses different speakers in his poems, "his craggy presence is everywhere present—the skeptic, the fanatic, the evasive metaphysician" (p. xix). Part I, "The Poet and His Craft," consists of two chapters. Chapter 1, "The Metaphysical Shudder" (pp. 3–36), attempts to distinguish metaphysical poetry from other modes, especially those of Milton, the Romantics, and the early modern poets (Yeats, Eliot, and so on). Maintains that the metaphysical poets "wrote ego poetry, that is, the poetry that expressed a conscious mind coming to terms with the reality about it" and argues that their poems "take place in a situation, a particular here and now to be assessed and worked with" and thus that the poem "is not a set-piece . . . but an event to be mastered" (p. 23). Comments on Donne's use of the lyric plot. Chapter 2, "John Donne" (pp. 37–61), presents a biographical sketch and a psychological analysis of Donne that later accounts for the arranging and interpreting of the poems. Stresses Donne's psychosexual development as projected in the voices in his poems. Part II, "The Early Poems," consists of four chapters: "The Promiscuity Poems" (pp. 65–83), "The Misogyny Poems" (pp. 84–96), "The Rejection Poems" (pp. 97–108), and "The Compromises of Love" (pp. 109–20), each of which analyzes individual poems according to amatory themes and gestures and according to the changing perspectives of the poet. Part III, "The Poems of Marriage," consists of five chapters: "The Structure of Love" (pp. 123–40), "The Marital Poems" (pp. 141–57), "Poems of Parting" (pp. 158–70), "The Mellow Progress of Love" (pp. 171–84), and "Love's Death" (pp. 185–97), each of which, based on biographical and psychological assumptions, explores different aspects of Donne's more mature attitudes toward love through the analysis of individual poems. Part IV, "Special Subjects," consists of two chapters: "The Fragility of Art" (pp. 201–14) and "Anniversaries" (pp. 215–27). Part V, "The Religious Poems," consists of five chapters: "The Early Devotions" (pp. 231–41), "Holy Sonnets: 1" (pp. 242–52), "Holy Sonnets: 2" (pp. 253–66), "Holy Sonnets: 3" (pp. 267–77), and "The Visionary Engagement" (pp. 278–88), each of which suggests a spiritual advancement on the part of the poet, the unfolding of the "I," as he moves through the various stages of the spiritual battle and finally in "A Hymne to God the Father" expresses his final self-surrender. Selected bibliography (pp. 287–92).

◄§ 268. STANWOOD, P. G. "Patristic and Contemporary Borrowing in the Caroline Divines." *RenQ* 23: 421–29.
Comments on the widespread practice among Caroline divines of drawing on patristic sources as well as from each other. Gives an example of Donne's and John Cosin's use of St. Gregory the Great and perhaps of the work of each other.

◄§ 269. STEIN, ARNOLD. "Metaphysical Poets." *YR* 59: 598–604.
Review article of Earl Miner, *The Metaphysical Mode from Donne to Cowley* (entry 123); A. L. Clements, *The Mystical Poetry of Thomas Traherne* (Cambridge: Harvard University Press, 1969); Ann E. Berthoff, *The Resolved Soul: A Study of Marvell's Major Poems* (Princeton: Princeton University Press, 1970); and Louis L. Martz, *The Wit of Love: Donne, Carew, Crashaw, Marvell* (entry 117).

◄§ 270. STRZETELSKI, JERZY. *The English Sonnet: Syntax and Style.* Krakow, Poland: Jagellonian University. 149p.
Employs descriptive linguistics to examine the contribution of syntax to the style of the English sonnet and attempts "to find out what describable formal syntactic features of the sonnets differentiate the style of the English sonneteers from one another" (p. 12). Comments in detail on the structure and syntax of Donne's "What if this present were the worlds last night?" (pp. 60–65). Identifies and illustrates certain chief characteristics of his "highly individualized and idiosyncratic style" (pp. 107–12) and observes that "as the most frequent and violent feature is the precipitation, Donne's sonnets are the most tense and consequently the swiftest of all, when it comes to releasing the tagmeme-filler" (p. 112). Suggests that, "because the piling up of the tension occurs both in the hard and in the soft structures, and because it is counteracted by series of slow, free units,

the overall resultant is balanced" and that "the violent pulsation of tension and release is, however, conspicuous and the general effect is that of generating and curbing very much energy" (p. 112). Suggests that Herbert's style is more involved and more complex than Donne's. Includes several illustrative tables and charts.

◆§ 271. SUMMERS, JOSEPH H. *The Heirs of Donne and Jonson.* London: Chatto and Windus; New York: Oxford University Press. 198p.

Argues that "most of the interesting poets of the period were in some sense heirs of both Donne and Jonson and that they wrote successfully a large number of different kinds of poetry" and maintains that "granted the general condition of the language, the literary and intellectual currents, the 'spirit of the age,' and other large and vaguely apprehended abstractions, for the seventeenth century as for other periods one can discover almost as many aesthetics as there are interesting poets" (preface). Rejects the notion of "schools" and finds the term *metaphysical poetry* less than satisfactory. Proposes that Herrick, Suckling, Carew, Henry King, George Herbert, Crashaw, Vaughan, and Marvell may best be seen as heirs of Donne and Jonson, "not with the implication that later poets had any familial or natural right or that either Donne or Jonson intended that they should inherit, but in the simple recognition that they came to occupy a good deal of the literary estate of their two great predecessors" (p. 15). Several parts of the book are reprinted from earlier works: Chapter 1, "The Heritage: Donne and Jonson" (pp. 13–40), first appeared as "The Heritage of Donne and Jonson (entry 272); several paragraphs in Chapter 3, "Gentlemen at Home and at Church" (pp. 76–101), appeared as part of the author's introduction to *The Selected Poems of George Herbert* (New York and London: The New American Library and The New English Library, 1967); the discussion of Marvell's "The Garden" in Chapter 5, "The Alchemical Ventriloquist: Andrew Marvell" (pp. 130–55), first appeared in *CentR* 13, no. 1 (1969); and several paragraphs from Chapter 5 and much of Chapter 6, "Private Taste and Public Judgement: Andrew Marvell" (pp. 156–81), were included in the author's essay, "Andrew Marvell: Private Taste and Public Judgement," in *Metaphysical Poetry*, edited by Malcolm Bradbury and David Palmer (entry 182), pp. 181–209. Shows in the individual studies of Suckling, Herrick, Carew (Chapter 2); Henry King and George Herbert (Chapter 3); Richard Crashaw and Henry Vaughan (Chapter 4); and Marvell (Chapters 5 and 6) that "Donne and Jonson's inheritance was less important as a fabulously rich collection of specific models than as a suggestion of the possibilities available for individual poets who were willing to explore varying, and even contrasting, speakers, modes, genres, and literary ideals" (p. 40).

◆§ 272. ———. "The Heritage of Donne and Jonson." *UTQ* 39: 107–26.

Reprinted as Chapter 1 (pp. 13–40) of *The Heirs of Donne and Jonson* (entry 271).

Distrusts the term *metaphysical poetry* because it "inevitably results in an emphasis on the influence of Donne and one kind of poetry at the expense of other influences and kinds" and suggests that *heirs of Donne and Jonson* is preferable because it correctly points out that later poets "came to occupy a good deal of the literary estate of their two great predecessors" (p. 108). Argues that the inheritance "was less important as a fabulously rich collection of specific models than as a suggestion of the possibilities available for individual poets who were willing to explore varying, and even contrasting, speakers, genres, and literary ideals" (p. 126). Outlines some of the major features of Donne's and Jonson's art, showing the differences as well as the similarities between the two. Argues that, when one compares the poets, one is tempted to set up a series of opposites but cautions that the "marshalling of abstractions can be misleading" (p. 125) and can obscure the similarities between the two poets.

◄§ 273. THORNBURG, THOMAS R. "Donne's *The Extasie*: A Definition of Love." *BSUF* 11: 66–69.
Argues that, although "The Extasie" "retains the trappings of the standard *invitation à l'amour*," it is essentially a serious disquisition on love, "a definition of earthly love considered as a manifestation of the metaphysic of Love" and therefore "what Dryden would call a 'nice speculation in philosophy'" (p. 66). Comments on Donne's use of the condensed conceit and analogy and suggests that his use of the conceit is "the controlling aspect" (p. 68) of his work.

◄§ 274. THORNE, J. P. "Generative Grammar and Stylistic Analysis," in *New Horizons in Linguistics*, edited by John Lyons, pp. 155–97. Harmondsworth, Eng.: Penguin Books; Baltimore: Penguin Books; Ringwood, Australia: Penguin Books Australia.
Reprinted many times.
Briefly comments on certain deep structures in "A nocturnall upon S. Lucies day" to show that "the poem has sentences which have inanimate nouns where one would usually expect to find animate nouns and animate nouns (or rather the animate first person pronoun) where one would expect to find inanimate nouns" (p. 193). Argues that "these irregularities are regular in the context of the poem" and that "these linguistic facts underlie the sense of chaos and breakdown of natural order which many literary critics have associated with the poem" (p. 193). Suggests that, in effect, Donne creates a new language and that, therefore, "the task that faces the reader is in some ways like that of learning a new language (or dialect)" (p. 194).

◄§ 275. TOMLINSON, T. B. "Donne and His Critics." *CR* 13: 84–100.
Evaluates Donne's vision of love and his love poetry, primarily by disagreeing with the opinions of several modern critics, such as Helen White, Rosemond Tuve, A. J. Smith, Douglas Peterson, and Louis Martz. Suggests that there is a tendency in Donne criticism to protect the poet and

his poetry from adverse criticism, to find highly questionable influences at work in his verse, and to sentimentalize both the poet and his poetry. Claims that Grierson, in the introduction of his two-volume edition of Donne's poetry (1912), opens up "more of Donne's truly radical and biting poetry than any critic before or since" (p. 100), while recognizing the limitations imposed on Grierson by his Georgian background. Maintains that the main thrust of Donne's love poetry "is to show the world of experience as in the end (and indeed at the age of twenty-five) as weighing more, and worth more, than the world where souls dwell or shall dwell" (p. 94). Points out that modern critics are bothered because Donne "can and does change from a lyrical love to a thoroughly carnal world with so little sense of personal upset or strain" but argues that, although Donne "attacks the dangers of and in the world, or in European fashion and behaviour," he can, at the same time, "take part in that world, on something of its own terms, and without being at all upset or disgusted or tired by it" (pp. 96–97).

◄§ 276. TUFTE, VIRGINIA. "Jonson and Donne," in The Poetry of Marriage: The Epithalamium in Europe and Its Development in England, pp. 207–29. (University of Southern California Studies in Comparative Literature, vol. 2.) Los Angeles: Tinnon-Brown.
Briefly compares and contrasts the epithalamia of Donne and Jonson, pointing out that both express the theme that perfection can be attained through marriage and that both are given to verbal and structural ingenuity. Maintains that Donne, however, is less conventional and that "in his hands, the epithalamium becomes a mixed mode in which humor, satire, philosophical observations, and commentary on men and affairs accompany the more customary topics and devices" (p. 219). Notes that Donne's epithalamia, like his other poems, are characterized by "extended conceits, bold metaphors, exaggeration, ambiguity, epigrams, puns, colloquial language, a strong dramatic element, and argumentative structure" (p. 219). Comments on the enigmatic nature of "Epithalamion made at Lincolnes Inne" and suggests that "An Epithalamion, Or mariage Song on the Lady Elizabeth" is "one of the most ingenius epithalamia after Spenser and one which best demonstrates Donne's major contribution to the mode, the restoration of humor" (p. 226). Criticizes "Ecclogue. 1613. December 26" for its farfetched, marinistic conceits and suggests that it is primarily interesting "for its form, a few brilliant passages, and its hint . . . of melancholy" (p. 226).

◄§ 277. VEAR, JOHN. "The Man Behind the Verse." Bolt 1, i: 23–27.
Comments on Donne's views on pleasure as reflected in "The Baite." Briefly compares the poem with Marlowe's "The Passionate Shepherd to His Love" and suggests that for Donne sensuous desirability of the woman would not be enough and that "he would also take along his intellectual

brilliance, satiric wit, for good company—in case the other went hard on him" (p. 24).

☙ 278. VICKERS, BRIAN. *Classical Rhetoric in English Poetry.* London: Macmillan and Co.; New York: St. Martin's Press. 180p.

Mentions Donne throughout this concise history of rhetoric. Gives examples of Donne's uses of various rhetorical figures: *anaphora* in "The Indifferent"; *parison* in "The Indifferent," "Twicknam garden," and "Loves Alchymie"; *asyndeton* in "Loves Usury" and "On his Mistris"; *auxesis* in "A Valediction: of the booke" and "On his Mistris"; *epanalepsis* and *epistrophe* in "The Extasie" and "The Indifferent"; *polce* in "A nocturnall upon S. Lucies day," "The Anniversarie," and "Song: Sweetest love, I do not goe"; *anadiplosis* in "A Valediction: of my name, in the window"; *antimetabole* in "The good-morrow"; *syllepsis* and *zeugma* in "The Canonization"; and *polyptoton* in "Twicknam garden" and "Loves exchange."

☙ 279. WARNKE, FRANK J. "Metaphysical Poetry and the European Context," in *Metaphysical Poetry*, edited by Malcolm Bradbury and David Palmer, pp. 261–76. (Stratford-Upon-Avon Studies, 11.) London: Edward Arnold; New York: St. Martin's Press.

Suggests that most scholars and critics today would agree that metaphysical poetry is "a kind of poetry created in England during the first two thirds of the seventeenth century, distinguished by a radical use of conceited imagery, rational or argumentative structure, a specifically intellectual emphasis manifesting itself usually in a non-sensuous texture, a language—sometimes colloquial, sometimes learned—from which all traces of special poetic diction has been purged, a markedly dramatic tone, and a preoccupation, in both amorous and devotional poetry, with themes of transcendence and aspiration" (p. 263). Attempts to point out "the connections between this poetry and a broader historical pattern, a more inclusive geographical scope" (p. 263) and thereby to challenge the notion that metaphysical poetry is a "school" (especially a "school of Donne") and to show that England shared certain literary traditions with the Continent and participated in certain historical developments that "make the existence of metaphysical poetry outside England inevitable" (p. 264). Sees metaphysical poetry as one of several versions of baroque literature and points out similarities between certain Continental poets (Jean de la Ceppède, Francisco de Quevedo, Lope de Vega, Constantijn Huygens, Tommaso Campanella, Paul Fleming, Jean Bertaut, Peter Motin, Théophile de Viau, Hofmann von Hofmannswaldau, and Marc-Antoine de Saint-Amant, among others) and the English metaphysical poets, especially Donne, Herbert, Vaughan, Traherne, and Marvell, in order to demonstrate that "metaphysical poetry is an international European phenomenon" (p. 276).

◄§ 280. WATSON, GEORGE. "The Language of the Metaphysicals," in *Literary English Since Shakespeare*, edited by George Watson, pp. 156–74. London, Oxford, New York: Oxford University Press.

First issued as an Oxford University paperback in 1970.

Argues that "there is no strictly linguistic way to take intellectual possession of metaphysical poetry, and that this judgment must apply, though in differing measure, to Renaissance and to modern methods of linguistic analysis" (p. 162). Chooses Donne's "Negative Love" and Herbert's "Vertue" to test certain "ancient and accepted assumptions about the ways that language works in them" (p. 162). Comments on a number of common (though not universal) aspects of metaphysical poems: the narrative quality, the use of dramatic monologue, the sense that the poet and the reader share an experience, the coterie nature of much of the language, the uses of argumentation, and so on. Argues that the history of metaphysical poetry "seems to be a progress toward public status" and notes that "this is a language that begins in relative secrecy among friends, and turns decisively toward public utterance with Herbert's *Temple*" (p. 170). Comments on a number of literary, philosophical, and moral reasons for the virtual demise of metaphysical poetry after 1660.

◄§ 281. WEDGWOOD, C. V. *Seventeenth-Century English Literature*. 2d ed. (Oxford Paperbacks University Series, no. 50, edited by D. R. Newth and Anthony Quinton.) London, Oxford, New York: Oxford University Press. 148p.

Revision of the 1950 edition (published in the Home University Library Series) with a new bibliography. Comments briefly on Donne's sermons (pp. 23–25, 71) and characterizes them as having "a compelling, dark, and difficult eloquence, a mixture of medieval logic with the sensual speculation of the Renaissance" (p. 23). In "John Donne and Caroline Poetry" (pp. 51–69) comments on the general characteristics of Donne's secular and sacred poetry, his fluctuating reputation over the centuries, and stresses his wit, genuine passion, logic chopping, complexity, and humor. Says that his attitude toward love is "satirical-sullen" (p. 23) and maintains that his love poetry comes from his personal experiences. Briefly compares him to Crashaw, Lovelace, Herbert, and Christopher Harvey.

◄§ 282. WEIDHORN, MANFRED. *Dreams in Seventeenth-Century English Literature*. (Studies in English Literature, 57.) The Hague and Paris: Mouton. 167p.

Discusses major theories of the dream from Homer to Hobbes, the uses of the dream in Western literature, and, in particular, seventeenth-century contributions to the traditional dream genres. Comments on how Donne uses the dream trance and cosmic voyage to hold together the varied material in *Ignatius his Conclave*, "a satire directly of the Jesuits and indirectly of the innovations wrought in medicine, cosmology, and political theory by the Renaissance" (p. 79). Comments also on the influence of

Kepler's *Somnium* and Galileo's *Sidereus* on Donne's Neoplatonic notion
that "in sleep the soul undertakes farflung voyages to obtain knowledge"
(p. 81). Discusses briefly Donne's use of love-dreams in his poetry, especially in "The Dreame" (in *Songs and Sonets*) and in "Elegy: The Dreame."
Suggests that the best love-dream lyrics in the English Renaissance are
Donne's dream lyrics, Herrick's "Vine," and Milton's Sonnet 23. Briefly
contrasts Dryden's use of the convention with Donne's.

◄§ 283. WINNY, JAMES. A *Preface to Donne*. (Preface Books, gen. ed.
    Maurice Hussey.) Foreword by Maurice Hussey. New York: Charles
    Scribner's Sons; Harlow: Longmans Group. 160p.
    Reprinted: Charles Scribner's Sons, 1972.
Primarily intended "for those who are fresh to the poetry of Donne and
realize that critical guidance is essential before this intricate verbal art can
communicate to us today" (foreword). Chapter 1, "John Donne" (pp. 9–
52), presents a biographical sketch of Donne and his times and traces the
development of Donne's critical reputation from the seventeenth century
to T. S. Eliot. Chapter 2, "The Religious Background" (pp. 53–67), surveys the religious history of England from the time of the Reformation to
the Commonwealth and presents a brief account of the controversies between the Established Church and the two major dissident groups, the
Catholics and the Puritans. Chapter 3, "The Intellectual Background"
(pp. 68–90), discusses the traditional Elizabethan world view and comments on the effect of the new science and philosophy on Donne's thought
and sensibility. Chapter 4, "The Literary Background" (pp. 92–119), outlines some of the major features of metaphysical style and compares and
contrasts Donne's poetic style with those of Shakespeare and Jonson. Discusses the influence of Donne and Jonson on later seventeenth-century
poets and concludes that Donne "forged a means of expression which was
both unmistakably characteristic of its time and an intimate reflection of
himself" (p. 119). Chapter 5, "A Critical Examination of Some Metaphysical Poems: Donne to Marvell" (pp. 120–52), illustrates major characteristics of Donne's love poetry and presents critical readings of "Womans
constancy," "The Apparition," "The Flea," "The Sunne Rising," "The Relique," and "A Valediction: forbidding mourning." Briefly comments on
Donne's religious verse by discussing "Batter my heart." Compares and
contrasts Donne with Herbert, Vaughan, and Marvell through an analysis
of Herbert's "Conscience," Vaughan's "Corruption," and Marvell's "To His
Coy Mistress." Short biographies of twenty-eight persons mentioned (pp.
153–57). Selected bibliography (p. 158). Index. Twenty illustrations.

◄§ 284. YAMAGATA, TAKASHI. "Shoron 'Hi-sonzai-teki Genson'—Shijin
    Donne, Sakuhin, Ai" ["Non-existential Existence"—An Essay on
    Donne the Poet, His Works, and Love]. *Metropolitan* (Tokyo Toritsu
    Daigaku), no. 14 (December): 77–84.
Discusses "The Extasie," "A Valediction: forbidding mourning," and "A

nocturnall upon S. Lucies day" to show that love exists in Donne's poetry only because it does not fully exist in reality. Comments on the "non-existential existence" of love in Donne's love poetry.

✒ 285. YOKOTA, NAKAZO. "Donne no 'The Extasie' ni tsuite" [On Donne's "The Extasie"]. *Kiyō* (Kyōyōbu, Tōhoku Daigaku), no. 11 (March): 1–18.
Argues that "The Extasie" is not a Platonic poem but rather an argument for the interdependence of body and soul.

1971

✒ 286. ANON. "Testing Time for Donne." *Cambridge Evening News,* 5 May.
Announces that Oliver Neville will read Donne's Sermon on Psalm 63 at the morning service in King's College Chapel on 9 May. Notes that the sermon was preached originally at St. Paul's when Donne returned to London after the plague.

✒ 287. AHRENDS, GÜNTER. "Discordia concors: John Donne's 'Nocturnall upon S. Lucies Day.'" *NS* 20: 68–85.
Presents a detailed analysis of "A nocturnall upon S. Lucies day." Argues that ambiguity and paradox are the organizing principles of the poem and claims that Dr. Johnson's description of metaphysical poetry as "discordia concors" is the very center of the message of the poem: "Die Einheit in der Zweiheit betrifft jedoch nicht nur die zentrale Aussage des Gedichts; diese ist vielmehr eingebettet in ein Geflecht von Doppeldeutigkeit, Doppelschichtigkeit, Doppelbezügen und Doppelsymbolik" (p. 69). Suggests that the modern reader is too inclined to reduce the paradox and ambiguity or at least to attempt to resolve them, whereas the seventeenth-century reader was content to allow them to remain ambiguous and intact.

✒ 288. AIZAWA, YOSHIHISA. "John Donne no Skūkyō-shi (1)—*La Corona* o megutte" [John Donne's Religious Poetry (1)—On *La Corona*]. *Bunkei Ronshū* (Jimbungakubu, Hirosaki Daigaku) 7, no. 1 (Bundaku-hen VII) (December): 1–17.
Discusses Donne's religious conversion and presents a critical analysis of *La Corona.* Comments on the devotional tradition of the sequence and on Donne's religious sensibility reflected in it.

✒ 289. ANSELMENT, RAYMOND A. "'Ascensio Mendax, Descensio Crudelis': The Image of Babel in the *Anniversaries.*" *ELH* 38: 188–205.
Argues that the image of the Tower of Babel in *The second Anniversarie* (line 417) is symbolically and structurally important to the meaning of both *Anniversary* poems. Points out that its traditional association with

human vanity, ambitious delusion, pride, and evanescence is used in both poems to describe Donne's assessment that all human achievement motivated by pride and worldly ambition will lead man ultimately to debasement, not to exaltation. Suggests that the image of the Watch Tower in *The first Anniversary* (line 294), "a perspective from which man can view true knowledge with clarity" (p. 203), contrasts with the Tower of Babel in *The second Anniversarie*. Argues that, paradoxically, the Christian reaches heaven through humility, as St. Augustine maintains, and that this lesson "is the essential wisdom of the *Anniversaries*" (p. 205). Maintains further that "the lesson of Babel, set in relief by the watchtower and the essential joys of heaven, warrants its position at the climactic moment" (p. 205).

◄§ 290. APPLEBAUM, WILBUR. "Donne's Meeting with Kepler: A Previously Unknown Episode." *PQ* 50: 132–34.
   Points out that, although it is certain that Donne read Kepler's *De Stella Nova*, "there is as yet no warrant for the speculation that he read anything else by Kepler in either printed or manuscript form" (p. 133). Points out, however, that Donne met Kepler in October 1619 at Linz. Notes that in an undated letter to an unnamed correspondent, Kepler notes that he met Donne, whom he calls a Doctor of Theology, and that Donne agreed to act as an intermediary for presenting dedication copies of Kepler's latest work in England. Argues that the work was Kepler's *Harmonica Mundi*, which he dedicated to James I in 1619 and not, as previously thought, the *De Stella Nova*, which Kepler had sent to James I in 1607.

◄§ 291. ARCHER, STANLEY L. "Donne's *Holy Sonnets IX*." *Expl* 30: Item 4.
   Maintains that Donne may have had St. Paul in mind (Romans 4: 4–5) when he wrote the variously interpreted final couplet of "If poysonous mineralls" and argues that he discredits an erroneous view of salvation based on good works. Suggests that the couplet ("That thou remember them, some claim as debt, / I think it mercy, if thou wilt forget") may be read as "That thou remember them for the merit of their works some claim as debt, salvation being their due; I think it merciful if thou wilt forget my works, good and evil." Notes that Donne, thus, stresses man's dependence on the mercy of God. For a reply, see Susan Linville (entry 1014).

◄§ 292. BALUTOWA, BRONISŁAWA. "Donne," in *Mały słownik pisarzy angielskich i ameriykanskich* [A Concise Dictionary of English and American Writers], edited by Stanislaw Helsztyński, pp. 144–45. Warsaw: Wiedza Powszechna.
   Presents a general encyclopedic account of Donne's life and works and outlines major features of his style. Comments on the nature of metaphysical poetry, especially viewing it as a reaction to Elizabethan poetry.

ᴥᴥᵹ 293. BENOIST, JEAN-MARIE. "La géometrie des poètes métaphysiques." *Critique* (Paris) 27: 730–69.

Uses the critical principles of Derrida to comment on Donne's imagery, especially his images of the tear, the specular stone, the glass, the flea, and the planisphere. Praises metaphysical poets because they recognized and accepted a universe in flux: they "bouleversent l'economie de la métaphysique, par lesquels ils réinstallent avec audace la discontinuité heraclitéenne d'un temps sans téléogie au sein même de orbe parmenidienne dans laquelle rien n'advenait" (p. 769). Explicates "Hymne to God my God, in my sicknesse," noting particularly the images of transgression, and briefly compares it to Marvell's "To His Coy Mistress."

ᴥᴥᵹ 294. BENSON, DONALD R. "Platonism and Neoclassic Metaphor: Dryden's *Eleonora* and Donne's *Anniversaries*." *SP* 68: 340–56.

Contrasts Dryden's uses of Platonism with the all-pervasive Neoplatonism underlying Donne's *Anniversaries* and shows that the "She" of the *Anniversaries* "is a figure of us, of our essence and nature's, now corrupted, whose purity can be restored only by grace, as a gift" whereas Eleanora "is a constructed idea of what we might make ourselves into, built up out of selected and heightened parts but given at least a semblance of divine origin and authority by allusive identification with divine persons" (p. 352). Suggests, therefore, that in the *Anniversaries* "the anatomy of the world is integral and necessary" but that in Eleanora it is "only a moralizing addendum" (pp. 352–53). Notes that the "She" of Donne's poems "is a figure of original virtue itself" (p. 349) whereas Eleanora is "a construction of virtues" (p. 348), more closely allied to Aristotelian moderation than to grace.

ᴥᴥᵹ 295. BICKFORD, SAMUEL S., JR. "A Note on Donne's 'The Apparition.'" *CP* 4, i: 13–14.

Points out that much of the dramatic and rhetorical appeal of "The Apparition" resides in the tension that results from the "disparity between the extraordinary nature of the things being asserted by the speaker and the quasi-rational manner in which he is speaking" (p. 13). Discusses the imagery, diction, tone, and mood of the poem. Sees in it the possibility of intended humor and even a touch of burlesque and thus argues that "the intent of the poem seems not as serious as what *prima facie* takes place in it" (p. 14).

ᴥᴥᵹ 296. BOSTON, ROSEMARY. "The Variable Heart in Donne's Sermons." *CSR* 2: 36–41.

Explores Donne's recurrent use of the metaphor or figure of the heart (based in large part on the language of the psalmists, prophets, and the Church Fathers) in some of his early and later sermons in order to illuminate "the maturation of his prose in substance, style, and art" (p. 36) and to show that, in later life, Donne "achieved a felt conviction that 'evenness' [of the heart and spiritual balance] need not be stasis, or require an impossibly rigid control over the heart's oblique declinations" (p. 41). Suggests that Donne moves "beyond emblem and into complex metaphor" and from "rigidity to flexibility in rhetoric and substance" and seems to reach "an emotional physics which can tolerate tension and stress so long as right orientation is maintained," an achievement that "results directly from his acceptance of the fact that the heart is, after all, subject to God's mercy and sometimes worthy even of our own" (p. 41).

⮵ 297. CHAMBERS, DOUGLAS. "'A Speaking Picture': Some Ways of Proceeding in Literature and the Fine Arts in the Late-Sixteenth and Early-Seventeenth Centuries," in *Encounters: Essays on Literature and the Visual Arts*, edited by John Dixon Hunt, pp. 28–57. New York: W. W. Norton & Co.; London: Studio Vista.
Discusses the iconographical and typological mode of Elizabethan and early seventeenth-century portraiture. Comments on the Lothian portrait of Donne (and reproduces it): "We do not look simply for the biographical Donne in his poems, and the Lothian portrait, suspended between wry wit and black gloom, is a way of telling us why we must not" (p. 31). Comments on Donne's love of "playing character roles for a moral purpose" (p. 31) both in his poetry and in his sermons and sees the portrait of Donne in the deanery at St. Paul's and the effigy of him in his winding sheet in the cathedral as proof of his continuing delight in the dramatic.

⮵ 298. CHANDOS, JOHN. "John Donne," in *In God's Name: Examples of Preaching in England from the Act of Supremacy to the Act of Uniformity, 1534–1662*, chosen and edited, with an introduction and annotations, by John Chandos, pp. 241–44, 270–74, 308–10. Indianapolis and New York: The Bobbs-Merrill Co.
Contrasts Donne with Lancelot Andrewes and disagrees with T. S. Eliot's evaluation of Donne's sermons. Says that, in the sermons, Donne "invites us to share in a subjective adventure in transcendental experience" and that "his spiritual transactions with God are as rapturous as his venereal ones formerly were with women" (p. 241). Suggests two reasons for Donne's success in the pulpit: "first, he brought to his sermons a public personality of ravishing charm; and second, a London Jacobean congregation came to church prepared to enjoy flesh-creeping thrills and theatrical rhapsodies as a legitimate part of a preacher's dispensation" (pp. 242–43). Reprints selections from Donne's sermons (pp. 242–43, 270–74, 308–10).

⮵ 299. DANIELS, EDGAR F. "Donne's 'Crucifying,' 8." *Expl* 30: Item 25.
Disagrees with Helen Gardner's interpretation of line 8 of "Crucifying," the fifth sonnet in *La Corona* ("Measuring selfe-lifes infinity to 'a span"). Defines *self-life* as Christ, the source and essence of all life, and *measuring* as equating or making commensurate. Suggests, therefore, that the line

means "equating the infinity of Christ with the finitude of human life, which is figuratively 'an inch.'"

✍§ 300. DATTA, KITTY. "Love and Asceticism in Donne's Poetry: The Divine Analogy." *The Jadaupur Journal of Comparative Literature* 9: 73–97.
Reprinted in *CritQ* 19, no. 2 (1977): 5–25.
Surveys Donne's attitude toward and expression of sexual love in his poetry and argues that "under his varying experiences of love, voluptuary and marital, admiring and flirtatious, ran his pursuit of Lady Virtue," whom he saw "shadowed forth in strange, even paradoxical places" until finally he "turned his amorousness rather fiercely upon God, as he had learnt from the Latin Doctors to do" (p. 92). Maintains that in the *Elegies*, *Satyres*, *Songs and Sonets*, certain of the verse epistles, and the *Anniversaries* Donne's attitude toward love and his expression of it are informed by the ascetic norms and practice of the Platonists and the Latin Fathers, especially St. Augustine, St. Ambrose, and St. Jerome. Points out how Donne's reading of the Latin Fathers shaped his own thinking on the relationship of love and chastity, marriage and virginity, eros and agape, and suggests that Donne's uses of erotic language to advocate a kind of asceticism in love reflect his Augustinian roots.

✍§ 301. DE SILVA, D. M. "John Donne—An Un-metaphysical Perspective." *Ceylon Journal in Humanities* 2: 3–14.
Challenges T. S. Eliot's criticism of Donne and argues that Donne "no more possessed 'a mechanism of sensibility which could devour any kind of experience' than did Tennyson or Browning" (p. 5). Comments on the limits of Donne's sensibility, especially his insensitivity to "beauty of most kinds" and "ugliness of all kinds" (p. 5). Suggests, for instance, that "Show me deare Christ" contains a "very grave defect in poetic sensibility" and calls the conceit of the poem "licentious" since it "makes of Christian faith a more than usually repulsive species of adultery with the Church in the role of a profligate wife and Christ as decadent wittol" (p. 6). Finds nothing particularly metaphysical about Donne's thought and maintains that his poetry "is primarily emotional, springing from the basic emotional need of self-expression, and addressing itself, unlike a mathematical or a philosophical treatise, primarily to our emotions rather than to our intellect" (p. 7). Discusses the ratiocinative and argumentative elements in Donne's poetry but warns that often "the formal argument is ancillary or subsidiary to the emotion" (p. 9). Notes that his arguments are interesting "not because of their validity in logic but because of that emotional truth they serve to stress" (p. 10) and concludes, therefore, that Donne's dialectical manner "is only a manner and does not imply an intellectual quality in his poetry" (p. 11) and that his ingenuity and learned images are merely "the brilliantly *effective* instruments of a very persuasive rhetoric" (p. 14).

◆§ 302. DEUBEL, VOLKER. *Tradierte Bauformen und lyrische Struktur. Die Veränderung elisabethanischer Gedichtschemata bei John Donne.* (Studien zur Poetik und Geschichte der Literatur, Band 14.) Stuttgart: Verlag W. Kohlhammer. 168p.

Offers a structural analysis of Donne's poetry that attempts to view it in the perspective of existing literary traditions and stresses that, although Donne's poetry developed within inherited traditions, he carried them in a new direction. Briefly reconstructs the literary situation in which Donne's lyrics were composed and appraises the stylistic ideals that determined both the possibilities and the limits of literary production around 1600. Points out the effects of contradictory stylistic ideals on Donne's poetry and notes that he often used new principles of construction (multidimensionality) and new structural forms (time frames, *coincidentia oppositorum*, value constellations). Suggests that Donne's artistry lies, in part, in his ability to manipulate conventional practices and to take them to their possible limits. Notes his talent in subjecting, even thematicizing, existing techniques to special semantic functions in individual poems. Concludes, therefore, that the actual innovations in Donne's lyrics are based on a fluid literary situation and that this process of renewal is best seen in the light of Donne's capacity to manipulate and vary standardized poetic traditions.

◆§ 303. DITSKY, JOHN. "Hemingway, Plato, and *The Hidden God.*" *SHR* 5: 145–47.

Calls Donne's influence on Hemingway "a fascinating and extensive critical paradox" (p. 147). Argues that in *For Whom the Bell Tolls* Hemingway may have had more of Donne in mind than merely the *Devotions upon Emergent Occasions* and suggests that the novel "is rich with the hot fusion of sexuality and spirituality found throughout Donne's poems . . . as well as that special form of consolation for the loss of the beloved which is another of his major themes" (p. 147). Disagrees with Cleanth Brooks in *The Hidden God* (1963) and argues that, "in view of the extended philosophical development a fuller reading of Donne makes possible, Jordan must be called much more than 'a naturalist in all the senses'" (p. 147). Briefly comments on Donne's Neoplatonism and on his view that spiritual union of lovers transcends death, especially in "To the Lady Bedford: You that are she" and "The Extasie." Maintains that in Donne, "there is no discrepancy between the sensual world and the spiritual" and that, "like the Christian mystics, he combined sexual and divine usage in a single grammar of life, an abiding metaphor of love" (p. 147).

◆§ 304. DONNE, JOHN. *John Donne: The Complete English Poems,* edited by A. J. Smith. (Penguin English Poets, gen. ed., Christopher Ricks.) Harmondsworth, Eng.: Penguin. 679p.

Reprinted, with minor corrections, in 1973; reprinted, 1975, 1976, 1977, 1978.

Reprinted in the United States: New York: St. Martin's Press, 1974.

First printed in hardback, 1974.

Contains a table of contents (pp. 5–12), a preface (pp. 13–15), a table of Donne's dates (pp. 17–25), a selective bibliography (pp. 27–31), a note on meter (pp. 33–37), the English poems (pp. 39–349), explanatory notes on the poems (pp. 351–667), an index of titles (pp. 669–74), and an index of first lines (pp. 673–79). Since the primary aim of this edition is "to make an old and difficult author as intelligible as is now possible to readers of today" (p. 15), the spellings have been modernized, the punctuation slightly modified, and some doubtful poems included. Follows no single copy text and presents the poems in the *Songs and Sonets* in alphabetical order. Records in the notes only variant readings that bear upon the sense of a line and keeps the notes primarily explanatory, not evaluative.

◄§ 305. ———. *Love Poems of John Donne*, compiled by Martha L. Moffet. (Great Love Poems.) New York and Cleveland: The World Publishing Co. xi, 111p.

Contains a brief biographical sketch of Donne and brief comments on his love poetry (pp. vii–xi). Considers "ingenious figures of speech and turns of wit, learned imagery, and fresh, original rhyme and rhythm" (p. vii) as Donne's major characteristics. Claims that "the depth and intensity of Donne's feeling for Anne [More] are clear in the poems known to be addressed to her, such as 'Sweetest love, I do not goe'" (p. x) and calls Donne's love philosophy "at once realistic and poetic, based on his brilliant insight into the love of man and woman" (p. x). Reprints (modern spellings) without notes or commentary forty-nine poems from the *Songs and Sonets*. Index of first lines (pp. 109–11).

◄§ 306. ———. *Poesie amorose. Poesia teologiche*. Introduction and translations by Cristina Campo. (Collezione di poesia, 79.) Turin: Giulio Einaudi. 123p.

Reprinted: 1973, 1977.

Introduction (pp. 7–16) presents a brief biographical sketch that stresses Donne's early Catholicism and discusses major characteristics of his poetry, focusing on the tensions and polarities in both his life and verse and on his attempts to reconcile these opposites. Bibliographical note (pp. 17–19) and a biographical chronology (pp. 21–22), followed by fourteen selections from the *Songs and Sonets*, seven of the *Holy Sonnets*, "A Hymne to Christ, at the Authors last going into Germany," "Hymne to God my God, in my sicknesse," and "The Crosse" (pp. 28–99). English and Italian on facing pages. Notes (pp. 103–17); index (pp. 121–23).

◄§ 307. FISCHER, HERMANN, ed. *Englische Barockgedichte: Englisch und Deutsch*. Stuttgart: Philipp Reclam Jun. 440p.

General introduction to English baroque poetry (pp. 5–18); fourteen selections from Donne's secular and religious poems (pp. 24–53) with German prose translations; a brief biographical note on Donne (pp. 371–

72); notes on the individual poems anthologized (pp. 372–75); and a selected bibliography (pp. 417–28).

◀§ 308. FISH, STANLEY E., ed. *Seventeenth-Century Prose: Modern Es-
says in Criticism*. (A Galaxy Book.) New York: Oxford University
Press. xi, 572p.
Collection of previously published essays, several of which contain references to Donne. Three items specifically on Donne: (1) Dennis Quinn,
"Donne's Christian Eloquence" (pp. 353–74) from *ELH* 27 (1960): 276–
97; (2) William J. J. Rooney, "John Donne's 'Second Prebend Sermon'—
A Stylistic Analysis" (pp. 375–87) from *TSLL* 4 (1962): 24–34; and (3)
Joan Webber, "Donne and Bunyan: The Style of Two Faiths" (pp. 489–
532) from *The Eloquent "I": Style and Self in Seventeenth-Century Prose*
(entry 59), pp. 15–52.

◀§ 309. FOX, RUTH A. "Donne's *Anniversaries* and the Art of Living."
ELH 38: 528–41.
Attempts to make clear "the extent to which the refinement of Elizabeth
Drury out of the *Anniversaries* enables us to conclude where the poems
themselves conclude, neither with Elizabeth Drury nor a vision of God
in heaven, but with the poet's voice speaking to men" (p. 528). Maintains
that the *Anniversaries* celebrate Donne himself and the worth of the good
soul and shows that the main focus of the poems is his intense reaction to
the goodness and death of Elizabeth Drury, a death that so inflames his
imagination that she becomes transformed by his verse into the very idea
of goodness. Concludes that the poems, therefore, "turn Elizabeth Drury's
death into the poet's life by giving him goodness to make into verse" (p.
529).

◀§ 310. FRIEDMAN, STANLEY. "Donne's 'The Apparition.'" *Expl* 30: Item
15.
Sees the last four lines of "The Apparition" as an "apparent rebuff that
is actually a strategem to win affection" by which the speaker of the poem
hopes "to play on feminine fear and contrariness." Argues that "the lack
of logicality reveals the speaker's desperation—whatever he professes for
strategic reasons, he still loves the lady."

◀§ 311. GABLER, HANS W., comp. *English Renaissance Studies in German 1945–1962*. (Schriftenreihe der deutschen Shakespeare-
Gesellschaft West, Neue Folge Band XI.) Heidelberg: Quelle &
Meyer. 77p.
A checklist of German, Austrian, and Swiss theses, monographs, and
books published between 1945 and 1967 on English literature from circa
1500 to 1650. Lists ten items on Donne, in addition to a number of
general studies on Tudor and Stuart literature.

ఆక్ష 312. GANG, TEA. "Donne," in *The Penguin Companion to English Literature*, edited by David Daiches, pp. 152–55. New York: McGraw-Hill Book Co.; Harmondsworth, Eng.: Penguin Books.

Encyclopedic account of Donne's life, works, and reputation—a highly selected bibliography.

ఆక్ష 313. GARDNER, HELEN. "Seventeenth-century Religious Poetry," in *Religion and Literature*, pp. 171–94. New York: Oxford University Press.

Surveys English religious verse of the seventeenth century and attempts to account for the fact that this period, perhaps more than any other, was propitious for religious poetry. Suggests three things that make seventeenth-century religious poetry appeal to readers of various persuasions: (1) the "poems are made poems, not effusions of feeling" (p. 192); (2) the poetry is highly intellectual; "though full of feeling, emotion, strength of devotion and personal faith, [it] is laced by, built upon, a scheme of thought, and a universe of discourse that is not the poet's own invention, but has the toughness of systems that have been debated and argued over for centuries" (p. 193); and (3) the poetry reflects "the unembarrassed boldness and naturalness with which these poets approach their subject, and the freedom with which they bring the experiences of daily life, their experience of art, their native powers of mind, their skill in argument and their wit, to play over religious doctrine, religious experience and religious imperatives" (p. 193). Maintains that Donne's influence on Herbert is not extensive and points out that "there are very few even possible borrowings from Donne in Herbert's poetry and none that are unquestionable" (p. 173). Argues that the seventeenth-century poets are linked primarily by their common religious tradition, such as that of discursive meditation. Praises Donne's ability to develop his divine poems dramatically and sees him as a "key witness to the limitations that the writing of religious verse lays upon the poet" (p. 190). Argues that Donne's religious poetry developed out of his moral poetry, not his love poetry, and that, although "we miss in the *Divine Poems* the élan of the *Songs and Sonnets*, their splendid hyperboles, the note of personal discovery, the virtuosity in the handling of argument, and the brilliance in the invention and manipulation of stanza forms" (p. 191), we find in them an intensity and an expression of the sense of human need that we do not find in the love poetry. Comments briefly on "A Hymne to God the Father," which "does not render the truth of a moment of passionate experience" but, with a sobriety that is unusual for Donne, "sums a life and has a painful honesty" (p. 192).

ఆక్ష 314. GEORGE, A[RAPARA] G[HEVARGHESE]. "Metaphysical Poetry," in *Studies in Poetry*, pp. 37–59. New Delhi and London: Heinemann.

Very general introduction to the nature of metaphysical poetry and to

Donne that relates both to the social and intellectual background of the seventeenth century. Surveys most briefly Donne's life, personality, and mind and outlines some of the most major characteristics of his poetry. Presents short analyses of "The Indifferent," "The good-morrow," "Loves Alchymie," "The Extasie," and "The Canonization."

🎜 315. GOLDBERG, JONATHAN S. "Donne's Journey East: Aspects of a Seventeenth-Century Trope." *SP* 68: 470–83.

Discusses the theological, poetical, and typological traditions behind Donne's trope of the journey to the west that becomes a journey to the east in "Goodfriday, 1613. Riding Westward." Shows that Donne's uses of traditional tropes normally and liturgically associated with the Nativity and the Epiphany in a poem on the Crucifixion support and illustrate his essential typological view of understanding historical events as well as man's place in them. Explains the theological and typological significances of this subtle collocation of seemingly diverse tropes in the poem and argues that the whole poem is "built around the tensions occasioned between two journeys: the outward physical journey west and the internal eastern journey" (p. 481). Suggests that the poem, therefore, shows that the self "becomes the instrument for the perception of the eternal in the temporal, and self-fulfillment resides in the internalization of Christ" (p. 483).

🎜 316. ———. "The Understanding of Sickness in Donne's *Devotions*." *RenQ* 24: 507–17.

Recognizes the *Devotions upon Emergent Occasions* as a unique work of Donne's imagination but challenges those who view it as the product of a disturbed or idiosyncratic mind. Shows how, in fact, his "devotional aims lead him to traditional themes and to a view of the self that tends to deny value to personal idiosyncrasies" (p. 507). Discusses the various commonplaces drawn from contemporary devotional literature that are at the center of Donne's understanding of the ultimate meaning of illness. Shows that the *Devotions*, far from being idiosyncratic, reveals "the continuities between private experience and the human condition" (p. 517). Explains that in the *Devotions*, as in most devotional literature of the time, sickness is seen as signifying sin and yet, at the same time, is seen as leading ultimately to salvation, for, "by punishing, God shows his election" and thus "ultimately sickness causes rejoicing because resurrection is implicit in the act of casting down" (p. 512). Maintains that Donne identifies his sickness with the continual human condition of sickness and sin and that by showing his transformation from sin-sickness to salvation-health he instructs his reader. Comments on the centrality of Christ to Donne's vision of sickness and salvation: "The Christocentricity of the *Devotions* serves at once its double nature: the examination of the self and the application of the commonplaces of the prayer book tradition as a prime tool in this process of self-scrutiny" (p. 517).

✍§ 317. GRANT, PATRICK. "Augustinian Spirituality and the *Holy Sonnets* of John Donne." *ELH* 38: 542–61. PN 603 R 642

Sees the *Holy Sonnets* as a synthesis of traditional Augustinian spirituality (as transmitted primarily by St. Bernard and the medieval Franciscans, such as St. Bonaventure, Jacopone da Todi, the Pseudo-Bonaventure, and others) and a "characteristically Latitudinarian desire to repudiate the harsh doctrinal derivations from Augustine, such as they were to be found, for example, among the Reformers" (p. 544). Discusses the hallmarks of medieval Augustinian piety that Donne expresses in the *Holy Sonnets*: (1) affective piety that evokes through the senses specifically biblical scenes, (2) a focus on the cross as a major devotional motif, (3) an emphasis on contrition rather than on penance and attrition, (4) an emphasis on the *felix culpa* concept of Christ's atoning through his Incarnation, Passion, and Cross for Adam's sin, and (5) a stress on the last four things in meditation in order to move man to contrition. Maintains, however, that although the *Holy Sonnets* may be seen as fundamentally Augustinian, they are also characterized by a religious sensibility that approaches that of the Cambridge Platonists. Argues, therefore, that the poems reflect "the tension of the young Renaissance latitude-man, attempting here to express himself in the mould of older models of devotion despite aspirations to achieve new" (p. 558). Points out that the "contorted and impassioned logic, the witty paradox, the flawed spirituality and note of sensationalism" (p. 560) are part of the appeal of the *Holy Sonnets* and concludes that they "are fundamentally traditional poems, and retain their identity as such even though the modes of devotion which they represent are, in the England of Donne's time, challenged" (p. 561).

✍§ 318. HALEY, MARTIN. "Donne and the Jesuits: A Satirist Goes Through His Paces." *Twentieth Century: An Australian Review* 26: 124–34.

Comments on Donne's Catholic upbringing and connections and suggests that both *Pseudo-Martyr* and *Ignatius his Conclave* are little more than Lucianic tours de force, written by Donne primarily to strengthen his position with James I, to assure the king that he was opposed to the Jesuits "as innovators, who had changed Catholicism from what it was in the good old pre-Tridentine days" (p. 129), and to dismiss any suspicion that he had Counter-Reformation leanings that would have disqualified him for secular preferment. Suggests that there is little solid theological content in either work and shows that after 1611 Donne was little concerned with the Jesuits, although he found Jesuit casuistry attractive and remained ever loyal to his recusant family. Points out that even in his Latin poem of 1622, "The Apotheosis of Ignatius," written on the occasion of Ignatius's canonization, Donne "does little beyond showing what a clever fellow its author was" (p. 134) and maintains that the same can be said of *Ignatius his Conclave*: "Donne cast himself and not Ignatius and the Jesuits in the chief role, and wanted secular preferment, not ecclesiastical" (p. 134).

◄§ 319. HASSEL, R. CHRIS, JR. "Donne's *Ignatius His Conclave* and the New Astronomy." *MP* 68: 329–37.

Challenges Charles Coffin's view of Donne's attitudes toward the new science (*John Donne and the New Philosophy*, 1937) and discusses how, in fact, *Ignatius his Conclave* not only complements Donne's view of the new science but also fits into his general intellectual and artistic development. Shows that Donne finds both the Jesuits and the astronomers foolish and dangerous. Argues that, although Donne confronts and inspects the discoveries of the new astronomers and fully explores the philosophical implications of their findings, he finally "rejects their discoveries as presumptuous, confusing, and inessential after they have passed through his consciousness" (p. 336). Sees *Ignatius, The first Anniversary*, and *The second Anniversarie* "as three steps in the process of confronting, evaluating, and dismissing consciousness" (p. 337) and concludes that "Donne's so-called disillusionment is actually a tightly controlled yet courageous free venture into consciousness by a mind which will always emerge again from that venture to transcend itself in unity" (p. 337).

◄§ 320. HEBAISHA, HODA. *John Donne: The Man and His Poetry. With an Anthology of Representative Poems*. Cairo: The Anglo-Egyptian Bookshop. 119p.

Preface (p. 5) suggests a close link between Donne's life and his poetry and maintains that Donne's "intellectual and emotional life formed such a marked pattern that his poetry can be divided into four distinct periods that coincide with four distinct phases of his life." Section 1 of the introduction (pp. 7–30) briefly discusses Donne's early life; his reaction against Petrarchism; his imitations of Ovid and uses of the tradition of the paradox, especially in the *Elegies* and in early love lyrics; and his place in the tradition of Renaissance satire. Section 2 (pp. 31–45) surveys his early religious crises, his connection with important patrons, and his marriage and comments on *Satyre III*, some of the verse epistles, and a number of the love poems that treat love with reverence and witty seriousness. Section 3 (pp. 46–56) discusses the years immediately after Donne's marriage, his occasional pieces, and especially the *Anniversaries*. Section 4 (pp. 57–67) comments on Donne's serious interest in religion and discusses *La Corona*, the *Holy Sonnets*, and the hymns. Section 5 (pp. 68–74) discusses the general characteristics of Donne's style, especially his uses of imagery, conceits, language, prosody, and dramatic elements. An anthology of selected poems (pp. 77–119), divided according to the divisions established in the introduction and based on the texts of Helen Gardner, Wesley Milgate, and Frank Manley.

◄§ 321. HERNÁDI, MIKLÓS. "Metaphysical Bards and Modern Reviewers." *Angol es Americai filologiai tanulmanyak* [Studies in English and American Philology] 1: 227–41.

Comments on the role that the "new criticism" played in the modern revival of interest in metaphysical poetry and suggests that Donne and the other metaphysical poets provided a "convenient hunting-ground for the 'new critics' who insist that the various ingredients of wit, so inherent in seventeenth-century English poetry, should be regarded as governing properties of all poetry" (p. 231). Notes that several of the most influential of the "new critics" were also practicing poets and sees a strong tie between their evaluative criticism and the directions of much modern poetry. Argues that the most unfortunate aspect of the "new criticism" has been its "extension of a Metaphysical doctrine of poetry over other kinds of poetry," an extension that "leads to the exclusion of all poetries that do not 'toe the line' of that doctrine" (p. 236), such as the poetry of Milton and of the Romantics.

⊷§ 322. HIRSH, JOHN C. "Donne's 'To His Mistris Going to Bed,' 35–38." *N&Q* n.s. 18: 286–87.
Argues that Donne's reversal of the sexual roles and his simile in lines 35–38 of "Going to Bed" may have been a conscious imitation of Catullus and not, as many editors have suggested, a blunder on Donne's part. Further suggests that lines 5–6 of the elegy may also have been inspired by Catullus and notes that the glosses in the 1521 Venetian edition of Catullus edited by A. Guarinus emphasize "precisely those elements which find expression in Donne's poem" but points out that there is no information on whether or not Donne knew this edition.

⊷§ 323. HÖLTGEN, KARL JOSEF. "Unpublished Early Verses 'On D: Donnes Anatomy.'" *RES* n.s. 22: 302–6.
Reproduces and comments on some verses in praise of Donne that may contain one of the few early references to *The first Anniversary*, written between 1635 and 1645 and found among the papers of the Isham family of Lamport, Northamptonshire. Suggests that the verses are important as "an example of contemporary Donne enthusiasm and for their interesting use of conceits, especially anatomical ones" (p. 303). Notes that the verses are written in the hand of Elizabeth Isham (1609–1654), daughter of Sir John Isham and unmarried sister of Sir Justinian Isham, and suggests that she may be the author of the verses. Praises various parts of Donne's body—brain, tongue, heart, hands and "all his other parts" (line 17)—and comments on their literal and figurative functions.

⊷§ 324. HUGHES, RICHARD E. "Metaphysical Poetry as Event." *HSL* 3: 191–96.
Argues for the development of a "mythico-religio-poetics" so that the twentieth-century reader might better understand and appreciate metaphysical poetry: "Writing in a time of anxiety amenable to myth; nurtured by a faith supportive of a sacramental response to reality; accepting the world as a panorama of symbol-saturated events rather than neuter objects: the poets of the earlier seventeenth century were involved in poem,

myth and religious insight all at once" (p. 196). Mentions Donne several times by way of illustration. Points out, for instance, that "The Sunne Rising" has as its central motif the myth of sacred time and notes that Donne's theology is fundamentally incarnational with an emphasis on the centricity of Christ.

◄§ 325. IWASAKI, SŌJI. *Eibungaku no Ishiki* [The Ethical and Aesthetic View in English Literature]. Tokyo: Kenkyūsha. xiii, 263p.
    Refers to Donne throughout. The major entry, "Love and Loneliness in the World" (pp. 160–77), contrasts the love poetry of Donne with that of John Wain. Translates into Japanese "Song: Sweetest love, I do not goe" and calls it Donne's easiest poem to understand. Presents brief critical comments on the poem and contrasts it with Wain's "Anecdote at 2 A.M." Suggests that Donne, in a Janus-like fashion, looks back to the troubadours and forward to the modern view of love. Maintains that Donne's love poetry is a blend of thought and passion, whereas Wain's lacks passion.

◄§ 326. JOSEPH, B[ERTRAM] L[EON]. *Shakespeare's Eden: The Commonwealth of England, 1558–1629*. (Blandford History Series, gen. ed. R. W. Harris.) London: Blandford Press. 368p.   /√
    Comments on seventeenth-century reaction to the "new philosophy" and suggests that much confusion has resulted from misreading Donne's famous lines from *The first Anniversary* ("And new Philosophy calls all in doubt, / The Element of fire is quite put out"). Argues that Donne was not expressing "consternation at the disappearance of old certainties crumbling into chaos; his consternation was at human pride, his own in particular" (p. 24). Suggests that likewise, in *Ignatius his Conclave*, Donne does not denounce the "new philosophy" but rather "denies that Copernicus was responsible for men coming to believe that there is no hell, or to deny the punishment of sin" (p. 25). Briefly comments also on Donne's obscurity in verse and suggests that the difficulty experienced by modern readers often comes from their "ignorance of the surface sense of Elizabethan words, and in half-ignorance or confusion over Elizabethan ideas" (p. 295). Questions whether one can say with any certainty that Donne imitated colloquial rhythms of speech in his poetry: "Guesses may be made about the colloquial rhythms of the sixteenth and seventeenth centuries (they may be dignified in academic jargon as 'conjectures'), but little is known for certain about the rhythms of daily speech in those times" (p. 297).

◄§ 327. KAWASAKI, TOSHIHIKO. "Donne's Microcosm," in *Seventeenth-Century Imagery: Essays on Uses of Figurative Language from Donne to Farquhar*, edited by Earl Miner, pp. 25–43. Berkeley, Los Angeles, London: University of California Press.
    Discusses Donne's use of microcosmic figures to show that "his micro-

cosm and macrocosm not only correspond to each other as two entities and symbolically reflect each other, but also that they represent a definite system of relative values: the smaller world is more valuable than the larger" (pp. 26–27). Points out that Donne's microcosmic figures are structurally multilevel, "a great chain of being whose links extend methodically from the largest to the smallest" (p. 27), and that in his microcosmic imagery Donne is "acutely conscious of the transference of identity by each link in the chain" (p. 29). Comments on Donne's obsession with the metaphysics of the unity of lovers in his love poetry, suggests that in these poems "the lovers' preoccupation with small things, with the microcosmic concept, and with the unity of the two are inseparable parts of the whole" (p. 33), and maintains that such figures represent a serious philosophical attitude on Donne's part and are "more than a conceited exaggeration of a Neoplatonic cliché" (p. 35). Discusses the microcosmic imagery in such poems as "The good-morrow," "The Sunne Rising," "A Valediction: of weeping," "The Canonization," and "The Flea." Points out, however, that "there are two Donnes in Donne's religious writing: the one microcosmic, the other macrocosmic" (p. 42): "The former seems to represent the man who withdraws into his private chamber in order to contemplate his dissolution into the Godhead; the latter is he who steps forth and tries to save the congregation in the Church" (p. 42). Shows that, as in his secular poetry, the microcosmic imagery in the religious poetry "served as a proper vehicle for expressing his fervent beliefs" (p. 43).

◄§ 328. KEAST, WILLIAM R., ed. _Seventeenth Century English Poetry: Modern Essays in Criticism._ Rev. ed. (A Galaxy Book, 89.) London, Oxford, New York: Oxford University Press. x, 489p.
Revision of the 1962 edition. From a total of twenty-nine previously published essays, there are five essays on the general nature of metaphysical poetry and poets: (1) Herbert J. C. Grierson, "Metaphysical Poetry" from _Metaphysical Lyrics & Poems of the Seventeenth Century: Donne to Butler_ (Oxford: Clarendon Press, 1921), pp. xiii–xxxviii; (2) T. S. Eliot, "The Metaphysical Poets" from _Selected Essays, 1917–1932_ (New York: Harcourt, Brace, 1932); (3) Helen Gardner, "The Metaphysical Poets" from _The Metaphysical Poets_ (London: Oxford University Press, 1961), pp. xix–xxxiv; (4) Earl Miner, "Wit: Definition and Dialectic" from _The Metaphysical Mode from Donne to Cowley_ (entry 123), pp. 118–58; and (5) Joseph Anthony Mazzeo, "A Critique of Some Modern Theories of Metaphysical Poetry" from _MP_ 50 (1952): 88–96. There are three items specifically on Donne's poetry: (1) J. B. Leishman, "Donne and Seventeenth-Century Poetry" from _The Monarch of Wit: An Analytical and Comparative Study of the Poetry of John Donne_ (London: Hutchinson, 1951), pp. 9–26; (2) George Williamson, "The Convention of _The Extasie_" from _Seventeenth Century Contexts_ (London: Faber & Faber; Chicago: The University of Chicago Press, 1960, 1961), pp. 63–77; and (3) Louis L. Martz, "John Donne in Meditation: the _Anniversaries_" from

The Poetry of Meditation: A Study in English Religious Literature of the Seventeenth Century (New Haven: Yale University Press; London: Oxford University Press, 1954), pp. 211–48.

◄§ 329. KERMODE, FRANK. "John Donne," in *Shakespeare, Spenser, Donne: Renaissance Essays*, pp. 116–48. New York: The Viking Press.

Reprinted as *Renaissance Essays: Shakespeare, Spenser, Donne* (London: Fontana, 1973).

Reprint of *John Donne*, which first appeared in the Writers and Their Works, no. 86 (London: Longmans, Green and Co., 1957), 48p.

◄§ 330. KISHIMOTO, YOSHITAKA. "Donne no Holy Sonnets" [Donne's *Holy Sonnets*]. *Kiyō* (Bungakubu, Baika Joshi Daigaku) no. 8 (December): 1–14.

Explores the uniqueness of the *Holy Sonnets*, especially Donne's uses of biblical language in them. Points out that Donne typically employs biblical language to achieve highly emotional and paradoxical effects, especially by using biblical language in very realistic contexts.

◄§ 331. KREPS, BARBARA I. "The Serpent and Christian Paradox in Donne's 'First Anniversary.'" *RLMC* n.s. 24: 198–207.

Argues that in *The first Anniversary* Donne's double purposes of praising a specific person and of anatomizing the corruption of a fallen world are united in his treatment of Elizabeth Drury, who is seen both as the human embodiment of perfection and as the very principle of Perfection itself: "Thus in her latter identity she is cause, where in the former she partakes of the effect" (p. 199). Points out that the image of the serpent reflects the dual directions of the poem and, in fact, becomes "a symbol which unites in itself the divergent concepts lying at the heart of 'The First Anniversary'" (p. 199). Surveys the complex and often paradoxical uses of the serpent in the unnatural natural history of the Renaissance and in the Old and New Testaments and concludes that in the poem the serpent is a figure both of Elizabeth and of Christ and that, by associating the two, Donne suggests that "as in studying Christ, so in studying the figure of the ideal Elizabeth can one learn to live well by learning properly to value the life of this world and that of the next" (p. 207). Argues that, although the serpent image is not pervasive in the poem, "the weight of tradition behind the figure gives it the power when it does appear to suggest the poem's most central concerns" (p. 207).

◄§ 332. KUSUNOSE, TOSHIHIKO. "John Donne—Henreki to Fukkatsu" [John Donne—Wandering and Resurrection] in *Shi to Shin—Donne o Meguru Shijin tachi* [Poetry and Faith—Poets around Donne], pp. 1–75. Kyoto: Keibunsha.

Maintains that Donne was deeply introspective and that certain of his poems are self-reflective meditations, such as *The second Anniversarie*, in which the real subject is Donne, not Elizabeth Drury. Discusses Donne's notion of the unity of body and soul and suggests that his poems that pursue this theme display a high level of intellectual and moral sensitivity. Notes that the sermons reveal much about his spiritual explorations and his attempts to come to terms with his inner tensions and contradictions and notes that they therefore often employ images taken from navigation. Suggests that Donne is a moralistic theologian, but not a logical dogmatist. Notes that Donne's sense of spiritual exploration and self-analysis led him to be preoccupied with death but that he regarded death not as an end but as the moment of resurrection.

333. LANDER, CLARA. "A Dangerous Sickness Which Turned to a Spotted Fever." *SEL* 11: 89–108.

Suggests that Donne's *Devotions upon Emergent Occasions*, while essentially devotional in nature and not merely the record of a private experience, mirrors in language and structure the pathogenesis of the typhus that afflicted Donne in 1623–1624. Examines the devotional, psychological, and clinical patterns of the *Devotions* to show how all three combine and are part of the whole. Suggests further that each of the three parts reflects different stages in the disease and maintains that the three parts of each meditation—the Meditation, Expostulation, and Prayer—correspond not only to the morning, afternoon, and evening services of the Book of Common Prayer but also to "the morning, afternoon, and evening entries on a medical case chart" (p. 94). Points out that the symptoms of typhus (deep melancholia, a tendency toward suicide, and so on) parallel many of the major psychological and metaphysical concerns of the age. Maintains that "like the Old Mystery, Miracle, and Morality Plays, intended to instruct but also to entertain, *Devotions* is part mummery, part declamation" and that "clinical realities are used to thread the narrative, lending immediacy and authenticity to the whole" (p. 103).

334. LEGOUIS, PIERRE. "Some Remarks on Seventeenth-Century Imagery: Definitions and Caveats," in *Seventeenth-Century Imagery: Essays on Uses of Figurative Language from Donne to Farquhar*, edited by Earl Miner, pp. 187–97. Berkeley, Los Angeles, London: University of California Press.

Reprinted in *Aspects du XVIIᵉ Siècle* (Paris: Librairie Marcel Didier, 1973), pp. 225–33.

Comments briefly on the confusion and ambiguous use of critical terms, such as imagery, metaphor, allegory, analogy, type, emblem, symbol, myth, ambiguity, puns, irony, and dramatic irony: "The modern tendency has been . . . to extend the meaning of critical terms beyond recognition" (p. 189). Mentions briefly his early study of Donne's imagery and comments on his study *Donne the Craftsman* (1928), which "at least made a stir (mostly protests)" (p. 187).

◀§ 335. LEVINE, GEORGE R. "Satiric Intent and Baroque Design in Donne's 'Go and Catch a Falling Star.'" NS 20: 384–87.

Explicates "Song: Goe, and catche a falling starre" as "a piece of baroque art" in which the major complications "consist of a series of closely linked antitheses and a series of related progressions—chronological, spatial, and rhetorical," all of which "are, in turn, themselves reflections of a central, controlling antithesis" (p. 385). Comments on the controlling elements of the poem, on the antitheses of time and space in it, and on the various progressions in its argument and suggests that the cynical speaker not only attempts to teach his friend about feminine infidelity but also tries to strengthen his own doubts about woman's unfaithfulness.

◀§ 336. LEWALSKI, BARBARA K. "Donne's Poetry of Compliment: The Speaker's Stance and the Topoi of Praise," in *Seventeenth-Century Imagery: Essays on Uses of Figurative Language from Donne to Farquhar*, edited by Earl Miner, pp. 45–67. Berkeley, Los Angeles, London: University of California Press.

Suggests that "if we set aside Donne's anniversary poems, which are altogether more complex in conception and treatment, the epithalamia, which are concerned to celebrate the occasion of a marriage rather than an individual, and those verse letters that offer advice on moral conduct or poetry in the forthright tones of manly friendship, Donne's remaining poems of compliment—almost all of them written in the period 1605–1614—display a remarkable stylistic similarity, who ever the person praised" (pp. 45–46). Discusses how these epideictic poems differ radically from the epideictic poetry of Donne's contemporaries and how the uniqueness of his poems of compliment arises "from the speaker's stance and from the symbolic value discovered in the persons addressed, both of which have profound implications for the ways in which the traditional topoi are developed" (p. 67). Shows that Donne's speaker usually assumes the stance of "studying or meditating upon, or contemplating the person he addresses or elegizes" (p. 47) and that often the speaker involves his audience in the experience. Points out that, since Donne sees the individual person praised "not as an image or reflection of an ideal Platonic form or idea but, more precisely, as an image of God," his meditations and compliments are "metaphysical praises of the possibilities of the human spirit acted upon by God" (p. 49) and are "recognitions of what Heaven can make of any piece of human clay, of what we can study and discern through any good Christian life, of the 'God' in the Countess of Bedford, or in any other person" (p. 50). Analyzes a number of the poems to show how Donne combines wit with high seriousness and argues that the wit of these poems "is compatible with—indeed it is the very vehicle for—serious metaphysical explorations of the bases of human worth" and that "the praises are not directed to the specific moral qualities of particular individuals (as with Ben Jonson), but to the potentialities of the human soul as image of God" (p. 67).

❧ 337. LISBETH, TERRENCE L. "Donne's 'Hymne to God my God, in my sicknesse.'" *Expl* 29: Item 66.

Discusses "several associative ideas concerning explorations, religious beliefs, and concepts of man as a microcosm" in Donne's highly witty conceit of the *mappa mundi* in "Hymne to God my God, in my sicknesse," specifically his uses of the phrases *South-west discoverie* and *Per fretum febris* and of the word *streights*.

❧ 338. McCANLES, MICHAEL. "Mythos and Dianoia: A Dialectical Methodology of Literary Form," in *Literary Monographs*, vol. 4, edited by Eric Rothstein, pp. 3–88. Madison, Milwaukee, and London: The University of Wisconsin Press.

Argues that "plot, considered in the Aristotelian manner as the ultimate principle of coherent form to which other parts of a literary mimesis are subordinated as to their final cause, is generated out of the attempt on the part of the agent of the plot to avoid and deny plot" and that "the logic which controls this generation of plot out of a 'refusal' of plot is a dialectic, the forms of which are themselves various corollaries to the principle of noncontradiction" (p. 3). Analyzes the dialectical plots in a number of Donne's poems and comments on the dialectical interactions that Donne sets up between his reader and his persona's argument. Notes that in "The Flea," for instance, the persona is shown to push "a single line of argumentation to such a narrow extreme that the reader is invited to reverse this direction with a simple negation" (p. 34) and that likewise in "Lovers infinitenesse" the reader is "called upon to make continual adjustments as he looks through (i.e., by means of) the poem at what the poem is referring to, grasping this reality just as the poem itself does, by a constant realignment of individual statements in relation to one another" (p. 35). Notes that in "Annunciation" (from *La Corona*) Donne invites the reader "to transcend discursive thought and to wonder at the mystery of the Incarnation" by rendering the mystery overtly "in language which communicates precisely its incommunicability" (p. 36).

❧ 339. MACDONALD, ROBERT H. *The Library of Drummond of Hawthornden*, edited with an introduction by Robert H. MacDonald. Edinburgh: Edinburgh University Press; Chicago: Aldine Publishing Co. xii, 245p.

Briefly comments in the introduction on William Drummond of Hawthornden's critical appraisal of Donne's poetry: "He could appreciate Donne, but not imitate him; he had an instinctive distrust of the way Donne broke the good rules of prosody" (p. 26). Lists Donne books (entries 753, 754) and manuscripts (entries 1346, 1347) found in Drummond's library.

❧ 340. MAHONY, P[ATRICK J]. "'She' and 'Shee' in Donne's *Anniversaries*." *AN&Q* 9: 118–19.

Presents additional arguments to refute Marjorie Nicolson's theory in

The Breaking of the Circle (1950; rev. ed., 1960) that Donne used *she* in the *Anniversaries* to refer to a real person and *shee* to refer to "the Idea of a Woman." Agrees with Joan Bennett (*MLR* 47 [1952]: 390–92) and Sir Herbert Grierson (*RES* 3 [1952]: 178–80), who note that the double *e* was used simply for emphasis, especially at the ends of lines.

◄§ 341. MANN, LINDSAY A. "Aquinas in Donne's Sermon Preached at Paul's Cross, 24 March 1616/17." *N&Q* n.s. 18: 287.

Notes that Donne's idea of love as a transforming power that appears in his early sermon on Proverbs 22:11 echoes the specific words and ideas of St. Thomas Aquinas found in his commentary on Peter Lombard's *Sentences*. Points out, however, that although Donne relies on Aquinas's definition of love, he merely "uses the definition to support his own high evaluation of love," since he goes beyond the expository purpose of Aquinas and, through his diction and metaphors, gives "to a traditional conception renewed and emotional force."

◄§ 342. ———. "The Marriage Analogue of Letter and Spirit in Donne's Devotional Prose." *JEGP* 70: 607–16.

Notes that for Donne, as for most seventeenth-century Christians, marriage was seen as a type or symbol of numerous kinds of relationships— between God and man, Christ and the Church, God and the individual, reason and faith, the prince and his people, and so on—and was also seen as contributing to and partaking in these relationships. Discusses in particular Donne's view of the relationship between the letter (the literary history) and the spirit (the spiritual significance) in Scripture and shows how his "conception of marriage as a union of mutual dependence and subordination seems to be reproduced in his vision of a close relation between letter and spirit in Scripture" (p. 610). Examines Donne's exegetical techniques to show that for him "the spiritual and the literal are married, but, in conformity with the Antiochene School of Chrysostom and the best Medieval exposition (Hugh of St. Victor, Aquinas), Donne stresses more heavily than usual in Medieval practice the absolute primacy of the literal level"—a distinctly Reformation emphasis that parallels "his insistence on the dignity of the human body and of marriage—though both in exegesis and in men's relations he is not content to rest merely with the body, with the natural" (p. 614). Discusses Donne's application of biblical texts and exegesis to human marriage, especially in his famous marriage sermon based on Hosea 2:19, to show that "the relation between the letter and spirit in Scripture, in which the letter is of fundamental importance for constituting spiritual meaning, but in which the spiritual meaning is more exalted, parallels the relationship between human marriage and spiritual marriage to Christ" (p. 616).

◄§ 343. MARINELLI, PETER V. *Pastoral*. (The Critical Idiom, no. 15, gen. ed., John D. Jump.) London: Methuen & Co. vi, 90p.

Relates "The Baite" to the pastoral tradition and shows how Donne "transfers the setting from a pastoral to a piscatorial setting" (p. 29). Notes that, unlike the use of fishermen and seashore settings in Theocritus and Sannazzaro, Donne's setting "is made with cunning and malice" (p. 29).

❧ 344. [MAXWELL, J. C., AND E. G. STANLEY], editors of *N&Q*. Replies to "Two Hitherto Unrecorded Imitations of Donne in the Eighteenth Century." *N&Q* n.s. 18: 346.

The editors append to their additions to Brijraj Singh's "Two·Hitherto Unrecorded Imitations of Donne in the Eighteenth Century" (entry 370), a further item, "On Chloe's Picture," an expansion of Donne's epigram, "Phryne," that appeared in *The Universal Spectator* (1 December 1733). See also Peter A. Tasch (entry 375).

❧ 345. MENDEL, SYDNEY. "Dissociation of Sensibility." *DR* 51: 218–27.

Discusses in a very broad sense the dissociation of sensibility in modern man—the tendency to engage in abstract thinking and thereby dissociate thought from the senses and from feelings—and concludes that "the mild form of dissociation of sensibility that Eliot discerns in Tennyson and Browning leads ultimately to that crisis of self-identity which threatens modern man" (p. 227). Briefly outlines Eliot's theory and mentions Donne by way of illustration.

❧ 346. MILES, JOSEPHINE. "Twentieth-Century Donne," in *Twentieth-Century Literature in Retrospect*, edited by Reuben A. Brower, pp. 205–24. (Harvard English Studies, 2.) Cambridge, Mass.: Harvard University Press.

Reprinted in *Poetry and Change: Donne, Milton, Wordsworth, and the Equilibrium of the Present* (Berkeley, Los Angeles, London: University of California Press, 1974), pp. 143–64.

Discusses major characteristics of Donne's poetry, especially the essential elements of his language and attitudes and "the simplicity and extremity of his conceptual construction": "A characteristic poem by Donne proposes an excess, by superlative or imperative, then negates the excess" (p. 205). Suggests that his poetry is "the poetry of effortful articulation of thought; it is spelling out of problems, analyzing of motives and situations, a learned exploring of extremes of the planes of existence now and hereafter, of the cosmos below and above" (p. 221). Argues that in fundamental ways Donne differs from the other metaphysical poets and from modern poets who claim to be influenced by him: "far more verbs and connectives than for anybody else, far less concretion than for most others, a far more persistent pattern of poetic construction" (p. 206). Calls W. B. Yeats "our greatest modern metaphysical poet" (p. 210) and compares and contrasts him with Donne. Discusses the nature and extent of Donne's influence on certain twentieth-century poets, especially T. S. Eliot,

W. H. Auden, E. E. Cummings, Robinson Jeffers, Wallace Stevens, and Robert Penn Warren, but concludes that few "have tried for or achieved that combination of values which makes for a whole likeness rather than a scattering of likenesses" (p. 221). Points out, however, that W. S. Merwin's long lyric "Fear" is a good example of a modern metaphysical poem and finds in it "a suggestion of the surviving power of Donne's thought in the twentieth century" (p. 224).

◄§ 347. MILGATE, WESLEY. "Donne, 1572–1631," in *English Poetry: Select Bibliographical Guides*, edited by A. E. Dyson, pp. 40–59. London and New York: Oxford University Press.
Evaluative bibliographical essay on Donne divided into five major sections: (1) texts, (2) critical studies and commentary, (3) biographies and letters, (4) bibliographies, and (5) background reading, followed by a listing of selected items according to the above categories.

◄§ 348. ———. "Donne and the Roman Triumph." *Parergon* no. 1: 18–23.
Comments on lines 177–246 of "Obsequies to the Lord Harrington" in which Donne employs conceits and notions based on the *ius triumphandi*, the rules governing the triumphal entry of victorious generals into ancient Rome, to describe Lord Harrington's entry into heaven. Tentatively suggests the *De Roma Triumphante* (1531) by Flavio Biondo (Blondus), perhaps supplemented by other accounts, as the most likely source for Donne.

◄§ 349. MILLER, DAVID M. *The Net of Hephaestus: A Study of Modern Criticism and Metaphysical Metaphor*. The Hague and Paris: Mouton. 173p.
Examines the accomplishment of the "new critics" (especially I. A. Richards, T. E. Hulme, William Empson, Allen Tate, John Crowe Ransom, Cleanth Brooks, W. K. Wimsatt, Jr., Philip Wheelwright, and Murray Krieger) by focusing on their theories and explications of metaphor, particularly as applied to metaphysical poetry. Comments in detail on the structure, satiric attitude, and metaphorical implications in Donne's "Epithalamion made at Lincolnes Inne" (pp. 140–53). Argues that "if the poem is successful, the broadly satiric reading should arise, not from Donne's biography, but from the poem itself" and presents a reading of the poem to show that there is "ample evidence for a broadly satiric reading in the structure of its metaphoric action" (p. 144). Comments also briefly on Tate's and Brooks's discussion of "A Valediction: forbidding mourning" (pp. 74, 88) and on Krieger's reading of "The Canonization" (p. 116). Discusses Donne's use of the pun (pp. 127–28), the tenor and vehicle of "Batter my heart" (pp. 131–33), and the metaphoric implications of lines 18 and 20 of "Goodfriday, 1613. Riding Westward" (pp. 138–40).

≥§ 350. MINER, EARL. *The Cavalier Mode from Jonson to Cotton.* Princeton: Princeton University Press. xiv, 333p.

Attempts "to discriminate Cavalier poetry from other seventeenth-century alternatives, and to discriminate the major features within it" as well as "to describe conceptions of the self, of life, and the world held by poets in the late sixteenth and seventeenth centuries, conceptions which one group, the Cavaliers, tended to set forth in terms of certain styles, certain recurring subjects, certain recurring approaches, and certain cultural assumptions" (p. vii). Mentions Donne throughout, primarily contrasting the private mode of his poetry with the social mode of such poets as Jonson, Cowley, Carew, Waller, and Suckling. Argues that "Donne's policy of exploring within the private world for what may belong to larger worlds was not followed by Jonson and his sons," but "they explored the social world in order to discover their own inner resources" (p. 155). Sees Donne as Petrarchan or anti-Petrarchan but argues that "Cavalier poetry was, so to speak, pre-Petrarchan in its major emphasis" (p. 118) and suggests that, "whereas Donne took and refashioned the conceited aspects of Petrarchanism, Jonson and the Cavaliers refashioned and revitalized the psychological conventions of Petrarchanism" (p. 225). Briefly comments on "Since you must goe, and I must bid farewell," a poem variously attributed to both Donne and Jonson (pp. 244–45).

≥§ 351. MINER, EARL, ed. *Seventeenth-Century Imagery: Essays on Uses of Figurative Language from Donne to Farquhar.* Berkeley, Los Angeles, London: University of California Press. xxi, 202p.

Contains eleven original essays, three of which discuss Donne. Each has been entered separately in this bibliography: (1) Toshihiko Kawasaki, "Donne's Microcosm" (entry 327), pp. 25–43; (2) Barbara K. Lewalski, "Donne's Poetry of Compliment: The Speaker's Stance and the Topoi of Praise" (entry 336), pp. 45–67; and (3) Pierre Legouis, "Some Remarks on Seventeenth-Century Imagery: Definitions and Caveats" (entry 334), pp. 187–97.

≥§ 352. MOORHEM, SISTER JOAN. "Two Explications—John Donne's Holy Sonnet XIV and Gerard Manley Hopkins' Sonnet 69." *Insight* (Notre Dame Joshi Daigaku, Kyoto) no. 3 (May): 62–71.

Compares and contrasts the poetry and spiritual temperaments of Donne and Hopkins through explications of "Batter my heart" and Hopkins's sonnet 69, both poems of spiritual conflict and anguish. Discusses the metaphoric structure of Donne's sonnet, its form, imagery, uses of paradox, logic, and rhythm. Shows that Donne and Hopkins express similar themes in their sonnets, share certain techniques, and create effective rhythms to convey human suffering yet concludes that essentially they are different: "Donne's development is discursive; Hopkins', contemplative" (p. 70).

⁓§ 353. MUELLER, JANEL M., ed. *Donne's Prebend Sermons.* Edited, with an introduction and commentary, by Janel M. Mueller. Cambridge, Mass.: Harvard University Press. xi, 361p.

Preface (pp. vii–xi) argues that the Prebend Sermons should be considered together because "as a unit they rank high among Donne's best and most representative productions" and also because the five sermons have "the advantage of wholeness" (p. x). Announces that this edition provides a more detailed and extensive introduction and commentary on the five sermons than Potter and Simpson provided; the correction of several minor textual errors of the Potter and Simpson text; and extensive examination of Donne's theory and practice of preaching, especially his notions on the use of Scripture in sermons; and a detailed study of Donne's references to the Fathers of the Church, the Scholastics, and other commentators and writers mentioned in the Prebend Sermons. Introduction (pp. 1–70) presents the biographical and historical contexts of the Prebend Sermons (mid-1624 to mid-1627); comments on Donne's views on preaching and on Scripture and discusses the influence of the Fathers, especially St. Augustine, and of the Scholastics, especially St. Thomas Aquinas, on Donne's notion of scriptural discourse and of the sermon patterned on these sources; gives an introduction to and brief analysis of each of the five sermons; and explains textual deviations from Potter and Simpson. Reproduces the five Prebend Sermons (pp. 72–179), followed by a detailed commentary, a listing of sources, and notes for each of the sermons (pp. 183–327). Appendix A, "The Date of the Fifth Prebend Sermon" (pp. 331–37), argues by means of topical allusions and textual parallels that the sermon was delivered in May or June 1627. Appendix B, "Table of English and Latin Citations of Scripture in the Prebend Sermons" (pp. 338–54), attempts to show Donne's "energetic and eclectic use of most of the English and Latin versions available and, above all, to document very graphically the material role of God's Word among the words of Donne the preacher" (p. 338). Index.

⁓§ 354. NAGOYA, YASUHIKO. "Donne no Shi no Engeiki-teki Seikaku" [The Dramatic Nature of Donne's Poems]. *Kiyō* (Gengo/Bungaku) (Gaikokugogakubu, Achi Kenritsu Daigaku) 6 (December): 85–109.

Discusses Donne's interest in the theater and suggests its influence on his highly dramatic poems. Explores in particular the dramatic settings of *Satyre II, Satyre IV*, "This is my playes last scene," "The Perfume," "The Dreame," "The Apparition," "The Extasie," "The good-morrow," and "Goodfriday, 1613. Riding Westward."

⁓§ 355. NAKAMURA, MINEKO. "A Ring Without the Stone: A Study of Baroque Quality in *The First Anniversary* (1)." *Insight* (Notre Dame Joshi Daigaku, Kyoto) no. 3 (May): 72–96.

First part of a two-part article; see also entry 477. Comments on the puzzlement and dissatisfaction that many readers of *The first Anniversary* have felt since the time of Ben Jonson and argues that it is a more difficult poem to understand than is *The second Anniversarie*. Discusses *The first Anniversary* in terms of a specialized definition of the baroque and calls it "a poem that gives a picture of the world like that of a ring that lost its jewel" (p. 76), Elizabeth Drury being the jewel and the world being the ring.

◆§ 356. ORGEL, STEPHEN. "Affecting the Metaphysics," in *Twentieth-Century Literature in Retrospect*, edited by Reuben A. Brower, pp. 225–45. (Harvard English Studies, 2.) Cambridge, Mass.: Harvard University Press.

Points out that the label *metaphysical* is largely the creation of critics, not of the poets themselves; yet "from the time 'metaphysical' was first formulated as a critical term its definition has remained relatively constant, but the list of poets whom critics regarded as metaphysical has varied wildly from generation to generation" (p. 226). Presents a brief history of the term and considers how a seventeenth-century reader would have regarded Donne's poetry. Points out, for instance, that "by Elizabethan standards Donne has most of the traditional virtues" and that he is "less an innovator than Sidney" (p. 230): "The things that have been most startling to readers since the eighteenth century—the far-fetched comparisons, the synthesis of disparate materials—are in fact the least new" (p. 231). Argues that what is truly new in Donne is "the intelligence, the sensitivity, the extraordinary command of language and emotive detail: what is new, in fact, is what is new about every great poet" (p. 231). Shows that "no theory of metaphysical poetry has proved adequate" because "'metaphysical' refers really not to poetry, but to our sensibilities in response to it" (p. 245). Discusses in particular Renaissance concepts of poetic images, especially emblems, stressing that even in emblem books the verbal element is basic: "Renaissance poets tended to think of images as tropes or rhetorical figures, that is, as verbal structures" (p. 238). Concludes, "What we find as critics in works of art is largely determined by what we are looking for, and it is one of the functions of criticism to make us look again and again at works of art in ways that are valid but untried," but warns that "we must beware of taking our responses for historical data" (p. 245).

◆§ 357. PARTRIDGE, A. C. "Donne," in *The Language of Renaissance Poetry: Spenser, Shakespeare, Donne, Milton*, pp. 231–60. (The Language Library, edited by Eric Partridge and Simeon Potter.) London: Andre Deutsch.

Discusses the general characteristics of Donne's poetic themes and style and contrasts his poetry to that of Spenser and Shakespeare. Presents detailed stylistic analyses of "To Sir Henry Wotton: Sir, more then kisses" (lines 1–8, 47–58, 63–70), "The Dreame" (from the *Elegies*), "The Dreame" (from the *Songs and Sonets*), "Twicknam garden," "The Litanie" (stanzas I, III, VI, VIII, XV), and "A Hymne to Christ, at the Authors last going into Germany." Suggests that the main ingredients of Donne's style are "paradox, conceits, syntactical fragmentation, and metrical originality, sometimes so daring that the pattern is in danger of annihilation" (pp. 258–59) and that his originality "lies largely in his introspective and analytical power," by which his poems become "logical patterns of association" (p. 259). Stresses that Donne's style is "the antithesis of Spenser's expansive method" (p. 259) and that his language, unlike Spenser's, "expands the speculative imagination" (p. 260).

◄§ 358. PITTS, ARTHUR W., JR. "Donne's *Holy Sonnets* VI." *Expl* 29: Item 39.
Argues that the face mentioned in line 7 of "This is my playes last scene" is not the face of God at Judgment Day, as most editors have suggested, but is rather the face of Satan. Points out that seeing the face as belonging either to God or to death "weakens the otherwise tight parallel structure and unity" of the sonnet. For replies, see Edgar F. Daniels (entry 403) and J. Max Patrick (entry 482).

◄§ 359. POWERS, DORIS C. *English Formal Satire: Elizabethan to Augustan.* (De Proprietatibus Litterarum, edited by C. H. van Schooneveld, Series Practica, 19.) The Hague and Paris: Mouton. 214p.
Argues that eighteenth-century formal satire directly descended from Elizabethan satire. Outlines major features of early English formal satire and shows that there is a continuous history of the genre throughout the seventeenth century that can be described "in terms of an early-established set of basic formal elements from which each writer in turn made his selection and which he handled in accordance with the gradually shifting emphases of his times" (p. 8). Comments throughout in some detail on Donne's satirical techniques in his five satires, commenting on such features as his uses of personae, colloquial diction and speech rhythms, setting, witty and hyperbolic language, and farce. Contrasts the rhetorical strategies of Donne's *Satyres II, III,* and *V* (pp. 177–83). Compares and contrasts Donne throughout with Wyatt, Lodge, Marston, Guilpin, Hall, Middleton, and Marvell.

◄§ 360. RING, STEPHEN D., S.J. "Donne's 'Loves Growth,' 25–28." *Expl* 29: Item 58.
Shows how Donne in the last four lines of "Loves growth" "presents his love as paradoxical: spring adds new heat to it, but no winter comes along in turn to chill it," and argues that the paradox "owes its success to Donne's use of 'spring' in a literal as well as a figurative sense." Suggests that he relates his love to spring "both as a symbol of warmth and as a fourth part of the yearly cycle" and thus "describes his love's irreversible growth in the

paradoxical terms of spring never giving way to winter." For a reply, see Alan Blankenship (entry 533).

↩ 361. ROCKETT, WILLIAM. "Donne's Libertine Rhetoric." *ES* 52: 507–18.

Discusses the dialectical strategy of the libertine personae that Donne creates in his early poems, especially in the *Elegies*, and shows how "the dramatic quality of several of the libertine poems is actually inseparable from their rhetorical quality" (p. 508). Points out that Donne often "speaks through the mask of stock characters—the naturalistic libertine, for example, the *miles amoris*, the *praeceptor amoris*, or the *exclusus amator*—and the purpose of his rhetoric, on one level, is to make his characters seem convincing, or to breathe life into old forms" (pp. 508–9). Discusses how Donne uses the traditional figures of rhetoric, such as *aetiologia, concessio, paromologia*, and *expeditio*, to create a narrative mask for his personae and shows how these etiological and dialectical figures are used "to reenforce the pretentiousness of the speaking voice by creating the impression of authority—making the libertine narrator not only a dialectician but a kind of imperious *magister* as well—and thereby implicitly threatening the opposing point of view with such eventualities as unorthodoxy, immorality, or perhaps even heresy" (p. 517). Points out that the fact that Donne "deliberately intended the libertine persona to be at once dramatic and dialectical is demonstrated . . . in the frequency of the figures which argue and the relative infrequency of those which, for lack of a better word, adorn" (p. 517). Says that "The Bracelet" is, among the libertine poems, "one of the most accomplished in its uses of rhetoric" (p. 514) and presents a detailed analysis of it to show that the dramatic and rhetorical structures "fuse and become indistinguishable as Donne builds a persona whose identity resides in the manner rather than the substance of his argument" (p. 517).

↩ 362. ROSTON, MURRAY. "John Donne and Mannerist Art," in *University Teachers of English Proceedings of the Conference Held at the University of Negev, Beer-Sheva, March 1971*, edited by Ruth Nevo, pp. 1–21. Beersheba: University of Negev.

Defines and defends mannerist art and contrasts it with the baroque and Renaissance. Points out certain manneristic features in Donne's poetry and argues that the reader gains a new perspective on his poetry by viewing it in the light of Counter-Renaissance mannerist art. Notes Donne's "*transmutation* of the physical world, whereby the material only gains its validity as the larger spiritual implications are grasped" and warns against the tendency to minimize the "underlying vein of seriousness which modifies and enriches his most irreverent sallies" (p. 6). Suggests, for example, that the inversion of the Copernican system in "The Sunne Rising" is not merely braggadoccio but is rather "a striking re-assertion of man's centrality in the universe" (p. 8). Challenges the notion that Donne is a strict practitioner of logic; argues that a close reading of most of his poems confirms the centrality of a lightly camouflaged illogicality, a kind of "intellectual acrobatics which subtly contradict the accepted laws of reasoning while yet achieving a new and revitalized rationale of their own" (p. 10); and raises Donne's "sparkling irreverence towards that idol of humanism, logic or 'right reason'" (p. 10) as one of the major delights of his poetry. Sees similarities between Donne's pseudo-logic and wit and the mannerist movement in art, for in both "the firmness of Renaissance perspective and the solidity of its three-dimensional realism have been rejected in favour of the hallucinatory, the fluid, and the unstable . . . through an awareness that syllogistic proofs are prosaic and nugatory beside the energizing power of paradox" (p. 10). Analyzes "The Flea" to show that its real theme is "the discrepancy between the apparently firm, rational argumentation and the obvious untenability of the conclusions at which it arrives" (p. 12). Maintains that Donne's increasingly serious uses of the metaphysical conceit and pun reveal his growing realization that "surface wordplay is in fact rooted in a cultural, rather than merely semantic identity and the reverberations of the profounder ambiguity eventually assert themselves to validate and confirm the apparent extravagance of the initial conceit" (p. 13). Points out, for instance, that the extravagance of "The Expiration" is not merely a display of wit and hyperbolic conceit but is a thoroughly sensitive description of genuine emotional reality and demonstrates how in "Batter my heart" the paradox "allows the spiritual meaning to dwarf the physical absurdity" (p. 14) of the imagery of the sonnet. Concludes that Donne, though thoroughly aware of and responsive to the new science, "is intrigued primarily not by the clear rules and indisputable proof science offers but by the contradictions it betrays which support his own conviction that the final answers are not to be found in the neatly organized world of empirical reasoning" (p. 15) and that, like the mannerists, he rejects prosaic limitations and strives to reach out imaginatively for verities beyond these restrictions. Records a question-and-answer period following the talk (pp. 16–21).

୶ 363. S., R. "John Donne's Autograph." *BLR* 8, no. 5: 234–35.
Announces the acquisition by the Bodleian Library of the autograph · manuscript of Donne's verse letter to Lady Carew, from the collection of the Duke of Manchester and identified by the staff of Sotheby's. Notes that it is "the only autograph manuscript of an English poem by Donne and one of the very few autograph manuscripts of an English poet before Milton" (p. 234). Thanks contributors who made the purchase possible.

୶ 364. SAKURAI, SHŌICHIRŌ. *"Songs and Sonnets* no Genjitsu" [The Reality of *Songs and Sonets*]. *Joshidai Bungaku* (Gaikoku Bungaku) (Osaka Joshi Daigaku) 23 (March): 37–54.
Discusses those poems in the *Songs and Sonets* described by Helen Gardner as "serious" love poems and notes that they are characterized by

a sense of ecstasy and joy. Examines in some detail "The Anniversarie" and "The good-morrow" and suggests that the motivation behind these lyrics is fear—a fear of the outside world, of love ending, and of the unfaithfulness of the beloved.

❧ 365. SANDBANK, SHIMON. "On the Structure of Some Seventeenth-Century Metaphors." *ES* 52: 323–30.

Discusses ways that a reader should approach seventeenth-century images and metaphors and challenges "the neutralization-of-the-vehicle doctrine, or the never-try-to-visualize-it rule" supported by certain modern critics of metaphysical poetry. Concentrates primarily on images found in character books and shows that often "the vehicle is not the faceless carrier of a logical truth" (p. 328) but must be visualized. Opens up questions about the "metaphysicalness" of metaphysical poetry. Argues that, whereas the Spenserian poet tends to relate sense impressions harmoniously to one another, the metaphysical poet typically sees "logical resemblances while being aware of sensory disparities" (p. 330). Uses Donne's compass image in "A Valediction: forbidding mourning," as well as selections from the sermons, to illustrate the general discussion.

❧ 366. SANDERS, WILBUR. *John Donne's Poetry*. London: Cambridge University Press. vi, 160p.

Reprinted: 1974.

Acknowledges that Donne the poet has achieved "classic" status in this century but suggests that modern criticism has "left us with a Donne whom every schoolboy knows is a great poet, whom many students of English literature suspect is not, but of whose classic status, anyway, we possess no cogent contemporary account" (p. 1). Points out that Dr. Johnson's criticism of Donne has never been adequately answered by modern critics and attempts such a reply. Dislikes in particular T. S. Eliot's approach to Donne, finds Coleridge's criticism engaging, and endorses essentially the critical approach of F. R. Leavis. Argues for an approach to Donne that examines more closely the persuasiveness of the authoritative, masculine, speaking voice in his poems. Maintains that Donne is most engaging when he does not play witty games, does not advertise his cleverness, and does not attempt to distance himself through a persona. Argues that in Donne's most successful poems "utterance is not for him a way of relieving his feelings: it is a way of discovering, creating, realising his feelings" (p. 13) and yet acknowledges that often Donne can sink to the level of "pure Clevelandism" (p. 17). Discusses Donne's uses of wit and humor through an examination of *Paradoxes*, the *Satyres*, and the *Elegies* and suggests that these early works are primarily "performances," which, in the final analysis, are "*inventive* rather than *creative*" (p. 39). Suggests that Donne's early poetry "makes one unfailing demand on its readers: agility" and that "we have to be awake to the endless self-betrayals the tone can surprise us into; and we must be very limber to handle those perversions of logic so flagrant that the guffaw dies in the throat, or to avoid falling for affectations of blunt good sense which rapidly reveal themselves to be intellectual booby-traps" (p. 44). Discusses "Womans constancy," "The Apparition," and especially "The Canonization" and "The Extasie" as unsuccessful poems that exhibit contradictory manifestations of wit. Argues for the superiority of such poems as "The good-morrow," "The Sunne Rising," "The Anniversarie," "A Valediction: forbidding mourning," "Song: Sweetest love, I do not goe," "Aire and Angels," and "Loves growth"—poems of fulfilled love that "offer something to our understanding of love which is not available elsewhere" (p. 61) and that do not indulge in pyrotechnical devices, excessive wit, manipulated irony, and mere cleverness. Comments on the curious and conscious relationship in Donne's poetry between idealized love and sexual love and notes that in a number of his poems Donne's "sense of the ridiculous punctures the idealisation, and his unquenched thirst for the ideal makes him restless with the merely fleshly" and suggests that in his most successful love poems he presents "a love so present that the desperate oscillation of spirit loses itself in the vastness of fulfillment" (p. 108). Comments on such poems as "The Extasie," "Going to Bed," "The Relique," and "Loves growth" to show that in his greatest poetry Donne does not create an antithesis between higher and lower love. Observes, likewise, that in Donne's religious poems "there is no shallow antithesis between the natural man and religious man, but a deep continuity" (p. 110), but, on the whole, finds the religious poems less engaging than the love poems. Suggests that "when Divinity is mystery, not love or wonder, we get doctrinal gymnastics like 'La Corona' and the majority of the *Holy Sonnets*—poems which know so well in advance what the range of possible feelings is, that they are incapable of feeling any of them" (p. 114). Finds "A nocturnall upon S. Lucies day," for instance, more effective on the subject of death than most of the *Holy Sonnets*, which are said to be at times overly controlled and "hysterically out of control" (p. 130). Dismisses the *Anniversaries* as "constrictingly and repressively pedantic" (p. 136) but finds "Since she whom I lov'd hath payd her debt," on the death of Donne's wife, a poem in which "divinity, love, and wonder are momentarily one" (p. 138). Praises the hymns as poems, like the best of the *Songs and Sonets*, that "use the voice of the whole man and draw upon his experience as a whole man" (p. 139) and do not resort to ironic evasiveness, self-parody, excess of wit, self-conscious play, nor need for a persona. (Does not comment on "Goodfriday, 1613. Riding Westward.") Concludes that Donne deserves the title *classic* and "need fear nothing from the vagaries of critical fashion, the apostasy of his prophets—or even from the industry of his expositors" (p. 159). Makes numerous comparisons between Donne and many other authors, especially Dostoevsky, D. H. Lawrence, Joseph Conrad, Henry James, Wordsworth, Coleridge, Keats, Dunbar, G. M. Hopkins, George Herbert, and George Eliot.

◀§ 367. SANO, NORITSUGU. "Donne no 'Primrose' ni tsuite" [On Donne's "Primrose"]. *Kenkyū Hōkoku* (Sasebo Kōgyō Kōtō Semmon-Gakkō) no. 8 (October): 181–86.
A close critical reading of "The Primrose."

◀§ 368. SCHWARZ, DANIEL R. "The Unity of Eliot's 'Gerontion': The Failure of Meditation." *BuR* 19, i:55–76.
Discusses T. S. Eliot's uses of Donne's *Anniversaries* in "Gerontion." Notes that Eliot's main character desperately attempts "to place his life within an eschatological context and to achieve the humility and passionate commitment to Christ on which his salvation depends" and that "by having Gerontion consciously quote Lancelot Andrewes and unconsciously parody a passage from *Second Anniversary*, Eliot implicitly juxtaposes Gerontion's monologue to the spiritual unity and concomitant rhetorical control of successful meditations within the tradition of *contemptus mundi*" (p. 55). Suggests that in the *Anniversaries* Donne is "dramatizing the process of discovering spiritual certainties amid excruciating and agonizing doubts that his Zeitgeist presented to him" (p. 60) and that Eliot intentionally juxtaposed Donne's efforts at successful meditation to Gerontion's ineffectual attempts at meditation as he moves toward greater fragmentation and doubt.

◀§ 369. SICHERMAN, CAROL M. "Donne's Discoveries." *SEL* 11: 69–88.
Discusses a common pattern of development observable in over a dozen of Donne's poems: "after a confident or at least decisive opening, the speaker moves from initial certainties to new perceptions and emerges finally to an assured conclusion, making discoveries about himself which neither he nor we his readers have fully anticipated" (p. 69). Points out that the speaker, although primarily confronting some interior crisis, carries out his self-examination by exploring his relationship to God or to a woman and that the language the speaker employs in his search is continuous and the metaphors "serve the development and may not be excised for separate scrutiny" (p. 69). Exemplifies the pattern through a detailed reading of "Goodfriday, 1613. Riding Westward" and "The Autumnall" and shows that in these poems "we hear a speaker forced by his own acuity and honesty to abandon a false confidence and to recognize and accept an unwelcome truth about his personal situation" (p. 78). Shows in a less detailed manner how a similar pattern obtains in "A Valediction: forbidding mourning," "A nocturnall upon S. Lucies day," the *Anniversaries*, and the twelve Holy Sonnets that form a sequence.

◀§ 370. SINGH, BRIJRAJ. "Two Hitherto Unrecorded Imitations of Donne in the Eighteenth Century." *N&Q* n.s. 18: 50.
Notes that two anonymous poems, "The General Lover" and "The Lover's Curse," which appeared in *The Universal Spectator* (no. 280) for 16 February 1736, are based on Donne's "The Indifferent" and "The Curse"

respectively. Notes that there are several imitations of Donne in *The Universal Spectator* of this period: (1) "To Sir Gimcrackle Noddy" (no. 258, 15 September 1733) is an expansion of "Antiquary"; (2) "The Man of Business no Lover" (no. 260, 29 September 1733) is based on "Breake of day"; and (3) "The Oxonian's Trip to the Drawing Room" (no. 278, 2 February 1734) draws on *Satyre IV*. See also J. C. Maxwell and E. G. Stanley (entry 344) and Peter A. Tasch (entry 375).

◀§ 371. STANWOOD, P. G. "'Essentiall Joye' in Donne's *Anniversaries.*" *TSLL* 13: 227–38.
Reprinted in *Essential Articles for the Study of John Donne's Poetry*, edited by John R. Roberts (entry 786), pp. 387–96.
Explores the essentially religious and Christian dimensions of the two *Anniversaries*, especially their teaching about sanctifying grace, and argues that the poems "mediate for God on behalf of Christ, with the poet himself acting a priestly office by turning his poetry and himself into a holy sacrifice, into which and out of which grace may flow" (p. 228). Maintains that Elizabeth Drury is not allegorical but is "the idealized, the saintly embodiment of God's free gift of sanctifying grace" (p. 229). Suggests that in *The first Anniversary* Donne anatomizes the decay and corruption of the world, "the fallen world in need of the grace which Elizabeth embodied" but that *The second Anniversarie* "is a poem about Elizabeth Drury, but it is also, and more important, about the creative power of the soul itself, above all about the power of the poet who interprets and prophesies and gives form to the highest truth"—and this truth is "the life of grace made possible by God, through the Incarnate Christ, in the Holy Spirit—and it infuses everything" (pp. 231–32). Argues that Donne, "who himself accompanies Elizabeth on a progress, and identifies himself with her, transforms, by means of grace available through Christ and embodied in Elizabeth Drury, the vulgar world; for he has made possible its transubstantiation" (pp. 237–38).

◀§ 372. STEELE, THOMAS J., S.J. "Donne's *Holy Sonnets*, XIV." *Expl* 29: Item 74.
Suggests that throughout "Batter my heart" Donne uses the second-person-plural form of the pronoun (you) and therefore finds untenable the suggestion that Donne singles out the Father, the Son, and the Holy Spirit in the first, second, and third quatrains respectively. Furthermore suggests that the word *ravish* (line 14) does not mean to rape but "to take away, to remove spatially, as when St. Paul is spoken of as being ravished into the third heaven." Notes that the soul, traditionally seen as feminine, is "primarily asking to be taken away from her bondage to the enemy of the three-person'd God."

◀§ 373. SUDŌ, NOBUO. "Christian Humanism to shite no John Donne" [John Donne as a Christian Humanist], in *Jūshichi seiki Eibunka ni okeru* Christian Humanism [Christian Humanism in Seventeenth-Century English Literature], pp. 5–40. Tokyo: Yugakusha.

Discusses the nature of Christian humanism and, through a survey of Donne's poetry and prose, shows how he reflects the basic tenets and attitudes of the Christian humanist. Comments on Donne's baroque sensibility and on his preoccupation with death.

✎§ 374. SUGIMOTO, RYŪTARŌ. *Keijijōshi no Sugata to Nagare* [Metaphysical Poetry—Its Forms and Development]. Tokyo: Shinozaki Shorin. 232p.

General critical introduction to metaphysical poetry. Chapter 1, "An Introduction to Metaphysical Poetry"—its historical background and uses of wit and the conceit; Chapter 2, "John Donne"—a study of the technical aspects of the *Songs and Sonets* as well as a survey of Donne's view of women as reflected in the secular poems; Chapter 3, "The Poems of Crashaw"—with attention to Crashaw's relation to Donne and Herbert; Chapter 4, "Metaphysical Poetry and Marvell"; Chapter 5, "Milton and Metaphysical Poetry"; Chapter 6, "Coleridge's Criticism of Metaphysical Poetry"; Chapter 7, "T. S. Eliot and the Metaphysical Poets"; and Chapter 8, "Donne in the Twentieth Century"—a review of criticism and scholarship. Stresses Donne's originality in style and his innovative experimentation with form and argues that by means of the conceit and the uses of dramatic techniques Donne was able to control the possibilities of emotional excess in his poetry. Suggests that Donne's fragmentary, complex, and often conflicting views of women perhaps are reflections of or projections of his complex personality.

✎§ 375. TASCH, PETER A. Replies to "Two Hitherto Unrecorded Imitations of Donne in the Eighteenth Century." *N&Q* n.s. 18:464.

Notes that "To a Lady, who lov'd angling, from a Hint, Out of Dr. Donne" by Aaron Hill (1753) is based on "The Baite." Suggests that this item, along with additions made by the editors in *N&Q* (entry 344), should be added to those by Brijraj Singh and the editors in *N&Q* (entry 370).

✎§ 376. THOMAS, JOHN A. "John Donne's *The Progresse of the Soule*: A Re-Evaluation." *BRMMLA* 25: 112–21.

Argues that the narrative of *The Progresse of the Soule* "is carefully wrought to give macrocosmic perspective to the poem" and that "each episode achieves its own balance or a balance with other episodes through structure and through witty *similia* interlaced with aphoristic pronouncements" and describes the poem as "considerations of heretical and orthodox opinions on creation derived from emblematic pictures, quickened by Donne's strong-lined poetry" (p. 112). Presents a reading of the poem and comments especially on its structure, allegorical qualities, witty and satiric tone, emblematic seriousness, symbols and language, and pseudo-logic and proverbial morality. Maintains that the poem reveals Donne's "originality and complexity, his mock seriousness, and his love of dramatic argument" and feels that, even though much of the material in it is commonplace, Donne's "partial and selecting genius finds a new way to develop a pro-verbial central theme—that this earth offers security neither to the weak nor the strong" (p. 121).

◄§ 377. WEBBER, JOAN. "Stylistics: A Bridging of Life and Art in Seventeenth-Century Studies." *NLH* 2: 283–96.

Argues that stylistics "is an excellent tool by which to refocus criticism so that it can work evenhandedly along the spectrum, gathering into the canon of works that have been thought too unliterary for serious consid-eration, reaching even beyond written works into men's lives, and yet at the same time continuing to assert for criticism the primary importance of esthetic and moral design" (p. 284). Concentrates primarily on literature of dissent written in the seventeenth century: "Because both in content and form it challenges accepted values, this literature forces one to attend to questions about the primacy of such values, the absoluteness of any literary criteria, and the automatic distinction between meaning and value of life and those of art" (p. 284). Comments primarily on John Lilburne, George Fox, and Milton but also mentions Donne's *Satyres*. Points out that the topicality of the poems has, for the most part, made them less interesting to modern readers, and thus "we have been pleased with Donne the sexual rebel, and with Donne the religious rebel, but Donne the po-litical rebel, as he was in his early twenties, has never stirred our interest" (p. 290). Suggests that in 1970 some of Donne's lines in the *Satyres* "sud-denly came alive" as students recognized similar contemporary political situations.

◄§ 378. WELLINGTON, JAMES W. "The Litany in Cranmer and Donne." *SP* 68: 177–99.

Discusses "The Litanie" primarily "in the light of that theology and the various forms of the English litany available to Donne in the seventeenth century" (p. 178). Argues that Donne's litany follows in both form and wording the litany composed by Archbishop Thomas Cranmer in 1544 and its successors, not the Roman Catholic litany, and that the theology that informs the poem is characteristically Anglican in all respects.

◄§ 379. WHITE, HELEN, RUTH WALLERSTEIN, RICARDO QUINTANA, and A. B. CHAMBERS, eds. "John Donne," in *Seventeenth-Century Verse and Prose, Volume I: 1600–1660*, pp. 73–131. 2d ed. New York: The Macmillan Co.; London: Collier-Macmillan.

Revision of the 1951 edition, with new introduction to Donne and with new notes, selections, and bibliography. General introduction to Donne's life, reputation, and poetry, followed by a selected bibliography (pp. 73–75). Suggests that Donne "is most to be admired as a celebrant of secular and sacred love" (p. 73) and calls him "the best representative of his time"

(p. 74). Maintains that "whatever the theme or form of Donne's writing, the basic matter of it is the same, the infinitely subtle and endlessly ramified self-awareness of one man, John Donne" (p. 74). Reproduces thirty-five poems (secular and religious), a selection from *The first Anniversary*, and selections from *Devotions upon Emergent Occasions* and from two sermons.

✎ 380. WILLY, MARGARET, ed. *The Metaphysical Poets*. (The English Library, edited by James Sutherland.) London: Edward Arnold; Columbia, S.C.: University of South Carolina Press. x, 149p.

An anthology of metaphysical poems divided into two sections: (1) poems of love and death and (2) divine poems. Contains a general introduction to metaphysical poetry (pp. 1–11) and includes fourteen of Donne's poems, each with a brief critical introduction and explanatory notes (pp. 12–40, 79–85). Includes "The good-morrow," "The Sunne Rising," "A Valediction: of weeping," "A Valediction: forbidding mourning," "Aire and Angels," "The Extasie," "A nocturnall upon S. Lucies day," "The Canonization," "The Relique," "The Anniversarie," "Batter my heart," "Death be not proud," "Hymne to God my God, in my sicknesse," and "A Hymne to God the Father." Selected bibliography.

✎ 381. WILSON, DAVID B. "*La Puce de Madame Desroches* and John Donne's 'The Flea.'" *NM* 72: 297–301.

Suggests that "The Flea" is a witty and dramatic reworking of French poetic conventions and puns. Points out certain similarities between the poem and the poems published in *La Puce de Madame Desroches* (1583), especially Etienne Pasquier's "La Puce de E. Pasquier." Argues that Donne's model is clearly French, not, as some critics have suggested, Italian, since the references to "maidenhead" and "mariage bed" suggest French puns on "puce," "pucelage," and "dépuceler." Argues that the poem is perhaps wittier than many critics have supposed—"in the sense that his seventeenth century audience would have been aware of the irony inherent in his refashioning of the flea motif and might also have been aware of the deliberate or accidental insertion of French puns into an English poem" (p. 301).

1972

✎ 382. ANON. "Diverging on Donne." *TLS*, 29 December, pp. 1581–82.

Review article of R. C. Bald, *John Donne: A Life* (entry 179); *John Donne: Ignatius his Conclave*, edited by Timothy S. Healy (entry 79); *John Donne: Satires, Epigrams and Verse Letters*, edited by Wesley Milgate (Oxford: The Clarendon Press, 1967); Peter Amadeus Fiore, ed., *Just So Much Honor* (entry 421); and A. J. Smith, ed., *John Donne: Essays in*

Celebration (entry 508). Suggests that the "numerous serious studies and centenary tributes prove that Donne's poetry continues to fascinate—as does the debate over what constitutes its essential qualities" (p. 1581). Comments on the general state of Donne's reputation and of Donne scholarship in the twentieth century and points out a number of difficulties and uncertainties that still confront the Donne specialist, such as certain areas of Donne's religious and political thinking, his immediate ancestry, details of his life during his middle period, and the dating and ordering of the poems.

383. ANON. "Donne at Cambridge." *TLS*, 29 December, p. 1588.
   Describes an exhibit held at the University Library, Cambridge, to commemorate the four-hundredth anniversary of Donne's birth. Notes that Cambridge conferred on Donne the honorary doctorate of divinity at the King's request in 1615, just weeks after his ordination, and calls attention to the first public showing of the University Grace Book E, which records the event. For a full description of the exhibit, see entry 393.

384. AKIBA, RYŪZŌ. "The 'Ecstasy' Reconsidered." *Ronsō* (Meijigakuin Daigaku), no. 188 (March): 207–16.
   Cited in "The 1972 Bibliography," *The Renaissance Bulletin* (The Renaissance Institute, Tokyo) 6 (1979): 18. Unavailable.

385. ANDERSON, DONALD K., JR. "Donne's 'Hymne to God my God, in my sicknesse' and the T-in-O Maps," in *Essays in the Renaissance in Honor of Allan H. Gilbert*, edited by Philip J. Traci and Marilyn L. Williamson. *SAQ* 71: 465–72.
   Argues that, in addition to using the two-hemisphere modern map to shape the argument and metaphorical content of "Hymne to God my God, in my sicknesse," Donne also "demonstrates a knowledge of the T-in-O maps and utilizes this knowledge to enhance the meaning of the poem" (p. 471). Shows how the medieval T-in-O map (a T circumscribed by an O), which divides the whole world among Europe, Asia, and Africa and places Jerusalem at the center, helps explain the allusions to Jerusalem and Gibraltar and the three sons of Noah in stanza 4 and "makes the transition to the next stanza much less confusing" (p. 469). Shows how the map functions metaphorically "to represent visually both the world and three dominant images in stanza 5: Christ on the cross, Adam's tree (the Tree of Knowledge), and the recumbent persona Donne on his deathbed" (p. 470).

386. ANGLO, SYDNEY. "More Machiavellian than Machiavel: A Study of the Context of Donne's *Conclave*," in *John Donne: Essays in Celebration*, edited by A. J. Smith, pp. 349–84. London: Methuen & Co.

Discusses the contemporary religio-political controversies that form the context of *Ignatius his Conclave*. Agrees with T. S. Healy that Donne's attack on the Jesuits was devised, in part at least, as a satirical mockery of Robert Bellarmine's attack on James I's defense of the 1606 Oath of Allegiance but argues that to understand fully the function of Donne's satirical mockery one must also consider his attack in the context of anti-Machiavellian literature of the time and its relationship to anti-Jesuit polemics. Points out that Donne's notions about Machiavelli were, for the most part, popularly held views and that he need not have read Machiavelli to have obtained them and suggests that Donne cleverly used contemporary anti-Machiavellian attacks as a means of showing that the Jesuits were perhaps more Machiavellian than Machiavelli. Discusses also various charges of Machiavellianism hurled by both Protestants and moderate Catholics against the Jesuits, commenting in particular on three anti-Jesuit works by the English secular priest William Watson. Argues that Donne's view of Ignatius in the *Conclave* is shaped and influenced by many of these contemporary sources, not just by the controversy surrounding the Oath of Allegiance, but that he goes even beyond the usual charges and finally pictures Ignatius as triumphing over Machiavelli in hell by claiming that Jesuits are committed not only to political murder but also to the overthrow of royal power itself for the benefit of the Roman Church.

◄§ 387. ARMSTRONG, RAY L. "Donne's 'A Jeat Ring Sent.'" *Expl* 30: Item 77.

In part, a reply to L. P.'s inquiry (entry 246). Explicates lines 7–8 of "A Jeat Ring sent": "Figure our loves? Except in thy name thou have bid it say, / I am cheap, and nought but fashion, fling me'away." Suggests that the pronoun references are as follows: "*our* (the lovers'); *thy, thou* (the woman); *it* (the ring); *I, me* (the woman)." Speculates that Donne may see the woman as saying that she is unworthy of his love, either as a maneuver in the game of love or as an unconscious revelation or factual self-reproach. See also Edgar F. Daniels (entry 402). For a reply, see Thomas J. Wertenbaker, Jr. (entry 967).

◄§ 388. BAIRD, JOSEPH L., AND LORRAYNE Y. BAIRD. "John Donne's Southeast Discovery." *RLV* 38: 254–62.

Argues that it is "only by recognizing Donne's calculated manipulation of the ambiguities of 'west' and 'southwest' and 'discovery'" (p. 254) that one can fully understand "Hymne to God my God, in my sicknesse." Explores various levels of meanings and possible traditional interpretations of these directions in the poem and attempts to show that the whole poem is a blending or harmonizing of contraries, of "eastness-westness—body-spirit, death-resurrection, degradation-regeneration, physical-metaphysical" (p. 261) and suggests that Donne's inspiration for the phrase *South-west discoverie* may have come from Saint Jerome.

✍§ 389. BAKER-SMITH, DOMINIC. "John Donne's *Critique of True Religion*," in *John Donne: Essays in Celebration*, edited by A. J. Smith, pp. 404–32. London: Methuen & Co.

Challenges T. S. Eliot's broad assertion that, unlike the more medieval Lancelot Andrewes, Donne in his sermons is more modern in his cultivation of personality and self-expression and argues that Donne's "modernity" is, "when analysed, the expression of a new mode of religious sensibility; one which differs from the 'medieval' certainly but is not less rooted in tradition" (p. 432). Discusses Donne's religious development from *Satyre III* to his sonnet on the Church to show that throughout his life he held that "the quest for true religion involves constant self-discipline, a refusal to settle for an idol or pseudo-Church which relieves the individual of his obligations" (p. 432). Argues that in his quest for authentic doctrine, in his debates with the extremes of both Rome and Geneva, in his approach to biblical exegesis, and in his final interpretation of the demands of faith, Donne freely admits an element of subjectivity, for to him "man is not saved by a system but by a personal relation with God expressed in assurance of mercy" (p. 413). Notes that "that awareness of the immediate and the momentary which has been so admired in Donne's secular poems plays an equally vital role here in his formulation of religious experience" (p. 413). Argues that Donne sought the authentic self, without which "divinity becomes an intellectual game and the Church a self-perpetuating system" (p. 418). Comments extensively on Donne's relationship with religious thinking of his time, especially on the Continent, as expressed by such notables as Paolo Sarpi. Discusses in the light of Donne's religious development a number of individual works, especially *Satyre III*, certain of the verse epistles, the *Anniversaries*, the sermons, and *Pseudo-Martyr*.

✍§ 390. BEER, PATRICIA. *An Introduction to the Metaphysical Poets.* London and Basingstoke: Macmillan Press; Totowa, N.J.: Rowman & Littlefield. 115p.

General introduction to metaphysical poetry designed primarily for students in their first year of reading for an English honors degree. Divided into seven chapters: (1) "The Term 'Metaphysical'" (pp. 1–12), (2) "The Chief Characteristics of Metaphysical Poetry" (pp. 13–33), (3) "John Donne" (pp. 35–54), (4) "George Herbert" (pp. 55–70), (5) "Henry Vaughan" (pp. 71–83), (6) "Andrew Marvell" (pp. 85–98), and (7) "The Metaphysical Poets and the Twentieth Century" (pp. 99–112). The chapter on Donne presents a biographical sketch and discusses "The Funerall," "Batter my heart," and "The good-morrow" as typical of Donne's themes and style. Says that "of all Metaphysical poetry Donne's is the richest and most diverse" (p. 53).

✍§ 391. BERNARD, JOHN. "Orthodoxia Epidemica: Donne's Poetics and 'A Valediction: Of My Name in the Window.'" *SAQ* 71: 377–89.

Argues that "the pose of the libertine or cynic in Donne's witty lyrics has never seemed quite convincing" (p. 378) and that even in the most erotic poems "we sense an underlying disillusionment with the very physical shortcomings, the sad finiteness, of the sexual act" (p. 379). Suggests that the libertinism in much of Donne's poetry is his own skeptical answer to his uncertainties about love. Notes, for example, that in such poems as "The good-morrow," "The Canonization," and "The Anniversarie" Donne presents a pattern "of venting a thirst for the infinite and then imposing rational limits on it" (p. 381). Comments in some detail on "A Valediction: of my name in the window," which is seen as "an important key to Donne's nature both as a man and as a Renaissance poet" because in it "the subliminal struggle of faith and doubt in the religion of poetry seems to surface" (p. 384). Suggests that the poem ultimately shows that "myth has not the power to metamorphose reality; that not magic but rules govern our lives" (pp. 387–88). Concludes, therefore, that Donne was skeptical of his own creative motions and that his uncertainties "are so profound, his mistrust of the merely fictive so ingrained, that it was inevitable he would come to rest where Authority was greatest: in orthodoxy, not paradoxy" (pp. 388–89).

✒ 392. BULLOUGH, GEOFFREY. "Donne: The Man of Law," in *Just So Much Honor: Essays Commemorating the Four-Hundredth Anniversary of the Birth of John Donne*, edited by Peter Amadeus Fiore, pp. 57–94. University Park and London: The Pennsylvania State University Press.

Comments on Donne's association with the Inns of Court during both his early years as a student and his later years as Reader of Divinity to the Benchers of Lincoln's Inn. Points out that Donne's legal studies, his continuing and wide-ranging interest in all kinds of law (divine, human, physical, and natural), and the intellectual and literary atmosphere of the Inns of Court greatly affected his poetry and prose. Suggests that Donne's fondness for and extensive use of the epigram, the paradox, the problem, and satire may be traced in part to his experiences at the Inns of Court, where these genres were very much in fashion and highly developed. Comments also on Donne's extensive use of legal references, allusions, and analogies in his literary works and especially notes his uses of his legal training and knowledge in the *Satyres, Biathanatos, Pseudo-Martyr, Essays in Divinity*, and the sermons, particularly those preached at Lincoln's Inn and those on the theme of death and judgment.

✒ 393. CAMBRIDGE UNIVERSITY. *An Exhibition to Celebrate the Work and Reputation of John Donne, 1572–1631*. Cambridge: Cambridge University Press. 12p.

Catalog of an exhibit held at Cambridge from 23 October to 23 December 1972 to commemorate the quatercentenary of the birth of Donne. Arranged by David McKitterick. Preface (p. 1) by E. B. Ceadel, librarian, notes that, in addition to books and manuscripts by Donne, the exhibit contains eight books from Donne's library (several in contemporary bind-ings), all four books dedicated to Donne as Dean of St. Paul's, Izaak Wal-ton's copy of *Six Sermons,* and, shown for the first time, the University Grace Book E, which records Donne's honorary D.D. degree, conferred by royal mandate in 1615. Introductory note (pp. 2–3) reproduces part of a page from the Grace Book and comments on the circumstances sur-rounding the event. Notes that the exhibit includes all editions of the *Poems* from 1633 to 1779 and also one of the two known copies of the 1611 *An Anatomie of the World.* Listings divided into sixteen sections: (1) The first and second Anniversaries (7 items); (2) Books including contri-butions by Donne (3 items); (3) Early manuscripts of Donne's poems (7 items); (4) Collected editions of the *Poems,* 1633–1779 (17 items); (5) *Ju-venilia* and *Essays in Divinity* (7 items); (6) *Pseudo-martyr* and its early reputation (4 items); (7) *Conclave Ignati* (8 items); (8) *Biathanatos* and its early reputation (8 items); (9) *Devotions upon Emergent Occasions* (10 items); (10) Sermons (27 items); (11) Letters (2 items); (12) Books dedicated to Donne (8 items); (13) Books from Donne's library (8 items); (14) The nineteenth century (7 items); (15) The twentieth century (7 items); and (16) Music (2 items).

≈§ 394. CAMPBELL, JANE. *The Retrospective Review (1820–1828) and the Revival of Seventeenth-Century Poetry.* (Waterloo Lutheran University Monograph Series.) Waterloo, Ontario: Waterloo Lu-theran University. 76p.

Outlines the history of the *Retrospective Review* (London, 1820–1828), comments on the literary background of the review, and assesses the im-portant role it played in the reevaluation of early seventeenth-century po-etry and poets during the Romantic period. Specifically outlines and com-ments on the contribution made by the *Review* to Donne's reputation (pp. 50–56). Discusses the critical attitudes of Southey, Coleridge, Lamb, Hazlitt, and DeQuincey toward Donne and primarily comments on John Spence's critical essay on Donne that appeared in the *Retrospective Review* 8 (1823): 31–35. Suggests that Spence's evaluation was generally influenced by Coleridge's comments and notes that it is "the only article to be devoted to Donne during the whole period" (p. 53).

≈§ 395. CARRITHERS, GALE H., JR. *Donne at Sermons: A Christian Ex-istential World.* Albany: State University of New York Press. x, 319p.

Proposes "to distinguish the genius of 'the sermon' among generic ways of relating to the world, . . . to explicate some Donnean existential con-victions in action," and "to document John Donne's achievement in put-ting his own world together" (p. ix). Notes that the approach "will be phenomenological in temper and existential in assumptions in ways anal-ogous to Donne's own assumptions" (p. 4). Divided into three parts. Part I, "The Sermonic World" (pp. 1–126), contains two general and analytic chapters. Chapter 1, "Donne and the Sermonic Muse" (pp. 3–35), de-

scribes the generic characteristics of the sermon and notes that, "like philosophical poetry, epic, and elements of all drama, it looks to the present"
and, "like comedy, the sermon has in the present some sort of heading
toward a bright future" (p. 8). Stresses that the sermon is a dramatic enter-
prise and is fundamentally "dialogic" in nature and suggests that Donne's
"dynamic efforts to make the sermon enlist its auditors in both optical and
acoustical space seem . . . demonstrably better executed than those of any
other Anglican" (p. 12). Notes that since it is "a communal, inclusive,
dramatic 'exercise,'" the sermon uses metaphor and allegory energeti-
cally and suggests that Donne's most pervasive metaphor is "*living* as *trav-
elling*" (p. 21). Chapter 2, "The Existential Order of Discourse" (pp. 37–
126), argues that "the obvious term to use for Donne's way of being-in-
the-pulpit and being-in-the-world is *existential*" (p. 38) and discusses
Donne's ontology under four major topics: "(1) several kinds of things are
real; (2) human life is characterized by *limitation*; (3) (a logical consequence of 1 and 2) the *relativity* of human perception, cognition, and
constancy; (4) men live not in the world as God sees it or as any measuring
instrument sees it but in a life-world of past, present, and future involve-
ments" (p. 39). Discusses in some detail Donne's uses of imaginative language, rhetorical figures, and dramatic elements in his sermons. Suggests
that at the end of a Donne sermon one senses that "he has kept the faith
of his calling by making himself present to an issue of ultimate significance as he develops it from biblical context or topical context to life
context" and that "he has shown his listeners a way through to a response
that can unite them all in more abundant life" (p. 126). Part II, "Single
Sermons" (pp. 127–89), presents a detailed analysis of four sermons in the
light of the preceding critical commentary, and Part III, "Sermon Texts"
(pp. 191–288), presents the texts of the four sermons analyzed. Notes (pp.
287–306) and index (pp. 307–19).

◄§ 396. COLIE, ROSALIE L. "'All in Peeces': Problems of Interpretation
in Donne's Anniversary Poems," in *Just So Much Honor: Essays
Commemorating the Four-Hundredth Anniversary of the Birth of John
Donne*, edited by Peter Amadeus Fiore, pp. 189–218. University
Park and London: The Pennsylvania State University Press.

Evaluates recent critical discussion of the *Anniversaries* and notes that
"the various interpretations have seemed especially selective and difficult
to modulate into a general understanding of the works" (p. 189). Points
out that, although the criticism of such scholars as Marjorie Hope Nicolson, Louis L. Martz, George Williamson, O. B. Hardison, Frank Manley, Northrup Frye, Earl Miner, and others helps in explaining the argument, imagery, philosophical doctrines, or structure of the poems, these
readings "conspicuously do not mesh with one another in mutually valuable contributions to interpretation" (p. 192). Argues, however, that "the
poems' hospitality to multiple readings is not a function of the author's
sloppiness so much as of his rigorous inclusiveness"; shows that, in fact,

the poems consciously "exploit playfully and seriously, a great many literary genres available to the Renaissance poet"; and suggests that it is precisely "this shiftiness that makes the *Anniversary Poems* so difficult for us to read, trained as we are to find unity of thought, structure, pattern and tone in the 'good' poems we read" (p. 193). Presents an overall interpretation of the two poems as well as the attached funeral elegy to show how the poems form, both conventionally and unconventionally, an elegaic collection that "transcends elegy, but in terms familiar to readers of Christian consolation" (p. 200). Argues that "by seeing into and wittily exploiting the various pieces of literary repertory, Donne has forced them beyond their own limits, toward a new coherence unspecified in the textbooks of mankind" (p. 214).

≈§ 397. ———. "Seventeenth-Century Manners." *YR* 61: 591–99.
Review article of Earl Miner, ed., *Seventeenth-Century Imagery: Essays on Uses of Figurative Language from Donne to Farquhar* (entry 351), and Frank J. Warnke, *Versions of Baroque: European Literature in the Seventeenth Century* (entry 524). Praises in particular Barbara Lewalski's essay on Donne (entry 336) in the Miner collection and suggests that "her analysis of why Donne wrote of actual people in ways Ben Jonson could not approve opens perspectives of clarity hitherto darkened by turbulence and stormy confusion in interpretation" (p. 595). Finds Warnke's book interesting and, at times, exciting but questions his notion that baroque can be viewed as a period-concept and suggests that the book "dares to do something that is (probably) impossible both logically and empirically" (p. 599).

≈§ 398. COLLINS, DAN S. "Donne's 'To the Countess of Bedford' ('T'have written . . . ')." *Expl* 31: Item 19.
Comments on the difficult reversal that begins in line 53 of "To the Countesse of Bedford: T'have written then." Points out that from lines 37 to 52 Donne describes the corrupting effect of the body on the soul and that the reader, expecting an elaboration on this point, is confused by the sudden praise of the body that begins in line 53 and continues through line 58. Explains that the confusion arises only if one fails to recognize that the main theme of the poem is virtue, not the rivalry of body and soul, and shows how this section of the poem fits into Donne's central argument that both body and soul can be corrupted if virtue is lacking and that it is only the absence of virtue that "converts the body from its dignity as palace or temple of the soul into a prison and school of vice."

≈§ 399. CRAWSHAW, ELUNED. "Hermetic Elements in Donne's Poetic Vision," in *John Donne: Essays in Celebration*, edited by A. J. Smith, pp. 324–48. London: Methuen & Co.
Points out that, although alchemy was losing ground quickly as experimental science developed during the seventeenth century, Donne's physics "is still very much in the alchemical tradition" (p. 324). Discusses

Donne's uses of alchemical images in his poetry and considers also "how some of the broader issues of Hermetism bear on Donne's vision of things" (p. 324). Notes that alchemy provided him with "a sort of symbolic short-hand whose terms evoke a certain way of approaching some of his major preoccupations, and when he uses its language he does it with the seriousness and precision of the alchemists themselves" (p. 348). Points out that in the secular love poems Donne often employs alchemical imagery "dramatically and flamboyantly and twists it into striking paradoxes" (p. 341). Suggests that Donne "derides the scientific mode of empirical enquiry because we lack the faculties for it" (pp. 338–39) and yet maintains that Hermetism, as such, was for him only a symbolic mode of reflecting his philosophical attitudes about such central issues as physical beauty reflecting inner beauty, death as a process of transformation and completion, the correspondences between the moral and physical planes of existence, the problem of transience and permanence, the need for regeneration, the problem of mutability and decay, and the levels of order and existence.

⋙ 400. CREWE, J. V. "T. S. Eliot: A Metaphysical Problem." *ESA* 15: 105–14.

Discusses Eliot's admiration for the metaphysical poets, especially Donne, and comments on Eliot's influence on and reflection of his times. Suggests that F. R. Leavis may be regarded as Eliot's "chief apostle or chief critic" and notes that "their common admiration of the metaphysicals is unquestionable" (p. 109). Briefly contrasts "Hymne to God my God, in my sicknesse" to Tennyson's "Crossing the Bar" to show how "the learned, religious, witty, allusive, strong-minded and highly-conscious metaphysicals cast their spell over a whole generation of the educated few, and gave some grounds for hope that the great Christian-Classical civilization might not be beyond redemption" (p. 114). Suggests that, in Donne, Eliot found "a vocabulary, imagery, and mode of argumentation that made the Christian standpoint tenable once again—at least on paper" (p. 114). Notes that "when we read a poem like 'Hymne to God my God, in my sicknesse,' we are conscious of how near it must have seemed to Eliot, and how far it actually was," for Donne "vividly renews a living tradition" whereas Eliot's "persistent note is one of nostalgia, after the ripe fruit of high-bourgeois civilization has dropped from the tree" (p. 114).

⋙ 401. DAICHES, DAVID. "A Reading of the 'Good-Morrow,'" in *Just So Much Honor: Essays Commemorating the Four-Hundredth Anniversary of the Birth of John Donne*, edited by Peter Amadeus Fiore, pp. 177–88. University Park and London: The Pennsylvania State University Press.

Explicates "The good-morrow" to show how the poem "moves from simple question to a complex 'metaphysical' argument" (p. 177) and how "the increase in the ratiocinative element as the poem moves forward in time is psychologically justified by the emotional cycle which the poem acts out" (p. 178). Suggests that Donne's greatest achievement in the poem is "the creation of a compelling world of psychological and chronological reality, a world of experience that actually works itself out in time within the poem" (p. 187) and praises the psychological plausibility of the poem, its union of passionate feeling with intellectual playfulness, and its intricate and subtle development of thought.

402. DANIELS, EDGAR F. "Donne's 'A Jeat Ring Sent.'" *Expl* 30: Item 77.
In part, a reply to the inquiry of L. P. (entry 246). Explicates lines 6–8 of "A Jeat Ring sent": "Oh, why should ought less precious, or lesse tough / Figure our loves? Except in thy name, thou have bid it say, / I'am cheap, and nought but fashion, fling me'away." Suggests that the word *except* in line 7 means *unless* and thus relates the idea of its clause to lines 6 and 8. Suggests, then, that "the poet asks, why should a substance less precious than gold be used to symbolize his love and that of his lady, unless (and here his afterthought answers the question) its very cheapness is appropriate to their loves?" Points out a parallel use of *except* in the last couplet of "On his Mistris." See also Ray L. Armstrong (entry 387).

403. ————. "Donne's *Holy Sonnets* VI." *Expl* 31: Item 12.
In part, a reply to Arthur W. Pitts, Jr. (entry 358). Argues that the face mentioned in line 7 of "This is my playes last scene" is that of God, not, as Pitts suggests, that of Satan. Concludes that in lines 6 and 7 Donne "is hesitating between the Moralist heresy, which holds that the soul will sleep until Judgment Day, and the orthodoxy that the soul will see God immediately after death." See also J. Max Patrick (entry 482).

404. DEAN, JOHN. "The Two Arguments of Donne's 'Aire and Angels.'" *MSE* 3: 84–90.
Argues that "Aire and Angels" moves on two distinct levels, the spiritual and the sexual, and suggests that "by explicating both levels one can delineate to what degree the two arguments jar or harmonize into a single poetic narrative" (p. 84). Points out numerous possible sexual references and metaphors in the poem and finds that these throw the spiritual argument out of balance and that finally the two arguments "are too disparate to coexist harmoniously in the same poem" (p. 88). Concludes, therefore, that the two arguments finally lead the reader into "irreconcilable incongruities" and that the poem "ends half finished and half complete" (p. 90).

405. DOEBLER, BETTIE ANNE. "Donne's Incarnate Venus," in *Essays in the Renaissance in Honor of Allan H. Gilbert*, edited by Philip J. Traci and Marilyn L. Williamson. *SAQ* 71: 504–12.

Discusses the relationship between the apparent libertine fleshiness and the idealized spirituality of Neoplatonic love in Donne's secular love poems. Argues that Donne's Neoplatonism is, "in its serious concern with union, flesh and spirit, closely related to the philosophic Neoplatonism of a Ficino or a Leone Ebreo and not simply a compendium of the rhetorical images of his time" and that Donne's thought "insists on love as process, or two-becoming-one, the movement within the poems which makes the images fluid and the poetic experience immediate" (p. 506). Points out that during the Renaissance the Florentine Neoplatonists, following the Stoic allegorists, attempted to interpret morally the often voluptuous and sensual classical figures and myths depicted in paintings and poetry and that "even the figure of Venus came to be understood in terms of a principle of love in the universe—an ideal of purity—that lay very close to Pauline *caritas*" (p. 506). Shows then how "the popular allegorical Neoplatonic reading of the Mars and Venus resolution of irritability and concupiscence exists in many of Donne's poems as a fundamental part of his poetic movement and his methodology" (p. 506). Argues that just as Mars and Venus were seen as a balance between and a rational control over human emotions, an integration of aggression and the softness of love, so Donne's love poems "present to us as readers the process of internal conflict moving and searching and finally arriving at harmony and balance" (pp. 510–11). Illustrates how the personae of "The Canonization" undergo conflict and finally arrive at such a harmony. Maintains that Donne implies in the poem that "man comes to the celestial presence by means of the terrestrial Venus," to a fully spiritual love that does not reject the flesh for the spirit but rather chooses "to transcend and to contain the flesh in the transcendent union of souls—a truly Neoplatonic goal" (p. 512).

⋙ 406. DONNE, JOHN. *Devotions upon Emergent Occasions*, 1624 *(excerpt)*. Charlottesville, Va.: Alderman Press. Folder c61 × 49cm fold. to 31 × 25cm.

One-page excerpt from *Devotions upon Emergent Occasions*. First issue of the Alderman Press, handset in Caslon types, and printed at the University of Virginia Library. Limited to twenty-five copies. Reimpression of 750 copies printed for the Associates of the University of Virginia Library as a Christmas greeting.

⋙ 407. ———. *John Donne. Poemas amorosos*. Selection, translation, and prologue by José M. Martin Triana. (Coleccíon Visor de Poesía, 22.) Madrid: Alberto Corazon / Visor Poesía. 83p.

The prologue (pp. 9–17), entitled "Notas para una primera lectura de John Donne," presents a general introduction to Donne's love poetry and love philosophy, a short biographical sketch, and a brief survey of his critical reception. Translates into Spanish twenty-four poems from the *Songs and Sonets*, five of the *Elegies*, and "Heroicall Epistle: Sapho to Philaenis" (pp. 19–83), without notes or commentary.

<s 408. DONOGHUE, DENIS. "Denis Donoghue Celebrates the Quater-centenary of John Donne." *Spectator*, 18 November, pp. 795–96.
Essentially a review of A. J. Smith, ed., *John Donne: Essays in Cele-bration* (entry 508). Suggests that in spite of modern critics "people still read Donne pretty much as he was read forty years ago" (p. 795) but notes that the real problem is "that Donne himself has been dislodged from the central position he held for English readers forty years ago" and that "it would be hard to name any substantial poets now flourishing to whom Donne's poems speak with unusual force" (p. 796). Finds the essays in the collection "admirable for being what they set out to be" but complains that the collection as a whole "lacks the exhilaration of perception" (p. 796) that one found several decades earlier in Empson's criticism.

<s 409. DUNDAS, JUDITH. "Levity and Grace: The Poetry of Sacred Wit." *YES* 2: 93–102.
Discusses the various inherent oppositions between wit and faith, at-tempts to identify those particular qualities that "distinguish poems that successfully marry wit and faith from those that merely yoke them to-gether," and suggests "the possible form that sacred wit may take in poetry today" (p. 93). Notes that in "The Litanie" (lines 188–89) Donne specifi-cally warns against using religion simply as an occasion for the exercise of wit. Compares the emblematic imagery and wit in "A Hymne to Christ, at the Authors last going into Germany" and in Quarles's Emblem XI of Book III in order to distinguish between true and false sacred wit. Points out that in his poem Donne "specifically repudiates games of wit as one of the false mistresses of his youth" (p. 100) and that, unlike Quarles, he does not simply elaborate on various points of correspondence between the earthly and divine but rather provides a context that gives meaning to his initial emblems. Shows that Donne employs paradox in his poem not simply as a form of ingenuity but rather as a means "to mediate between the rational mind and the irrational, transcendent experience," that his wit perceives the discrepancy between earthly and heavenly values, and that it is "in the vital awareness of this discrepancy that real faith and real wit find their meeting-ground" (p. 100).

<s 410. EDDLEMAN, FLOYD E. "Donne's 'The Computation.'" *Expl* 30: Item 71.
Points out that in "The Computation" Donne ingeniously flatters his mistress by likening each hour of her absence to a century. Shows that the total time mentioned in the poem is 2,400 years, the time "since yester-day" (line 1).

<s 411. EDINGER, WILLIAM. "Johnson on Conceit: The Limits of Partic-ularity." *ELH* 39: 597–619.
Surveys Dr. Johnson's concept of the extended conceit and comments in detail on his probable objections to the compasses in the late three

stanzas of "A Valediction: forbidding mourning." Notes that Johnson, unlike the modern reader, "seems habitually to have visualized the referents of concrete language in metaphor and to have expected the resulting image to contribute to the effect of the whole passage or poem" (p. 604). Suggests that, judging Donne's extended metaphor by these standards, Johnson would have found the compass image both irrelevant and distracting.

•§ 412. EDWARDS, ANTHONY S. G. "Libertine Literature." *TLS*, 18 February, p. 189.
Asks for information on the earliest specific reference to a pornographic book in English literature. Notes that Donne refers to Aretino's "licentious pictures" in *Ignatius his Conclave* (1610), a reference to Guilio Romano's pictures that accompanied Aretino's *Sonnetti Lussuriosi* (1527). Rejects Donald Thomas's suggestion in *A Long Time Burning: The History of Literary Censorship in England* (entry 161) that Donne's reference to Aretino in a letter of 1600 addressed to Sir Henry Wotton is a specific reference to the *Sonnetti*. See also entry 413.

•§ 413. ———. "Libertine Lit." *TLS*, 2 June, p. 633.
Continuation of an inquiry about the earliest specific reference to a pornographic book in English literature; see entry above. Suggests that Donne's allusion to "Aretines postures" in *Satyre IV*, line 9, antedates Jonson's reference in *Volpone* by ten years.

•§ 414. ELLIOTT, EMORY B., JR. "Persona and Parody in Donne's *The Anniversaries*." *QJS* 58: 48–57.
Suggests that if "we separate the speakers of *The Anniversaries* from John Donne, we can recognize that the poems are not only elegies on the death of Elizabeth Drury but that they are also dramas in which Donne joins with the reader to try on masks and to examine attitudes and responses toward the problems of death and man's relationship to his fellows and to God" (p. 49). Sees the speaker of *The first Anniversary* as "puritanical and pedagogical" and as employing "rhetorical tricks and scientific thinking in an effort to draw for his audience or congregation a reasonable moral from the fact of the girl's death" and views the so-called poetic failures of the poem "as strokes of dramatic brilliance and parody" (p. 49). Sees the speaker of *The second Anniversarie* as a mystic who "attempts to escape the trials of human experience, that is, by transcending them in the mystical experience of meditative poetry" (p. 53). Suggests that, by adopting these masks, Donne parodies Puritan preaching in the first and Jesuit mystical sacred poetry in the second. Argues that, by looking at the poems as highly dramatic parodies, we can recognize their "full dramatic complexity . . . , their rich humor, and their high degree of poetic and rhetorical achievement, for they become Donne's homily on the value of

the *via media*" (pp. 49–50). Concludes, therefore, that, when seen together, the two poems present "a highly complex dramatic comment upon two extreme and inadequate responses to the human condition, symbolized by the death of the girl," and that Donne's use of personae "allows us to appreciate better the dramatic power through which Donne persuasively presents his arguments for the middle way of Anglicanism" (p. 57).

◄§ 415. ELLRODT, ROBERT. "De Platon à Traherne: L'intuition de l'instant chez les poètes métaphysiques anglais du dix-septième siècle," in *Mouvements Premiers: Études critiques offertes à George Poulet*, pp. 9–25. Paris: Librairie José Corti.

Copyright 1972; actually printed in 1973.

Relates Donne's view of the "instant" or "moment" in his poetry to those of Plato, Plotinus, Aristotle, and Kierkegaard. Suggests that "l'intuition de l'instant situe Donne à un carrefour" (p. 18): he values both the moment that contains the eternal and the sensual pleasures of the moment because these pleasures are valid in and for themselves. Suggests, then, that "malgré des divergences profondes on peut donc déceler chez Donne un mouvement de l'esprit qui correspond à l'effort romantique «d'incarner l'éternité dans le temps» tel que l'a dépeint George Poulet . . . mais Donne, en certains de ses poèmes profanes, semble déjà saisir l'éternité dans son «expérience personnelle du temps»" (p. 18).

◄§ 416. EMPSON, WILLIAM. "Rescuing Donne," in *Just So Much Honor: Essays Commemorating the Four-Hundredth Anniversary of the Birth of John Donne*, edited by Peter Amadeus Fiore, pp. 95–148. University Park and London: The Pennsylvania State University Press.

Argues that Donne needs to be rescued from "the habitual mean-mindedness of modern academic criticism, its moral emptiness combined with incessant moral nagging, and its scrubbed prison-like isolation," and, in particular, argues that "the text of the love poems does literally need rescuing, at a small number of crucial points, from the recent edition edited by Professor Helen Gardner (*The Elegies and the Songs and Sonnets* [Oxford, 1965])" (p. 95). Disagrees with a number of Gardner's interpretations of the manuscripts and proceeds to defend older readings of Donne's text, primarily those found in Grierson's edition and in the first edition. Defends the Group V manuscripts, claiming they were copied by a group of late and apparently slovenly copyists who deliberately included in the manuscripts words and phrases that Donne in his later life attempted to correct or erase in order to avoid personal embarrassment. Suggests that in his love poetry Donne was influenced by ideas derived from the Family of Love and from the fanatical millenarians and rejects the "scholarly misrepresentation" that Donne "never experienced love, but only engaged in daydreams about it after his marriage, so as to sulk and insult his wife" (p. 141).

◄§ 417. ERSKINE-HILL, HOWARD. "Courtiers out of Horace: Donne's *Satyre IV*; and Pope's *Fourth Satire of Dr John Donne, Dean of St Paul's Versifyed*," in *John Donne: Essays in Celebration*, edited by A. J. Smith, pp. 273–307. London: Methuen & Co.

Argues that Donne's *Satyre IV* is both a conscious imitation of and a deliberate departure from Horace's *Satire I, ix*. Notes that "not only is the first half of *Satyre IV* a recognisable imitation of Horace's encounter with the Talker, but there are several small though clear echoes of Horace's text" (p. 276). Among the differences between Donne's and Horace's poems, stresses Donne's fearful attitude toward the law, which is perhaps a reflection of his recusant background. Points out that, although there were numerous English translations and imitations of Horace's poem between the 1590s and the first decade of the eighteenth century, none was "so bold, extravagant and significant an adaptation as Donne's *Satyre IV*" (p. 293). Discusses in detail "the impressive human complexity" of Donne's poem and argues that, "far from being a shapeless and over-long denunciation, this satire possesses an expressive unifying structure" (p. 306). Comments on Pope's brilliant, if not fully successful, imitation and suggests reasons for Pope's choosing to express his own satiric comments on the court through his imitation of Donne's poem, noting, in particular, the attraction of Donne's political daring, his uses of Christianity, and his comic wit.

◄§ 418. EVERETT, BARBARA. *Donne: A London Poet*. (Chatterton Lecture on an English Poet.) London: Oxford University Press. 31p. Reprinted in *PBA* 58 (1974): 245–73.

Argues that Donne was—"despite the abstract habits of thought which might appear to dissociate him from place—a Londoner by nature as well as by birth and breeding . . . at that crucial phase in the city's history when it took on the character by which we recognize it now" (p. 3) and that his being a Londoner adds "something to our understanding of him as a writer" (p. 5). Maintains, however, that in a less obvious and simple sense London had for Donne a metaphorical meaning, since the city was preeminently familiar to him. Shows, for instance, that in *Satyre I* Donne not only makes detailed social observations on contemporary London life and manners but also makes "full imaginative use of the most metropolitan of Roman poets" (p. 7), the satirists. Suggests that Horace and Juvenal "helped Donne towards the half-casual re-creation of London in the image of Rome nearly a century before the Augustans were to do it again" (p. 7) and that Persius provided Donne with models of imaginary and internalized dialogue. Examines a number of poems (especially *Satyre I*, "On his Mistris," "A Valediction: forbidding mourning," "A Lecture upon the Shadow," "The Canonization," and "The Extasie") to show how Donne's consciousness of London and its life shaped his vision and sensibilities. Sees many of the *Songs and Sonets* as London poems, "first, because of their hold on the dense medium of actual experience, which qualifies all romantic abstracts; second, because of their author's self-consciousness as an artist, his extreme awareness of himself in relation to a surrounding audience" (p. 26). Notes that the complex tone and sense of tension in many of his poems has earned for Donne "the right to be called our first (perhaps our only) real master of the poetry of urban anxiety" (p. 13).

◄§ 419. EVETTS-SECKER, JOSEPHINE. "Henry Hawkins, S.J., 1577–1646: A Recusant Writer and Translator of the Early Seventeenth Century." *Recusant History* 11: 237–52.
Suggests that the Jesuit Henry Hawkins, translator and writer of devotional literature, best known for his *Partheneia Sacra*, was familiar with Donne's poetry. Points out that in his poems, *Fuga Saeculi*, Hawkins borrowed directly from Donne.

◄§ 420. FIORE, PETER AMADEUS. "John Donne Today," in *Just So Much Honor: Essays Commemorating the Four-Hundredth Anniversary of the Birth of John Donne*, edited by Peter Amadeus Fiore, pp. 1–8. University Park and London: The Pennsylvania State University Press.
Discusses Donne's appeal to twentieth-century readers, especially "the remarkable subtlety with which he achieves an effect in a poem, and the grotesque images and metaphors which he uses at the most unlikely moments" (p. 3). Illustrates Donne's ability to connect "diverse elements of a poem by the slightest manipulation of words and images which result in a development of sensibility" (p. 3) by commenting on "A Valediction: forbidding mourning," "The Apparition," and "A Valediction: of weeping." Illustrates Donne's unique uses of the grotesque by commenting on the imagery of *Deaths Duell*, "Batter my heart," and several sermons.

◄§ 421. FIORE, PETER AMADEUS, ED. *Just So Much Honor: Essays Commemorating the Four-Hundredth Anniversary of the Birth of John Donne*. University Park and London: The Pennsylvania State University Press. 291p.
Collection of eleven original essays, each of which has been separately entered in this bibliography: (1) Peter Amadeus Fiore, "John Donne Today" (pp. 1–8); (2) Edward Le Comte, "Jack Donne: From Rake to Husband" (pp. 9–32); (3) Roger Sharrock, "Wit, Passion and Ideal Love: Reflections on the Cycle of Donne's Reputation" (pp. 33–56); (4) Geoffrey Bullough, "Donne: The Man of Law" (pp. 57–94); (5) William Empson, "Rescuing Donne" (pp. 95–148); (6) Wesley Milgate, "'Aire and Angels' and the Discrimination of Experience" (pp. 149–76); (7) David Daiches, "A Reading of the 'Good-Morrow'" (pp. 177–88); (8) Rosalie L. Colie, "'All in Peeces': Problems of Interpretation in Donne's Anniversary Poems" (pp. 189–218); (9) David Novarr, "'The Exstasie': Donne's Address on the States of Union" (pp. 219–43); (10) John T. Shawcross, "All Attest His Writs Canonical: The Texts, Meaning and Evaluation of Donne's Satires"

(pp. 245–72); and (11) Josephine Miles, "Ifs, Ands, Buts for the Reader of Donne" (pp. 273–91).

🖎§ 422. FISH, STANLEY E. *Self-Consuming Artifacts: The Experience of Seventeenth-Century Literature*. Berkeley, Los Angeles, London: University of California Press. xiv, 432p.
Paperback edition: 1974.
Contends that it is characteristic of certain seventeenth-century literary works, such as Donne's *Deaths Duell*, Bacon's *Essays*, Burton's *The Anatomy of Melancholy*, Herbert's *The Temple*, Bunyan's *Pilgrim's Progress*, Milton's *The Reason of Church Government*, and Browne's *Religio Medici*, "first to involve the reader in discursive activities—evaluating, deducing, interpreting—and then to declare invalid or premature the conclusions these activities yield," thus resulting in "a disturbing and unsettling experience in the course of which a reader is continually revising his understanding, until, in some cases, the very possibility of understanding is itself called into question" (abstract, in paperback edition only). Argues, therefore, that "these works are self-consuming in two directions, for in the course of unbuilding their own structures, they also unbuild the structure of the reader's self-confidence" (abstract, in paperback edition only). Mentions Donne throughout, especially his sermons, and briefly contrasts or compares him with Bacon, Burton, Herbert, Browne, and Bunyan. Chapter 1, "The Aesthetics of the Good Physician" (pp. 1–77), contains a subsection entitled "Donne: The Word As All" (pp. 43–77), in which *Deaths Duell* is analyzed to show that the sermon is a self-consuming artifact. Maintains that the sermon succeeds "by calling attention to what it is not doing, by transferring the burden it first assumes (the burden of containing and communicating the truth) from the words on the page (which are contradictory and circular) to the Word that is inscribed on the fleshly tables of the reader's or auditor's heart," that is, it reveals the Word "by removing from our line of vision the structures that obscure it and cause us to forget it" (p. 69). Shows that *Deaths Duell* "serves us by refusing to serve us, by failing" and points out that Donne, no less than the reader, is "the beneficiary of this failure; for by fashioning words and sentences that point only to their insufficiency, he displaces attention from his own efforts to the Spirit which informs them; and by emptying his art of its (claims to) power, he acknowledges his own powerlessness, becoming like us and like the shell of his sermon a vessel filled by and wholly dependent on the Lord" (p. 69). Contrasts Donne's seemingly theatrical but essentially self-effacing art in the sermon with the stylistically self-deprecating but finally self-glorifying art of the Puritan sermon.

🖎§ 423. FREEDMAN, WILLIAM. "Donne's 'Lovers Infinitenesse.'" *Expl* 31: Item 6.
Explicates the extended financial conceit in "Lovers infinitenesse" and

notes how Donne plays it off against a secondary and antithetical metaphor of organic growth and how he "achieves a conceptual synthesis (in both senses, i. e. of concept and conceit) in the final lines," in which the persona explains to his mistress that, "although a heart may not be completely given, a body may be, and although the mechanical exchange of hearts will not join them, will not make them a single organic unit, the animate joining of bodies will." Points out that, although the final transaction is still made in financial terms, the language and the spirit of the marketplace have been "superseded by a liberality more appropriate and more adequate to the organic infiniteness of true love."

٭٭§ 424. FULLER, JOHN. *The Sonnet.* (The Critical Idiom, no. 26, gen. ed. John D. Jump.) London: Methuen & Co. 58p.

Comments on Donne's experimentation with the sonnet form and suggests that, like Milton, Donne "presided over the general blurring of the sonnet's musical form" (pp. 22). Discusses very briefly the structure of "Death be not proud" (p. 23) and comments on the unity of *La Corona* (pp. 41–42).

٭٭§ 425. GARDNER, HELEN. "Donne's Verse-letter." *TLS*, 21 January, pp. 68–69.

Disagrees with A. J. Smith's conclusions about the significance of the text of the holograph of Donne's verse letter to Lady Carey (entry 507). Argues that the variants in the holograph do not establish or call into question the manuscript groupings and that the holograph "supports editorial confidence in the readings of Groups I and II against Group III and, consequently in the edition of 1633, which, as Grierson demonstrated, was based upon manuscripts of these two groups" (p. 68). Comments on the substantive and accidental variants between the holograph and the other texts and suggests that perhaps Donne himself may have made a copy of the original and that it is the copy that is the source of the manuscript texts. See also A. J. Smith (entry 506) and P. L. Heyworth (entry 437).

٭٭§ 426. ———. *John Donne's Holograph of "A Letter to the Lady Carey and Mrs Essex Riche."* London: Scolar Mansell, in conjunction with The Bodleian Library, Oxford. 11p.

Contains (1) a facsimile reprint on a separate sheet of Donne's holograph of "A Letter to the Lady Carey, and Mrs Essex Riche, From Amyens" (title in 1633 edition) discovered in 1970 by Peter Croft of Sotheby's among the family papers of the Duke of Manchester, which had been formerly deposited in the Public Records Office and is currently in the Bodleian (MS. Eng. Poet. d. 197) and (2) a separate eight-page introduction by Helen Gardner with a typescript of the manuscript. Describes the manuscript and its history and evaluates its relationship to other manuscripts and printed texts. Argues that the poem is not a fair copy but was written out as it was composed and suggests that Donne very likely kept a copy in his letter-book and that it is the copy that became the ultimate source of the copies of the poem in surviving manuscripts and in the 1633 edition. Suggests that, although the variants are slight, the holograph confirms editorial confidence in the 1633 edition and the manuscripts it followed and that "the main interest of the holograph for an editor lies less in its substantive readings than in its accidentals" (p. 5), such as the uses of eye-rhymes, elision marks, capital letters, and punctuation. Notes that for lovers of Donne's poetry the holograph "throws light on his attitude to his art, his character as a poet, and his character as a man": "The poem, so beautifully and fluently written, so adequate to its occasion, so full of intelligence and wit, which mingles with the necessary flattery Donne's own convictions, reveals a poet so much the master of his art that he can on request and at need produce a finely wrought verse-epistle that combines courtly compliment with moral seriousness" (p. 7).

427. ———. "The 'Metempsychosis' of John Donne." *TLS*, 29 December, pp. 1587–88.

Sees *Metempsychosis* as "a much more high-spirited affair than has been assumed" and suggests that Donne originally conceived it as "a political satire disguised as the beginning of a mock epic" (p. 1587). Argues that the grandiose dedication and the cryptic prefatory epistle are parts of the satiric jest, not a seriously intended outline of a projected work, and that the poem as we have it is a complete work. Rules out the suggestion that Donne intended to end the poem with an attack on Elizabeth I and argues that, more likely, the poem "is an attack on some contemporary, disguised as the first canto of an epic, with impressive dedication and a parody of an explanatory epistle, and that Donne threw himself with gusto into an elaborate fiction that served the purpose of protecting him as a satirist touching on affairs of state at a particularly sensitive time, and gave him the opportunity to parody epic solemnity, display some curious learning, and exercise his invention and imagination" (p. 1587). Recognizes that, in part, the poem is a literary jest but does not deny that there is a fundamental moral seriousness behind its parody, invention, and wit.

428. ———. *The New Oxford Book of English Verse*, 1250–1950. Chosen and edited by Helen Gardner. New York and Oxford: Oxford University Press. xii, 974p.

When Arthur Quiller-Couch edited *The Oxford Book of English Verse*, 1250–1900 (1900), he chose to include seven poems by Donne. The present edition, not a revision but an entirely new anthology, includes nineteen of Donne's poems or selections therefrom. Includes lines 72–110 of *Satyre III*, "On his Mistris," "The Storme," eleven poems from the *Songs and Sonets*, four of the *Holy Sonnets*, and "To Christ." Brief textual notes (p. 948).

↩§ 429. GILL, ROMA. "*Musa Iocosa Mea*: Thoughts on the *Elegies*," in *John Donne: Essays in Celebration*, edited by A. J. Smith, pp. 47–72. London: Methuen & Co.

Suggests that labeling Donne's *Elegies* as "Ovidian" or even "Roman" can obscure their unique qualities. Discusses the differences between the *Elegies* and those of Ovid and suggests that Donne is most Ovidian when he is witty and unfeeling. Calls "Loves Warr" the most Roman of all Donne's elegies, notes his uniqueness even in this poem, and concludes that it is little more than "an example of the slavish following of a convention which, when there is not enough personal pressure to revivify it, becomes tedious imitation" (pp. 59–60). Sees "Natures lay Ideot" as a more successful Roman imitation that "catches the spirit, half-amused and half-resentful, of Ovid and adds to this the witty and mimetic but non-Roman reminder of the lady's social and amatory inadequacies" (p. 62). Challenges Leishman's view that "Going to Bed" was suggested by Ovid's *Amores*, I, v, and suggests Propertius's *Elegies*, II, xv, as a more likely model, but even then finds Donne's poem very un-Roman in most respects. Argues that "The Perfume" best exemplifies "Donne's mastery, even at this very early stage in his career, of language, and his sensitivity at once to the rhythms of speech and to those of the couplet" (pp. 67–68) and notes Donne's almost obsessive use of religious language in the *Elegies*, specifically the language of Roman Catholicism. Suggests that of all the *Elegies* "On his Mistris" stands apart by its very un-Ovidian passionate tenderness and sense of privacy: "it is Donne's own emotion, imagined with sincerity and communicated with honesty, that makes the poem so moving" (p. 72). Concludes, therefore, that the *Elegies* "are a mongrel breed, numbering among their ancestors the Latin elegists, Marlowe as translator of Ovid and sponsor of the heroic couplet and, especially in their use of language to display character, the native dramatic tradition" (p. 70).

↩§ 430. GILLIE, CHRISTOPHER. *Longman Companion to English Literature*. London: Longman Group. 885p.

Mentions Donne throughout under different headings. See especially (1) "Donne, John" (pp. 487–88), a brief biographical sketch and introduction to Donne's poetry and prose; (2) "*Songs and Sonnets*" (p. 799); (3) "Metaphysical Poets" (pp. 648–49), an outline of the history of the term *metaphysical poets* and major features of metaphysical poetry; and (4) "Nocturnall upon St Lucy's Day" (pp. 675–76), a brief critical analysis of the poem.

↩§ 431. HAMILTON, HORACE. *The Cage of Form: Likeness and Difference in Poetry*. Encino and Belmont, Calif.: Dickenson Publishing Co. viii, 272p.

Mentions Donne throughout. Notes specifically how in "Song: Goe, and catche a falling starre" Donne "combines hyperbole with paradox to tease the listener's incredulity" (p. 110) and suggests that "the quality of the hyperbole is such that the speaker seems vulnerable to his own disillusionment rather than a worldly cynic" (p. 111).

⌐§ 432. HANSCOMBE, GILLIAN. "John Donne and the Writing of Lyrics." *Studies in Music* 6: 10–26.

Discusses how most of Donne's poems break with the traditional values of lyric poetry and argues that most of them are "unsuitable for melodic treatment for reasons other than whether or not they are good poems" (p. 26). Discusses in some detail "The triple Foole" to show that "if Donne did not write lyrics, it was not necessarily because he did not understand the requirements of a singing line, but perhaps more because he wished to explore other avenues, the power of poetry to yield awareness and its property of regulating into consciousness the mute demands of strong feelings" and also to show Donne's "method of sustaining one set of attitudes—nonchalance, whimsy, playfulness—while at the same time delivering a seriously considered point," a method quite different from the lyricist, who "looks to a melodic line to establish the point" (p. 14). Comments also in detail on "Song: Sweetest love, I do not goe" along with the musical setting of the poem found in MS 1018 (f.44b) of St. Michael's College to show that the music is only a dramatic setting for a poem that is "already complete within its own terms" and "therefore does not need a melodic expansion" (p. 25).

⌐§ 433. HARDING, D. W. "The *Devotions* Now," in *John Donne: Essays in Celebration*, edited by A. J. Smith, pp. 385–403. London: Methuen & Co.

Argues for the relevancy of the *Devotions upon Emergent Occasions* for the twentieth-century reader, even if he does not share Donne's religious faith and sensibilities. Points out that the *Devotions* offer a convincing picture "of an intellectually subtle and a strongly emotional man struggling with problems that still assail us" and argues that Donne's encounters with sickness, sin, and death "can be recognised as human experiences by people of different religious faith or of none" (p. 385) but will still speak most directly to those "who have felt despair and horror at themselves and their waste of life" (p. 386). Presents a critical reading of the *Devotions*, commenting on structure, imagery, tone, and themes. Likens Donne's method of free association to modern psychoanalysis and his technique to that of seventeenth-century sermons and stresses Donne's emotional honesty, his capacity for personal self-revelation, his robust and vigorous mind, his respect for the body, and his intense fear of separation from those that he loved coupled with a keen awareness of his need for others. Emphasizes throughout that, although expressed in his own Christian idiom, "the whole plan of the *Devotions* gives the religious concepts a firm anchorage in human events and emotions" (p. 401). Concludes that, for

Donne, faith in redemption convinced him "that his self-condemnation need not and must not be total and final" (p. 401).

◄§ 434. HARDY, BARBARA. "Thinking and Feeling in the Songs and Sonnets," in *John Donne: Essays in Celebration*, edited by A. J. Smith, pp. 73–88. London: Methuen & Co.

Reprinted in *The Advantage of Lyric: Essays on Feeling in Poetry* (Bloomington and London: Indiana University Press, 1977), pp. 18–32.

Points out that Donne's dramatic lyrics "renew, recreate, and accessibly record the life of the passions, keeping faith with the way the passions grow, move, shift, combine, and relate to intelligence and sensation" (p. 73). Argues that "lyric creates a language for the passions by not naming, by showing those limits and falsities of naming" (p. 73). Examines three groups of Donne's poems to show the range, variety, and complexity of his passionate lyrics: (1) "Loves growth," a poem of satisfied and secure love that shows Donne's "capacity for dropping and picking up wit and fancy, or to put it another way, for using flights of wit and fancy audaciously, simply, and always passionately" (p. 77); (2) several poems of hostility and frustration, such as "Loves diet," "The Blossome," and "The Legacie," in which "destructiveness is shown as the other side of love, in the poetic process" (p. 80); and (3) "A Valediction: of my name, in the window," a poem representative of those poems which possess "a rare and highly disturbing quality, which belong to and imprint that kind of passionate experience which joins extremes, which feels the momentary truth of possession with the possibility of loss, the expectation of denial at the time of recognition" (p. 84). Shows that in Donne's poems "we have a special sense of the exposure of human beings in their relationships"; that we find a "sense of pride, triumph, delight and power, felt by the artist but on behalf of a prowess and energy larger than the experience of art"; and that we sense "wit as the overflow of artistic power, creativity exulting and scattering its energies, in a virtuosity which is never merely virtuosity" (p. 75).

◄§ 435. HAWKES, TERENCE. "Donne and the Compasses," in *Metaphor*, pp. 18–22. (The Critical Idiom, no. 25, gen. ed. John D. Jump.) London: Methuen & Co.

Comments on Elizabethan attitudes toward metaphor and suggests that, for them, the main function of metaphor was "to reinforce an established view of the world, certainly not to challenge or question that view by means of particular 'local' or 'singular' insight" (p. 20). Points out that the main concern of the Elizabethan metaphor "seems to have been to involve its audience in an *abstract* process, and to make it participate therein," unlike modern metaphors, which "try to deliver their good in one immediate 'handing over' which is complete in itself" (p. 22). Discusses briefly Donne's use of the compass in "A Valediction: forbidding mourning" to show that the metaphor is decorous and suited to the subject of the poem and is in no way shocking or original.

◆§ 436. HENRICKSEN, BRUCE. "Donne's Orthodoxy." *TSLL* 14: 5–16.
   Maintains that an examination of Donne's sermons reveals that he was not a mystic and that he "repeatedly presents an orthodox and conservative message which he himself sees as being opposed to any religious position that would embrace mysticism" (p. 5). Suggests that, like St. Augustine, Donne came to realize that mysticism "is a threat to orthodox religious institutions, to the established church" (p. 10). Points out that Donne's extensive use of marriage symbolism in his sermons, as well as in certain of the divine poems, "reveals a fundamental difference between Donne and the mystics, for he speaks of the marriage of Christ to the Church, not to the individual soul directly" (p. 8). Notes that, although the persona in "Batter my heart" seems to yearn for mystical experience, this does not mean that Donne actually had one and notes further that in "Show me deare Christ" Donne "clearly expresses the idea that Christ is married to the church rather than to the individual soul" (p. 9). Stresses that Donne, like Hooker, consciously defended the established Church against private and schismatic forms of prayer and worship and that he "spends much of his time in his sermons defending the specific merits of the sacraments and ceremonies of his Church" (p. 14). Argues that rejecting the images of Donne as the "naughty boy" of the secular poems and as the mystic will allow us "to see and appreciate what is continuous in Donne's work—the examination and acceptance of the traditional values of his society, first on the private level and then on the public level as Dean of St. Paul's" (pp. 15–16).

◆§ 437. HEYWORTH, P. L. "Donne's Verse-Letter." *TLS*, 24 March, p. 337.
   Comments on A. J. Smith's account of Donne's holograph verse letter to Lady Carew (entry 507) and regrets that Smith resigned the field so promptly in his reply (entry 506) to Helen Gardner's objections (entry 425). Questions Gardner's assumption that the holograph "may be not a fair copy but the original, written in *currente calamo*." Suggests that perhaps Donne sent a copy to Lady Carew and kept the original and thus the Bodleian holograph would not be the single source of all variant versions (as Smith suggested) but rather itself a variant version.

◆§ 438. HIRABAYASHI, JIRŌ. "John Donne to Sono Anglicanism" [John Donne and His Anglicanism]. *Kiyō* (A: Jimbun / Shakai) (Kyoto Kyōiku Daigaku), no. 40 (February): 77–95.
   Argues that Donne's conversion to and defense of Anglicanism was entirely sincere and that he would not have considered his conforming to the English Church as an act of apostasy from the apostolic, Catholic Church. Points out that, although his sense of personal unworthiness and

of sin became more apparent to him as he grew in the spiritual life, there is nothing to suggest that he was a very wicked person nor an apostate. Surveys Anglican attitudes during the period on the nature of the Church and concludes that Donne's views are in harmony with Anglican thought.

⌘ 439. HOLLANDER, JOHN. "Donne and the Limits of Lyric," in *John Donne: Essays in Celebration*, edited by A. J. Smith, pp. 259–72. London: Methuen & Co.

Reprinted in *Vision and Resonance: Two Sources of Poetic Form* (New York: Oxford University Press, 1975), pp. 44–58.

Considers the unmusicality and roughness of Donne's lyrics and comments on "certain features of his rhythmic style, strophic patterning and rhetorical tonality which make the 'songs' of their title so hard to take with an older, Elizabethan literalness" (p. 261). Compares, for example, Alfonso Ferrabosco's setting of "The Expiration" (1609) with an anonymous setting of the same poem at about the same time to show that "even the most musicianly attention to word-stress . . . will frequently not suffice to accentuate correctly the textual syntax" (p. 263). Points out that in the *Songs and Sonets* "the modulation of personal speech makes the sounds of sense, and makes sense of the sound patternings of the metre" (p. 270) and that they "embody a constant process of dialectic between modalities, conducted by an ingenuity masked as a reality principle, juggling hyperbole and abuse, insisting that the truest tenderness is the most feigning, that the most faithful caresses are those of wit and will combined" (p. 272). Concludes that it is no wonder, then, that "art song could not begin to treat such complexity musically until Schumann began to set Heine *Lieder*" (p. 272).

⌘ 440. IKUNO, SETSUKO. "Aubade ni tsuite—Chaucer to Donne" [On Aubade—Chaucer and Donne]. *Kiyō* (Tsurumi Joshi Daigaku), no. 10 (December): 49–54.

Compares and contrasts Chaucer's *Troilus and Criseyde* and Donne's "The Sunne Rising," especially noting their mutual borrowings from Ovid's *Amores*. Suggests that Donne's talent was so great that even when he borrowed subjects and metaphors from others, they were completely assimilated and presented as something uniquely his own.

⌘ 441. JENSEN, EJNER J. "The Wit of Renaissance Satire." *PQ* 51: 394–409.

Argues that "in its exuberance and youthful self-delight, in its variety of techniques and tactics, and above all in its impulse toward the dramatic," Renaissance satire "offers its own sorts of literary pleasures" and that "the poems in which this wit operates most successfully deny by their very brilliance the boundaries of genre criticism" (p. 409). Comments on Donne's skillful handling of wit, character development, dialogue, and other dramatic techniques in *Satyre I* and *Satyre IV* and argues that in Donne's poems Renaissance satire "appears at its brilliant best: playing directly to the reader's responses, making vivid and particular instances of folly which in lesser poems are mere items in a catalogue, presenting the infectious idiocies of the contemporary scene with a vitality that remains persuasive" (p. 407).

✑ 442. JHA, MOHAN. *The Phoenix Riddle: An Interpretation and Critical Treatment of Donne's Love Poems*. New Delhi: Arya Book Depot. vi, 147p.

Chapter 1, "Donne's Reputation as a Love Poet" (pp. 3–21), briefly traces Donne's reputation as a love poet from the seventeenth century to the 1930s. Chapter 2, "Classification of Donne's Love Poems" (pp. 25–30), reviews various attempts to classify the love poems (Grierson, Leishman, Redpath, and Gardner) and concludes that on the basis of tone they can be divided into three groups, as they are in chapters 3, 4, and 5. Chapter 3, "Poems: Cynical or Outrageous" (pp. 31–47), discusses briefly those poems in which Donne deals with love as physical passion and suggests that Ovid may have been his starting point but that his uses of dramatic techniques, argumentative structure, paradoxical wit, and irony give these poems a distinctive Donnean independence. Chapter 4, "Poems: Courting or Intimidating" (pp. 48–83), discusses those poems in which the lover attempts "to bring round his mistress entirely to himself through flattery, compliment or threat" (p. 48) and stresses that, although Donne uses Petrarchan elements, he gives them his own particular slant. Chapter 5, "Poems: Happy or Contented" (pp. 84–112), comments on poems that "celebrate the glory of mutual love" (p. 84). Chapter 6, "Conclusion" (pp. 113–17), summarizes the preceding chapters; defends Donne against the charge of being pedantic, obscure, cynical and antifeminist; stresses that Donne's poems are a unique blend of tradition and individual talent; and maintains that "the uniqueness of Donne's love poetry lies in its combination of variety and intensity, in its association of thought and feeling" (p. 117). Appendix (pp. 121–24) surveys the scholarship of Grierson and Gardner on whether or not "Julia," "A Tale of a Citizen and his Wife," "Selfe Love," "The Expostulation," "Variety," "Sonnet. The Token," and "His parting from her" should be attributed to Donne. Notes and references (pp. 127–43) and selected bibliography (pp. 144–47).

✑ 443. JURAK, MIRKO, ed. "The Stuart Age," in *English Poetry: An Anthology with A Critical and Historical Introduction for Foreign Students*, pp. 53–90. Ljubljana: Državna Založba Slovenije.

Presents a brief general introduction to seventeenth-century nondramatic poetry, especially metaphysical poetry (pp. 53–55), followed by eight selections from Donne (pp. 55–69) with brief notes, glossaries, and questions. Includes "Song: Goe, and catche a falling starre," "The Sunne Rising," "Twicknam garden," "The Dreame," "The Apparition," "Going to Bed," "Death be not proud," and "Since she whom I lov'd."

❧ 444. Kawamura, Jōichirō. "Christ no Hanayome wa Dare ka?— Donne no Shūkyō-shi Ippen o ronzu" [Who Is Christ's Spouse?— An Essay upon Donne's Holy Sonnet "Show me . . ."]. *Gengo Bunka* (Hitotsubashi Daigaku), 9 (November): 49–66.

Presents a survey of recent criticism on Donne's "Show me deare Christ" and offers a detailed critical reading of the poem, commenting especially on Donne's concept of the Church.

❧ 445. Keeble, N. H. "The Love Poetry of John Donne." *Lang&L* (Copenhagen) 1, iii: 7–19.

Believes that modern critics have overrated Donne as a love poet. Argues that, although Donne's love poetry "gives fine expression to a great variety of experiences and reveals the working of an extremely subtle mind, the subtlety of that mind never extends to evaluating those experiences" (p. 17). Admits that "no other English poet has treated so many kinds of sexual relationship, nor dealt with so many moods of affection" (p. 9) but concludes that, although Donne is "capable of intense seriousness, cynical frivolity and piercing insight," he is "uncapable of sustained thought" and is "never so bold as to reflect, select, prefer" (p. 17). Claims that Donne's love poetry is flawed by a kind of "moral isolation" and that for all his superficial uses of learning, he "was intellectually indifferent to all metaphysics" (p. 15). Maintains that Donne actually shows little interest in a true love relationship but rather focuses almost entirely on himself and that his dominating masculine tone actually tends to degrade women.

❧ 446. Kirkpatrick, Hugh. "Donne's 'Upon the Annunciation and Passion Falling upon One Day. 1608.'" *Expl* 30: Item 39.

Shows how "The Annuntiation and Passion" is built upon a series of paradoxes and ambiguities and suggests that the major paradox is symbolized and resolved in the figure of the circle, "perfect and yet paradoxical in that it has no beginning and no end." Explains how finally the figure of the circle becomes a "symbol of Christ's life and man's life, of the unity of birth and death and of all beginnings and endings, and of the destruction of time by eternity."

❧ 447. Kishimoto, Yoshitaka. "Donne no Holy Sonnet (1633) 10-Giko to Kanjo no Chowa" [Donne's Holy Sonnet 10—On the Harmony of Its Technique and Feeling]. *Baika Review* (Baika Joshi Daigaku), no. 5 (March): 1–11.

Presents a close critical analysis of "Batter my heart" and stresses the relationship between its structure and technique and its unusually powerful emotional intensity.

❧ 448. ———. "Donne no The First Anniversary Shiron" [An Essay on Donne's The First Anniversary]. *Kiyo* (Bungakubu, Baika Joshi Daigaku), no. 9 (December): 1–17.

Presents a general critical reading of *The first Anniversary* and points
out that Donne performs an "autopsy" on the world, the cosmos, the new
philosophy, and himself in his search for the ideal spiritual world.

❧ 449. KRASAVCHENKO, TATYANA N. "T. S. Eliot i Dzhon Donn" [T.S.
Eliot and John Donne], *Sbornik nauchnykh rabot aspirantov KBGU*
[*An Anthology of Scholarly Works by Graduate Students at the
Karbinian-Balkarian State University*], vol. 3, part 3 (Nalchik, n.p.),
pp. 53–95.
Discusses Eliot's service in bringing about the belated recognition of
Donne and relates the similarities in their poetry to similarities in their
social and intellectual milieux.

❧ 450. KREMEN, KATHRYN R. *The Imagination of the Resurrection: The
Poetic Continuity of a Religious Motif in Donne, Blake, and Yeats.*
Lewisburg, Pa.: Bucknell University Press. 344p.
Discusses the continuity of the resurrection motif in the works of Donne,
Blake, and Yeats and shows that the motif, which begins as a religious
doctrine that reveals the mystery of man's redemption, becomes for the
Romantic poets a recreation of the imagination. Maintains that "without
ontological certainty of divine redemption and without shared (across time
and across persons) access to its public forms (the Bible, liturgy, and doctrine) authoritative symbolization of an essentially religious subject (salvation) is not successful" (p. 320), as exemplified by Yeats. Chapter 1,
"The Origins and Development of the Resurrection Doctrine" (pp. 29–
79), surveys the origin and development of the doctrine of resurrection in
the Old and New Testaments, the Apocrypha and Pseudoepigraphia, and
in post-Apostolic theology from the first century to Luther and Calvin.
Chapter 2, "The First Resurrection in Donne's Religious Prose and Poetry: The Whole 'World's Contracted Thus'" (pp. 80–129), discusses Donne's
view of resurrection as reflected in his religious prose, divine poems, and
love poetry and maintains that he is quintessentially representative of post-
Reformation theology and Christian symbolism. Argues that in his love
poems he incorporates the doctrine of resurrection by presenting erotic
love as a *figura* of eschatological reality and shows how his development
of the relationship between the erotic and the eschatological differs from
that of Shakespeare and Marvell. Suggests that the main difference "arises
from Donne's essentially religious view of sexual love" and notes that for
him "the resurrection in soul and body to heavenly union with the Trinity
sanctifies both sacred and profane love relationships" (p. 96). Comments
on Donne's theology of love and marriage as seen in his sermons and
poetry and shows how "the Christian doctrine of resurrection not only
sanctions Donne's incorporating the erotic into the eschatological in an-
amnetic relation, but also gives him 'metaphors for poetry'" (p. 98). Comments on the relationship of the erotic and eschatological specifically in
"A Valediction: forbidding mourning," "The Extasie," "The Sunne Ris-

ing," and "The Canonization." Comments on the resurrection motif in Donne's specifically religious works, especially "Batter my heart," "Show me deare Christ," "Hymne to God my God, in my sicknesse," "At the round earths imagin'd corners," "Goodfriday, 1613. Riding Westward," the two *Anniversaries*, and *Devotions upon Emergent Occasions*. Chapter 3 (pp. 129–259) and Chapter 4 (pp. 260–307) discuss respectively the resurretion motif in the poetry of Blake and Yeats and contain comparisons between them and Donne. Chapter 5, "'Post-Mortem': Very Last Things" (pp. 308–24), summarizes the basic argument of the study and stresses again that Donne and Blake are Christian poets whose symbolism is authentic because they believed in eschatological reality while Yeats failed "because his secular system includes no transcendent divine reality and no eschatological symbol, which participates in it" (p. 318). Bibliography (pp. 325–37) and index (pp. 339–44).

451. KUSUNOSE, TOSHIHIKO. "The Satires ni okeru John Donne" [John Donne in *The Satires*]. *Ronkō* (Kanseigakuin Daigaku), no. 21 (December): 95–115.
Cited in "The 1972 Bibliography," *The Renaissance Bulletin* (The Renaissance Institute, Tokyo) 6 (1979): 18. Unavailable.

452. LEACH, ELSIE. "T. S. Eliot and the School of Donne." *Costerus* 3: 163–80.
Summarizes the shifts in Eliot's critical position toward the metaphysical poets and argues that "the changing emphases of Eliot's criticism parallel developments in his own verse" (p. 163). Shows how after 1931 Eliot evidences an increasing enthusiasm for Herbert as his interest in Donne, Marvell, and Crashaw diminishes. Shows that at first Eliot regarded Herbert as Donne's inferior but from 1944 on he championed Herbert as a major poet; stressed Herbert's affinities to Donne, not his differences; and finally preferred Herbert to Donne.

453. LEBANS. W. M. "Donne's *Anniversaries* and the Tradition of ✓✓
Funeral Elegy." *ELH* 39: 545–59.
Regards "A Funerall Elegie" as important to an understanding of the *Anniversaries* and argues that an examination of the elegy and Donne's *Epicedes and Obsequies* in general in relation to the *Anniversaries* "suggests strongly that both the latter arise, at least in part, out of the tradition of funeral elegy based on classical models which Donne adapted to his own purposes and modified in his characteristic way" (pp. 545–46). Examines Donne's funeral elegies of a private character, written before and after the *Anniversaries*, to show that they "are conceived and written in terms of the conventions of non-pastoral elegy which Donne derived from his knowledge of the classical models of such elegies and from the prescriptions of the classical rhetoricians" and that in all of them "the three basic elements of all funeral elegies are easily observable: lament, eulogy

and consolation" (p. 546). Presents a close reading of "A Funerall Elegie" to show how Donne "manipulates a series of traditional themes to his own advantage" (p. 547) and outlines the structure of the two *Anniversaries* to show that it "confirms their relationship to Donne's funeral elegies and thus to the classical predecessors" (p. 550). Suggests that the death of Elizabeth Drury was an occasion for Donne to give "poetic form to his attitudes to a world that was going to pieces around him and to his ideas of eternity and eternal life" (p. 556). Argues that the "she" of the poem is not *sapientia creata*, Elizabeth I, idealized woman, the Virgin Mary, nor any of the other possibilities suggested by modern critics but is Elizabeth Drury, transformed and real, and thus the poems "weave back and forth between transfiguration and reality in an extraordinary but nevertheless recognizable seventeenth-century fashion" (p. 559). Suggests that Donne was "deliberately setting out to upset the convention that a public elegy could only be written on a public figure" (p. 559).

454. ———. "The Influence of the Classics in Donne's *Epicedes and Obsequies*." *RES* n.s. 23: 127–37.

Argues that the direct influence of classical sources on the structure of Donne's nonpastoral funeral elegies, written between 1596 and 1625, is highly probable since the poems, "in spite of their conceits and other typical characteristics of the metaphysical mode, use as their basic principle of structure the classical organization into lament, panegyric, and consolation, and exploit these elements in a fashion which fully demonstrates his knowledge of the classical models and the prescriptions of the rhetorical treatises" (p. 128). Argues further that the direct influence of the classics on specific words, phrases, images, and allusions in the funeral elegies is likely only in some cases, since "the greater part of these allusions are either Renaissance commonplaces or derived at second or third hand from their original classical sources" (p. 130). Maintains, however, that Donne's governing conceit of a Roman triumph in the second half of "Obsequies to the Lord Harrington" suggests very strongly that he consulted directly several classical sources for his details. Notes that "in those cases when classical influences can be proved or reasonably assumed, the classical authors on whom Donne relies are not those regularly drawn on by contemporary poets," which, in itself, gives "additional credibility to the argument for classical influences" (p. 197).

455. LE COMTE, EDWARD. "Jack Donne: From Rake to Husband," in *Just So Much Honor: Essays Commemorating the Four-Hundredth Anniversary of the Birth of John Donne*, edited by Peter Amadeus Fiore, pp. 9–32. University Park and London: The Pennsylvania State University Press.

Reprinted in slightly revised form in *Poets' Riddles: Essays in Seventeenth Century Explication* (Port Washington, N.Y., and London: Kennikat Press, 1975), pp. 44–66.

Conjectures that Donne and Ann More were not married secretly in December 1601 (N.S.), as Donne's letter to his father-in-law, George More, states, but that the marriage actually took place sometime in January 1602 (N.S.), at which time Ann was already pregnant. Suggests that Donne predated the marriage in order to protect his wife's honor and also to guarantee the legitimacy of their first child, Constance. Argues that Richard Swale, the judge who finally validated the marriage on 27 April 1602, left the exact day in January purposefully vague so as to allow the couple as much leeway as possible. Suggests also that the premarital union of the couple was "not an evasion of, but a way into marriage" since "it strengthened their legal claim on each other" (p. 20). Reviews various aspects of Donne's youthful libertinism but questions whether these justify calling Donne a rake.

❧ 456. LEVER, WALTER. "Phallic Fallacies in the Bower of Bliss." *WCR* 7, no. 1: 62–63.

Points out that the word *eye* could mean "testicle" in Elizabethan English and suggests that in "The Extasie" (lines 7–8) "'eye' signifies testicle and 'eye-beam' the erected penis" (p. 63). Concludes, therefore, that the lines mean that, "with intertwined genitalia, frozen on the high plateau of excitement like climbers on some Alpine ledge, Donne and his boyfriend could neither get up or down, but were fixed in a state of sexual immobility" (p. 63). Suggests also that "a new concoction" (line 27) refers to orgasm.

❧ 457. MCADAMS, JAMES R. "A Mixed Success." *JGE* 24: 206–13.

Review article of Peter Amadeus Fiore, ed., *Just So Much Honor: Essays Commemorating the Four-Hundredth Anniversary of the Birth of John Donne* (entry 421). Finds the collection "disappointing in details of conception and execution but well-intentioned and valuable overall" (p. 206).

❧ 458. MACCOLL, ALAN. "The Circulation of Donne's Poems in Manuscript," in *John Donne: Essays in Celebration*, edited by A. J. Smith, pp. 28–46. London: Methuen & Co.

Surveys in detail the existing seventeenth-century manuscripts of Donne's poems and also the manuscript miscellanies in which his poems appeared to show that few of Donne's poems reached a very large audience in his own lifetime and that the majority of them scarcely began to circulate to any great extent until well into the second decade of the century. Points out that only the *Satyres*, *Elegies*, and "The Storme" and "The Calme" were very much circulated in the first decade of the century. Suggests, therefore, that "it should no longer be possible to speak without qualification of Donne's 'great popularity' as a poet" (p. 43) during his own lifetime. Notes that Donne rarely gave out copies of his single poems, except for the verse letters and occasional pieces; that he consciously avoided public attention as a poet from the beginning; that he fully regretted the publication of the *Anniversaries*; and that he was fully "aware of the dangers of exposing poems written for a circle of like-minded readers to the public gaze" (p. 44) and only twice allowed large collections of his poems to leave his hands. Shows that it was only from about 1625 until the mid-1640s (and especially after the first edition of 1633) that the poems show up in any great numbers in the manuscript miscellanies and then only certain poems were regularly reproduced. Points out that after 1650 "the flood dwindles to a trickle" (p. 45). Concludes, therefore, that Donne was, in a sense, "a 'coterie poet' not because the public did not appreciate his work but because for a long time it was available only to a small number of readers" (p. 45).

≈§ 459. McGOWAN, MARGARET M. "'As Through a Looking-glass': Donne's Epithalamia and their Courtly Context," in *John Donne: Essays in Celebration*, edited by A. J. Smith, pp. 175–218. London: Methuen & Co.

Argues that Donne's verse letters and especially two of his epithalamia "should be studied not as anomalous and extravagant pieces but as the natural expressions of a highly self-conscious and literate society which genuinely believed itself to be exactly as its spokesmen depicted it" (p. 175). Argues that "the particular character of Donne's *Epithalamia* emerges only when the poems are studied within the context which inspired them" and that, conversely, "this context can only be defined with any accuracy by a study of the individual works which comprised it at any one moment of time" (p. 217). Discusses in detail the structure, tone, language, and imagery of "An Epithalamion, Or mariage Song on the Lady Elizabeth" and "Ecclogue 1613. December 26" to show that, although the two poems are quite different, they are both very much "products of the robust atmosphere of James I's Court" (p. 176). Attempts "to convey an idea of the spirit of James I's Court, and of the criteria of expectation assumed by poet and audiences alike" and examines the epithalamia "against the background of other poems, plays, and masques written to celebrate the same occasions" (p. 177). Concludes that "participation and celebration are key concepts for a proper understanding of any poetic work of this period when it was the social context, above all, which determined the form" (p. 217), that during the period "poet and reader consciously shared certain assumptions about language and metaphor, so that images could simultaneously provide not only a vehicle for general expression which could be immediately comprehended, but also a means of making more private comment" (p. 217), and that "the technique of generalising . . . was the principle way in which 'court' poets—and Donne is one of them—solved the problems posed by being bidden to write for a particular occasion" (p. 218).

 ≈§ 460. MAHONY, PATRICK. "The Structure of Donne's *Anniversaries* as Companion Poems." *Genre* 5: 235–56.

Calls the *Anniversaries* "the most spectacular companion poems of high caliber in English literature" (p. 235) and attempts to show that their interrelationship "is manifest in their general thematic balance and, even more remarkably, in the similarities and antitheses of their corresponding sections" (p. 235). Shows that "not only are there correspondences between the introductions and conclusions of both poems, but there is also a respective correspondence between the five meditations, eulogies and morals of *FA* with the first five meditations, eulogies and morals of *SA*," resulting in "a network of modulations, internal allusions, and ironic echoes, without which the bipartite masterpiece has never been fully understood or aesthetically appreciated" (p. 236). Suggests that in some ways the poems "parallel Petrarch's *Canzonieri*, in which the earthly Laura, who is a given social stress, stands off against the heavenly Laura, who is given an individual accent" (p. 252).

⊷§ 461. MARTIN, F. DAVID. "Literature and Immanent Recall," in *Art and the Religious Experience: The "Language" of the Sacred*, pp. 183–227. Lewisburg, Pa.: Bucknell University Press.
Comments briefly on Donne's use of various poetic devices in the first four lines of "Batter my heart" to show that "the cumulative power of these devices is iconic with the central designative meaning of the quatrain and the poem as a whole" and to demonstrate that "all the meanings, with their extremely tight interrelationships, converge around the symbol of the 'three person'd God'" (p. 206). Maintains, however, that Masaccio's visual symbol of the three-personed God in his painting *Trinity* "is likely to hold our attention more strongly than Donne's verbal symbol" (p. 207).

⊷§ 462. MEDINE, PETER E. "Praise and Blame in Renaissance Verse Satire." *PCP* 7: 49–53.
Suggests that the central aesthetic problem facing the Renaissance verse satirist "lay in resolving his basic impulse to praise and blame into an integrated poetic scheme" (p. 49) and argues that Donne, through the thematic and structural integrity of his satires, solves the problem. Maintains that "in combining the positive and negative statements within each satire, Donne integrated the entire design of his collection" and that "with one impulse strengthening the other the conception of truth and virtue is not blurred but sharpened by the analysis of falsehood and vice" (p. 52). Contrasts Donne with Thomas Drant.

⊷§ 463. MENASCÈ, ESTHER. "Note su «Ignatius his Conclave»", in *Studi Machiavelliani* (Università degli studi di Padova, Facoltà di economia e commercio in Verona), pp. 473–521. Verona: Palazzo Giuliari.
Examines *Ignatius his Conclave* in relation to contemporary interpretations of Machiavelli's works. Attempts to determine what knowledge Donne could have had and what opinion he held concerning Machia-

velli. Suggests three possible sources: his studies at the university; his contact with certain persons who were familiar with Machiavelli's theories, especially Sir Walter Ralegh; and the theater, in which the pseudo-Machiavelli was a popular character. Discusses in detail Donne's relationship with and opinion of the Jesuits. Analyzes the text of *Ignatius*, compares speeches by Machiavelli in the satire with passages from *I Discorsi* and *Il Principe*, and attempts to determine, by means of the accusations of the character of Ignatius, whether Donne had first-hand knowledge and/or an accurate understanding of Machiavelli's doctrines. Concludes that Donne probably had read both *I Discorsi* and *Il Principe*, at least in part. Indicates that since *Ignatius* is a satire, it is difficult to determine what attitude Donne actually had toward Machiavelli. Maintains, however, that despite his representation of Machiavelli as a villainous politician for artistic purposes, Donne appears to have understood and respected many of his ideas.

⏴⧸ 464. MERCHANT, W. MOELWYN. "Donne's Sermon to the Virginia Company, 13 November 1622," in *John Donne: Essays in Celebration*, edited by A. J. Smith, pp. 433–52. London: Methuen & Co.
Presents the historical context of Donne's sermon to the Virginia Company on 13 November 1622. Comments especially on Donne's letter to Sir Thomas Roe of 1 December 1622 as helpful in estimating the tone and temper of Donne's sermon. Shows that, although Donne was always willing to be judicious in theological matters where that was demanded of his office and always diplomatic in regard to political powers where that did not in any way compromise him as a Christian preacher, he was never willing to suppress the truth as he saw it. Comments on the careful rhetorical structure of the sermon to the Virginia Company, its restraint in the light of the emotionally charged issues confronting the company, and its extraordinary wit: "Donne was walking delicately: he spoke in a situation in which his anti-papal feelings, focussed upon Spanish relations in the New World, were engaged in making a political statement which could scarcely please the king; and at the same time he preached words of comfort to the businessmen of the Virginia plantation while yet deploring their harsh reaction to the massacre [of white settlers by Indians]" (p. 444). Shows how skillfully Donne weds in complete sincerity sound Christian teaching and support of the king by urging the company to lead the Indians to a love of the king who has sent such honest, loving men to civilize them and to teach them to adore the King of Kings: "Rhetoric was here the temporary servant of a political situation, as in the great preachers it regularly has been" (p. 452).

⏴⧸ 465. MILES, JOSEPHINE. "Forest and Trees: The Sense at the Surface." *NLH* 4: 35–45.
Reprinted as "The Sense at the Surface," in *Poetry and Change: Donne,*

Milton, Wordsworth, and the Equilibrium of the Present (Berkeley, Los Angeles, and London: University of California Press, 1974), pp. 7–22.

Contrasts briefly the elements of design in Donne's "Oh, to vex me, contraryes meet in one" with those in Milton's "When I consider how my light is spent" to show that in Donne's sonnet "surface design is a steady tool throughout: line-ends enforced by rhymes; the rhymes parallel in meaning . . . ; a structure shifted between octave and sestet" (p. 39). Points out Donne's use of parallelism, repeated subordinate clauses, and irony, and maintains that for him "a tight design is part of the air he breathes, the art he works in" (p. 39).

466. ———. "Ifs, Ands, Buts for the Reader of Donne," in *Just So Much Honor: Essays Commemorating the Four-Hundredth Anniversary of the Birth of John Donne*, edited by Peter Amadeus Fiore, pp. 273–91. University Park and London: The Pennsylvania State University Press.

Reprinted in *Poetry and Change: Donne, Milton, Wordsworth, and the Equilibrium of the Present* (Berkeley, Los Angeles, London: University of California Press, 1974), pp. 65–83.

Comments on the characteristic patterns of usage, the simple content, the major vocabulary, and the structures of Donne's poetry in an attempt to show that a quantitative and structural analysis will "show the reader on what firm ground of actuality in the text some of his reactions may rest" (p. 274). Argues that an analysis of Donne's vocabulary and structure indicates "how the specialization of his structure in subordinate propositions and the specialization of his reference in cognitive terms makes a bond which relates sixteenth century poetic substance of Wyatt and Sidney to the seventeenth century poetic grammar of Jonson and Herrick, Carew and Cowley, and goes beyond it all to an encompassable realm, where it is no wonder no one follows" (pp. 275–76). Discusses such matters as Donne's use of "a vocabulary of concept distinguished by its concern with time, cognition, and truth, positive and negative" (p. 274); his uses of the terms of formal logic, descriptive relative clauses, and active prepositions; his use of strong verbs and clausal connectives for verbs, which separates him from "all other poets by its singularity and also affords a scale of approximation for affinitives, by which we may see Jonson, Herrick, and later Coleridge as closest to him" (p. 275); and his extraordinary ability to use the complexities of logical argumentation. Maintains that "his chief connectives are *and, but, that, to,* in disjunction, relation, and direction, and the rest of his connectives support mainly the logic of alternatives or consequences, so his substantive vocabulary also establishes a world of arguable inference" (p. 289). Concludes that in the *Songs and Sonets*, as well as in Donne's art in general, one finds "a persistent characterizing abstract structure" (p. 289) and suggests that to ask how Donne *feels* his thought will be unsuccessful: "rather to ask how Donne thinks his feeling is to seek and find the pattern of exuberant superlative questions and imperatives compellingly tempered by conditionals, adversatives, and straight denials, a pattern that emerges as a simple downright statement of the actuality of language and of life" (p. 291).

❧ 467. MILGATE, WESLEY. "'Aire and Angels' and the Discrimination of Experience," in *Just So Much Honor: Essays Commemorating the Four-Hundredth Anniversary of the Birth of John Donne*, edited by Peter Amadeus Fiore, pp. 149–76. University Park and London: The Pennsylvania State University Press.

Calls "Aire and Angels" a truly metaphysical poem because "it studies its subject in large perspectives of time, showing how a passionate experience arises out of the past and opens upon a never-ending future" and because "it presents and defines the contours of human experience in relation to the spiritual substance of the universe itself" (p. 175). Suggests that we are now capable of better understanding and appreciating the poem than any previous readers have been, even in Donne's lifetime. Reviews the metaphysics upon which "Aire and Angels" is built and suggests that much of its richness is "due to the tension and interaction between a view of the universal frame of things as static and a view of human experience as dynamic" (p. 152). Presents a detailed reading of the poem and stresses the sense of dramatic progression the poem reveals "as the speaker vividly recalls and assesses the movements of complex experience to the present, or desired state of mutual adjustment of which he now speaks to his lady" (p. 152). Suggests finally that the speaker of the poem concludes that "though love passes through the stages of wonder and worship, and various kinds of physical attraction and desire, love can find its only appropriate fulfillment when it relates to the love that the woman gives in return, not to the woman herself" (p. 170).

❧ 468. MILLS, LLOYD L. "The Literary Character of Donne's References to Specular Stone." *HAB* 23: 37–41.

Argues that Donne's references to specular stone in "To the Countesse of Bedford: Honour is so sublime" and in "The undertaking" are purely literary references and do not refer to a particular material to be found in either the ancient or the modern world. Suggests that the references are used primarily in a poetically complex way and that the descriptive detail and metaphorical implications of a passage about specular stone in Donne's Sermon 16 are the best means for illuminating his meaning. Shows that the reference to specular stone in "To the Countesse of Bedford" is used to illustrate her spiritual perfection and that in "The undertaking" it is used to illustrate the difficulty of being Platonic in an un-Platonic age and the "inability of the poet to teach (or indeed practice) his art where there is no subject" (p. 40).

◄§ 469. MIROLLO, JAMES V. "The Mannered and the Mannerist in Late Renaissance Literature," in *The Meaning of Mannerism,* edited by F. W. Robinson and S. G. Nichols, pp. 7–24. Hanover, N.H.: University Press of New England.

Reviews the state of scholarship on and various theories about the concept of mannerism in literature and suggests ways to improve the present confusion concerning the application of the term. Distinguishes between mannerist art and mannered style. Suggests that "literary mannerism is, on the whole, parasitic and parodic in nature," that "it does seem to mark a break from the esthetic assumptions and the representational style of High Renaissance art, but, incongruously, it still depends upon that art for its effects," and that "the overwhelming impression one has is that of a failure to be genuinely revolutionary in saying something new . . . and of a nearly total reliance on representational *means*" (p. 17). Notes that "in mannerism the *mannered* is never far off because it is too easy to fall into mere quotation of one's predecessors, however exaggerated" (p. 17) and that, although mannerism produced a number of unquestionable masterpieces, it did not produce many great works. Argues that, "for Renaissance writers seeking alternatives, the traditional codified esthetic imperative was *wit*, which in its literary sense means verbal or imagistic or formal complexity, distortion, compression, enlargement, enigma, obscurity, displacement—in sum, all the deviations from the norm of clear, rational, coherent, and balanced presentation or structure"; and thus, mannerism "is the art that reveals art" (p. 17). Mentions Donne throughout by way of example.

◄§ 470. MONTGOMERY, LYNA LEE. "The Phoenix: Its Use as a Literary Device in English from the Seventeenth to the Twentieth Century." *DHLR* 5: 268–323.

Comments on selected uses of the phoenix legend in English literature from the seventeenth to the twentieth century. Notes that, "from its full splendor and vitality as a literary device in the seventeenth century the phoenix sank into the nest of eighteenth and nineteenth century literature, relatively dead, to arise once more in contemporary literature, renewed and vigorous, as a rich and almost endlessly versatile symbol—of love, of the soul of the poet, of the unconquerable spirit of whatever it is that men value and long to believe has permanence" (p. 321). Notes that, although the actual existence of the phoenix was debated in the seventeenth century, Donne denies its historical reality in "An Epithalamion, Or mariage Song on the Lady Elizabeth" and points out that he was "among the first to appropriate the phoenix as a symbol of sexual love" (p. 277). Discusses briefly Donne's uses of the phoenix in "The Canonization," where the man and woman, "uniquely gifted in love, re-enact and indeed give fresh meaning to the phoenix myth," and in the aforementioned epithalamion, where "he first uses the phoenix as a symbol of excellence in a compliment to the bridal pair" (p. 277).

🍃 471. MORGENSTERN, CHARLES. "John Sparrow's 'Manuscript Corrections in Two Issues of Donne's *Biathanatos*.'" *BC* 21: 557.

Reply in part to John Sparrow (entry 510). Notes that the St. John's copy of the undated issue of *Biathanatos* has all the manuscript emendations that Sparrow notes in his two copies of the first issue and that they are in the same hand. Questions also Sparrow's comment about an erased comma and the careless overlooking of a second "t" in *written*. See also John Sparrow (entry 607).

√ **🍃 472.** MORRIS, BRIAN. "Not, Siren-like, to tempt: Donne and the Composers," in *John Donne: Essays in Celebration*, edited by A. J. Smith, pp. 219–58. London: Methuen & Co.

Notes that, although Donne knew musicians and caused his "Hymne to God the Father" to be set to music, he "was not interested in music either as listener or performer, that he thought of it (when he did) primarily in scientific, cosmological terms, and that it moved his imagination only in the most obvious ways" (p. 223). Notes the relatively few references to music in Donne's poems and points out that apparently Donne "never conceived his poems in musical terms, and never delivered them as material for a marriage of the arts" (p. 224). Discusses in detail surviving contemporary settings of seven of Donne's poems: "Song: Goe, and catche a falling starre" (anonymous); "Song: Sweetest love, I do not goe" (anonymous); "The Message" (by Giovanni Coperario); "Breake of day" (by William Corkine); "The Expiration" (one setting by Alfonso Ferrabosco; the other anonymous); "A Hymne to God the Father" (one setting by John Hilton; another by Pelham Humfrey), and his paraphrase of *Lamentations* (by Thomas Ford), the latter of which is reproduced for the first time (pp. 252–58). Suggests that the anonymous setting of "The Expiration" is "certainly the most perceptive setting of any of Donne's secular verse" (p. 234) but notes that the comparative failure of the other settings of the secular poems arose from attempts to fit the poetic rhythms to set musical phrases. Points out that the composers, on the whole, failed to understand that Donne "was treating stanzaic construction in a wholly new way, and a radically anti-musical way" (pp. 241–42) and that his "accent and rhythm was dictated by the passionate speaking voice rather than by the regular lyric metre" (p. 243). Notes that Donne was ignored by composers in the eighteenth and nineteenth centuries and that Benjamin Britten's *The Holy Sonnets of John Donne* (1945), the first important twentieth-century setting, was a success because Britten "saw that the essence of drama in music is the single emotional impact of thematic material to be developed" and also "realised that it was not necessary for the rhythms of his vocal line to be limited by those of the poem" (p. 245). Notes other twentieth-century attempts to set Donne's poems to music by amateurs at the universities and especially by Elizabeth Maconchy, who is said to be "fully alive to all the complexities and opportunities which Donne's resolutely unmusical voice provides"—in fact, "much more alive, it seems, than Donne's own contemporaries were" (p. 251).

◄§ 473. MORRIS, WILLIAM E. "Donne's Use of Enallage in 'The Good-Morrow.'" AN&Q 11: 19–20.
First appeared in *LangQ* 8; see entry 126. Reprinted with only minor word changes.

◄§ 474. MUELLER, JANEL M. "Donne's Epic Venture in the *Metempsychosis.*" *MP* 70: 109–37.
Surveys the critical history of the *Metempsychosis* and suggests that in the twentieth century Donne's poetic fragment has been generally misunderstood as being primarily a satire and thus has been misinterpreted and underevaluated. Discusses the form and content of the poem and argues that in it Donne, unlike the writers of the usual Ovidian mythical-erotic narrative poems that are based on single episodes from the *Metamorphoses*, evolved "an epic design that reflected the larger contours and substance of Ovid's epic" (p. 115). Does not insist on direct parallels between Ovid and Donne but stresses "the continuing consonance of the two poets in treating their very similar themes of metamorphosis and metempsychosis" (p. 116). Argues that, although Donne creates an original, even an idiosyncratic, poem based on a myth of his own devising, the thematic core of his poem was influenced by the views of Carpocrates and Epiphanes, whom Donne likely found in the Latin works of Clement of Alexandria and in Tertullian, from whom he "evidently got the 'Pithagorian' association for Carpocrates as well as the title for his poem" (p. 125). Maintains that the Gnostic raw materials from which Donne drew show that the *Metempsychosis* "is not a satire in the basic or usual sense: the vision is of a world so bad . . . that it is to be rejected, not reformed" and further suggests that Donne chose an epic mode because of the gravity of the subject and that he "was following (individualistically, as always) the Ovidian model of the epic" (p. 135), a fact recognized by the seventeenth-century editor, who placed the poem at the head of the 1633 edition. Argues that Donne abandoned the poem because he came to recognize the impossibility "of an approach to life grounded in anything other than personal moral responsibility and an orthodox belief in salvation through Christ as the one hope of that life in the body and the world" (p. 137). Argues that, like St. Augustine, Donne "came to adopt an intensely subjective approach to experience, one which shifted emphasis from the metaphysics of the universe to the morality and spirituality of the self" and thus "as a transition piece by which Donne found his true personal and poetic direction, the *Metempsychosis* is well placed at the head of his poems" (p. 137).

◄§ 475. ———. "Exhuming Donne's Enigma." *MP* 69: 231–49.
Review article of five books: (1) R. C. Bald, *John Donne: A Life* (entry

179)—"chiefly valuable as a compendium and a synthesis" in which, "while a number of new facts do appear, a greater amount of information impresses itself anew upon the reader because it is placed in a developed context where its importance and its implications can be gauged" (p. 235); (2) Winfried Schleiner, *The Imagery of John Donne's Sermons* (entry 261)— "the most solid contribution to our understanding of Donne the preacher that we have had to date" (p. 237); (3) Judah Stampfer, *John Donne and the Metaphysical Gesture* (entry 267)—"the worst faults of this book lie not in details but in the primacy of the psychological approach" (p. 243) and its most engaging feature "is the enthusiasm with which it was overwritten" (p. 244); (4) Robert S. Jackson, *John Donne's Christian Vocation* (entry 219)—a book that "in general repudiates the ordinary standards of precision, discrimination, and coherence that obtain in historical and literary study" (p. 245) and yet makes good points about doctrine and scripture; and (5) Earl Miner, *The Metaphysical Mode from Donne to Cowley* (entry 123)—a study that, with its presentation of "some certainties, some surmises, some close examination of evidence, some sweeping statements, some questions left hanging—epitomizes our present situation with regard to the Donne enigma" (p. 249).

⋙ 476. MURPHY, AVON JACK. "The Critical Elegy of Earlier Seventeenth-Century England." *Genre* 5: 75–105.
Discusses the seventeenth-century critical essay as a subgenre of the funeral elegy. Delineates its distinctive features, the range and varieties of its techniques, and its tradition. Comments briefly on Lord Herbert of Cherbury's and Arthur Wilson's elegies on Donne and discusses Henry King's "Upon the Death of my ever Desired Freind Dr. Donne Deane of Paules" to show how King imitates Donne's tone, prosody, and imagery. Calls King's elegy "literary criticism of the highest order" (p. 93) and says that Carew's elegy on Donne exhibits "critical brilliance unsurpassed by any contemporary Englishman" (p. 94). Contains a selected, annotated checklist of critical elegies written in England between 1600 and 1670 (pp. 97–105) and lists seven on Donne.

⋙ 477. NAKAMURA, MINEKO. "A Ring without the Stone: A Study of Baroque Quality in *The First Anniversary* (2)." *Insight* (No're Dame Joshi Daigaku, Kyoto), no. 4 (May): 59–75.
Second part of a two-part essay; see entry 355. Discusses the baroque qualities of *The first Anniversary*, especially massiveness and movement in both matter and form, and distinguishes this definition of baroque from that offered by Odette de Mourgues in *Metaphysical Baroque & Précieux* (1953). Compares and contrasts *The first Anniversary* and Crashaw's "The Weeper." Suggests that Donne's poem could be called "an epic of smaller size, a sort of post-Paradisean epic" (p. 71), and maintains that "massiveness, movement, structure and metaphor are all united to show one direction: upward" and that "distorted vision, disproportion, and irregularity

are all its components" (p. 72). Concludes that "the seemingly excessive lamentation and emotional agitation is planned to give immediate impact of desolation and depression, and to bring out, in a negative paradoxical way, the hope and aspiration to virtuousness, to get to Heaven, to move upward" (p. 73).

~§ 478. NOVARR, DAVID. "'The Exstasie': Donne's Address on the States of Union," in *Just So Much Honor: Essays Commemorating the Four-Hundredth Anniversary of the Birth of John Donne*, edited by Peter Amadeus Fiore, pp. 219–43. University Park and London: The Pennsylvania State University Press.

Discusses both the advantages and the limitations of interpreting Donne's poetry in the light of the history of ideas and, in particular, evaluates the approaches to and the interpretations of "The Extasie" by Helen Gardner and A. J. Smith. Maintains that their critical insights are valuable and reveal "a foundation upon which a resolution of the controversy about the tone of the poem and its attitude toward human love can be built, given three assumptions: that Donne did not research 'The Exstasie' as he did *Biathanatos* and *Pseudo-Martyr*; that in 'The Exstasie' he was not only interested in casuistry of love but even more interested in a poetic construct; that he was not only the first poet in the world in some things, but also that the level of his customary achievement is so high that 'The Exstasie' is a fine poem" (p. 221). Disagrees with Gardner, who "seems to feel that unless Donne is serious about ecstasy in this crucial poem, the precursor of the great love poems, he has somehow compromised the integrity of his basic belief about love" (pp. 226–27) and points out that "it is frequently the committed man who dares to explore and exploit alternatives and that it in no way undercuts a man's integrity if he chooses to be witty about a subject that matters to him" (p. 227). Agrees with A. J. Smith that "The Extasie" is a remarkably witty poem but thinks that Smith "does not seem to find the wit very remarkable when he discusses it" (p. 227) and also is too inclined to push Donne "too far into the Aristotelian camp" (p. 230). Presents a reading of the poem that underscores aspects of its wit that have been neglected or misinterpreted in the past and finds Donne's clever uses of a hypothetical listener and a "dialogue of one" as "the keystone of Donne's arching wit" (p. 232). Argues that through these devices Donne is able to deliver an authoritative, dispassionate, and almost scientifically objective justification of bodily love as compatible with spiritual love. Sees the poem not as a celebration of mutual love but points out that its "arid air of refined doctrine provides a fertile atmosphere for crisp argument and dry wit" (p. 240).

~§ 479. NYE, ROBERT. "The body is his book: the poetry of John Donne." *CritQ* 14: 345–60. AP 4 C887

Argues that, if Donne's poetry, both the secular and the sacred, is read as a whole, the reader will find "a consistent and credible Donne, much concerned with the problem of how to exist well, in whatever worlds may be, and how to love well, beyond the fact of self" (p. 352). Attempts to answer the objections of those modern readers who are put off by Donne's religious verse because they find it too witty, find it lacking in mystical and visionary impetus, or suspect that it is perhaps insincere or, at best, half-hearted. Surveys Donne's biography, attitude toward love, and his religious sensibilities to show that he was consistently serious about his commitment to love and that his religious development was achieved by great moral effort, hard intellectual searching, and absolute honesty. Discusses "The Canonization" and "The Extasie," for example, to show that there is no radical division between Donne's love poetry and his religious verse since both are serious, albeit witty, explorations of the nature of love, which is fundamentally a religious issue. Discusses the *Holy Sonnets* as a meditative sequence and suggests that their major appeal is that they present Donne "as an ordinary man down on his knees before God" (p. 357). Briefly comments on the effectiveness of "The Litanie" and "The Crosse," but suggests that it is in "Goodfriday, 1613. Riding Westward," "A Hymne to God my God, in my sicknesse," and "A Hymne to God the Father" that the reader will see "the height of his powers and the depth of his seriousness as a poet, wringing every drop of meaning from his experience" (p. 358).

◄§ 480. PARFITT, GEORGE A. E. "Donne, Herbert and the Matter of Schools." *EIC* 22: 381–95.
   Recognizes the influence of Donne on George Herbert, especially on certain of Herbert's best poems, but distrusts the label *School of Donne*, which "conceals more than it reveals" (p. 395). Contrasts Donne and Herbert as religious poets and sees Donne primarily as "the great religious poet of self-dramatisation" (p. 382), who objectifies his experience in order to come to a personal understanding of his relationship to God and who projects in his poetry a great lack of confidence and sense of uncertainty in his beliefs. States that Donne "is better as a poet of individual faith and doubt than as a celebrator of the communion of Christian belief and of the great occasions of the life of the Church" (p. 386). Maintains that Herbert's poems are less egocentric than Donne's, less imbued with doubt and rebellion, for Herbert sees his own experience as analogous to that of all Christians.

◄§ 481. PARKS, EDNA D. *Early English Hymns: An Index.* Metuchen, N.J.: The Scarecrow Press. viii, 168p.
   Presents an index of early English hymns, in part to challenge the assumption that English hymn writing dates from Isaac Watts (1674–1748). Includes much religious poetry of the seventeenth century, since "much which was suitable was soon adapted and joined with a tune" (p. iv), even though it was not originally designed for congregational singing. Includes poems that were never set to music if they conform to the definition of

the hymn. Arranges the hymns in alphabetical order by first line and also presents (1) the meter, (2) the number of lines or stanzas in the earliest publication of the poem, (3) the name of the author, (4) date of publication and page or line numbers where the hymn can be found, and, when possible, (5) information about the tune and composer. Lists five items for Donne. Contains bibliography (pp. 143–54), author index (pp. 155–62), composer index (pp. 163–65), and tune index (pp. 166–68).

◆§ 482. PATRICK, J. MAX. "Donne's *Holy Sonnets* VI." *Expl* 31: Item 12.

In part, a reply to Arthur W. Pitts, Jr. (entry 358). Argues that the face mentioned in line 7 of "This is my playes last scene" is the face of God, not that of Satan, as Pitts suggests, and that lines 11–14 are "a plea or prayer to God for purgation from sin and for the imputation of righteousness" and not, as Pitts maintains, about resisting temptation and welcoming death with a confident tone. Shows how Donne emphasizes the "unjointing" of body and soul and of the soul from sin and how the speaker pleads in the final lines of the sonnet that, just as his flesh will be unjointed from his soul at death, so may his sins be unjointed from his soul and fall to hell as his freed soul flies to heaven, where it may view the face of God without fear. See also Edgar F. Daniels (entry 402).

◆§ 483. PIRIE, ROBERT S., comp. *John Donne 1572–1631: A Catalogue of the Anniversary Exhibition of First and Early Editions of His Works Held at The Grolier Club February 15 to April 12, 1972.* Foreword by John Sparrow. New York: The Grolier Club. xv, 41p.

Limited to 650 copies.

Describes briefly in the foreword (pp. ix–xi) the exhibit; notes that, except for a few unique items, the contents of the exhibition were from public and private sources in the United States and comments on the extensive interest in Donne by modern scholars and critics. States in the compiler's note (pp. xi–xiii) that "only seven items by Donne printed before 1700 and listed in Keynes were not included in the exhibition" (p. xiii). Lists lenders to the exhibition (p. xiv–xv) and lists 157 annotated main entries divided into five major sections: (1) prose works; (2) letters; (3) sermons; (4) poetry (with three additional subdivisions: John Donne and the Grolier Club, musical settings, and translations); and (5) miscellany (including Donne's seals, books dedicated to Donne, books from Donne's library, biography, iconography, memorial verses, modern editions, bibliography, and memorabilia). Contains five illustrations.

◆§ 484. POWER, HELEN W. "The Speaker as Creator: The Voice in Donne's Poems." *XUS* 11, no. 1: 21–28.

Discusses Donne's use of dramatic devices in a number of poems, including "The Flea," "The Sunne Rising," "A Valediction: forbidding mourning," "The Canonization," "The Indifferent," and several of the *Holy*

Sonnets, to show that the speaker of the poems "controls the poetic activity in the poem" while "Donne controls the poem" (p. 28). Disagrees with critics who see the speaker as typically presenting an evolution of his own thoughts and feelings within the poem or as proceeding in such a manner as to enlarge his own perceptions of his experiences. Maintains rather that the speaker consciously creates a speech, a verbal construct, in order to manipulate a given situation. Sees the speaker, then, as primarily a highly conscious performer and warns that, although the audience within a poem should be fooled, the audience outside it should not be.

◄§ 485. REEVES, TROY DALE, ed. *Donne: 1967–1971; Steinbeck: 1962–1971; Shakespeare: Films and Recordings: Two Author Bibliographies and an Audio-Visual Checklist*. Prepared by students of English 6391. San Angelo, Texas: Angelo State University. 141p.
An unannotated checklist of criticism on and editions of Donne for 1967–1971 (pp. 7–20). Lists 142 items, excluding reviews.

◄§ 486. ROLFE, SUE, AND ANDREW HILTON, eds. *A City Tribute to John Donne, Poet and Dean of St. Paul's, To Celebrate the 400th Anniversary of his birth, 1st-8th October 1972*. Portsmouth: Grosvenor Press. 25p. + 5p.
Contains a foreword by Martin Sullivan, Dean of St. Paul's (p. 1) and a chronological list of Donne's life and major publications (1572–1640) (p. 2). Lists three commemorative events held at St. Paul's Cathedral: (1) a commemorative service, including readings from the sermons on 1 October; (2) a reading by Bernard Miles from the sermons and *Devotions upon Emergent Occasions* at the North Door on 3 October; and (3) a program of music and readings, including a talk by Helen Gardner, a reading from the poems and sermons by Alan Dobie, and a musical presentation by the Campian Consort, playing seventeenth-century settings of Donne's poems by Coperario, Ferrabosco, Hilton and others, along with Duncan Robertson accompanied by Brian Vickers singing Britten's *The Holy Sonnets of John Donne* (p. 3). Announces a program of words, music, and pictures, entitled "John Donne: An Illumination," given by Frank Kermode, William Empson, Roy Strong, and Andrew Hilton at the Mermaid Tavern on 6–8 October (p. 3). Separate program attached. In "The Donne Revival" (pp. 4–5) Geoffrey Keynes comments briefly on the revival of interest in Donne in the twentieth century, mentions how he was introduced to Donne's poetry by Rupert Brooke, and comments briefly on his textual and bibliographical publications. In "Donne in a World of Crisis" (pp. 6–9) Jack Lindsay presents a brief biographical sketch of Donne and a general introduction to his works and sensibility. In "Donne: A London Poet" (pp. 10–13) Barbara Everett comments on Donne's London roots and his affection for the city and briefly discusses London during the lifetime of Donne (from *Donne: A London Poet*, entry 418). Brief com-

ments on Donne by Dryden, Coleridge, Yeats, Eliot, and Pound (pp. 14–15). In "Donne the Preacher" (pp. 16–20) Helen Gardner discusses Donne's concept of and practice of preaching and general characteristics of his sermons and illustrates her comments by an analysis of Donne's sermon preached before King Charles I at St. James on 3 April 1625. In "Donne Set to Music" (pp. 21–23) Ian Harwood discusses the early musical settings of Donne's poems and comments briefly on Donne's attitude toward music. Reproduces a selection from *Benjamin Britten: A Commentary on His Works* by Peter Pears that discusses Britten's settings for the *Holy Sonnets* (pp. 23–24). A selection from Walton's *Life* that describes Donne's orders for his monument (p. 25). Several illustrations.

🎜 487. ROUSSEAU, GEORGE S., AND NEIL L. RUDENSTINE, eds. *English Poetic Satire: Wyatt to Byron.* New York: Holt, Rinehart and Winston. xvi, 599p.
   Surveys in the introduction (pp. 1–43) the development of satire from the ancients to the Romantic era. Calls Donne the foremost English satirist of the 1590s and maintains that, although differing in tone and theme, all five of his satires have resemblances one to another: "their satiric personae are not primarily malcontents or cynics, but adventurous, witty, and bewildered moral spirits engaged upon journeys that serve as occasions for evaluating and choosing among conflicting kinds of experience and modes of life" (p. 14). Points out major features of Donne's satirical art, especially his uses of the dramatic monologue in combination with open pentameter couplets and his introduction of Horatian and Ovidian materials into satire. Briefly compares and contrasts Donne to John Marston and Joseph Hall. Selected bibliography on satire (pp. 44–46). The section on Donne (pp. 55–77) includes a brief biographical sketch and a short introduction to the *Satyres*, a selected bibliography of works on the *Satyres*, and reproduces the five satires (Milgate's text) with explanatory notes (pp. 57–77).

🎜 488. ROWSE, A. L. *The Elizabethan Renaissance: The Cultural Achievement.* New York: Charles Scribner's Sons. xiv, 412p.
   Comments on Donne's reaction against Elizabethan poetry: "He is a singular, isolated phenomenon, with no obvious affiliations; of extraordinary originality, emotional intensity, intellectual vitality, he is already on his way to the next age, a forerunner, a precursor" (p. 80). Discusses major characteristics of Donne's poetry and comments on his Catholicism. Points out his eroticism and suggests that the skepticism, cynicism, and relativism of his poetry show that "he is finding his way out of Catholicism" (p. 81). Discusses *Pseudo-Martyr*, particularly Donne's attack on the Jesuits and especially on Robert Persons (pp. 345–48).

🎜 489. RUFFO-FIORE, SILVIA. "Donne's 'Parody' of the Petrarchan Lady." *CLS* 9: 392–406.

Reprinted as Chapter 2 of *Donne's Petrarchism: A Comparative View* (entry 863), pp. 23–38.

Analyzes "Song: Goe, and catche a falling starre," "Womans constancy," "Communitie," and "The Indifferent" to show that Donne, a true innovator, did not reject Petrarchism but adapted it subtly to his own poetic temperament and needs and to show that, "whereas Petrarch took the first steps toward humanizing Dante's totally spiritual conception of woman, Donne extended Petrarch's partially humanized view into an even more down-to-earth situation" (p. 397). Reevaluates Donne's uses of parodic and satiric devices to show that "it is too facile to conclude that his poems are un-Petrarchan because they show mistrust, cynicism, or sarcasm toward women" (p. 396) and maintains that Donne's use of the cynical mask in his poetry is perhaps his major contribution to the development of the Petrarchan tradition. Concludes that Donne neither uncritically accepts the idealized view of woman projected by Petrarch's imitators nor denies the ideal with satiric attack; rather he satirizes the abuses of the ideal while at the same time redefining it in a more realistic context.

◆§ 490. ———. "The Unwanted Heart in Petrarch and Donne." *CL* 24: 319–27.

Reprinted as Chapter 1 of *Donne's Petrarchism: A Comparative View* (entry 863), pp. 11–22.

Discusses Donne's complex adaptation of the motif of the unwanted heart in "The Blossome" and "The broken heart" to show Donne "could express himself creatively within the conventional limits of Petrarchanism" (p. 327). Argues, therefore, that Donne, unlike many lesser Petrarchan imitators, "neither imitates nor rejects Petrarchan conceits, language, or situations, but rather builds on their implications by probing how its code and idiom relate to his experience" (p. 327). Claims that, by taking Petrarchan thought and expression a step further, Donne "made an original contribution to the mode, and thus can be rightly called as much an innovator as Petrarch was in his day" (p. 327).

◆§ 491. RUOFF, JAMES E., ed. "John Donne, 1572–1631," in *Major Elizabethan Poetry and Prose*, pp. 863–919. New York: Thomas Y. Crowell Co.

Brief biographical and critical introduction to Donne (pp. 863–72) followed by selections (with notes) from the secular and sacred poems (pp. 873–919). Suggests that even when writing of love Donne is essentially a religious poet: "his recurring fascination is with the great central paradoxes of Christian doctrine" (p. 863). Discusses major characteristics of the poetry, such as Donne's intellectualism blended with passion, his uses of metaphor and the conceit, and his rhetorical strategy of colloquial argumentation. Notes that the sermons, like the poetry, show a "curious exhibitionism, a deliberate theatricality" (p. 870). Comments very briefly on Donne's reputation and presents a selected bibliography.

❧ 492. SAKAMOTO, MITSUHARU. "John Donne: 'The Exstasie'—Hitotsu no Kaishaku" [John Donne: "The Extasie"—An Interpretation]. *Shuryū* (Doshisha Daigaku), no. 34 (November): 1–19.
Presents a critical reading of "The Extasie" and suggests that Donne's intention in the poem is to develop a more complete depiction of human beings in love, which he does through the use of alchemical imagery. Maintains that Donne shows that the sublimation of the flesh refines love and spirit and that flesh is ultimately displaced as sexual energy and is sublimated into religious fervor.

❧ 493. SCHAAR, CLAES. "'Balme' in Donne's 'Extasie.'" *ES* 53: 224–25.
Suggests that in the phrase "With a fast balme" ("The Extasie," line 6) *balme* refers to a fragrant garden herb, not to sweating palms. Maintains that "if *balm* is taken in this sense, *fast* is used in a natural way ('firmly tied'); *thence did spring* refers back to *banke*; *balme* continues the flower theme and connects with the thread-and-string image of lines 7–8; figures on tombs can be overgrown with herbs, and *ciment* can simply mean 'join'" (p. 225). Suggests that such an interpretation is strengthened if one examines stanzas 8 and 9 of Lord Herbert of Cherbury's "Ode Upon a Question moved, Whether Love should continue for ever?"—an imitation of "The Extasie." See also Charlotte F. Otten (entry 685) and Susan C. Kemper (entry 837).

❧ 494. SCHLÜTER, KURT. "Die Lyrik der englischen Renaissance," in *Renaissance und Barock*, vol. 10, edited by August Buck et al., pp. 216–56. (Neues Handbuch der Literaturwissenschaft, vols. 9 & 10, edited by Klaus von See.) Frankfurt am Main: Akademische Verlagsgesellschaft Athenaion.
General historical survey of English lyric poetry of the Renaissance. Comments on Donne's position in the tradition and outlines certain general features of his poetry, such as dramatic intensity; uses of wit, argument, and the conceit; and conventional speech patterns, through brief critical discussions of "The Extasie," "A Valediction: forbidding mourning," "Song: Goe, and catche a falling starre," "Hymne to God my God, in my sicknesse," and "Batter my heart." Presents German translations of each of the poems.

❧ 495. SCHRICKX, W. "John Donne in Lille, Courtrai and Ghent in May 1619." *ES* 53: 225–27.
Maintains that a letter, dated 17 May 1619, from William Trumball, English ambassador to the Court of Archduke Albert of Brussels, to Monsieur de la Faille, the archduke's councilor and secretary of state, confirms that Donne, as chaplain to Viscount Doncaster's embassy to Bohemia, traveled with the ambassador's train through Lille, Courtrai, and Ghent, en route from Calais to Antwerp. Suggests that the embassy may

have chosen to visit Antwerp, rather than proceeding directly from Lille to Brussels, in order to allow a member of the embassy to visit the workshop of Rubens and/or to allow Donne and William Trumball to visit their old friend, Sir Tobie Mathew, who was residing at the time in Flanders.

❧ 496. SCUPHOLME, A. C. "Anglican Wit: An Anniversary Study of John Donne: I." *Theology* 75: 21–26.

Points out that Donne, "with all his naturalist passion, knowingness, obscenity indeed, is *anima naturaliter theologica*" (p. 23) and discusses Donne's interest in and witty uses of theology in his early love poems, such as "Going to Bed" and "The Bracelet." Notes that the same wit is apparent in the sermons but observes that in them the reader "does not feel the same strain in following the conceit as he feels when reading the poems" and also "does not find there mere illustrations which are complex rather than valuable" (p. 23). Presents a brief biographical sketch of Donne. (Continued in entry 497.)

❧ 497. ———. "'Fraited with Salvation': An Anniversary Study of John Donne, II." *Theology* 75: 72–78.

Continuation of entry 496. Suggests that the *Divine Poems*, on the whole, show "a sense of strain which seems to arise from Donne's deliberate attempt to force his imagination to conform to the traditional Christian doctrine and the liturgical practice of the Church" (p. 72) but praises Donne's three major hymns as classics of religious poetry, noting that in them the liturgical and theological constraints are moved far into the background. Discusses Donne as a preacher and notes that his sermons are distinguished "by wit, apt and vivid illustration, and here and there by unrivalled passages of grave and musical prose" (p. 77).

❧ 498. SEYMOUR-SMITH, MARTIN. *Longer Elizabethan Poems*. Edited with an introduction and notes by Martin Seymour-Smith. (The Poetry Bookshelf, gen. ed., James Reeves.) London: Heinemann Educational Books; New York: Barnes & Noble. 261p.

Includes *The Progresse of the Soule* (pp. 133–53) with notes (pp. 240–48). Presents a very brief survey of Donne's life and works (pp. 28–29) and a critical discussion of the poem (pp. 29–33). Sees the poem as "vital to an understanding of Donne's humourous, unhappy, sceptical position in the months prior to his materially disastrous marriage" and as "a piercingly intelligent comic and satirical fragment" (p. 2). Surveys various critical interpretations of the poem—from Jonson to W. A. Murray, H. W. Janson, and Wesley Milgate—and concludes that it is probably impossible to say exactly what Donne's intention was in composing it but that clearly he directed his satire against public life. Suggests that readers have often taken the poem too seriously and solemnly and have failed to see it simply as "an ambivalent comic poem, by an undecided man" (p. 32) and thus have failed to appreciate it as "ingeniously brilliant and irreverent," with much "nervous sexual self-criticism"; a poem that served "as an exercise for re-lieving immediate and subjective tension" (p. 33). Selected bibliography (pp. 53–58).

◆§ 499. SHARROCK, ROGER. "Wit, Passion and Ideal Love: Reflections on the Cycle of Donne's Reputation," in *Just So Much Honor: Essays Commemorating the Four-Hundredth Anniversary of the Birth of John Donne*, edited by Peter Amadeus Fiore, pp. 33--56. University Park and London: The Pennsylvania State University Press.
Briefly traces the cycles of Donne's critical reputation and challenges certain recent approaches to the love poems. Suggests that recent "well-bred indifference to autobiography or metaphysics leaves unanswered the yawning gap of question as to what this poetry is about" and fears that the history of Donne's reputation has now come full circle: "What began as praise of sheer wit, the ingenuity of tropes detected by his contemporaries . . . seems likely to return it to a similar position after the revolutions of more ambitious judgments" (p. 37). Finds inadequate purely rhetorical interpretations of Donne's love poems and insists that they should not be seen simply "as exercises in argument in which commonplaces of amatory compliment are polished and rearranged" (p. 38). Argues, on the contrary, that behind the wit of the poems lie much genuine passion, tenderness, and serious love philosophy and maintains that recent historical, textual, and internal evidences point to the fact that Donne developed his style methodically in order to communicate his complex attitude toward love. Recognizes a development in Donne's love poetry—from early light-hearted, cynical, erotic poems to a group of highly complex, serious poems that define and celebrate mutual love as miraculous union. Suggests that in these latter poems, informed by a sophisticated Christian Neo-Platonism, Donne "achieved a fusion of the naturalism of atmosphere of the Latin love elegy, of dramatic timing and pause, and of a dynamic philosophy of love, that maintains an emotional authority unlike anything in poetry since the troubadours" (p. 54). Concludes that it may be his "astonishing subjectivism, this reduction of all experience within the chosen amatory field of play of individual will and consciousness, that makes Donne an ancestor of the modern mind in a sense different from that employed by the new critics of the past" (p. 55).

◆§ 500. SHAWCROSS, JOHN T. "All Attest His Writs Canonical: The Texts, Meaning and Evaluation of Donne's Satires," in *Just So Much Honor: Essays Commemorating the Four-Hundredth Anniversary of the Birth of John Donne*, pp. 245–72. University Park and London: The Pennsylvania State University Press.
Discusses the textual history, ordering, and dating of Donne's satires as well as their themes, prosody, and style. Points out that, since the texts are not definitive, "a diplomatic text drawn from various printed and manu-script sources seems to be the best that can be achieved" (p. 250) and

supports the notion that all five satires may have been written in 1597–1598, when Donne first entered the service of Egerton. Discusses how the satires expose five basic, universal problems or dilemmas that beset man; pose "the constant duel between the id and the superego, the problem of change in this world, the need for a guiding philosophy of life, the pride man shows in externalities, and the avaricious nature of man"; and thus depict "a full range of deadly sin" (p. 262). Notes that, although Donne offers no definitive solutions to these dilemmas, he "hopes that his satires will at least be recognized as proposing true doctrine for the world of moral men" (p. 262). Suggests that the satires progress "from the problem of self to the problems of law courts and lawyers . . . to the problems of religious belief to the problems of the aristocratic world . . . to the problems which greed breeds in both the haves and the have-nots" (p. 269). Sees *Satyre I* as a dialogue between the body and soul and notes that *Satyre V* "has lost some of the spleen of the others and is almost pervaded with pity" (p. 260). Finds the prosody and style of the satires perfectly suited to their themes and intentions and observes that the style "seems different from others' because of the satires' techniques, their humor, and, beneath the jibes, their compassion for man" (p. 266).

〰§ 501. SHERWOOD, TERRY G. "Reason in Donne's Sermons." *ELH* 39: 353–74.

Argues that reason was more central to Donne's beliefs than has been realized by modern critics and shows that reason informs both the content and the literary form of his sermons. Maintains that his notion of reason is based upon St. Augustine's view that reason is a prior and continuing aspect of belief and that Donne attempted "to create a role for reason consistent with both his intellectual nature and his sense of human limitations" (p. 358). Argues that Donne's notion of reason also "accounts for many elements necessary for assessing the sermons as literature" (pp. 358–59) and discusses the rational content, logical argumentation, language of logic, syllogistic structures, and analogical metaphors in the sermons. Notes that for Donne meditation is fundamentally a rational process and that he was always interested in the logical dimension of Scripture. Argues, therefore, that his notion of reason "does not contradict other elements of his Augustinianism, but is, on the contrary, explained most fully by the Augustinian rubric: man as rational creature must reason before and after belief" (p. 366). Examines specifically the imagery, emotion, logic, structure, and stylistic features of Donne's Easter sermon of 1626 and his Second Prebend sermon to show how they are fully informed by his notion of reason. Maintains that Donne is not a rationalist nor does he claim that reason can comprehend the whole experience of belief, but argues that Donne's "aesthetic is the offspring of reasoned belief" and that for Donne, "spiritual experience is not free from the restrictions of rational understanding but is dependent upon understanding" (p. 374).

●⊰ 502. SIMPSON, LOUIS. "Reading the Poem," in *An Introduction to Poetry*, pp. 13–33. 2d ed. New York: St. Martin's Press.

Comments on "The Sunne Rising" (pp. 15–18) and suggests that its major theme is "the centering, controlling power of love" (p. 17). Agrees with Leishman (*The Monarch of Wit*, 1951) that the most striking characteristics of Donne's poetry are "wit, self-dramatization, and the use of the colloquial" (p. 16). Sees a dead seriousness in much of Donne's playfulness and says that the metaphysical poets exhibit such variety "that perhaps their only resemblance is in the use of metaphysical conceits" (p. 18).

●⊰ 503. SLIGHTS, CAMILLE. "'To Stand Inquiring Right': The Casuistry of Donne's 'Satyre III.'" *SEL* 12: 85–101.

Presents a reading of *Satyre III* in the context of seventeenth-century Anglican casuistry. Suggests that in tone, structure, and theme the poem is "a dramatization of a case of conscience" and that the persona is "a casuist trying to deal with the problems of a doubting conscience" (p. 86). Surveys Donne's interest in and reservations about casuistry, especially his disagreement with Roman Catholic approaches based on the concept of probabilism, an approach most clearly identified with the Jesuits. Outlines basic differences between Anglican and Catholic casuistry, noting primarily differences on the question of authority and individual responsibility. Sees Donne in *Satyre III* playing the role of a casuist "advising a young man whose confusion over the complexities and contradictions of institutionalized religion is apparently leading to cynicism, accompanied, perhaps, with swaggering bravura" (p. 94). Argues that, like a good Anglican casuist, Donne does not suggest a solution to the problem of choosing the right religion but rather offers a method for discovering a solution. Suggests that the poem exhibits Donne's "independence and originality as a moralist and churchman" (p. 100) and that, since it was written before the flowering of Anglican casuistry in the seventeenth century, the poem shows, in a sense, how Donne himself "helped create the Anglican tradition" (p. 101).

●⊰ 504. SMITH, A. J. "The Dismissal of Love or, Was Donne a Neoplatonic Lover?," in *John Donne: Essays in Celebration*, edited by A. J. Smith, pp. 89–131. London: Methuen & Co.

Reviews the arguments both of those who maintain that Neoplatonic attitudes "crop up" in many of Donne's love poems and that the serious love poems are clearly Neoplatonic, and of those who suggest that Donne's love poetry "offers no coherent view of love at all but only a variety of local impulses, felt in the senses as any virile man feels them and carried with subtle erotic life in the texture of the verse" (p. 89). Maintains that wit, not sex, is the distinctive quality of Donne's love poetry and that "his wit is purposeful and expresses a settled way of encountering experience which *is* his philosophy of love" (p. 90). Proposes that Donne is "wholly

pragmatic, exploratory" and that "in feeling his way to an understanding
of his own proven experience he inevitably fastened on ideas already current which seemed to define and clarify it" (p. 90). Argues that in the
Songs and Sonets Donne "expressed a sexual consciousness undefined till
then" (p. 90) and surveys and then compares Donne's attitudes with those
of other great European love poets, including Dante, Guinizelli, Fresco-
baldi, Cavalcanti, Petrarch, Serafino, Tasso, Sidney, Spenser, and especially Ficino and Pico. Sees Michelangelo as "the one great European
love poet who unmistakably tried to live out this superhuman metaphysic
of love in his art, and in a sense redeems its flights from academicism" (p.
106). Maintains that Donne does not belong in this company and argues
that, instead of a preconceived philosophy of love, "what holds Donne's
love poetry together is not the pattern of his sentimental life, such as it
may be, but a coherent vision of human nature and a consistent temper
of mind" (p. 124). Presents a detailed reading of "Farewell to love" as an
example of Donne's handling of "one sensitive motif in Renaissance love
poetry, the renunciation of love" (p. 90). Argues that the poems themselves show Donne "consciously formalising his experience in a precise
scholastic way" and that "he'd have been chagrined to find people talking
of neoplatonic ideas in his verse" (p. 131).

₰ 505. ———. "Donne's Reputation," in *John Donne: Essays in Celebration*, edited by A. J. Smith, pp. 1–27. London: Methuen & Co.
Traces the history and development of Donne's reputation as a poet
from his own time to the early twentieth century and notes that a history
of Donne's reputation "is a vivid index of changing critical attitudes over
three hundred years" (p. 1). Accounts for the decline of interest in Donne
in the last half of the seventeenth century and during the eighteenth century and notes that "some of the best things ever said about Donne come
from the nineteenth century" (p. 1). Points out that Grierson's edition of
the poems (1912) did not "burst like a bomb upon an unsuspecting literary
world" but came rather "as the completion of a process which started with
Coleridge and Lamb a century before" (p. 20). Points out that T. S. Eliot's
endorsement of Donne in 1921, "which inaugurated modern criticism of
Donne" (p. 27), and his notion of Donne's unified sensibility were also
part of a long process. Notes, however, that in 1972 critics are "as far
removed in time from those formulations [of Eliot] as Saintsbury was from
Southey" (p. 27).

₰ 506. ———. "Donne's Verse-letter." *TLS*, 4 February, p. 129.
Thanks Helen Gardner for her observations (entry 425) on his account
of Donne's holograph verse letter (entry 507). See also P. L. Heyworth
(entry 437).

₰ 507. ———. "A John Donne Poem in Holograph." *TLS*, 7 January,
p. 19.

Reproduces in facsimile, describes, and discusses Donne's holograph "To the Honorable lady, the lady Carew" found by P. J. Croft of Sotheby's in April 1970 among the family papers of the Duke of Manchester that were formerly in the Public Records Office. Suggests that the poem was probably written in early February 1612 and is "the only English poem of Donne which we certainly have as he wrote it." Comments on the importance of the discovery for textual scholars of Donne's poetry since "all our texts of Donne's poems depend on seventeenth-century transcripts made at several removes from the original copies" and points out that "none of the early manuscripts or printed texts gives the poem exactly as Donne wrote it here." For various replies, see Helen Gardner (entry 425), A. J. Smith (entry 506), P. L. Heyworth (entry 437), and William C. McAvoy in *Manuscripta* 16 (1972): 131–44.

◄§ 508. SMITH, A. J., ed. *John Donne: Essays in Celebration.* London: Methuen & Co. viii, 470p.
Collection of sixteen original essays on Donne, with a preface by A. J. Smith (pp. vii–viii), an index to the writings of Donne (pp. 453–56), and a general index (pp. 457–70). Each of these essays has been entered separately in this bibliography. Contains the following items: (1) A. J. Smith, "Donne's Reputation" (pp. 1–27); (2) Alan MacColl, "The Circulation of Donne's Poems in Manuscript" (pp. 28–46); (3) Roma Gill, "*Musa Iocosa Mea*: Thoughts on the *Elegies*" (pp. 47–72); (4) Barbara Hardy, "Thinking and Feeling in the Songs and Sonnets" (pp. 73–88); (5) A. J. Smith, "The Dismisal of Love or, Was Donne a Neoplatonic Lover?" (pp. 89–131); (6) Brian Vickers, "The 'Songs and Sonnets' and the Rhetoric of Hyperbole" (pp. 132–74); (7) Margaret M. McGowan, "'As Through a Looking-glass': Donne's Epithalamia and Their Courtly Context" (pp. 175–218); (8) Brian Morris, "Not, Siren-like, to tempt: Donne and the Composers" (pp. 219–58); (9) John Hollander, "Donne and the Limits of Lyric" (pp. 259–72); (10) Howard Erskine-Hill, "Courtiers out of Horace: Donne's *Satyre IV*; and Pope's *Fourth Satire of Dr John Donne, Dean of St. Paul's Versifyed*" (pp. 273–307); (11) Patricia Thomson, "Donne and the Poetry of Patronage" (pp. 308–23); (12) Eluned Crawshaw, "Hermetic Elements in Donne's Poetic Vision" (pp. 324–48); (13) Sydney Anglo, "More Machiavellian than Machiavel: A Study of the Context of Donne's *Conclave*" (pp. 349–84); (14) D. W. Harding, "The *Devotions* Now" (pp. 385–403); (15) Dominic Baker-Smith, "John Donne's *Critique of True Religion*" (pp. 404–32); and (16) W. Moelwyn Merchant, "Donne's Sermon to the Virginia Company 13 November 1622" (pp. 433–52).

◄§ 509. SOUTHALL, RAYMOND. "Love Poetry in the Sixteenth Century." *EIC* 22: 362–80.
Discusses the decline of courtly love poetry in England after the death of Wyatt and relates this phenomenon to the shift in forms of economic association: "The break between the plain style of Wyatt and his fellows

and the rich ornate style of the Elizabethans marks an important change of poetic sensibility, the 'rich esteeming' of the new style reflecting a new, because normative, respect for expensiveness" (pp. 378–79). Briefly comments on Donne's uses of commercial images and his employment of business transactions as a vehicle for expressing love. Points out, for example, that in "Lovers infinitenesse" Donne's love "is realized in the marketplace; the lover is a would-be purchaser whose lack of thrift prevents him from paying the agreed price for his lady" (p. 376). Suggests that this "bazaar appreciation of love" suggests "the consequence of particular constraints which have been imposed not primarily by intellectual, religious, or aesthetic opinion, but by the forms of economic association which have come to dominate English life in the course of the sixteenth century" (p. 379). For replies, see Stanley Gardner (entry 552) and F. W. Bateson, *EIC* 23 (1973): 440.

≈§ 510. SPARROW, JOHN. "Manuscript Corrections in the Two Issues of Donne's *Biathanatos*." *BC* 21: 29–32.
Compares and discusses the bibliographical implications of several minor corrections found in a copy of the undated issue (1646 or 1647) of *Biathanatos*, a Bodleian duplicate from the Rawlinson collection, and those found in a copy of the 1648 issue. 3 plates. See also Charles Morgenstern (entry 471) and Sparrow (entry 607).

≈§ 511. STEIG, MICHAEL. "Donne's Divine Rapist: Unconscious Fantasy in Holy Sonnet XIV." *HSL* 4: 52–58.
Argues that "Batter my heart" "appeals to us on a fundamental psychological level, and that the explications that have been given to it are perhaps in part defenses against an awareness on this level" (p. 54). Points out that within the sonnet there are numerous intertwined and juxtaposed images or key words of sex and violence and suggests that the basic unconscious content of the poem can be paraphrased: "'Punish me, father, for your mild attempts at correction fail to purify me or give me a sense of potency [1–4]. I strive to be morally and sexually submissive to you, as my conscience and sense of guilt tell me I should be, but my attachment to my mother is still powerful—I still love the one with whom I have seen you locked in combat [5–10]. But I shall submit myself to be raped by you, for in that way I can both gain your love by taking the woman's role; I shall submit myself to be raped by you, for in that way I can gain both your love and free myself of guilt'" (p. 55). Suggests that the "fantasy material" in the sonnet is carefully disguised by a host of defenses—the religious meaning, intellectualization, biblical associations, the rhyme scheme, the metrical pattern, and so on. Concludes that awareness of these basic fantasy materials helps the reader, especially one who does not share Donne's religious experience, to recognize "the basic human elements Donne is dealing with" (p. 57).

⊷ᆼ 512. SUGIMOTO, RYŪTARŌ. "Genjitsu to Hi-genjitsu—Donne no Style ni kansuru Ichi Kōsatsu" [Reality or Not Reality?—A Study of Donne's Style]. *Jimbun Kenkyū* (Osaka Shiritsu Daigaku) 24, no. 9 (November): 3–13.

Comments on Donne's tendency to employ very concrete imagery to represent supranatural elements, such as ghosts, and his opposite tendency to employ highly abstract logic in the discussion of concrete matters. Focuses upon "The Apparition."

⊷ᆼ 513. SUZUKI, KŌZŌ. "John Donne no 'Divine' na Ren-ai-shi to 'secular' na Shūkyō-shi" [John Donne's "Divine" Love Poetry and "Secular" Religious Poetry]. *Eigo Eibungaku Kenkyū* (Yamagata Daigaku), no. 16 (February): 19–34.

Discusses how secular images function in Donne's religious poems and how religious images function in his secular love poetry.

⊷ᆼ 514. SZENCZI, MIKLÓS, TIBOR SZOBOTKA, AND ANNA KATONA. *Az angol irodalom története* [The History of English Literature]. Budapest: Gondolat. 699p.

General survey of Donne's poetry (pp. 165–72) that stresses the unconventionality and uniqueness of his style, sensibility, and life. Discusses major characteristics of his poetry, especially his uses of realism and conversational tone, his employment of dramatic techniques and argumentative analysis, and his transformation of Elizabethan conventions into new forms and for new uses. Briefly compares Donne and Browning and comments on Donne's complex interest in philosophy and science and briefly compares him to Giordano Bruno. Discusses the metaphysical mode, both its themes and distinctive style. Suggests that in his religious poetry Donne returns to more traditional Christian orthodoxy but emphasizes that in all respects he best represents the transitions of thought and sensibility that took place in the late sixteenth and early seventeenth centuries. Mentions Donne in relation to George Herbert, Lord Herbert of Cherbury, Vaughan, and Marvell and relates English metaphysical style to the Gongorism of Spain and the Marinismo of Italy. Comments also on Donne's influence on later poets, such as Gerard Manley Hopkins, T. S. Eliot, and the post–World War I poets.

⊷ᆼ 515. TARLINSKAYA, M. G. "Evoliutsiia slogovoi i aktsentnoi struktury angliiskogo sillabo-tonicheskogo stikha" [The Evolution of the Syllabic and Accentual Structure of English Syllabo-tonic Verses]. *Sbornik nauchnykh trudov Moskovskogo pedagogischeskogo instituta inostrannykh yazykov* 66: 75–84.

Discusses the evolution of the syllabic and accentual structure of English syllabo-tonic verses. Includes Donne and suggests that John Suckling learned his poetry not so much from Ben Jonson as from Donne.

≤§ 516. TATSUMA, MINORU. *Eishi no Ritsudō* [Rhythms in English Poetry]. Tokyo: Shohakusha. 529p.

Briefly discusses the flexibility and complexities of Donne's use of rhythm in his poetry and points out how he abandoned the regularly repeated beat of the line and adjusted the pace and emphasis to fit his meaning and to reflect the accents of speech. Discusses ways in which Donne overstepped the conventional patterns in blank verse, sees a number of resemblances between Donne's experimentations and those of Gerard Manley Hopkins, and suggests that Donne's rhythms might profitably be examined in the light of sprung rhythm. Briefly compares and contrasts Donne to Browning.

≤§ 517. TAYLOR, ROBERT. "The Seasons of His Mercies: John Donne at St. Paul's, Christmas, 1624." *SCN* 30: 35.

Reviews a liturgical play by Martin Robbins (with musical settings) that was produced at Emmanuel Church of Boston on 19 December 1971, with William Lacey as Donne and John R. Tobinski as a young curate. Consisted of two parts: (1) a discussion of theological matters by Donne and his supposed curate and (2) the delivery of Donne's sermon (cut and condensed) given at St. Paul's on Christmas evening 1624.

≤§ 518. TAZAKI, KENZŌ. "John Donne to Umi [John Donne and the Sea]. *Eigo Eibeibungaku* (Chūō Daigaku), no. 12 (March): 19–40.

Presents a brief biographical sketch of Donne, placing him in the chaotic context of seventeenth-century Europe and emphasizing his spiritual struggles. Shows how in his poetry and prose Donne often uses the sea as a metaphor for death, conflict, scripture, the world, the Church, and so on.

≤§ 519. THOMAS, GILBERT. "John Donne." *Aryan Path* 43, no. 8 (October): 347–51.

Very general appreciative sketch of Donne that stresses his ultimate reconciliation of various psychological and religious tensions. Claims that Donne, more than any other writer of his time, "helped to release truth from its theological, academic, literary, and other straitjackets" and substituted a sincere "searching for a merely formal approach" (p. 351). Suggests that other revolutionaries of his day are now either dated or forgotten, but Donne, "because he strove after vital balance and harmony, lives on" (p. 351). Reproduces "Goodfriday, 1613. Riding Westward" without notes or commentary.

≤§ 520. THOMSON, PATRICIA. "Donne and the Poetry of Patronage: The *Verse Letters*," in *John Donne: Essays in Celebration*, edited by A. J. Smith, pp. 308–23. London: Methuen & Co.

Discusses the importance of the relationship between poet and patron during the Elizabethan and Jacobean periods and notes that, although poets obviously tried to please their patrons, "it is not true that mere flattery of patron or mere pandering to their tastes always followed" (p. 308). Points out that many patrons and patronesses were themselves literary people who played important roles in shaping taste. Focuses on the verse letters of Donne, Jonson, and Daniel to show that all three "rarely use the verse letter merely to pay compliments" and that "there are differences between the three poets, differences which correspond to their differing experiences of and attitudes to patrons, and as might be expected, even more to their differing individualities" (p. 310). Stresses that Donne, unlike the other two, was not a professional writer and thus "had his place in a scheme of social rather than literary patronage" (p. 310). Suggests that Donne's verse letters are distinguishable "as being exceedingly witty discourses showing at once the patron's worth and the poet's skill" (p. 311) and reflect his intellectual restlessness, coming as they do during his middle period (from about 1601 to 1615), a period in which his future was far from secure. Shows that Donne's verse letters are not all of one piece; compares those addressed to friends, such as Sir Henry Wotton, with those addressed to patronesses, such as the Countess of Bedford; and notes differences among those addressed to patronesses such as the Countess of Huntington and the Countess of Bedford.

⋙ 521. VARMA, R. S. *Imagery and Thought in Metaphysical Poets: With Special References to Andrew Marvell*. New Delhi: S. Chand & Co. xiii, 234p.

Mentions Donne frequently in this critical study of metaphysical thought and imagery, primarily comparing and contrasting Donne to Marvell. Part 1, "Method—Nature and Function of Poetic Imagery and Method of Studying It" (pp. 1–24), surveys approachs to the study of imagery in general with an appeal for an "organic method" of approach. Part 2, "Theory—An Approach to Metaphysical Imagery" (pp. 25–80), attempts to define the nature and function of metaphysical imagery and critiques previously held theories, such as concettismo, emblem, baroque, Ramist logic, and unified sensibility. Part 3, "Application—Marvell's Imagery in Relation to Thought" (pp. 81–212). Appendix 1, "Longer Notes" (pp. 213–19), and Appendix 2, "Authenticity of the Satires Attributed to Andrew Marvell" (pp. 220–24). Selected bibliography (pp. 225–34).

⋙ 522. VICKERS, BRIAN. "The 'Songs and Sonnets' and the Rhetoric of Hyperbole," in *John Donne: Essays in Celebration*, edited by A. J. Smith, pp. 132–74. London: Methuen & Co.

Comments on the novelty of Donne's love poetry in his uses of language and rhetoric, his treatment of love and the relationship between lovers, his celebration of full sexual relationships, his masculine assertion and reversal of traditional love situations and roles, and his emphasis on the unity of lovers, especially the way in which he "presents the two lovers as a race apart" and creates this separation "by use of the rhetorical figure hyperbole" (pp. 136–37). Surveys the history of the rhetorical tradition of the hyperbole from Aristotle to the eighteenth century and stresses that, among other things, hyperbole is a special kind of language used "to express a supra-normal idea or experience" and is "an encoding that expects from the reader a decoding" (p. 143). Discusses the ingenious, complex, and even bawdy and blasphemous uses of hyperbole in the *Songs and Sonets*, in particular in "two main groups of subjects to which hyperbole is applied: the lovers, and love, considered first as values in themselves; and then considered in relation to the rest of the world" (p. 148). Discusses in the first group "The good-morrow," "The Anniversarie," "A Valediction: of my name, in the window," "A Feaver," "Lovers infinitenesse," "Loves growth," "A Valediction: of weeping," "A nocturnall upon S. Lucies day," and especially "The Sunne Rising"; and under the second category, "Twicknam garden," "A Valediction: forbidding mourning," "The Extasie," "Loves exchange," "A Valediction: of the booke," "The Dreame," "The Relique," "The Funerall," and especially "The Canonization." Disagrees with Wilbur Sanders's reading of Donne's love poetry, especially "The Canonization," in *John Donne's Poetry* (entry 366) and attributes his misreading in part to a failure to understand and appreciate Donne's uses of hyperbole. Maintains, in response to Sanders, that Donne "used hyperbole in a variety of ways, demanding that we should decode the internal conventions which he set up in full awareness that this 'figure of excess' needs to be, in Joseph Priestley's words, 'so circumstanced' that 'we are led into no mistake by such terms' and perceive their unique economy" (pp. 173–74).

~§ 523. WAGNER, CHARLES A., ed. "The 62nd Annual Dinner" and "Found—A Donne Holograph!" *The Poetry Society of America Bulletin* (May): 3–19, 30–31.

(1) Reports a celebration of the four-hundredth anniversary of Donne's birth held on 20 April 1972 by the members of the Poetry Society of America at the Plaza in New York (pp. 1–19). Contains an address by John T. Shawcross, in which he evaluates modern interest in Donne, regrets the "kidnapping" of Donne by scholars, and argues for a reexamination of his poetry as poetry, not as a repository for ideas and philosophical concepts. Notes that, following Shawcross's address, Arnold Moses read from Donne's poems and Thomas Bogdon sang a number of the *Holy Sonnets* set to music by Virgil Thomson and Benjamin Britten. (2) Reproduces the first six tercets from the holograph of Donne's "To the Lady Carew" that was recently sold at Sotheby's and also reprints the same six tercets from Shawcross's edition of the poems (1967).

~§ 524. WARNKE, FRANK J. *Versions of Baroque: European Literature in the Seventeenth Century*. New Haven and London: Yale University Press. xi, 229p. P N 741 W3
Chapter 3, in different form, first appeared in *CollG* 1 (1967): 38–48.
Most of Chapter 4 first appeared as "The World as Theatre: Baroque

Variations on a Traditional Topos," in *Festschrift für Edgar Mertner*, edited by Bernard Fabian and Ulrich Suerbaum (Munich: Wilhelm Fink Verlag, 1968), pp. 185–200.

A portion of Chapter 5 was first published as "Das Spielelement in der Liebeslyrik des Barock" (entry 166).

Uses the term *baroque* "to denote not a precisely definable style but a period complex made up of a whole cluster of more or less related styles— a complex which, in its earlier phases (approximately 1580–1610), contains significant survivals of the preceding complex, or period style (i.e. the Renaissance), and, in its later phases (approximately 1650–90), anticipations of the subsequent complex (i.e. Neoclassicism)" (pp. 1–2). Maintains that a "literary period cannot be conceived of as a time span populated by authors expressing themselves in virtually identical styles, style itself being too individual a phenomenon to allow for such a conception. A literary period is, rather, a time span in which underlying shared spiritual preoccupations find expression in a variety of stylistic and thematic emphases" (p. 9). Isolates a number of these emphases, preoccupations, and topoi of baroque literature in nine chapters: "Terms and Concepts," "Appearances and Reality," "The Experience of Contradiction," "The World as Theatre," "Art as Play," "Metaphysical and Meditative Devotion," "The Baroque Epic," "The Sacrificial Hero," and "The End of the World." Considers Donne as representative of the "spare, witty, conceptual Metaphysical style" (p. 32) of baroque art and points out baroque characteristics of his art and sensibility throughout. Chapter 2, "Appearances and Reality" (pp. 21–51), argues that "the contradictory vision and the attempt to capture absolute reality constitute the unifying elements of Baroque poetry" (p. 23). Contrasts lines 179–218 of *The second Anniversarie* with passages from Spenser's "Hymne to Heavenly Beautie" and Crashaw's "In the Glorious Assumption of Our Blessed Lady" to show differences between both baroque and Renaissance style and between two major subdivisions of baroque style. Comments on the cerebral and paradoxical quality of Donne's art and sensibility and notes that "the isolation of the individual sensibility is the point of departure for the Baroque imagination" (p. 30). Mentions Donne's highly dramatic, personal, and colloquial voice and the variety of stanzaic forms in his love poetry. Briefly compares Donne to Góngora, Jean-Baptiste Chassignet, Montaigne, Pascal, Giles Fletcher, Shakespeare, and others. Chapter 3, "The Experience of Contradiction" (pp. 52–65), suggests that Donne, like Marvell, explores wittily the related phenomenon of erotic and religious experience, as, for example, in "Lovers infinitenesse" and "Batter my heart," and that he "uses logic and argumentation to subvert the bases of logic and argumentation, establishing thus the validity of opposed propositions in the realm of thought itself" (p. 64). Chapter 5, "Art as Play" (pp. 90–129), discusses the serious playfulness in much baroque art, especially in devotional poetry and in love lyrics, and notes that Donne "creates an atmosphere of play, almost of joke, without in the least degree compromising the seriousness of his statements" (p. 98). Suggests that the *Songs and Sonets* "constitute a compendium of Baroque amorous attitudes" (p. 104) and notes that the playfulness of baroque love poetry "shows itself in four distinct but related features: the imposition of a double view, through which the speaker simultaneously voices his personal passion and distances himself from it in a half-amused way; the formulation of the speaker's relation to the beloved in quasi-dramatic terms; the use of comic hyperbole; and the practice of insulting or showing aggression toward the beloved, with the consequent creation of a kind of amorous agon, or erotic flyting" (pp. 98–99). Discusses the playfulness of "The Canonization" as an example of baroque comic hyperbole and compares Donne to numerous Continental poets, such as Góngora, Marino, Hofmannswaldau, Quevedo, Saint-Amant, Paul Fleming, and others. Chapter 6, "Metaphysical and Meditative Devotion" (pp. 139–57), deals with the baroque religious and devotional lyric, both English and Continental. Relates the features of the devotional lyric to the art of discursive meditation and suggests reasons for the decline of baroque sensibility during the last half of the seventeenth century. Comments specifically on the paradoxical and dramatic elements of the *Holy Sonnets* and suggests that *Devotions upon Emergent Occasions* shows "the degree to which orthodox Renaissance scientific thought permeated Baroque meditation" (p. 142).

☞ 525. WASWO, RICHARD. *The Fatal Mirror: Themes and Techniques in the Poetry of Fulke Greville*. Charlottesville: University of Virginia Press. ix, 181p.

Refers to Donne throughout. Compares and contrasts Greville's ironic Petrarchism and style with those of Donne: "In directly denouncing women, both in general and in particular, he can evoke a frank and bitter sensuality that would do Donne credit" (p. 63). Suggests that Greville is superior to Donne as a religious poet because he "rises through the experiences in which Donne is perpetually engaged, the fears of judgment and hypocrisy, the passionate outcries for true contrition, to that experience which Donne, in verse, never reached: the complete renunciation of self" (p. 131). Comments on Donne's "The Crosse" and suggests that its style "functions not as a sensuous apprehension of thought or experience, but as a sensuous avoidance of both" (p. 132). Suggests that, unlike Donne, Herbert "dealt adequately with redemptive psychology" (p. 133) by modifying the metaphysical style.

☞ 526. WHITE, GERTRUDE M., AND JOAN G. ROSEN, eds. "John Donne (1572–1631)," in *A Moment's Monument: The Development of the Sonnet*, pp. 51–55. New York: Charles Scribner's Sons.

Traces the history and development of the sonnet in the Renaissance (pp. 1–14) and anthologizes five of Donne's *Holy Sonnets*: "Thou hast made me," "At the round earths imagin'd corners," "Death be not proud," "What if this present were the worlds last night?" and "Batter my heart,"

introducing each with a brief critical paragraph. Suggests that in form
Donne adapts Wyatt and calls the *Holy Sonnets* "unrivalled by any religious poetry in their extraordinary mixture of qualities" (p. 51).

✎§ 527. ZINS, HENRYK. "Echa odkryiica Kopernika w literaturze Angiel-
skiej na poczatku XVII wieku" [Echoes of Copernicus's Discovery in
English Literature at the Outset of the XVIIth Century], in *Mikołaj
Kopernik w kulturze umysłowej epoki Szekspira* [Nicholas Copernicus in English Intellectual Culture in Shakespeare's Epoch], pp.
119–41. Wroclaw: Zaklad Narodowy Imienia Ossolinskich Wy-
dawnictwo Polskiej Akademii Nauk.
  Notes that in England more than in other countries Copernicus's thought
was readily accepted in the late sixteenth and early seventeenth centuries.
Discusses the reception of Copernican theory in England and its influence on both scientific thinking and literary vision. Comments specifically on Donne's interest in the new science and points out that he uses
scientific terminology in his poetry (pp. 129–34). Stresses that Donne
tried to reconcile his theological vision of the world with the changing
scientific knowledge and suggests that he was one of the few English poets
of his time who had an awareness of the scientific intellectual revolution.
Cites a few examples from Donne's poems and especially from *Ignatius
his Conclave* to show that Donne's attitude toward Copernican thought
was basically positive. Points out that in his satire on the Jesuits Donne
views Copernicus as an intellectual hero and predicts that the Roman
Catholic Church will put his works on the Index of Forbidden Books.

1973

✎§ 528. AKIBA, RYŪZŌ. "Donne no Light Verse" [Donne's Light Verse].
Ronsō (Meijigakuin Daigakuin Daigaku), no. 208 (June): 121–40.
  Reviews briefly the current state of Donne studies and comments in
particular on the criticism of T. S. Eliot on the metaphysical poets. Argues that there is a tendency to read the *Songs and Sonets* too seriously
and suggests that many of the poems should be read as "light verse," citing
as an example "Lovers infinitenesse."

✎§ 529. ALTIZER, ALMA B. *Self and Symbolism in the Poetry of Michelangelo, Donne, and Agrippa d'Aubigné.* (International Archives of
the History of Ideas, Series minor 10.) The Hague: Martinus Nijhoff.
xi, 117p.
  Discusses the increasing awareness of an alienated self in the poetry of
Michelangelo, d'Aubigné, and Donne and argues that each of the three
poets moves from a witty rhetorical mode to a profound symbolic one.
Maintains that, "increasingly, the work of each poet centers on a need to
analyze or abolish the gulf separating subject and object, self and other"
and that "underlying most of their poems is a profound self-consciousness—

a heightened awareness of self as a powerful, separate entity, with a corresponding objectification of all reality outside of self" (p. vii). Analyzes this progressive movement by distinguishing between the uses of "conceits" in their earlier poems and the uses of "concetti" in their later poems, the first simply witty, highly ingenious verbal techniques but the latter a way of profoundly apprehending truth. Devotes Chapter 3 (pp. 69–100) to Donne's poetry. Traces the movement from "conceit" to "concetti" in his poetry and argues that the later poetry embodies "a poetic-religious vision of the paradoxical self at the center of a human community whose dimensions are at once historical and mythic" (p. 69). Demonstrates this development by commenting on "The good-morrow," "The Sunne Rising," "The Extasie," "The Canonization," "The Relique," "A Valediction: forbidding mourning," *La Corona*, "The Litanie," the *Holy Sonnets*, the two *Anniversaries*, "Goodfriday, 1613. Riding Westward," and "Hymne to God my God, in my sicknesse." Stresses that the profound poems—"though not necessarily the 'best'—are those in which the poet's imagination searches for new ways to symbolize the individual's relation to the world, new images of the relation between self-consciousness and its exterior ground" (p. 101) and that these poems are "primarily symbolic, rather than rhetorical or expressive" (p. 101). Emphasizes the inwardness of Donne's poetry as he searches for unity, which he ultimately finds in his vision of Christ, "who is at once the cosmic center and the center of human consciousness" (p. 108) and thus the self becomes the place where the two Adams mentioned in "Hymne to God my God, in my sicknesse" finally converge.

⋙ 530. ARAKAWA, MITSUO. "*Songs and Sonnets*—Donne no Ai no Tetsugaku" [Donne's Philosophy of Love—On *Songs and Sonets*]. *Ronshū* (Ippan Kyōiku) (Tōhōkugakuin Daigaku), no. 59 (June): 187–207.

Cited in "The 1973 Bibliography," *The Renaissance Bulletin* (The Renaissance Institute, Tokyo) 6 (1979): 46. Unavailable.

⋙ 531. BARKER, NICOLAS. "Donne's 'Letter to the Lady Carey and Mrs. Essex Riche': Text and Facsimile." *BC* 22: 487–93.

Comments on the discovery in 1970 of the only Donne holograph poem in English to survive, "A Letter to the Lady Carey, and Mrs Essex Riche," and on its acquisition by the Bodleian for 25,000 pounds. Describes the facsimile, with its transcription and introduction by Helen Gardner (entry 426). Discusses in detail "eight undeniable errors in 63 lines" (p. 493) in the transcription—"all in accidentals, but not insignificant" (p. 488). Suggests that Donne "took the most minute care with this copy, a care which is not reflected in the many manuscript collections and the early printed editions on which the text has hitherto been based" (p. 489). Disagrees with Helen Gardner's assumption that Lady Carew and Essex Rich were not particularly virtuous and were unknown to Donne, questions her suggestion that the verse epistle was accompanied by a covering letter composed by their brother, Sir Robert Rich, and argues that the manuscript is not a first draft, as Helen Gardner suggests, but "a copy made from an earlier text" (p. 492). Three plates: (1) recto of the manuscript, (2) verso of the manuscript, and (3) a photographic enlargement of the opening of lines 40–42.

≈§ 532. BATESON, F. W. "As We Read the Living? An Argument. II. Editorial Reply." *EIC* 23: 175–78.
Reply to Roma Gill (entry 554), who asks how teachers "can prevent the too easy reading of poets of the past, reading them 'as we read the living,' without at the same time destroying the meanings that come from the recognition and identification of what is traditional" (Gill, p. 175). Argues that all great poetry must communicate some matter of essential human interest and questions if a poem can be read separately as "art" and as "life." Suggests that "the answer must surely be that a properly literary response combines both attitudes" (pp. 177–78). Uses examples from "The good-morrow" to exemplify his premise.

≈§ 533. BLANKENSHIP, ALAN. "Donne's 'Love's Growth.'" *Expl* 31: Item 73.
In part, a reply to Stephen D. Ring, S.J. (entry 360). Shows how "Loves growth" can be read in three different ways and how it "works forcefully and defensively, obscuring the tone so that each person hears what Donne wants him to hear." Sees the poem as dividing into two balanced halves: in the first stanza, the speaker praises spiritual love, compliments his mistress, and introduces the theme of the second stanza; in the second, the speaker displays his libertine wit and sexual passion. Maintains that "the beauty of the poem is that Donne means all of these things and has proven that his love is pure by the truth of his poem, which has demonstrated the inextricable commingling of the spiritual and the physical."

≈§ 534. BRADBROOK, MURIEL. "John Donne." *Dome* (Friends of St. Paul's Cathedral) 10: 4–9.
Comments on Donne's personal conflicts and struggles and presents a general sketch of his life. Notes that Donne "conducted a great bridging operation between medieval and modern modes of thinking, and achieved a difficult re-integration" (p. 5). Suggests that Donne's greatest strength "lay in the depth and sensitiveness of his relationships" and stresses that his religion also "took a form intensely personal" (p. 9).

≈§ 535. BRANTS, J. "Bladerend in John Donne." *Dietsche Warande en Belfort* 7: 507–15.
Discusses Constantijn Huygens's seventeenth-century translations of

nineteen of Donne's love poems into Dutch and comments on critical attention paid to him by various modern Dutch critics and translators. Suggests that Donne's usual combination of religious devotion and eroticism reminds one of Jacob Cats but notes that in Cats's work one will not find Donne's profundity of thought, penetrating expressiveness, and fine sense of humor. Reprints Huygens's translation of "The Flea" and J. Eijkelboom's translation of "The Perfume" and suggests that in the latter Donne expresses his hatred of his parents-in-law. Praises in particular "The Will," "The Extasie," "The Legacie," and "The good-morrow." Reproduces three selections from Eijkelboom's translations of one of Donne's sermons delivered at The Hague, part of "A Hymne to God the Father," and the sestet of "If poysonous mineralls" translated by Theun de Vries.

◄§ 536. BRAY, ROBERT. "Interpretation, Criticism, and the Problem of Poetic Structure." *MQ* 14: 318–38.

Argues that interpretation differs from and should precede criticism and uses several stanzas from "A Valediction: forbidding mourning" to illustrate the theory. Stresses the importance of recognizing that the poem is about the parting of lovers, not death, as one might be led to believe from the opening stanza, and suggests that Donne creates his elaborate compass conceit because he "values love" (p. 337).

◄§ 537. BRUMBLE, H. DAVID, III. "John Donne's 'The Flea': Some Implications of the Encyclopedic and Poetic Flea Traditions." *CritQ* 15: 147–54.

Discusses "The Flea" in the light of two major sources of flea lore to show "an approximation of the intellectual equipment a Renaissance reader might have brought to the poem" (p. 149): (1) that of the Renaissance encyclopedists and grammarians, who obtained their notions primarily from classical and medieval naturalists, such as Pliny, Aristotle, and Bartolomeus Anglicus, who "defined the flea as copulating without conceiving and as being born of dust, without parents" (p. 149), and (2) the long-established tradition of the flea poem, originating with the pseudo-Ovidian "Elegia de Pulice" (attributed to Ofilii Sergianii) and found in Marlowe's *Dr. Faustus* as well as in a host of Latin, English, French, and Arabic poems. Presents a stanza-by-stanza analysis of Donne's poem to show that, by using the tradition of the encyclopedists, the flea poem, and wrong reason, he creates a persona who "uses reason, perverse reason, for wrong ends" (p. 152) and who reflects a type of spiritual aridity. Suggests, therefore, that the poem, although indeed witty, is also something more and notes that the wit in the poem resides in its "use of tradition rather than in any disregard of tradition" (p. 153) and perhaps is intended to instruct as well as delight the reader.

◄§ 538. CARLSON, NORMAN E. "Donne's 'Holy Sonnets, XIX.'" *Expl* 32: Item 19.

Suggests that in "Oh, to vex me, contraryes meet in one" the syntactically difficult lines 7–8 ("As ridling distemper'd, cold and hott, / As praying, as mute; as infinite, as none") become clear if one recognizes that they amplify lines 5–6, "cataloguing further points of similarity between his 'contritione' and his 'prophane love,' and that the phrase 'cold and hott' in line 7 is both logically and grammatically parallel to praying-mute and infinite-none in line 8." Paraphrases the lines thusly: "My contrition is as riddlingly distempered, as cold or as hot, as my profane love was, and it [contrition, again] is as praying, sometimes, and as mute, other times, as my profane love was, and it [my contrition] is as infinite, sometimes, and as none [which is to say, non-existent] other times, as my profane love was." Suggests that by reading lines 5–8 "as an extended, multifold comparison between Donne's contrition and his profane love not only *dispels* the syntactical ambiguity, but also, by suggesting an ironic series of possible allusions to his own earlier work, makes the sonnet a more interesting poem than critics have apparently considered it to be."

꣯ 539. CHATTERJEE, A. B. "John Donne's *Twicknam Garden*: An Interpretation." *VQ* 39: 172–83.
Argues that "Twicknam garden" is not, as commonly thought, a poem in the courtly love tradition and, furthermore, that it has nothing to do with Lucy, Countess of Bedford: "Someone gave a title—rather unwarrantedly—to a poem to which the poet had given none, and then all began to interpret the poem in the light of that title!" (p. 179). Sees the poem as typical of Donne, "one of broken assignation" (p. 180) and of "mock-anger (like *The Apparition*), lightheartedly cynical and touched by a spirit of fun behind its show of passion" (p. 177). Argues that the aim of the poem is to "convince the beloved that the union of lovers is the most normal thing and there is no sense in trying to avoid it" (p. 177) and tentatively suggests that the poem may have been addressed to Ann More before she married Donne.

꣯ 540. CLARK, JOHN R., AND ANNA MOTTO, eds. "Toward the Appreciation of Satire," in *Satire—That Blasted Art*, pp. 1–23. New York: G. P. Putnam's Sons; New York: Capricorn Books.
Discusses "Song: Goe, and catche a falling starre" (pp. 7–10) as an example of paradoxical disruption and parodic debunking. Notes that even the title of the poem has a parodic function, since the poem is only superficially a song. Concludes that Donne's success "lies in his deliberate disruptions: He promises a song but delivers a jeremiad; he advises a knighthood flower, only to divest him of his vocation and ideals"; and his audience "is hit for liking little songs, women are rapped for not being impossible romantic ideals, the vacillating speaker himself is incriminated, and knighthood (long after its demise) is heartily deflowered" (p. 10).

◄§ 541. CLINE, GLORIA STARK, AND JEFFREY A. BAKER. "Donne," in *An Index to Criticism of British and American Poetry*, pp. 38–41. Metuchen, N.J.: The Scarecrow Press.

Lists eighty items on Donne from 1960 to 1970. Primarily intended for undergraduate students.

◄§ 542. COX, GERARD H., III. "Donne's *Devotions*: A Meditative Sequence on Repentance." *HTR* 66: 331–51.

Argues that *Devotions upon Emergent Occasions* is not only a series of meditations on Donne's physical and spiritual condition but also "a prose sequence on repentance that is aimed at a public audience" (p. 331). Discusses how Donne treats his recovery from illness "as a return to a state of grace that would in turn look forward to eternal life" and· how "the resulting sequence of meditations, expostulations, and prayers leads into the stages of repentance on the purgative way to spiritual perfection" (p. 335). Shows that, although the work is highly ordered and is based on a tripartite meditational structure, it is not specifically Ignatian, as has been alleged. Argues that Donne uses neither the allegorical nor the fourfold method of scriptural interpretation but rather employs "the equally old figural method of interpretation used by the Church fathers" (p. 332). Suggests that Hooker's treatment of repentance in *Of the Laws of Ecclesiastical Polity* "is valuable for reading the *Devotions* because it establishes how an Anglican might understand this subject and how he might use certain principles to order the 'way or method' of repentance" (p. 337). Traces the carefully ordered progression toward repentance in the *Devotions* and concludes that "the figural method relates Donne's physical sickness and recovery to his spiritual sinfulness and recovery through repentance" while "the meditative structure moves the emotions appropriate for attaining the stages of contrition, confession and satisfaction" (p. 350).

◄§ 543. CROFT, P. J. "John Donne," in *Autograph Poetry in the English Language: Facsimiles of original manuscripts from the Fourteenth to the Twentieth Century*, compiled and edited with an introduction, commentary and transcripts by P. J. Croft, 1: 25–26. New York: McGraw-Hill Book Co.; Oxford: Oxford University Press.

Limited edition of 1,500 copies.

Reproduces a facsimile of the manuscript of Donne's verse letter that appears in the 1633 edition under the title "A Letter to the Lady Carey, and Mrs Essex Riche, *From Amyens*" (Bodleian Library, MS. Eng. poet. d. 197), with transcription. Presents a history of the transmission of the manuscript and a detailed bibliographical description of it. Says that it is the only known English poem in Donne's hand and comments on features of his handwriting. Argues that, although Donne clearly drafted the poem before writing the present final version, he was still obviously engaged in polishing his text, as is indicated by several revisions and deletions, especially the significant revision of line 14. Notes that, in addition to two small verbal variants, the manuscript copy contains many differences in punctuation, use of capital letters, and layout from the text presented by Wesley Milgate (1967).

⋙ 544. DIVINE, JAY DEAN. "Compass and Circle in Donne's 'A Valediction: Forbidding Mourning.'" *PLL* 9: 78–80.

Shows that the figure of the compass and that of the circle underlie the whole structure of "A Valediction: forbidding mourning" and together "give it its thematic unity and make it, indeed, a great poem" (p. 80). Argues that the figure of the circle, "a universal symbol of eternity, of God, and of the beginning and end of all created things," is reinforced by the visual figure of the compass, which re-creates visually the Alpha and Omega of the Greek alphabet and reminds the reader "of the wide use of 'Alpha and Omega' in ecclesiastical literature as a term signifying both 'completeness' and the omnipotence of God" (p. 79). Suggests that the visual image of the compass reinforces and affirms "the presence of God in a love whose soul is spiritual" (p. 80). Further suggests that, since the Alpha is a phallic or male image and the Omega is a female image, the compass suggests that physical love is a necessity of human love and that love, even if spiritual, "becomes complete only with the acceptance of the physical" (pp. 79–80).

⋙ 545. DONNE, JOHN. *Deaths Duell; a sermon delivered before King Charles I in the beginning of Lent 1630/31 by Dr John Donne, late Dean of St. Paul's*, edited, with postscript, by Geoffrey Keynes Kt. London: Bodley Head; Boston: David R. Godine. 54p.

Text of *Deaths Duell*, based primarily on the 1660 folio, with modernized spellings and the elimination of italics (except for quotations, Latin words, and proper names) (pp. 1–26). A postscript by the editor (pp. 27–52) followed by a list of readings taken from the quarto of 1632 in preference to those of the folio of 1660 (pp. 53–54). Discusses Donne's effectiveness as a preacher in general and comments on contemporary accounts of his sermons. Examines the circumstances in which Donne preached, the usual seventeenth-century practices in composing and delivering sermons, and outlines the history of how Donne's sermons came to be preserved. Discusses in particular circumstances surrounding the delivery and publication of *Deaths Duell* and presents an analysis of the substance, language, and rhetorical strategy of the sermon. Discusses also the history and design of Donne's monument in St. Paul's Cathedral and the engraving executed by Martin Droeshout that was prefixed to *Deaths Duell* when it was first printed in 1632. Five illustrations.

⋙ 546. ———. *Dzhon Donn—Stikhotovoreniia*, edited by B. Tomashevskii. Translations and introduction by B. Tomashevskii. Leningrad: "Khudozhestvennaia literatura" Leningradskroe otdelenie. 168p.

Anthology of Donne's secular poems in Russian. Presents a brief biographical sketch of Donne, surveys his early critical reputation, and comments on his modern discovery (pp. 5–16). Divides the poems into three
categories, suggesting that each parallels a period in Donne's life: the love
lyrics and elegies, the satires and verse epistles, and the religio-philosophical
poems and sonnets. Comments on Donne's rejection of Petrarchism and
his uses of metaphors and images drawn from the new science. Suggests
that Donne's major theme is love and maintains that in his love poetry he
voices a protest against the morality of bourgeois society and the restrictions of the medieval Church. Suggests that the *Elegies* contain sharp
social criticism and present vivid details of London life and maintains that
Satyre I (the only one included in the anthology) is an attack on London
society, particularly on the Puritans, whom Donne is said to have seen as
representing the hated bourgeois society. Notes that the new science sig-
naled to Donne the end of the medieval world view. Sees him as moving
from Renaissance optimism and individualism to a later baroque pessimism as he turned from the world about him to religion. Notes that Soviet
readers are familiar with Donne only in brief passages. Translates into
Russian selections from the *Songs and Sonets*, the epigrams, the *Elegies*,
Satyre I, and several of the verse letters (pp. 19–157). Notes (pp. 158–
68).

✒§ 547. ———. *Lucie in the Sky or Darkness Before Light*. Printed and
published at the Ixion Press, Loughborough for the Beaupertuys So-
ciety by Frances Mary White, Susan Margaret Shuetter, Catherine
Shaw, Alan Robert Phillips. 8p.
Limited edition of nine numbered copies.
Reprints "A nocturnall upon S. Lucies day" (pp. 3–5) and Herbert's
"Easter Wings" (pp. 6–7). No notes or commentary.

✒§ 548. ———. *Ten Love Poems by John Donne*. Original etchings by
Christine Tovey. Exeter: The Octavo Book-Press. 47p.
Contains a brief biographical introduction (p. 3); a short introduction
to the love poems (p. 5); and reproduces ten poems with modern spelling,
each of which is accompanied by an etching: "The Baite," "A Jeat Ring
Sent," "The Blossome," "Aire and Angels," "His Picture," "The Sunne
Rising," "Song: Sweetest love, I do not goe," "The Flea," "Elegy: The
Dream," and "A Lecture upon the Shadow."

✒§ 549. FLYNN, DENNIS. "Irony in Donne's *Biathanatos* and *Pseudo-
Martyr*." *Recusant History* 12: 49–69.
Suggests that Donne's obsession with suicide and martyrdom evidenced
in his poetry and prose may be attributed, in part, to his Catholic background and education that finally led him "not into the path of righteous
fidelity, but to a bemused fascination with death by self-murder, a cavalier
irony that is one of the hallmarks of his style" (p. 49). Reassesses Donne's

intent in *Biathanatos* and *Pseudo-Martyr*, "two diverse though related books" that express "a display of outward indifference or cynicism, an appearance of scepticism toward both sides" (p. 49), an attitude common among former Catholics of the Jacobean period. Maintains that both works are fundamentally satires on religious controversy, that in both Donne employs examples and citations that "seem to cut with a double edge and to jest while they appear to argue" (p. 50), that both consciously parody techniques employed by the controversialists "by making use of conventional prefatory apparatus to conceal their satiric barbs," that "both were presented by Donne in letters to his like-minded friends as ironical comments on the religious controversy in England from a point of view of apparent scepticism toward both sides," and that both, "while they protest their own straightforwardness, evoke from serious disputants charges of lightness and insincerity" (p. 66). Suggests that *Biathanatos* is an ironic blend of learning and cynicism, a satire that contains specious and irrelevant arguments and absurd examples and that toys ironically with orthodoxy and scripture. Considers *Pseudo-Martyr* as a satire specifically on the controversy surrounding the Oath of Allegiance and as a parody of partisan writers such as Sir Edward Coke, the attorney general, who had disputed the primacy of the church in ecclesiastical jurisdiction with the Jesuit Robert Persons. Points out that "consideration of only a few aspects of *Pseudo-Martyr* shows that the King's cause in serious controversy was certainly not served well by this book" (p. 66). Concludes that both *Biathanatos* and *Pseudo-Martyr* suggest that Donne's attitude toward religious controversy "was one of wry and ironical detachment, expressed in the same sort of scepticism that can be found in other writings of '*Jack Donne*'" and that they "cast a peculiar light on the sincerity of Donne's nominal Anglicanism from 1607 to 1610" (p. 67).

⋙ 550. ———. "The Originals of Donne's Overburian Characters." *BNYPL* 77: 63–69.
Suggests that the satiric attack on the dunce in Donne's "The True Character of a Dunce" may have been directed toward Thomas Coryate, the court jester of Prince Henry, or, "if not personally at Coryate, then at the kind of person he exemplified at the Court of James I" (p. 67) and that Donne's "The Character of a Scot at First Sight" may have been a satiric attack on King James I. Suggests also that the Tom. Thorney referred to in the character of the Scot may have been one of James's gentlemen of the Privy Chase.

⋙ 551. FRIEDMAN, DONALD M. "Memory and the Art of Salvation in Donne's Good Friday Poem." *ELR* 3: 418–42.
Presents a detailed analysis of the argument, the rhetorical and dialectical figures, the syntax and rhythms, and the dramatic persona and structure of "Goodfriday, 1613. Riding Westward" to show that Donne skillfully dramatizes "the specious appeal of rationalizing intelligence and the

creations of verbal artifice" (p. 437) and shows "how true devotion kindled by God's grace can lead a sinful, but self-conscious, soul from the prideful grip of inadequate knowledge to the light and clarity of 'remembered' wisdom" (p. 426) and toward "the restorative path of confession and prayer" (p. 437). Traces how, through his projected persona, Donne dramatizes "the speaker's discovery of the soul's deeply embedded power to recognize truth no matter how skillfully, or for however apparently beneficent motives, it has been disguised and distorted by the self-protective reason" and reveals how the speaker, through the use of memory, descends "from the heights of intellectual sophistication, through the dawning realization of his weakness, to the final acceptance both of his sin and his sole culpability" (p. 439). Maintains, however, that the poem is not simply an attack on poetic artifice and the rational intellect but is a dramatic exposition of "the futility of relying upon them" to obtain salvation and a disabusing of the human conscience "of a mistaken pride in the power of the mind unaided by God's grace" (p. 442). Concludes that for Donne "to use the powers of reason and imagination to reveal their incompleteness for the tasks of faith is to come very close to solving the problem of devotional poetry" (p. 442).

🖝 552. GARDNER, STANLEY. "Love in the Sixteenth Century." *EIC* 23: 435–40.
A reply to Raymond Southall (entry 509). Suggests that there is an essential link between Elizabethan ostentatious display of wealth and power and the rich, ornate style of Elizabethan poetry but rejects the notion that the cause is incipient capitalism, as Southall's article might imply. Argues that when Elizabethan poets "extolled their mistresses in terms of 'superlative expansiveness' they were surely seeing them as conveying or exemplifying status" (p. 436). Suggests that in his poetry Donne, perhaps more than in most, is questioning relationships and values and thus it would be "misguided, and misguiding, to suggest a formula which associates Donne uncritically with the jewel-box poetry" (p. 436). For a reply, see F. W. Bateson's editorial comment (*EIC* 23 [1973]: 440).

🖝 553. GÉRARD, ALBERT. "John Donne et le maniérisme: La structure scolastique de *The Extasie*," in *Approaches de l'art: Mélanges d'esthétique et de sciences de l'art offerts à Arsène Soreil, Professeur émérite de l'Université de Liège, Professeur à l'Institut supérieur d'histoire de l'art et d'archéologie de Bruxelles*, pp. 171–83. Brussels: La Renaissance du Livre.
Explicates "The Extasie" and explains in particular the shifting relationships between the body and the soul in the poem. Observes that in lines 1–20 the emphasis is on the body, which has a soul; in lines 21–48 the emphasis changes to the soul, which has a body; and finally in lines 49–76 the body and soul are viewed as co-equal partners. Suggests that this shifting is characteristic of mannerist style, which often consists in an

acute consciousness of a split between body and soul, the real and the ideal.

❧ 554. GILL, ROMA. "As We Read the Living? An Argument." *EIC* 23: 167–75.
Questions F. R. Leavis's premise that poets of the past should be read as if they were living. Argues that, although a poem like "The good-morrow" may seem at first quite contemporary, "we must allow the poem to lead us back—back from the initial impact when we read 'as we read the living'— to considerations of the period when it was written, when medieval and modern modes of thought were in collision" (p. 170). Expresses concern about those undergraduate students who demand "sincerity" in poetry, who insist on biographical interpretations, and who have lost a sense of tradition in poetry. Points out that it is not enough to read "The Sunne Rising" without understanding the tradition that informs the poem: "the fullest enjoyment of the poem is dependent on a recognition of the *tradition* to which it belongs—and which it proudly rejects" (p. 173). Poses the question, which she cannot answer: "How can we prevent the too easy reading of poets of the past, reading them 'as we read the living', without at the same time destroying the meanings that come with the recognition and identification of what is traditional?" (p. 175). For replies, see F. W. Bateson (entry 532) and S. W. Dawson, Harriet Hawkins, and Robert Elliott (entry 632).

❧ 555. GRANT, PATRICK. "Donne, Pico, and Holy Sonnet XII." *HAB* 24: 39–42.
Comments on Donne's knowledge of and indebtedness to the theological writings of Giovanni Pico della Mirandola and notes his many references to and uses of Pico in *Essays in Divinity* and *Biathanatos.* Argues that Pico's *Heptaplus* (1489), especially Book 5, chapters 6–7, may be the source of "Why are wee by all creatures waited on?" Shows that "not only are the broad outlines of the argument and the particular ordering of its parts similar [to Pico's], but to a significant degree details of the wording also" (p. 41). Suggests that recognition of the source confirms Donne's interest in Pico at the time he was writing the *Holy Sonnets*; that it "illuminates a point of detail in the poem by directing our attention through the 'greater wonder' to the implied answer made explicit in the *Heptaplus*, of man's reason as his special gift, marking him off as the 'magnum miraculum' of God's creation"; and also shows that, like Pico, Donne "is fascinated by the paradox that man is special to God's creation, and yet is a rebel against that very creation by his sinfulness" (p. 41). Notes that Donne's dramatizing of Pico's argument "poetically complicates the reader's reaction," for "man is shown as a great wonder despite himself; the questions he asks are evidence of his special status, while the very fact that he feels compelled to ask them reveals the flaw of his fallenness" (p. 41).

Points out that "the process of the poem thus extends our experience beyond the comprehension of its dramatized speaker" (p. 41).

🥚 556. GREENBLATT, DANIEL L. "Generative Metrics and the Authorship of 'The Expostulation.'" *Centrum* 1: 87–104.

Employs the method of metrical analysis developed by Halle and Keyser and uses metrical data obtained from a computer-aided scansion of "The Expostulation" and other elegies by Donne and Jonson to show that Donne did not write "The Expostulation" and that Jonson possibly did. Notes that "the possibility of 'The Expostulation' and the sample of Donne's elegies coming from the same population is less than .01 according to several statistical tests" and that "all control tests comparing the Donne sample with a Donne elegy of comparable length yielded values of p greater than .10 that the samples were drawn from the same population" (p. 87). Points out, however, that "all tests comparing 'The Expostulation' with a sample from Jonson's elegies also yielded values of p greater than .10" (p. 87).

🥚 557. GUPTA, O. S. "Donne's 'A Valediction: Of Weeping'—A Reappraisal." *PURBA* 4, ii: 59–67.

Disagrees with the critical positions of Empson, Gransden, and Leishman on "A Valediction: of weeping" and considers the poem an expression of "genuine grief and sincere emotion on the eve of parting" (p. 60). Finds the poem simultaneously witty and passionate and informed by much tenderness, sincerity, and reciprocity between lovers. Argues that the poem is no more ingenious than "A Valediction: forbidding mourning" and maintains that the wit is the very vehicle used to convey tender emotion. Suggests that the shift of attention in the middle of the poem "from his own weeping to that of his mistress renders the poem excellently dramatic" (p. 65). Sees two phases or situations in the poem, the second of which arises naturally and dramatically from the first: (1) the lover weeps at parting unmindful of the emotional state of the beloved, but (2) when he notices her weeping, he forgets his own and wittily tries to dissuade her from further tears and sorrow.

🥚 558. HATTORI, AKIO. "Donne's Sacred Eloquence." *Dōshisha Literature* (Dōshisha Daigaku) 27 (November): 13–27.

Discusses various literary aspects of Donne's sermons, particularly in the light of St. Augustine's views on Christian oratory and eloquence. Comments on Donne's uses of rhetorical devices, metaphor, and analogy in his sermons, especially on his ability to create concrete, personal situations. Analyzes *Deaths Duell* and suggests that it "represents the norm of his preaching" (p. 23). Argues that Donne "employs various rhetorical devices to support his personal mode of thinking" and that his style, "which often lacks grammatical coherence, imitates the mode of his suffering conflict itself" (p. 27). Concludes that the primary feature of Donne's sermon style "is the perfect coincidence of style and mode of thinking, which is found, Donne says, in St. Paul's 'elegant language'" (p. 27).

↭§ 559. HOLLANDER, JOHN, AND FRANK KERMODE, eds. "John Donne," in *The Oxford Anthology of English Literature*, vol. 1: The Middle Ages through the Eighteenth Century, pp. 1015–64. New York: Oxford University Press.

Reissued in a separate volume: *The Literature of Renaissance England* (The Oxford Anthology of English Literature, vol. 2), pp. 515–64. New York: Oxford University Press, 1973.

Contains a brief biographical sketch, a general introduction to Donne's poetry (and to a lesser degree to the prose), an analysis of his religious development and sensibility, and a brief survey of his followers and his critical reputation (pp. 1015–19), followed by selections from *Juvenilia*, the *Elegies*, *Songs and Sonets*, *Satyre III*, *The second Anniversary*, *Holy Sonnets* and other *Divine Poems*, *Devotions upon Emergent Occasions*, and "A Sermon Preached at St. Paul's for Easter-day, 1628," all with notes (pp. 1019–64). Suggests that combinations—"of apparent spontaneity and fine drawn ratiocination, of amorous élan with verse forms of wantonly ingenious difficulty—characterize the finest of the poems to a degree that sets them apart from all predecessors and imitators, no matter how cogently resemblances are argued" (pp. 1016–17).

↭§ 560. HÖLTGEN, KARL JOSEF. "Donne at Aix-la-Chapelle." *Anglia* 91: 485–86.

Notes that in one of his sermons delivered at Lincoln's Inn, Donne presents an amusing description of a house of Anabaptists in which he stayed during a visit to Aix-la-Chapelle. Argues that Donne visited the German town in 1612, during his tour with Sir Robert Drury, not in 1619 when, as chaplain, he accompanied Lord Doncaster's Embassy to the princes. Notes that after 1614 the Spaniards occupied the town, restored Catholicism, and ordered all Protestant ministers and Anabaptists to leave.

↭§ 561. HUGHES, K. J., AND PETER M. HOROWITZ. "Organic Biography: The Death of an Art." *JBS* 12, no. 2: 86–104.

Suggests that biographies written from 1640 to 1851, such as Walton's *Lives*, are "universally regarded as works of art but castigated in varying degrees for the alleged unreliability of their facts and thus for their departure from the straight and narrow path of truth" (p. 86). Argues that they are, in fact, "part of a tradition that critics have consistently failed to understand" (p. 86). Reviews twentieth-century concepts of biography and challenges those critics who, while supposing an evaluation independent of any preconceived conceptual scheme, actually impose one that perhaps simply differs from that of the early biographers. Argues, for instance, that Walton's *Life of Donne* was written from a pre-Restoration, Anglican-Royalist point of view and based on a conceptual scheme that differs from but is not necessarily inferior to those of modern critics. Challenges, therefore, those critics who charge Walton with having "created great art but that his facts are wrong," or who claim that he "strayed from the path of truth," or that he simply transformed Donne "into a species of Anglican saint" (p. 97). Argues that Walton chose to emphasize exactly those aspects of Donne's life that he considered important and that, even though modern critics may wish to know more about Donne as a poet or a lover, Walton was "much more concerned with the Doctor of the Church and the lover of God" and thus attempted "to catch the Dean of St. Paul's as an Anglican Royalist type" (p. 97). Discusses Walton's *Life of Donne*, as well as several other pre-1851 biographies, as examples of "organic biography" and lists twelve characteristics of the type, such as unity of style and thought, the presentation of the subject as an embodiment of a social type, the biographer's direct or indirect acquaintance with the subject, the biographer's willingness to make value judgments, and the close relation of biography to other literary modes of the times.

📖 562. IZUMI, KEIKO. "John Donne no Sermonic World—Liberality no Shakugi to Sono Metaphor" [The Sermonic World of John Donne— An Exegesis of 'Liberality' and Its Metaphor]. *Kenkyū Hōkoku* (Shoken Jogakuin Tanki Daigaku), no. 20 (October): 49–58.
Discusses the historical and social background of Donne's sermon given on Easter, 15 April 1628, and comments on its theological content and especially on its uses of the idea of "liberality."

📖 563. JOHNSON, JOSEPH A., JR. "Donne's Reconciliation of Opposites in 'Love's Growth.'" *LangQ* 11, nos. 3–4: 21–22, 50, 56.
Argues that in "Loves growth" Donne examines both the spiritual and physical aspects of love but attempts "not to assert the one over the other but to reconcile the two apparent opposites—that is, to find unity in difference" (p. 21). Examines the structure, point of view, tone, syntax, uses of paradox, and figurative language—all of which "move toward a common end and together lead the reader to that end" and argues that "each part points toward Donne's poetic attempt to present a reconciliation of spiritual and physical love, a union of opposites" (p. 22). Points out that, by so doing, Donne "may also be poetically affirming, if not establishing, the essential unity of his world" (pp. 22, 50).

📖 564. KAWAMURA, JŌICHIRŌ. "Donne Kenkyū no Chihei—Seitan 400-nen Kinen ni yosete" [Horizon in the Study of Donne—Commemorating His 400th Anniversary]. *EigoS* 119: 42–44.
Review article of A. J. Smith, ed., *John Donne: Essays in Celebration* (entry 508), and Peter Amadeus Fiore, ed., *Just So Much Honor: Essays Commemorating The Four-Hundredth Anniversary of the Birth of John*

Donne (entry 421). Particularly approves of William Empson's essay in the Fiore collection (entry 416).

◆§ 565. KELLY, T. J. "A Burial for John Donne." *CR* 16: 91–104.
Essentially an unfavorable review article of A. J. Smith, ed., *John Donne: Essays in Celebration*, (entry 508). Calls the collection a "monumentally depressing book" and suggests that primarily it celebrates "pedantic triviality, the mystery religion of academia" (p. 91). Disagrees especially with the essays of A. J. Smith (entries 504, 505), Brian Vickers (entry 522), and Eluned Crawshaw (entry 399) and thinks that the best essays are those by Roma Gill (entry 429), Barbara Hardy (entry 434), and especially D. W. Harding (entry 433). Presents an interpretation of "Aire and Angels," calling it "a minor triumph of wit and tone" and praising its "beautifully light, flexible, poised control of awareness of so many things at once—a high degree of awareness that never gets smothered in its own multiplicity, a high degree of poetic self-awareness that never falls into self-consciousness" (p. 96). Comments, less fully, on "The Sunne Rising" and "The Canonization" as well as a number of other poems.

◆§ 566. KEYNES, GEOFFREY. *A Bibliography of Dr. John Donne, Dean of St. Paul's*. 4th ed. Oxford: Clarendon Press. x, 400p.
First published in 1914; 2d ed., 1932; 3d ed., 1958.
Much enlarged and revised, with new bibliographical prefaces to bring all important information up to date. The "Biography and Criticism" section (in collaboration with Wesley Milgate) is greatly enlarged with many new seventeenth- and eighteenth-century items listed as well as more recent ones up to and including 1971. An inventory of books from Donne's library (with assistance from John Sparrow) has been extended from 197 to 213 titles. Full collations of all early editions of Donne; facsimile reprints of title pages of the early editions; a catalog of portraits of Donne; twelve reproductions from engraved portraits and manuscripts. Contains (1) list of twelve illustrations (pp. ix–x); (2) abbreviations (p. ix); (3) prose works (pp. 1–159): *Pseudo-Martyr* (pp. 1–9), *Conclave Ignati* (pp. 11–24), sermons (pp. 25–77), *Devotions upon Emergent Occasions* (pp. 79–90), *Juvenilia* (pp. 91–107), *Biathanatos* (pp. 109–22), *Essays in Divinity* (pp. 123–29), letters (pp. 131–59); (4) poetical works (pp. 161–236): occasional pieces (pp. 161–68), *Anniversaries* (pp. 169–80), collected poems (pp. 181–216), selected poems and prose, including translations and musical settings (pp. 217–36); (5) Walton's *Life of Donne* (pp. 237–42); and (6) Appendixes: works by John Donne, D.C.L. (pp. 245–51), works by John Done (pp. 252–54), books dedicated to Donne (pp. 255–57), books from Donne's library (pp. 258–79), biography and criticism (an unnumbered checklist) (pp. 280–371)—divided into four groups: 1594–1700, 1701–1800, 1801–1900, and 1901–1971, the first three of which are arranged chronologically and the fourth alphabetically, and iconography (pp. 372–

76); (7) libraries consulted (pp. 377–80), (8) printers and publishers, 1607–1719 (pp. 381–82); and (9) index (pp. 383–400).

567. ———. "A Footnote to Donne." *BC* 22: 165–68.

Suggests that the twenty-line unsigned elegy, "An Epitaph on Donne," that was first printed in the first edition of *Deaths Duell* (1632) and was later entitled "On the death of Dr. Donne" and signed "Edw. Hyde" in the 1633 edition of the poems should be attributed to Sir Edward Hyde, later Lord Chancellor, and not to Edward Hyde (1607–1659), a Royalist divine, whom Grierson, following the suggestion of Charles Eliot Norton, identified as the author. Futher suggests that *MS EH* of Donne's poems has a signature on the flyleaf that matches Sir Edward Hyde's signature in the Matriculation Subscription Book of Oxford University under the date 31 January 1622; that on the flyleaf is also written "On the death . . . ," "On the death . . . ," "On the . . . ," the first two or three words of the heading of the elegy as it was printed in 1633; and that the number of doddles on the flyleaf—many *m*'s plus the words *mame, may*—perhaps suggests Hyde's awareness of the awkward repetition of sounds in line 15 of the elegy. Concludes, therefore, that Sir Edward Hyde "was thinking about Donne with his poems in front of him, when he wrote 'On the death' among the doodles covering the fly-leaf" (p. 167).

568. KOBAYASHI, SAKAE. "Washi to Hato no iru Buntai" [Emblematic Style with Eagle and Dove]. *Oberon* 14: 48–61.

Discusses Donne's use of the emblem tradition, especially in "The Canonization." Suggests that his direct borrowing of imagery from the emblem books of his day is fairly limited, but acknowledges their indirect and general influence on his poetry.

569. LABRIOLA, ALBERT C. "Donne's 'The Canonization': Its Theological Context and Its Religious Imagery." *HLQ* 36: 327–39.

Interprets "The Canonization" in the light of Donne's sermons and Christian iconography to explain the theological context of the poem, to illuminate its religious images, and to elucidate the range of Donne's wit that "moves freely between playful daring on the one hand and breezy blasphemy on the other" (p. 327). Argues that the two lovers of the poem "will be venerated as saints because their relationship resembles the divinely 'mysterious' Idea of love that is trinitarian unity"; that, "like the Divine Persons, Donne's lovers exemplify unity, wholeness, and self-sufficiency"; and that "each lover, in short, becomes identical with the other, like the Father and Son are depicted alike in some iconographical representations of the Trinity" (p. 330). Discusses in detail how the images of the dove, eagle, and phoenix relate specifically to the theological context of the poem. Notes, for example, that "the subtle interplay between erotic and religious connotations of the dove is ironically exploited" and how "this allusive image enables the speaker to liken sensualism to spiritual

love and to suggest resemblances between his loving relationship and trinitarian unity" (p. 333). Argues that the speaker of the poem contends that
"the lovers have achieved sainthood because of their unitive relationship—through which they have become alike by exchanging identities;
through which each is joined to the other and both, in turn, will be united
with God; and through which both, like saints, will ascend toward heaven"
(p. 337).

◆ぅ 570. LEGOUIS, PIERRE. "Donne Through French Eyes," in *Aspects
du XVIIᵉ Siècle*, pp. 33–54. Paris: Librairie Marcel Didier.
Surveys Donne's reputation in France during the past fifty years or so
(written originally in 1953) and points out that Legouis is the only French-
man to have written a volume solely devoted to Donne (*Donne the Craftsman*, 1928). Discusses the reception of this study among Donne scholars
and attempts to answer some of the criticism that was leveled against it by
certain English and American critics. Comments in particular on his reading
of "The Extasie" as a seduction poem and the subsequent debate that it
occasioned, especially Merritt Hughes's "The Lineage of 'The Extasie'"
(*MLR* 27 [1932]: 1–5). Postscript I (written in 1963) surveys the more
recent additions to the debate on "The Extasie," and Postscript II (written
in 1972) surveys yet newer comments on the debate.

◆ぅ 571. LEWALSKI, BARBARA K. "A Donnean Perspective on 'The Extasie.'" *ELN* 10: 258–62.
Reviews briefly the critical debate and controversy surrounding Donne's
shift from the celebration of Neoplatonic love to physical lovemaking in
"The Extasie" and notes that "the issue is whether this shift constitutes a
sharp and illogical disjunction in the poem's argument or whether the
apparent inconsistency can be explained in terms of some generally coherent metaphysical position" (p. 259). Argues that the conclusion of the
poem emphasizes "that the body is the soul's proper organ, its only means
of *acting* in the world in this our human condition, with the further suggestion that the lovers have a profound responsibility for such action in
the human community" (pp. 260–61). Points out that the basis of Donne's
argument can be found in his own resurrection sermon on 1 Corinthians
15:29, in which he enunciates characteristic Protestant assumptions "about
the life of action and social responsibility which is proper to our created
nature" (p. 262). Concludes that in "The Extasie" (but not in the sermon)
Donne obliquely suggests "that the Christian mysteries of the Incarnation
and of scripture revelation are proper models for these spiritual lovers in
their decision to manifest the perfections attained in the realm of the spirit
in the less exalted domain of the body" (p. 262).

◆ぅ 572. ——. *Donne's* Anniversaries *and the Poetry of Praise: The
Creation of a Symbolic Mode.* Princeton: Princeton University Press.
ix, 386p.

Proposes "to identify and analyze some of the traditions and habits of thought in sixteenth- and seventeenth-century epideixis, in Protestant meditation, in biblical hermeneutics, in funeral sermons (and specially in Donne's own practice in these arts) which gave rise to the *Anniversary* poems and their distinctive symbolic mode" (p. vii). Introduction (pp. 3–8) outlines the basic organization and purpose of the study and stresses that central to the study is how the *Anniversaries* transformed conventional praise into a symbolic mode. Divided into four major sections: (1) "Literary Contexts and Donnean Innovations" (pp. 9–70), (2) "Theological Contexts and Donnean Developments" (pp. 71–215), (3) "The Symbolic Mode of Donne's *Anniversaries*" (pp. 217–303), and (4) "The Legacy of Donne's Symbolic Mode" (pp. 305–70). Chapter 1, "Contemporary Epideictic Poetry: The Speaker's Stance and the *Topoi* of Praise" (pp. 11–41), surveys the theory and practice of English occasional epideictic poetry from 1595–1616, pointing out "what is unique about the *Anniversary* poems, what traditional assumptions and poetic conventions they call upon, and what strikingly new directions they define" (p. 14). Notes that the *Anniversaries* in many ways resemble contemporary poems of compliment but observes that their striking differences "reveal that in just the most fundamental matters, and notably in regard to the conception of praise itself, Donne seems to be marking out a new direction" (p. 40). Chapter 2, "Donne's Poetry of Compliment: Meditative Speaker and Symbolic Subject" (pp. 42–70), examines Donne's *Epicedes and Obsequies* and verse epistles to patronesses in order "to define the kind of praise Donne characteristically accords his subjects, whoever they are," and to identify "just what is significantly new in Donne's conception and practice of poetic praise" (p. 43). Notes that Donne's speaker characteristically takes a meditative stance toward his subject and that "the praises are not directed to the specific moral qualities of particular individuals (as were Ben Jonson's) but rather to the potentialities of the human soul as image of God" (p. 70). Chapter 3, "Protestant Meditation and Protestant Sermon" (pp. 73–107), surveys contemporary English Protestant theory and practice of meditation (in contrast to Catholic) and the development of the Protestant sermon and argues that Donne's "conception of meditation, as evidenced by his sermons and his own meditative exercise, the *Devotions upon Emergent Occasions*, appears to have been shaped by these Protestant emphases" (pp. 83–84) and that they inform the conception of meditation that can be found in his complimentary poems as well as in the *Anniversaries*. Notes that the Protestant fusion or near identification of meditation and the sermon accounts, in part, for the public voice in Donne's poetry of compliment and observes that in the *Devotions* and in the *Anniversaries* Donne fuses Protestant occasional and deliberate meditation. Stresses that Protestant meditation, unlike Catholic, seeks to apply and to locate the subject of meditation in the self and suggests that in Donne's complimentary poems, especially the *Anniversaries*, "the subject is located, embodied, in the person who is praised in the poem and then it is apprehended by the speaker (and his auditory) through meditation on that person" (p. 107). Chapter 4, "The Ordering Symbol: The Restored Image of God in Man" (pp. 108–41), surveys Protestant theology on the notion of the Christian as the restored image of God and argues that Donne's ordering symbol in the *Anniversaries* is Elizabeth Drury as the regenerate Christian, "who in some essential ways recapitulates the original innocence but also surpasses it in respect to the nearness her regenerate condition has to heavenly perfection and the purchase that state gives her upon heavenly glory" (p. 140). Chapter 5, "Symbolism and Hermeneutics" (pp. 142–73), suggests that Donne's typological symbolism is closely related to Protestant hermeneutics as reflected in his own sermons and theological writings that reflect Protestant theory about allegory and figurative language in Scripture. Notes that Elizabeth Drury "is made a type both of the condition of original created perfection and of the heavenly glory to come; her untimely death is a type (recapitulation) of the death brought upon us all by original sin; her religious death is an event (like the illness which occasions Donne's *Devotions*) in which the speaker finds a figure of his own renunciation of the world; her actual ascension to heaven is a *figura* of Christ's ascension, even as the imagined flight of the speaker's own soul is a *figura* of hers, and the projected spiritual progress of the fit audience of the poems will recapitulate both her progress and his" (p. 173). Chapter 6, "The Funeral Sermon: The Deceased as Symbol" (pp. 174–215), surveys the theory and practice of the Protestant funeral sermon, especially Donne's, and discusses the relationship between the *Anniversaries* and this mixed genre of instruction, meditation, and praise. Notes that Donne "characteristically . . . extends and exploits as only a master poet could the rich potential for paradox, psychological analysis, and symbolism inherent in these Protestant developments" and that his sermons provide important analogues to the *Anniversaries* "in regard to conception, structure, stance of the speaker, and exploration of the symbolic meaning of the deceased" (p. 215). Chapter 7, "*The First Anniversarie*" (pp. 219–63), and Chapter 8, "*The Second Anniversarie*" (pp. 264–303), analyze the two poems and "A Funerall Elegie" in the light of the preceding discussion of Protestant meditation, doctrine, hermeneutics, and the funeral sermon focusing primarily on the theological ideas and generic forms that give substance and structure to their central metaphysical argument. Stresses that in the poems Donne "transfigured occasional poetry, making this conventional form the vehicle of a new metaphysical symbolic mode and audaciously developing that mode in the extended format of a major poetic sequence" (p. 303). Chapter 9, "The Tradition of the *Anniversary* Poems: Tributes, Echoes, and Imitations" (pp. 307–36), discusses the influence of the poems on subsequent poetry of compliment and on future poetic symbolism, noting various tributes, echoes, and imitations. Chapter 10, "The Tradition of the *Anniversary*

Poems: Major Poetic Responses and Re-Creations" (pp. 337–70), surveys the influence of the *Anniversaries* on Jonson, Dryden, and especially Marvell's "Upon Appleton House." Index (pp. 371–86).

✒ 573. LEWALSKI, BARBARA K., AND ANDREW J. SABOL, eds. *Major Poets of the Earlier Seventeenth Century: Donne, Herbert, Vaughan, Crashaw, Jonson, Herrick, Marvell.* Indianapolis and New York: The Odyssey Press, a Division of Bobbs-Merrill Co. xxxv, 1330p.

Contains a general introduction to earlier seventeenth-century lyric poetry (pp. xix–xxxi); a selected bibliography of studies of seventeenth-century poetry and its backgrounds (pp. xxxiii–xxxv); an introduction to Donne's life and poetry (pp. 1–15); a selected bibliography of editions of and studies on Donne's poetry and his life (pp. 16–17); extensive selections from Donne's poems (including the complete *Songs and Sonets*), with explanatory notes (pp. 21–170); an introduction to and selections from musical settings of Donne's lyrics (pp. 1209–21); textual notes on the Donne poems included in the anthology (pp. 1269–79); and an index of titles and first lines (pp. 1301–30). The general introduction (by Barbara Lewalski) outlines major modern critical trends in the study of early seventeenth-century poetry; notes the modern tendency to break down the rigid dichotomy between metaphysical and early neoclassical poetry as well as to relate English poetry to Continental poetry of the period; comments on the trend to reevaluate the poetry in terms of genre and individual authors, "diverting attention away from broad generalizations about common features of style toward the unique poetic experience which each of these poets can offer" (p. xxvii); and discusses the relationship between the lyric and music. The introduction to Donne (by Andrew J. Sabol) briefly outlines Donne's life and comments on the major characteristics of his poetry. Stresses that it "is ordered to display the variety of human experience rather than to define a unified perspective on it" and that "the range of Donne's poetic and imaginative sensibility is revealed in the way he perceives and treats these human experiences of love and religious devotion" (p. 5). Discusses Donne's achievement and sources in various poetic genres—the satire, the love elegy, panegyric verse, the love-lyric—and surveys his essential philosophy of love. Comments also on his religious sensibility. Suggests that "at the heart of Donne's surprising and daring and witty effects is an imagination that constantly conflates and incarnates the great universals into the particulars of human experience" (p. 14).

✒ 574. LOVELOCK, JULIAN, ed. *Donne: Songs and Sonets: A Casebook.* (Casebook Series, gen. ed. A. E. Dyson.) London: Macmillan. 256p.

Introduction (pp. 11–29) presents a biographical sketch of Donne, comments on the essential characteristics of metaphysical poetry in general, and considers Donne's poetic individuality, especially as it is revealed in the *Songs and Sonets.* Notes that his originality stems primarily "from his freedom to draw on a number of different conventions and to adapt them to his own peculiar voice" (p. 18) and suggests that, although original, Donne is at the center of English poetic tradition. Defends Donne against the charge of being obscure, too learned, and often unrealistic and notes that, "because the *Songs and Sonets* are so grounded in the turmoil of the real world, they are unable to transcend it to that higher, timeless reality where human love is purified and made spiritual, and human lovers enjoy the assurance, the peace, and even the immortality, which are the normal reserve of Christians and other religious believers" (p. 23). Briefly outlines the history and development of Donne criticism and explains the selections included in the casebook. Part 1, "Early Comments" (pp. 33–46), reproduces two extracts from Donne and selected critical commentary from Carew, Dryden, an anonymous reviewer in the *Guardian* (1713), Lewis Theobald, Richard Hurd, Joseph Warton, an anonymous contributor to the *Monthly Review*, and Dr. Johnson. Part 2, "Selection of Nineteenth-Century and Early Twentieth-Century Criticism" (pp. 47–109), includes extracts from Coleridge, Hazlitt, an anonymous contributor to the *Retrospective Review* (1823), George Saintsbury, a 1900 review possibly by J. A. Symonds, Sir Herbert Grierson, W. B. Yeats, Rupert Brooke, and T. S. Eliot. Part 3, "Recent Studies" (pp. 111–248), reprints C. S. Lewis, "Donne and Love Poetry in the Seventeenth Century," and Joan Bennett, "The Love Poetry of John Donne—A Reply to Mr. C. S. Lewis," both of which first appeared in *Seventeenth Century Studies Presented to Sir Herbert Grierson* (1938); a section on "The good-morrow" from Arnold Stein, *John Donne's Lyrics: The Eloquence of Action* (1962); a selection from Louis Martz, *The Wit of Love* (1969), entitled "John Donne: Love's Philosophy"; an original essay by A. E. Dyson and Julian Lovelock entitled "Contracted Thus: 'The Sunne Rising,'" reprinted in A. E. Dyson and Julian Lovelock, *Masterful Images* (entry 817); a selection from J. B. Leishman, *The Monarch of Wit* (1951); Michael F. Moloney, "Donne's Metrical Practice" from *PMLA* 65 (1950); and Helen Gardner, "The Argument About 'The Ecstasy'" from *Elizabethan and Jacobean Studies* (1959). Selected bibliography (pp. 249–50); list of contributors to Part 3 (pp. 251–52); and index (pp. 253–56).

◆§ 575. McCann, Garth A. "Dryden and Poetic Continuity: A Comparative Study." *SAQ* 72: 311–21.
Argues that Dryden "is a poet not only of the Restoration but also of the Renaissance" and "belonged not only to the last half but also the first half of his century" (p. 311). Compares and contrasts his poetry with the theories of Sidney and the poetry of Spenser, Jonson, Donne, and Herbert to show a continuity between Dryden and his predecessors and to demonstrate that "he differs . . . more in degree than in kind" (p. 321). Suggests many differences between Dryden and Donne but sees Donne's and Dryden's didacticism, their combining the general with the concrete, and their using poetry as a vehicle to teach and to delight as linking them both with Renaissance poetic theory and practice. Comments on the element

of didacticism in Donne's poetry, his uses of particularized images, and
his dramatic uses of argument. Briefly compares Donne and Herbert.

◄§ 576. MANLEY, FRANK. "Formal Wit in the *Songs and Sonnets*," in
   *That Subtile Wreath: Lectures Presented at the Quatercentenary
   Celebration of the Birth of John Donne*, edited by Margaret W. Pepperdene, pp. 5–27. Atlanta: Agnes Scott College.
   Discusses how Donne often "took certain traditional lyric genres defined not by metrical form but by content, and by a sudden flash of wit
turned them upside-down so that while remaining recognizably themselves, they became vehicles for an entirely new and original experience"
(p. 8). Suggests that modern readers frequently miss the audacity and brilliance of Donne's formal wit (that is, a wit that is located within the form
of the poem itself) because they fail to recognize the lyric types. Briefly
discusses Donne's uses of the carpe diem theme in "The Relique" and of
the pastoral invitation in "The Baite" as well as mentions his uses of the
reverie or song of awakening of spring in "Twicknam garden," the classical
dirae in "The Curse," the *adunata* or catalog of impossibilities in "Song:
Goe, and catche a falling starre," the *tenso* or *débat d'amour* in "The
Canonization," and the valediction in a number of poems. Explicates "The
Sunne Rising" and "The Anniversarie" to show how by using two traditional forms, the *alba* and the *epitaphium anniversarium*, Donne "revi-
vifies them, or at least the essential impulse that gave rise to them in the
first place" and "makes them over into something uniquely his own"
(p. 8).

◄§ 577. MARTZ, LOUIS L. "Donne's *Anniversaries* Revisited," in *That
   Subtile Wreath: Lectures Presented at the Quatercentenary Celebration of the Birth of John Donne*, edited by Margaret W. Pepperdene,
   pp. 29–50. Atlanta: Agnes Scott College.
   Briefly reviews recent critical commentary on the *Anniversaries* and revises his earlier position (first stated in "John Donne in Meditation: *The
Anniversaries*," *ELH* 14 [1947]: 247–73, and repeated in *The Poetry of
Meditation* [1954]) that *The first Anniversary* fails as a formal religious
meditation. Suggests that the coalescence of the satiric, religious, and
didactic in the poem has a special appeal to modern literary scholars but
argues that the basic cause for modern interest is that "Donne now seems
to speak directly to us, explaining what it is to live in a world that seems
to be dying in the throes of some mysterious renewal" (p. 31). Sees the
poem as standing "at the watershed between ancient and modern," as pro-
nouncing "a valediction or elegy upon the Renaissance quest for an ideal
harmony of body and spirit," and as holding "the past in memory, while
the speaker's understanding and will move toward the future" (p. 33). Discusses the structure and imagery of *The first Anniversary* and sees the
poem as a "powerfully successful satire" that consciously "enacts a failure
in the meditative process" and uses the forms of meditation "for denunci-

ation, not devotion" (p. 38). Views the "Shee" of the poem not as simply a dead girl but as "the image of ancient virtue struggling vainly for life in a twilight world of decay" (p. 40). Discusses also the structure and theme of *The second Anniversarie* and argues that it, unlike the first, enacts "the progress of the restoration of the three-fold Image of God within man, in accordance with the theology set forth by St. Augustine in his great treatise on the Trinity and after him by St. Bernard" while the image of the idealized girl becomes "a symbol of that interior Image" (p. 46). Sees the two poems as companion pieces "in which the sadness of untimely death is converted to the consolation of a religious death, while the speaker himself is transformed from the bitter, angry voice of the public satirist into a gentler, inward voice of one who has learned how to see, and judge, and follow worthiness" (p. 48).

*§ 578. ———. "A Selected Bibliography of Writings on Donne's Anniversaries, 1942–1972," in *That Subtile Wreath: Lectures Presented at the Quatercentenary Celebration of the Birth of John Donne,* edited by Margaret W. Pepperdene, pp. 51–55. Atlanta: Agnes Scott College.
Lists twenty-seven critical works on the *Anniversaries,* written between 1942 and 1972. Partially annotated.

*§ 579. MORRIS, HARRY. "John Donne's Terrifying Pun." *PLL* 9: 128–37.
Suggests that in a number of his poems Donne employs *paranomasia* (punning on names) and specifically comments on Donne's punning on his wife's name, Ann More. Suggests the possibility of a pun on either his father-in-law's name or perhaps his wife's name in "The Canonization" (line 15) and argues that there is definitely a pun on his wife's name in "A Valediction: of weeping" (line 7). Notes that in the secular poems the puns tend to be "frivolous, witty, or mirth-provoking" but that in the divine poems they become increasingly "sober, profound, and ultimately terrifying" (p. 132). Suggests that Donne, following St. Augustine's notion that sin is a *conversio ad creaturam,* came to regard his love for his wife as a form of idolatry disallowed by a jealous God and that in certain of his sacred poems he explores this conflict: Lines 9–10 of "Since she whom I lov'd," lines 21–22 of "A Hymne to Christ, at the Authors last going into Germany," and especially throughout "A Hymne to God the Father," perhaps Donne's last poem, which pivots on "the polarity in which the names of Donne and More seem at opposite ends of a teeter-totter" (p. 136). Suggests if the reading of the 1633 edition of the last line is maintained ("I feare no more"), then Donne is saying that "his only hope for salvation lies in Christ's redemptive act, which atones for the sin even when the poet appears before him in judgment with love for Anne deep in his soul" (p. 137).

◆§ 580. NAKAMURA, TŌRU. "Donne to Eikoku Kokkyōkai [Donne and the Church of England]. *Eigo to Eibei Bungaku* (Yamaguchi Daigaku), no. 8 (December): 17–32.

Outlines and discusses the spiritual struggle that Donne experienced in renouncing Roman Catholicism and embracing the Church of England. Examines, in particular, the state of Donne's religious spirit and conscience as reflected in the *Anniversaries*.

◆§ 581. NISHIYAMA, YOSHIO. "John Donne no Teishin-kan no Ichimen—Teishin no Bitoku to shite no Kichi no Gainen" [One Aspect of John Donne's View of the Courtier—The Idea of Wit as a Virtue of the Courtier]. *Kiyō* (Eigo Eibungaku Kenkyūjo, Tōhokugakuin Daigaku), nos. 3–4 (in one volume) (February): 13–46.

Considers Donne's general view of courtiers, with special reference to the relationship of his *The Courtier's Library* and Castiglione's *Il libro del Cortegiano*. Notes that Donne was fond of parodying the notion of "indifferent judgment," one of the standards presented by Castiglione for the courtiers of Urbino.

◆§ 582. ———. "Nicholas Breton to John Donne" [Nicholas Breton and John Donne]. *Ronshu* (Tohokugakuin Daigaku), no. 60 (September): 67–81.

Discusses similarities between those poems of Donne and of Nicholas Breton that were apparently inspired by Castiglione's *Il libro del Cortegiano* and notes that Donne often parodies the Italian work.

◆§ 583. OKADA, HIROKO. "John Donne no Fukkatsu—Devotions o Chūshin ni" [John Donne's Resurrection: With References to the *Devotions*]. *SELit* 50, no. 1: 15–28.

Traces Donne's spiritual growth from a deep sense of sin and damnation bordering on despair to his later religious maturity and sees this transition taking place in the *Devotions upon Emergent Occasions*, in which Donne comes to view the cure of his illness as a sign of God's forgiveness and also as a promise of final resurrection. Suggests that from 1623 on Donne's best sermons result, in part, from this reassuring experience and points out that in his last sermon, *Deaths Duell*, Donne eloquently states his firm belief in eternal life as promised by Christ's death.

◆§ 584. PEPPERDENE, MARGARET W., ed. *That Subtile Wreath: Lectures Presented at the Quatercentenary Celebration of the Birth of John Donne*. Atlanta: Agnes Scott College. v, 80p.

Contains a foreword (pp. i-iii) by Pepperdene, introducing a symposium held at Agnes Scott College on 24–25 February 1972, in honor of the quatercentenary celebration of Donne's birth; a welcoming address by Wallace M. Alston, president of Agnes Scott College; three lectures on Donne (each of which has been separately entered in the bibliography):

(1) Frank Manley, "Formal Wit in the *Songs and Sonnets*" (pp. 5–27), (2) Louis L. Martz, "Donne's *Anniversaries* Revisited" (pp. 29–50), followed by a "Selected Bibliography of Writings on Donne's *Anniversaries*, 1942–1972" (pp. 51–55), and (3) Patricia G. Pinka, "The Autobiographical Narrator in the *Songs and Sonnets*" (pp. 57–76); a program of seventeenth-century music for lute and voice (including several songs by Donne) given at Agnes Scott College on 25 February 1972 (pp. 77–79); and a list of lecturers (p. 80).

585. PHILLIPS, JOHN. "Transition," in *The Reformation of Images: Destruction of Art in England, 1535–1660*, pp. 140–56. Berkeley, Los Angeles, London: University of California Press.

Discusses the prevailing views of Jacobean Anglicans and Puritans on religious images and ceremonies and comments briefly on Donne's conciliatory position on such matters (pp. 149–51). Suggests that, like Lancelot Andrewes, Donne "believed that ceremonies in themselves are 'indifferent,' but where there is no obedience nor ritual, religion necessarily will vanish" (p. 149) and notes that, "though Donne felt that existing disagreements with the English Church should be settled by lawful authority, he was quite put off by the Puritans' refusal to accept images" (p. 150). Notes that Donne, like Thomas More, rejected the notion that ceremonies and images should be abandoned simply because they had been abused in the past.

586. PINKA, PATRICIA G. "The Autobiographical Narrator in the *Songs and Sonnets*," in *That Subtile Wreath: Lectures Presented at the Quatercentenary Celebration of the Birth of John Donne*, edited by Margaret W. Pepperdene, pp. 57–76. Atlanta: Agnes Scott College.

Discusses Donne's skillful manipulation of the autobiographical narrator in a small group of his love poems in which he "sets the reporter's version of himself in collision with the discrepancies and ironies which arise from the reporter's performance as a narrator" (p. 59). Shows how the point of view of the narrator, his often authoritarian relationship with his listeners, and his movement away from the present "subtly interweave to modify the meanings of the autobiographical narratives in the *Songs and Sonnets*" (p. 63). Presents a detailed analysis of the interaction of these elements in "Farewell to love" and "The Relique" to demonstrate Donne's art in handling the narrative mode.

587. POLLARD, ARTHUR. "John Donne: 'Show me deare Christ, thy spouse, so bright and cleare.'" *CritS* 6: 16–20.

Gives a close reading of Donne's "Show me deare Christ" and regards it as both "a mark of his literary power and a measure of his religious commitment" (p. 20). Suggests that the sonnet presents Donne's view of the Church "not as an earthly and visible institution, not even perhaps as an allegorical city, but as a spiritual mystery expressed through the most tender and also ineluctable of human relationships, a mystery whose greatness is emphasized in that, for Donne, it can only be adequately expressed by inverting the normal order of that relationship, by substituting for a jealously protected exclusiveness a comprehensive inclusiveness" (p. 19). Concludes that perhaps the sonnet was not published in Donne's lifetime nor in the early editions because "Donne the churchman was himself outraged by this more daring exploit of Donne the poet and felt it best that, though most appropriate and most telling in its truth, this sonnet, for its expression, was best confined to a small audience with strong literary stomachs" (p. 19).

☙ 588. POLLOCK, JOHN J. "Reply to Elisabeth Schneider's 'Prufrock and After: The Theme of Change' in *PMLA*, 87 (1972), 1103–18." *PMLA* 88: 524.

Disagrees with Schneider's mention of Donne's "Batter my heart" in her essay on Eliot's religious conversion and his preoccupation with change, in which she suggests that in Donne, God "seizes possession of man's self and will," whereas in Eliot "the coming of God is willed within the human self" (Schneider, p. 1103). Argues that the images in Donne's sonnet are more violent than those in Eliot's poetry and that the persona wills to be seized by God but has not been seized. Maintains that the main difference between Eliot and Donne "is not that Eliot is active where Donne is passive, but that Eliot wills to believe in God where Donne wills to serve Him" or, "in other words, Eliot, unable to presuppose a basic belief in God either for himself or for his twentieth-century reader, must begin at an earlier stage in the conversion process, that is, at the initial stage of willing to believe." Points out similarities between Donne and Eliot in their rendering of Christian experience, especially their acute self-consciousness and fear that their public avowal of faith is perhaps not matched by their private beliefs. For a reply by Schneider, see *PMLA* 88 (1973): 525–26, in which she agrees in part with Pollock's points but insists that the contrast she intended between Donne and Eliot was that Donne "either had or longed to have and asked for an intense and intimate *personal* relationship with God or Christ, whereas Eliot, or at any rate the Eliot of the poems, does not appear to think or feel in these terms" (p. 525).

☙ 589. PRITCHARD, ALLEN. "Donne's Mr. Tilman." *RES* n.s. 24: 38–42.

Comments on five letters in the D'Ewes papers among the Harleian MSS. in the British Library that provide additional information on Edward Tilman, to whom Donne addressed his poem "To Mr Tilman after he had taken orders." One letter is addressed by Simond D'Ewes to his father, Paul D'Ewes, recommending Tilman for a position as advowson of Stowlangloft in Suffolk, and four letters are by Tilman to his patron, Paul D'Ewes. Notes that, although the letters do not prove that Donne knew Tilman personally, they do suggest that Tilman had achieved some prominence at Cambridge in 1618 and, thus, increase the likelihood that Donne had some knowledge of his character. Also notes that Tilman's letters are excessively flattering and indicate his worldly ambitions and that Donne's poem, as Helen Gardner points out, addresses the problem of the unattractiveness of the life of a cleric from a worldly point of view.

◄§ 590. QUENNELL, PETER, AND HAMISH JOHNSON. "The Seventeenth Century," in A *History of English Literature*, pp. 93–201. London: Weidenfeld and Nicolson; Springfield, Mass.: G. C. Merriman Co.
   Hamish Johnson does not appear on the title page of the American edition.
   Presents a brief biographical sketch of Donne's life and works (pp. 118–23). Outlines major characteristics of his poetry and prose and stresses the originality and complexity of his thought and expression: he "adapted and rarified the kind of elaborate conceits that sixteenth-century poets favoured, giving them an entirely new and often striking individual twist" (p. 120). Notes that Donne's prose style "is no less complex and energetic than the use he made of verse" (p. 121).

◄§ 591. RAMSARAN, JOHN A. "English Metrical Psalms, Donne's *Holy Sonnets* and Tulasī Dāsa's Vinaya Patrikā," in *English and Hindi Religious Poetry: An Analogical Study*, pp. 141–63. (Studies in the History of Religions, 23.) Leiden: E. J. Brill.
   Briefly comments on Donne's poem on the translations of the Psalms by Sidney and the Countess of Pembroke and suggests that the colloquial directness of Wyatt's metrical versions of the Psalms reminds one of Donne. Notes that, although Donne rendered *The Lamentations of Jeremy* into English, his poetic temperament, "which inclined towards a concentration of argumentative thought and passion, could not find ample scope in the mere versification of biblical laments" (p. 159). Points out, however, that there are numerous echoes from the Psalms in Donne's religious poems, such as in "A Hymne to God the Father" (which has its starting point in Psalm 51: 3–5) and in the *Holy Sonnets*. Compares and contrasts the *Holy Sonnets* with the *padas* of Tulasī Dāsa in the *Vinaya Patrikā* and suggests that "the feelings, emotions and divine aspirations expressed in these works are, at one and the same time, the means and the end of a religious poetry inspired by the true spirit of bhakti" (p. 163).

◄§ 592. REEVES, CAROLYN H. "Donne's 'The Calme,' 3–4." *Expl* 32: Item 3.
   Points out that Donne was familiar with the descriptive tradition in which the calm and the storm represent respectively the good and evil aspects of Fortune. Suggests that in lines 3–4 of "The Calme" Donne not only refers to Aesop's fable but also calls attention to his "juxtaposition of the events of the storm and calm, in his paired poems the calm following

instead of preceding the storm." Suggests that Donne "was aware that he was 'inverting' tradition by making the calm just as destructive as the storm, thereby presenting Fortune as completely malevolent." Notes further that in the two poems Fortune is presented as capricious, just as Zeus is presented as capricious in Aesop's fable. Suggests, therefore, that when the sailors in Donne's poem, confronted by a malevolent, mocking, and annihilating Fortune, are said to "forget to pray" (line 48), they may be recalling the fate of the frogs that petitioned Zeus and, "having just passed through the horrors of the storm, may find it wiser not to play the part of suppliant."

593. REYNOLDS, E. E. "A Note on John Donne." *Moreana* 37: 41–43.
Discusses Donne's relationship to the family of Thomas More. Notes that John Donne, Jr., in his will of 1661 bequeathed a portrait of More to his friend Sir Christopher Guise, who, in turn, bequeathed it to Christ Church, Oxford. Suggests that the portrait (now lost) came to John Donne, Jr., from his father, who probably inherited it from his mother, Elizabeth Heywood, daughter of Joan Rastell, More's niece. Discusses Elizabeth Heywood's recusancy and marriages. Notes that she arranged for Fr. William Weston, S.J., to visit her brother, Jasper Heywood, S.J., in the Tower and suggests that Donne probably met his uncle and also Robert Southwell, S.J.

594. RICHMOND, H. M. "Donne's Master: The Young Shakespeare." *Criticism* 15: 126–44.
Argues that many of Donne's lyrics contain precedents, echoes, and analogues derived from Shakespeare, especially from the early comedies, and that "it is scarcely an exaggeration to say that as distinctive a personality as Donne appears to have been psychologically conditioned by his master, and that he is less capable of grasping and extending the sweep of the dramatist's genius, than of excerpting, elaborating, and delicately perfecting a few flashes of character from among the many sparkling showers of personae thrown off by Shakespeare's virtuosity" (pp. 143–44). Maintains, therefore, that, rather than being uniquely inventive, as has often been held, "Donne and his supposed 'followers' look increasingly like a charming but derivative appendix to the Elizabethan drama" (p. 144). Suggests, for example, that such early plays as *Love's Labour Lost*, *The Two Gentlemen of Verona*, *The Comedy of Errors*, and *The Taming of the Shrew* provided Donne with models for his "lively and sardonic yet passionate personae" (p. 130) as well as precedents for his images and conceits. Notes also that Shakespeare's "parody of affectations provides the specific models for many of the hyperbolic conceits of Donne" (p. 131), who often plays straight the sentiments or roles that Shakespeare ridiculed or censured in his plays. Finds specific Shakespearean precedents, echoes, and analogues in "A Valediction: of weeping," "The good-morrow," "The

Sunne Rising," the two poems entitled "The Dreame," "A nocturnall upon S. Lucies day," "The Extasie," "Womans constancy," and "The Canonization."

❧ 595. ROBERTS, JOHN R. *John Donne: An Annotated Bibliography of Modern Criticism, 1912–1967*. (University of Missouri Studies, 60.) Columbia: University of Missouri Press. 323p.

Lists alphabetically by year and fully annotates 1,280 books, essays, monographs, and notes written on Donne from 1912 through 1967. Includes extended discussions of Donne that appear in books not centrally concerned with him, editions that contain significant critical discussion, and many items in languages other than English. Excludes mentions of Donne in books and articles, references in encyclopedias and literary histories, book reviews, and doctoral dissertations. Contains three indexes—author, subject, and Donne's works mentioned in the annotations.

❧ 596. ROSENTHAL, M. L., AND A. J. M. SMITH. "Metaphysical Poetry," in *Exploring Poetry*, pp. 280–304. 2d ed. New York: The Macmillan Co.

Comments generally on the qualities of Donne's poetry. Explicates "The Sunne Rising" and "Goodfriday, 1613. Riding Westward" (pp. 280–85), pointing out that the two poems "are indeed unlike in their literal themes and in their feeling toward the central images of universal authority, but the similarity in technique should be apparent" (p. 283). Stresses the changes and development of tone in the first and the movement of thought, projected through the images, in the second. Comments briefly on "The Apparition," the *Holy Sonnets*, and "The Extasie," calling the later "the Metaphysical poem *par excellence*" (p. 288). Brief references to Donne throughout.

❧ 597. SAKURAI, SHŌICHIRŌ. "Curing Like by Like—Donne to Paracelsus (1), (2)" [Curing Like by Like—Donne and Paracelsus (1), (2)]. *Jimbun* (Kyōyōbu Kyoto Daigaku), no. 19 (March): 45–72; *Eibungaku Hyōron* (Kyoto Daigaku), no. 31 (December): 1–45.

Discusses the prevalence of Paracelsian medical theories in Donne's poetry and prose and suggests that these theories may be a unifying principle in Donne's works. Applies Paracelsus's theory of using poison to eradicate poison to Donne's poetry, especially to the *Divine Poems*, in which he discusses sin as a means of purifying sin.

❧ 598. SAMARIN, R. M. "Tragedija Džona Donna" [The Tragedy of John Donne]. V*Lit* 17, no. 3: 162–90.

Reprinted in *"This Honest Method": A History of Realism in Western European Literature* (Moscow: Moscow University, 1974), pp. 221–44 [in Russian].

Presents a broad survey of Donne's life and poetry. Laments that a poet who in his earlier life and poetry celebrated the body and humanity so fully, a poet dedicated to the Renaissance concepts of freedom, individuality, reason, and learning, should have renounced all these important human values and embraced both in his life and in his poetry a religious asceticism that dampened his creative genius. Sees the change in Donne first fully articulated in *The Progresse of the Soule* and outlines the spiritual metamorphosis of Donne that culminated in the *Holy Sonnets*, poems that are filled with interior anguish and fear of death. Concludes that because of his spiritual agony and his inability to transcend his inner conflicts Donne, unlike Shakespeare and Cervantes, failed to realize the possibilities of his creative genius.

🦢 599. SCHLÜTER, KURT. "Die Lyrik der englischen Renaissance," in *Englische Dichtung des 16. und 17. Jahrhunderts*, by Horst Oppel and Kurt Schlüter, pp. 54–94. (Athenaion Essays, 3). (Studienausgaben zum «Neuen Handbuch der Litteraturwissenschaft», edited by Klaus von See.) Frankfurt am Main: Akademische Verlagsgesellschaft.

Outlines major characteristics of Donne's love poetry and sacred poetry and links them by their uses of wit and the Neoplatonic Petrarchan tradition. Notes that Donne's attitude toward love varies greatly in the *Songs and Sonets*: Love can be "unnatüraliche und erniedrigende Versklavung des Mannes," as seen in "The Curse," "The Indifferent," and "Loves Usury," in which woman, too, is "von dem Postament herabgeholt, auf das die echten Jünger Petrarcas sie gestellt hatten" (p. 77). Notes, however, that love may also be described as pure and the highest good, as in "The Extasie," in which spiritual union, as experienced by the lovers, compensates for the imperfections of the individual souls and includes the need for physical union between lovers as the soul's medium for communication. Suggests that Donne follows the Aristotelianism of Padua, not the Florentine Neoplatonic tradition. Notes certain stylistic features of Donne's love poetry—dialectic development of thought; uses of dramatic devices; conversational tone; the uses of conceit, wit, and paradox—all of which are found also in his religious poems, especially the *Holy Sonnets*. Comments on Donne's use of Petrarchan motifs in his religious poetry and relates him to Jonson and especially to George Herbert, who "scheint der wichtigste Vermittler zwischen Donne und den späteren «metaphysicals» gewesen zu sein" (p. 84).

🦢 600. SHERWOOD, TERRY G. "Reason, Faith, and Just Augustinian Lamentation in Donne's Elegy on Prince Henry." *SEL* 13: 53–67.

Maintains that an understanding of "Elegie upon the untimely death of the incomparable Prince Henry" increases one's understanding of the coterie element in Donne's poetry and prose and shows further his profound debt to St. Augustine. Argues that Donne's elegy, though a public poem, is also specifically addressed to his two friends, Edward Herbert and Henry Goodyere, both of whom had written elegies on the occasion of the death of the prince. Points out, through a detailed comparison between Donne's poem and those of his friends, that Donne adapted Edward Herbert's epistemological approach and ironic mode but amplified and complicated his Platonic philosophical formulations by examining mortality in a much broader theological context and that, similarly, he extended Goodyere's Augustinian discussion of suffering, grief, and lament in order to show the profound theological implications of their mutual grief. Notes that Donne's elegy, written just after his expression of great intellectual doubt in the *Anniversaries*, "flatly refutes ultimate rational skepticism and hence marks an important point in Donne's intellectual history" (p. 53). Shows that one of his principal assertions is "that the problem of skepticism is inseparable from other problems of mortality, such as grief, love, and social ties," problems dealt with together in *The City of God*, and thus he "adapts the Augustinian discussion to an ironic mode, which is a basic means of treating epistemological issues raised by Henry's death" (p. 54). Argues that Donne's central Augustinian assertion "is that the rational mind can begin to reconstruct value, which is threatened by mortal catastrophe, through reasoning itself" and that "affirming its own existence, reason leads outward for confirmation from other rational beings, ending finally in love and faith" (p. 53). Concludes, therefore, that the fact that Donne "chose a major occasion to affirm the importance of reason, for a select corterie as well as a wider public audience, and that he worked out this affirmation using an Augustinian vocabulary make the elegy necessarily a significant Donne work" (p. 67).

601. SHURBANOV, ALEXANDER. "Donne's 'Dramatic' Imagery." *Annuaire de l'Université de Sofia*. Faculté des Lettres. 67, ii: 201–20.

A continuation of "A Study of John Donne's Reform of Elizabethan Imagery" (entry 263). Analyzes the dramatic elements of the *Songs and Sonets*, especially the dynamic and dramatic function of Donne's images, as seen in such poems as "The Flea," "The Dreame," "A Valediction: of weeping," "A Valediction: forbidding mourning," "Twicknam garden," "The Indifferent," "Loves Deitie," "The Prohibition," "Lovers infinitenesse," "Womans constancy," "The Canonization," "The good-morrow," and "The Extasie." Concludes that "the dramatic character of some of Donne's poems, expressed in an action capable of changing the initial situation as well as the psychological state of the participants, makes many of the images flexible and dynamic" and that "poems in which there is no explicit action, but the attitude and mood of the speaker changes from stanza to stanza or from line to line also tend to produce developing images," although some of the poems have "disjointed heaps of figures with nothing to keep them together apart from the personality of the emotionally disturbed speaker" (p. 219). Notes also that there is a "search-for-a-fitter-image" pattern in the *Songs and Sonets*, which is often "responsible for the general impression Donne's poems make of improvised monologues" (p. 219). Summary in Russian (p. 220).

⋙ 602. SMITH, DON NOEL. "The Artistry of John Donne's Devotions." *UDR* 10, i: 3–12.
Comments on the critical history and reputation of the *Devotions upon Emergent Occasions*, surveys modern criticism on the work, and analyzes it as a work of art, "as an intensely realized dialectic of the soul, embodied in a finely controlled dramatic action" (p. 11). Suggests that the unity and coherence of the parts and of the whole, the careful structure, the controlled limitations imposed to guarantee relevancy and effectiveness, the concern for rhetoric and the unifying progression of the action, and the high level of intensity and suspense maintained throughout the development of the action—all indicate that Donne gave careful attention to the artistry of the work.

⋙ 603. SMITH, M. VAN WYK. "John Donne's *Metempsychosis*." *RES* n.s. 24: 17–25, 141–52.
Argues that an examination of Donne's sources in *Metempsychosis* supports Helen Gardner's notion (entry 427) that the poem is complete in itself and is a satirical mock allegory that "presents a perfect inversion of the moral progress traditionally associated with the soul's upward movement from plant through beast to man" (p. 17), a scheme that gave Donne an ideal pattern in which to develop the corrupt attributes of the person he wished to satirize—Robert Cecil. Suggests that Donne's most likely sources are Tertullian's *De Anima*, which not only discusses transmigration and moral degeneracy but also links these notions with the heresies of Simon Magus and Carpocrates; the writings of the neo-Pythagoreans, from Pico della Mirandola to Archangelus Burgonovo; and Hermetic and Cabalistic writings. Mentions, in particular, the works of Franciscus Georgius, Fridericus Balduinius, Johannes Reuchlin, Juan Vives, and Pierre de la Primaudaye. Suggests that, in addition to classical and Renaissance theories on transmigration and moral order, Donne "added the narrative and metaphoric substance of the traditional beast allegory, so that the poem finally issues as a series of brief beast satires with the continuum of degenerative metempsychosis" (p. 141). Finds that both Spenser's *Mother Hubberd's Tale* and Richard Niccol's *The Beggar's Ape* (? 1607) provide clues to Donne's intent, since both were political satires directed against the Cecil family and both used beast satire to camouflage their criticism. Outlines the historical context to show that by 1601 Donne, like Ralegh and many others, had reason to resent the immense power and influence of Cecil. Points out, for instance, that the death of the whale episode may be Donne's account of Essex's fall. Suggests, then, that in *Metempsychosis* "the narrative moves on two levels at once: while the work as projected

purports to be a history of the growth of havoc from Genesis to Donne's own time, with the adversary as the epitome of all evils the 'great soule' would acquire in the course of its long history, the poem as we have it actually consists of a series of brief beast satires, some referring directly to Cecil, others only glancing at him, and some, indeed, being no more than witty inventions in the narrative continuum of a progress in decadence" (p. 148). Suggests that Donne may have later regretted his support of Ralegh and possibly resolved to suppress the poem.

604. SNYDER, SUSAN. "Donne and Du Bartas: *The Progresse of the Soule* as Parody." *SP* 70: 392–407.

Surveys critical opinion on *The Progresse of the Soule* from the time of Jonson to the present and points out that modern critics disagree about the subject matter of the poem and about the kind of poem it is. Argues that Donne was consciously parodying Du Bartas's divine epic, the *Sepmaines*, which was first published in 1578 and 1584, was widely known and greatly admired among English Protestants, and was translated in part by Sidney, James I, and others, and finally in its entirety by Joshua Sylvester. Maintains that, if regarded as a mocking parody of *Sepmaines*, Donne's poem "acquires a sharper focus and its peculiarities begin to form a pattern" and that "a comparison with the Bartasian model also makes sense of the poem's puzzling incompleteness" (p. 396). Compares the two poems to show that Donne not only ridiculed and parodied certain literary devices employed in Du Bartas's poem but also attacked Du Bartas's whole point of view. Notes that, although Du Bartas's poem has certain surface similarities to the metaphysical mode of wit, a comparison with Donne's poem only "accentuates the difference between Du Bartas' heavy-handedness and Donne's agility, between the one's bent for elaboration and expansion and the other's for selection and compression" (p. 398). Concludes, therefore, that "most critics have been taking the poem too seriously" and have failed to see it as a "high-spirited cynical parody, more complicated than the 'Epithalamion Made at Lincolns Inne' but essentially in the same vein" and as a work of a "clever, 'advanced' young man having fun at the expense of the literary and religious Establishment" (p. 407).

605. SOUTHALL, RAYMOND. "The Little World of John Donne," in *Literature and the Rise of Capitalism: Critical Essays mainly on the Sixteenth and Seventeenth Centuries*, pp. 86–95. London: Lawrence & Wishart.

Maintains that Donne's poetry and prose reflect his closed, circular, and paradoxical world of medieval thought, especially in his uses of the image of the circle and of images of small, enclosed containers (a room, a tear, a face, an eye) and in his uses of riddles, paradoxes, and orthodox dialectic and ratiocination by which "he pokes fun at the gyrations of the mind as it explores the medieval universe" (p. 90). Suggests that Donne's greatness "lies in his capacity to integrate what we, in the normal course of things, too readily accept as disparate" (p. 86) and that it is "in terms of its attempts to create a human world, that one ultimately distinguishes the poetry of Donne from what we usually think of as Elizabethan" (p. 87). Concludes that the tightly integrated and closed medieval world that Donne's poetry reflects, a world in which "man's relationships to mankind and his relationships to nature are essential aspects of man himself" and in which "he stands in relation to the world about him not as an object amongst objects, but as an intrinsic part of one great whole, of which he is the consciousness and centre" (p. 94), was ultimately destroyed by the rise of capitalistic society, "in which men came to be seen as freely competing individuals: and the new individualism produced its own image of the world, in which natural objects appear as things-in-themselves acted upon by powerful external forces—just such a vision as Hobbes has of the social life of man" (p. 95).

◄§ 606. ———. "Love Poetry in the Sixteenth Century," in *Literature and the Rise of Capitalism: Critical Essays mainly on the Sixteenth and Seventeenth Centuries*, pp. 21–85. London: Lawrence and Wishart.

Examines the imagery and sentiment of sixteenth-century love poetry from a broadly Marxist perspective to show that the rise of capitalism in England profoundly changed society and human relationships and that that change was reflected in the love poetry of the period. Argues that seemingly far-fetched conceits of love poets "are the natural expressions of minds so perfectly attuned to their social surroundings that their erotic enthrallment is most aptly defined by the convergence of the account book and the billet-doux" (p. 60). Briefly comments on Donne's use of economic and commercial terms to express personal affection and points out that in "Lovers infinitenesse" love "is realized in the market-place; the lover is a would-be purchaser whose lack of thrift prevents him from paying the agreed price for the lady," and that "in the remainder of the poem the conceit develops into a legal quibble concerning the pre-emptive right of a land purchaser to the future products of his purchase" (pp. 51–52). Notes that even the Elizabethan view of heaven and the blessed is presented in terms of conspicuous wealth and treasure and suggests that Donne, like Sidney, Spenser, and others, equates wealth with virtue and honor.

◄§ 607. SPARROW, JOHN. "John Sparrow's 'Manuscript Corrections of Two Issues of Donne's *Biathanatos.*'" *BC* 22: 235–36.

In part a reply to Charles Morgenstern (entry 471). Presents additional information on uncorrected and corrected copies of the undated and the 1648 issues of *Biathanatos*. Emends and amplifies his earlier comments (entry 510) on several corrections.

✒§ 608. SPRINGFIELD, ASALEAN. "John Donne's 'The ecstasy': A Formal Analysis." *Faculty Journal* (Tennessee State University, Nashville) (1973–1974): 20–26.

Paraphrases the argument of "The Extasie" and comments on its organizing structure, uses of paradox, and key words (*love, soul, language*). Argues that it is a "unitary poem in that it may be partly realized through its argument, since its organizing structure supports this form of discourse" (pp. 25–26), that "the total poem may be partly understood as paradox, since it seems to spring from the key words as they expand in meaning to include their opposites," that "the argument and the paradox entail a two-part analysis," and that when they are combined with the paraphrase they reach "for both the 'ostensible' as well as the 'latent' meaning of the poem" (p. 26).

✒§ 609. STAPLETON, LAURENCE. "John Donne: The Moment of the Sermon," in *The Elected Circle: Studies in the Art of Prose*, pp. 17–44. Princeton: Princeton University Press.

Shows that Donne regarded the sermon as an active literary form and as "a mode of art that exalts art" (p. 19). Discusses how the sermon both liberated and, to a lesser extent, restricted the full play of Donne's imagination. Comments on his command of language and his scrupulous respect for precision and accuracy of word choice; his careful and artistic uses of logic and rhetoric for specific purposes and effects; and his awareness of the subtlest elements of style. Suggests that rhythm is Donne's "most fundamental resource, in his prose as in his poetry" (p. 26). Examines the vitality and variety of Donne's images and metaphors in the sermons and concludes that "it is the purpose of analogy, rather than that of opening a sudden new insight into experience, that Donne's metaphors in the sermons chiefly serve—that, and the pleasure of concreteness in an otherwise abstract discourse" (p. 27). Argues that, although Donne's themes are somewhat preordained and constrained by his orthodox Christian theology, he often strikes a note of individuality in the handling of themes that are especially important to him personally, such as the notion of calling and the mercy and sociableness of God. Presents analyses of many individual passages from the sermons and discusses as a whole Donne's sermon on the text, "Therefore the Lord shall give you a signe; Behold a Virgin shall conceive and beare a son, and shall call his name Immanuell" to show that he was aware of the advantages and disadvantages of the sermon as a form of literature. Maintains that, "if the sermons do not 'equal' the poetry as art," it is partly because they are not comparable, for, "although only the poet could have written these sermons, it was a different kind of work, and the writer knew it to be" (p. 40). Contends that the sermons, like the essays of Emerson and D. H. Lawrence, "appeal powerfully for assent" and treat themes "that penetrate the contours of experience, whatever the form of the reader's belief" (pp. 40–41), in part because they express vividly the experience and imagination of a masterful preacher and artist.

610. STRINGER, GARY. "Learning 'Hard and Deepe': Biblical Allusion in Donne's 'A Valediction: Of My Name, in the Window.'" *SCB* 33: 227–31.

Discusses Donne's use of biblical allusions in his love poems and specifically shows how "A Valediction: of my name, in the window," is a "dramatic monologue informed by an elaborate, though somewhat elusive, metaphor drawn from Holy Writ" (p. 227). Suggests that the poem is "a secular anti-type, an ectype, of Jesus' departure from His disciples" and that it "identifies the lover with Christ, the mistress with a disciple (or the Church), and generally recalls Christ's parting from His disciples at the Ascension" (p. 228). Argues that this scheme of biblical allusion "largely determines the conceptual and imaginal structure of the poem" and that "this elaborate metaphor greatly increases the poem's affective power and range" (p. 231). Notes that all four of the valediction poems contain religious language and allusions.

611. TARLINSKAYA, MARINA. "The Syllabic Structure and Meter of English Verse from the Thirteenth through the Nineteenth Century." *Lang&S* 6: 249–72.

Defines the meter of Middle English rhymed verse and traces certain aspects of the syllabic structure of English verse from the thirteenth through the twentieth century. Specifically discusses the syllabic structure of Donne's verse (pp. 268–70) and notes the relatively high number of dissyllabic intervals, "even though his frequent use of author's marks suggests that he intended to preserve the syllabic regularity of the line" (p. 268). Compares and contrasts Donne to Pope and postulates that, "if it is assumed that the boundary line between syllable-stress meters and the *dol'nik* is fixed at 10 percent of the lines having a dissyllabic interval, then it can be stated that Donne, like the early Chaucer, used loose syllable-stress verse, while Lydgate and Skelton employed the *dol'nik*" (p. 271). Concludes, therefore, that "among the modern English poets whose verse has been analyzed, Donne approaches the closest to the boundary for the *dol'nik*" (p. 271).

612. WHITING, ANTHONY. "Donne's 'A Valediction: Forbidding Mourning.'" *Expl* 31: Item 56.

Suggests that the circle made by the compass in "A Valediction: forbidding mourning," which symbolizes the perfect and infinite nature of Donne's love, is reinforced by his mention of gold in line 24. Points out that the alchemists used the image to symbolize gold, and thus, "by his exploitation of this fact, Donne further enforces his conception of the essential quality of his love."

◀§ 613. YOKOTA, NAKAZŌ. "John Donne no Elegies ni tsuite" [On John Donne's *Elegies*]. *Kiyō* (Kyōyōbu, Tōhoku Daigaku), no. 18 (March): 18–42.
Discusses the dramatic elements in the *Elegies* and maintains that the speaker of each poem is the center of the dramatic situation and the dominant force in that poem.

1974

◀§ 614. AHMAD, IQBAL. "Woman in Donne's Love Poetry," in *Essays on John Donne: A Quater Centenary Tribute*, edited by Asloob Ansari, pp. 39–58. Aligarh: Department of English, Aligarh Muslim University.
Argues that Donne in his love poetry rarely presents detailed physical descriptions of women but rather concentrates on their evocative power over men and thus allows them to become concrete, lively participants in the poems. Notes that, on the whole, Donne presents women as rational beings who are forthright, practical, self-respecting individuals who see through the pretenses of Petrarchan conventions and other exaggerated forms of love. Suggests that Donne's females, as realists in love, insist upon a male lover who is assertive and aggressive but who is also committed to a relationship that is mutually self-fulfilling. Analyzes Donne's portrayal of women in a number of the *Songs and Sonets* and in the *Elegies*, especially "Breake of day," "Selfe-love," "Womans constancy," "The Indifferent," "The good-morrow," "The Sunne Rising," "The Primrose," "Aire and Angels," and "The Extasie." Discusses also Donne's general attitude on love and on Renaissance theories of love and notes that in his complex uses of Petrarchan conventions "he transformed, or extended, or even inverted, also dramatized these myths of love, and thus showed them as hollow or worthless, and thereby, through proxy, established a healthier truth, or else extracted more meaning from them, than their stock responses could by themselves yield" (p. 49). Points out, however, that even though the presence of women is strongly felt in most of Donne's love poems, his primary emphasis is on the self-exploration of the male speaker.

◀§ 615. ALMASY, RUDOLPH. "John Donne's 'Air and Angels' Again." *WVUPP* 21: 17–22.
Disagrees both with those critics who see "Aire and Angels" as "the search for and final discovery of the true object and meaning of love" (p. 17) and with those who see the poem as moving from "exaltation to insolence" (p. 18). Argues that "many critics have been too eager to assign the poem a definite category and, ignoring the speaker and the intricate maneuvering of his mind, have allowed the category to precede the poem" (p. 18). Traces the basic argument of the poem, noting first the speaker's rejection of idealization, then his rejection of an overemphasis on physi-

cal experience, and finally his defining of love "not in the realm of ideas or the realm of physical experiences but in the realm of human relationships" (p. 19). Maintains that Donne's use of analogy between angels' purity and air and man's love and woman's love, as well as the analogy of the intelligences and spheres, explains the relationship. Argues that the speaker concludes that "woman's love is inferior but as he considers this idea and adds the final lines to his monologue, emphasizing that the disparity 'will ever be', . . . he is not content with this situation" (p. 21) but accepts it as inevitable. Warns that "readers need to remember to be open at all times to the unpredictable thoughts and feelings of Donne's speakers, most urgently when they do not fit neatly into categories as is the case of the lover in 'Air and Angels'" (p. 22).

⋖§ 616. ALTON, R. E., AND P. J. CROFT. "John Donne." *TLS*, 27 September, pp. 1042–43.

Reply to Nicholas Barker (entry 620). Asserts that the copy of the Goodfriday poem and several prose pieces in the Huntingdon Record Office and the Hofman copy of the poem are in the handwriting of Sir Nathaniel Rich (?1585–1636). Presents a brief biographical sketch of Rich and accounts for the papers appearing in the Manchester collection. Notes that, although the two copies of the poem are flawed, they are very early, probably before 1617. See also R. S. Thomson and David McKitterick (entries 673 and 710), along with Michael Horsnell (entry 654), Theodore Hofman (entry 652), and J. Max Patrick (entry 688).

⋖§ 617. ANSARI, A[SLOOB] A[HMAD]. "Two Modes of Utterance in Donne's Divine Poems," in *Essays on John Donne: A Quater Centenary Tribute*, edited by Asloob Ahmad Ansari, pp. 139–56. Aligarh: Department of English, Aligarh Muslim University.

Presents a general survey of Donne's divine poems and comments on the changes in his religious thinking reflected in them. Sees *La Corona* and "The Litanie" as devotional poems of a communal and liturgical nature that are "more ingenious than witty" (p. 140). Finds most of the *Holy Sonnets*, with their expression of deeply felt emotion, dramatic intensity, and egocentric assertiveness, reminiscent of Donne's secular poems, in which one finds similar examples of wit, images of violence, and a "kind of picture-making" (p. 155). Presents a more detailed reading of "I am a little world," "Goodfriday, 1613. Riding Westward," and "Hymne to God my God, in my sicknesse" and finds in them "a new kind of humility along with an elaboration of conceits and symbolic correspondences" and "a certain relaxation of tension and a tenacious clinging to hope in the midst of utter despair" (p. 155). Notes that it is only in a few of the *Holy Sonnets* and in the hymns "that the citadel of exclusiveness is broken and the persistent doubts are resolved into resignation and hope" (p. 155).

◄§ 618. ANSARI, ASLOOB AHMAD, ed. *Essays on John Donne: A Quater Centenary Tribute.* Aligarh: Department of English, Aligarh Muslim University. 185p.
Collection of ten original essays by members of the Department of English at Aligarh Muslim University originally read at a celebration in honor of the quatercentenary anniversary of Donne's birth, preceded by the editor's preface. Each of the essays has been separately entered in this bibliography: (1) B. K. Kalia, "John Donne in His Own Age" (pp. 1–24); (2) Z. A. Usmani, "Some Aspects of Donne's Love Poetry: With Special Reference to *The Relique*" (pp. 25–38); (3) Iqbal Ahmad, "Woman in Donne's Love Poetry" (pp. 39–58); (4) Masoodul Hasan, "Donne's *Verse Letters*" (pp. 59–85); (5) M. K. Lodi, "Donne's Epithalamic Verse" (pp. 86–99); (6) Harish Raizada, "Donne as a Satirist" (pp. 100–116); (7) Jafar Zaki, "Pope's Adaptations of Donne's Satires" (pp. 117–38); (8) A[sloob] A[hmad] Ansari, "Two Modes of Utterance in Donne's Divine Poems" (pp. 139–56); (9) Naresh Chandra, "John Donne the Preacher" (pp. 157–72); and (10) P. K. Ghosh, "The Problem of Sin and Salvation in the Sermons of Donne" (pp. 173–85).

◄§ 619. ANZULOVIC, BRANIMIR. "Mannerism in Literature: A Review of Research." *YCGL* 23: 54–66.
Reviews research on the concept of mannerism in literature from 1920 onward. Notes that Donne "competes with Shakespeare as the favorite example for '*Angst*-Mannerism,' although his name did not appear in this context until 1956, when Wylie Sypher and Rudolf Stamm, independently of each other, described him as a prominent representative of this style" (p. 58). Briefly notes and comments on the work on Donne by Stamm (1957), Daniel B. Rowland (1964), Arnold Hauser (1965), Mario Praz (1964, 1970), and Frederick B. Artz (1962). Selected bibliography (pp. 64–66).

◄§ 620. BARKER, NICOLAS. "'Goodfriday 1613': by whose hand?" *TLS*, 20 September, pp. 996–97.
In part a reply to two articles by R. S. Thomson and David McKitterick (entries 673 and 710) on a copy of Donne's Goodfriday poem and various prose pieces, all in the same hand, in the Huntingdon Records Office. Argues that the poem and the prose pieces were written by a copyist, not by Donne. Outlines the characteristics of Donne's handwriting noted by P. J. Croft in his *Autograph Poetry in the English Language* (entry 543). Notes that there was a second manuscript copy of the poem by the same hand in the Manchester papers, which were sold at Sotheby's on 23 June 1970 in a separate lot, and notes the variants between the two copies. Observes that, although the Huntingdon copyist was often inaccurate and careless, it is interesting to note that in both copies line 18 reads "tune" (as Helen Gardner suggests in her edition), not "turne." Points out a num-

ber of interesting questions that are raised by the Manchester manuscript. See also Michael Horsnell (entry 654), Theodore Hofman (entry 652), R. E. Alton and P. J. Croft (entry 616), and J. Max Patrick (entry 688).

⊷§ 621. BARRELL, JOHN, AND JOHN BULL, eds. "The Seventeenth–Century Pastoral," in *The Penguin Book of Pastoral Verse*, introduced and edited by John Barrell and John Bull, pp. 139–219. London: Allen Lane.

In the United States published under the title A *Book of English Pastoral Verse* (New York: Oxford University Press, 1975).

In the introduction (pp. 141–48) surveys the development of pastoral poetry during the seventeenth century. Observes that the metaphysical poets were rarely interested in the pastoral and that Donne's "The Baite" "is little more than an exercise-piece, one in a long and ever more tedious series of replies to Marlowe's 'Passionate Sheepheard'" (p. 141). Points out that "in place of a vision of a simple, harmonized society, the metaphysicals looked for a resolution of contemporary problems in terms of the individual, be it in the area of the religious or the secular" and that "a pastoral tradition which had arisen in reaction to an awakening of an individualist philosophy in the Renaissance had little to offer a writer intent on exploring the new world of scientific rationalism" (pp. 141–42). Notes that "the poetry of the metaphysical period is largely that of an urban culture which no longer feels sufficient connection with a rural alternative, an alternative which had anyway become ever more an artifice and a way of avoiding the contemporary and the threatening" (p. 142). Reproduces "The Baite" and a selection from "Ecclogue. 1613. December 26" (pp. 149–50), without notes or commentary.

⊷§ 622. BLACK, MICHAEL. "Stylistics and Donne's *The Sunne Rising.*" *Lang&L* 2, iii: 55–58.

Supports the notion of stylistics as "a semantic theory of performance, part of literary criticism: the interpretation, but not evaluation, of utterances (performance of language as opposed to abstract knowledge of language)" (p. 55) and offers a detailed stylistic analysis of "The Sunne Rising" to illustrate this concept. Examines the phonetic, graphetic, phonological, graphological, grammatical or syntactical, lexical, and semantic features and/or structures of the poem. Points out that the relationship of all the features constitutes the meaning of the poem and warns that "they cannot be reduced to statements such as 'The Sunne Rising is a poem about love in relation to time and the world'" for "such statements are simply a part of the semantic analysis, contributing to the total meaning but distinct from it" (p. 67). Concludes that perhaps it is finally impossible to say what the poem means because "we lack a semantic theory that could ensure cohesion and determine the relevance of every observation" but offers the present analysis to help the reader "in his own understanding of this poem, and indeed of any other utterance" (p. 67).

✍ 623. BLAMIRES, HENRY. *A Short History of English Literature*. London: Methuen & Co. 536p.

Discusses Donne's poetry (pp. 113–17) and prose (pp. 138–39). Comments very briefly on Donne's life and on his influence on T. S. Eliot. Outlines certain features of Donne's poetry, such as his uses of the dramatic argument and extravagant, far-fetched imagery. Maintains that he "is at his finest in his short poems" (p. 116) and suggests that his high point is "Goodfriday, 1613. Riding Westward," where the paradoxical theme of rising by dying is handled with subtlety of image and intensity of personal devotion" (p. 117). Briefly mentions Donne's uses of argumentation, striking imagery, and rhetorical strategies in his religious prose.

✍ 624. BLANCH, ROBERT J. "Fear and Despair in Donne's *Holy Sonnets*." ABR 25: 476–84. ⅔ 7 ⅃.⌐05 ⩘ 3⌐

Discusses the elements of fear and despair in the *Holy Sonnets* (following Grierson's ordering) and argues that Donne's shifting devotional attitudes in the *Holy Sonnets* and their apparent lack of strict thematic ordering and of consistent patterns of imagery may be conscious attempts to depict realistically his difficult search for God and spiritual peace and to show his willingness to draw upon any source in the search. Suggests that Donne deliberately conjured up fearful images "as chastening devices to drive him to God just as contemplation of God's beauty soothed him into complacency" (p. 484). Suggests, therefore, that Donne welcomed fear as an important spiritual means and that the *Holy Sonnets* do not portray "a soul so tortured by fear as to be in a state of mental or emotional disintegration" (p. 484).

✍ 625. BRINK, ANDREW. "On the Psychological Sources of Creative Imagination." QQ 81: 1–19.

Presents a psychoanalytic interpretation of Donne's attitudes toward women in the *Songs and Sonets* and maintains "that Donne was ambivalently testing the emotional viability of relations with his objects," a strategy that "cannot be doubted by anyone familiar with the obsessional defence" (pp. 15–16). Argues, therefore, that his love poetry, "famed for its erotic daring, is ironically a testing device originated by a son whose mother had psychologically dominated his life" and that "its mode is that of avoidance of women as much as it is a hopeful engagement with them, the situation being one of latent homosexual ambivalence" (p. 16). Suggests that Donne's religious struggle in midlife represents his search for a father and that his "shift to religion founded on a masculine God eased conflict" (p. 16).

✍ 626. BROADBENT, JOHN, ed. *Signet Classic Poets of the 17th Century*, vol. I. (The Signet Classic Poetry Series, gen. ed.⌐ John Hollander.) New York and Scarborough, Ontario: New American Library; London: The New English Library. xviii, 377p.

Introduces and anthologizes the poetry and prose of Jonson, Donne,

Herbert, Crashaw, Vaughan, Marvell, and Dryden. Notes that Donne's poems are grouped by theme: sex and platonic love; valedictions; sensual and ironic poems; epithalamia; poems on church and state; poems, letters, and sermons to or about patrons; religious poems; and poems on dying. Quotes several passages to show that, in addition to the theme of love, Donne was "obsessed with change, transubstantiation, conversion, metamorphosis, hence with dying" and suggests that his "overriding quality is density" (p. 4). Presents a chronological table of Donne's life (pp. 77–78); selections from Walton's *Life* and Coleridge's *Lectures* (pp. 78–79); and selections from the poems, both secular and sacred, along with selections (with notes) from three sermons and *Devotions upon Emergent Occasions* (pp. 81–135).

◄§ 627. Brooks, Cleanth. "Religion and Literature." *SR* 82: 93–107.
    Argues that the functions of religion and literature must be distinguished, disagrees with those who hold that poetry can perform the same function in an age of disbelief that religion performed in an age of belief, and argues further that poetry, in order to perform its special function, needs religion. Comments on Donne's use of religious imagery in his love poems and his use of erotic images in his divine poems. Notes that he "knew the difference between religion and poetry since he so obviously makes use of a tension between the two in his profane love poetry and in his Holy Sonnets" (p. 98).

◄§ 628. Campbell, Gordon. "Words and Things: The Language of
    Metaphysical Poetry." *Lang&L* 2, iii: 3–15.
    Challenges critics, such as Rosemond Tuve, who attempt "to experiment with the analytical tools of the Renaissance in an attempt to recreate the sixteeenth- and seventeenth-century readers' understanding of the poetry" and argues that "these methods, although historically justified, are ultimately destructive, and that an appreciation of Renaissance poetry, particularly metaphysical poetry, is predicated on a knowledge of the poets' ideas about the nature of poetry rather than an ability to implement the philosophers' ideas on how a poem should be analysed" (p. 3). Challenges also the notion that Ramism accounts for metaphysical poetry and summarizes the long debate among poets and philosophers of the Renaissance about the primacy of words or things. Points out that Donne certainly uses logic in his poems but that one need not immerse oneself in the technicalities of Renaissance logic in order to follow the argument or to note the fallacies. Maintains that a genuine appreciation of Donne's love poems "must be firmly rooted in an enthusiasm for his language" and that "we do not serve ourselves or the poetry if we look for the 'ideas' which the language is cloaking" (p. 10). Concludes that metaphysical poetry is "primarily a poetry of words rather than things" and that "it is the glorification of the power of words as words, and we should be content to admire it at that level" (p. 11).

᪐ 629. CHANDRA, NARESH. "John Donne the Preacher," in *Essays on John Donne: A Quater Centenary Tribute*, edited by Asloob Ahmad Ansari, pp. 157–72. Aligarh: Department of English, Aligarh Muslim University.

Suggests that only Anglican preachers of the seventeenth century "have a secure place in English literary history" (p. 158). Comments on Donne's distinctiveness as a preacher: (1) his conversion from a life of excesses to one of piety that allowed him to "visualize and personify a sin or temptation, stalking on its silent feet and knocking at the heart of the would-be sinner" (p. 159); (2) his deeply held belief in the importance of preaching grounded in scripture and his conviction that public worship was preferable to private devotion; and (3) his effective prose style, "a most judicious balance between arguments and similitudes, exposition and expostulation, concentration and extension, attaining to something like Allen Tate's theory of tension in poetry" (p. 164), along with his concern to make himself fully understood by his congregation. Praises Donne's prose style in general terms and regrets the decline after Donne of the eloquent style of preaching.

᪐ 630. CHINOL, ELIO. *English Literature: A Historical Survey*. Vol. 1: To the Romantic Revival. (Le lingue e le civiltà straniere moderne collana diretta da Elio Chinol.) Naples: Liguori. 686p.

Reproduces "The Baite" (pp. 169–70); presents a brief introduction to Donne's life, personality, and poetry (pp. 278–80), together with seven selections from the *Songs and Sonets* and four selections from the *Holy Sonnets* (pp. 281–96), and a selection from *Devotions upon Emergent Occasions* (pp. 303–5). All texts and the introduction are in English; notes are in Italian. Comments on Donne's reaction against the decorative and melodic poetry of Spenser, his realism and uses of colloquial speech, his rejection of poetic diction and uses of the conceit, and his blend of thought and passion. Suggests that his poetry should not be called "metaphysical," strictly speaking, but rather "the poetry of wit," "taking wit to mean what in seventeenth-century Italy was meant by *argutezza*" (p. 280).

᪐ 631. COLLMER, ROBERT G. "Another Look at 'The Apparition.'" *CP* 7: 34–40.

Maintains that "The Apparition" "exhibits what Northrup Frye (in another context) calls a 'demonic epiphany'" (p. 34) and explains the poem "as a precise, though blasphemous construction employing religious conventions" (p. 35). Argues that the keys to the poem are the connotations of *ghost* and *apparition* and shows that, since in the seventeenth century the term *apparition* "could refer to a manifestation, an action of revealing, an epiphany, an advent," Donne "may not be talking about a specter; he may be promising a manifestation of a spirit to a scornful mistress" (p. 37). Suggests that "the twist in the poem involves a transfer of the role of the poet from Second Advent figure to Devil figure" (p. 38) in which he says to his rejecting mistress, "Like Christ, I shall appear; like the Devil, I shall plague you; since you have by your scorn killed me and my love is too little to aid you, you must lie unprepared and unassisted to meet my avenging spirit" (p. 39). Concludes that the poem "proves that eschatology, wittily employed, excels even the power of scatology to vilify" (p. 39).

⌐§ 632. DAWSON, S. W., HARRIET HAWKINS, AND ROBERT ELLIOTT. "As We Read the Living?" *EIC* 24: 94–104.
    Three replies to Roma Gill (entry 554). (1) Dawson agrees that the teacher of Donne should "draw attention to the use of traditional themes, ideas and images when it is possible to turn related passages to critical effect" and must also "bring . . . students to understand the ways in which poetry of the past *belongs* to its time" (p. 96). Maintains, however, that "to read Donne 'as we read the living' is the only way to grasp such of the past as we find in him, not as information, but as experience" (p. 96). (2) Hawkins, without mentioning Donne specifically, argues against all closed systems of criticism and maintains that "the first step in teaching our students to read the literature of times past and present alike is to encourage them to recognize and interpret for themselves the great and enduring problems posed, and the great and enduring realities exhibited in literature," and that, although "these recognitions may require a knowledge of relevant historical information, a knowledge of related works of art, and a knowledge of interesting critical discussions of the literature," still "*no source of knowledge has any final authority* so far as our individual interpretations of and responses to literature are concerned" (p. 100). (3) Elliott challenges certain of Gill's assumptions about poetry, especially her comments on "The good-morrow" and "The Sunne Rising," and disagrees with F. W. Bateson's attack on F. R. Leavis in his response to Gill's essay (entry 532).

⌐§ 633. DEITZ, JONATHAN E. "Donne's 'To His Mistress Going to Bed,' 33–38." *Expl* 32: Item 36.
    Suggests that Donne's allusion to Atalanta's "balls" in line 36 of "Going to Bed" may not be a confusion of classical myth but may refer to female breasts. Cites several Renaissance sources to show that breasts were referred to as "balls" or "globes." Suggests, therefore, that "Donne knew what he was about" and is saying that all distracting baubles, be they clothes, gems, or breasts, should not distract one from tasting the "whole joyes." For replies, see Richard F. Giles (entry 750) and Edgar F. Daniels (entry 737).

⌐§ 634. DEMING, ROBERT H. "Love and Knowledge in the Renaissance Lyric." *TSLL* 16: 389–410.
    Discusses the concept of the self in the Renaissance love lyric and comments on "the functional relationship . . . between self-conscious lyricism and a kind of knowledge that would be acceptable to the posthumanistic

English Renaissance" (p. 389). Argues that "if we wish to learn the 'why and how' Renaissance poets made their poems, we must consider poetry as a means of knowing (an epistemological structure) rather than as an object of knowledge" and "we must further consider the poetry as models of self-discovery and self-knowing and as models descriptive of the process of gaining self-knowledge" (p. 391). Maintains that the Renaissance love poet tried to reconcile the inherent dilemma of his dual existence and attempted to harmonize his rational and his passionate nature. Points out that Donne's "Loves growth" is a good example of how love involves both knowing and loving and suggests that the *Elegies*, though often seen as purely libertine, "presents a tension between the claims of the celestial and the natural forms of love" (p. 396). Observes that "all the varieties within human love that Donne expresses in his poetry are expressed in psychological paradoxes because Donne alternately hopes for both loves, the contemplative and the active, but argues poetically only for the achievement of human love" and thus should be seen as "a poet in conflict with the demands of the flesh hoping for the dream of *mens angelica*" (p. 396). Notes that, since Donne "cannot tell us what love is, he tells us in the poem 'Negative Love' what it is not" and that "in using the rhetoric and dialectic of negatives and extremes, Donne acknowledges his literary debt to his predecessors—Petrarch, Wyatt, Sidney, Spenser, and Shakespeare—who had all discovered conflict and dialectical opposition at precisely those points in their own statements of 'human love' where their 'thinking consciousness' questions itself and its ways of knowing" (p. 397). Comments also on "The triple Foole," in which Donne shows that "he is wise because he has loved and because he knows that in 'loving' and 'saying so' in verse he has achieved power over love" (p. 398).

⋅⋅⋅ 635. DE STASIO, CLOTILDE. "*Loves Sweetest Part, Variety*," in *Studi Inglesi: Raccolta di saggi e ricerche*, 1, edited by Agostino Lombardo, pp. 51–73. Bari: Adriatica Editrice.
Analyzes in some detail "The Indifferent" and sees the poem not as a celebration of infidelity but as a rebellion against prevailing concepts of courtly love and Petrarchism and suggests that in it Donne substitutes a new, freer sensuality for the older ideal. Points out that Shakespeare and others shared some of the same notions and discusses the systematic destruction of traditional concepts of love through irony and humor in such poems as "Womans constancy," "Song: Goe, and catche a falling starre," "Loves diet," "Change," "The Message," and "The Apparition." Suggests that the contrast of such poems to Donne's other love poems may be a kind of "discordia concors" or a parallel to Shakespeare's use of comic or pseudo-comic scenes in his tragedies. Notes that themes of instability and uncertainty are reflected also in the religious and scientific thought of the time.

⋅⋅⋅ 636. DIRCKS, P. T. "The Dramatic Structure of 'Loves Alchymie.'" *English Quarterly* (Toronto) 7, no. 1: 7–9.

Maintains thal in "Loves Alchymie" there are two distinct speakers and that "the bulk of the poem is addressed by one speaker to a fictitious listener, who eventually questions the speaker" (p. 8). Argues that Donne's use of two personae explains the two markedly different attitudes toward love in the poem and that "notable differences in language, rhythm and tone distinguish the ironic bitterness of the first persona from the bemused query of the second in ll. 3–17" (p. 8). Presents a brief reading of the poem to show that it is an organic whole and that it effectively re-creates the drama of conflicting ideas. Maintains that "the contrast between the language, rhythm, and tone of the two personae provides a dramatic illustration of Donne's intellectual analysis" and suggests that in the poem Donne "dichotomizes, for purposes of examination, the elements of physical passion and spiritual love which he fused in his great love poetry" (p. 9).

᪵ 637. DOEBLER, BETTIE ANNE. *The Quickening Seed: Death in the Sermons of John Donne.* (Salzburg Studies in English Literature, Elizabethan & Renaissance Studies, edited by James Hogg, no. 30.) Salzburg: Institut für englische Sprache und Literatur, Universität Salzburg. vii, 297p.

Discusses Donne's sermons in the light of seventeenth-century attitudes toward death and from his own personal perspective of the subject. Chapter 1, "The Quickening of the Seed" (pp. 1–86), challenges the notion that Donne is preoccupied with death in his poetry and prose and the idea that he presents death through morbid concepts and images. Argues that his treatment of the subject must be seen in the light of seventeenth-century traditions, especially biblical eschatology; Greek and Roman views on death, which Donne often used to support Christian orthodoxy and to deepen his own vivid sense of death; and the mainstream of early Christian and medieval thought on death. Notes that Donne "was an heir of this tradition which focused on death and analytical consideration of it as a crucial human and religious experience" and that he employed themes and images that "arose out of the long history of thought concerning death" (p. 86). Chapter 2, "Doctrine and Poetry" (pp. 87–145), discusses seventeenth-century theology of death, particularly as it was related to the doctrine of atonement; comments on devotional literature of the period, as reflected in various sermons, meditations, and tracts; and shows how Donne saw these ideas and attitudes in the light of his experience as a poet. Analyzes the theme and images of "Goodfriday, 1613. Riding Westward" because Donne "includes within it the experience which is the core of Christianity—the experience of one sinful human being, moved to repentance by a confrontation with God Incarnate" (p. 144) and because it reflects Donne's personality, "which rests upon a universal view of human nature and which seeks out the essences through the personality and particularity of the intelligible world" (p. 145). Chapter 3, "Donne's Debt to the Great Tradition" (pp. 146–88), examines Donne's attitudes toward Christian history and tradition, noting in particular his debt to the Psalms and to St. Paul and analyzes the themes, tone, images, and structure of several funeral sermons. Chapter 4, "The Long Art" (pp. 188–228), explores Donne's treatment of death in the sermons as a whole and discusses how he handled traditional and conventional materials and themes, such as those arising from the *ars moriendi* tradition. Suggests that the sermons as a whole show his "constant effort to balance and to synthesize material and spiritual reality—an effort characteristic of the growth by death into a better life" and as it were "contain the record of spiritual growth towards death and the life to come" (p. 227). Chapter 5, "The Long Meditation" (pp. 229–63), comments on Donne's views on judgment, hell, and heaven as reflected in his sermons, noting that he tends not to emphasize the visual details in portrayals but achieves passionate feeling through the intensity of his thought. Chapter 6, "The Quality of Mercy" (pp. 264–89), concludes that Donne's "experience of mercy and the depth of thanksgiving that accompanies it—a thanksgiving from the heart of one who has searched the depths of his own sin—gives form to the internal structure which paradoxically encloses the external architecture of Donne's writing and preaching on death" (p. 265). Argues that, although he owed a great debt to traditions that formed him, Donne's distinctive expression and poetic vision cannot be underestimated. Discusses Donne's view on the role of the preacher and analyzes his sermon preached at St. Paul's on Christmas 1622 as an example of his theological position on atonement and his three sermons on the resurrection preached in 1626 as examples of his joy in the resurrection. Bibliography of works cited (pp. 290–97).

◆§ 638. DONNE, JOHN. *Letters to Severall Persons of Honour* (1651). (Anglistica & Americana: A Series Selected by Bernhard Fabian, Edgar Mertner, Karl Schneider, and Marvin Spevack, no. 148.) Hildesheim and New York: Olms Verlag. 318p.
Facsimile of the copy of *Letters to Severall Persons of Honour* (1651) in the Library of the University of Göttingen (shelfmark: 8° Hist. lit. biogr. VII 3582). Frontispiece reproduced from copy in the Library of Trinity College, Cambridge (shelfmark: Grylls, 16.162). No notes and no commentary.

◆§ 639. ———. *Pseudo-Martyr.* A Facsimile Reproduction with an Introduction by Francis Jacques Sypher. Delmar, N.Y.: Scholars' Facsimile & Reprints. [viii], 392p.
Facsimile reprint of a copy of *Pseudo-Martyr* (1610) in The British Library, London (1009.c.33). Presents a concise historical introduction to Donne's defense of King James I's *Triplici Nodo, Triplex Cuneus, or an Apologie for the Oath of Allegiance, against the two Breues of Pope Paulus Quintus and the Late Cardinall Bellarmine to G. Blackwell the Arch-Priest* (London, 1607). Points out that Donne's defense "resembles more a legal brief than a work of imaginative literature" but that "it nevertheless

has the rhetorical and literary virtue of being both precise and moderate" and avoids the tone of "the raging tirades and vicious personal accusations that were then the staple of controversialists and pamphleteers" (p. iii). Notes Donne's uses of vivid images of physical corruption, disease, and death; his uses of metaphors drawn from a wide range of sources—alchemy, astronomy, natural history, navigation and geography, rhetoric, etymology, and warfare; and his uses of startling comparisons and puns. Lists modern critical studies of *Pseudo-Martyr* and notes copies of the first edition available in American libraries. Offers a modern table of contents.

⋙ 640. FARLEY-HILLS, DAVID. *The Benevolence of Laughter: Comic Poetry of the Commonwealth and Restoration.* Totowa, N.J.: Rowman and Littlefield; United Kingdom: The Macmillan Press. viii, 212p.

Mentions Donne throughout this study of comic poetry of the Commonwealth and Restoration. Notes that comic poetry during the Commonwealth "increasingly comes to mean something more disruptive even than Jonsonian comedy" and is "often no longer play-acting" (p. 185) as it is in Donne and the metaphysicals. Notes also that Donne's cynicism, in such poems as "The Indifferent," "seems to be rather the result of a *jeu d'esprit* than an expression of settled conviction" (p. 23) and that his uses of the *carpe diem* theme are mostly a game. Comments on Donne in relation to Cleveland, Dryden, and Rochester and briefly discusses Donne's views on sexuality, especially as revealed in such poems as "Variety," "The Relique," and *The Progresse of the Soule.*

⋙ 641. FERNÁNDEZ SUÁREZ, JOSÉ RAMÓN. "Repercusiones de la obra de Fray Luis de Granada en los Sermones de John Donne." *ES* (Valladolid) 4: 111–31.

Briefly comments on the enormous popularity of Fray Luis de Granada in England and on his influence on English poets of the late sixteenth and early seventeenth centuries, including Donne. Notes that Donne knew Spanish, had traveled to Spain, and was familiar with Spanish literature, especially the religious literature. Presents parallel passages from the works of Luis de Granada and Donne's sermons to show that on such topics as the relationship of creatures to the Creator, the miseries of man, divine grace, prayer, fear of the Lord, and penitence the two share similar ideas and often use similar words and images. Maintains that, although there is no evidence to show that Donne specifically read Luis de Granada and although no one parallel proves a direct borrowing from his works, the number of parallels, when taken together, strongly provide evidence of the Spanish writer's influence on Donne.

⋙ 642. FLEISSNER, ROBERT F. "Frost's 'Moon Compasses.'" *Expl* 32: Item 66.

Suggests that Robert Frost had in mind Donne's "A Valediction: forbidding mourning" when he wrote "Moon Compasses." Points out that "by referring to 'a masked moon' covering a 'cone mountain' with light, he utilizes geometric imagery with emphasis upon circularity in a manner similar to that suggested in Donne's poem, though without the necessity of introducing an alchemical allusion."

✥ 643. FUJII, TAKEO. "Donne's 'Canonization' and 'Extasie.'" *Kenkyū Ronshū* (Kansai Univ. of Languages) no. 21 (February): 1–9.
Cited in *The Renaissance Bulletin* (The Renaissance Institute, Tokyo) 7 (1980): 20. Unavailable.

✥ 644. GHOSH, P. K. "The Problem of Sin and Salvation in the Sermons of Donne," in *Essays on John Donne: A Quater Centenary Tribute*, edited by Asloob Ahmad Ansari, pp. 173–85. Aligarh: Department of English, Aligarh Muslim University.
Suggests that Donne has little original to say about sin and salvation in his sermons but considers his treatment of them to be distinguished by his "confessional truth" and "the way he grapples with them to seek a resolution to the paradoxes and the pessimism that accrued to him from his own experiences of life" (p. 173). Discusses Donne's preoccupation with sin (both original and actual) and his overriding sense of guilt and comments generally on his views on salvation and grace, especially his belief that Christ is the only guarantee of salvation.

✥ 645. GILL, R. B. "Another Reference to Donne's 'Satire III', ll. 79–82." *AN&Q* 13: 53–54.
Points out that Richard Niccol's "Epig. III. In templum honoris" in *Vertue's Ecomium: or, the Image of Honour* (1614) contains verbal echoes of Donne's description of the hill of Truth in *Satyre III* (lines 79–82). Suggests that, since Niccol had little connection with Donne, the epigram leads one to believe that Donne's manuscripts circulated outside the circle of his immediate friends.

✥ 646. GRANT, PATRICK. *The Transformation of Sin: Studies in Donne, Herbert, Vaughan, and Traherne*. Montreal and London: McGill-Queens University Press; Amherst: University of Massachusetts Press. xiii, 240p.
Discusses the poetry of Donne, Herbert, Vaughan, and Traherne "in terms of a hypothetical encounter between guilt culture and enlightenment" (p. 38), or, in other words, in terms of a conflict between traditional Augustinian theology and sensibility and a new ethical view of man. Although Donne is mentioned throughout, Chapter 2, "Augustinian Spirituality and the Holy Sonnets of John Donne" (pp. 40–72), is devoted entirely to a discussion of Donne's medieval and Augustinian spirituality in the Franciscan tradition and argues that the *Holy Sonnets* are greatly informed by a tradition that is both basically Catholic and peculiarly English. Compares St. Bonaventure's hymn, *Laudismus de Sancta Cruce*,

with Donne's *Holy Sonnets* and shows that Donne's sonnets are, in fact, "a synthesis of, on the one hand, a traditional Augustinianism . . . and, on the other, a characteristically seventeenth-century latitudinarian desire to repudiate the harsh doctrinal derivations from Augustine, such as were found, for example, among the Reformers" and thus the *Holy Sonnets* dramatically present a struggle that attempts "to discover a middle way not simply between Catholicism and Protestantism (which the Anglican via media is often represented as espousing) but between the traditional guilt-culture inheritance of Augustine, represented by Franciscan spirituality, and a typically enlightenment Neoplatonist latitude" (pp. 42–43). Shows specifically how the *Holy Sonnets* are informed by Augustinian theology and sensibility, noting that they are "centrally concerned with contrition and the twice-born experience of regeneration, stressing the centrality of the cross to salvation and using techniques of affective piety to stimulate fear of last things as well as awe of the crucifixion itself, and informed throughout with a profound sense both of the fallen nature of man in Adam and of the link between Adam and the blood sacrifice of the Atonement" (pp. 64–65). Suggests also that in the *Holy Sonnets* Donne is, in a sense, a precursor of the Cambridge Platonists, such as Henry More. In Chapter 3, contrasts Donne's turbulence in the *Holy Sonnets* with George Herbert's quiet assurance in *The Temple* and finds that the main reason for the differences is that Herbert is "a more assuredly Protestant theologian than Donne, as his acceptance of the typically Calvinist doctrines of predestination and the Convenant attests" (p. 75). In Chapter 6, contrasts Donne with Traherne to show that they are unlike as devotional poets and to observe that in Traherne the Augustinian tradition no longer predominates.

৺§ 647. GREGORY, MICHAEL. "A Theory for Stylistics—Exemplified: Donne's 'Holy Sonnet XIV.'" *Lang&S* 7: 108–18.

Defines a theory of interpretative stylistics, based primarily on the linguistic model of John Rupert Firth, and notes that "when the language of a text is examined, not as a source of information about plot, character, vision, etc., but as the major focus of attention in the dialectical process of criticism—that is, when the response and the statement are primarily involved with the use of language itself in the text—then the critic is pursuing *interpretative stylistics*, a very central kind of literary criticism because it concentrates on the medium of the art of literature, language" (p. 110). Agrees with Susan Sontag in *Against Interpretation* (1967) that "to confront a work of art with 'what does it mean?' as the initial question too often means that it ceases to be treated as a work of art, as *artefact*, and is looked at as though it were something else—a piece of theology, sociology, philosophy, or political theory" (p. 110). Describes the lexical, grammatical, and situational features of "Batter my heart." Maintains that an "examination of the language of the poem, its internal patterns and their external relevance, shows it to be linguistically dynamic, coherent yet complex" (p. 116) and that such an examination "leads us to know that for Donne the religious commonplace was no commonplace but a thought that had been felt, proved upon his pulses," primarily because "he sees it in relation to known experiences" and because "he reveals patterns of similarity amongst diverse experiences" (p. 117). Concludes that in dealing with the poem "lexically, grammatically, and situationally, discerning its internal and external patterns, we can enter into a developing response to it; and in articulating a statement about 'what it is' and 'how it is' make a statement of meaning about it that leaves it as a poem, a work of art using the medium of language" (p. 117).

⊷§ 648. HAMMOND, GERALD, ed. *The Metaphysical Poets: A Selection of Critical Essays*. (Casebook Series, gen. ed. A. E. Dyson.) London and Basingstoke: The Macmillan Press. 254p.

Collection of previously published essays. Contains the general editor's preface (p. 9); a general introduction that outlines the reputation of metaphysical poetry and metaphysical poets from the seventeenth century to the present (pp. 11–32); a collection of twenty-four essays or parts of essays (pp. 34–241); a selected bibliography (pp. 243–45); notes on contributors to part three (pp. 247–48); and an index (pp. 249–54). Part 1, "Seventeenth- and Eighteenth-Century Criticism" (pp. 34–54), contains selections from Thomas Sprat, Edward Phillips, William Winstanley, Giles Jacob, the anonymous editor of *Select Hymns Taken out of Mr Herbert's Temple* (1697), Joseph Addison, John Oldmixon, the anonymous author of *A Dialogue on Taste* (1762), and Samuel Johnson. Part 2, "Nineteenth- and Early Twentieth-Century Criticism" (pp. 59–88), contains selections from Coleridge, Hazlitt, De Quincey, Emerson, George Macdonald, Alexander Grosart, Arthur Symons, and T. S. Eliot. Part 3, "Recent Studies" (pp. 89–241), contains selections from Rosemond Tuve, "The Criterion of Decorum," from *Elizabethan and Metaphysical Imagery* (1947); Leo Spitzer, "'The Extasie,'" from *A Method of Interpreting Literature* (1949); S. L. Bethell, "The Nature of Metaphysical Wit," from *Northern Miscellany of Literary Criticism* (1953); Joseph H. Summers, "George Herbert: The Conception of Form," from *George Herbert: His Religion and Art* (1954); Josephine Miles and Hanan C. Selvin, "A Factor Analysis of the Vocabulary of Poetry in the Seventeenth Century," from *The Computer and Literary Style* (1966); Earl Miner, "The Metaphysical Mode: Alteration of Time," from *The Metaphysical Mode from Donne to Cowley* (entry 123); and Rosalie L. Colie, "Andrew Marvell: Style and Stylistics," from *'My Ecchoing Song'—Andrew Marvell's Poetry of Criticism* (1970).

⊷§ 649. HARRISON, JAMES. "Syntax in Donne's 'The Dreame.'" *HAB* 25: 141–45.

Analyzes "The Dreame" to show that in the poem Donne examines and explores a very personal love, "which, initially perfect and subsequently flawed, is in the end left tantalizingly in the balance" and argues that "these characteristics are inherent in the very texture of the language used" (p. 142). Discusses various syntactical and rhetorical features of the poem, such as the complex uses and close proximity of personal pronouns (nineteen instances of the second-person singular in thirty lines), the uses of repetition and of objective complement and inversions, the employment of antithetical balances, and the creation of certain verbal equations in order to demonstrate how "the lines move from affirmation of perfection to exploration of imperfection" (p. 143). Shows how, for example, the whole second stanza is "a single sentence of mounting complexity" and how the concluding couplet of the stanza is "one of the most superb of all Donne's many bragging overstatements of love" (p. 143). Considers also the theological argument of the poem, which is inextricably bound up with its syntactical and rhetorical features. Concludes that in the third stanza the poem recovers some of the syntactical and rhetorical aplomb of its first two stanzas, but much less dogmatically, with new tentativeness, and asserts that the poem is thus "one of Donne's more interesting and candid comments on the business of loving" (p. 144).

◄§ 650. HASAN, MASOODUL. "Donne's *Verse Letters*," in *Essays on John Donne: A Quater Centenary Tribute*, edited by Asloob Ahmad Ansari, pp. 59–85. Aligarh: Department of English, Aligarh Muslim University.

Briefly traces the history and development of English epistolary verse and suggests that Donne's informal, personal verse letters, modeled upon those of Horace, made original contributions to the genre. Comments on the high opinion Donne's verse letters enjoyed not only among his contemporaries, such as Thomas Pestell, Jonson, and Dekker, but also among the eighteenth-century poets, especially Pope and Dr. Johnson. Reviews the major themes of Donne's verse epistles and argues that, although one may fail to find in them the vision, intensity, dramatic realism, and the subtler shades of thought and emotion that characterize the best of the *Songs and Sonets* and his religious poems, the verse epistles mark an important stage in Donne's development in the handling of prosody, structure, and certain major themes. Suggests that Donne as writer of verse letters may have influenced Jonson but points out that "in depth of thought, subtlety of wit, range of subjects and technical virtuosity, Donne's pieces have a distinct advantage over Jonson's epistolary verse" (p. 81). Compares Drayton to Donne and concludes that Drayton's expression is perhaps "more smooth and racy, and the couplets more refined than Donne's; but in the breadth of his interests, artistic manipulation of argument, and structural variety the latter is decidedly the more attractive and influential poet" (pp. 81–82).

ॐ 651. HEDETOFT, ULF. "The Contracted Universe of *Songs and Sonets*: A Dialectical Analysis." *Lang&L* 2, iii: 32–54.

Presents a Marxist dialectical analysis of the *Songs and Sonets* in order "to lay bare certain connections and structures, certain dynamic developments both within the *Songs and Sonets* themselves and between them and 'their' society" (p. 33). Concentrates on the influence of various societal and historical factors on Donne's aesthetic consciousness, such as the class struggle, the breakdown of feudal and aristocratic society, the rise of early capitalism, the collapse of the order and stability of a hierarchical view of the cosmos, and so on, and suggests ways "in which the ideological structuring of the *Songs and Sonets* points beyond itself, into Donne's later life" (p. 33). Comments on Donne's adherence to an aristocratic and academic viewpoint and notes that "it is precisely this class context that both makes the *Songs and Sonets* possible *and* limits their scope and their consciousness" (p. 35). Discusses four major ways in which the aristocratic framework of the poem is manifested: "(i) imagery ('Court' images, 'Chain of Being' images), (ii) exclusion of material and consequent delimitation of themes, (iii) the element of non-work, leisure, and (iv) tone(s) (cynicism, off-hand manner, wit, defeatism, etc.)" (p. 36). Discusses how Donne incorporates images from the "new world" (geographical expansion, discoveries, trade, and so on) but uses them only as images and how "the same world is made to contrast according to the rules determined by an 'I' who in important respects is the ideological-social product of this world" (p. 41). Argues that Donne's society, then, is present in the *Songs and Sonets* "both in the poetic expansion and in the ideological contraction" (p. 41) and that ultimately "the aim of the process of contraction is the re-establishing of a personal realm of order and harmony . . . which directly corresponds with (the loss of) the collective order of the Chain of Being—whose destruction is mirrored in Donne's use of it—whereas his personal search is triggered by certain historical and social developments, mirrored in the 'new world' imagery" (p. 42). Maintains that Donne's search for ideal love, which is ultimately frustrated, leads to further idealization of love as Love, and finally results in his search for transcendence in religion, his final attempt to escape the material reality of his crumbling world.

ॐ 652. HOFMAN, THEODORE. "John Donne." *TLS*, 20 September, p. 1018.

Replies to David McKitterick and R. S. Thomson (entry 673). States that the copy of the Goodfriday poem in his possession is definitely not in Donne's hand. See also Michael Horsnell (entry 654), R. S. Thomson and David McKitterick (entry 710), Nicolas Barker (entry 620), R. D. Alton and P. J. Croft (entry 616), and J. Max Patrick (entry 688).

ॐ 653. HÖLTGEN, KARL JOSEF. "A Nuremberg Book in the Bodleian Library and Its Owners." *Anglia* 92: 177–79.

Comments on two German books, Sebastian Munster's *Cosmographey* (Basel, 1578) and *Der Stat Nürmberg verneute Reformation* (Nuremberg, 1564), given by Edward Parvis (or Parvish) to the Bodleian Library in 1603. The first contains an inscription and a signature that shows it was originally owned by Donne. Suggests that Donne may have given it to Parvis in acknowledgment of assistance given to him during his travels abroad. Comments briefly on Parvis, a London merchant who had business connections in Germany and Venice.

◆§ 654. HORSNELL, MICHAEL. "Manuscript find throws new light on the poetry of John Donne." *The Times* (London), 16 August, p. 16.

Announces that the copy of Donne's Goodfriday poem, discovered by R. S. Thomson and David McKitterick in the Huntingdon Records Office (formerly in the stables at Kimbolton Castle until 1952) is in Donne's hand and valued at about 100,000 pounds. Suggests that the Bodleian Library is expected to be interested in purchasing the manuscript. Further suggests that five other documents found in the collection are by Donne. Reports various comments on the importance of the discovery by Mc-Kitterick and by Sir Geoffrey Keynes. For a full account by Thomson and McKitterick, see entries 673 and 710. For replies, see Nicolas Barker (entry 620), Theodore Hofman (entry 652), R. E. Alton and P. J. Croft (entry 616), and J. Max Patrick (entry 688).

◆§ 655. HOUGH, GRAHAM. "An Eighth Type of Ambiguity," in *William Empson: The Man and His Work*, edited by Roma Gill, pp. 76–97. London and Boston: Routledge & Kegan Paul.

Suggests that "behind Empson's seven types of ambiguity there lurks an eighth—ambiguity between intended and achieved meaning" and that it is "in the interplay between intended and unintended meaning that interpretation finds most work to be done" (p. 78). Comments on "Song: Goe, and catche a falling starre" to illustrate this kind of ambiguity and to show that to interpret the poem one must consider "not only lexical and syntactical meaning, but connotative meaning, associated suggestions, rhythmical and auditory effects" (p. 83). Argues that in such a poem there is no one best reading. Analyzes the intended and achieved meaning in the poem and shows the differences between its intended and unintended effects: "The achieved effect is not one of bitterness and disappointment, but of energy, curiosity, intellectual and emotional life, even if enclosed within a recognition of limits and frustrations" (p. 84). Observes that "answers to questions about what the poet empirically believed will not necessarily yield answers to questions about what he is doing in a poem" (pp. 86–87).

◆§ 656. JOHNSON, C. D. "Bedroom and Landscape in Donne's *The Songs and Sonnets.*" *Cresset* 37, no. 4: 6–9.

Suggests that by studying the physical settings in the *Songs and Sonets* one can view "these poems of love and death in an unusual perspective, one which reveals some things about the craft and the themes of individual poems, as well as Donne's attitude toward the world around him" (p. 6). Points out that "Donne has his lovers act out their parts in carefully chosen interior and exterior settings which are almost without exception—encompassed in little rooms" (p. 6). Notes that the "sole interior settings are the rooms of love and the rooms of death, the latter including the deathbed and tomb," and further discovers a thematic balance between the two: "there are ten poems set in the rooms of love and ten in the rooms of death" (p. 6). Notes that "in all the deathbed poems, love and death are connected visually because the deathbed constantly recalls the lovebed" and that, "for the most part, when Donne writes dramatically of the negation of physical love—denial, platonic love, grief—he chooses the grave for setting" (p. 8). Points out that only five poems in the *Songs and Sonets* have an out-of-doors setting and that even in these Donne "manages to take the walls of the room with him" and creates "roofless rooms" (p. 8). Suggests that Donne's very limited use of natural settings indicates his general discomfort "with the geocosm, plain and unadorned" (p. 9) and notes that, even when he does use a natural setting, he does very little with it.

◆§ 657. KALIA, B. K. "John Donne in His Own Age," in *Essays on John Donne: A Quarter Centenary Tribute*, edited by Asloob Ahmad Ansari, pp. 1–24. Aligarh: Department of English, Aligarh Muslim University.

Comments on Donne's reputation and influence during the late sixteenth and early seventeenth centuries. Discusses Donne's audience and the few scattered contemporary references to his poetry. Stresses that, although Donne published very little of his poetry during his lifetime, he was widely read and admired as a wit among a discriminating minority of important readers and hence influenced the direction that poetry was subsequently to take. Suggests that Jonson's appreciation of Donne is fairly representative of this intelligent minority of readers. Points out that Donne's contemporary reputation rested primarily on his two *Anniversaries*, the *Satyres* and the *Elegies*, and a few amatory poems and notes that there are no contemporary references to Donne's religious poems.

◆§ 658. KAWAMURA, JŌICHIRŌ. "Counter-Renaissance with Donne as the Central Figure," in *Renaissance to Han-Renaissance* [Renaissance and Counter-Renaissance], by Haruhiko Fujii, Shūji Takashima, Takashi Sasayama, Susumu Kawanishi, and Jōichirō Kawamura, pp. 159–214. Tokyo: Gakuseisha.

Presents comments by five Japanese critics (Haruhiko Fujii, Shūji Takashima, Takashi Sasayama, Susumu Kawanishi, and Jōichirō Kawamura) on the relationship between Renaissance and anti-Renaissance literature, dissociation of sensibility versus unified sensibility, love lyrics, mannerism, and baroque poetry. Translates into Japanese "Going to Bed," explicates it, and uses it as a primary example of anti-Renaissance literature. Notes that anti-Renaissance literature is a continuation of Renaissance literature in both style and theme, but that these are used differently, with a highly conscious emphasis on the individual's point of view. Points out, for instance, that the Renaissance stock images and the analogy of love and faith are present in Donne's elegy but stresses that Donne uses stock images to achieve the reverse of the effect they had in Renaissance literature and that he rejects Neoplatonic love theory by saying that the achievement of faith through love is more difficult than the Neoplatonists think. Relates Donne's poetry to mannerism and to the baroque and suggests that his love lyrics are more manneristic and his religious poems more baroque.

🍋 659. ———. "Donne to Mannerism mata wa Baroque" [Donne and Mannerism or Baroque]. *EigoS* 119: 748–50.

A lecture sponsored by the Italian Embassy in Japan on baroque literature in Europe. Discusses the changes in literature and art from mannerism or "proto-baroque" to the baroque, focusing on the year 1590. Suggests that Donne's poetry contains both manneristic and baroque characteristics. Argues that there is little point in trying to decide whether "dissociation of sensibility," as described by T. S. Eliot, actually began with Donne's poetry or later.

🍋 660. KELLIHER, W. HILTON. "The Latin Poetry of George Herbert," in *The Latin Poetry of English Poets*, edited by J. W. Binns, pp. 26–57. London and Boston: Routledge & Kegan Paul.

Reprinted in *Essential Articles for the Study of George Herbert's Poetry*, edited by John R. Roberts (Hamden, Conn.: Archon Books, 1979), pp. 526–52.

Notes Herbert's friendship with Donne and comments, in particular, on the several Latin epigrams on the device of the cross-anchor that Donne adopted as his seal at about the time of his ordination in 1615. Notes that Donne gave Herbert a ring with this device on it not long before his death. Observes also that Herbert's "La Natales et Pascha Concurrentes" may have been suggested, in part, by Donne's "Upon the Annuntiation and Passion falling upon one day. 1608." Points out that Donne, unable to officiate at the funeral of Magdalen Herbert, preached "A Sermon of Commemoration of the Lady Danvers" at Chelsea on 1 July 1627 and that the following week the sermon, along with Herbert's Latin commemorative verses on his mother, was entered at the Stationer's Hall. Notes several possible borrowings of metaphors from Donne in Herbert's Latin poetry.

🍋 661. KERINS, FRANK M. "Donne's 'A Valediction: Of Weeping,' 10–19." *Expl* 32: Item 71.

Suggests that in "A Valediction: of weeping" the "round ball" (line 10) "which was nothing" (line 13) is transformed into "All" (line 13), that is, the world, and that "it is only at line 14 and following that the tear image enters the stanza," thus making the globemaker image simply a "necessary preparation for the image of the tear's becoming a world when reflecting the beloved's face." Points out that in line 14 "it is this tear wearing an image of her, which grows into a world just as the 'round ball,' wearing copies of continents, grows into a globe." Argues that lines 17–18 further develop the conceit: "His tears are mixed with hers because her face is being reflected in his tear. Thus as she weeps, her weeping becomes superimposed upon his tear, and the 'world' of his tear is flooded by her weeping." Notes also that "his 'heaven' is 'dissolved,' firstly, since she is his heaven 'from which these floods pour down'" (as noted by Helen Gardner in her edition, Oxford, 1965, p. 198) and, "secondly, since these floods are dissolving the image of her in his tear, they are paradoxically dissolving her, his 'heaven' also."

◄§ 662. KERMODE, FRANK, STEPHEN FENDER, AND KENNETH PALMER. *English Renaissance Literature: Introductory Lectures.* London: Gray-Mills. vi, 145p.

Contains two university lectures on Spenser (by Kermode and Fender), five lectures on Donne (by Kermode), and six lectures on Milton (four by Palmer and two by Kermode) given between October 1972 and March 1973. Contains a short preface by Kermode (pp. v–vi) in which he stresses that the lectures are "purely routine" and "were not what the authors would have *written.*" In Chapter 2, "Donne: Lecture One" (pp. 30–40), Kermode outlines some of the literary and intellectual concerns of Donne's time; stresses Donne's interest in humanist and scientific works but notes also his medieval mode of apprehending the world about him; comments on major characteristics of his poetry (especially argument, hyperbole, wit, obscurity, use of the conceit, and stanzaic experimentation) and illustrates these by a brief reading of "The Dreame." In Chapter 4, "Donne: Lecture Two" (pp. 41–53), Kermode discusses in more detail Donne's uses of wit and the conceit and suggests approaches to his poetry by explicating "Loves Alchymie," "A Valediction: of weeping," and "The Extasie." Stresses the range of Donne's love poetry and rejects the notion that a consistent philosophy of love emerges in it. In Chapter 5, "Donne: Lecture Three" (pp. 54–67), Kermode surveys Donne's Catholic background and his profound interest in religion; discusses the *Elegies,* especially "The Anagram," "On his Mistris," "Natures lay Ideot," and "Going to Bed," to illustrate Donne's libertine poetry; and comments on the *Satyres,* especially I and III. In Chapter 6, "Donne: Lecture Four" (pp. 68–82), Kermode discusses several of the verse epistles and especially the *Anniversaries* and explains briefly the influence of discursive meditation on Donne's poetry. In Chapter 7, "Donne: Lecture Five" (pp. 83–95), Kermode surveys Donne's religious poetry and comments briefly on his prose; outlines Donne's religious development; discusses in some detail the *Devotions upon Emergent Occasions* and selected passages from the sermons and in a more cursory way *Pseudo-Martyr, Biathanatos, Essays in Divinity,* and *Ignatius his*

Conclave; regards the *Holy Sonnets* as Donne's most important religious poems, "Goodfriday, 1613. Riding Westward" as his best occasional poem, and "Hymne to God my God, in my sicknesse" as his most significant hymn.

๙§ 663. KERRIGAN, WILLIAM. "The Fearful Accommodations of John Donne." *ELR* 4: 337–63.

Observes that "Batter my heart" and "Show me deare Christ" often disturb the modern reader who finds the anthropomorphism of Donne perplexing and notes that the sonnets "raise the larger question of how and why Donne thought of man while thinking of God": "Approving the theological tenor, we suspect the anthropomorphic vehicle" (p. 340), especially Donne's effort to have the reader imagine in some detail the sexuality of God. Outlines the history of Christian accommodation and considers its psychological implications in order to explain "the strategy of these two sonnets, clarifying both the logic which informs them and the ambivalence which they inspire" (p. 340). Presents a detailed reading of the two sonnets to show that Donne "alone explored the difference between God as we know him and God as we must believe him to be, compelling us to recognize the conjunction of vice and virtue as the necessary condition of our knowledge of the deity" (p. 361). Suggests that the paradoxes in the two sonnets "reenact, within the particular terms of their anthropomorphism, this concealment: behind chastity is violation, behind fidelity is adultery" and that, "mysteriously, our love of God is linguistically and psychologically inextricable from our lust" (pp. 361–62). Concludes that the sonnets, therefore, should not be seen as "the pathological impositions of a terror-stricken convert nor the doctrinal expositions of a stolid conformist" but rather as examples of Donne's "permitting the traditional language of devotion to mean what it does mean and opening that language until, having proposed a fallen God, he raised his healing paradox" (p. 363).

๙§ 664. KNIGHTS, L. C. "All or Nothing: A theme in John Donne," in *William Empson: The Man and His Work*, edited by Roma Gill, pp. 109–16. London and Boston: Routledge & Kegan Paul.

Notes that in Donne there is a "conflict between his sense of the enormous importance of his own immediate experience and the sense of his own inadequacy and unimportance," that is, "the immoderate and hydroptic thirst for 'all' (or at any rate for a very widely inclusive experience) clashing with the feeling of being 'nothing'" (p. 109), especially notable in his letters, verse epistles, *Biathanatos*, and the *Anniversaries*. Notes that this conflict is often expressed in terms of the *contemptus mundi* theme or through a rejection of a fragmentary, disappointing world and suggests that Donne found an adequate solution to his sense of nullity only in "a life of austere devotion and duty" (p. 113). Observes that it is only in "The Litanie" that Donne "comes to terms with the all or nothing antithesis in a sober recommendation," and yet it is "his confrontation of nothingness that results in one of his greatest poems" (p. 114)—"A nocturnall upon S. Lucies day," a poem that "by the very energy of the account of 'how it feels to reach absolute zero' and 'how it feels to *think* when you are there', becomes a kind of affirmation . . . a victory over chaos and the sense of nothingness that is its theme" (p. 115).

◄§ 665. KOLIN, PHILIP C. "Donne's 'Obsequies to the Lord Harrington': Theme, Structure, and Image." SoQ 13: 65–82.

Reviews briefly the critical reception of and various critical responses to "Obsequies to the Lord Harrington," maintaining that the poem should be given a higher place than most critics give it. Presents a brief sketch of Harrington's life but argues that the poem is more than a biographical sketch of a promising young gentleman and suggests that it "provides the occasion for some serious meditation by the poet" (p. 69). Points out that "the idea of a corrupt world and the problems of securing corrective information in order to recover virtue are the major issues behind the 'Obsequies,'" shows how the poem "moves through a dialectic of doubt and belief," and illustrates how, "through appropriately created images of measurement and direction, Donne explores the nature and consequences of Harrington's death while setting him up as the symbol of the heavenly guide, much as he did for Prince Henry" (p. 70). Sees the poem as a meditational devotion, structured by a series of eight questions, in which Donne "agonizingly searches for the guideposts of man's spiritual knowledge and for proper ways of acquiring virtue" (p. 70) and notes how Donne alternates between despair and hope until he reaches a final solution. Shows how, "employing a series of images stressing the human instruments of physical measurement—maps, mirrors, compasses, scales, sun dials, and clocks—Donne represents Harrington's potential power to instruct earth-fettered man" and "establishes earthly correspondences for divine wisdom and spiritual assistance" (p. 75). Concludes that, "through his meditations enriched by these images, Donne has arrived at his own accommodated truth," for "he learns that the virtuous man, however brief his stay on earth may be, is still equal to the potential we see in him"(p. 82).

◄§ 666. LEIN, CLAYTON D. "Donne and Ronsard." N&Q n.s. 21: 90–92.

Identifies the possible sources and contexts of Donne's only specific reference to Ronsard, which occurs in prefatory sentences to Problem Four, "Why is there more Variety of Greene than of other Colours?" in MS Ashmole 862. Notes several passages in various of Ronsard's works in which he mentions green eyes (*l'oeil verd*), the figure that Donne refers to. Suggests that Donne may have known several of Ronsard's works and that he may have been influenced by Ronsard's experimentation with stanzaic forms as well as by his exploration of a wide range of amorous attitudes.

⊷§ 667. ————. "Donne's 'The Storme': The Poem and the Tradition."
ELR 4: 137–63.

Maintains that "The Storme" is "a sustained variation upon a standard
rhetorical theme, an adaptation far more extensive, in fact, than even its
most thorough critic to date suspects" (p. 137). Traces the rhetorical tradition that informs the poem and juxtaposes it with classical and Renaissance examples of storm accounts to show "the rigorous classicism of
Donne's poem" that can be observed not only in its theme but also "in
virtually every significant aspect of structure and descriptive detail" (p.
138). Argues that Ovid is the primary model but comments on how Donne
also modified the tradition he borrowed. Notes especially his range of
personification in the poem, which gives it "a grand movement of epic
proportions" (p. 151), and which, in effect, creates "a Christian adaptation
of the type of cosmic, apocalyptic struggle in which Virgil, for example,
placed Aeneas at the beginning of his epic" (p. 152). Suggests that in the
poem Donne explores himself as well as celebrates the expedition: "The
occasion of the storm becomes another opportunity for Donne to contemplate his death, to indulge in another immersion into the void, to marshall his experience in terms of the clashing tensions of Chaos and Creation—all fundamental patterns in his poetry" and argues that "these desires
truly control the poem, create its unique tone, and most easily serve to
differentiate it from its ancestors" (p. 152). Points out that the biblical
allusions to Jonas and Sarah "clarify the psychological center of the poem,"
"create a fascinating modification of the storm tradition and perform complex functions" (p. 159). Concludes that the poem "magnificently demonstrates the pressure Donne's predilection for self-definition placed upon
a formulaic genre and superbly displays his subtlety at coordinating the
two dimensions of form" and that his "craftsmanship brilliantly wove ordinarily discrete descriptive details into a gorgeous unified tapestry of an
unexpected entry into a nightmare realm of chaos with an equally unexpected divine resolution" (p. 163).

⊷§ 668. LEVER, J. W., ed. Sonnets of the English Renaissance. Selected
and edited by J. W. Lever. (Athlone Renaissance Library, gen. ed.,
Geoffrey Bullough.) London: Athlone Press (University of London).
186p.

Briefly outlines the history of the sonnet, especially in England, during
the Renaissance and discusses its major themes, forms, and conventions
(pp. 1–30). Maintains that, although the sonnet was used for a variety of
purposes, its main function was "to chart the intimacies of personal experience" (p. 1). Comments on some of the outstanding characteristics of
the sonnets of Wyatt, Surrey, Sidney, Spenser, Daniel, Drayton, Shakespeare, Greville, William Drummond, William Alabaster, and Donne.
Discusses the Holy Sonnets (pp. 28–30) and notes in them an "intellectual
curiosity and strong sensuous response, together with a characteristic im-

patience with prescribed attitudes" (p. 28). Suggests that "the restless play of thought in these sonnets makes them unique as devotional poems" (p. 28) and points out that "in form Donne's sonnets follow Sidney; both reflect the conflict of reason and emotion, affirmation and doubt, through the duality of octave and sestet, often with a paradoxical conclusion hammered home by the couplet" (p. 30). Fifteen selections from the *Holy Sonnets* (pp. 130–37) with notes (pp. 179–83).

৵§ 669. LINDEN, STANTON J. "The Breaking of the Alembic: Patterns in ✓ Alchemical Imagery in English Renaissance Poetry." *WascanaR* 9: 105–13.
   Contrasts two literary uses of alchemy during the Renaissance. Points out that, from Chaucer onward to Donne and Jonson, alchemy was presented with a satirical intent and became synonymous with greed, deceit, self-delusion, and all kinds of moral depravity. However, before this satirical tradition died out, there also developed (between 1580 and 1630) a new pattern of alchemical usage, one in which alchemy was used metaphorically to suggest growth, change, and even regeneration. Maintains that the poetry of Donne and Herbert gives us the best examples of the way that alchemy was utilized during the transitional period, since they "tend to use alchemy with an awareness and understanding of its full range of denotations, connotations, and associational nuances" (p. 109). Comments briefly but specifically on the range of Donne's uses of alchemy and, while commenting on *The first Anniversary*, notes that "not since the assessment of philosophical or spiritual alchemy occurring near the end of *The Canon Yeoman's Tale* . . . has the art been treated with such respect and nobility" (p. 111).

৵§ 670. LODI, M. K. "Donne's Epithalamic Verse," in *Essays on John Donne: A Quater Centenary Tribute*, edited by Asloob Ahmad Ansari, pp. 86–99. Aligarh: Department of English, Aligarh Muslim University.
   Briefly outlines the history, development, and major conventions of the epithalamion and argues that Donne, though indebted to the tradition and especially to Spenser, made his own original contributions to the genre, especially through his uses of intellectual conceits, extravagant paradoxes, and satire. Outlines the theme and content of each of Donne's three epithalamia and argues that in the "Epithalamion made at Lincolnes Inne" the wit is "too close to effrontery" and the tone lacks "the usual cavalier geniality of Donne" (p. 96) and thus the poem can best be understood as a satire meant to entertain the young wits at the midsummer revels at Lincoln's Inn in 1595.

৵§ 671. MCFARLAND, RONALD E. "Thanksgiving in Seventeenth Century Poetry." *Albion* (Washington State University Press) 6: 294–306.

Surveys the background and tradition of Christian poems of thanksgiving and comments on representative examples written during the seventeenth century in England. Suggests that *La Corona* should be included in a list of major thanksgiving poems but chooses to discuss only three poems in detail that suggest the range and variety of the poem of thanksgiving—Marvell's "Bermudas," Herrick's "A Thanksgiving to God," and Herbert's "The Thanksgiving."

⋙ 672. McGuire, Philip C. "Private Prayer and English Poetry in the Early Seventeenth Century." *SEL* 14: 63–77.

Discusses the influence of private prayer, as opposed to formal discursive meditation, on poetic practice in the early seventeenth century as reflected in six poems by Donne, Jonson, and Herbert. Outlines various contemporaries' attitudes toward, and definitions of, prayer and points out that Renaissance devotionalists "divided private prayer into a preface (which could also be a conclusion) and three major components—confession, invocation, and thanksgiving—which were organized either to praise God or, more frequently, to persuade him" (p. 65). Analyzes Donne's "Thou hast made me" to show that it fits all the rules for a prayer of petition, such as found in Elrathan Parr's *Abba Father*; notes that "Hymne to God my God, in my sicknesse" follows exactly the usual instructions for prayer on one's deathbed found in the devotional manuals and the treatises on *ars moriendi*; that "A Hymne to God the Father" follows the rules for a deathbed confession, as outlined, for instance, in John Clarke's *Holy Incense for the Censers of the Saints*; and that "A Hymne to Christ, at the Authors last going into Germany" is directly linked to prescribed Renaissance prayers before making a journey, such as one discovers in Hieron's *A Helpe unto Devotion*. Concludes that the art of private prayer "functioned as a set of extra-literary 'conventions,' providing subjects, attitudes, and formal principles which poets could join to appropriate poetic forms and conventions" (p. 77).

⋙ 673. McKitterick, David, and R. S. Thomson. "A Donne Discovery." *TLS*, 30 August, p. 930.

Corrects and modifies several points in their previously published article (entry 710). (1) Notes that in the light of orthographic and paleographic evidence the papers in the Huntingdon Records Office can only be most tentatively ascribed to Donne and states that "there must be some doubt as to whether these are by Donne himself or by a copyist with a remarkably similar hand." (2) Suggests that, apart from the draft version of the Goodfriday poem, the "literary quality of the papers suggests a hand other than Donne's" and that, although in the same hand as the poem, the other items "obviously bear little relation to Donne's known work, but as papers associated with the poem they cannot be ignored completely." (3) Notes that Nicolas Barker in a review of the Scolar Press facsimile had already noted that Donne composed with less ease than is ordinarily thought, had cast doubt on Helen Gardner's assumption that Lady Carew and Mrs. Essex Rich were unknown to Donne, and had noted that the poem was written only to Lady Carew, not to the two women, as suggested by the title of the poem in the printed version of 1633. See also Michael Horsnell (entry 654), Nicolas Barker (entry 620), Theodore Hofman (entry 652), R. E. Alton and P. J. Croft (entry 616), and J. Max Patrick (entry 688).

⋙ 674. MAROTTI, ARTHUR F. "Donne and 'The Extasie,'" in *The Rhetoric of Renaissance Poetry: From Wyatt to Milton*, edited by Thomas O. Sloan and Raymond B. Waddington, pp. 140–73. Berkeley, Los Angeles, London: University of California Press.

Offers a detailed reading of "The Extasie." Sees the poem primarily as a defense of conjugal love, "written originally, perhaps, as an exercise in literary imitation, but, nevertheless, rooted in Donne's deepest personal experiences and designed for a coterie audience familiar with *both* his life and his art" (p. 143). Calls the poem Donne's "most complexly argued lyric" (p. 144) and discusses the narrative, dramatic, and rhetorical devices that he employs to manipulate the reader's response. Views the first seven stanzas as an "attention-getting device, the effect of which is to draw us into the poem's world while, at the same time, making us self-conscious about our aesthetic act" (p. 147) and sees the last twelve stanzas as "yet-more-subtle slights of hand" which, after a false start, return the reader, "by masterful indirections, to the erotic situation with which the poem began" (p. 148). Notes that Donne "turns his sceptical intelligence on the philosophical and literary conventions he inherits" and that "no number of citations of Plotinus or Neoplatonic love-philosophers can obscure the basic fact that he could not take seriously the idea of amorous ecstasy as love's supreme expression" (p. 155). Suggests, therefore, that the poem actually "mocks its reader's suspension of disbelief, his too-easy acceptance, as a civilized man of the Renaissance, of love conventions and their philosophical and pseudo-philosophical vocabularies" (p. 155). Holds that the poem is not simply a speculative poem about the relation of the body and soul but also publicizes Donne's own marriage and that he "projects into it his personal experiences and conflicts in such a way that he involves the audience in the poem's emotional dynamics" (p. 158). Concludes that the poem offers the reader "a vision of incarnate, conjugal love set in a rich frame of reference that extends from the bloodstream to the heavenly spheres, from atoms to their Creator, from Plato to the seventeenth century, a love that can be treated comically as well as seriously because it is both profoundly human and wittily self-aware" (p. 173).

❧ 675. MESSENGER, ANN P. "'Adam Pos'd': Metaphysical and Augustan Satire." *WCR* 8, no. 4: 10–11.

Discusses Anne Finch, Countess of Winchilsea's, "Adam Pos'd," a rewriting of part of Donne's *Satyre IV.* Argues that she "took considerable liberties with her model and produced a brief, almost epigrammatic Augustan satire with moral implications, for all its brevity, nearly as wide-ranging as Donne's" (p. 10).

❧ 676. MILLER, CLARENCE H., AND CARYL K. BERREY. "The Structure of Integrity: The Cardinal Virtues in Donne's 'Satyre III.'" *Costerus* n.s. 1: 27–45.

Argues that the major reason for the clarity and integrity of *Satyre III* is that it is carefully structured according to the framework of the cardinal virtues (fortitude, temperance, prudence, and justice), "one of the most persistent patterns in Western ethical thought" (p. 28). Comments on how the basic underlying philosophical concept is based on Plato's division of man's ethical faculties into concupiscible, irascible, and rational powers of the soul, a concept later developed and elaborated on by Christian medieval and Renaissance philosophers and writers in their discussions of the four cardinal virtues. Notes that from the time of St. Augustine Christians focused their attention on "the relationship between virtue conceived naturally according to pagan philosophy and supernatural virtue springing from grace infused by God through Christ" (p. 34), the issue that Donne explores in lines 1–15 of *Satrye III.* Suggests that after this introduction, in which Donne states that "neither compassion nor derision seems effective in instilling religious values," he notes that "it is shameful that pagans should outstrip Christians in attaining religious goals" (p. 37). Sees the remainder of the satire as dividing into four major parts: (1) lines 16–32— a depiction of irreligious and irrational "courage" exhibited by adventurers, soldiers, and duelists; (2) lines 43–69—the portrayal of the tendency of man to seek religion as superficially as he seeks sexual pleasure; (3) lines 69–88—a description of the rational effort needed to find religious truth; and (4) lines 89–110—the depiction of the dangers to the individual conscience posed by unjust claims of civil power. Notes that in *Satyre III* "only prudence is treated quite practically," whereas "the other three virtues are treated mostly in terms of their opposites" (p. 33). Points out also that the diction, imagery, and sentence structure reflect the structure of the whole poem and help explain both the conflicting emotions and the moral integrity of the satiric persona. Suggests that, "before Dryden, perhaps only Donne recaptured the unity of Roman satire" (p. 64).

❧ 677. MINER, EARL. *The Restoration Mode from Milton to Dryden.* Princeton: Princeton University Press. xxiv, 587p.

Mentions Donne throughout this study of the "public mode" of seventeenth-century poetry from Milton to Dryden, contrasting it with the "private mode" of Donne and the "social mode" of Jonson. Defines the public mode and notes that it "tends to suspect what is valuable only apart from all others and to prize what men and women share" (p. xvii). Part I presents an extended definition of the "public mode"; Part II discusses the developments in narrative poetry from 1640 onward; and Part III deals with values (honor, praise, virtue), with a chapter each devoted to libertine poetry and satire. Calls Donne "radically private" and Dryden "radically public" (p. 6) with Jonson occupying a middle ground. Notes that Donne "wrote of the world to reject it" (p. 45) and observes that to Donne "the reality of consciousness and private psychological need is so great that the universe contracts itself to his chamber and the world's last night to a picture in his heart" (p. 7). Briefly comments on Donne's poetic uses of alchemy and discusses in some detail his attempts to alter radically poetic language and prosody and yet sees some likenesses and differences in Donne's attempt to reproduce the rhythm of natural speech and Dryden's experiments along the same line. Points out that Donne, like Rochester, mingles song and satire; that certain lines in Oldham's *Satyr Upon the Jesuits* remind one of "Loves Alchymie"; that Marvell's *Fleckno, an English Priest at Rome* is in the manner of Donne but lacks his dramatic power; and that Dryden's *Eleonora* is modeled on the *Anniversaries*.

⋘§ 678. MONTES DE OCA, MARCO ANTONIO, ed. *El surco y la brasa: Traductores mexicanos.* Selection and prologue by Marco Antonio Montes de Oca. (Letras mexicanas.) Mexico City: Fondo de Cultura Económica. 446p.
Contains Spanish translations of Donne's poetry and prose: (1) two selections from the sermons by Octavio G. Barreda (pp. 50–51); (2) "A Hymne to God the Father" by Jorge Cuesta (p. 69); (3) "Going to Bed" by Octavio Paz (pp. 116–17); (4) "The Sunne Rising" by Jaime García Terrés (pp. 223–24); and (5) "The Flea" by Gerardo Deniz (pp. 344–45).

⋘§ 679. MORILLO, MARVIN. "Donne's 'The Relique' as Satire." *TSE* 21: 47–55.
Discusses "The Relique" as "an altogether consistent and witty piece of anti-'Platonic' satire" (p. 47) and argues that such a reading brings "apparent tonal discrepancies into harmony" (p. 54) and also brings the poem "into that distinguished family of Donne's lyrics that justify and celebrate the perfection of human love, poems that reconcile body to spirit and sanctify sexual union" (p. 55). Comments on each of the stanzas to show that by statement and implication Donne rejects the kind of neuter love extolled by the Petrarchan sonneteers through the uses of erotic images, cynicism, irony, and hyperbolic compliment. Calls the poem a mock encomium that obliquely insists "that 'desire without fruition' does not belong to the world of nature" and that "a sexual love misconstrued through

the blindness of misdevotion" is a "love that belongs to a supernatural realm and requires a Christ as lover" (p. 54). Suggests further that the last stanza may be, in fact, an oblique celebration of sexual love as truly miraculous and that "the culminating irony is that the love celebrated is quite other than what those misled by devotion think it is" (p. 55).

❧ 680. MÜLLER, WOLFGANG G. "Anrede und Selbstgespräch in John Donnes 'Songs and Sonnets.'" *GRM* n.s. 24: 305–23.

Argues that the description of lyric poetry as expressing emotion in a songlike, subjective monologue does not apply to Donne's *Songs and Sonets*. Shows that the lyrical speech in Donne's poetry differs from this classification either because poetic address is used to present self-scrutiny in a dramatic form, or because subjective monologue serves as a medium of analytical self-definition rather than as a medium of giving voice to emotion. Demonstrates with "Womans constancy" that poetic address fulfills the subjective functions of lyric monologue and is not one-half of a dialogue that expects an answer. Classifies five basic types of monologue: theater monologue in front of an audience, monologue for an audience on stage (political speech, persuasion), soliloquy, monologue with one listener (love poem, ode), and monologue in which the poet plays a role as a dramatis persona (Donne's "Breake of day"). Discusses the tradition of poetic address in English lyric poetry and demonstrates that the dramatic form of poetic address in Donne (such as in "The Expiration") has an "authentische, unverwechselbare Ichqualität" (p. 317). Compares Donne's poems of poetic address with his poems of monologue (such as "Loves growth"), in which the affected lover taxes his own feelings. Locates the step from a *semper idem* expressing emotion to a changeable self defining itself as the transition from Renaissance to baroque. Defines the lyrical self as "die Delegation des authentischen Personalen in die Sprachmächtigkeit" (p. 322), and applies this definition to Keats, Gerard Manley Hopkins, Dylan Thomas, the French symbolists, R. M. Rilke, and Gottfried Benn.

❧ 681. NEWTON, RICHARD C. "Donne the Satirist." *TSLL* 16: 427–45.

Argues that the *Satyres* reveal "an intense critical interest on Donne's part in his own character as satirist" and that "the sequence of five Satyres presents the unfolding drama of Donne's exploration of the satiric character, together with the record of his own discoveries" (p. 429). Discusses each of the satires and shows how, in *Satyre V*, the two major themes of all five satires paradoxically come together: "On the one hand we have the character of the satirist—anarchic, destructive, iconoclastic—a character which is to the poet a burden like original sin yet which is at the same time a necessary condition of life," while "on the other hand we have the necessary search for 'constancy' and security, the search for a safe and unafflicted vision of truth" (p. 440). Notes that "the truth discoverable by the satiric character, however, is a truth only of uncertainty" and that, "if we need this truth in order to free ourselves of blindness and anguished suffering, we still cannot find in it the security and clarity which it seems to promise" (pp. 440–41). Points out that "in Satyre I constancy is a joke; in Satyre II it disappears ambiguously; in Satyre III it shows itself necessary to be sought after and at the same time necessarily unattainable"; and then "in Satyre IV we see Donne come to terms at last with the satiric character and the uncertainty it entails" and finally, "in Satyre V, while giving up the search for constancy, Donne shows us that the satirist's uncertainty is the condition of all society" (p. 441). Concludes that "it is in the Satyres that the early Donne most completely encounters that doubting, questioning, and critical aspect of his character and makes it part of his wisdom as a poet and as a man" (p. 445).

682. NICHOLS, OLIVIA MURRAY. "Donne's 'A Lecture upon the Shadow.'" *Expl* 32: Item 52.

Argues that "A Lecture upon the Shadow" is "an intellectual, well-wrought piece of rhetoric" based on Cicero's classical arrangement of *exordium* (lines 1–2), *narratio* (lines 3–8), *expositio* (lines 9–11), *propositio* (lines 12–13), *confirmatio* and *refutatio* (lines 14–24), and *peroratio* (lines 25–26).

683. ONG, WALTER J., S.J. "Gospel, Existence, and Print." *MLQ* 35: 66–77.

Essentially a review article of Gale H. Carrithers, Jr., *Donne at Sermons: A Christian Existential World* (entry 395), and James Gray, *Johnson's Sermons: A Study* (Oxford: Clarendon Press, 1972). Finds Carrithers' approach to Donne's sermons exciting, promising, and enlightening. Agrees that the "present existential frame of mind does enable us to talk more directly than before of such things as the denseness of human existence, the irreducibility of existence to a series of concepts, no matter how numinous or numerous, the uniqueness and isolation of personal consciousness, the deep inarticulate ground of being in all of us, which is in some ways luminous . . . and in other ways dark" (p. 71). Contrasts the sermon with purely literary texts by showing its connection with the liturgy: "it looks to results, to conversion, *metanoia*" (p. 68).

684. OSMOND, ROSALIE. "Body and Soul Dialogues in the Seventeenth Century." *ELR* 4: 364–403.

Discusses the revival of interest in body-soul dialogues in the first half of the seventeenth century and presents a number of reasons for "this apparently anachronistic literary form" making "a sudden and brief appearance between 1602 and 1651 only to die out completely after that date" (p. 364). Suggests that "careful examination of the characteristics of both the form and content of the medieval debates makes it clear that they have much more in common with at least certain aspects of early seventeenth century thought and literature than one might suppose" and yet notes that seventeenth-century writers of body-soul dialogues "can be seen adapting themselves to the demands and influences of the new age" (p. 364). Discusses briefly Donne's view of body-soul relationship in his sermons. Reviews the complexities of seventeenth-century thinking about the roles and responsibilities of the body and soul in sin and notes that, while seventeenth-century writers "can think of body and soul as abstract philosophical concepts, it is not primarily in abstract terms that they write about them" but as "characters playing their roles in the drama of life and death" (p. 377). Comments on Donne's personification of the soul and points out that, although he and his contemporaries "did not consciously believe the soul to be visible, they just as certainly did imagine it to be so" (p. 379) in their poems. Cautions that, although poetic images cannot be literally taken as statements of belief, they do subtly help to form certain theological attitudes and influence the general understanding of certain theological concepts.

⋙ 685. OTTEN, CHARLOTTE F. "Donne's 'The Extasie,' 6." *Expl* 32: Item 58.

Agrees with Claes Schaar (entry 493) that *Balme* (line 16) in "The Extasie" refers to a plant but disagrees with Schaar's notion that the plant simply entangles the lovers' hands and holds them firmly tied. Suggests that "the clue to Donne's allusive use of the plant *balme* and to the meaning of *fast* lies in the Renaissance herbals." Discusses the description of *balme* in several popular herbal manuals, especially John Gerard's *The Herball or Generall Historie of Plantes* (1597, enlarged and amended by Thomas Johnson in 1633, 1636), to show that, "since the juice of the leaves of the *balme* plant rubbed on the hives attracts and nourishes bees, causing them to stick together, *fast* in Donne's poem describes the property of the *balme* which cements the lovers' hands together in a nourishing and sustaining union." Notes further that *entergraft* (line 9) "reinforces this image, since grafting requires an adhesive substance to make the graft and the tree stick to each other, as the Renaissance agricultural manuals show." Concludes, therefore, that Donne "uses the leaves of *balme* as a fragrant glue rubbed on lovers' hands to form an indivisible graft; that is all the cement required to graft the image to a poem which is a 'dialogue of one.'" For a reply, see Susan C. Kemper (entry 837).

⋙ 686. OUSBY, HEATHER D. "Donne and Gilpin: Another Conjecture." *N&Q* n.s. 21: 89–90.

Suggests that perhaps two passages about painting in "Of Nigrina. 57" and "Of the Same. 62" in Everard Guilpin's *Skialetheia* (London, 1598) may have been suggested by Donne's epigram "Phryne," in which he says, "Thy flattering picture, *Phryne*, is like thee, / Onely in this, that you both painted be." Cautions that a definite chronological relationship between the epigrams of Guilpin and that of Donne cannot be made since Donne could have written his epigram any time between the early 1590s and 1619.

◄§ 687. ———. "Donne's 'Epithalamion Made at Lincolnes Inne,' 90."
    Expl 32: Item 49.
Agrees with John Shawcross in *The Complete Poetry of John Donne* (1967) that in line 90 of "Epithalamion made at Lincolnes Inne" the word *t'embowell* may be a pun, meaning "to hide in the inward parts," but suggests a second possible pun on the word *embowell*, meaning "off-spring." Notes that, since Renaissance epithalamia traditionally refer to the birth of children and since Donne specifically refers to motherhood in line 87, line 90 may mean "that the bridegroom will engender an heir."

◄§ 688. PATRICK, J. MAX. "A Donne Discovery." *SCN* 32: 72–73.
Calls attention to and summarizes an article by R. S. Thomson and David McKitterick (entry 710). Calls the documents discovered by Thomson and McKitterick "significant Donne discoveries" but warns that in this case, just as in the case of the so-called Robert Herrick Commonplace Book, "one must be cautious about accepting attribution of the handwriting of these 17th-century authors and about crediting them unhesitatingly with full responsibility for these materials, if only because, in both instances, some radical changes in standard conceptions of these authors would be necessitated" (p. 73). See also David McKitterick and R. S. Thomson (entry 673), Michael Horsnell (entry 654), Nicolas Barker (entry 620), Theodore Hofman (entry 652), and R. E. Alton and P. J. Croft (entry 616).

◄§ 689. POLLOCK, JOHN J. "Donne's 'Lamentations of Jeremy' and the
    Geneva Bible." *English Studies* (Amsterdam) 55: 513–15.
Argues that, although Donne may have used the Vulgate for his translation of Tremellius's Latin in "Lamentations of Jeremy," "the actual textual evidence indicates that it is more likely he used the Geneva Bible, if not in place of, at least in addition to the Vulgate" and that, although he probably used the Authorized Version also (noting that "the frequency of words and phrases identical to that translation suggests the poem was written after 1611"), Donne "apparently turned to the Geneva Bible considerably more often" (p. 513). Notes that Donne "appears to turn to the Geneva Bible roughly two or three times more often than to the Authorized Version in choosing equally suitable nouns and verbs to translate Tremellius's Latin"; that "adjectives, adverbs, tense, and number also favor the Geneva Bible, though by much smaller and statistically insignificant percentages"; and that "particular sections of Donne's paraphrase (lines 249–66, for example) show a fairly large density of Genevan nouns and verbs, which also suggests that Donne had the Geneva Bible before him" (p. 514). Argues that the recognition of these facts is important in arriving at a more accurate text and in determining the nature and extent of Donne's

own poetic contribution. Lists and compares notations from the Geneva Bible with those of Grierson and Gardner to show that, "although in a number of places Donne's poem is closer to the Vulgate than to the Tremellius text, in each of these cases either the Geneva text or the Authorized Version can 'explain' the deviation from Tremellius just as well as, and often better than, the Vulgate can" (pp. 513–14).

ᵛᶳ 690. ———. "A Note on Donne's 'Elegie on the L. C.'" *N&Q* n.s. 21: 92–93.

Rejects John Shawcross's suggestion in *The Complete Poetry of John Donne* (1967) that in "Elegie on the L. C." (lines 9–13) Donne alludes to the popular fable about an oak tree and a briar that is found in Aesop and exemplified by Spenser in the February eclogue of *The Shepeardes Calender*. Argues that, "since Donne's poem deals with the fact that a good and holy man has died and left his family and friends to honour his memory, the moralistic theme of Spenser and Aesop could not possibly be relevant" (p. 92). Suggests that Donne had in mind the common metaphor, found in Latin and English love poetry (Horace, Catullus, Shakespeare), of comparing husbands and wives to a tree and vine. Argues that Donne perhaps transformed the popular metaphor of marriage into a religious one "to indicate the spiritual love, as well as dependence, which characterized the gentleman's relationship with those about him while he lived" (p. 93).

ᵛᶳ 691. PORTER, PETER. "Thomas Campion (1567–1620), Sir Walter Raleigh (?1552–1618), Fulke Greville (1554–1628), John Donne (1572–1631)," in *The English Poets from Chaucer to Edward Thomas*, compiled by Peter Porter and Anthony Thwaite, pp. 95–107. London: Secker and Warburg.

Briefly comments on Donne's life, personality, and poetry (pp. 102–7), calling him, "except for Shakespeare, the greatest poet of the age," and points out that his poetry "changed the entire course of English poetry" (p. 102). Comments briefly on certain major features of Donne's poetry, such as its blend of intellectual power and passionate feeling, its union of cleverness with sincerity, its uses of rhetoric and hyperbole, and its conceits. Suggests that as both a secular and a sacred poet Donne primarily casts himself in the role of a wooer. Comments briefly on "The Flea," especially its reflection of the intensity of Donne's regard for physical love; on "The Perfume," especially its dramatic effects; and on "Since she whom I lov'd," especially its quiet tone and euphonious language. Suggests that "England was not unaffected by the Counter-Reformation and Donne's baroque poems are full of the hysteria which accompanied the return to faith on the Continent" (p. 107).

ᵛᶳ 692. RAIZADA, HARISH. "Donne as a Satirist," in *Essays on John Donne: A Quater Centenary Tribute*, edited by Asloob Ahmad Ansari, pp.

100–116. Aligarh: Department of English, Aligarh Muslim University.

Surveys the themes, content, and major stylistic features of Donne's *Satyres*. Finds *Satyre I* more realistic and dramatic than other Elizabethan satires, see *Satyre II* as least individualistic, praises *Satyre III* for its use of the extended conceit and for its focus, finds *Satyre IV* the least interesting and without plan and dominant mood, and rejects *Satyre V* as the least brilliant and the most self-consciously witty. Suggests that, although the satires are often "marked by an unusual energy and a richness of contemporary references," they "do not escape the weaknesses of the general run of Elizabethan satires" (p. 107), such as metrical roughness, piling up of details, and lack of focus. Comments on the satiric impulse in Donne that finds better expression in some of the *Songs and Sonets* and notes that several of Donne's major satirical targets, such as corrupt courtiers and court life, greed, inconstancy, corrupt lawyers, and so on find their way into his love poetry and that to these favorite targets he adds such abuses as Petrarchan adoration and other extravagant, sentimental forms of love. Suggests that Donne's use of a satirical, comical, and ironical tone in his love poetry often makes it difficult for his readers to determine the mood and tone of individual poems.

◆§ 693. Ricks, Christopher. "Empson's Poetry," in *William Empson: The Man and His Work*, edited by Roma Gill, pp. 145–207. London and Boston: Routledge & Kegan Paul.

Discusses how Empson's poetry was influenced by his critical appreciation and understanding of Donne's poetry and comments on Empson's criticism of Donne and how it reflects his own personal concerns. Notes that, "for Empson, and for his poems, Donne's love-poems embody a defiance of church and state" and "celebrate freedom and independence" (p. 167) and "are alive with thought and feeling about begetting and posterity and about the relation between a true worldliness and a true unworldliness" (p. 171). Calls Donne "the poet who means most to Empson's poems" (p. 147) and observes that Empson's metaphors, like Donne's, "are not reduced to blank obedience but are allowed to ask for themselves a richer presence" (p. 186). Comments especially on Empson's views on Donne in his essay, "Donne the Space Man" (*KR* 19 [1957]: 337–99).

◆§ 694. Roston, Murray. *The Soul of Wit: A Study of John Donne*. Oxford: The Clarendon Press. 236p. PR 41 D65 A67

Attempts to show the unity between Donne's secular and religious poetry and compares his techniques, attitudes, and perspectives to those of mannerist artists. Chapter 1, "The Two Worlds" (pp. 1–20), comments on modern critical evaluations of and approaches to Donne's poetry and maintains that "the terminology so widely applied to Donne since T. S. Eliot's essay [of 1921] needs to be readjusted" (p. 13). Objects to modern efforts to regard Donne's poetry as an amalgamation of disparate experiences "as though he were joining two equally valid worlds, the factual and the emotional, to create the poetic artefact" and argues that the poetry "constitutes rather a transmutation of the actual, as its spiritual significance is perceived" (p. 13). Stresses the interrelatedness of Donne's secular and religious poetry and argues against "any attempt to separate human experience into neatly divided categories" (p. 12). Suggests that the key to the underlying unity of the earlier and later poems is wit. Presents a reading of "The Sunne Rising" to show that even in his lighthearted amorous verse Donne's levity and wit have a serious undercurrent and that in his playfulness he is fully commited to the world of the spirit. Chapter 2, "The Mannerist Perspective" (pp. 21–70), surveys and defends the nature and function of mannerist art, distinguishing it from both Renaissance and baroque art. Uses mannerist religious art to explain Donne and suggests that "the common denominator of religious mannerism is the dematerialization of the physical universe and the tormented striving towards a more satisfying spiritual reality beyond the empirically verifiable world" (p. 69). Finds parallels in perspective and technique between Donne's poetry and the art of such mannerists as El Greco and Tintoretto. Chapter 3, "Shimmering Logic" (pp. 71–107), argues that Donne is much less logical than most critics think and suggests that the complex movement of a Donne poem "is constructed with extraordinary subtlety specifically in order to create a spring-board for the leap into the mysterious or transcendental" (p. 75). Sees a connection between Donne's use of pseudo-logic and mannerist illusion and suggests that his various witty uses of logic simply underscore his faith in a world that is beyond the limited physical and rational world of man. Argues that Donne's "poetic wit, with its grotesque juxtaposition and deceptive reasoning, offered a perfect medium for expressing that mistrust of the objective" (p. 107) that pervaded Counter-Renaissance thinking. Notes also that "the disconcerting element in Donne's writing is his unique capacity for embracing both mannerist extremes—the teasing and the solemn—often within the same poem" (p. 90). Observes that Donne's love poems and his religious poems share "a penchant for erecting a façade of superficial wit or fortuitous word-play through which some more lasting truth is gradually perceived" (p. 97) and finds parallels between this technique and those of the mannerists. Chapter 4, "The Wit of Illusion" (pp. 108–49), presents a reading of "The Flea" to show that Donne typically "loves to coax us into a novel, unconventional viewpoint by means of a speaker whose adroit inversion of cliché and intellectual vitality is hard to resist; but once coaxed into that viewpoint, we discover to our amused chagrin that we have been duped, and the speaker has already swung off in a new direction, leaving us beached on a dialectical sandbank" (p. 108). Analyzes "Loves growth" and "Song: Sweetest love, I do not goe" to show that Donne's subtle shifts in logic, uses of deceptive reasoning, sliding metaphors, and illusory wit are distinctively his and yet reflect the illusory perspective of mannerist art. Argues that Donne is not a Neoplatonist, even in "The Extasie," and that his world is "too perverse, as well as too fascinating in its contradictions, delights, and sorrows to be neatly fitted into any idealized, harmonious scheme" (p. 142). Discusses in detail "The Dreame" to show that, although the poem is light and fanciful, it embodies, as do most of the poems in the *Songs and Sonets*, a serious viewpoint. Chapter 5, "The Paradox of Faith" (pp. 150–220), discusses Donne's religious poetry, especially the *Holy Sonnets*, "Goodfriday, 1613. Riding Westward," and the hymns, and argues that there is an "inner continuity which, belying surface differences, unites the secular with the devotional poetry" (p. 151). Maintains that in the religious poems Donne did not repudiate his earlier concerns "but allowed those themes submerged in his secular verse to rise to the surface and gain a new prominence in their religious setting" (p. 150). Discusses his uses of secular and sexual imagery in his religious poetry and comments on how his "natural penchant for the perverse, complex, and the contradictory afforded him a rare protection against that pietism which has spoilt so much religious verse" (p. 154). Finds parallels between Donne's disruption of traditional norms and similar tendencies in the art of Caravaggio, Tintoretto, Rosso, and Zurburan. Compares the spiritualized eroticism of Bernini's *Ecstasy of St. Teresa* and Donne's sense of unity between divine and human love. Denies that Donne is a "sacred parodist" but sees him rather as belonging to the Counter-Reformation tradition "with its encouragement to cultivate the bodily senses imaginatively, as a means of glimpsing the celestial" (p. 182). Discusses Donne's views on death, time, space, and eternity to show how they reflect his mannerist perspective. Comments on his interest in science and notes that "in his sympathetic response to scientific thought and experimentation, he is intrigued primarily not by the clear rules and indisputable proofs which such investigation provides, but by the inner contradictions it discloses" and points out that "he seizes upon such anomalies in order to justify his own belief that, in the final analysis, the answers to man's pressing problems are not to be found in the neatly organized world of empirical reasoning" (p. 209).

৵§ 695. RUFFO-FIORE, SILVIA. "A New Light on the Suns and Lovers in Petrarch and Donne." *FI* 8: 546–56.
    Reprinted as Chapter 5 in *Donne's Petrarchism: A Comparative View* (entry 863), pp. 70–79.
    Argues that in "The Sunne Rising" Donne "presents a dramatic reconciliation of the sterile world of Petrarchan adoration with the fruitful world of reciprocated love" and adjusts "the remote and passive Petrarchan vision of love to the necessities of actual existence" (p. 546). Notes that the subject matter of the poem is neither original nor revolutionary but that "what *is* innovative is the unusual way that Donne combines Petrarchan ingredients, extending and refining them to produce a poem offering an insight into his mature vision of love as a feasible reconciliation of time with eternity" (p. 546). Argues that "the situation it dramatizes, the solu-

tion it offers, and the language by which both are projected can be understood more clearly once viewed within the context of Petrarchan motifs, idiom, and behavior which the poem reshapes" (p. 546). Compares Donne's use of the *alba* form and sun image with Petrarch's use to show "how Donne assimilated and transmogrified the Petrarchan mode" (p. 546). Suggests that such a comparison indicates that Donne's debt to Petrarch may be greater than traditional criticism has previously acknowledged and, at the same time, "offers some insight into the precise relationship between the imitative and unique elements of Donne's poetry, while suggesting alternate readings of his *Songs* as a whole by comparison with the broader Petrarchan context" (pp. 546–47).

≥§ 696. SCHEER-SCHÄZLER, BRIGITTE. "Zur Tradition von John Donnes *The Sunne Rising.*" *Arcadia* 9: 235–50.
Argues that many of Donne's themes are often less original than many critics assume and suggests that his true originality emerges in his skillful handling of traditional themes. Examines in detail "The Sunne Rising" to show that its themes are anticipated in the works of Ovid, Antonius Flaminius, Prudentius, Giraut de Bornelhs, and Spenser.

≥§ 697. SEGEL, HAROLD B. *The Baroque Poem: A Comparative Survey.* New York: E. P. Dutton & Co. xx, 328p.
Presents "a comprehensive survey of the Baroque: the state of scholarship in the field, problems in the definition and use of Baroque as a term and concept, the relationship of mannerism to Baroque, the political, religious, scientific, and philosophical background of the age, the possible impact of non-literary events on the evolution of Baroque taste, art, and outlook, the various types of Baroque poetry and aspects of Baroque poetic style" and illustrates "points made in the first, or survey, part of the book by giving a broad selection of representative poems, mostly lyrics, in the original languages and accompanying English translations" (pp. xix–xx). Contains 150 poems from the following literatures: English, American, Dutch, German, French, Italian, Spanish, Mexican, Portuguese, Polish, Modern Latin, Czech, Croatian, and Russian. Mentions Donne throughout and regards him as a baroque poet. Notes that, "allowing for essential theological incompatibilities, a stylistic comparison of sermons by the Protestant John Donne and his counterparts in Spain and Orthodox countries of Eastern Europe discloses far more similarities than differences" (p. 58). Notes that love in baroque poems often becomes either a poeticized eroticism or an elaborate wit. Includes three of the *Holy Sonnets* (pp. 147–48) as well as "Going to Bed," "A Valediction: of weeping," "The Flea," and "The Extasie" (pp. 261–65).

≥§ 698. SELDEN, RAMAN. "Hobbes and Late Metaphysical Poetry." *JHI* 35: 197–210.
Reevaluates Hobbes's aesthetic and psychological theories to provide a

basis for a reconsideration of his relationship with poetry and suggests that "it is possible to perceive certain historically significant analogies between Hobbes' mechanico-materialism and some late metaphysical poetry" (p. 197). Suggests that the notion of a School of Donne is too simplistic and that "the conventional placing of the poetry of Benlowes, Cleveland, Randolph, and Cowley as a decadent form of Donne's poetry needs to be reconsidered, not necessarily with a view to disturbing established *valuations* of these poets (though this may occur), but rather to substituting a more positive and particular description for the conventionally attributed 'decadence'" (p. 209). Notes that in Donne's poetry scholastic terms "still possess the ambiance of their original 'meanings,' whereas in Cleveland, that ambiance has been scoured of its deposits: scholasticism has become mock-scholasticism" (p. 209). Suggests, therefore, "that the decade of the 1640's is marked by a hectic revaluation of older modes of thought, not only in philosophy, but in other 'worlds' too (fictional, political, social)," and that Hobbes's mechanical conception of nature "represents an aggressive reaction to older conceptions, and, in effect, deflects the complex levels of royalist thought into a lower (more naturalistic) trajectory" (p. 210).

◄§ 699. SELLIN, PAUL R. "The Hidden God: Reformation Awe in Renaissance English Literature," in *The Darker Vision of the Renaissance: Beyond the Fields of Reason*, edited, with introduction by Robert S. Kinsman, pp. 147–96. (UCLA Center for Medieval and Renaissance Studies, Contributions VI.) Berkeley, Los Angeles, London: University of California Press.
Contrasts the theology found in *Everyman* with that of the Reformers: "unlike much art following the advent of the Reformation, *Everyman* exhibits a great deal of sureness about how God relates to man" (p. 150), whereas, unlike "the anthropocentric benevolence exhibited in the play, the 'new' irrationality places the main emphasis on the absolute majesty and sovereignty of God, and for most of the great figures of the Reformation those attributes were the cornerstone of their theology" (p. 153). Discusses the transforming effects of Reformation thinking on literature of the period, especially on Elizabethan and Jacobean tragedy and on serious lyric poetry. Suggests that Donne's *Holy Sonnets*, as well as *La Corona*, reflect "the impact that Reformation preoccupation with the arcane 'irrationality' of God exercised on the materials and imaginations of English poets and on the minds to which they attempted to appeal" (p. 195). Comments in some detail on "As due by many titles" and "If poysonous mineralls," and, to a lesser extent, on "At the round earths imagin'd corners," "Spit in my face you Jews," and "Batter my heart," as well as on *La Corona*. Suggests that whether or not he agreed theologically with the doctrine of double predestination, "it is easy to imagine Donne, for instance, tailoring personae to the prepossessions of his audience" (p. 195). Concludes that "to the 'lunacy' of the northern Renaissance, then, one can

pay this tribute: in the concept of the hidden God, the sense of awe at fate and destiny which antiquity once felt and used was brought back into the experience of Western man and placed at the service of poetry" (p. 196).

📖 700. SHAWCROSS, JOHN T. "The Poet as Orator: One Phase of His Judicial Pose," in *The Rhetoric of Renaissance Poetry: From Wyatt to Milton*, edited by Thomas O. Sloan and Raymond B. Waddington, pp. 5–36. Berkeley, Los Angeles, London: University of California Press.

Discusses the use of the forensic mode through the rhetorical technique of *distributio-recapitulatio* ("the citing of a series of specific facts or arguments followed by a summing up or restating of these same facts or arguments in brief form" [p. 7]) in various Renaissance poems, including Donne's "The Message" and "The Prohibition." Suggests that such a study will demonstrate "(1) that this technique, employed in various poems of the period, offers another approach to rhetorical analysis of literature, (2) that the forensic mode is employable in 'creative' literature, (3) that the poems employing this technique must be read differently from the way they usually are, and (4) that recognition of this mode of persuasion in poetry of the English Renaissance reinforces the view of the poet as maker, not poet as philosopher or poet as emotionalist" and that "this awareness in turn goes a long way in separating the lyric from the epic, from dramatic poetry, and from didactic poetry . . . and . . . from other kinds of poems which are often categorized under the catch-all word 'lyric'" (pp. 6–7). Points out that, in his use of the forensic mode in "The Message," Donne becomes, as it were, "the prosecuting attorney in iambic" (p. 24) and gives the reader a portrait of a poor loser who asks not for a judgment from his mistress but rather for the reader to judge the worthiness of his plaint. Points out that, although Donne mixes the deliberative and forensic modes in "The Prohibition," "his stance is that of the forensic orator who hopes to achieve his ends by justifying the action he recommends" (p. 25). Notes, however, that neither poem can be easily categorized. Concludes, from a study of the forensic mode, that a lyric can be defined as "a shorter poem in which the author intends to produce a successful literary creation by specific, chosen techniques, devices, form, language, and the like, in a competitive spirit (ultimately) for evaluation by his readers"—a definition that "assumes the poet's function as rhetor and his recognition of that function" (p. 35). Suggests that arguments about Donne's sincerity in such poems as "The good-morrow" or "The Extasie" are "meaningless and beside the point when 'lyric' is viewed in this way" (p. 35).

📖 701. SHIBLES, WARREN. "John Donne," in *Death: An Interdisciplinary Analysis*, pp. 365–68. Whitewater, Wis.: The Language Press.

Comments on Donne's views on death, immortality, and resurrection and briefly notes the pervasive use of images, conceits, and metaphors on death in his poetry. States that Donne "was preoccupied with the sensual aspects of physical death and even jellied putrefaction" (p. 366), that he links love and death in his poetry, and that he often pictures himself as dead. Maintains that he did not believe in the immortality of the soul nor in resurrection: "His final view was one of doubt" (p. 368).

⋘ 702. SLOAN, THOMAS O. "The Crossing of Rhetoric and Poetry in the English Renaissance," in *The Rhetoric of Renaissance Poetry: From Wyatt to Milton*, edited by Thomas O. Sloan and Raymond B. Waddington, pp. 212–42. Berkeley, Los Angeles, London: University of California Press. *PR 533 S5*
Discusses the importance of rhetoric in Renaissance poetry, especially *inventio*, and its radical transformation in English rhetorical theory between Wyatt and Milton—"when the Ramists revised rhetorical theory in such a way that they made the orator's creative process totally unlike the poet's" and "when rhetorical theory converged with devotional theory and once more established common ground, for a while at least, between orators and poets" (p. 214). Sees Donne as at odds with the "new rhetoric." Comments on "To E. of D. with Six Holy Sonnets" (pp. 223–25) and argues that Donne analyzes the creative process, which, to him, is neither impersonal nor systematic. Argues that in Donne's poems invention and judgment are not creative arts but are only the passive, "feminine" elements that need the "hot Masculine Flame" of wit to transform them into true poetry.

⋘ 703. SLOAN, THOMAS O., AND RAYMOND B. WADDINGTON, eds. *The Rhetoric of Renaissance Poetry: From Wyatt to Milton*. Berkeley, Los Angeles, London: University of California Press.
A collection of ten original essays by various hands that considers the effects of rhetoric on English Renaissance poetry. Although Donne is mentioned in several of the essays, see primarily the following, each of which has been separately entered in this bibliography: (1) John T. Shawcross, "The Poet as Orator: One Phase of His Judicial Pose" (pp. 5–36); (2) Raymond B. Waddington, "Shakespeare's Sonnet 15 and the Art of Memory" (pp. 96–122); (3) Arthur F. Marotti, "Donne and 'The Extasie'" (pp. 140–73); and (4) Thomas O. Sloan, "The Crossing of Rhetoric and Poetry in the English Renaissance" (pp. 212–42).

⋘ 704. SLOANE, MARY COLE. "Emblem and Meditation: Some Parallels in John Donne's Imagery." *SAB* 39, ii: 74–79. *PB 156*
Points out that emblem and meditation "meet as interior drama" in Donne's poetry and that this meeting "helps to account for the peculiar kind of sensuosity one finds in Donne's imagery" (p. 74). Notes, for instance, that in the opening lines of "A Valediction: of weeping" "the symbols are either acting or being acted upon" and "it is, therefore, not merely the figures in the poem but the objectified ideas themselves that are doing the acting" (p. 75). Finds Quarles's emblems especially useful "as an aid

to the understanding of the emblem's relationship to the 'Holy Sonnets' as meditations" and suggests that "at least part of the importance of these pictures [of Amor and Anima] lies in the fact that they are visual manifestations of the tendency to transfer the iconography of profane love to the province of divine love" (pp. 75–76). Shows that, just as the erotic imagery and dramatic elements that can be found in the religious emblem were attempts to involve the reader emotionally through his senses, so the meditation was an attempt to involve the meditator dramatically in a vividly realized religious scene. Illustrates this concept by examining a number of passages from the *Holy Sonnets* and concludes that, when viewed in combination, the emblem and meditation "provide both iconographical tradition and situational milieu consistent with Donne's 'metaphysical' conceits" (p. 79).

🥬 705. STRINGER, GARY A. "Donne's 'The Primrose': Manna and Numerological Dalliance." *EIRC* 1: 23–29.

Comments on certain technical features of "The Primrose," specifically on the significance of the manna image in lines 1–4 and the cynical enigma of lines 18–20: "Since there must reside / Falshood in woman, I could more abide, / She were by art, then Nature falsify'd." Argues that an understanding of these two cruxes and the relationship between them "will lead us to a fuller understanding of 'The Primrose' and show that this poem typifies Donne's poetic technique as well as a significant strain in his philosophy of human love" (pp. 23–24). Explains the manna image by suggesting that, "since women are equated with primroses in the poem, the image of dew drops transformed into provender anticipates and forms a paradigm of Donne's subsequent sophistical transmutation of men into sexual victuals for ravenous women of the last stanza of the poem" and claims that in lines 18–20 Donne is saying "that since true loves, both flowers and women, are falsifications, perverse mutations of nature, and since the normal woman, represented by the five-petaled rose, is inevitably false, promiscuous, in nature, he prefers the ordinary to the unusual kind of falseness and proposes to justify his preference by *his own poetic art*" (p. 25). Suggests that by lines 18–20 Donne "announces his intention to do for woman what the imagined shower of rain would do for the primroses at his feet" and, consequently, in the third stanza "disperses a shower of wit upon women that provides them with ample food for their lust" (p. 26). Suggests that the numerology in the last stanza should thus be seen as the art that Donne has promised and "not merely as an arcane philosophy of numbers he jumped into without warning" (p. 26). Argues, then, that "The Primrose" is "partly about art and the relationship of art to truth" and is "not primarily about Pythagora's numerology and does not derive its validity from it" (p. 27). Points out that the poem is typical of Donne's art in two ways: (1) it exemplifies that many of his conceits are 'self-explanatory or, as one might say, auto-exegetical," that their language is "reflexive rather than referential" (p. 27), and that Donne "characteristically extends the conceit to shape an organic poem that reveals its own internal structure and meaning" (p. 28) and (2) it exemplifies the dramatic quality of many of Donne's lyrics, which have about them the appearance of "a spontaneous, self-directed logic" (p. 29).

◆§ 706. SULLIVAN, ERNEST W., II. "Post Seventeenth-Century Texts of John Donne's *Biathanatos.*" *PBSA* 68: 373–90.

Argues that all post-seventeenth-century texts of *Biathanatos*, both selected passages from the work and complete editions, are unreliable and unauthoritative. Maintains that the only known extant manuscript, given to the Bodleian Library in 1642 by Lord Herbert of Cherbury (shelfmark Ms. e Musaeo 131), which contains extensive notes and one correction of sixteen words in Donne's hand, is the most authoritative text. Argues that post-seventeenth-century texts are unreliable, "not just because they rely on the quarto [first edition] as their copy text (even Jessopp introduces Bodleian manuscript readings into his copy of the quarto rather than vice versa), but because they (1) misrepresent their faithfulness to their copy text (Simpson, Hayward, Hebel, Gardner and Healy), or (2) rely on one of these unfaithful texts (as do Hillyer, Garrod, Coffin, and Mark) or (3) are much more incomplete than their editor (Jessopp) states" (p. 390). Refers the reader to his doctoral dissertation, "A Critical, Old-spelling Edition of John Donne's *Biathanatos*" (UCLA, 1973, University Microfilms order #73–16, 704).

◆§ 707. SULLIVAN, MARTIN. "Voice from the past." *Spectator*, 12 January, p. 39.

As current Dean of St. Paul's, calls attention to a moving passage about the existence of God from a sermon that Donne delivered at Old St. Paul's on the Feast Day, 25 January, in 1628 or 1629. Comments on the relevance of the passage to modern times and detects in it "an autobiographical unveiling of Donne's own soul." Notes also that the famous portrait of Donne by an unknown painter still hangs in the dining room of the Deanery of St. Paul's. Reproduces some unfavorable comments on Donne by Dean Inge and disagrees with them.

◆§ 708. SWIFT, ASTRID, ed. "John Donne," in *Die englische Satire*, pp. 41–48. (Uni-Taschenbücher, 381.) Heidelberg: Quelle & Meyer.

Reproduces *Satyre II* (in English). Briefly describes Donne's development as a satirist and places him within the historical context of the English tradition of satire. Compares and contrasts Donne with Roman models, especially Persius, Horace, and Juvenal.

◆§ 709. TARLINSKAYA, M. G. "Rim Stroki i netr angliyskogo Ryatistopnogo yanba." *Moskovskii gosuudarstriennyi pedegogisheskii Instituta inostrannykh* 73: 305–13.

Presents a comparative statistical study of the accentual line structure of nineteen poets, including Donne. Notes the number and distribution of strongly stressed syllables on the ictic and non-ictic positions of an iambic line-scheme and comments on rhythmical line variants and the meter of English pentameter verse. Regards Donne and Jonson as unique among seventeenth-century poets and notes that Donne's poetry reflects a "loosening of assimilated forms."

∾§ 710. THOMSON, R. S., AND DAVID MCKITTERICK. "A Donne Discovery: John Donne's Kimbolton Papers." *TLS*, 16 August, pp. 869–73.

Notes that in 1952, through the cooperation of the Duke of Manchester, a large collection of Montague family papers that had previously lain undisturbed in the stables of Kimbolton Castle was deposited in the Huntingdon Records Office. Observes that in 1881 the Historical Manuscript Commission removed some of the important items in the collection to the Public Records Office, including the holograph of Donne's "A letter to the Lady Carey, and Mrs Essex Riche, From Amyens," which was not recognized as Donne's until 1970 and which is now at the Bodleian Library. Announces that in the present collection in the Huntingdon Records Office the authors have discovered six important documents: (1) an early draft of "Goodfriday, 1613. Riding Westward," entitled "Meditation upon a Goodfriday, ryding from London towards Exceter, westward"; (2) a draft of a letter by Donne to a lady who was a mutual friend of the Earl of Southampton; (3) a draft of an unpublished devotional essay on preparations for receiving Holy Communion; (4) some notes on the subject of conscience; (5) a fragment of some notes from an unidentified book; and (6) a broken quotation and note from Matthaeus Westmonasteriensis entitled *Flores historicarum* (London, 1570). Suggests that the first four items were corrected and amended by Donne. Suggests also various possibilities for how these documents came to be in the possession of the Montague family and postulates that Robert Rich, who visited Donne in Frankfurt in 1612, may have taken the entire bundle back with him to England. Presents transcriptions of the first five items (along with photocopies of items 3 and 4). Tentatively suggests that the draft of the Goodfriday poem was Donne's own copy that he later developed and notes variants between it, the printed version in the 1633 edition, and the texts offered by Grierson and Gardner. Proposes that the title in the Manchester manuscript suggests that the poem may have been written in 1610 and that the mention of Exeter may suggest that Donne is alluding to a visit he made to Exeter in that year to meet with Matthew Sutcliffe, Dean of Exeter, who only a month later received a charter from James I to establish a new college at Chelsea to combat papist controversialists. Supports this notion by observing that the distress and anguish in the poem are more than that of being forced to travel on Good Friday and suggests that Donne may also be recording his still troubled conscience about entering the Church. Proposes also that the second item in the collection may have been written in 1612 to Elizabeth Vernon, Southampton's wife, while Donne was in Germany. Comments very briefly on items 3 and 4, suggesting that the latter may have been written between 1609 and 1612, when Donne was seriously engaged in theological controversy. Suggests that the documents show that Donne found writing difficult and composed very slowly. See also David McKitterick and R. S. Thomson (entry 673). For replies, see Nicolas Barker (entry 620), Theodore Hofman (entry 652), R. E. Alton and P. J. Croft (entry 616), and J. Max Patrick (entry 688).

෴ 711. TOURNEY, LEONARD D. "Convention and Wit in Donne's *Elegie* on Prince Henry." *SP* 71: 473–83.
Regards "Elegie upon the untimely death of the incomparable Prince Henry" as "one of the more curious specimens of Renaissance funeral poetry" and tries to show "how Donne adapted the traditional matter of its genre to produce one of the great funeral poems of the seventeenth century" (p. 473). Discusses the main characteristics of the Renaissance funeral elegy and argues that, "while the poem is properly located in this venerable poetic tradition, it is wrought with such rhetorical verve, molded by such originality in handling standard elegiac formulas, that its conventional base is likely to be missed in what most moderns will consider an inordinately dense matrix of extravagant praise and fantastic speculation" (p. 474). Outlines the argument of the poem, points out its conventional themes and Donne's original treatment of traditional topoi, and maintains that, although Donne's praise is indeed lavish, "it is not senseless," for he exhibits "both insight and genuine feeling" (p. 475). Shows that the poem is more than simply a lament for a dead prince and becomes "an act of contemplation or meditation, with just that subjectivity, gravity, and logical rigor characteristic of such an exercise" and that for Donne the untimely death of the prince "is not pathetic but an intellectual problem" (pp. 476–77). Argues that "it is Henry's role as Christian Prince that is the intellectual fulcrum of the poem" (p. 478) and shows that Donne's argument, then, "is both an original version of a traditional topos and a vivid demonstration of the tenuousness of faith and reason in a fallen world" (p. 480) and that his conclusion "modifies a familiar elegiac topos, the deceased's pre-possession of heaven," which he does "by redefining the nature of heaven and its bliss" and "by boldly spiritualizing human love in the neo-Platonic fashion of his love lyrics" (p. 481). Concludes, therefore, that, while the poem "memorializes a great prince and the devotion of his people, the craftsmanship of the poem remains a fitting, if long-neglected, monument to a great poet" (p. 483).

෴ 712. TSUR, REUVEN. "Poem, Prayer & Meditation: An Exercise in Literary Semantics." *Style* 8: 404–24.
Discusses the relationship between devotional and aesthetic value in religious poems. Distinguishes between a poem, a prayer, and a meditation and uses Roman Jakobson's model of linguistic function "to show

how these three 'deep structures' *can* be conveyed by the same words, as well as . . . map out the points of similarity and of difference between these three" (p. 410). Presents a detailed analysis of the content, grammar, semantic features, tone and emotional intensity, figurative language, dramatic and rhetorical elements, and linguistic multivalence of "Batter my heart." Argues that the unbeliever can appreciate Donne's sonnet because he "does not necessarily undergo the experience embodied in the poem with the intensity of a mystic or a meditating believer," but simply "contemplates a speaker who addresses God and undergoes the experience" and thus "*may* emotionally respond to it" (p. 417). Suggests that the sonnet has "the shape of an 'emotive *crescendo*' (with a beginning, a middle, and an end), with a high degree of vividness, multiple relationship of imagery (bestowing *unity* upon *multiple* imagery), and mounting intensity" but denies that the poem is a meditation (or mystical experience) since "the reader *perceives* the process of mounting emotion, whereas in meditation or ecstasy he is supposed to *experience* it" (p. 421).

⋙ 713. USMANI, Z. A. "Some Aspects of Donne's Love Poetry: With Specific Reference to 'The Relique,'" in *Essays on John Donne: A Quater Centenary Tribute*, edited by Asloob Ahmad Ansari, pp. 25–38. Aligarh: Department of English, Aligarh Muslim University.

Discusses the wide range of paradoxical mysteries and miracles associated with love that Donne explores in his love poetry and notes that typically he enriches, deepens, and makes visible the paradoxical nature of love rather than attempting to resolve the paradoxes through logical analysis. Presents a reading of "The Relique" to show that the poem is built upon a series of paradoxes that attempts to illuminate a central paradox about love and that in the poem Donne "brings about a concrescence of the perspectives of religion, art and science" (p. 31) that reveals his mythic consciousness. Suggests that the major argument of the poem is that "if you have an eye for genuine miracles that are happening around you, you can apprehend the miraculous, paradoxical nature of existence that reveals transcendental realities in the temporal and the mundane" (p. 34).

√ ⋙ 714. WADDINGTON, RAYMOND B. *The Mind's Empire: Myth and Form in George Chapman's Narrative Poems*. Baltimore and London: The Johns Hopkins University Press. xi, 221p.

Mentions Donne throughout, primarily contrasting him with Chapman. Suggests that one effect of the twentieth-century revival of interest in Donne was to create renewed interest in Chapman but notes that, while the revival "caused Chapman to be read more widely than at any time since the enthusiastic appreciation of the Romantics, it also established a mental set which ensured that much of the reading was a misreading" (p. 1). Compares and contrasts Donne and Chapman primarily to show how different they are and thus to establish Chapman's poetic identity. Specifi-

cally notes the differences by contrasting their so-called obscurity and by
pointing out that, unlike Donne, Chapman was an allegorist. Contrasts
also their uses of Platonism, noting that "beneath Donne's veneer of platonism lurks a strong strain of medieval Christianity in the tradition of the
contemptus mundi," whereas Chapman's Platonism "runs deep in his
thought, committing him to a view of life perceived as wholeness and
harmony" (p. 195).

●§ 715. ———. "Shakespeare's Sonnet 15 and the Art of Memory," in
The Rhetoric of Renaissance Poetry: From Wyatt to Milton, edited
by Thomas O. Sloan and Raymond B. Waddington, pp. 96–122.
Berkeley, Los Angeles, London: University of California Press.
  In the process of analyzing in detail Shakespeare's Sonnet 15, discusses
memory as one of the five major divisions of classical rhetoric and comments on its importance, not only in the sonnet, but also in Donne's
sermons. Points out that Donne's theory of memory was derived essentially from Cicero through St. Augustine and notes that "the importance
assigned to memory by these three eloquent men . . . springs in large part
from their common Platonic philosophical orientation" (p. 106). Points
out that hundreds of years after St. Augustine, "but in an unbroken line
of intellectual descent, Donne preached sermons on the belief that 'The
art of salvation, is but the art of memory'" (p. 106).

●§ 716. WALLER, G. F. "John Donne's Changing Attitudes to Time."
SEL 14: 79–89.
  Reprinted in *The Strong Necessity of Time: The Philosophy of Time in
Shakespeare and Elizabethan Literature* (De proprietatibus litterarum, Series
practica, 90, edited by C. H. Van Schoonveld) (The Hague and Paris:
Mouton, 1976), pp. 67–78.
  Traces Donne's radical intellectual development from the 1590s to 1631,
primarily focusing on his shifting attitudes toward time. Suggests that in
his early poems Donne "draws heavily on many medieval traditions, but
his independence of any systematic metaphysical implications is a marked
feature of his more serious love poems," whereas in his later works "his
solution to the problems raised by time and mutability becomes the traditional Christian one" (p. 81). Notes that in the love poems two attitudes
toward time conflict: "either time is redeemable from outside, by values
that lie beyond time's grasp, or else time is something that must be used
or exploited from within" (p. 83). Sees the period from 1605 to 1615–
1617 as a distinct turning point in Donne's intellectual development, a
time of great personal turmoil, doubt, and frustration, evidenced, for example, in the *Holy Sonnets* and the *Anniversaries*. Notes that, whereas
Donne saw mutability and change as "the medium of life's variety," now
they "are evidence of its fragmentariness" (p. 84), and thus Donne's "fascination with time is slowly becoming a deep despair in the face of un-
bearable tensions, necessitating a search for less fragile certainties" (p. 85).

Shows that in the sermons and *Devotions upon Emergent Occasions* Donne "interiorizes the commonplace observation on the brevity of time in comparison with eternity" and embarks on "a quest for the permanent beyond time" that can only be found in "God's eternity, not man's temporal achievements" (p. 85). Concludes, therefore, that "Donne's apprehension of time and mutability in his love poems is, however striking and powerful, oddly limited by its very intensity; and his later intellectual development and his surrender to religious orthodoxy may paradoxically have their roots in the very strength of independence and isolation that his love poems demonstrate" (p. 89).

❦ 717. WHITE, GAIL. "Last Days of Donne." SCN 32: 72.
An original poem on Donne's death.

❦ 718. WOODHEAD, M. R. "A Mid-Seventeenth Century Allusion to 'The Extasie.'" N&Q n.s. 21: 413.
Finds a possible allusion to "The Extasie" in a prose essay in *Dia, a Poem* (1659) by William Skipton, in which he attacks the "Platonicks." Notes that Skipton shows little understanding of Donne's poem as a whole and may have read only the opening lines or perhaps only remembered them.

❦ 719. YOSHIDA, SACHIKO. "Jinsei no Tabi no Tojō ni atte—John Donne no 'Anniversaries' no Kaishaku" [Through the Street of This Life— A Reading of Donne's *Anniversaries*]. *Kenkyū Nenpō* (Nara Women's College), no. 18: 25–41.
Cited in "The 1974 Bibliography," *The Renaissance Bulletin* (The Renaissance Institute, Tokyo) 7 (1980): 20. Unavailable.

❦ 720. ZAKI, JAFAR. "Pope's Adaptations of Donne's Satires," in *Essays on John Donne: A Quater Centenary Tribute*, edited Asloob Ahmad Ansari, pp. 117–38. Aligarh: Department of English, Aligarh Muslim University.
Discusses Pope's acquaintance with and admiration of Donne's satires. Comments on specific details of Pope's adaptations of *Satyres II* and *IV* and notes that, although Pope followed the general plan and structure of Donne's poems, he refined the couplets, chose contemporary targets for his attacks, modified allusions to fit his contemporary scene, and often introduced differences in tone. Argues that Pope may have sincerely wanted to make Donne's satires available and intelligible to his contemporaries by modernizing them and that he may have wanted to stress the notion of the continuity of the satiric tradition, but stresses that Pope's primary motive in publishing his adaptations was "to carry on his campaign against the people he had come to dislike for one reason or the other" (p. 131). Maintains that in his satiric campaign Pope "was fighting *his* battle him-

self and with *his* own weapons; he was simply using Donne as a stalking-horse" (p. 131).

1975

⋙ 721. AKIBA, RYŪZŌ. "*Songs & Sonnets* ni okeru 'Giron'" [The Function of 'Argument' in Donne's *Songs & Sonets*]. *Ronsō* (The Meiji Gakuin Review, The Literature and Economics Society, Meiji Gakuin University), no. 225 (March): 45–59.
Cited in "The 1975 Bibliography," *The Renaissance Bulletin* (The Renaissance Institute, Tokyo) 7 (1980): 36. Unavailable.

⋙ 722. ANAND, SHAHLA. "John Donne—An Article in Encyclopedia Style," in A *Potpourri of Thoughts on English Literature*, pp. 45–58. New York: Vantage Press.
Presents a general biographical sketch of Donne and a critical survey of his poetry and prose along with a highly selected bibliography. Intended for the reader who has no previous acquaintance with Donne or metaphysical poetry. Calls Donne "one of the most popular poets of his times" and maintains that "aesthetically his poems belong, with others of his period, to the baroque art, but it is his impassioned ardour and wit that set him apart" (p. 49). Agrees with Joan Webber in *Contrary Music* (1963) that "it was in the pulpit that Donne achieved his fullest artistic expression" (p. 55).

⋙ 723. ———. "Women and Donne," in A *Potpourri of Thoughts on English Literature*, pp. 59–65. New York: Vantage Press.
Comments briefly on Donne's highly idealized views on noble women in his poetry, especially in his verse epistles, one-third of which were addressed to highborn ladies. Discusses Donne's patronesses, especially Magdalen Herbert and Lucy Harrington, Countess of Bedford. Points out that, in addition to simply praising noblewomen, the verse epistles express Donne's ideas "of womanhood exalted—exalted to the point that the ideas become intellectual concepts" (p. 59). Points out that for Donne virtue "is almost a religion, integrity itself" and that thus "his great ladies are virtuous not only in goodness, in their honour, in talents, in physical grace' and beauty, but they are virtuous in active goodness" (p. 61). Sees that, in spite of his often mundane thoughts, elaborate conceits, and uses of the courtly love tradition, these poems reveal Donne's serious piety: "the young courtier-lover progresses to a divine [love]" (p. 64). Highly selected bibliography.

⋙ 724. BAKER, HERSCHEL. "John Donne," in *The Later Renaissance in England: Non-dramatic Verse and Poetry, 1600–1660*, pp. 56–86, 544–61, 680–82, 717–18. Boston: Houghton Mifflin Co.
General introduction to Donne's life, poetry, and prose (pp. 56–59)

with a selected bibliography (pp. 59–60). Selections from Donne's poetry (pp. 60–86); selections from *Essays in Divinity, Devotions upon Emergent Occasions,* and *LXXX Sermons* (pp. 544–61); selections from *Juvenilia* (pp. 680–82), and "The Dunce" (pp. 717–18)—all with notes. General bibliography (pp. 945–48).

√ ✒ 725. BAKER-SMITH, DOMINIC. "Donne's 'Litanie.'" *RES* 26: 171–73.
   Notes that in a letter to Sir Henry Goodyere concerning "The Litanie" Donne mentions two monk-poets associated with St. Gall, Ratpertus (died circa 885) and Notker Balbulus (circa 840–912) and suggests that Donne obtained his information from the *Antiquae Lectiones* (or *Promptuarium Ecclesiasticum*) compiled by Henricus Canisius (1557–1610), a nephew of St. Peter Canisius, a canonist from Nijmegen, and a professor at Ingolstadt from 1590 to 1610. Points out that in the second part of the five-volume collection (published in 1608) Canisius printed "Epigrammata seu Hymni sacri illustrium virorum antiquorum patrum monasterii S. Galli," which he obtained from Dom Jodocus Metzler, a monk of St. Gall, and which contains several litanies (with notes by Metzler). Maintains that these litanies "throw a good deal of light on Donne's references in the letter to Goodyer" (p. 172) and shows similarities and differences between Donne's "The Litanie" and those of the two St. Gall poets. Points out, in particular, Donne's "highly personal handling of the litany" (p. 173). Suggests that evidence indicates that Donne's poem was written late in 1608.

✒ 726. BARBIERI, RICHARD E. "John Donne and *Richard II*: An Influence?" *SQ* 26: 57–62.
   Points to a passage in the eighth meditation of the *Devotions upon Emergent Occasions,* in which Donne is visited by the King's physician and speculates on the paradox of royalty being subject to frailty; recalls the deposition scene in Shakespeare's *Richard II* (IV.1.287–97), in which, calling for a mirror, Richard speculates on his state. Notes similarities in the verbal and pictorial details of the mirror image and the use of the image. Suggests that it is unlikely that Donne read the play, but argues that it is perhaps possible that he saw it performed when it was presented by the Lord Chamberlain's Men at the request of the Essex faction on 7 February 1601.

✒ 727. BARKAN, LEONARD. "Natural Philosophy: The Human Body and the Cosmos," in *Nature's Work of Art: The Human Body as Image of the World,* pp. 8–60. New Haven and London: Yale University Press.
   Discusses Donne's views on the human body as a microcosm of the cosmos, his general analogical world view, and his complex attitudes toward the new science. Suggests that, "even when Donne specifically mentions the new philosophy, clearly referring to the science that will discredit the system of universal analogies, his fears seem as much responses to that

proliferation of the analogical system which he saw in Cusanus, Pico, and Paracelsus as they are to the more contemporary discrediting of the Ptolemaic cosmology" (p. 48). Maintains, therefore, that in Donne "there are as many tensions between harmony and diversity within the old system as there are between the old system and the new" (p. 49). Discusses in some detail *Devotions upon Emergent Occasions* and suggests that "no work of the English Renaissance illustrates more fully the close connections between literary metaphor and the belief in a universal system of analogies" (p. 51). Sees the *Devotions* as "a late Renaissance, self-conscious, and baroque version of the medieval world view," a work that combines cosmological security with personal insecurity and makes " a startling use of some very familiar tensions implicit in the old analogical world view" (p. 53). Suggests that "Hymne to God my God, in my sicknesse" epitomizes the Renaissance traditions of corporeal transformation and *homo omnis creatura*: "Cosmology, self-knowledge, and knowledge of God unite in the poetic metamorphosis of the human body" (p. 60).

≈§ 728. BELLETTE, ANTONY F. "Art and Imitation in Donne's *Anniversaries*." *SEL* 15: 83–96.

Argues that Donne's controlling principle in the *Anniversaries* is "not to be found in any particular symbolic identification which we might give to Elizabeth Drury, nor in the traditional meditative pattern he uses" but that our full understanding of the poems "depends on our recognizing the essentially *poetic* use he makes of both the central figure and the formal framework of the poems" (p. 84). Discusses Donne's concept of imitation and shows that the poems "are (like Elizabeth Drury herself) an embodiment of the Idea in the Word, and thus directly imitative of God's creative Act" (p. 85). Notes that "it is the action of her soul, potential in the *Anatomy*, realized in the *Progress*, which our own actions must, however imperfectly, imitate"; that "it is this action which these poems themselves imitate in their inner structure; this action which governs the movement and development of each poem and makes it a consistent and unified whole"; and that "it is through this action and the poems' imitation of it that Donne leads us to a contemplation of the original creative Act" (p. 85). Points out that the reader is to see Elizabeth Drury not only as a worthy object of praise but, more importantly, also as a model of virtuous action. Shows how the internal structure of each poem and the variations on the refrain in each suggest "a movement from death to life, from earth to Heaven, from stasis to action, from unfulfilled to fulfilled potential" (p. 89). Maintains that Donne clearly "intends us to go beyond Elizabeth Drury to the poetic act that embodies her, as she embodied all virtue" and that the poems together "are finally a celebration not so much of Elizabeth Drury as of the undying creative power of the soul itself, and particularly of the power of the poet who interprets and prophesies and gives form to the highest truth" (p. 94). Concludes, therefore, that Donne attempts "to repeat the act of Elizabeth Drury and to give the new world a

pattern and form, in his celebration of her who gave pattern and form to
the old world" (p. 95) and that the poems themselves embody the very
message that they attempt to convey.

◄§ 729. ———. "'Little Worlds Made Cunningly': Significant Form in
    Donne's *Holy Sonnets* and 'Goodfriday, 1613. Riding Westward.'"
    SP 72: 322–47.   405   ST94
Argues that "we should approach Donne's religious verse with at least
as much regard for its form and structure as for its intellectual and emotional content" and that "we must attend not only to the words and lines
themselves, but to the way they are arranged on the page" (p. 325). Discusses Donne's adaptation of the traditional sonnet form for his own purposes and examines several groups of the *Holy Sonnets* to show how their
forms reinforce and articulate the thematic development of movement
from despair to consolation, noting that in the sonnets of despair the structure, syntax, and rhythm reflect the theme and that in the sonnets of
consolation the figure of Christ becomes the very principle of organization
and the structure reflects the order and harmony of the theme. Comments
on "Goodfriday, 1613. Riding Westward" to show "its faultless structure as
a meditation on the figure of Christ" and to suggest that, "as with the *Holy
Sonnets*, awareness of form is integral to our understanding of meaning"
(p. 342). Points out that the *Holy Sonnets* "depict the process of spiritual
disintegration, or of reintegration through Christ, but only a longer poem
less tied to a traditional form, less teleological in nature than the sonnet,
can suggest the mysterious simultaneity of the processes" (p. 346) and
concludes that the Goodfriday poem, "the most carefully and deliberately
wrought of all Donne's devotional poems, shows that final fusion of form
and content which the *Holy Sonnets* so impressively anticipate" (p. 347).

◄§ 730. ———. "The Originality of Donne's *Satires*." *UTQ* 44: 130–
    40.
Points out that Donne "at once initiated and departed from the norms
of Roman satire as it was understood and rendered into English in the last
decade of the sixteenth century" and argues that his departures "not only
reveal Donne's own practices in the art of poetic imitation, but clarify, at
the very beginning of his career, certain central preoccupations which
recur throughout his writing" (p. 131). Focuses on "the presence of the
poet himself in the scene he depicts, and with the personal, moral issues
which arise from this presence" (p. 131) in *Satyres I, II,* and *IV*. Notes
that in all three satires the religious terminology "is applied primarily to
the speaker himself, and reveals a degree of religious trepidation and guilt,
a degree of personal involvement with the subject of the satire that is
unique to Donne" (p. 133). Points out that in the three satires Donne
argues that "one must encounter the world, know all its subtleties, recognize one's own involvement in it through the common fall, yet strive to
remain free from its contagion" (p. 136). Suggests that Donne's particular

way of resolving the problem of living responsibly and knowingly in the world "has little to do with the conventional role of satirist" (p. 137) and that his sense of being in some way responsible not only for his own sins but also for the sins of others suggests that Donne sees his role as satirist as both a priestly and a Christ-like function. Concludes that it is this sense of personal involvement in the sin and vice that he sees about him that distinguishes Donne from other Renaissance satirists and that "enables us to place both the conventional and unconventional elements of the poems within a larger context of his poetic and spiritual development" (p. 139).

◆§ 731. BOZANICH, ROBERT. "Donne and Ecclesiastes." *PMLA* 90: 270–76.

Suggests that during the years at Mitcham following his marriage Donne became increasingly overwhelmed by an awareness of his own vanity, a state reflected, for example, in his well-known letter to Sir Henry Goodyere in September 1608, and that he turned to Ecclesiastes to find some insight into his situation, since vanity is the major theme of Solomon's book. Shows that, from that time on, Ecclesiastes "exerted a profound and life-long influence on Donne himself" and that "its effects can be seen through virtually the entire range of his work—including the ostensibly nonauto-biographical and nonreligious" (p. 275). Notes the influence of Ecclesiastes on a number of Donne's later works—the letters, sermons, *Devotions upon Emergent Occasions, Biathanatos,* and especially the *Anniversaries.* Calls the poems "Donne's Ecclesiastes" (p. 272) and comments on the dependence of the two poems on Solomon's book, especially calling attention to the importance of the theme of repudiation of the vanity of human learning and the futility of human knowledge. Points out that the *Commentarii in Ecclesiasten* by Johannes Lorinus is the only modern authority on Ecclesiastes that Donne mentions and maintains that this commentary "explains virtually every statement that Donne ever made about the book" (p. 271). Notes, for example, that Lorinus's commentary throws new light on the complex imagery of lines 207–13 of *The second Anniversarie,* imagery anticipated in "The Funerall."

◆§ 732. CATHCART, DWIGHT. *Doubting Conscience: Donne and the Poetry of Moral Argument.* Ann Arbor: The University of Michigan Press. 199p.

Argues that much of Donne's poetry, especially the *Songs and Sonets,* is informed by methods of reasoning and by habits of thought that are quite similar to those employed by seventeenth-century casuists in their examination of cases of conscience. Chapter 1, "Donne and Casuistry" (pp. 1–12), points out that the *Songs and Sonets,* more than any other one collection of Renaissance poems, are "poems whose motive, subject, structure, setting, tone, and premises are those of argument" and that the speakers of the poems "use the varieties of logic to defend and finally to support their private and vulnerable views" (p. 2). Discusses casuistry as a method of reasoning and as a habit of thought and argues that "in associating the casuistry of the seventeenth century, both Catholic and Protestant, with the *Songs and Sonets*, one can find a unifying principle that clearly relates the early to the late, the secular to the religious, the skeptical to the committed, the feeling to the thinking, and something that explains to some degree the special response to Donne" (p. 10). Chapter 2, "The Dramatic Grounds of Moral Argument" (pp. 13–32), discusses the dramatic elements of Donne's love poems and especially comments on how he creates and develops the "you" of the poems and allows his speaker to respond to the assumed views and attitudes of the addressed "you." Shows how in such poems as "The Prohibition," "The Legacie," "The good-morrow," "The Expiration," "A Valediction: of weeping," "A Valediction: of my name, in the window," "The Sunne Rising," "The Canonization," "The Extasie," and "The Flea" "the distance between the person to whom the poem is spoken and the reader is wide but not infinite, and the latter's response to the poetic experience includes his understanding of the spoken as well as the unspoken words supplied by imagination" and that, "as the imaginative experience must constantly be renewed, as with each reading, one must resupply the response of the 'you,' one is forced back each time into those possibilities of the drama of the poem which never are exhausted, never become actualities" (pp. 31–32). Chapter 3, "Truth and the Speaker" (pp. 33–88), stresses that Donne's speaker, whether serious or flippant, attempts to articulate a moral truth that is an exception to the general moral law and that he does this by reasoning that is quite similar to that of the casuists. Surveys a number of poems, especially "The Canonization," "The Flea," "The good-morrow," and "The Extasie," to show that the speaker primarily argues with a "you" in the poems "who apparently represents for him all that is public and all the speaker finds restrictive of his individuality; in short, the 'you' seems to stand for all that is normal" (p. 37). Maintains that in the *Songs and Sonets* Donne chose "to write poems about those hard questions which also give rise to casuistry—when he saw or forced a disjunction between his own view and the general one" and that "the truth they drive toward is essentially paradoxical" (p. 39). Analyzes Donne's special kind of skepticism and discusses how in moral matters he is primarily a probabliorist rather than a probabilist. Argues that in Donne's poems there exists a tension between a desire for certainty and an acceptance of uncertainty and that "this unfulfilled need in the face of uncompromising reality and the compromise that arises from that hard dichotomy illustrate the near kinship of the speaker of the poems with the casuists of the seventeenth century" (p. 88). Chapter 4, "The Speaker's Means to His Ends" (pp. 89–140), discusses how, as the speaker "argues again and again with his various listeners, defending his strange views against what he knows to be 'moral,' asserting that fornication is virtuous or that the separation of bodies is not all that it appears to be, arguing slyly at some times and solemnly at others, his voice and the way he speaks become familiar, as does the method of argument which he employs without regard to the kind of relationship between himself and his listener, to the issue at hand and without regard to the tone he takes with respect to that issue" (pp. 89–90). Discusses also Donne's uses of logic, imagery, and metaphor in a number of poems to show how they reinforce his reasoning and suggests that, at times, Donne's extreme method of reasoning is quite close to that of the Jesuit casuists. Chapter 5, "The Sound of the Speaker's Voice" (pp. 141–52), comments on the intensity of the speaker's voice and the sense of doubt and conflict in it as he makes his moral arguments. Notes that much of the wit in the poems "is not merely a response to that doubt but is also an expression of it" (p. 147). Chapter 6, "The Mind of the Poet" (pp. 153–72), surveys briefly how the doubting conscience and the uses of casuistry pervade much of the rest of Donne's canon. Notes that in the religious poems "it is the speaker who asserts the reasonable and understandable view" and that "the paradoxes which close the religious poems assert his communion with God, for these paradoxes are, most of them, the central truths of Christianity" (p. 163). Discusses how Donne is both like and unlike his modern readers and warns that "our difficulties are not Donne's" and suggests that "the separation is epistemological," for Donne, unlike us, "knows that truth exists, that inductive reasoning does not necessarily lead to truth, that the private view is not paramount, and that truth does exist separate from its application" (pp. 170–71). Notes (pp. 173–84), selected bibliography (pp. 185–91), and index (pp. 193–99).

➷ 733. CHAMBERS, A. B. "Christmas: The Liturgy of the Church and ✓ English Verse of the Renaissance," in *Literary Monographs*, vol. 6, edited by Eric Rothstein, pp. 109–53. Madison: University of Wisconsin Press.

Discusses the history, theology, and symbolism of the liturgy of the Christmas cycle, comments on how seventeenth-century divines interpreted these materials, and shows how an understanding of the Christmas liturgy is useful in interpreting late sixteenth- and early seventeenth-century poems on the birth of Christ. Comments in detail on "Nativitie," the third sonnet in *La Corona*, to show that the chronology of Donne's poem "is faithful to the demands of liturgical time, even though its résumé of past history, from a liturgical point of view, is peculiarly straightforward," that Donne is also "faithful to liturgy and theology in his consistent use of oxymoron," and that, since the poem is limited by the sonnet form to fourteen lines, his lines "resemble a compressed and difficult shorthand, which, in longhand, would fill many pages and poems" (pp. 120–21). Notes that in his sonnet Donne "refused to limit his vision of the Nativity to events of Christmas Day" and concludes that "Nativitie" is "atypical of Christmas poems only in its heavy dependence on a narrative survey of the cycle as a whole" (p. 125). Compares and contrasts Donne's poem with nativity poems by Rowland Watkyns, Crashaw, Southwell, John Collop, Alabaster, Herbert, Vaughan, Jonson, Milton, and others.

◄§ 734. CLARK, JOHN R., FRANK FABRY, FRANK MASON, WILLIAM E. MORRIS, AND FLORA ZBOR. "Satire: A Selective Critical Bibliography." *SCN* 33: 1–10.

Offers a selected survey of books and articles on satire published from 1940 to 1974 in order to show the development of modern critical trends. Argues that the period "dramatizes for us the enormous burgeoning of critical interest in satire, and itself constitutes a new period in the life of satire—a period when satire in all its diversity is coming to be known" (p. 5). Comments briefly on several major critical studies published between 1944 and 1974 of Donne's *Satyres* and his uses of the satiric mode and suggests that future Donne studies should consider in more detail the satiric intent of his love poems, religious poems, and sermons.

◄§ 735. CLAYES, STANLEY A., AND JOHN GERRIETTS. "John Donne," in *Ways to Poetry*, pp. 181–95. New York: Harcourt Brace Jovanovich.

Presents a general introduction to Donne's poetry with some biographical information. Discusses "The Sunne Rising" as a typical metaphysical poem and shows that it "illustrates the audacity of the metaphysical conceit in initially appealing to the senses, but ultimately to the intellect" (p. 183). Reproduces (with notes and study questions) "Song: Goe and catche a falling starre," "Loves Deitie," "Lovers infiniteness," "The Canonization," and "A Valediction: forbidding mourning"; reproduces with commentary "The Extasie" and two of the *Holy Sonnets*: "At the round earths imagin'd corners" and "Wilt thou love God, as he thee!" In other parts of the book, five Donne poems are reproduced, including "Batter my heart" with study questions and notes (p. 171).

◄§ 736. CRAGG, GERALD R. *Freedom and Authority: A Study of English Thought in the Early Seventeenth Century.* Philadelphia: The Westminster Press. 334p.

Surveys the numerous intellectual concerns of the first forty years of the seventeenth century as these are reflected in the philosophical, scientific, political, and religious life of the times, especially the central and persistent issue of freedom and authority. Mentions Donne throughout and views him as "a particularly illuminating figure; in his early work he reflected the growing awareness that the cohesion of the familiar intellectual world was threatened if not already shattered," but "by resorting to paradox he held in tension elements that were in danger of appearing as stark opposites—confidence and pessimism, body and soul, skepticism and faith, worldliness and otherworldliness, humanism and antihumanism" (p. 33). Maintains that Donne's sermons "provide an unusually revealing clue to the forces shaping the thought of his period," for "nowhere else do we find so clearly reflected the concepts that occupied the minds of his more thoughtful contemporaries" (p. 33). Comments on Donne's attitude on the new science, Neoplatonism, Paracelsus, death, witchcraft, alchemy, saints, Jesuits, Catholicism, papal authority, Calvinism, and the Gunpowder Plot. Extensive primary and secondary bibliographies.

737. DANIELS, EDGAR F. "Donne's 'To His Mistress Going to Bed,' 33–38." *Expl* 33: Item 71.

Reply to Jonathan E. Deitz (entry 633). Disagrees that "balls" in line 36 of the elegy refers to female breasts. Finds such a suggestion inconsistent with the argument of lines 33–38 and with the myth of Atalanta. Notes that "to use the possessive ('Atalanta's balls') does not require us to believe that she cast the golden apples but merely that they are traditionally associated with her." Points out that Donne's uses of the image in a reversal of the sex roles (women diverting men rather than a man diverting a woman) is a characteristically witty implied paradox." See also Richard F. Giles (entry 750).

738. DAVIES, HORTON. *Worship and Theology in England: From Andrewes to Baxter and Fox, 1603–1690*. (Worship and Theology in England, vol. 2.) Princeton: Princeton University Press. xxiii, 592p.

Surveys four major religious traditions in England from 1603 to 1690—the Anglican, the Roman Catholic, the Puritan, and the Quaker. Discusses not only the theological differences among the groups and their resultant differences in public and private worship but also such topics as their characteristic architecture, modes of preaching, and attitudes toward sacred music. Mentions Donne throughout, but primarily as a "metaphysical" preacher, those preachers "who emphasized the paradoxical character of Christian revelation, who used far-fetched analogies to create surprise and interest, and whose word-play was dazzling, while their erudition and culture were wide" (p. 143). Compares and contrasts Donne with a number of preachers—Thomas Adams, Joseph Hall, Jeremy Taylor, Richard Baxter—and especially with Lancelot Andrewes. Maintains that "brilliant in his psychological penetration and wide-ranging imagination that garners from a wide direct experience, as well as from unusually exotic sources of knowledge derived from reading, Donne yet incurs a suspicion of the impure motive, of the exhibitionist" (p. 101). Suggests that Donne's strengths as a preacher are his incisively powerful and dramatic ability to bring alive scriptural texts, his striking uses of images and figures of speech, his ability to make his points relate to the practical lives of his audience, and, above all, his passionate subjectivity; yet sees his weaknesses as well, especially his obscurity, his uses of far-fetched allegorical interpretations, his tendency to meander, and his sometimes tasteless uses of melodrama. Notes the Ignatian influence on Donne's spirituality, his translation of the Psalms, and his contribution to the development of the hymn. Extensive bibliography.

739. DITTMAR, WILFRIED. "Holy Sonnets" and "An Anatomie of the World," in *Hauptwerke der englischen Literatur: Einzeldarstellun-*

gen und Interpretationen, mit einem einlitenden Essay von Rudolf Stamm, edited by Manfred Pfister, pp. 95–96, 99–100. Munich: Kindler.

Two handbooks entries on Donne: (1) "Holy Sonnets" (pp. 95–96) and (2) "An Anatomie of the World" (pp. 99–100). Each presents a general historical and critical introduction to the works, with a selected bibliography for each.

740. DONNE, JOHN. *Devotions upon Emergent Occasions*. Edited, with Commentary by Anthony Raspa. Montreal and London: McGill-Queen's University Press. lvi, 192p.

Preface (pp. ix–x). Introduction (pp. xiii–lvi) is divided into five sections: (1) The illness and occasion (pp. xiii–xix) presents the known facts about Donne's illness of 1623 that was the occasion for his writing the *Devotions upon Emergent Occasions*; (2) Meditation and metaphysics (pp. xix–xl) outlines the metaphysical, theological, and literary influences on the *Devotions*; discusses the style, imagery, and structure of the work; and shows how Donne adapted Ignatian meditation in such a way as to leave him free "to devise a meditational structure of his own choosing, conforming to his theology and the tenets of his church" (p. xxxii) and how he created "a literary work fusing biblical prototypes and their copies in the Book of Creatures into a literary form that had an aesthetic effect on the reader akin to the ascetic experience of Ignatius" (p. xxxix); (3) Seventeenth-century copies (pp. xl–xliv) lists by date known extant seventeenth-century copies of the *Devotions*; (4) The editions (pp. xliv–liii) discusses the first five seventeenth-century editions and, in less detail, the three nineteenth-century and four twentieth-century editions; (5) The text (pp. lii–lvi) explains and defends the choice of the copy-text used in this edition (first edition of 1624) and explains minor textual additions, corrections, and changes. The text of the *Devotions*, with textual notes (pp. 1–127). Commentary (pp. 129–87). Selected bibliography (pp. 188–92) lists Renaissance works on theology, medicine, and astrology used more than once in the commentary. Stresses that the *Devotions* is an autobiographical and devotional series of meditations in which Donne synthesized his ideas "about metaphysics and literature, medicine and cosmology, and the relationship of man to God" and shows how Donne "uses one incident in his life to pursue the significance of its whole" (p. xii).

741. ———. *John Donne's Devotions upon Emergent Occasions: A Critical Edition with Introduction and Commentary* by Sister Elizabeth Savage, S.S.J. (Salzburg Studies in English Literature; Elizabethan & Renaissance Studies, vol. 21.) 2 vols. Salzburg: Institut für englische Sprache und Literatur. cxxiii, 269p.

Volume 1 consists of four main parts: (1) References and Abbreviations (pp. iii–v); (2) Literary Traditions and Style (pp. vi–cii); (3) The History of the Text (pp. ciii–cxviii); and (4) The Text of This Edition (pp. cxix–cxxi) and a list of sigla (pp. cxxii–cxxiii). Part 2, "Literary Traditions and Style," is subdivided into five sections: (1) Previous Criticism (pp. vi–xiii), which surveys critical commentary on the *Devotions upon Emergent Occasions* from Donne's time to 1971, with special emphasis on works published from 1950 to 1971; (2) The Use of Scripture (pp. xiii–xxxi), which comments on Donne's adaptation of the Bible (as well as biblical commentary and Patristic sources) in the *Devotions* and contrasts his approach with that reflected in the sermons to show that "rather than being emphasized or 'built up to,' the word of God becomes incorporated into and subordinated to Donne's own words" (p. xxxi); (3) The *Ars Moriendi* Tradition (pp. xxxii–lvi), which surveys Donne's attitudes toward death and time, comments on his adaptation of the art-of-dying genre in the *Devotions*, and suggests that, "although not *ars moriendi* literature in the strict sense, the *Devotions* clearly and consistently reflects the influence of the genre" (p. lvi); (4) The Ignatian Meditative Tradition (pp. lvii–lxxx), which comments on Donne's adaptation of discursive meditation and Ignatian spirituality in the *Devotions* and suggests that his variations upon and departure from *The Spiritual Exercises* "do not place his work outside the Ignatian tradition" (p. lxxix); and (5) Prose Style (pp. lxxxi–cii), which surveys Donne's various styles in the *Devotions* and shows that he adapts "distinct and apt styles for each of his three subdivisions" (p. cii). Part 3, The History of the Text, is subdivided into three sections: (1) Bibliographical Descriptions (pp. ciii–cx), descriptions of the first five editions; (2) Seventeenth-Century Editions (pp. cx–cxvi), a discussion of the first five editions and the bibliographical history of their printing; and (3) Modern Editions (pp. cxvii–cxviii), a survey of the various editions from 1839 to 1959. Volume 2 consists of the text of the *Devotions* (pp. 1–181), based on the first edition of 1624, with a list of variant readings in seventeenth-century editions; commentary (pp. 182–237); glossary (pp. 238–42); a bibliography of secondary works (pp. 243–56); a scriptural index (pp. 257–63); and a general index (pp. 264–69).

⊷§ 742. FERRARI, FERRUCCIO. *La poesia religiosa inglese del Seicento.* Florence: Casa editrice G. D'Anna. 202p.

Divided into two major parts: (1) "Un secolo di poesia religiosa" (pp. 9–125), which consists of a series of essays on English religious poetry of the seventeenth century, and (2) "Robert Herrick, poeta religioso" (p. 127–79). Mentions Donne throughout the first part and briefly compares and contrasts him with Herrick in the second. Discusses Donne especially in the following: (1) "Introduzione" (pp. 11–22) presents a brief sketch of the religious situation and temperament in England during the first half of the seventeenth century and discusses how sacred poetry of the time reflects the religious conditions of the period. Calls Donne the most representative poet of the century and notes that "il suo lirismo ragguinge punte di fervore mistico e devozionale, ma il linguaggio è realistico e colloquiale" (p. 13). (2) "La poesia metafisica. John Donne e i suoi imitatori" (pp.

34–48) comments on the influence of Donne and Jonson on the development of English poetry and suggests that "dalla felice combinazione
delle scuole di Jonson e di Donne deriva la poesia profana e religiosa del
Seicento inglese" (pp. 34–35); discusses briefly Donne's religious background and sensibility, his major characteristics as a poet, and his influence on his followers, especially George Herbert. (3) "L'arte della medi-
tazione e i poeti contemplativi" (pp. 74–98) discusses the development
and importance of discursive meditation on early seventeenth-century
English religious poetry and the influence of the "literature of tears"; comments on Donne's Christology, noting that "la chiave dell'esperienza mistica di Donne è proprio la struttura cristologica della sua fede, è l'intenso
amore per Cristo" (p. 86); discusses his religious temperament as reflected
in the *Holy Sonnets*, "Hymne to God the Father," and "Goodfriday, 1613.
Riding Westward"; and comments briefly on Donne as a preacher, calling
him "il più insigne rappresentante dell'oratoria sacra e barocca inglese"
(p. 95). (4) "Il culto mariologico in Inghilterra dopo la Riforma" (pp. 99–
110) comments briefly on Donne's attitude toward the Virgin Mary as
reflected in "The Litanie," "Goodfriday, 1613. Riding Westward," *La Corona*, and "The Annuntiation and Passion." Bibliography (pp. 183–93).

⋙ 743. FERRY, ANNE. *All in War with Time: Love Poetry of Shakespeare, Donne, Jonson, Marvell.* Cambridge, Mass., and London:
Harvard University Press. 285p.

Chapter 2, "Donne" (pp. 65–125), discusses Donne's attitude toward
the Renaissance concept of the power of poetry to immortalize the beloved and to preserve love in a world of change and loss and notes that his
ways of defying time are distinguishable from those of other poets. Points
out that Donne typically rejects the role of the poet-lover and argues that
love can be immortalized by aligning it with the immutable laws of nature, not by poetry. Shows that Donne develops "a kind of anti-conven-
tional eternizing poetry" (p. 84) and points out that "throughout his poetry, by echoing, imitating, parodying, transforming recognizable poetic
styles and conventions, he habitually sets off the special nature of his
poems" (p. 67). Presents detailed readings of "The good-morrow," "The
Sunne Rising," "A Valediction: of weeping," "A Valediction: forbidding
mourning," "The Anniversarie," "The Relique," "A Valediction: of the
booke," and "The Canonization" to show how Donne treats the conventions of "eternizing verse." Comments especially on Donne's originality in
the aubade and the valediction. Discusses in much detail "The Canonization," sees it essentially as an elaborate joke, and suggests that it is "ultimately different in kind from the *Songs and Sonets* with which it is
usually grouped, and yet, like them, it defines itself in relation to conventional eternizing poetry, which seems to have embodied for Donne attitudes toward which his imagination was deeply hostile" (p. 125). Notes
that in "The Canonization," as in many of his love poems, Donne rejects
and satirizes the convention of eternizing poetry "in favor of a kind of

poem that does not 'Beg from above / A patterne' of the ideal, but finds it in the 'Mysterious' and mutable experience of mortal lovers" (p. 125). Compares and contrasts Donne to Shakespeare, Jonson, and Marvell. Notes that, "when Donne argues the power of his lover to give shape to experience by making his language conform to the facts of the timebound world rather than to alter them miraculously, he is newly defining poetry" and yet suggests that Donne's love poems "express a belief in an almost magical efficacy of language to impose order on the flux of experience, even if its workings are said to be like those of natural, not miraculous forces" (p. 255).

◆§ 744. FLYNN, DENNIS. "Donne's Catholicism: I." *Recusant History* 13: 1–17.
Discusses Donne's Catholic heritage, early background, education, and associations and finds inadequate R. C. Bald's account in *John Donne: A Life* (entry 179). Particularly disagrees with Bald's emphasis on Donne as an ambitious place-seeker and, while noting that Bald greatly modifies Walton's account of Donne's life, insists that his "modifying of Walton simply reinforces Walton's view that Donne was, but was not really, a Catholic," since Bald "in the end agrees with Walton's less elaborately documented view, somehow inferring that Donne's Catholicism must have been 'continued until he had the independence of mind to make his decisions for himself'—a point in time Bald seems to think coincided roughly with Donne's inheritance at twenty-one" (p. 5). Disagrees also with Bald's suggestion that the death of Donne's brother, Henry, led to his apostasy, resentment against the Jesuits, and later skepticism and cynicism. Argues that Donne's abjuration of Catholicism was a slow process and that he maintained many of his Catholic sympathies and associations well into his middle years. Disagrees also with Bald's notion that Donne's early travels to Italy and Spain were not intricately bound up with his religious sympathies and stresses that Donne's life "exemplifies the religious dilemma faced by successive generations of conforming English Catholics in the sixteenth and early seventeenth centuries" and that his final conformity, "accompanied by detached, private Catholic sympathies, bears witness to a significant feature of Tudor and early Stuart English life" (p. 14). For a continuation, see entry 825.

◆§ 745. FOWLER, ALASTAIR. "The Shakespearean Conceit," in *Conceitful Thought: The Interpretation of English Renaissance Poems*, pp. 87–113. Edinburgh: Edinburgh University Press.
Discusses the complexity of the uses of figurative language in Elizabethan poetry, especially in Spenser's *Amoretti*, Sidney's *Astrophil and Stella*, and Shakespeare's sonnets, and argues that critics who regard Elizabethan use of figurative language as "easy" in comparison to the intricacies of the metaphysical conceit have oversimplified the situation. Argues that "in the earlier period, wider reliance on familiar metaphors in fact made pos-

sible more complex figurative construction" and that "these familiar metaphors have themselves, in some cases, become obscure" and thus "communication may break down and leave us unimpressed by poetry of an apparently jejune simplicity" (p. 106). Notes that compound metaphors are much less characteristic of metaphysical poetry and suggests that the figurative structures of many of Donne's secular poems are, in fact, much simpler than those employed by his immediate predecessors. Suggests that in the *Songs and Sonets* "the figurative structure seems to be simplified by a baroque unification and intensification of effect" (p. 104). Illustrates this concept by analyzing the figurative language of the conclusion of "A Valediction: forbidding mourning," especially the compass conceit, to show that the poem "remains simple and easily grasped, in spite of a series of more or less subdued puns" (p. 104). Points out, however, that Donne's religious poems, for example, "Batter my heart," contain fairly complex metaphors. Concludes that "the different styles not only overlapped, but coexisted in the same author" and that "it would be nearer the truth (though still an oversimplification) to say that one sort of complexity, suitable for sustained meditation and large imaginative construction, gave way to another sort, adaptable to quick striking effects" (p. 113).

◄§ 746. FREITAG, HANS-HEINRICH. *John Donne: Zentrale Motive und Themen in seiner Liebeslyrik.* (Studien zur englischen Literatur herausgegeben von Johannes Kleinstuck, Band 14.) Bonn: Bouvier. 172p.

The first four chapters classify Donne's love poems into groups by motifs and themes. Points out the great variety within these groups as well as common characteristics, such as the basic attitude of skeptical distance and the absence of defined values and ideals, and compares Donne's motifs and themes with those of his Elizabethan contemporaries as well as his dynamic tone of argumentation to their static tone of lament. Chapter 1, "Farewell," argues that environment may be either integrated into the situation of farewell, or else negated, or completely rejected; and notes that the death-motif prevails throughout. Chapter 2, "Death," subdivides the central death motif according to three basic situations: imagined death of the speaker, imagined death of both lovers, or the imagined or real death of the beloved. Chapter 3, "Dream," discusses in particular "Elegie X: The Dreame" and "The Dreame" (from *Songs and Sonets*) and observes that, though different in content, both poems view the dream as a source of perception for the lover. Chapter 4, "Love Philosophy," identifies four aspects of Donne's love philosophy: "erotic love" is presented with playful arguments about passion and promiscuity; in "complaints and problems" the critical lover explains the Petrarchan one-sidedness of unfulfilled, rejected love with an alleged intention of the beloved to kill her lover; "love's fulfillment" is mixed with a tone of skepticism, indirectly in poems expressing the bliss of love and directly in poems theorizing about love; and "criticism and renunciation" shows erotic disillusionment with playful wit or bitter cynicism. Chapter 5, "Petrarchism in Diction Only: The Homage," discusses how Donne uses elements of the Petrarchan tradition but places the motifs, metaphors, and themes in the form of an argument. Shows, in an appendix, that "A Valediction: of the booke" combines all four aspects of Donne's love philosophy.

◄§ 747. FRENCH, ROBERTS W. "Donne's 'Elegie XVIII' (Loves Progress), 38." *Expl* 34: Item 5.
Suggests that the difficult phrase "as infinite as it" in line 38 of the elegy may be a reference to the doctrine of the resurrection of the body. Argues that in the elegy Donne insists "that the body is no less worthy for love than the soul—and surprisingly—no less *infinite* than the soul" and that, although he has the female genitals in mind in lines 33–38, they, as an organ of the body, will also share in the immortality of the body, which "is part of the point, and part of the joke." For a reply, see Edgar F. Daniels (entry 912).

◄§ 748. GALDON, JOSEPH A., S. J. *Typology and Seventeenth-Century Literature.* (De proprietatibus litterarum, Series Maior, 28.) The Hague and Paris: Mouton. 164p.
Explains biblical typology to those not trained in theology and comments on the pervasiveness of typological images and themes in seventeenth-century literature. Discusses specifically but briefly Donne's uses of typology in "Hymne to God my God, in my sicknesse," *Devotions upon Emergent Occasions, Essays in Divinity*, several sermons, several of the *Holy Sonnets, The first Anniversary*, and especially in *The second Anniversarie*. Suggests that in the *Anniversaries* Elizabeth Drury can be seen as a type of Christ, Mary, and Queen Elizabeth I and that Eve can be seen as a type of the Ideal Woman reflected in Elizabeth Drury, the Queen, and Mary. Mentions Donne throughout and suggests that his manipulation of typological images is more complicated and involved than that of Milton and less traditional than that of Herbert.

◄§ 749. GALLANT, GERALD, AND A. L. CLEMENTS. "Harmonized Voices in Donne's 'Songs and Sonets': 'The Dampe.'" *SEL* 15: 71–82.
Argues that "the various tones which have been used to define and categorize individual 'Songs and Sonets' often may exist in a single poem— not as an obfuscating ambiguity that diminishes meaning but in mutual support as a kind of orchestration that enhances meaning" (p. 72). Notes that, "in such multitonal poems, one or another voice at times may be in the foreground with others clustered behind" and that "the total effect is a multi-leveled, enriched, and integrated poem, which is composed of the overlapping voices" (p. 72). Analyzes "The Dampe" to show "this orchestration of voices—broadly speaking, (1) the voice of a cynical, false, or anti-Petrarchan lover, (2) the voice of a sincere, true lover, and (3) the

voice of a complimentary, Petrarchan lover" (p. 72). Demonstrates that
the inextricably interwoven voices of the poem are almost completely in
harmony, even though their motives differ, that they create a subtle interplay throughout the poem, and that the center of interest in the poem is
"a collection of motives which are resolved musically rather than in a
single rational proposition" (p. 82).

◥◤ 750. GILES, RICHARD F. "Donne's 'To His Mistress Going to Bed,'
    33–38." *Expl* 33: Item 71.
    Reply to Jonathan E. Deitz (entry 633). Disagrees that in line 36 of the
elegy "balls" refers to female breasts. Emphasizes that Donne is not mistaken in his use of the myth of Atalanta but rather refers the reader to "the
time after the famous footrace has occurred, after Atalanta has 'stooped'
to retrieve the golden balls, after they have become (literally) Atalanta's
balls." Points out that in lines 33–38 Donne argues that there is "the danger of inanimate gems drawing attention away from the 'real' gems of
women: their nude bodies" and asks "if, as Mr. Deitz insists, the mistress's
'balls' are her breasts, how could they possibly act as distraction from her
nude body, since it is inconceivable that flesh should distract from itself?"
See also Edgar F. Daniels (entry 737).

◥◤ 751. GOLDBERG, JONATHAN. "Hesper-Vesper: Aspects of Venus in a
    Seventeenth-Century Trope." *SEL* 15: 37–55.
    Notes that the star Venus was called both Hesper and Vesper in the
Renaissance, a double naming that not only occasioned one of Donne's
Paradoxes and Problemes but that he also later used seriously in *The second Anniversarie* (lines 98–99). Analyzes poems by Milton and Marvell
that employ the Hesper-Vesper trope in order "to understand the rich paradoxes implicit in Donne's couplet" and to show that, "in the broadest
sense, that understanding involves an investigation of seventeenth-century
imagery in its relationship to philosophical and religious questions of the
greatest significance" (p. 39). Shows how the Hesper-Vesper trope "is a
limited yet significant example of the relationships between seventeenth-
century imagery and thought" and notes that "the neoplatonism of these
poems reaches back as far as the Florentine Academy and their typology
has roots in the writings of St. Paul" (p. 54). Suggests, however, that "their
combination in English poetry occurs first in the seventeenth century"
and that this combination reflects the peculiar quality of the seventeenth-
century mind and stands "at the center of any discussion of the nature of
its poetry" (p. 54). Concludes that "in the Elizabethan skies one star went
by two names and signified opposite times of day; but daybreak and sunset
meet in Christ, alpha and omega; youth and age meet in Him and in our
souls; the world, the flesh, and the devil (what Donne saw in the multi-
nominous Venus) and heaven, soul and Christ, are reconciled in the *con-
cordia discors* of Hesper and Vesper" (pp. 54–55).

≈§ 752. GRANQVIST, RAOUL. *The Reputation of John Donne 1779–1873.* (Acta Universitatis Upsaliensis, Studia Anglistica Upsalensia, 24.) Uppsala: [Universitet]; Stockholm: distributed by Almqvist & Wiksell International. 212p.

Surveys available data about Donne and his works, both poetry and prose, and charts his critical reception from 1779 (Dr. Johnson's "Life of Cowley") to 1873 (Grosart's second volume of Donne's poetry). Finds three basic attitudes toward Donne and his work during the eighty-four years surveyed: "one derogatory (a continuation of the adverse criticism of the eighteenth century); a second ambivalent and apologetic; and a third laudatory (containing the seeds of the twentieth-century appraisals of Donne)" (p. 171). Notes that the modern Donne revival was underway from about 1830 and points out that "there was a wider recognition of Donne in his functions as a literary personality, orator, moralist, and churchman" (p. 173), that approaches to Donne's work were greatly expanded, and that, in addition to being evaluated as a satirist, Donne's other works were increasingly taken seriously, especially his religious poetry and prose. Calls the twentieth-century "discovery" of Donne a myth and argues that "the resurrection of Donne started much earlier, about 1800," that "it gained in vigour and impetus throughout the century," and that, "if we wish to commemorate single individuals in the restitution of Donne's fame, it should be Coleridge and his immediate successors rather than Gosse and Eliot" (p. 174). Contains a preface (pp. 11–15), an introduction (pp. 17–24), and a conclusion (pp. 171–74). Divided into two major parts, each of which contains five chapters: Part I, 1779–1830 (pp. 25–79), contains (1) "Johnson on Donne," (2) "Literary Historians and Antiquarians on Donne" (with comments on the appearance of Donne's poetry and prose in anthologies), (3) "Walton's *Life of Donne*: A Source of Information and Inspiration" (with comments also on various paraphrases and editions of the *Life*); (4) "Donne in the *Retrospective Review*," and (5) "S. T. Coleridge and Some Romantic Essayists on Donne" (especially the Lamb Circle, William Hazlitt, and Walter Savage Landor); and Part II, 1830–1873 (pp. 101–70), contains (1) "Views on Donne's Prose" (including a discussion of Donne's influence on Coleridge's sermons and on the Oxford Movement), (2) "Literary Historians and Scholars on Donne's Poetry" (noting the exclusion of Donne from *The Golden Treasury* and certain other standard anthologies while also pointing out the increasing appearance of his secular and sacred poems in many other anthologies), (3) "Donne's Biography," (4) "Three Victorians on Donne" (especially Leigh Hunt, Coventry Patmore, and Robert Browning), and (5) "Transcendentalists on Donne" (especially Emerson, Thoreau, and James Russell Lowell). Contains a bibliography of primary sources, arranged chronologically and including sixty-four new items (pp. 175–88) and a bibliography of secondary sources, arranged alphabetically (pp. 189–94), as well as an index (pp. 195–212) and seven illustrations of eighteenth- and nineteenth-century engravings.

◆§ 753. GRAY, BENNISON. *The Phenomenon of Literature.* (De proprietatibus litterarum, Series Maior, 36). The Hague and Paris: Mouton. xiii, 594p.

Argues that literature can best be defined and analyzed as fiction. By
way of defining the phenomenon of literature, notes briefly that "The
Canonization" contains rhetorical elements, but because it lacks specific
characteristics of a space-time event, it is not literature" (p. 281). Argues
that the lesson to be learned from Murray Krieger's attempt to define literature in *The New Apologists for Poetry* (1956) is that "no adequate theory
of literature can be based on Metaphysical poems like 'The Canonization'" and that "the reason is simple: it has an element of direct address
but not sufficiently sustained and particularized to be an act of utterance,
a fictional event" (p. 290). Maintains that "The Flea," however, is literature because in it "we are provided with a clearly particularized act of
utterance" and thus "it is an unequivocal Monolog" (p. 291).

◆§ 754. HENRICKSEN, BRUCE. "The Unity of Reason and Faith in Donne's
Sermons." *PLL* 11: 18–30.

Argues that in his sermons and elsewhere Donne, by affirming the
Thomistic unity of faith and reason, "takes a position between the extreme
elevation of reason by the scientists and its extreme denigration by the
radical Protestants" and that, "despite the frequent polemics against Catholics in his sermons, Donne adopts the Tridentine injunction against 'subtle
disputation,' and in the central problem of reason and faith he confidently
asserts that no separation exists" (p. 19). Notes that Donne "stresses those
aspects of Augustinianism that are compatible with Thomism" and that,
although he rarely mentions St. Thomas by name, the sermons and *Essays in Divinity* "reveal a thorough knowledge of Aquinas and they often
make silent use of arguments and propositions derived from him" (p. 21).
Points out that, although Donne knew the scientific theories of his day,
"the truth of these theories is not of great importance compared to the
devotional truths of God's Church" and that, able to use either the old or
the new in his poetry and prose, "his attitude toward secular knowledge is
a logical extension of his method of reconciling the claims of reason and
faith" (p. 29). Concludes that "at a critical juncture in this historical
movement from medieval unity to contemporary absurdity one finds Donne
as a person aware of the dangers of the new theology, ambivalently fascinated and threatened by the new science, and somewhat nostalgically
attempting, like Milton's educator, to repair the ruins" (p. 30).

◆§ 755. HILL, J. P., AND E. CARACCIOLO-TREJO, eds. *Baroque Poetry.*
Selected and translated, with an introduction by J. P. Hill and E.
Caracciolo-Trejo. London: J. M. Dent & Sons; Totowa, N.J.: Row-
man and Littlefield. xx, 276p.

The introduction (pp. xi–xvii) defines *baroque* as a literary term and
explains the rationale and organization of this anthology of English, French,

Spanish, Italian, and German baroque poems of the sixteenth and seventeenth centuries. Suggests that, although individual poets and national literatures differ, baroque poetry is characterized by its uses of the conceit; the manipulation of syntax that creates ambiguity or drama; excess, exaggeration, and a relatively uncontrolled energy; individualism; and certain similar themes. Divides the anthology into five major sections, each of which is introduced by a brief critical essay: (1) "Vision of Nature"; (2) "Artifice," which includes "The Anagram" (pp. 105–6) and "The Autumnall" (pp. 138–39); (3) "Love," which includes "The Dreame" (p. 148); (4) "On Life, Time and Death," which includes three of the Holy Sonnets: "This is my playes last scene" (p. 188), "Oh my blacke Soule" (p. 196), and "Death be not proud" (p. 220); and (5) "The Love of God," which includes two Holy Sonnets: "At the round earths imagin'd corners" (pp. 264–65) and "Batter my heart" (p. 265). Literal translations of foreign poems with text of the original. Selected bibliography (p. xviii).

≈§ 756. HOLLANDER, JOHN. *Vision and Resonance: Two Senses of Poetic Form.* New York: Oxford University Press. xiii, 314p.

Mentions Donne in several previously published essays and in one new one. "Donne and the Limits of Lyric" (pp. 44–58) first appeared in A. J. Smith, ed., *John Donne: Essays in Celebration* (entry 508). Contrasts between Donne and Thomas Campion and comments on Donne's poems as texts "whose musical settings can best be thought of as the 'verbal' music of their own, intense speech cadences" (p. 73) appear in "The Case of Campion" (pp. 71–90), most of which first appeared as an introduction to *Select Songs of Thomas Campion*, selected by W. H. Auden (Boston: David R. Godine, 1973). Comparisons of Donne and Jonson in "Ben Jonson and the Modality of Verse" (pp. 165–85) first appeared as an introduction to *Selected Poems of Ben Jonson* (New York: Dell Laurel Editions, 1961). Comments on Donne's songs as written texts for study in contrast to Elizabethan songs for singing in "Romantic Verse Form and Metrical Contract" (pp. 187–211) appeared in *Romanticism and Consciousness*, edited by Harold Bloom (New York: W. W. Norton, 1970), which, in turn, was expanded from an earlier version of a Blake essay that appeared in *From Sensibility to Romanticism*, edited by Frederick W. Hilles and Harold Bloom (New York: Oxford University Press, 1965). Discusses in a new essay, entitled " 'Haddock Eyes': A Note on the Theory of Titles" (pp. 212–26), "various species of titles and the different kinds of relations they bear to, and effects they exercise on, certain literary texts" (p. 123), especially the short lyric. Notes that "it will be hard to find a group of short poems antedating Donne's *Songs and Sonnets* of 1633 that contains a significant number of examples of what we loosely think of as modern titling" (p. 220) and suggests that even Donne's titles "seem often to bear an indirect or almost perverse relation to the poem when considered as mere labels of subject or topic" (p. 221). Suggests that Donne's titles often function as if they were emblems and "provide a conventional literary context against which dramatic and dialectical qualities of the poems themselves may work, in this case to produce a new sort of lyric, neither song nor emblem nor occasional piece nor dramatic musical dialogue, but a mixture of all of these" (p. 223).

⊷§ 757. ISHII, SHŌNOSUKE. "Keijijōshijin to Shūkyō—yonin no Keishi-jōshijen—Donne, Herbert, Crashaw, Vaughan" [Metaphysical Poets and Religion—Four Metaphysical Poets—Donne, Herbert, Crashaw, Vaughan], in *Eikoku Renaissance to Shūkyō* [Renaissance and Religion in England], edited by Shōnosuke Ishii and Peter Milward, pp. 113–58. Tokyo: Aratake Shuppan.
Discusses the religious sensibility and theological views of Donne, especially as these are reflected in his poetry (pp. 115–21). Includes discussions also of Herbert, Crashaw, and Vaughan.

⊷§ 758. JASON, PHILIP K. "Donne's 'Elegie XIX (To His Mistress Going to Bed).'" *Expl* 34: Item 14.
Suggests that in the final couplet of the elegy the speaker, by offering himself as a proper "covering" for his mistress, not only presents her with an example and tries to shame her into undressing, but perhaps also "argues that the desired consummation of two bodies (and perhaps two souls) can be thought of as the unification of body and soul into a perfected individual." Argues that "this concept of the new, rarified individual born of love and/or sexual consummation, an idea that runs through many of Donne's earlier poems, provides a witty, reverberating conclusion to the adversary relationship which the poem's opening announced."

⊷§ 759. JONES, MYRL G. "Donne's 'The Good-Morrow.'" *Expl* 33: Item 37.
Points out Donne's uses of various rhetorical figures of word-repetition in "The good-morrow" (*epanalepsis, paroemion, diaphora, epanaphora, antanaclasis*) and shows how they form an integral part of the argument. Explains how the poem "is almost an exercise in the mathematics of love" through its skillful uses of singular and plural pronouns.

⊷§ 760. KERINS, FRANK. "A Contemporary Variation on John Donne's 'The Flea' by John Davies of Hereford." *N&Q* n.s. 22: 539–41.
Comments on John Davies's admiration for and association with Donne and points out that in his *Scourge of Folly* (1611) appears a Shakespearean sonnet, entitled "The Flea," that seems indebted to Donne's poem but "is quite different in its tonality and emphasis" (p. 540). Suggests that Davies probably obtained a manuscript copy of Donne's poem and composed "his variation as both an exercise of his own wit and a tribute to his friend" (p. 541). Agrees with Gardner that Donne's poem was likely written before 1601.

761. KIPARSKY, PAUL. "Stress, Syntax, and Meter." *Language* 51: no. ✓✓
3: 576–615.

Maintains that "the way stress is patterned in English depends on word and phrasal structure, according to strict rules which are not accounted for by either traditional or more recent metrics," and proceeds to explore these rules in detail and to develop "a formal metrical theory capable of expressing them" (p. 576) based on an inventory of basic patterns, a set of metrical rules, an index of metrical tension, and a set of prosodic rules (pp. 580–86). Specifically comments on Donne's metrics (pp. 602–3, 605–6). Scans several lines, drawn primarily from *La Corona*, the *Holy Sonnets*, and the *Elegies*, to show that "what so bothered the contemporary champions of 'correctness' [such as Ben Jonson] was that Donne's poetry contains in numbers too great to blame on carelessness or textual inaccuracy, lines that violate the monosyllabic condition of MR2" (p. 605), that is, that the odd-numbered syllables of the line cannot be occupied by stressed syllables unless the stresses are in monosyllabic words. Suggests that Donne's "metrical rules are thus different from those of the main tradition of English poetry" (p. 605).

762. KISHIMOTO, YOSHITAKA. "Donne no Shi no Hiyu—Sono Fūshi ni tsuite" [John Donne's Metaphor—On the Satirical Feature in It]. *Kiyō* (Baika Literary Bulletin, Baika Women's College), 12 (December): 57–66.

Cited in "The 1975 Bibliography," *The Renaissance Bulletin* (The Renaissance Institute, Tokyo) 7 (1980): 36. Unavailable.

763. KORKOWSKI, EUGENE. "Donne's *Ignatius* and Menippean Satire." *SP* 72: 419–38. ✓

Argues that *Ignatius his Conclave* is an early English example of neoclassical Menippean satire. Traces the development of the Menippean tradition and compares *Ignatius* with satires written for and against the Jesuits during the late sixteenth and early seventeenth centuries to show that when Donne wrote his satire there already existed "a strong current of other works much like his own; written in Latin (the *Ignatius* appeared twice in Latin before it was published in English), aimed at the Jesuits (or involving them), set in the next world, describing a secret gathering, and judging the philosopher, savant, or theologian who deserved, better than his rivals and antagonists, the dubious distinctions of some fit niche in Hell, or some similar otherworldly locus" (p. 431). Points out numerous parallels between anti-Jesuit Menippean satires and Donne's, such as the elaborate effort to be anonymous, the use of the victim's name in the title along with an ironic epithet, the mixing of prose and verse, and the ironic uses of the "printer's statement" (which in Donne's case is himself). Suggests that Donne followed the model of Curione's *Pasquillus Ecstaticus* (1545). Notes that Donne's mention of Macer (actually Caspar Schoppe), Reboul, Lucian, Pasquil, and Erasmus shows his familiarity with recent

Continental Menippean satire and notes that in *The Anatomy of Melancholy* (1621) Robert Burton lists *Ignatius* among other Menippean satires. Suggests that Donne may have written his satire at the suggestion of Sir Henry Wotton, the King's ambassador in Venice, who informed James I that Casper Schoppe (a pro-Jesuit Menippean satirist) was preparing an attack on the King's book of theology, *Ecclesiasticus*. Surmises that Donne, in order to win the King's favor, decided to take advantage of the moment, "not only by satirizing Schoppe and the Jesuits, but also by ridiculing them in a genre which had long been an embarrassment to Catholicism—a genre which the Jesuits had attempted to appropriate for their own purposes with dubious success" (p. 438).

꜏ 764. LA BELLE, JENIJOY. "Martyr to a Motion Not His Own: Theodore Roethke's Love Poems." *BSUF* 16: 71–75.

Discusses the influence of Donne on Roethke's love poems and suggests that Roethke's methodology "is consistently in the tradition of Donne" (p. 74). Points out that Roethke directly refers to Donne in "The Swan," that in the elegy "The Dream" he "adopts both the title and theory of one of Donne's love elegies" (p. 72), that he borrows the title "Love's Progress" from Donne, and that in "I Knew a Woman" he uses an image ultimately derived from St. Augustine but that "the master of the method which Roethke uses to handle this image is Donne" (p. 74). Also suggests that, "although usually we do not think of Yeats as essentially in the Donne tradition, Roethke responds to him in a way which does point out the sympathies between the love poems of Yeats and the tradition of Donne" and that "by bringing Yeats into association with Donne, Drummond, Jonson, Marvell, and Lawrence, . . . he offers us a new perspective on a major tradition in English love poetry" (p. 75).

꜏ 765. LERNER, LAURENCE. "The Dream," in *An Introduction to English Poetry: Fifteen Poems Discussed by Laurence Lerner*, pp. 42–51. London: Edward Arnold Publishers.

Explicates the highly intellectual argument of "The Dreame" and contrasts its wit and complexity with Thomas Campion's melodious and direct "Come, O! my life's delight." Also compares "The Dreame" with "The Relique." Shows how Donne mingles lyric, narrative, and dramatic elements and suggests that his originality as a love poet "consists essentially of two things: his wit . . . and his dramatic power" (p. 50). Briefly compares *The second Anniversarie* to Browning's "Johannes Agricola in Meditation" (pp. 161–62) and notes that, while "both poets tell us how the soul journeys through the firmament, impatient to arrive at its goal . . . , what Donne strives toward, Browning simply states" (p. 162).

꜏ 766. LOTTES, WOLFGANG. "'On this *Couch* of *tears*': Meditationen in Schwerer Krankheit von Donne, Wotton, Latewar, Isham und Philipot." *LWU* 8: 56–71.

Discusses the "poem of severe sickness" as a specific genre written within the *meditatio mortis* and *ars moriendi* traditions. Explicates "Hymne to God my God, in my sicknesse" and calls it the high point of Donne's religious poetry. Relates the poem to ideas found in sermons, especially *Deaths Duell*, and compares and/or contrasts Donne's brilliant treatment of severe sickness and impending death with "poems of severe sickness" by Henry Wotton, Richard Latewar (or Latworth), Sir Justinian Isham, and Thomas Philipot—all of whom see suffering and death as meaningful steps toward eternal life.

⁂ 767. McCANLES, MICHAEL. "The Dialectical Structure of the Meta-physical Lyric: Donne, Herbert, Marvell," in *Dialectical Criticism and Renaissance Literature*, pp. 54–117. Berkeley, Los Angeles, London: University of California Press.

Discusses a dialectical method of analyzing Renaissance literary works and demonstrates the method by commenting on specific poems by Donne, Herbert, and Marvell. Examines the highly paradoxical nature of meta-physical poetry and especially comments on how the poems "exhibit paradox in their personae's attempts to exhaust a multi-faceted reality in a single intuition or proposition" (p. 54) and thus how the reader "must make continual adjustments as he grasps the reality through the poem—through in the sense both of instrument, and of a movement beyond it" (p. 56). Suggests that typically Donne "speaks to the reader both through his personae and over their heads, detailing such accommodation of dialectic as the lyric—indigenously a nondialectical genre—can afford" (p. 57) and that Donne attempts "to reduce the interrelations of objects and persons in time and space to a single moment of intuitive, transdiscursive vision" (p. 57). Discusses the dialectic logic, uses of paradox, and inter-penetration of dynamism and stasis in lines from "Obsequies to the Lord Harrington," "Lovers infinitenesse," "A Lecture upon the Shadow," "The Canonization," "The Anniversarie," "The Extasie," "Oh, to vex me, con-trayes meet in one," and "Hymne to God my God, in my sicknesse." Shows that "in both sacred and profane poems Donne engages to best purpose the intimate confrontation between demands for unchanging cer-titude, and a human or divine reality that can be seen only in continually modified perceptions" (p. 72).

⁂ 768. MacCOLL, ALAN. "A Note on Donne's 'Loves Growth.'" *ES* 56: 314–15.

Suggests that in lines 15–18 of "Loves growth" Donne may be referring to the medieval notion that all heavenly bodies, including stars, owe their light to the sun and, therefore, the lines mean that "the stars (including the planets, often spoken of as 'stars') are visible to us only by virtue of the light from the sun which they reflect and which thus 'shows' them without of course altering their actual size" and that, "similarly, love does not really become greater in the spring—the influence of spring is rather to make it 'more eminent,' causing it to reveal itself (by eliciting the 'gentle love deeds' of line 19)" (p. 315). Notes several possible objections to such a reading but maintains that it seems "more characteristic of Donne that he should have constructed his analogy from an item of traditional scientific lore than that he should have got it from some idiosyncratic natural observation" (p. 315).

√√ ◄§ 769. MORTIMER, ANTHONY. *Petrarch's Canzoniere in the English Renaissance.* Edited with introduction and notes by Anthony Mortimer. Bergamo: Minerva Italica. 157p.
Documents the direct influence of Petrarch on English poets of the Renaissance and attempts to show which of the poems in the *Canzoniere* they read and imitated. Points out that Donne demonstrates the continuing vitality of the Petrarchan tradition in the early seventeenth century, not only in his parodies of the conventions but also in his serious use of them. Points out direct borrowings from Petrarch in "Twicknam garden." Notes that Donne extends the range of Petrarchan imagery and devices by using them for non-Petrarchan ends, such as the erotic love poem and the religious sonnets. Presents an anthology of English translations and/or imitations of specific Petrarchan poems (pp. 35–105) followed by the Italian originals (pp. 109–40). Selected bibliography (pp. 143–46).

◄§ 770. MUELLER, JANEL M. "Death and the Maiden: The Metaphysics of Christian Symbolism in Donne's *Anniversaries.*" MP 72: 280–86.
Review article of Barbara K. Lewalski, *Donne's Anniversaries and the Poetry of Praise: The Creation of a Symbolic Mode* (entry 572).
Calls the study a first-rate contribution not only to Donne studies but also to an understanding of seventeenth-century literature in general. Especially praises Lewalski's presentation of the theological and biblical underpinnings of seventeenth-century English Protestantism that inform Donne's poems and finds the presentation of the tradition of eulogistic and complimentary verse also especially helpful. Does not share fully Lewalski's judgment on the final success of Donne's poems and finds Elizabeth Drury a somewhat inadequate symbol.

◄§ 771. NAHDI, SALAH AL. "John Donne's Love Lyrics: A Study in Dramatic Structure." *JEn* 1: 67–76.
Cited in *PMLA Bibliography,* 1980, item #5516. Unavailable.

◄§ 772. ŌI, SŌICHIRO. "John Donne—Sono Ai no Shisei ni tsuite" [John Donne—His Attitude toward His Loves]. *Kenkyū Ronshū* (The Review of Inquiry and Research, Kansai University of Foreign Studies), no. 21 (February): 39–67.
Cited in "The 1975 Bibliography," *The Renaissance Bulletin* (The Renaissance Institute, Tokyo) 7 (1980): 36. Unavailable.

◄§ 773. OTTEN, CHARLOTTE F. "Donne's 'Elegie upon the Untimely Death of the Incomparable Prince Henry.'" *Expl* 33: Item 59.

Suggests that Donne's reference to the mandrake in lines 53–54 and obliquely in lines 79–82 of "Elegie upon the untimely death of the incomparable Prince Henry" is to a sacred tradition concerning mandrakes, not to the magico-medieval one. Notes that in the sacred tradition the mandrake is a "poignant mortuary symbol," as evidenced, for example, in Philo of Carpasia's *Commentary on the Canticles*. Maintains that Donne likens the mourners in the elegy to mandrakes because, "as creatures who sprang from the dark earth and who will return to it, they wear the image of death." Thus, it is mortality that "unites mourners and mandrakes" and both are "nourished and sustained by Prince Henry's 'putrefaction' (1. 56)." Shows that Donne's reference serves to praise the Prince's superior state since he has risen above mortality.

◄§ 774. OWENS, ROBERT R. "The Myth of Anian." *JHI* 36: 135–38.

Notes that the straits of Anian, mentioned in "Hymne to God my God, in my sicknesse" (line 18), are "not a place but an idea that was transformed into an image and for nearly two centuries masqued as a physical location" (p. 135). Disagrees with Grierson and Clay Hunt, who identify the straits as the Bering Straits, since the Bering Straits were not known in Donne's time and since Donne's intention in his poem "is not to identify places on earth, but to assert a spiritual unity symbolized finally by Jerusalem" (p. 135). Points out that after Magellan discovered the straits named for him in 1520 "the existence of a northwest passage became 'necessary' to show the approximate mirror-image and perfect balance of the northern and southern hemispheres" and that the name *Anian* "was associated with the western terminus of the passage, or lands adjacent to it, wherever or whatever they were" (p. 135). Shows that at various times and on various maps Anian was located in different places in North America and Asia and was retained on maps well into the eighteenth century, until Vitus Bering's map of 1730 showed the straits bearing his name and "forced a curious conception in mythography to defer to empirical geography" (p. 138).

◄§ 775. PARKER, BARBARA L., AND J. MAX PATRICK. "Two Hollow Men: The Pretentious Wooer and the Wayward Bridegroom of Donne's 'Satyre I.'" *SCN* 33: 10–14.

Analyzes the structure, content, technique, and imagery of *Satyre I*. Argues that the structure and content "are interrelated and together elucidate the dual themes of inconstancy and self-deception around which all the poem's elements revolve," that the two major parts of the poem (lines 1–52 and 67–112) "are respectively dominated by a spiritual-intellectual and secular-physical character, two antithetical extremes," and that the "fondling motley humorist" serves as a foil and counterpart to the speaker, who "remains the primary butt and focus of the satire through which his character is progressively revealed, first by means of his attitudes in part one and secondly by means of his responses to the events in part two" (p. 13). Maintains that "the structural and thematic parallelism of the two parts is manifested in the overblown self-image of each character; in the correlated stages of their inconstancy, both of which culminate in the metaphorical adultery resulting from the desertion of their respective consorts; in the instability and 'improvident pride' motivating the behavior of each; . . . in the love motif; and in the movement of each part from a higher to a lower moral plane" (p. 13). Points out that in the transitional section of the poem (lines 53–66) the two characters "are equated and finally reduced to the same level" and argues that especially clothing "becomes a metaphor not only for inconstancy but for the illusion and self-deception which it here thematically embraces" (p. 13). Sees both characters in the poem, therefore, as caricatures. Suggests that *Satyre I* "exhibits the tension between the spirit and the flesh which was to engage Donne for the rest of his life" and that "it also adumbrates the concern with constancy that was to become the theme of so many of his later poems" (p. 13). Concludes that Donne probably did not believe in the possibility of constancy, unless, as *Satyre I* suggests, one chooses self-imprisonment.

◄§ 776. PARKER, DEREK. *John Donne and His World.* London: Thames and Hudson. 127p.

Presents a popular account of Donne's life, times, and literary works and reproduces 111 illustrations (portraits of Donne and his associates and contemporaries, maps, legal and literary documents, book illustrations from the period, pictures of places associated with Donne, and so on). Reads Donne's poetry and prose as autobiographical: notes, for instance, that in "The Canonization" Donne "sees Ann [More] and himself as one being, the Phoenix" (p. 39) and suggests that "Goodfriday, 1613. Riding Westward" (perhaps written in 1610) "certainly seems to comment on Donne's perplexities and worries about whether or not to enter the Church" (p. 51). Considers the *Elegies* and certain of Donne's other early poems as reflecting his personal libertinism and his erotic urgings at the time. Acknowledges, however, that "in the love poems one finds a radical moral tone illuminated by experiments in prosody and form, by images which could never have occurred to any poet before him as being possible, and which perhaps only in our own time have seemed natural and have their full effect" (p. 113). Calls the *Satyres* "uncomfortable works, as they were meant to be" (p. 21) and sees them as "obvious examples of his pioneering spirit as far as social criticism goes" (p. 112). Praises Donne's religious poetry for its complexity and sincerity and admires the power of his sermons. Chronology (pp. 115–16), list of sources and bibliography (p. 117), annotated list of the illustrations (pp. 118–23), and index (pp. 124–27).

◄§ 777. PARRISH, PAUL A. "Donne's 'A Funerall Elegie.'" *PLL* 11: 83–87.

Demonstrates how "A Funerall Elegie" "serves as an effective transitional piece between the two longer Anniversary poems" and comments on how "it calls attention, in explicit fashion, to the dominant images and point of view of the *Anatomy*" while, at the same time, hinting "at several concerns to be developed in the *Progres*" (p. 87). Maintains that, perhaps more importantly, "in its recognition and union of two quite distinct yet supportive perspectives on the death of a young girl, 'A Funerall Elegie' anticipates the ultimate and more complete union and reconciliation of the two poems to be achieved in the imaginative responses of the audience" (p. 87).

✒ 778. ———. "Donne's 'The First Anniversarie.'" *Expl* 33: Item 64.

Suggests that the word *retir'd* in line 161 of *The first Anniversary* is crucial to a proper understanding of the image created in lines 147–54 and should be read as "re-attired," a reading that emerges from the immediate context and that requires only a slight orthographical adaptation. Argues that such a reading "allows us to pick up immediately the clothing image with which Donne concludes his concern with the physical size of mankind" and reinforces the notion that man has not only shrunken in physical size but that his mind has been also impaired and crammed into this "tight-fitting garment."

✒ 779. PEACOCK, A. J. "Donne's Elegies and Roman Love Elegy." *Hermathena* 119: 20–29.

Discusses Donne's borrowings in the *Elegies* from Ovid and from other Roman elegiac poets, especially Tibullus, Propertius, and Catullus, and attempts to show that, "in considering Donne's *Elegies*, we should not look simply for borrowings from the *Amores*, but from the wider ethos and conventions of the Roman elegiac tradition" (p. 28). Argues for "a certain independence and eclecticism in Donne's elegaic borrowings" and points out that his "individual and imaginative re-working of certain motifs from the love-elegy" (p. 20) highlight his originality. Stresses that Donne "is in a position to survey love-elegy in its entirety and intelligently derive what is useful to him from every phase of its development" (p. 26).

✒ 780. POP-CORNIS, MARCEL. "Early Seventeenth Century Poetry and the Tradition of Modern Verse," in *Modern English Poetry: A Critical and Historical Reader*. Vol. 1: From Donne to Alexandre [*sic*] Pope (1590–1730), pp. 1–33. Timisoara, Rumania: Timisoara University Press.

Suggests that any survey of modern English poetry must begin with a study of seventeenth-century poetry and comments briefly on a metaphysical tradition from Donne to T. S. Eliot and Edith Sitwell. Surveys the political, intellectual, and religious history of the seventeenth century and comments on how the temper of the times is reflected in the poetry. Outlines major characteristics of metaphysical poetry and briefly surveys the history of the term, especially commenting on Dr. Johnson's criticism of metaphysical poetry. In "John Donne (1572–1631)" (pp. 14–22) discusses Donne's harsh realism, uses of conceits, colloquial language and natural rhythms, "masculine" expression, satirical and comical intentions, self-dramatization, and his love of playfulness and paradox. Comments on "The Sunne Rising"; "A Valediction: forbidding mourning," especially the compass image; and "If poysonous mineralls" to illustrate the major characteristics of Donne's poetry, especially its dramatic elements. Selected bibliography (pp. 51–54).

⋙ 781. POTTER, MABEL. "A Seventeenth-Century Literary Critic of John Donne: The Dobell Manuscript Re-examined." HLB 23: 63–89.

Describes the Dobell Manuscript (Dob) at Harvard (fMS Eng 966.4), which contains a large collection of Donne's works as well as miscellaneous notes written on blank pages and in the margins. Notes that the manuscript is unique among seventeenth-century collections of Donne in that it contains both his poetry and three sermons and especially calls attention to the important first sermon (Psalms 38: 9). Reviews the inconclusive evidence for the original owner of the manuscript and concludes that the Herbert family "is a tempting possibility" (p. 70). Points out that the marginal notes in Dob are by William Balam of Ely (1651–1726) and gives a brief biographical sketch of this admirer of Donne. Surveys the eclectic nature of Balam's notes and evaluates in particular his critical comments on Donne's poems. Surveys also Donne's popularity at the end of the seventeenth and the beginning of the eighteenth century and suggests that Dob "reveals an absorbing interest in John Donne at a time when the development of literary taste was counter to Donne's style" (p. 89) and also reveals Balam as a meticulous and astute literary critic who perhaps deserves to be called "a precursor of analytical criticism" (p. 86).

⋙ 782. REES, DAVID. "Marino and Donne," in Essays in Honour of John Humphreys Whitfield presented to him on his retirement from the Serena Chair of Italian at the University of Birmingham, edited by H. C. Davis, D. G. Rees, J. M. Hatwell, and G. W. Slowey, pp. 181–97. London: St. George's Press.

Contends that, although Marino had no direct influence on Donne and their personalities and careers were dissimilar, the two poets were both, in their own ways, poets in revolt and "major representatives in their respective countries of a move away from the broad Petrarchan tradition which had dominated the lyric in the sixteenth century" (p. 182). Stresses Donne's rejection of and paradoxical uses of the Petrarchan tradition and prevailing poetic fashions; his intensely colloquial, personal, and dramatic tone; his directness and the range of his love poetry; his wit; and his extensive experimentation with form. Suggests that Donne's ability to portray love "as a complex phenomenon involving the whole of the human personality and not as a literary myth organized along conventional, literary lines, combined with his stylistic originality and his intensely dramatic conception of the dynamics of a poem, makes Donne's an utterly distinctive voice" (p. 195). Compares and contrasts Donne and Marino, noting, for instance, that "the world of Marino is brilliantly sensuous, outward, visual, audible, tactile," while that of Donne "is dramatic, personal, inward" (p. 191). Concludes that "Marino, confronted with a declining poetic idiom, aims to revive it by a potent injection of rhetorical violence," whereas "Donne's reaction is to reject it and to substitute for it a style which is sinewy, colloquial, and in any traditional sense 'unpoetic'" and that, whereas "Marino's verse invites the reader to wonder at the musical and decorative quality of language and the virtuosity of the craftsman-poet," Donne's poetry "introduces him with monosyllabic urgency to drama, to argument, and to human predicament" (p. 196).

783. REEVES, TROY DALE. "Donne's 'A Nocturnall upon S. Lucies Day,' 35." *Expl* 34: Item 26.
 Points out that in "A nocturnall upon S. Lucies day" Donne says that the death of presumably Lucy, Countess of Bedford, has reduced him to nothing but insists that "the *ordinary nothing* (line 35) must be distinguished from the *first nothing* (line 29) in order for the reader to understand the perplexing final sentence of the fourth stanza, 'If I an ordinary nothing were, / As shadow, a light, and body must be here' (lines 35–36)." Comments on Donne's understanding of these two kinds of nothing by quoting from several of the sermons. Maintains that Donne, "sunk to the first nothing, to the chaos and non-being which preceded creation itself, has no body to cast a shadow were there light" and "has become, indeed, less than nothing, less than *ordinary nothing*, the 'Elixir,' the very essence, of the *first nothing*."

784. RICHMOND, HUGH M. "Personal Identity and Literary Personae: A Study in Historical Psychology." *PMLA* 90: 209–21.
 Discusses "historical psychology" and sees it as "a whole valid discipline parallel to literary criticism and reinforcing it, which studies the evolution of human sensibility and mental processes in ways also analogous to and largely including such more selective disciplines as the History of Science, or even the History of Ideas" (p. 209). Illustrates its procedures by suggesting that "partly as a result of nonliterary pressures in the Renaissance the human mind acquired certain possibilities for self-definition and heightened performance which were not as fully recognized in the literature of previous periods, so that the study of the uses of these resources in Renaissance literature is still essential to the full development of modern personal identity, as our continued admiration suggests" (p. 209). Discusses the Renaissance "legitimizing of a truly private individuality free equally" from a "growing revulsion from orthodox public roles and services, above all in the ecclesiastical hierarchy to which politics remained nominally subordinated throughout the Renaissance" (pp. 209–10). Among many

examples, discusses briefly Donne's "virtuosity in striking distinctive poses" in his poems and notes that the poems often "reject public office and rewards, while attempting to vindicate the worth of the private sexual satisfactions" (p. 211), as observed, for example, in "The Canonization." Suggests that the social discrimination that Donne suffered because of his Catholicism only served to intensify his rejection of fame, honor, and public roles. Compares Donne and Shakespeare and suggests that Donne created, "both in and out of his lyrics, a persona as complex, subjective, and volatile as any of Shakespeare's more gifted heroes" (p. 216). Maintains that, under the inspiration of Shakespeare, poets such as Donne, Milton, and Marvell "mapped out our modern sense of dimensions of personality" (p. 218).

⋙ 785. RISSANEN, PAAVO. "The Background of Experience Behind Donne's Secular and Religious Poetry." NM 76: 282–98.

Argues that, by examining the emotional background and experience that lie behind Donne's poetry and relating his ways of thinking and feeling in the poems to known biographical information, one can reconcile the seemingly separate personages of Jack Donne, the young libertine lover of the *Elegies*, and Doctor Donne, the divine of the hymns. Shows that in both secular and religious poems one can detect a common denominator: "the search for love and security, for emotional and existential fulfillment" (p. 282). Traces Donne's search for true human love in the *Elegies* and the *Songs and Sonets* and his equally difficult search for security and the fulfillment of God's love in his religious poems. Finds "The Extasie" an important turning point in Donne's quest, for in it he expresses new and different attitudes about love and "expounds his experience that love is not a static thing, but a dynamic process that expands and grows, finding new levels and dimensions" (p. 288). Disagrees with those who approach such poems on purely formalistic grounds and regard them as merely witty, rhetorical performances built on Renaissance theories of love or conventional models. Suggests that Donne's major crisis came in 1617, with the death of his major support, Ann More, and that following her death he turned more earnestly to finding security and fulfillment in God. Argues that "the fact that Donne sought and found a religious solution to his problems does not necessarily mean that they were religious in their nature, nor that peace with God was the only possible answer" (p. 297) but it was Donne's solution. Concludes that "at the core both Jack Donne and Doctor Donne lose their masks, and their story becomes that of John Donne, which in itself, at the deepest level, is the universal story of man, on his search for, and reaching of fulfillment" (p. 298).

⋙ 786. ROBERTS, JOHN R., ed. *Essential Articles for the Study of John Donne's Poetry.* (The Essential Articles Series, gen. ed. Bernard N. Schilling.) Hamden, Conn.: Archon Books, an imprint of The Shoe String Press. xiii, 558p.

Contains a foreword by Bernard N. Schilling (pp. ix–x) that explains the purpose of the series; a preface (pp. xi–xiii) that explains the guiding principles behind the selection of essays; thirty-nine previously published essays (reprinted without editorial changes) divided into eight major categories—(1) Donne's Reputation, (2) Donne and the Development of English Poetry, (3) Donne's Uses of Tradition, (4) Prosody and Rhetorical Tradition, (5) Love Poetry, (6) Religious Poetry, (7) The Anniversaries, and (8) Miscellaneous Poems (pp. 1–474); notes from the individual essays (pp. 475–553); and a selected bibliography of modern criticism (pp. 555–58). Essays published between 1968 and 1978 have been annotated in this bibliography; for annotations of the others, see John R. Roberts, *John Donne: An Annotated Bibliography of Modern Criticism, 1912–1967* (Columbia: University of Missouri Press, 1973). The following essays are included: (1) Mario Praz, "The Critical Importance of the Revived Interest in Seventeenth-Century Metaphysical Poetry," from *English Studies Today*, edited by C. L. Wrenn and G. Bullough (London: Oxford University Press, 1951), pp. 158–66; (2) William R. Keast, "Johnson's Criticism of the Metaphysical Poets," from *ELH* 17 (1950): 59–70; (3) Kathleen Tillotson, "Donne's Poetry in the Nineteenth Century (1800–72)," from *Mid-Victorian Studies*, edited by Geoffrey and Kathleen Tillotson (London: Athlone Press, 1965), pp. 278–300, which first appeared in *Elizabethan and Jacobean Studies* (Oxford: The Clarendon Press, 1959), pp. 307–26; (4) Merritt Y. Hughes, "Kidnapping Donne," from *Essays in Criticism* (2d series), University of California Publications in English 4 (1934): 61–89; (5) F. W. Bateson, "Contributions to a Dictionary of Critical Terms. II. Dissociation of Sensibility," *EIC* 1 (1951): 302–12; (6) Frank Kermode, "Dissociation of Sensibility," from *KR* 19 (1957): 169–94; (7) Beatrice Johnson, "Classical Allusions in the Poetry of Donne," from *PMLA* 43 (1928): 1098–1109; (8) Don Cameron Allen, "John Donne's Knowledge of Renaissance Medicine," from *JEGP* 42 (1943): 322–42; (9) Josef Lederer, "John Donne and the Emblem Practice," from *RES* 22 (1946): 182–200; (10) W. A. Murray, "Donne and Paracelsus: An Essay in Interpretation," from *RES* 25 (1949): 115–23; (11) Robert Ornstein, "Donne, Montaigne, and Natural Law," from *JEGP* 55 (1956): 213–29; (12) Louis L. Martz, "Donne and the Meditative Tradition," from *Thought* 34 (1959): 269–78; (13) Donald L. Guss, "Donne's Petrarchism," from *JEGP* 64 (1965): 17–28; (14) Arnold Stein, "Meter and Meaning in Donne's Verse," from *SR* 52 (1944): 288–301; (15) Michael F. Moloney, "Donne's Metrical Practice," from *PMLA* 65 (1950): 232–39; (16) A. J. Smith, "An Examination of Some Claims for Ramism," from *RES* n.s. 7 (1956): 348–59; (17) Thomas O. Sloan, "The Rhetoric in the Poetry of John Donne," from *SEL* 3 (1963): 31–44; (18) R. L. Colie, "The Rhetoric of Transcendence," from *PQ* 43 (1964): 145–70; (19) Michael McCanles, "Paradox in Donne," from *Studies in the Renaissance* 13 (1966): 266–87; (20) Helen Gardner, "The Argument about 'The Ecstasy,'" from *Elizabethan and Jacobean Studies Presented to F. P. Wilson*, edited by Herbert Davis and Helen

Gardner (Oxford: The Clarendon Press, 1959), pp. 279–306; (21) Merritt Y. Hughes, "Some of Donne's 'Ecstasies,'" from *PMLA* 75 (1960): 509–18; (22) William J. Rooney, "'The Canonization'—The Language of Paradox Reconsidered," from *ELH* 23 (1956): 36–47; (23) John Freccero, "Donne's 'Valediction: Forbidding Mourning,'" from *ELH* 30 (1963): 335–76; (24) Clarence H. Miller, "Donne's 'A Nocturnall Upon S. Lucies Day' and the Nocturns of Matins," from *SEL* 6 (1966): 77–86; (25) Douglas L. Peterson, "John Donne's *Holy Sonnets* and the Anglican Doctrine of Contrition," from *SP* 56 (1959): 504–18; (26) M. E. Grenander, "Holy Sonnets VIII and XVII: John Donne," from *Boston University Studies in English* 4 (1960): 212–17; (27) A. B. Chambers, "Goodfriday, 1613. Riding Westward: The Poem and the Tradition," from *ELH* 28 (1961): 31–53; (28) A. B. Chambers, "The Meaning of the 'Temple' in Donne's *La Corona*," from *JEGP* 59 (1960): 212–17; (29) Harold Love, "The Argument of Donne's *First Anniversary*," from *MP* 64 (1966): 125–31; (30) Patrick Mahony, "The *Anniversaries*: Donne's Rhetorical Approach to Evil," from *JEGP* 68 (1969): 407–13; (31) Dennis Quinn, "Donne's *Anniversaries* as Celebration," from *SEL* 9 (1969): 97–105; (32) Carol M. Sicherman, "Donne's Timeless *Anniversaries*," from *UTQ* 39 (1970): 127–43; (33) P. G. Stanwood, "'Essentiall Joye' in Donne's *Anniversaries*," from *TSLL* 13 (1971): 227–38; (34) A. LaBranche, "'Blanda Elegeia': The Background of Donne's 'Elegies,'" from *MLR* 61 (1966): 357–68; (35) N. J. C. Andreasen, "Theme and Structure in Donne's *Satyres*," from *SEL* 3 (1963): 59–75; (36) Thomas O. Sloan, "The Persona as Rhetor: An Interpretation of Donne's *Satyre III*," from *QJS* 51 (1965): 14–27; (37) David Novarr, "Donne's 'Epithalamion Made at Lincoln's Inn': Context and Date," from *RES* n.s. 7 (1956): 250–63; (38) Laurence Stapleton, "The Theme of Virtue in Donne's Verse Epistles," from *SP* 55 (1958): 187–200; and (39) W. A. Murray, "What Was the Soul of the Apple?" from *RES* n.s. 10 (1959): 141–55.

✎§ 787. ROCKETT, WILLIAM. "John Donne: The Ethical Argument of *Elegy III*." *SEL* 15: 57–69.

Notes that, just like Sophia in Bruno's *Spaccio de la bestia trionfante*, the narrator of "Change" believes "that movement or 'change' is the cause of pleasure, though what he means is the change from one woman to another rather than from one state or condition to another" (p. 57). Discusses Donne's libertine version of the Epicurean notion that the most certain way to pleasure is to imitate the constant movement found in nature and suggests that "the sense of equilibrium which Donne finds in the moving waters of his conclusion, a *via media* between the stagnant pool and the 'vast sea,' has something in common with the imagery in which later proponents of Epicurus described the effect of stability or constancy in the ethical life conceived of from the Epicurean point of view" (p. 58). Notes that Donne's narrator tries to avoid both the motionless pool of constancy and the indiscriminate lechery of animals and looks to a sexual mode of carefully selected change from one woman to another. Observes that what one feels in Donne's conclusion "is an opening out and a liberation, however precisely controlled, from states of putrefaction (either motionless or random movement) through purity (the moving water and musical harmony) to illumination (the discovery of eternity in generation)" and that "to cultivate a sexual mode which imitates the continuity of a world of ceaseless changes would seem to be the motive of Donne's argument" (p. 67). Notes that such a notion approximates a norm of constancy in movement but excludes the intensity of pleasure described in "The Extasie."

≈§ 788. Ruoff, James E. "John Donne," in *Crowell's Handbook of Elizabethan & Stuart Literature*, pp. 115–20. New York: Thomas Y. Crowell.

Published in England as *Macmillan's Handbook of Elizabethan & Stuart Literature* (London: Macmillan, 1975).

Presents a biographical sketch of Donne and comments on the major characteristics of his poetry and prose, such as his major themes, his uses of conceits and metaphors, his rhetorical directness and colloquial language, his uses of dramatic and argumentative elements, and his metrical roughness. Notes, for instance, that Donne's "relentless pursuit of exactness, coupled with a white-hot wit, breathtaking capacity for speculation, and contempt for conformity allow for few compromises with shallow-minded readers or with those sentimentalists who insist upon a conventional vocabulary for love poetry" and that "no single phrase can be omitted, no metaphor relinquished, without impairing the poem as a steadily unfolding process" (p. 117). Suggests that the tone of Donne's prose often "invokes the Augustinian and Counter-Reformation anxieties attendant upon recalling man's physical decay, disease, death, and depravity" and that his prose style "is characterized by open-ended coordinating conjunctions that pile up phrases as if into limitless expanse" (p. 119). Briefly traces and comments on Donne's critical reputation from his own time to the present and lists major editions and bibliographies.

≈§ 789. Selden, Raman. "John Donne's 'Incarnational Conviction.'" *CritQ* 17: 55–73.

Discusses Donne's "mixed style" in the light of Erich Auerbach's account of the Christian mixed style and suggests that metaphysical wit "may be regarded as the effect of incongruity and of paradox which results from the clash of the sublime and the low, an effect which had already been implicit in early Christian literature, and which becomes the focus of a distinctive new style in metaphysical poetry" (p. 57). Argues that, if the reader is prepared to read Donne's secular poems for their deep structures rather than settling for their superficial structures, then it can be shown that many of the poems "turn upon one transformation or another of . . . his *incarnational conviction*" (p. 59). Shows, for example, that

"The Extasie" is an anti-Platonic poem and that "the metaphor of incarnation is structurally determining at the deepest level" (p. 64) when the lovers decide to return to their bodies so that love may be manifested to others. Finds transformations of Donne's incarnational conviction also in "A Valediction: of the booke," "Aire and Angels," "Loves growth," and "A Valediction: forbidding mourning," all poems in which spiritual love is manifested through the body. Notes that "The Dissolution" and "A nocturnall upon S. Lucies day" both "explore the spiritual effects of bereavement in highly corporeal terms" (p. 68); that "The Primrose" presents "a restless intellectual search for an adequate psycho-physical medium, in which love may inhere" (p. 69); and that in *The second Anniversarie* "the image of the word incarnate is close to the surface" (p. 71) as Donne praises Elizabeth Drury for figuring forth divine beauty. Acknowledges that not all of Donne's poems depend upon a transformation of his incarnational conviction but maintains that in many he presents "an explicit or implicit critique of Platonism and Word-Flesh theology" (p. 70).

❧ 790. SERPIERI, ALESSANDRO. "Sull'uso del modello comunicativo nella poesia di John Donne: *The Funerall* e *The Relique.*" *SCr* 9: 275–308.

Approaches text analysis through semiotics to demonstrate relationships between "The Funerall" and "The Relique." Comments on the presence of both thematic and structural parallels and indicates that both poems contain and constitute a "signal" to be decoded. Constructs double communicative models for each poem to demonstrate parallels between the romantic interplay of sender and receiver of the message codified in the wreath of hair and the interplay of wit between poet and reader-recipient of the poetic message. Rejects critical interpretations of either poem as representing Platonic love and points out erotic implications of both signal and communicative process, whether desire is acted upon or maintained at a subliminal level.

❧ 791. SHAABER, M. A. *Check-list of Works of British Authors Printed Abroad, in Languages other than English, to 1641*. New York: The Bibliographical Society of America. xx, 168p.

Lists two works by Donne (p. 56): (1) *Conclaue Ignati. Siue eius in nuperis inferni comitiis inthronisato* . . . [Germany? after 1611] and (2) *Problematorum miscellaneorum antaristotelicorum, centuria, dimidiata,* . . . a Ludouico Rouzaeo . . . Lugduni Batauorum, ex officina Godefridi Basson . . . 1616.

❧ 792. SMITH, A. J., ed. *John Donne: The Critical Heritage*. (The Critical Heritage Series, gen. ed. B. C. Southam.) London and Boston: Routledge & Kegan Paul. xvii, 511p.

Presents critical commentary on Donne's poetry from his own time to the 1880s "to show what people have made of Donne's poetry over several hundred years and how opinions of it have shifted in that time" (p. xv). Includes general discussions on metaphysical poetry only when Donne is mentioned specifically and includes comments on Donne's prose only when they relate to the poetry. Introduction (pp. 1–28) surveys Donne's critical reputation from the seventeenth through the nineteenth centuries. Points out that his poetry was not widely read in his own day and that there is little evidence to show that he led a new poetic movement in the early seventeenth century. Discusses the appearance of Donne's poems in manuscript collection and in collections of manuscript miscellanies as well as references to them in printed books. Notes, however, that "for more than thirty years following the first publication of his poems [1633] Donne's supremacy among English poets was generally acknowledged" (p. 11) but that in the 1660s and in the following three decades his poetry "had become a mere curiosity which the amateur might indifferently patronise or discount" (p. 12). Suggests that by the early eighteenth century "Donne was a dead issue, a historical specimen only, and no dramatic fluctuations of his fortune were remotely in prospect" (p. 13), partly because relatively few readers knew his poetry, or if they did, they knew only the satires. Surveys Dr. Johnson's critical evaluation of Donne's poetry and concludes that Johnson's greatest disservice to Donne is that "he reduces Donne's poetry to wit and wit to a random trick of style" (p. 17). Comments extensively on the role Coleridge played in reviving interest in Donne among certain important nineteenth-century writers and evaluates the importance of new editions of and selections from Donne's poems, especially Grosart's edition of 1872, but notes that throughout the nineteenth century the reaction to Donne was quite mixed and that he was not widely read and acknowledged. Comments also on Donne's reception in America, noting in particular the criticism of James Russell Lowell. The main text is divided into three major sections: seventeenth, eighteenth, and nineteenth centuries; each separate entry is introduced by and commented on by the editor. "The Seventeenth Century" (pp. 31–163) contains a list of quotations, imitations, and echoes of Donne's poems from 1598 (Everard Guilpin's partial paraphrase of *Satyre I*) to 1700 (Dryden's adaptation of certain ideas from the *Anniversaries* for a funeral poem); has four lists of general references to Donne's poems or to Donne as a poet (circa 1608–1630; the 1630s and 1640s; 1650s; and 1660–1700); offers critical extracts from and commentary on various Donne manuscripts and editions; and presents critical commentary on Donne's poetry or poems addressed to him or about him from Ben Jonson (circa 1610) to Christian Wenicke (1697)—a total of 61 entries. "The Eighteenth Century" (pp. 165–259) lists references to Donne's poetry or to Donne and quotations from his poems from about 1700 (an anonymous marginal comment in a 1633 edition of the poems: "Donne is a dull ass") to about 1795 (Blake's reference to *Metempsychosis* in his notebook) and presents critical commentary on Donne from individuals and from anonymous reviewers (from Jeremy Collier in 1701 to Nathan Drake in 1798, 1817) as well as accounts in dictionaries and encyclopedias, both English and foreign—a total of 49 entries. "The Nineteenth Century" (pp. 261–491) lists critical commentary on the poems from 1795–1796 (Coleridge's notebooks) to 1889 (a letter of Sarah Orne Jewett), including anonymous reviews, the first publication of "Loves Warr" (1802), comments from and on various editions and selections of the poems published during the period, and references to the poems (such as George Eliot's use of Donne stanzas as chapter headings in *Middlemarch*)—a total of 110 entries. Appendix A (pp. 492–94) lists publications of Donne's poems from 1609 (the first stanza of "The Expiration" in Ferrabosco's *Ayres*) to 1912 (Sir Herbert Grierson's two-volume edition); poems reprinted in miscellanies are mentioned in the main text but are not listed in the appendix unless of special importance. Appendix B (p. 495) lists poems by Donne known to have been set to music down to the nineteenth century (from Ferrabosco to Browning). Selected bibliography (pp. 496–97) lists chief works that list references to Donne's poetry or trace the currency of his poems. Two indexes (pp. 499–511): (1) Donne's writings and (2) general index.

꧁ 793. SPENKO, JAMES L. "Circular Form in Two Donne Lyrics." *ELN* 13: 103–7.

Notes that George Puttenham in *The Arte of English Poesie* (1589) discusses two methods of composing a spherical or circular pattern poem that requires a distinctive ordering of subject matter but does not require a shaping of its typographical design. Suggests that Puttenham's second method of moving from outward statement to central point to outward statement again is the structural principle behind Donne's "The Undertaking" and "A nocturnall upon S. Lucies day" and that in the process Donne also exploits the symbolic meaning of the circle in the two poems. Shows how the structure of "The Undertaking" reflects its content and how Donne "has composed an exaltation of spiritual love within a form that represents the highest manifestation of the spiritual" (p. 106)—the circle—and how the circular form of "A nocturnall upon S. Lucies day" "represents eternity and everything that is spiritually transcendent" and thus "supports the feeling that there may be a new beginning at the end of the poem rather than a futile return to the old one" (p. 107).

꧁ 794. STULL, WILLIAM L. "Elizabethan Precursors of Donne's 'Divine Meditations.'" *Comitatus* 6: 29–44.

Argues that various techniques employed in the *Holy Sonnets* are foreshadowed, in varying degrees, by English sonneteers from Wyatt onward, especially by Elizabethan religious sonneteers such as Barnabe Barnes, Henry Constable, and Henry Lok, and suggests that recent critics have paid attention too exclusively to the meditative tradition and have discounted the literary ancestry of the poems. Comments on Donne's experiments with the rhyme scheme and structure of the sonnet to show that he is in the mainstream of the English tradition that continued Wyatt's

experimentations. Discusses the four-part structure and dramatic metaphors in "O my blacke Soule!" and points out similarities between it and
Lok's "I justly am accusde." Concludes that in the *Holy Sonnets* Donne
"was *un*original in everything but genius" and that "the fourfold logical
structure he uses with such effectiveness originated with Wyatt's translations of Petrarch and was transmitted to Donne by a substantial group of
minor religious sonneteers of the 1590's who anticipated his application
of the secular form to religious thought" (p. 40).

≼§ 795. SULLIVAN, ERNEST. "Authoritative Manuscript Corrections in
Donne's *Biathanatos.*" *SB* 28: 268–76.
Notes that the seven manuscript corrections (six in the Epistle Dedicatory and one in the main text) recorded by John Sparrow in one or the
other of the first issues of *Biathanatos* (entries 510 and 607) can be found
in a single copy of the first issue at Yale University Library. Argues that
"the presence of all corrections in a single copy of the first issue, the near
certain authority of the corrections, the clustering of the corrections in the
Epistle Dedicatory, the existence of the corrections (many in the same
hand) in at least three copies of the first edition, and the likelihood that
the need for corrections was recognized before the sheet containing sig.
Ee2 was cut even though the corrections were not actually made until
after the sheets in these three copies had been cut and bound, all imply
that the corrections represent an effort by the younger Donne, acting through
the publisher, to improve the readings in some copies of the first issue"
(p. 275).

≼§ 796. SUTHERLAND, JAMES, ed. *The Oxford Book of Literary Anecdotes.* Oxford: Clarendon Press. ix, 382p.
Contains three anecdotes relating to Donne: (1) Gives an account (pp.
19–21) by Logan Pearsall Smith of discovering some poems by Donne; a
copy of *Paradoxes*, along with a letter that Donne sent with them; and
several early unpublished letters by Donne at Oakham in a manuscript
volume, which he later had copied at Oxford. Notes that Grierson came
to Oxford to examine the poems in the volume, which was later destroyed
when the house burned down. (2) Notes (p. 21) that shortly after his marriage to Ann More, Donne wrote on a pane of glass "John Donne / An
Donne / Undone" and that the words were still visible in 1749. (3) Recounts (p. 22) the story of Donne's having his picture drawn in his wind-
ing-sheet.

≼§ 797. THOMAS, D. M. *Poetry in Crosslight.* London and New York:
Longman Group. xiv, 246p.
Reproduces poems and other related texts with the hope that "in seeing
a poem under crosslight from other connected but unique texts, readers
will . . . begin to breathe some of the poet's metaphoric excitement" (p.
xiii). Discusses Donne in three separate parts of the book: (1) Reproduces

a selection from *Sermon LXVI* along with "A Hymne to God the Father" (pp. 24–26) to show that, although both "express the same emotion: the ultimate, self-destructive fear that he has 'fallen out of the hands of the living God'" (p. 25), they differ in their uses of rhetoric and tone. Comments also briefly on Donne's pun on his own name in the hymn and suggests that there may also be a pun on Ann More in Donne's use of the word *more*. (2) Places together two dream songs by an American Indian, Papago, along with selections from "On his Mistris" and from Christopher Smart's *Rejoice in the Lamb* (pp. 170–72) to show that, although "there are no dream-songs in English," the three passages "have something of the same mixture of simplicity and symbolic mystery" (p. 172). (3) Reproduces together "A Spell to Destroy Life" by an American Cherokee Indian and "The Apparition" (pp. 174–75) to suggest that, although Donne's incantation in his poem "does not go quite as far, and perhaps it is more literary than literal," it is, nonetheless, like the Indian incantation, "flesh-creeping enough" (p. 175).

✒ 798. TRAUTMANN, JOANNE, AND CAROL POLLARD, eds. *Literature and Medicine: Topics, Titles, and Notes.* Hershey, Pa.: Department of Humanities, Hershey Medical Center. x, 209p.
Annotated bibliography of literary works related to medical topics, with a topical index. Lists fifteen annotated items by Donne (pp. 17–18)—poems and prose works that treat sexuality and sex roles, suicide, the body, disease and health, doctors and the medical profession, death, aging, body-mind relationships, grief, madness, homosexuality, women as healers, and venereal disease.

✒ 799. WALTER, JAMES. "Donne's 'Holy Sonnet XVIII' and the Bride of Christ." *Innisfree* 2: 4–7.
Presents a line-by-line reading of "Show me deare Christ." Notes that the questions posed in the sonnet, "although expressing the agonizing doubt that is part of the search for religious truth, express more significantly Donne's indirect criticism of certain recurrent religious attitudes" and that "receiving the brunt of his criticism is that attitude which demands rationalistic purity in all matters of worship and doctrine" (p. 4). Suggests that the epigrammatic closing couplet of the sonnet implies that all the preceding questions should be answered affirmatively and that Donne argues, therefore, that the true Church "is for men everywhere" and that, "like the City of God described by St. Augustine, she remains constantly 'open' to all lovers despite the bickerings of those who would possess her privately" (p. 7).

✒ 800. WANAMAKER, MELISSA C. *Discordia Concors: The Wit of Metaphysical Poetry.* (National University Publications: Literary Criticism Series, gen. ed. John E. Becker.) Port Washington, N.Y., and London: Kennikat Press. x, 166p.

Employs the philosophical concept of *discordia concors* as a means of explaining wit in the poetry of Donne, George Herbert, Henry Vaughan, Andrew Marvell, and Milton. Distinguishes two types: (1) unity in multiplicity and (2) a violent yoking of opposites. Maintains that the metaphysical poets "found the philosophical concept of *discordia concors* as a yoking of opposites expressive of their own disturbingly discordant world" (p. 13). Although Donne is mentioned throughout the book, Chapter 2, "John Donne: Yoking of Opposites" (pp. 14–36), is devoted exclusively to his attempts to reconcile opposites. Notes that "Donne's secular lyrics may perhaps be best characterized by *discordia concors*, wherein the poet attempts to reconcile opposites, especially those of body and soul, sense and spirit" and that, "when such opposites meet, however, they either clash violently and resist resolution, or they achieve a paradoxical resolution without transcendence of the body" (p. 14). Discusses "The Dampe," "The Flea," "Loves Alchymie," "Aire and Angels," "The Canonization," "The Undertaking," and "The Extasie" to show that the wit of these poems "may be characterized by the manner in which human love itself reflects a kind of *discordia concors*, a harmony of dissonant emotions" (p. 19). Maintains that in the devotional poetry, such as "A Hymne to Christ, at the Authors last going into Germany," Donne "employs *discordia concors* not merely to mirror the harmonious tension between contrary emotions, but to be the dynamic means of translating the earthly into an apprehension of the heavenly" (pp. 19–20). Notes that "by the time Donne was composing his lyrics, metaphor had changed from its traditional role, in which it dressed concepts with words, to one in which it dressed words with concepts" (p. 21). Briefly comments on *Devotions upon Emergent Occasions* to illustrate how "in metaphysical verse the conceptual and divine metaphor mediates between heaven and earth" (p. 23) and presents an analysis of the *Anniversaries* to show that "by changing from an earthly to a divine perspective, the two contraries, heaven and earth, are yoked together" (p. 31) and that Elizabeth Drury herself becomes "the divine mediating metaphor that links with considerable difficulty the extremes of heaven and earth" (p. 32). Notes that later metaphysical poets, unable to effect concord in the Donnean manner, "deal with a discordant world in ways quite foreign to John Donne" (p. 36). Compares and contrasts Donne in subsequent chapters with Herbert (pp. 37–39, 49–50, 53), Vaughan (pp. 55–56), Marvell (pp. 71–73, 90–91, 97), and Milton (p. 98) and summarizes the differences among them (pp. 125–27).

801. WRIGHT, MARGARET. "Donne's Book of Stars." *Communications* (University of Manchester), 5 November, pp. 20–21.

Describes a hitherto unrecorded book from Donne's library that was discovered in the John Rylands Library, a first edition of Johann Kepler's *De stella nova* (1606) that contains Donne's signature, motto, and marginal jottings. Notes that in a marginal note in his *Biathanatos* Donne refers to the book and comments on Donne's interest in astronomy and

especially his familiarity with Kepler's works. Discusses the possible significance of Donne's motto, "Per Rachel ho servito e non per Lea," which
he borrowed directly from Petrarch. Points out that in medieval symbolism Rachel often stood for the contemplative life and Leah for the active
life and suggests that Donne, who was so fully involved in the active life,
may have chosen the motto as "an admonition to himself, not [as] a true
affirmation of his natural inclination" (p. 21). Reproduces the title page
that contains the signature and motto.

1976

ᴥᔥ 802. AIZAWA, YOSHIHISA. "Keijijōshihin to Nihon—Oboegaki" [The
Metaphysical Poets in English—A Note] in *Keijijōshi Kenkyū*
[Metaphysical Poetry Studies], pp. 243–49. Tokyo: Japan Society of
17th-Century English Literature.
Discusses the interest in and study of the metaphysical poets in Japan.
Appends a bibliographical listing of Japanese books and articles and re-
views on metaphysical poets from 1927 to 1975 (pp. 1–32). All available
1968–1978 Donne items are entered and annotated in this bibliography.

ᴥᔥ 803. ARAKAWA, MITSUO. *Shinpishiso to Keijijoshijintachi* [Mystical
Thought and Metaphysical Poets]. Tokyo: Shohakusha. 203p.
Discusses Donne's mystical thought and his attitude toward God (pp.
55–82) through an analysis of a number of his religious poems, especially
several of the *Holy Sonnets*, "Goodfriday, 1613. Riding Westward," "A
Hymne to Christ, at the Authors last going into Germany," "The Annuntiation and Passion," "The Litanie," *La Corona*, and "A Hymne to God
the Father." Stresses that Donne's mystical attitude is fundamentally
Christocentric and that his religious poems are dominated by the image
of Christ as Savior. Follows, for the most part, the views of Itrat Husain
in *The Dogmatic and Mystical Theology of John Donne* (London: SPCK;
New York: The Macmillan Co., 1938).

ᴥᔥ 804. AYRES, PHILIP J. "Donne's 'The Dampe,' Engraved Hearts, and
the 'Passion' of St. Clare of Montefalco." *ELN* 13: 173–75.
Points out that the image of a woman's picture in the lover's heart in
"The Dampe" probably came from an image in Serafino's Strambotto 126.
Notes that Serafino, and perhaps Donne, may have had in mind the story
of St. Clare of Montefalco, whose heart was said to bear formations of
Christ's Passion. Notes that Anthony Munday in *English Romayne Life*
(1582) reports on a visit to Montefalco and that Donne, with his interest
in relics, may have known of the famous shrine and its saint.

ᴥᔥ 805. BACHRACH, A. G. H. "Constantijn Huygens's Acquaintance with
Donne: A Note on Evidence and Conjecture," in *Neerlandica
Manuscripta: Essays Presented to G. I. Lieftinck*, edited by J. P.

Gumbert and J. M. de Haan, 3: 111–17. Amsterdam: A. L. van Gendt.

Discusses the personal relationship between Donne and Constantijn Huygens (1596–1637), the Dutch poet-diplomat and first translator of four of Donne's poems into Dutch (1640). Presents autobiographical evidence to show tht Huygens "knew Donne personally and knew him well" (p. 115). Notes that when he was eighty-two years old, Huygens apostrophized Donne as "Thee, greatest Donne, / I place thee before all others, man divine, best Orator, / First of all Poets: O to how many of your words, / Those golden words, have I listened, / Uttered among friends or from the pulpit . . . " (quoted on p. 116). Suggests also that the inscription on the flyleaf of the copy of *Biathanatos* sent to Huygens by Donne the younger in 1649 indicates a genuine friendship existed between Huygens and Donne. Notes that, at his father's explicit request, Lodewyck Huygens, the poet's son, visited Donne's tomb in St. Paul's in 1632.

◆§ 806. BEALE, WALTER H. "On Rhetoric and Poetry: John Donne's 'The Prohibition' Revisited." *QJS* 62: 376–86.

Disagrees with Thomas O. Sloan's interpretation of "The Prohibition," especially his attempts to correlate the structure of the poem with Ramist rhetoric ("A Rhetorical Analysis of John Donne's 'The Prohibition,'" *QJS* 48 [1962]: 38–45, reprinted in *The Province of Rhetoric*, edited by Joseph Schwartz and John A. Rycenga [New York: Ronald Press, 1965], pp. 528–38, and in *Rhetorical Analyses of Literary Works*, edited by Edward P. J. Corbett [New York: Oxford University Press, 1969], pp. 3–15). Argues that the structure and the meaning of "The Prohibition" are derived from the common Renaissance rhetorical figure of "dilemma" or "horned argument" and shows how this classical and Renaissance rhetorical device informs the poem. Argues that the third stanza is an overturning of the argument of the poem, not a conclusion to it, as suggested by Sloan. Maintains that the poem may be a burlesque of conventional love poetry: "Reduced to absurdity and finally deflated altogether in this poem is not merely the convention of the lover's dilemma, but also an entire poetic language, embodied in the extravagant metaphors of conventional Renaissance love poetry" (p. 386). Notes that Donne partially parallels the logic of the poem in "A burnt ship" and compares Donne's uses of dilemma in "The Prohibition" with Spenser's use of it in *Amoretti*, XLII.

◆§ 807. BEAVER, JOSEPH C. *The Prosody of John Donne*. [Chicago: s.n.] √ v, 142p.

Presents a detailed linguistic analysis of Donne's metrics that is, in part, based upon the metrical theory of Halle-Keyser. Discusses such issues as syneresis or multiple position occupancy (pp. 8–48); diaeresis (pp. 49–50); other aspects of position occupancy: zero occupancy and extrametrical syllables (pp. 51–53); stress prominence in Donne (pp. 54–57); lexical stress in Donne (pp. 58–72); the compound stress rule (pp. 73–82); phrasal stress (pp. 83–108); contrastive stress in Donne (pp. 111–15); and metrical statistics in Donne (pp. 116–24). Appendix A (pp. 125–27) presents a formal summary of rules for Donne's metrics; Appendix B (p. 128) lists some unmetrical lines in Donne's poetry; Appendix C (pp. 129–36) offers sample scansions; Appendix D (pp. 137–39) is an index to titles of poems cited (based on *The Complete Poetry of John Donne*, edited by John T. Shawcross [1967]); and Appendix E (pp. 140–42) lists references.

⋙ 808. BERRY, BOYD M. *Process of Speech: Puritan Religious Writing and Paradise Lost.* Baltimore and London: The Johns Hopkins University Press. xi, 305p.

Chapter 13, "Two Spiritual Autobiographies" (pp. 191–210), compares and contrasts the theology, psychology, religious sensibility, and style of Donne and John Bunyan, as reflected in *Devotions upon Emergent Occasions* and *Grace Abounding to the Chief of Sinners.* Notes that "the idiosyncracies of these men, of their spiritual development, and of their works" clearly "prevent us from labelling them Puritan or Anglican in neatly partisan terms" (p. 192). Mentions Donne throughout. Contrasts Donne's religious sensibility to that of the Puritans and presents a reading of "At the round earths imagin'd corners" to show how Donne brings together "Puritanic" eschatology and a personal sense of sin. Also discusses Donne's uses of the circle in *Devotions upon Emergent Occasions* and in "Hymne to God my God, in my sicknesse."

⋙ 809. BROADBENT, JOHN. "Conceits and consciousness." *TLS*, 16 July, p. 873.

Reviews Anne Ferry, *All in War with Time: Love Poetry of Shakespeare, Donne, Jonson, Marvell* (entry 743), and Dwight Cathcart, *Doubting Conscience: Donne and the Poetry of Moral Argument* (entry 732). Questions the value of new commentaries on Donne's poetry: "I am not convinced that we need another published rehearsal by an individual on Donne's 'The Canonization' but if so it had better be in terms that generate further ideas."

⋙ 810. CALLARD, JOHN, comp. *A Catalogue of printed books (pre-1751) in the Library of St. George's Chapel, Windsor Castle.* (Historical Monographs relating to St. George's Chapel, Windsor Castle, vol. 15.) Printed and published for the Dean and Canons of St. George's Chapel in Windsor Castle by W. S. Maney and Sons, Hudson Road, Leeds. 282p.

Lists five volumes by Donne: (1) the 1640 edition of *LXXX Sermons* (STC 7038); (2) a 1611 copy of *Ignatius his Conclave* (STC 7027); (3) another edition of *Ignatius his Conclave* (1635) (STC 7030); (4) a copy of the 1633 edition of *Juvenilia* (STC 7043); and (5) the 1654 edition of *Letters to Severall Persons of Honour* (Wing D 1865).

◄§ 811. CAMERON, ALLEN BARRY. "Donne's Deliberative Verse Epistles." *ELR* 6: 369–403.

Provides a context for and an analysis of a group of seven of Donne's deliberative verse epistles to show their intrinsic merits as epistolary poems and to demonstrate that "an understanding of the rhetorical conventions of the verse epistles renders the poems immediately accessible" (p. 370). Comments on Donne's attitude toward the letter and maintains that he does not simply regard it as a "self-contained literary artifact, created merely for aesthetic contemplation without ends beyond itself" but rather as "a singularly valuable means of human discourse—a rhetorical structure that may be in fact, by its very existence, both a literal and symbolic witness of affection between the writer and recipient" (p. 371). Centers attention on seven deliberative epistles that were "written in three overlapping rhetorical traditions: the epistolary, the epideictic, and the paraenetic traditions of oratory and literature" (p. 372) and that concern the values of self-knowledge, the wisdom of virtue, and the inner life: (1) "To Sr Henry Wotton: Sir, more then kisses," (2) "To Sr Henry Wotton: Here's no more newes," (3) "To Sr Henry Goodyere: Who makes the Past," (4) "To Sr Edward Herbert. at Julyers: Man is a lumpe," (5) "To Mr R. W.: If, as mine is," (6) "To Mr Rowland Woodward: Like one who," and (7) "To Mr Tilman after he had taken orders." Argues that the verse epistle is "the occasional poem *par excellence*, for it enables the poet simultaneously to mark the occasion with propriety and to transcend it with freedom and in no other occasional poetic type can the poet be so unrestrainedly discursive" and thus the form is "a particularly useful medium for the presentation of tentative conclusions, for arguing rhetorically, that is, on the grounds of probability, and for charting the letter's own thought processes" (p. 402).

◄§ 812. CHAMBERLAIN, JOHN S. *Increase and Multiply: Arts-of-Discourse Procedure in the Preaching of Donne.* Chapel Hill: The University of North Carolina Press. xvi, 197p.

Discusses "the several most notable procedures in the church's preaching up to the time of Donne for developing a scriptural text into a discourse by relating doctrines of the trivium with particular theories and techniques for homiletic invention" and then analyzes sermons "to illustrate how these principles work in practice" and "to accumulate a critical vocabulary with which to discuss Donne's sermons in terms of the traditions upon which he drew" (p. xiv). Divided into two major parts: (1) The Arts of Discourse (pp. 1–91) and (2) Donne's Preaching (pp. 93–158). Chapter 1, "Grammar" (pp. 3–43), discusses the basic principles of the art of discourse "as formulated in treatises on the subject and as assumed by the ancient commentators" and discusses St. Augustine's views on language, their relation to "his procedure for exegetical invention that he sets out in *De doctrina Christiana*" (p. xiv), and their influence on early medieval preaching. Chapter 2, "Dialectic" (pp. 44–66), discusses the divisions of the text prescribed in the *ars praedicandi* of the medieval schoolmen and the dialectical doctrine that informed their procedures of invention and illustrates their practice by analyzing part of a sermon by St. Bonaventure on Psalm 106:8–10. Chapter 3, "Rhetoric" (pp. 67–91), discusses Renaissance treatises on ecclesiastical rhetoric, especially William Perkins's *The Art of Prophecying* (English translation, 1606); surveys the course of Protestant preaching of the English Reformation; and analyzes Perkins's sermons on Matthew 5–7 to illustrate the Puritan methods of discourse that Donne likely heard and later reacted against. Chapter 4, "Procedure" (pp. 95–108), shows that Donne's procedures for developing a text "were adopted in reaction to Puritan reduction by topical logic and were drawn instead from the patristic and medieval practice of taking up Scripture grammatically" (p. 102), a position he shared with the High Church. Chapter 5, "The Sermon" (pp. 109–54), discusses how Donne develops a scriptural text into a sermon; notes that characteristically "the division of the text— the point at which the words of Scripture are made into the structure of the preacher's discourse—is set out in the *divisio* of each sermon" and that this structure is then "filled out by grammatical means of multiplying the signification and consignifications of words" (p. xv); and analyzes in detail Donne's sermon on Psalm 32:1–2 as an example of his characteristic method. Conclusion (pp. 155–58) summarizes the main points of the study and stresses Donne's preference for patristic and scholastic arts-of-discourse procedures. Maintains that Donne "does not unravel his text but complicates it by his reading" and "does not reduce the sense from the verbal medium but lets the meaning of the sacred words realize itself" (p. 157). Notes (pp. 161–77), bibliography (pp. 179–92), and index (pp. 193–97).

> 813. CLEMENTS, ROBERT J., AND LORNA LEVANT, eds. *Renaissance Letters: Revelations of a World Reborn.* Edited with introductions, commentary, and translation by Robert J. Clements and Lorna Levant. New York: New York University Press. xxvi, 468p.
    Anthology of Renaissance letters with a historical survey of the development of the epistle (pp. ix–xiv). Reprints two letters by Donne (with headnotes and explanatory notes): (1) a letter to Sir Henry Wotton (?1599) in which Donne expresses his annoyance with Dante for having condemned Pope Celestine to Purgatory (actually Dante condemns him to Hell) (pp. 79–80); and (2) a conciliatory letter to Sir George More (2 February 1602) in which Donne asks his father-in-law to approve of his marriage (pp. 415–16).

> 814. COGNARD, ROGER A. "The Structural Unity of Donne's 'Lecture Upon the Shadow.'" *The Nebraska English Counselor* 21, no. 2: 15–18.
    Discusses the closely knit structural unity of "A Lecture upon the Shadow" and demonstrates how its "almost mathematically proportioned" (pp. 16–17) structure reinforces the serious argument of the poem. Outlines the

basic argument and comments on thematic and metrical patterns, especially noting Donne's skillful uses of spondee to emphasize major elements. Points out that the poem consists of twenty-six lines, which may represent twenty-six weeks, or one-half year, and suggests that "the primary observation to make, if such structural speculation were true, would be that the end of June marks the midyear, dividing it exactly in half" and that "what Donne may have intended, therefore, is the suggestion of the grandest 'noon' of all—the summer solstice—in an attempt to lend to his concept of mature love of mid-life the nobility he thought it deserved" (p. 18).

✍ 815. DAVIDSON, ALAN. "An Oxford Family: A Footnote to the Life ✓✓
    of John Donne." *Recusant History* 13: 299–300.
    Notes several possible Recusant connections for John and Henry Donne while they were students at Hart Hall, Oxford: (1) their father's sister was married to a Recusant, Robert Dawson, who kept the Blue Boar on the corner of St. Algate's and Blue Boar Lane, and (2) their stepfather, John Syminges, was acquainted with Roger Marbeck, son-in-law of Thomas Williams (and perhaps with Williams himself), whose son, Alexander, ran the Star until 1600. Notes that Marbeck and John Donne went on the Cadiz expedition together in 1596. Notes also that Thomas Williams's son and namesake was one of the first English Jesuits. Concludes that it is likely that John and Henry "knew that one of their uncle's fellow-Jesuits was a brother-in-law of one of their step-father's colleagues, and his family near neighbors to their aunt and uncle at the Blue Boar, and, given that knowledge, almost certain that they visited the Star" (p. 300).

✍ 816. DONNE, JOHN. *John Donne*. Kettering, Eng.: J. L. Carr. 18p.
    Cited in *British National Bibliography*. 1976. Vol. 1: Subject Catalogue, p. 987. London: The British Library Bibliographic Services Division, 1977. Unavailable.

✍ 817. DYSON, A. E., AND JULIAN LOVELOCK. "Contracted Thus: Donne's
    'The Sunne Rising,'" in *Masterful Images: English Poetry from Metaphysicals to Romantics*, pp. 21–28. London: The Macmillan Press; New York: Barnes & Noble Import Division of Harper & Row Publishers.
    First appeared in *Donne: "Songs and Sonets": A Casebook*, edited by Julian Lovelock (entry 574).
    Explicates the rhetorical strategy, dramatic techniques, imagery, tone, and other features of "The Sunne Rising" and suggests that it "thrives on extremes and quintessences, on paradoxes which look at one moment like intellectual scaffolding round simple emotions, at the next like internal complexities threatening the emotions themselves" (p. 27). Questions whether or not Donne effectively unites erotic and spiritual love in the poem: "When Donne projects religious assurance into merely sensual ex-

perience, he sets up tensions hard to resolve" and concludes that "it is because 'The Sunne Rising' celebrates Eros as a true Immortal that it has a real, as well as rhetorical nonsense at the heart" (p. 28).

◆§ 818. ELDER, DAVID. "L'image de l'épine dans la poésie métaphysique anglaise: Exergue et analyse," in *Études anglo-americaines*, pp. 21–35. (Annales de la faculté des lettres et sciences humaines de Nice, 27.) Paris: Minard.

Discusses the wide-ranging uses of the figure of the thorn in poetry, notes its appearance in metaphysical poetry, but warns that it is not found with obsessional frequency in metaphysical poems. Notes briefly Donne's use of the image in his verse epistle "To Mr Rowland Woodward: Like one who," in which he "met en relief le côté corrosif et infécond de des «épines satiriques» . . . où nous sommes incités à devenir les «fermiers de nous-mêmes»" (p. 26). Notes that "l'image de celui qui laboure convenablement son champ et qui acquiert des fruits pour l'éternité est souvent reprise dans la Bible" (p. 26).

◆§ 819. EL-GABALAWY, SAAD. "Aretino's Pornography and Renaissance Satire." *BRMMLA* 30: 87–99.

Comments on how Aretino's notorious book, *Ragionamenti*, and his sonnets, *I Sonnetti Lussuriosi* (with their accompanying pictures of sexual positions designed by Guilo Romano and engraved by Marcantonio Raimondi) became "functional as a medium of social, moral, and political satire in the later Renaissance" (p. 87) and shows that English satirists often refer to Aretino and his obscene manuals as a way "to smear the reputation of literary enemies or in moral and political satire to libel the Roman Catholics, condemn the Italians, expose the licentiousness of court life, denounce the sinfulness of the flesh, or reveal the corruption of human nature" (p. 99). Points out that in *Ignatius his Conclave* Donne links Machiavelli, Aretino, and St. Ignatius as "a triangle of evil" (p. 91) and as "models of depravity, villainy, unscrupulousness, and political expediency placed above morality" (p. 92) and also comments on Donne's references to Aretino in a letter of 1600 and in *Satyre IV*, where the allusion functions "as an emblem of vice to exhibit the poet's 'loathing' in his exposure of sin" (p. 96).

◆§ 820. ———. "Aretino's Pornography in the Later Renaissance." *EM* 25: 97–118.

Comments on the reactions of English writers during the sixteenth and seventeenth centuries to the works of Aretino, especially his *Ragionamenti* and *I Sonnetti Lussuriosi*, which were regarded as pornography, "perhaps the first of their kind in Christendom" (p. 97). Calls Donne's "Going to Bed" and Carew's "A Rapture" "English equivalents—without obscene words—of Aretino's sonnets" (p. 108). Notes, however, that in *Satyre IV* and in *Ignatius his Conclave* Donne "echoes the moral platitudes of his day about the Italian's pornography since they serve his purpose of satire" (p. 108). Notes also that in a letter of 1600 Donne makes a disapproving reference to Aretino. Argues that "not even Donne, in his most intense moments of passion, has celebrated sex in the uninhibited erotic terms of [Carew's] 'A Rapture'" (p. 117).

◄§ 821. ELLIOTT, EMORY. "The Narrative and Allusive Unity of Donne's *Satyres.*" *JEGP* 75: 105–16.

Argues that Donne intended all five of his satires to be read as a whole, that *Satyre III* serves to focus attention on the central ethical and religious meaning of the entire collection, and that Donne employed conventions of narrative and formal structure found in the classical and Renaissance traditions of satire to unify and deepen their meaning. Points out that Donne uses biblical allusions, especially to Matthew's account of the Sermon on the Mount, to focus attention upon the theme of his five poems, "providing them with an underlying unity and enhancing their dramatic power" (p. 110) and providing a "key to the internal conflict of the speaker-protagonist whose moral development the poems trace" (p. 106). Suggests that all five poems, taken together, "present a probing examination of the ideal of Christian charity as a fundamental principle for a life of social action and reform" (p. 106). Also suggests that the experience of the persona parallels Donne's own search for an acceptable vocation in which he could exercise his Christian ideals. Notes that, "from a moral standpoint, the poems are about the dilemma of the Christian humanist," but that, "from a literary standpoint, they are about the problem of satire as a poetic form" (p. 110) that would accommodate the Christian ideals of charity. Through a reading of the five poems shows that the persona finally abandons the role of satirist, deciding that he can have little effect on a wicked world in that role, and finally chooses to become secretary to one of the queen's most honored servants, a role in which, without deserting his religious and ethical ideals, he can redress wrongs and engage in constructive social action and reform. Concludes, therefore, that in the *Satyres*, Donne "appears to have left us a partial record of his search in the form of a collection of poems with unified narrative structure enforced by thematic allusion" (p. 116).

◄§ 822. ELLRODT, ROBERT. "Le fabuleux et l'imagination poétique dans l'oeuvre de John Donne," in *De Shakespeare à T. S. Eliot: Mélanges offerts à Henri Fluchère*, edited by Marie-Jeanne Durry, Robert Ellrodt, and Marie-Thérèse Jones-Davies, pp. 141–52. (Études anglaises, 63.) Paris: Didier.

Discusses Donne's fascination with and uses of unnatural natural history and the fabulous in his poetry, especially his uses of the phoenix. Suggests that Donne had a predisposition to the fabulous but points out that his critical mind tempered or even contradicted his appetite for the marvelous: "ce qui caractérise l'esprit de Donne, c'est moins la croyance ou le doute que le partage entre les deux" (p. 146). Maintains that, although the fabulous inspires interest in Donne's poetry, it is not the center of interest.

◄§ 823. FAULKNER, ELEANOR, AND EDGAR F. DANIELS. "Donne's *Holy Sonnets* XVIII (Since she whome I lovd), 1–2." *Expl* 34: Item 68.

Suggests that lines 1–2 of "Since she whom I lov'd" simply mean that Donne's wife "has paid her debt to Nature as a human being (all must die) and to her own nature as a woman (the danger peculiar to all women of dying in childbirth)" and that "the remainder of line 2 ('and my good is dead') means what it appears to mean: 'All that has been good in my life is dead.'"

◄§ 824. FLUCHÈRE, HENRI. "Fragment d'un «Donne»: Reflexions sur *Songs and Sonets.*" *RLC* 50, 1–2: 32–49.

Emphasizes Donne's modernity and presents a general survey and evaluation of his poetic themes and techniques. Focuses primarily on Donne's uses of images: "L'originalité fondamentale de Donne dans le domaine des images, c'est qu'il assigne à chacune une fonction à la fois discriminative dans le détail et déterminante dans mouvement créateur de la pensée" (p. 37). Notes that Donne's images are not simply illustrative and therefore static but rather are means by which he apprehends the multifaceted complexity of truth.

◄§ 825. FLYNN, DENNIS. "Donne's Catholicism: II." *Recusant History* 13: 178–95.

Continuation of entry 744. Surveys the circumstances surrounding Donne's marriage and suggests that he may have assumed that Egerton, himself a former Recusant, would support him in a difficult time. Finds particularly objectionable Bald's dismissal of Catholicism as a shaping force on Donne's poetry and thinking during his so-called middle years and notes that, although Donne publicly announced himself an Anglican during this time, "'A Litanie' and the other religious poems written at Mitcham, including most of the 'Holy Sonnets,' are the products of his private devotion" and "show that the tone of this devotion was essentially Catholic" (p. 188). Comments on the sense of spiritual isolation in many of Donne's devotional poems and traces briefly his slow, painful steps toward accepting Anglican holy orders.

◄§ 826. FRENCH, ROBERTS W. "Donne's 'Dissolution': What Does a Poem Mean, and Is It Any Good?" *CEA* 38, no. 2: 11–15, 46.

Presents a critical discussion of "The Dissolution" in the form of an imaginary conversation among three students—Volumnia, Cassius, and Antonio. Discusses the tone and structure of the poem; its uses of imagery, language, and conceits; and its relation to Petrarchan tradition and its genre. Focuses on the issue of how one can judge the effectiveness and/or success of a poem that triggers very disparate responses.

✒§ 827. FRIEDMAN, DONALD M. "Thomas Adams and John Donne." *N&Q* n.s. 23: 229–30.

Notes that the well-known preacher Thomas Adams, who perhaps met Donne in 1618 or 1619, was apparently acquainted with the *Anniversaries* before that time, as indicated by remarks in the Epistle Dedicatory of one of his 1614 sermons and again a little later in another sermon. Points out that Adams's treatise *Disease of the Soule* (1616) clearly echoes lines 91–92 of *An Anatomie of the World*.

✒§ 828. FROST, KATE. "John Donne's *Devotions*: An Early Record of Epidemic Typhus." *JHM* 31: 421–30.

Points out that, in addition to being a unique literary work, the *Devotions upon Emergent Occasions* is also "a first-hand account of early efforts to treat typhus fever" (p. 421). Comments on the work as a case history that contains Donne's "knowledgeable observations on the symptoms, crisis, and recuperation from typhus, as well as an accurate description of his doctor's attempts to save him" (p. 422). Discusses Donne's physicians, Simeon Foxe and especially Theodore Turquet de Mayerne, the King's physician, who treated Donne and who, shortly after his recovery, composed in Latin a series of treatises on diseases, including "spotted fever" or typhus.

✒§ 829. FUZIER, JEAN. "Donne sonnettiste: Les Holy Sonnets et la tradition européene," in *De Shakespeare à T. S. Eliot: Mélanges offerts à Henri Fluchère*, edited by Marie-Jeanne Durry, Robert Ellrodt, and Marie-Thérèse Jones-Davies, pp. 153–71. (Études anglaises, 63.) Paris: Didier.

Argues that Donne participated in a tradition of religious sonnet writing that began with Petrarch and compares Donne with Petrarch, DuBellay, Ronsard, La Cèppede, Michelangelo, Lazare de Selve, and Jacques Grévin. Comments on Petrarchan themes and imagery in sacred poetry of the time and discusses the appearance of sensual love imagery in religious poetry. Maintains that Donne's handling of conventional themes and images is original: he is "capable de contracter en l'espace étroit de moins de vingt sonnets tout l'univers de thèmes et d'images de la poésie sacrée de son temps, et de faire de cet univers, qui chez d'autres est aboutissement, le point de départ de sa propre méditation" (p. 167).

✒§ 830. GALE, STEVEN H. "An Analysis of John Donne's 'Love's Growth.'" *Horizontes* 20, nos. 39–40 (October 1976–April 1977): 41.

Paraphrases "Loves growth" to show that it is "an expression of the paradox of love—the mystery of how already complete love can continue to grow." Notes that Donne concludes that "love is not abated by time, but expanded by it—love increases on love, and therefore complete love can be added to unto infinity, yet the addition is just a different way of expressing what is already there, one stage being no less complete than that which follows it except in degree of manifestation."

ᴥᴥ§ 831. GREENFIELD, CONCETTA C. "Principles of Coherence in Spenser and Donne." *LeS* 11: 427–38.

Discusses the structural coherence of Donne's poetry based on its "operative content" and contrasts Donne's principles of coherence with the narrative or Aristotelian coherence found in Spenser's poetry. Summarizes and finds wanting basic trends of much traditional criticism of Donne's poetry and argues that "the identification of the type of coherence characterizing a poetical composition is fundamental for differentiating poetical schools" and that "the consideration of other elements as the social, political, economic, etc., the themes, the imagery, etc. will enrich our understanding of poetical language but are not suitable as tools for differentiating poetical languages from each other" (pp. 437–38). Points out that much early criticism of Donne failed to recognize that his poems were structured on a principle quite different from the one underlying Spenser's poetry. Presents a detailed structural and linguistic analysis of the first nine lines of "A nocturnall upon S. Lucies day." Argues that the "operative content" of the first eight statements (the title plus lines 1–4) is darkness and scarcity of light and points out that these statements "do not cohere in terms of any causal sequence" (p. 436). Suggests that the "operative content" of lines 5–9 is "a descending movement transmitted by the quasi-*gradatio* sunk-drunk-shrunk," a "movement downward, symbolizing here the fact that the life of the poet has been swallowed" (p. 437).

ᴥ§ 832. GRELLER, MARY ALICE. "Donne's 'The Autumnall': An Analysis." *LWU* 9: 1–8.

Presents a detailed critical analysis of "The Autumnall," commenting on its complex uses of language, images, rhetorical figures, tone, verbal wit, rhythms and meter, and structure. Notes, for instance, that cyclical images predominate in the poem and that "the syntactic structure repeats, in a concentric manner, the patterns set up by the sounds" (p. 5). Points out that the whole pattern of the poem "is built on a succession of fifteen negatives, accented by the imperative mode at crucial points in the elegy" (p. 5) and that the poem is structured on two frameworks, one analytical and one dialectical. Concludes that "close examination of the interrelatedness of language and structure suggests that Donne intended the elegy as a compliment to Mrs. Herbert's intellectual and aesthetic perceptiveness, to her sense of humor, her appreciation of wit, her relish for irony, above all, to her realistic and mature acceptance of the stage of life in which both poet and patroness found themselves" (p. 7).

ᴥ§ 833. GRUNES, DENNIS. "John Donne's 'The Good-Morrow.'" *AI* 33: 261–65.

Says that "The good-morrow" is "the one great morning after the wedding night poem in our language" and yet notes that "it speaks with a deeply troubled voice, for all its verbal dexterity and fashionable wit" (p. 261). Presents a psychoanalytical reading of the poem in which the speaker is identified as Donne himself, the person addressed is his wife, and the central conflict is Donne's fear that his oneness with his wife will be destroyed as was his oneness with the other omnipresent woman in his life, his mother. For example, reads "suck'd on countrey pleasures" (line 3) as reflecting infantile dependency and suggests that the major conflict in the first stanza is "that that early paradise of oral contentment must come to an end for all of us, but not as a sudden break though, but with a series of breaks whereby the mother removes her child from her nurturing teat" (p. 262). Reads stanza two as Donne's insistence "on his 'oneness' with his love in defense against the precariousness—the possible transience—of that oneness" and "on the freshness and reality of that love to try to distinguish it from that former bond whose conclusion, he fears, it may be doomed to repeat" (p. 263). Reads the third stanza as primarily Donne's strategy "to persuade the one he is addressing—and himself—that their relationship's ideality removes it from the realm of danger and vulnerability whose continually echoing precedent has been set in his infantile experience" (p. 264). Notes that in the conclusion of the poem Donne breaks the fulfillment of his wish by replacing the earlier image of resurrection with a conditional hope for love's oneness and immortality.

◈ 834. HAYA, KENICHI. "Hito to Shizen to Shinkō: John Donne to Dylan Thomas ni Furete" [Man, Nature, & Faith: Poems by John Donne and Dylan Thomas], in *Keijijōshi Kenkyū*, pp. 124–38. Tokyo: Japan Society of 17th-Century English Literature.

Compares and contrasts "A nocturnall upon S. Lucies day" and Dylan Thomas's "Ceremony After a Fire Raid" and suggests that both poems have the common theme of seeking salvation in the world of medieval Catholicism.

◈ 835. HESTER, M. THOMAS. "John Donne's 'Hill of Truth.'" *ELN* 14: 100–105.

Argues that "the spiraling motion of the mind of the pilgrim, as a contrast to the rectilinear movement of the adventurers and amorists which the poet ridicules, is the most significant feature of Donne's image" (p. 100) of the Hill of Truth in lines 79–84 of *Satyre III*. Shows how the diction, syntax, meter, and rhythm of the lines reinforce the image-emblem. Examines the image in the context of the whole poem and suggests that "the circularity of the progress around the hill in combination with the gradual rectilinear movement up it by the pilgrim reproduces that spiral motion which ancient, medieval, and Renaissance philosophy alike delineated as emblematic of the rational soul of man" (p. 101). Points out striking similarities between Donne's image and one used by Petrarch in his "Ascent of Mont Ventoux" in *Le Familiari* (Basel, 1581). Suggests that, although Petrarch may not be Donne's ultimate source, Petrarch's use is "one of the most famous examples in the Renaissance of the artistic application of a traditional motif" (p. 104). Notes other possible sources as well, such as Matthew 7:12–15 and Dante, to name but two. Stresses that "it is as a Christian humanist concerned with what man can (and should) do to save his soul that Donne writes" (p. 105).

✒ 836. ISHII, SHŌNOSUKE. "John Donne," in *Eishi no sekai: rikai to kanshō* [The World of English Poetry], pp. 163–65. Tokyo: Daishūkan.
Contains a translation of "Death be not proud" in Japanese along with a very brief introduction to Donne's poetry and notes on the sonnet.

✒ 837. KEMPER, SUSAN C. "Donne's 'The Extasie,' 6." *Expl* 35, ii: 2–3.
Reply to Charlotte Otten (entry 685) and to Claes Schaar (entry 493). Maintains that, when Donne mentions "balme" (line 6) in "The Extasie," he is referring to perspiration, not to plants. Suggests that "thence" (line 6) refers to "our hands," not to "A Pregnant banke." Paraphrases the line to mean that "the sweat from the lovers' hands cements their hands, even as the beams from their eyes thread their eyes" (p. 3).

✒ 838. KERMODE, FRANK, AND A. J. SMITH. "The Metaphysical Poets," in *English Poetry*, edited by Alan Sinfield, pp. 54–72. (Sussex Books.) London: Sussex Publications.
Reprinted: 1976.
Reproduces a discussion of the metaphysical poets between Kermode and Smith taken from recordings of an unscripted talk. The speakers attempt to define the nature of metaphysical poetry and discuss the similarities and differences among the various poets. Smith tends to see a common mode of apprehension, a shared sensibility, as uniting the poets, while Kermode stresses the individual differences between Donne, Herbert, Vaughan, and Marvell. Discusses in some detail "Goodfriday, 1613. Riding Westward" and "A Valediction: of weeping" but also mentions many other poems, especially "Jealosie," "Womans constancy," "Aire and Angels," "Hymne to God my God, in my sicknesse," "A nocturnall upon S. Lucies day," and "The Extasie," the latter of which Kermode says "is not to my mind a very good poem" (p. 58).

✒ 839. KRONENFELD, JUDY Z. "The Asymmetrical Arrangement of Donne's 'Love's Growth' as an Emblem of Its Meaning." *CP* 9: no. 2: 53–58.
Argues that the asymmetrical typographical arrangement of "Loves growth" into three groups of six, eight, and fourteen lines respectively (as found in the 1633 edition, in some of the manuscripts, in Grierson's 1912

edition, and in Clements's edition) "bears out a logical paradox on which the poem turns, and thus provides an emblem of the poem's meaning" (p. 54). Shows that the logical argument of the poem rests primarily upon the difference between appearance and reality: "his love has actually remained stable; its inherent nature has not changed, but only become more conspicuous or manifest" (p. 57). Maintains, therefore, that "this paradox provides a rationale for the exceptional asymmetry: two stanzas are presented *as if* they were three" and thus shows that "the groups of lines appear to grow, as the manifestation or greater conspicuousness of his love gave it the appearance of growth, but, in fact, the rhyme scheme of two identical fourteen-line stanzas tells us, as the poet's words do, that this is only an appearance which contradicts the actuality; the essential form of his love has not changed" (p. 57).

✑§ 840. KUSUNOSE, TOSHIHIKO. "Donne to *Fūshishishū*" [Donne and the *Satyres*], in *Keijijōshi Kenkyū*, pp. 83–110. Tokyo: Japan Society of 17th-Century English Literature.
Analyzes the *Satyres* and suggests that, although they are obviously influenced by and based upon classical models, they represent primarily Donne's own soul-searching during a particularly critical period of his life.

✑§ 841. LAURITSEN, JOHN R. "Donne's *Satyres*: The Drama of Self-Discovery." *SEL* 16: 117–30.
Suggests that the rough lines and "tortured verse" of the *Satyres* "are ultimately inseparable from their meaning and an accurate reflection of the sensibility of the speaker," whose mind "perceives a fallen world," "is deeply uncertain of its relationship to the evils of that world," and, in short, "is profoundly riddled with anxiety" (pp. 118–19). Points out resemblances between Browning's dramatic monologues and the *Satyres*, which "tell us more about the satirist than the things satirized" and suggests that "the full effect and meaning of Satire I through IV depend upon dramatic irony, upon our perception of the speaker's unconscious or preconscious relationship to his subject" (p. 120) and that only in *Satyre V* does the speaker himself at last realize the final irony that the sins of a fallen world are those of all men, including the satirist. Argues, therefore, that the *Satyres* reveal a progress in self-discovery and traces that progress from *Satyre I*, in which the speaker satirizes fallen nature; to *Satyre II*, in which he examines "the rather broader matter of the perversion of the word, whether this be law, theology, or poetry" (p. 123); to *Satyre III*, the least satiric, in which the speaker begins to recognize "his own diminished possibilities in a fallen world" (p. 127); to *Satyre IV*, in which the speaker, discovering his own fallen humanity, finds humanity itself; to *Satyre V*, in which he discovers a oneness with humanity and sees that "it is only by recognizing and accepting one's fallen state that one can begin to rise above it" and that only "by recognizing one's essential identity with other

men can one summon the compassion and care . . . necessary to alleviate the wretchedness of the human condition" (p. 130).

⌘ 842. LEWALSKI, BARBARA K. "Donne's Epideictic _Personae._" _SoQ_ 14: 195–202.

Notes that Donne wrote a wide range of epideictic poems—verse epistles to male friends and to patronesses and ladies of high birth, epithalamia, funeral elegies, and the two _Anniversaries_—and maintains that "these poems seem to display a dazzling array of _personae_, in an amazing diversity of stances toward audience and subject, nicely adjusted to the literary and personal requirements of specific occasions" (p. 195). Argues that "if we focus upon the diversity of stances and roles in Donne's epideictic poems we might well argue that there is a distinct _persona_ for each individual poem" but that "if we respond to the unmistakably Donnean voice, wit, and energy which almost all these poems display, we might conclude that there is but one persona who plays, as literary circumstances dictate, a dazzling variety of roles" (pp. 201–2). Surveys the epideictic poems and concludes that it is possible to discriminate "a few very fundamental _personae_ accommodated to Donne's specific genre requirements, some of whom assume for different poems quite different stances and roles" (p. 202), such as the familiar friend, a city wit, the Spenserian Hymen priest, _Idios_ the private man, and the unworthy praiser of women. Shows that in the _Anniversaries_, however, Donne created his most complicated and complex persona, one "who fuses into a single self the manifold dimensions of public teacher and preacher, rhetorical and surgical anatomist, Mosaic judge and prophet, hymnist, meditator, spiritual pilgrim, trumpet of doom and of spiritual awakening, and apocalyptic proclaimer of a new revelation" (p. 202). For a reply, see Michael Smalling (entry 872).

⌘ 843. LOW, ANTHONY. "The Gold in 'Julia's Petticoat': Herrick and Donne." _SCN_ 34: 88–89.

Calls attention to a possible parallel between Herrick's metaphor of gold in "Julia's Petticoat" (lines 1–10) and Donne's image of gold in "A Valediction: forbidding mourning" (lines 21–24). Notes that Herrick's poem echoes both the words _airy_ and _expansion_ and suggests that perhaps Herrick is making a double allusion, comically contrasting both the creation (as L. C. Martin's gloss on _expansion_ suggests) and the airy, expanding souls of Donne's lovers with the situation described in his poem. For a reply to Low's interpretation of the image of gold (but with no reference to the possible connection between Herrick's poem and Donne's), see J. Max Patrick in _SCN_ 34 (1974): 89–91; and for a reply to Patrick, see Low in _SCN_ 36, no. 1 (1976): 9.

⌘ 844. MCFARLAND, RONALD E. "The Rhodian Colossus in Renaissance Emblem and Poetry." _EM_ 25: 121–34.

Discusses various emblematic and poetic uses of the Rhodian Colossus during the sixteenth and seventeenth centuries and suggests that in the poetry of Donne and Carew "the pictorial tradition of the Colossus during the Renaissance achieves its most extravagant development" (p. 134). Notes that Donne puts the Colossus into a context that "allows for sexual or erotic implications" (p. 131). For instance, in "The Perfume" the Colossus "first receives some genuine metaphoric extension" and is made to represent "an obstacle to sexual indulgence" (p. 131) and "a guardian of love's port" (p. 132). In *Metempsychosis* (stanza 16) Donne's description of the aphrodisiacal mandrake as a Colossus "suggests undirected sexuality or elemental libido" (p. 132).

⋙ 845. MAUER, MARGARET. "John Donne's Verse Letters." *MLQ* 37: 234–59.

Discusses what Donne considered appropriate to the form of the verse epistle and applies this information to his more problematic works in that genre. Suggests that, if one reads his epistles to the Countess of Bedford, for instance, "as examples of a genre Donne practiced with deliberate art," then "much that readers have found puzzling or shocking makes sense as an extension of his characteristic method" (p. 235). Maintains also that, since the letter typified for Donne the problems of decorum, "an understanding of how Donne proceeds in a verse letter may illuminate his method in other occasional writings" (p. 235). Comments on Donne's theory and practice of letter writing and stresses that his verse epistles are highly conscious literary productions, not simply straightforward statements, and are usually intended for a wider audience than merely the person immediately addressed. Discusses how Donne typically develops and projects a specific speaker in his epistles that is consistent and appropriate to the occasion and to the person addressed. Examines early, middle, and late examples to show how Donne "develops and uses the images of himself writing the poems" (p. 243) and how he "proceeds in terms that his readers are expected to recognize" (p. 259). Suggests that in the verse epistles "the dramatic self-presentation that renders a love poem so compelling is, if anything, more accessible" (p. 259).

⋙ 846. MERRILL, THOMAS F. *Christian Criticism: A Study of Literary God-Talk.* Amsterdam: Rodopi. 201p.

Chapter 9, "The Sermon as Sacrament" (pp. 159–77), first appeared as "John Donne and the Word of God" (entry 33). Chapter 10, "Performative Preaching" (pp. 179–95), argues that, since Donne saw his preaching "not primarily as a rhetorical but a kerygmatic act," his sermons "comprise a system of utterances committed to *doing* rather than *saying*" (p. 179). Presents a detailed analysis of the "God-talk" content of Donne's sermon preached at St. Paul's on Christmas evening of 1624 and shows how the structure of the sermon "necessarily varies from the structure of the disquisition" (p. 187) and how the sermon "virtually manipulates the devotee into a state of consciousness receptive to an awareness of the presence of

God" (p. 194). Concludes that the distinctiveness of Donne's preaching style does not result primarily from his unique personality nor from his literary ingenuity but comes from his ability to present "a well-functioning, superbly-rendered God-talk" and suggests that "our most fruitful approach to the celebrated enigma of Donne's sermons may be simply to understand them not as specimens of religious art, but as religious instruments, that we become, in a word, 'worthy hearers'" (pp. 194–95).

৵§ 847. MILLIGAN, SHIRLEY. "Two elegies on the death of Donne." *Hermathena* 120: 25–29.

Compares and contrasts Carew's "An elegy upon the death of Dr. Donne, Dean of Paul's" and Henry King's "Upon the death of my ever-desired friend, Doctor Donne of Paul's" to show that Carew's elegy is a first-rate funeral elegy that effectively comments on Donne's art and, through imitation, displays Donne's art for the reader's appreciation, while King's elegy is a weak poem, either because King "lacks the perception to discern the elements of Donne's style or simply does not have sufficient skill as an imitator" (p. 25). Concludes that Carew "created a major critical poem that can stand alone as poetry on its very real merits" and that, "stylistically, his elegy is a fine tribute to Donne, and a far more knowing one than King's" (p. 28).

৵§ 848. MILLS, GORDON. "The Nonrational," in *Hamlet's Castle: The Study of Literature as Social Experience*, pp. 195–227. (The Dan Danciger Publication Series.) Austin and London: University of Texas Press.

Presents a reading of "The Canonization" (pp. 211–16) to show that Donne's intention "was to capture in artistic form the generally experienced fact that the relationships between sexual and divine love *are* ambiguous" (p. 216) and not to present a logical description of a process by which sexual intercourse actually leads to canonization. Maintains that the logic of emotion in the poem "is not somehow mysterious and foreign to the thoughtful mind" but "is understandable, even if it is not logical in the same way that arithmetic is" (p. 216).

৵§ 849. MILWARD, PETER, S. J. "Keijijogaku to Meiso" [Metaphysical Studies and Meditation], in *Keijijoshi to Meisoshi* [Metaphysical Poetry and Meditative Poetry], edited by Peter Milward and Shōnosuke Ishii, pp. 3–38. Tokyo: Aratake.

Translated into Japanese by Yamamoto Hiroshi. Discusses the influence of the tradition of discursive meditation on seventeenth-century English poetry, including Donne's divine poems and love poetry.

৵§ 850. MILWARD, PETER, S. J., AND SHŌNOSUKE ISHII. "John Donne no 'Seinaru Sonnet' Hyōshaku" [Commentary on John Donne's *Holy*

Sonnets]. *EigoS* 122 (1976–1977): 17–19, 138–40, 222–24, 413–15, 541–44; 123 (1977): 21–43.

Translates into Japanese, with historical and critical commentary on each in Japanese (by Ishii) and in English (by Milward), "Annuntiation" from *La Corona* (pp. 17–19); "Oh my blacke Soule!" (pp. 138–40); "Spit in my face you Jewes" (pp. 222–24); "I am a little world" (pp. 413–15); "Since she whom I lov'd" (pp. 541–44); and "Show me deare Christ" (pp. 21–23).

᪐ᶳ 851. MORTON, LENA BEATRICE. "The Sea Poetry of John Donne," in *The Influence of the Sea Upon English Poetry from the Anglo-Saxon Period to the Victorian Period*, pp. 93–98. New York: Revisionist Press.

Briefly comments on the description of the sea in "The Storme" and "The Calme" and notes that Donne's description of the calm, which made the sea so motionless that neither feathers nor dust would move, so impressed Ben Jonson that he committed to memory this figure of speech. Notes Donne's use of the sea as an analogy for death in "Elegie on the Lady Marckham"; his uses of the whale and sea in several stanzas of *The Progresse of the Soule*; his uses of a sea analogy to teach a moral lesson in his verse epistle "To Sr Henry Wotton: Sir, more then kisses"; and his references to the depth of the sea in *An Anatomie of the World*. Observes that in Donne's poetry the sea is found mostly in the form of witty analogies that "show little or no emotion" (p. 98).

᪐ᶳ 852. MÜLLER, WOLFGANG G. "Die Definition in John Donnes Liebesdichtung." *Anglia* 94: 86–97.

Discusses various kinds and functions of definition in Donne's love poetry, especially as seen in "The triple Foole," and relates his tendency toward definition to the argumentative and intellectual nature of his poetry. Sees the definition of the "I," that is, the character of the narrator, as centrally important, suggests that this emphasis on the "I" reflects the egocentric nature of the poetry, and stresses Donne's interest in self-exploration and self-representation. Points out that Donne often employs the intricate "I" definitions established within the poems as an occasion for exploring the paradoxical relationship between lovers.

᪐ᶳ 853. NISHIYAMA, YOSHIO. "Donne no Renaishi to Paradox no Dentō" [Donne's Love Poetry and the Tradition of Paradox], in *Keijijōshi Kenkyū*, pp. 59–82. Tokyo: Japan Society of 17th-Century English Literature.

Discusses Donne's elaborate and functional uses of paradox in the *Songs and Sonets*, especially in "The Flea," "Witchcraft by a picture," and "A Feaver."

᪐ᶳ 854. NOVAK, LYNN TAYLOR. "Response to G. T. Wright's 'The Personae of Donne's Love Poems.'" *SoQ* 14: 179–81.

Reply to George T. Wright (entry 890). Questions Wright's suggestion that Donne's love poems as a whole reveal a conscious attempt to explore and understand the nature of love and argues that "we should regard the poems in the light of what they are obviously doing" and that "the very degree of Donne's personae's involvement seems to becloud the possibilities of any real 'exploration' of a subject for the purposes of understanding or clarification" (p. 180). Maintains that in most of the love poems the emphasis "rests not so much with the various subjects and their explorations . . . as with the personae's intense, immediate and often turbulent dramatizations of and responses to them, which can be successively or simultaneously mocking, self-mocking, scornful, wounded, tender, brutal, sustaining, despairing, hating or loving" (p. 180). Suggests that, although Donne's love poetry may be a type of exploration of the nature of love, "it certainly brings no clarity or sense of order or meaning to that exploration, and as such, would result in being an exploration without discovery" (p. 180). Praises Wright's organization, his subtle distinctions concerning the relationship of the poems to Donne's life, and particularly his introduction of the concept that the speakers of the poems are virtual persons, not actual ones.

855. OTTEN, CHARLOTTE F. "Donne's Manna in 'The Primrose.'" *ELN* 13: 260–62.
    Notes that in the writings of seventeenth-century agriculturists, biblical commentators, natural historians, and poets there are descriptions of manna and that Donne's reference to it in line 4 of "The Primrose" would not have surprised his readers. Notes that Conrad Heresbachius in *Fovre Bookes of Hvsbandry* (1601) and Sir Thomas Pope Blount in *A Natural History* (1693) comment on manna and assume that it is a natural phenomenon. Points out also that the starlike primrose in Donne's poem does not glisten because it is watered with manna but rather because of its form. Notes that both Hieronymous Bok (known as Tragus) in 1577 and John Rea in 1665 comment on the "terrestrial Galaxie" formed by starlike primroses. Shows that in the light of seventeenth-century botany the puzzling references in the first seven lines of "The Primrose" dissolve.

856. OUSBY, HEATHER DUBROW. "Donne's 'Epithalamion made at Lincolnes Inne': An Alternative Interpretation." *SEL* 16: 131–43.
    Disagrees with David Novarr's intepretation of "Epithalamion made at Lincolnes Inne" as a parody of Spenser's *Epithalamion* (*RES* n.s. 7 [1956]: 250–63, reprinted in John R. Roberts, ed., *Essential Articles for the Study of John Donne's Poetry* [entry 786], pp. 439–50). Attempts to show that the poem is not a parody but that its oddities, infelicities, and incongruities are the result of a young, inexperienced poet's carelessness, haste, and/or clumsiness. Suggests that, rather than parodying Spenser's poem, Donne imitated it badly and half-heartedly and that the oddities come from "the tension between Donne's interest in Spenser and his need to reject him"

(p. 141). Disagrees that Donne's poem was written for a mock nuptial given at the Inns of Court and speculates that it is more likely an unsuccessful exercise written to celebrate the marriage of a friend. Argues that "Epithalamion made at Lincolnes Inne" should be seen in the light of Donne's other early poems, in which he often explored conventional genres in unconventional ways. Concludes that, seen thus, the poem "helps us to remember that Donne's innovative poetry grew out of his imitation of his predecessors as well as his rejection of them" (p. 143).

∽§ 857. ———. "John Donne's Versions of Pastoral." *DUJ* n.s. 37: 33–37.

Surveys Donne's uses of the pastoral mode, from his outright rejection of it in "Ecclogue," to his half-hearted exploration of it in "To Mr E. G.: Even as lame things thirst," to his genuine concern with it in "The Baite." Points out that, since critics agree that Donne did not find the pastoral mode congenial, they often tend to ignore or misread those poems that contain a pastoral vision. Argues that a study of Donne's pastoral poems, especially "The Baite," can be helpful in reassessing his attitude toward Elizabethan literary traditions and may help us "to qualify the conventional image of Donne as an iconoclast, the unrelenting enemy of the golden world of Elizabethan poetry" (p. 33). Presents a critical analysis of "The Baite" and calls it Donne's "one complete exploration of pastoral" (p. 34). Shows how Donne deviates from Marlowe's model and how he examines the pastoral mode itself within the poem. Concludes that the poem demonstrates that Donne "could be interested in and involved with pastoral, however briefly," and that "his indisputable originality and iconoclasm did not preclude a real interest in literary traditions" (p. 36).

∽§ 858. PARISH, JOHN E. "'Sun, Stand Still!' Secular Parody of Sacred Wonders." *EM* 25: 191–209.

Comments on the secular parody, primarily in Renaissance love poetry, of the biblical account of Joshua commanding the sun to stand still (Joshua 10:12–14) and of similar astronomical marvels both in the Bible and in Greek and Roman legends. Briefly notes the use of both traditions (sometimes simultaneously) in Herrick, Marvell, Marlowe, Milton, Carew, Waller, and Donne, as well as in Pope, Ben Franklin, Blake, and Elizabeth Akers Allen. Discusses in some detail Donne's uses of Ovid's humorous aubade, as well as his story of Phaeton from the *Metamorphoses*, in "The Sunne Rising," and his references to Joshua's story in "An Epithalamion, Or mariage Song on the Lady Elizabeth," "Epithalamion made at Lincolnes Inne," and "A Lecture upon the Shadow."

∽§ 859. PERRINE, LAURENCE. "On Donne's 'The Apparition.'" *CP* 9, no. 1: 21–24.

Argues that "The Apparition" is basically a seduction poem, an expression "of thwarted love and unspent desire in which the speaker is making a desperate effort to obtain his lady's favors" (p. 21). Explains that, instead of wooing and pleading, the speaker attempts to frighten the mistress so that she will yield to his desires.

◄§ 860. ———. "Seduced by a Flea? Not She!" *The CEA Forum*, 8 April, p. 8.
Shows how "The Flea" resembles a miniature drama. Disagrees with those who assume that the lady of the poem would be successfully seduced by the sophistry of Donne's male persona and concludes that, "if we extrapolate from the evidence given *in* the poem as to her past behavior, intelligence, and morality, we must conclude that she is a sensible young lady, no more deceived by the young man's sophistry than are the scholarly critics of the poem, and that she is holding out for honorable marriage, whether with this young man or another."

◄§ 861. POPE, MYRTLE PIHLMAN. "Donne's 'A Jeat Ring Sent.'" *Expl* 34: Item 44.
Paraphrases each of the three stanzas of "A Jeat Ring sent" to show how Donne weaves numerous ambiguities into his argument. Suggests that stanzas one and three are addressed to the present ring and stanza two to the absent lady. Maintains that, "because the great wit of Donne's poetry lies in its enigmatic naughtiness, shrouded in a defensible decency, it is still necessary to determine which of his ambiguous terms are representative of single elements and which representative of composite metaphors." For a reply, see Thomas J. Wertenbaker, Jr. (entry 967).

◄§ 862. ROBERTS, D. H. "'Just Such Disparity': The Real and the Representation in Donne's Poetry." *SAB* 41, iv: 99–108.
Attempts to define and explore the gap between the real and the representation of the real in Donne's poetry in order to show that Donne was much concerned about the epistemological crisis of the seventeenth century, to explain his use of unconventional images to examine age-old realities, and to demonstrate the close, inherent connection between the real and the representation. Argues that there are "at least three distinct types of relation based on the degree of identity or nonidentity between the real and representation in John Donne's poetry" and that they demonstrate his "recognition of the crisis in epistemology and his attempts to come to terms with just how we can know": (1) "an ultimate denial of identification, reached after an exploration of the possibilities of identification"; (2) "an imagistic or correspondential relationship," in which "partial identity is established"; and (3) "an affirmation of identity in which the representation is so closely akin to the real that any distinction is lost" (p. 100). Sees "A Valediction: of my name, in the window" as an example of the first category and shows that ultimately the poem seems "to conclude the mind can find no single image that corresponds exactly to any universal concept" (p. 102). Sees the compass image in "A Valediction: forbid-

ding mourning" and the overriding conceit in "The Canonization" as examples of the second category, in which he compares unlike things and "demonstrates how they may resemble each other at some point or points," and, "though absolute identity of the real and the representative is never claimed, we have moved a step closer toward being able to define a universal in terms of a concrete, a tentative affirmation of the possibility of gaining knowledge" (p. 103). Sees the image of the phoenix riddle in "The Canonization," the global and mapmaking images of "The good-morrow" and "The Sunne Rising," and especially the cartographic image of himself as a flat map in "Hymne to God my God, in my sicknesse" as examples of the third category, in which Donne affirms the real existence of universals in the mind and clothes them with concrete images that embody their essence. Notes that the three categories are not rigidly separated so that only one is exhibited in a given poem and shows how, in fact, Donne often manipulates the categories, "sliding or progressing from one to another, or placing them in conflict to see which will emerge victorious, or simply seeing in how many ways he can balance them" (p. 105). Discusses "The Flea" and "Aire and Angels" as examples of this interaction and manipulation.

◆§ 863. RUFFO-FIORE, SILVIA. *Donne's Petrarchism: A Comparative View.* Florence: Grafica Toscana. 130p.

Presents a critical reading of selected poems in the *Songs and Sonets* in terms of their relationship to Petrarch's *Canzoniere*, defines the nature of Donne's debt to Petrarch, and suggests ways that Donne deviated from the style and love ethic of Petrarch. Proposes not to show the direct influence of Petrarch on Donne "but simply to offer a reading of Donne which takes into account one of the most profound and pervasive literary forces of the Renaissance" (preface). Chapter 1, "The Unwanted Heart" (pp. 11–22), is a reprint of "The Unwanted Heart in Petrarch and Donne" (entry 490). Chapter 2, "Donne's 'Parody' of the Petrarchan Lady" (pp. 23–38), is a reprint of an essay by the same title in *CLS* (entry 489). Chapter 5, "Suns and Lovers" (pp. 70–79), is a reprint of "A New Light on the Suns and Lovers in Petrarch and Donne" (entry 695). Chapter 6, "Petrarchan Imagery in 'The Canonization'" (pp. 80–86), is a reprint of "Donne's Transformation of Petrarchan Imagery in *The Canonization*" (entry 864). Chapter 3, "Amorous Aberrations" (pp. 39–59), discusses the motif of the evil effect of love in the poetry of Petrarch and Donne, especially the "amorous aberrations" of excessive grief, perversity, overindulgence, and self-deception, and suggests that "the negative attitude toward love that many of Donne's speakers express, either directly or unconsciously, "is a common Petrarchan stance, even though Donne's lovers sometimes show a perverse cynicism untypical of Petrarch generally" (p. 40). Discusses "A Valediction: of weeping," "Twicknam garden," "Loves diet," "The Baite," "Loves Alchymie," and "Farewell to love" to show that "often the ideals and the effects of Petrarchan love prevail in Donne's *Songs* relatively unchanged" but that "the uniqueness of Donne's treatment of these stock motifs resides in his dramatic juxtaposition of Petrarchan ideals to the real world, in his frequent use of an ironic persona, who seemingly accepts but may undercut Petrarchan values, and in his making new associations or combinations between the world of ideal love and the world of reality which did not appear in Petrarch" (pp. 58–59). Chapter 4, "Dream, Memories, and Fantasy" (pp. 60–69), discusses how in "The Dreame," "The Apparition," and "Elegy X: The Dreame" Donne adapts the Petrarchan motif of the power of the lover's imagination to his own ends and that, unlike Petrarch, his "flights into fantasy do not perpetuate the irreconcilable chasm between the real and imagined" but rather "he effects an acceptable adjustment of real and ideal, of actual and imagined" (p. 62). Chapter 7, "Fools, Heroes, and Saints: The Petrarchan Hope for Fame" (pp. 88–98), compares Petrarch's attitude toward fame to Donne's, especially as reflected in "The triple Foole," "The undertaking," and "The Relique," and shows how Donne adapts Petrarchan ideals to his own creative purposes. Chapter 8, "Donne's Ironic Reversals of Petrarchan Death Motifs" (pp. 99–109), examines "The Will," "The Funerall," and "The Dampe" to show that Donne's originality in adapting the prevading Petrarchan theme of death resides "in his use of ironic reversal whereby he explores and reevaluates the nature and effects of Petrarchan love" (p. 109). Suggests that his intention is "to comment incisively on the aspect of Petrarchan love under scrutiny in a particular poem by the use of extension, exaggeration, and reversal of stock materials" (p. 109). Chapter 9, "Donne's Place in the Petrarchan Tradition: A Retrospective Commentary" (pp. 110–17), summarizes the argument of the study, stressing that Donne did not reject Petrarch but absorbed, adapted, and applied him to his own ends. Presents a reading of "A Valediction: of my name, in the window" to show how Donne assimilated Petrarchan themes and devices. Notes (pp. 118–25), selected bibliography (pp. 126–28), and index (pp. 129–30).

◄§ 864. ———. "Donne's Transformation of Petrarchan Imagery in *The Canonization*." *IQ* 19, nos. 73–74: 53–61.

Reprinted as Chapter 6 in *Donne's Petrarchism: A Comparative View* (entry 863), pp. 80–86.

Argues that Donne's originality lies more in his subtle adaptation, assimilation, and transformation of the Petrarchan tradition than in his celebrated rejection of overused Petrarchan elements. Points out specific examples of Donne's synthesis and manipulation of several Petrarchan images and themes in "The Canonization," especially in the third stanza. Notes, for example, Petrarchan analogues for Donne's use of the taper-fly image but stresses that in Donne's poem the image "functions as the basis of an elaborate defense the speaker builds to assert the exclusive nature of his love and how it differs from an irrational, unstable Petrarchan love whose evil effects are grief and self-destruction" (p. 57). Similarly notes that the phoenix image is informed, in part, by Petrarch's use of the same image in the *Canzoniere* but stresses again that Donne uses the image in his own way: "in Petrarch the phoenix symbolizes the hopeless cyclical pattern of his thwarted love, while in Donne the image expresses how the lovers transcend the immediately deadening physical effects of their consummated love" (pp. 57–58).

❧ 865. Sanesi, Roberto, ed. *Poeti metafisici inglesi (XVII secolo)*. Introduzione, traduzione e note di Roberto Sanesi. Teste inglese a fronte. (La Fenice.) 2d ed., revised and augmented. Parma: Ugo Guanda Editore. xix, 363p.
First published in 1961. Contains several new translations of Donne's poems: "Song: Sweetest love, I do not goe," "Aire and Angels," "Twicknam garden," "Witchcraft by a picture," "The Funerall," "The Dampe," "This is my playes last scene," "At the round earths imagin'd corners," "Death be not proud," and "Oh, to vex me, contraryes meet in one." New notes for the new inclusions, but others only slightly revised. Introductory essay, bibliography, and headnote on Donne unrevised.

❧ 866. Satterthwaite, Alfred W. "Donne's 'The Good-Morrow.'" *Expl* 34: Item 50.
Maintains that the most important aspect of the allusion to the Seven Sleepers of Ephesus in line 4 of "The good-morrow" is their awakening, not their long sleep. Recounts the legend and suggests that the speaker is saying that to awake to love is for him as miraculous and wonderful as it must have been for the young Christians to have awakened to find themselves in a Christian world.

❧ 867. Sayama, Eitarō. "John Donne no 'Holy Sonnets': Seinaru Mokusō." [John Donne and the *Holy Sonnets*: Divine Meditations], in *Keijijōshi to Meisōshi*, edited by Peter Milward and Shōnosuke Ishii, pp. 39–81. Tokyo: Aratake.
Presents a detailed analysis of the *Holy Sonnets* as poems of meditation. Shows how the tradition of discursive meditation is particularly reflected in the structure, tone, and religious sensibility of Donne's sonnets.

❧ 868. ———. "John Donne no *Shūnen Tsuitōshi* Saikō" [John Donne's *Anniversaries* Reconsidered], in *Keijijōshi Kenkyū*, pp. 111–23. Tokyo: Japan Society of 17th-Century English Literature.
Reviews various critical interpretations of the *Anniversaries* and concludes that fundamentally the poems are a bold expression of the struggling spirit that seeks God's love.

❧ 869. Schleiner, Winfried. "The Hand of the Tongue: Emblematic Technique in One of Donne's Sermons." *EM* 25: 183–90.
Discusses Donne's use of the emblematic tradition and the fable in his

sermon on Isaiah 65:20 (Simpson and Potter, vol. 7, no. 14) to illustrate his "way of referring to the tradition of emblems or hieroglyphs, his extended application of emblematic exegesis to a scriptural text, and his way of illustrating an important point (about the function of the preacher) by referring to a story popular in both literary and visual traditions" (p. 184). Notes that, although, unlike the Catholic baroque preachers, Donne does not structure his sermons around emblems, he does use them to communicate with his audience. Shows that in the sermon Donne "stresses spatial relationships between parts of the body mentioned in scripture and reads them emblematically" (p. 190).

◄§ 870. SELLIN, PAUL R. "John Donne: The Poet as Diplomat and Divine." *HLQ* 39: 267–75.
    Argues that Donne played the role of an important diplomat-divine in the special embassy of James Hay, Viscount Doncaster, sent in May 1619 by King James to mediate between Catholic and Protestant factions over the contended throne of Bohemia and to avert the Thirty Years' War. Bases this conclusion on the fact that, when Donne arrived with the embassy in the Hague in December 1619, he was received by the Dutch as an important representative of the English King and was given a gold medal commemorating the Synod of Dort, the same kind of medal given to the King's two official representatives to the Synod. Suggests that in terms of gifts offered Donne ranked third in the embassy, preceded only by Doncaster and Sir Francis Nethersole, the Secretary of the Embassy. Concludes, therefore, that Donne accompanied Doncaster in an official capacity, not merely as a private chaplain.

◄§ 871. SEYMOUR-SMITH, MARTIN, ed. "John Donne," in *The English Sermon: Volume I: 1550–1650: An Anthology*, pp. 333–90. Cheadle: Carcanet Press.
    Briefly outlines Donne's life and personality, calling him "a most unusual, complex, eclectic and introspective man," and gives a general introduction to the sermons: "His dramatic sermons—in terms of language the greatest ever preached—were simply an extension of the private spiritual exercises . . . in which he had been indulging during the years of his poverty and despair" (p. 336). Reproduces (with brief notes) "A Sermon of Valediction at My Going into Germany, Preached at Lincolnes Inne on April 18, 1619," "A Lenten Sermon Preached to the King at Whitehall," and *Deaths Duell* (pp. 338–90).

◄§ 872. SMALLING, MICHAEL. "The Personae in Donne's Epideictic Verse: A Second Opinion." *SoQ* 14: 203–6.
    Reply to Barbara K. Lewalski (entry 842). Basically agrees with Lewalski and simply offers further evidence "that the persona construct is requisite in appreciating the entire canon of Donne's poetry and that properly understood it is consistently applicable from the Ovidian songs to the pious

meditations" (p. 203). Primarily shows how the personae of the verse epistles "are no more the 'real' Donne than those of the love poems" (p. 203) but observes certain important distinctions. Comments on four of Donne's verse epistles to show that each confirms the presence of a persona.

᪐᪑ 873. SMITH, HALLETT. "The Permanence of Curled Metaphors." *SR* 84: 684–95.
Review article of several books on Donne: (1) Anne Ferry, *All in War with Time: Love Poetry of Shakespeare, Donne, Jonson, Marvell* (entry 743); (2) Dwight Cathcart, *Doubting Conscience: Donne and the Poetry of Moral Argument* (entry 732); (3) Michael McCanles, *Dialectical Criticism and Renaissance Literature* (entry 767); (4) Josephine Miles, *Poetry and Change: Donne, Milton, Wordsworth, and the Equilibrium of the Present* (Berkeley, Los Angeles, and London: University of California Press, 1974; see also entry 465); (5) John R. Roberts, ed., *Essential Articles for the Study of John Donne's Poetry* (entry 786); and (6) Thomas O. Sloan and Raymond B. Waddington, eds., *The Rhetoric of Renaissance Poetry: From Wyatt to Milton* (entry 703).

᪐᪑ 874. STORHOFF, GARY. "Metaphors of Despair in Donne's 'The Storme' and 'The Calme.'" *CP* 9, no. 2: 41–45.
Suggests that in "The Storme" and "The Calme" Donne is not recording his own psychological state so much as "exploring the consciousness of the man without faith, the man who does not turn to God in times of trouble," and notes furthermore that "the trouble the persona encounters becomes, through the metaphors Donne employs, images of spiritual catastrophes the person without faith must face: first a destructive turbulence, then a spiritual stagnation" (p. 41). Notes that the images of "The Storme" "convey a sense of chaos," while those of "The Calme" "evoke a sense of loss, of emptiness, inspired by the persona's pervading feeling of aimlessness" (p. 44). Concludes that the two poems show Donne's ability to depict psychological states and that his main point is that in times of stress the nonbeliever "will see the natural world as a destructive force" while in times of calm "he will lose all sense of meaning and direction" (p. 44).

᪐᪑ 875. STRINGER, GARY. "Donne's Religious *Personae*: A Response." *SoQ* 14: 191–94. 051   S099 35
Reply to Helen S. Thomas (entry 881). Disagrees with Thomas's approach of trying to read the divine poems as spiritual autobiography and argues that the reader must "first come to terms with them as esthetic objects" and that "a necessary part of this understanding . . . is the recognition within the poems of a *persona* or speaker, some personality-construct distinct from John-Donne-man-and-thinker" (p. 191). Maintains that the changing spiritual condition of the speaker of *La Corona* suggests that the poems are presented by a persona and argues that the highly

orchestrated and dramatic sonnet sequence formed by the first twelve of the *Holy Sonnets* strongly suggests "A Donne behind the scenes—an artist who has set a *persona* on stage to act out a parable of conversion" (p. 193). Questions Thomas's argument that the personal elements of the verse letters argue against the presence of personae in Donne's religious poetry and finds her discussion of the possible uses of personae in the sermons unconvincing.

◄§ 876. SULLIVAN, ERNEST W., II. "The Genesis and Transmission of Donne's *Biathanatos." Library* 31: 52–72.
Presents a detailed history of the genesis and transmission of *Biathanatos*. Argues that Donne wrote the work not before 1607 and not after 1609. Describes in detail and discusses the relationship among the three extant seventeenth-century texts: (1) a transcribed manuscript given to the Bodleian by Lord Herbert of Cherbury in 1642; (2) the quarto first edition printed by John Dawson with an undated title page, which was reissued unchanged by Humphrey Moseley and dated 1648; and (3) the octavo second edition dated 1700 and printed anonymously. Presents evidence to show that a copy of *Biathanatos* sent to Sir Robert Ker (now lost) was probably a holograph and the one used by the printer for the first edition. Suggests also that the Bodleian manuscript may have been copied from the manuscript sent to Ker before it was sent to the printers. Maintains that the second edition derives from the first, not from any of the manuscripts.

◄§ 877. ————. "The Presentation Letter in the Earl of Oxford Copy of Donne's *Biathanatos." PBSA* 70: 403–5.
Reproduces and describes the presentation letter in the Earl of Oxford's copy of *Biathanatos*, one of at least ten copies of the undated first issues published in 1647 by Donne's son and sent to friends and possible patrons. Notes that Keynes in *A Bibliography of Dr. John Donne, Dean of St. Paul's* (entry 566), pp. 113–16, printed all but this one. Notes also that the Shakespeare Folger Library acquired the Earl of Oxford's presentation copy in 1943. Briefly outlines the connection between the families of the patron of the first edition, Philip Herbert, Earl of Montgomery and Fourth Earl of Pembroke, and Aubrey de Vere, Earl of Oxford, and suggests that the presentation letter indicates that Donne the younger published *Biathanatos* against his father's wishes not for the professed reason of preserving the text but out of financial need.

◄§ 878. ————. "Reader's Queries." *N&Q* n.s. 23: 559.
Notes that in his 1647 edition of *Biathanatos* Donne the younger closes his "Epistle Dedicatory" with a proverb in Spanish ("Da vida osar morir") and that in the British Library copy of the first issue of the first edition of *Biathanatos* someone (not Donne's son) has written beneath the Spanish

the same phrase in Latin ("dat vitan, audere mori"). Asks for information about the source of the proverb, which may be Latin rather than Spanish.

❧ 879. TARLINSKAJA, MARINA. *English Verse: Theory and History.* (De Proprietatibus Litterarum, Series Practica, 117, gen. ed. C. H. van Schooneveld.) The Hague and Paris: Mouton. vii, 351p.

Discusses through induction the theory and history of English form from the thirteenth to the nineteenth centuries. Mentions Donne throughout, especially in Chapter 6, "The Nondramatic Iambic Pentameter" (pp. 138–58), in which various aspects of the syllabic and accentual structure of verse are discussed, and in Chapter 7, "The Transition from Iambics to Syllabics" (pp. 183–98), in which a methodology is proposed "for identifying the meter of a transitional verse form, Donne's *Satyres*" (p. 15). Argues that the *Satyres* "are an intermediary form between syllabo-tonic and syllabic verse" and defines their meter, "first, by a quantitative comparison of its verse structure with the canonical iamb, and second, by a comparison with a speech model of quasi-syllabic verse" (p. 15) to show that the poems are "a *typical transitional form*" (p. 198). Several charts and figures; see in particular Table 14 (pp. 252–53), Fig. 10 (p. 324), Fig. 13 (p. 326), Fig. 22 (p. 331), Fig. 23 (p. 332), Fig. 24 (p. 333), Fig. 27 (pp. 336–37), Fig. 28 (pp. 338–39), and Fig. 30 (p. 340).

❧ 880. TEPPER, MICHAEL. "John Donne's Fragment Epic: 'The Progresse of the Soule.'" *ELN* 13: 262–66.

Argues that, although *The Progresse of the Soule* fails to carry out Donne's announced intention of tracing the progress of the soul among the foremost heretics of the world, its conclusion suggests that it is a finished work. Notes that the soul in the fragment epic "makes fourteen distinct movements through all phases of life on three general planes—the vegetable, the animal, and the human" and that it is "last fixed in woman, who embraces elements of all three planes" (pp. 264–65). Suggests that Donne "seems confident of the poem's integrity as a complete whole" and that "the last stanza, written almost as an afterthought, distracts attention from the original design of the poem by drawing a moral and tying all the preceding stanzas to a common theme," namely that good and evil "are relative, and their understanding rests with comparison and opinion" and that "even though the soul's progress is in the direction of evil, we should not assume that evil is inevitable" (p. 266).

❧ 881. THOMAS, HELEN S. "The Concept of the *Persona* in John Donne's Religious Poetry." *SoQ* 14: 183–89.

Surveys recent critical approaches to the concept of the persona and longs for the days "before the advent of the *persona* craze in criticism, when Helen Gardner and two and a half centuries of critics before her could actually and unabashedly talk about John Donne, about the author, the poet, or the poet's imagination, without feeling that they had to interpose either a 'speaker' or a *persona* between the man and his religious poetry" (p. 185). Argues that Donne's religious poems seem "intensely personal, essentially individual, seeking and even begging for active divine aid in reaching assurance of salvation for John Donne" and that thus "to interpose a 'speaker' or a *persona* between him or his soul and me is a device that dilutes my experience of listening to the essence of John Donne attempting to fit himself into the public myth of the age, the revealed religion inherited from the middle ages" (p. 186). Suggests that Donne's revelations of his personal feelings in the verse letters support the notion that in the divine poems he is likewise conveying his own personal experience and feelings. Finds persona criticism of the sermons more acceptable, for in them one finds a speaker, an audience, and a situation that are quite different from those found in the religious poems. Concludes, therefore, that, "if some poems have a *persona*, others do not to any significant degree"; that "postulating a mandatory *persona* does not serve to dissipate the uncertainty, the 'tensions,' of Donne's *Holy Sonnets*"; and that in the religious poems "it is Donne's struggle that interests us" (p. 189). For a reply, see Gary Stringer (entry 875).

🔖 882. THOMAS, JOHN A. "The Circle: Donne's Underlying Unity," in *"The Need Beyond Reason" and Other Essays: College of Humanities Centennial Lectures 1975–76*, pp. 89–103. Provo, Utah: Brigham Young University Press.
Discusses Donne's fondness for circularity and his extensive use of the circle "as an image capable of expressing what is meant by man, the world and the universe, love and the inexpressible expansiveness of Deity" (p. 91) in his sermons, essays, letters, and devotions as well as in his poetry. Argues that Donne's use of the circle as image, metaphor, and symbol reflects his "medieval-inspired vision of the essential unity of God and the universe" (p. 92) and maintains that "the perfection of the circle allows Donne, the poet, to see God encompassing the pale of his valued creations" (p. 101). Sees Donne as seriously committed to an ordered, ethical vision of reality and maintains that by examining his uses of the circle "one can fully comprehend the serious voice of a Christian poet who preaches a pervading unity" (p. 101).

🔖 883. TJARKS, LARRY D. "Donne's 'Loves Usury' and a Self-Deceived Persona." *SoQ* 14: 207–13.
Presents a reading of "Loves Usury" to show how the submissive speech of the persona "signals the audience to resist his views and find better reasons against them" and how Donne at the same time "invites his audience to notice how the poem's allusions to Ovidian literature, the *senex amans* tradition, and Renaissance love theories expose this persona as a self-deceived fool" (p. 208). Points out that in both "Loves Usury" and "Loves Deitie" Donne uses his personae "to dethrone the tyranny of Cupid" but that in the latter "he has his persona directly condemn the tyranny of

Cupid and call for Cupid's dethroning," whereas in "Loves Usury" he deposes Cupid "by illustrating the folly, self-deception, and comedy of his persona's worship of Cupid" (p. 213). Argues that such a reading of the poem would suggest that Donne's other libertine poems and his supposedly rakish youth should perhaps be reevaluated.

◄§ 884. ———. "John Donne and the Concept of the *Persona.*" *SoQ* 14: ii–iii.

Introduces six essays in this special issue of *SoQ* devoted to Donne's uses of personae. Notes that all of the essays, with some later modifications, were originally presented at an MLA seminar held in San Francisco on 28 December 1975. Includes George T. Wright, "The Personae of Donne's Love Poems" (entry 890); Lynn Taylor Novak, "Response to G. T. Wright's 'The Personae of Donne's Love Poems'" (entry 854); Helen S. Thomas, "The Concept of the *Persona* in John Donne's Religious Poetry" (entry 881); Gary Stringer, "Donne's Religious *Personae*: A Response" (entry 875); Barbara K. Lewalski, "Donne's Epideictic *Personae*" (entry 842); and Michael Smalling, "The Personae in Donne's Epideictic Verse: A Second Opinion" (entry 872). In addition to the seminar papers, includes an essay by Larry D. Tjarks, "Donne's 'Loves Usury' and a Self-Deceived Persona" (entry 883), and an original poem by George T. Wright (entry 889).

◄§ 885. TRAISTER, BARBARA. "Donne's 'Love's Growth.'" *Expl* 34: Item 60.

Suggests that the final image of comparing increased love to increased taxes in "Loves growth" stresses "not only the unflagging increase of love but also the price which ever-increasing love extracts" and notes that "the constant emphasis in the last stanza on growth, budding, eminence, and addition suggests not only the swelling of a phallus but also that of pregnancy, the visible, tangible evidence of love's growth." Maintains that such a reading fits the tone of the last stanza: "Love is not static; it does increase and, along with its pleasures and heats, it 'gets' progeny which, come winter, will not disappear, even though the spring will bring still another swelling of love."

◄§ 886. TRIVEDI, R. D. "The Puritan Age: Poetry (1)," in *A Compendious History of English Literature*, pp. 129–39. New Delhi: Vikas Publishing House.

Comments unfavorably on the general features of Donne's poetry and maintains that, although Donne was "aiming at originality he achieved only novelty" (p. 135). Suggests that "Going to Bed" and "The Apparition" are "in bad taste and show a putrid, not a poetic mind" and asserts that the argument of "The Extasie" is "tortured into such ethereal shapes that only a reader gifted with a special sixth sense can grasp them" (p. 135). Dislikes Donne's "unsavoury realism," his "fanaticism" and "coarseness," and his "extravagant hyperboles and preposterous conceits" and sees the modern interest in Donne as "a passing phase" (pp. 135–36).

◄§ 887. WALL, JOHN N., JR. "Donne's Wit of Redemption: The Drama of Prayer in the *Holy Sonnets.*" *SP* 73: 189–203. ♥5 ST9 4
Disagrees with the notion that the *Holy Sonnets* present a continuous movement by the speaker toward God and argues that, in fact, the speaker "constantly changes his strategy of approach to God" and that "he alternately laments and aspires, but never rests long in any one stance" (p. 191). Sees the movement as circular, not linear, and suggests that the central subject of the *Holy Sonnets* is "not a movement of the speaker toward resolution of his relationship with God, but instead an exploration of the paradoxes of the Christian life on earth" (p. 191). Attempts to clarify the various stances taken by the speaker in the drama of redemption, indicates "the close affinity between these dramatic stances and the various forms of Christian prayer, especially as they are illustrated in the Psalms" (p. 191), and shows how the sonnets present Donne's particular Anglican understanding of the Christian life. Analyzes in detail "As due by many titles" and suggests that it fully "exhibits a pattern of shifting tone and dramatic stance which is carried out in many variations in the succeeding eighteen *Holy Sonnets*" (p. 194). Shows how the speaker "explores dramatically the complexities and paradoxes of redemption, both in its general sense as a promise of God for His people and its specific sense as an action which must take place in the life of every man" (p. 197) and demonstrates how each of the sonnets is "a sharply realized dramatic monologue in the testing drama through which the speaker hopes to pass into the inclusion in the last act of the salvation history" and that, to achieve this end, the speaker "calls on God, by assuming several roles identifiable with the five basic types of prayer," and "moves constantly from hope in God's promises to despair of his own inclusion, and back again" (p. 202).

◄§ 888. WELCH, DENNIS M. "The Meaning of Nothingness in Donne's 'Nocturnall upon S. Lucies Day.'" *BuR* 22, i: 48–56.
Applies certain modern phenomenological inquiries into the relationship between nonbeing and human awareness to "A nocturall upon S. Lucies day." Argues that the poem is serious, not sentimental, and that in it Donne confronts, and finally transcends, the experience of nothingness that he felt at the death of his wife. Notes Donne's precise scholastic distinctions between being and nonbeing and shows that he "confronted nothingness and transcended it through the poem's cautious sensualism, its creativity, and its Christian resolution as well as through his life as a clergyman" (p. 48).

◄§ 889. WRIGHT, GEORGE T. "Mummy." *SoQ* 14: iv.
An original poem on Donne in a special issue of *SoQ* devoted to Donne's uses of personae.

᠅ᢒ 890. ———. "The Personae of Donne's Love Poems." *SoQ* 14: 173–77.

Argues that Donne's love poems as a whole are dramatic efforts to explore the nature of love and that, at the same time, they present his own personal experiences of love. Though reluctant to connect the poems to specific circumstances or persons in Donne's life, agrees with Helen Gardner that there is a development in his personae—"from the masterful, arrogant young man about town of the *Elegies*, through the earlier lyrics' lover who is partly a 'licentious young amorist' and partly a 'lover who loves without reward,' to the more intimate, subtler, truer lover of the later songs and sonnets who can with tenderness show love as the 'bliss of fulfillment' and agonize over the conditions that perpetually threaten it" (p. 175). Observes that Donne presents "occasions of passionate feeling that reflect his own developing sense of love and that express, at a level deeper than Donne probably had any clear idea of, his own lifelong struggle for harmony" and notes that "the composite persona of Donne's love poems is a strong man in a weak position—our position as it turns out, that of subtle, passionate, energetic suitors in turn irritated, soothed, baffled, and appalled by women, change, time, death, by the nature of sublunary experience" (p. 176). Concludes, therefore, that the lovers in Donne's poems are, after all, only virtual speakers, roles that Donne adopted, masks that he put on; but since they all use the same idiom and style and see life from a particular perspective, they are all also recognizably Donne. For a reply, see Lynn Taylor Novak (entry 854).

᠅ᢒ 891. WYKE, CLEMENT H. "Edmund Gosse as Biographer and Critic of Donne: His Fallible Role in the Poet's Rediscovery." *TSLL* 17: 805–19.

Surveys and assesses Gosse's contribution to the twentieth-century revival of interest in Donne and in his poetry. Points out that in his *Life and Letters of Donne* (1899) Gosse, "in his faltering fashion, raised the torch to brighten the way to Donne's reemergence as a reputable poet, although it was Grierson who through his scholarly and literary perspicacity increased the glow of that torch and established the public recognition and popularity of the leading Metaphysical poet" (p. 805). Presents a brief biography of Gosse to show how his personal background affected his biography of Donne, traces the various motives and steps behind the actual publication of the biography, and comments on the contemporary critical reaction to its publication. Shows that, in spite of its many factual errors and inaccuracies, Gosse's biography presented Donne to a wide and important contemporary audience, provoked scholarly debate about Donne the man and about his poetry, made available Donne's letters and some of his heretofore unpublished poems, and, at a time when Browning's popularity was at a zenith, his comparison of Donne and Browning contributed immensely to making Donne more acceptable. Shows also that Gosse's evaluation of Donne's poetry, though often fallacious and misleading, stimulated critical interest and that "after the evidence was heard and evaluated the final judgment was in Donne's favor" (p. 819). Concludes, therefore, that "Gosse's part in that judgment, though rightly overshadowed by the scholarly accomplishment of Sir Herbert Grierson and clearly diminished by Gosse's own plethora of mistakes, is worthy of proper and impartial recognition" (p. 819).

❧ 892. YOKLAVICH, JOHN M. "Sir Ashton Cokayne Praises Donne's 'Satyres.'" N&Q n.s. 23: 552.
Notes that in a poem entitled "To my learned friend Mr. Thomas Bancroft" in his *Small Poems of Divers Sorts* (1658) Sir Ashton Cokayne, son of Donne's friend, Mrs. Thomas Cokayne, and a minor poet, wit, and playwright, praises Donne's *Satyres* and calls Donne "our prime wit."

❧ 893. YOKOTA, CHŪZO. "John Donne no *Song* to *Sonnet*: Sono Gikō no Ichimen" [John Donne's *Songs and Sonets*: An Assessment of Their Literary Technique], in *Keijijōshi Kenkyū*, pp. 42–58. Tokyo: Japan Society of 17th-Century English Literature.
Discusses how Donne's complex and skillful uses of a speaker in the *Songs and Sonets* contribute to the argumentative and dramatic elements in the poems.

1977

❧ 894. AIZAWA, YOSHIHISA. "John Donne no 'Shūnen tsutō shi' kō" [A Study of John Donne's *Anniversaries*]. Pt. 1. *Bunkei Ronsō* (Hiromae Daigaku Bungakubu) 12, no. 2 (February): 1–14.
Part I of a three-part series of articles. Translates into Japanese *An Anatomie of the World* and "A Funerall Elegie." Contains a general introduction to the series and to the *Anniversaries*. For Part 2, see entry 972.

❧ 895. ARCHER, STANLEY. "The Archetypal Journey Motif in Donne's Divine Poems," in *New Essays on Donne*, edited by Gary A. Stringer, pp. 173–91. (Salzburg Studies in English Literature, Elizabethan & Renaissance Studies, edited by James Hogg, no. 57.) Salzburg: Institut für Englische Sprache und Literatur, Universität Salzburg.
Points out that Donne is the first major English poet of the Renaissance to write a substantial collection of religious poems. Examines Donne's use of the archetypal journey motif and its associated metaphors, especially in the *Divine Poems*, and notes four major categories: (1) human life as a journey toward death, (2) the soul's journey to heaven, (3) Christ's journeys to earth, while on earth, and ultimately to heaven, and (4) journeys associated with the Church passing through time or with religious vocation. Notes that that the motif of the journey is the most frequently used figure in the *Divine Poems* yet observes that "journey metaphors and im-

ages are highly limited in time and distance, even in the longer poems which have the journey as the central metaphor" (p. 188). Points out that Donne's use of the journey motif "as it relates to human life is reductive" (p. 189) and "often represents either movement toward that fixed goal of rest or movement that serves as dramatic contrast to a celebration of religious truth" (p. 190). Shows that eschatology dominates Donne's thinking in the *Divine Poems* and stresses that, "by limiting the possibilities of the journey motif as he does, Donne succeeds in creating an intensity of tone that his poems would not otherwise have" (p. 190).

⋘ 896. ARMSTRONG, ALAN. "The Apprenticeship of John Donne: Ovid and the *Elegies*." *ELH* 44: 419–42.

Argues that Donne's *Elegies* "admirably support the Renaissance belief in imitation as the friend of invention" and "though devoid of 'translations' or even precise verbal echoes of Ovid, nevertheless, recreate Ovidian attitudes and techniques" and therefore "testify to Donne's discovery in the *Amores*, not only of a kindred spirit, but of a valuable textbook for the poet" (p. 419). Examines Donne's debt to Ovid, especially his adoption of Ovidian rhetorical techniques in creating a self-conscious persona. Argues that the *Amores* "showed Donne the way to use the established tradition of the erotic elegy as a counter-weight to the sonnet sequence tradition" (pp. 433–34). Discusses a number of the elegies in detail, especially "Loves Warr," "Jealosie," "The Bracelet," and "The Autumnall." Concludes that the *Amores* "presented Donne a richly elaborated poetic convention which he was peculiarly suited to revive," that "the Ovidian themes of the *Elegies*, however, may represent an inheritance less important to Donne than the finer art of the Ovidian self-conscious persona," and that, although Donne is one of the earliest and best of English elegists, it is later, in the *Songs and Sonets*, that he "pushed beyond the limits of the genre of elegy, while continuing to use the lessons he had learned from Ovid" (pp. 439–40).

⋘ 897. ASALS, HEATHER. "David's Successors: Forms of Joy and Art." *PPMRC* 2: 31–37.

Argues that St. Augustine's *Enarratio in psalmos* served as a major *ars poetica* for seventeenth-century poets and provided them with a theory of form and "a system of thinking about the language of religious poetry which was particularly appropriate to their own apologetic" (p. 31). Suggests that the role of the poet as prophet, announcer, and demonstrator of the word of God "found its precedent in Augustine's David, a figure who linked himself, in turn, with both John the Baptist and the blessed Virgin" (p. 31). Shows how seventeenth-century Anglican understanding of Augustine's exegesis of the psalms led to "a complex of convictions about the nature of poetry" (p. 31) and comments, in particular, on Donne's Augustinian views of the outward voice (*vox*) and the inward voice (*verbum*) as expressed in his sermons, *La Corona*, and "Upon the Translation of the

Psalms." Notes how Donne used the figures of John the Baptist and the Virgin Mary to explain the role of the poet. Comments briefly on Donne's Marian theology and observes that "poetic form, according to Donne's theology of art (based as it is in his theology of the pulpit) resembles by virtue of its outwardness and fleshiness the virgin womb in which Christ was conceived" (p. 34). Notes that Mary Sidney in Donne's poem on the Sidney psalms is seen as "the type of all 'Successors' of David, making her Maker, 're-revealing' the new within the old song, the *verbum* in the *vox*, in a 'forme' that is both 'joy and art'" (p. 36).

⋙ 898. BAUER, ROBERT J. "Donne's Letter to Herbert Re-Examined," in *New Essays on Donne*, edited by Gary A. Stringer, pp. 60–73. (Salzburg Studies in English Literature, Elizabethan & Renaissance Studies, edited by James Hogg, no. 57.) Salzburg: Institut für Englische Sprache und Literatur, Universität Salzburg.

Reads Donne's "To Sr Edward Herbert. at Julyers: Man is a lumpe" as a reply to Herbert's satiric "The State Progress of Ill" and primarily as a "cryptic statement of the literary ideals to which Donne himself aspired" (p. 62). Sees lines 1–32 as outlining Donne's position on morality; lines 33–44 as reassessing the office of the poet; and lines 45–50 as offering praise to Sir Edward as a fellow poet. Suggests that, like Sidney, Donne is primarily concerned about the effects of poetry on morality but that he goes further than Sidney in suggesting that poetry has the power to redeem the nature of man, to facilitate his pursuit of perfection, and to correct and restore what was lost in the fall of Adam—rational control and wisdom. Points out that the ultimate paradox in the epistle is that, though Donne attempted to write his theory of aesthetics in verse, "his very compulsion to achieve the moment of aesthetic fruition in his verse letter was precisely what jeopardized this letter's aesthetic wholeness" (p. 71).

⋙ 899. BELL, SRILEKHA. "John Donne: A Symbol of the Middle Ages." EAS 6, no. 2: 68–77.

Disagrees with those twentieth-century critics who regard Donne as a revolutionary or as a great innovator of sexual liberation and argues that Donne's love philosophy is basically medieval and, by the standards of his contemporaries, reactionary. Maintains that Donne's allegiance is to the love philosophy of the poets of the "dolce stil nuovo," although "his allegiance to that system he hardly dare confess even to himself, for its values were at odds with those of the circles in which he chose to move, but it is an allegiance that persists everywhere beneath the surface of his verse, occasionally breaking into expression and always supplying the imagination with a wealth of figures, images, and conceits" (p. 76). Points out that Donne considered poetry essentially a social grace but that his attitude does not preclude sincerity. Stresses that in his witty and cynical poems Donne "complied to the demands of the society of gay blades he sought out but below the level of consciousness he seems to have rebelled against their insincerity and inadequacy" (p. 72), as, for instance, in "Loves Deitie" and "Aire and Angels." Maintains that Donne's attitudes toward love, as well as many of his specific images and conceits, are similar to those of the Florentine school and especially to those of Guido Cavalcanti, Guido Guinizzelli, and the younger Dante.

◄§ 900. BEVAN, JONQUIL. "Izaak Walton and His Publisher." *The Library* 32, series 5: 344–59.
Discusses Walton's dealings with his publisher, John Marriot, and later with his son, Richard Marriot. Notes that Walton's first publication was his elegy on Donne that he contributed to John Marriot's edition of the *Poems* (1633) and that Walton's copy of the fifth edition of the poems (1650), published by Marriot and edited by Donne's son, contains, in addition to Walton's corrections, an inscription that indicates that the volume (now at Harvard University) was presented to Walton by Marriot. Observes that Richard Marriot's first imprint and Walton's first substantial publication, his *Life of Donne*, appeared in the same year as the 1640 edition of *LXXX Sermons* and that their association continued for forty-three years. Points out that throughout Richard Marriot's career Walton took an active, if unofficial, part.

◄§ 901. BROWN, ASHLEY, AND JOHN L. KIMMEY, eds. "John Donne: 'The Baite,'" in *Satire: An Anthology*, pp. 118–20. New York: Thomas Y. Crowell, Harper & Row Publishers.
Reprints "The Baite" and briefly comments on how it is a witty parody of Marlowe's "The Passionate Shepherd to His Love." Presents a very brief biographical sketch of Donne and says that his satirical verse "is marked by a jaunty, colloquial tone, far-fetched conceits, clever wordplay, and a brilliant display of paradox and irony" (p. 118).

◄§ 902. BURCHMORE, SUSAN. "A Note on the Date of 'The Canonization.'" *N&Q* n.s. 24: 200–202.
Suggests that "reall" in line 7 of "The Canonization" probably refers to King James I's "ryall" or his more valuable "Rose Ryal," coins struck in 1606 that bear his image. Maintains, therefore, that the reference to the coins suggests that the poem was written after 1606. Points out that such a dating strengthens the possibility of autobiographical references in the poem and that perhaps the whole poem may be a defense of his marriage. Notes also that the religious imagery may reflect Donne's contemplating Holy Orders between 1606 and 1614 and that, if the poem was written as late as 1606, the speaker's references to his gout and palsy may reflect Donne's illness in that year. For a reply, see Marvin Morillo (entry 1023).

◄§ 903. BYARD, MARGARET M. "Poetic Responses to the Copernican Revolution." *Scientific American* 236, no. 6: 120–29.
Discusses the impact of the Copernican revolution on seventeenth-cen-

tury poets, including Donne. Mentions Donne's possible connection with Thomas Hariot, the first English astronomer to use the telescope, and notes Donne's scientific sophistication. Discusses briefly the uses of cosmic images, allusions, and metaphors in Donne's poetry and prose. Notes that in his love poems "his imagery is almost always Ptolemaic" (p. 122) and comments on how Donne celebrates and flatters women with cosmic references, how his cosmic references in the religious poems become more serious, and how he laments the breakdown of the Ptolemaic world view in the *Anniversaries*. Notes that the *Anniversaries* are, in fact, "an interweaving of the old and the new" and that "at the same time they lament the old model of the universe, they carry the reader out toward the uncertain boundaries of space" (p. 123).

⋙ 904. CARLETON, FRANCES BRIDGES. "The Meditative Recitative," in *The Dramatic Monologue: Vox Humana*, pp. 61–71. (Salzburg Studies in English Literature, Romantic Reassessment, edited by James Hogg, no. 64). Salzburg: Institut für Englische Sprache und Literatur, Universität Salzburg.

Discusses Donne's contribution to the tradition of the dramatic monologue and comments, in particular, on resemblances and differences between Donne's metaphysical lyrics and Browning's dramatic monologues. Also contrasts Donne's "dramatic stance" with the more "cultivated simplicity" (p. 62) of Sidney's sonnets. Points out that Donne's dramatic mode is characterized by immediacy, a private and personal tone, the presentation of individual experiences as representative of the universal drama of life, dialectical argumentation, realism, and a sense of play. Considers briefly "The Extasie," "The Canonization," and several of the *Holy Sonnets* as representative of Donne's connections with monologue tradition. Notes, however, that Donne's art is "one of personal self-scrutiny, whereas Browning's wider range over many personalities and situations reduces the possibilities of biographical intervention" and suggests that Donne's characteristic "dramatic stance" is, in some ways, "a foretaste of things to come in the monologue tradition after Browning; specifically, the completely inner voice developed by Joyce and others in the interior monologue" (p. 69). Claims that Donne's "metaphysical voice epitomizes the basic ingredient of almost any dramatic verse from the psalmic ritual to the elliptical dialogue: the perplexing duality of flesh and spirit" (p. 71).

⋙ 905. CHAMBERS, A. B. "*La Corona*: Philosophic, Sacred, and Poetic Uses of Time," in *New Essays on Donne*, edited by Gary A. Stringer, pp. 140–72. (Salzburg Studies in English Literature, Elizabethan & Renaissance Studies, edited by James Hogg, no. 57.) Salzburg: Institut für Englische Sprache und Literatur, Universität Salzburg.

Discusses the historical, philosophical, religious, literary, and especially the liturgical contexts of Donne's religious poems, such as "The Annuntiation and Passion," "The Crosse," "Goodfriday, 1613. Riding Westward," and especially the seven sonnets of *La Corona*. Explains in particular the complex uses of time in the liturgical day and liturgical year and shows how the liturgy provides poets of the time with a rich source of "meaningful images for the essential unity of time past, present, and future, images which suggest that all of time celebrates, anticipates, even participates in the arrival of that which is timeless, images of that which otherwise would be unimaginable" (p. 159). Discusses *La Corona* "as a remarkably complete exposition of the themes and images of the liturgical year and day" and "as a remarkable poem" (p. 160). Points out, for example, how Donne in the third sonnet, "Temple," which recalls a seemingly minor event in Christ's life, fulfills the intent of liturgy in a most subtle way and, in fact, epitomizes the life of Christ between the Nativity and the Passion. Discusses how *La Corona* "weaves an endless circle of prayer and praise" (p. 167) and comments on the particular significance of Donne's symbolic uses of seven, the infinite number.

⋙ 906. CONTE, GIUSEPPE. "Mistica e retorica: a proposito di un sonetto di John Donne." *RSLR* 13: 127–33.

Discusses Donne's use of oxymoronic structure in "Batter my heart" as a reflection of the conflicting relationship of magic (that is, art) and mysticism to language. Describes the metaphoric violence of the text as purified by the oxymora of its carnal and sensuous force, but indicates that the self-destructive terms in which the relationship with God is framed are a linguistic representation of the paradox posed by the mystic's need for silence and the poet's reliance on words. Concludes that the antithesis of mysticism and art is the paradox articulated in the sonnet's oxymoronic juxtaposition of chastity and rape.

⋙ 907. COOPER, ROBERT M. "The Political Implications of Donne's *Devotions*," in *New Essays on Donne*, edited by Gary A. Stringer, pp. 192–210. (Salzburg Studies in English Literature, Elizabethan & Renaissance Studies, edited by James Hogg, no. 57.) Salzburg: Institut für Englische Sprache und Literatur, Universität Salzburg.

Notes in the *Devotions upon Emergent Occasions* the prevalence of political images and allusions, especially to King David, and also the curious fear of relapsing, expressed in images of idolatry, that appears in the conclusion of the work. Argues that "within the complex structure of the *Devotions* there is a strain of political advice which lies just beneath the themes of Donne's personal sickness and cure and man's sin and salvation," which "delineates both the general duties of the king and, in its final fear of relapse, suggests the dangers that the 'Roman Church' holds for that king" (p. 193). Notes that in 1622–1624 English Protestants were disturbed by King James I's dalliance with the courts of Spain and France and feared that Prince Charles would be married to a Catholic queen. Suggests that Donne, who had previously incurred the king's displeasure by criticizing his inclinations toward Catholicism, offers subtle advice in the *Devotions* to the king, advising him to be like David, a king obligated by God to protect his people against the threat of idolatry, and to save his people from the danger of the Catholic Church.

⋙ 908. Couper, John M., and William D. McGaw. "Aire and Angels." *AN&Q* 15: 104–6.

Paraphrases the argument of "Aire and Angels" and suggests that the wit of the poem is serious and sincere. Argues that the sexual connotations of the second stanza make it clear that the speaker has been overtaxed by lovemaking, has allowed his desire for his lady to spoil his love, has found his lovemaking inadequate for such a desirable mistress, and decides to reduce her from the level of a love goddess to that of a mere woman so that he can succeed with her. Suggests that in the concluding lines of the poem the mistress is the sphere that the speaker puts on and maintains that "there is nothing necessarily profane in dealing thus with love," for "if the emphasis is on the carnal side of love it is because ideal love must work carnally too" (p. 106). Maintains that the speaker "has genuinely sought and found an excellent woman only to be confounded by his performance" and that "it is precisely because he values her that he must get things right" (p. 106).

⋙ 909. Cruttwell, Patrick. "The Metaphysical Poets and Their Readers." *HAB* 28: 20–42.

Discusses the unusually close cooperation required between the metaphysical poet and his intended reader and argues that, since metaphysical poets intended their poems for a very specific, limited, and, in a sense, elitist audience, the modern critic is able "to investigate outwards, from the poems themselves, and from them to deduce the nature of the chosen reader" (p. 22). Examines a number of specific poems from this perspective and concludes that the metaphysical poets seemingly imagined their readers to be persons very much like themselves, both in their general knowledge and education and in their willingness to accept certain traditional attitudes. Points out that the metaphysical poets and their readers apparently shared a "sort of classical derivativeness" (p. 23) but did not hold with certain heroic pretensions about poetry or about poets that can be observed in earlier Renaissance poetry. Notes that, although metaphysical poets and their readers evince an interest in scientific discoveries and philosophical speculations of their time, they "never think them of primary importance" since the poetry itself characteristically "moves through a triangle formed by body, soul, and God" and since, "within that triangle, it really did not make any difference whether the sun goes down or the earth comes up" (p. 29). Argues, however, that the metaphysical poets did "expect from their readers not only a considerable familiarity with the scholastic method, but a respect for it, a willingness to accept its procedures": "Hence the well-known tendency of this poetry to organize its material in the tripartite structure of a syllogism even when the material is blatantly untheological" (p. 30). Notes also that the learning embedded in the metaphysical poem is "there if you want to find it or happen to recognize it, but your knowledge is neither asked for or essential" (p. 33) since it functions primarily as a vehicle only for exploring the central concerns or themes of the poem. Maintains that, since metaphysical poetry is not propagandistic and since both poet and intended reader shared accepted norms of morality, the reader is expected and even encouraged by the poet to develop a sense of deliberate disengagement, an ability "to let one's moral imagination out for a gallop and not feel uncomfortable afterwards" (p. 37).

◆§ 910. CUNNAR, EUGENE R. "Donne's 'Valediction: Forbidding √ Mourning' and the Golden Compasses of Alchemical Creation," in *Literature and the Occult: Essays in Comparative Literature*, edited by Luanne Frank, pp. 72–110. (University of Texas at Arlington Publications in Literature.) Arlington: The University of Texas at Arlington.

Argues that "Donne's knowledge and use of alchemy were much more central to both his intellectual and poetic endeavors than has previously been claimed or demonstrated" and discusses in detail Donne's uses of alchemical concepts in "A Valediction: forbidding mourning" in order to demonstrate "how Donne found in alchemical ideology a symbolic paradigm for his creative imagination" (p. 73) and to show how he employed hermetic and alchemical concepts "as the central means of integrating and understanding his existential experience in terms of his theological goals" (p. 74). Presents a detailed analysis of the alchemical and numerological structure of the poem to show that Donne "equates his creative imagination with the Paracelsian archeus and internalizes its force within the very poetic structure of the poem" (p. 78) and argues that Donne's use of the alchemical compass enables him to unify all the analogies of the poem. Maintains that "unless one sees the unified alchemical analogy controlling the poem, one is likely to conclude that the poem is based on superficial wit" (p. 96) and to fail to perceive that Donne is, in fact, exploring in the poem his own poetic creativity. Argues that Donne "transmutes the traditional genre of the valediction into a seriously provocative poem" (p. 109) and that what he is "forbidding" ultimately is "mourning over his love affair with the imagination because he sees it functioning as the Philosophers' Stone in transmuting his existence into celestial gold" (p. 110). Concludes that "Donne's ability to project himself into the role of the spiritual alchemist and incorporate his discoveries into an understanding of the purpose of his life and poetry suggests his success in reconciling the disparate aspects of his life" (p. 110).

◆§ 911. DANE, PETER. "The Figure of Lovers' Parting in the Poetry of John Donne." *Parergon* 19: 23–26.

Discusses Donne's uses of the familiar analogy of lovers' parting to death in his love poetry and shows that the way he employs the analogy for a temporary separation of lovers reflects "a system of thinking shaped by his familiarity with medieval theology and modified by his experience of love as the love between equals" (p. 23). Notes, for instance, that the very argument of "A Valediction: forbidding mourning" lies in the parting-death analogy established in the first two stanzas: "If, for all the horrors of the body's decay in death, the dying man [referred to metaphorically in stanza one] can so calmly accept the parting of body from soul because his faith assures him of a reunion, the lovers' faith should enable them to so calmly part the one from the other in the assurance of a reunion, if not in time then beyond time" (p. 24). Notes that in "The Extasie" the body and soul are described as lovers and that the two lovers in the poem yearn "to relate to each other more precisely in the way body and soul interlock in each of them" (p. 25). Suggests that some of Donne's notions can be found specifically in St. Bernard's commentary on the *Song of Songs* and suggests that the most prevalent theme in Donne's love poetry is precisely "that the love relation creates a new world and a new life that makes the familiar world and the familiar life fade into insignificance" (p. 25). Notes that in "The Relique" Donne uses wittily the same notion of reunion of body and soul after death that he expounds more seriously in his sermons. Notes also that Donne believed that the soul after death would be joined to a perfected body and that "the redeemed will still be able to know each other as Adam knew Eve" (p. 26). Concludes, therefore, that Donne "can so increase the precision of the familiar analogy between the temporary parting of lovers and of body and soul in death because for him these two relations—of love and individual life—are precisely congruent, equally carnal, or incarnational" (p. 26).

912. DANIELS, EDGAR F. "Donne's 'Elegy XVIII' (Loves Progress), 37–38." *Expl* 35, iv: 2.
Rejects Roberts W. French's notion (entry 747) that Donne suggests in lines 37–38 of "Loves Progress" that the body will achieve infinitude at the Day of Judgment. Argues that the lines should be read as: "it is no more true that the soul is worthier or fitter for love than the body, than it is true that the body is as infinite as the soul" and that, "in context, just as the earth is inferior to the celestial bodies yet worthy of our love and tillage, and just as we admire the superiority of a woman's heart and mind yet love her body, so we acknowledge the superiority of the soul in respect to its infinitude yet maintain the equal worthiness and fitness of the body for love" (p. 2).

913. DONALD, ROSLYN L. "Another Source for Three of John Donne's Elegies." *ELN* 14: 264–68.
Discusses Donne's debt to the blazon tradition and notes that numerous analogues and sources have been suggested for "The Anagram," "The Comparison," and "Loves Progress." Points out that, although Donne was

obviously indebted to the Roman elegy, the paradoxical *encomium*, anti-Petrarchan burlesques, and numerous other blazons, he may have been influenced also by the *Song of Songs* (4:1–7, 5:10–17, 7:1–9) and by Sidney's "What tongue can her perfection tell" in the *Arcadia*. Notes that chapters 4 and 7 of the *Song of Songs* contain full-length, erotic blazons and that chapter 7 contains a foot-to-head catalog, an order crucial to the wit of "Loves Progress." Observes that Sidney's blazon is one of the longest and fullest catalogs of a woman's body in English poetry and contains the journey motif that Donne uses in "The Comparison," "Loves Progress," and "Going to Bed." Suggests that "The Anagram" draws heavily on Continental models, but notes that Donne handles the blazon much differently than do either Berni or Tasso. Points out that the comparison blazons in Robert Greene's *Menaphon* (1589) may be a source for "The Comparison." Stresses that Donne "uses literary models only as a place to begin, and his wit turns the conventional into something bizarre" (p. 267).

⊷ 914. DONNE, JOHN. *The Flea*. Design in relief by Willow Legge. Guildford: Circle Press. [8]p.
Limited edition: 75 copies.
The poem with a design of a flea in relief.

⊷ 915. ———. *Ignatius His Conclave* (London, 1611). (The English Experience, no. 868.) Amsterdam: Theatrum Orbis Terrarum; Norwood, N.J.: Walter J. Johnson. 143p.
Facsimile edition of the Cambridge University Library copy of the first edition of *Ignatius his Conclave* (Syn. 8.61.170), with leaf G1 from Emmanuel College Library, Cambridge (S. 10.5.93¹) and page B₂r from British Library (C. 111.a.12). STC: 7027. No introduction or commentary.

⊷ 916. ———. *Letters to Severall Persons of Honour* (1651). A Facsimile reproduction with an introduction by M. Thomas Hester. Delmar, N.Y.: Scholars' Facsimiles & Reprints. xxii, 318p.
Facsimile reprint of 128 letters written by Donne between 1600 and 1631 that were collected and published by John Donne the younger in 1651. Notes that the letters illustrate Donne's character during these years, his relationships with his family and patrons, his religious views and attitudes toward contemporary events, and his increasing involvement in the world of public affairs. Points out that many of the same subjects that engaged Donne in his poetry continue to attract him in his letters and that in them he retains that quality of wit that distinguishes his poetry. Suggests that one of the most impressive features of the letters is the portrait of Donne as a family man that emerges. Notes that the most common subject in the letters is the truth of religion and discusses Donne's developing religious attitudes as they are reflected in the letters. Comments on the poor editorial practices of Donne's son in preparing the volume for publication and suggests some of his motives for making the letters available.

Presents a chronological list of the letters and their known recipients to correct the misdirections set out by Donne's son.

⋘ 917. EL-GABALAWY, SAAD. "Aretino's Pornography and English Renaissance Satire." *HAB* 28: 9–19.
First appeared in *BRMMLA* (entry 819); reprinted here with minor revisions.

⋘ 918. EVETTS-SECKER, JOSEPHINE. "*Fuga Saeculi* or Holy Hatred of the World: John Donne and Henry Hawkins." *Recusant History* 14: 40–52.
Compares *The first Anniversary* with Henry Hawkins's metrical "Treatise on the Holy Hatred of the World" that he affixed as a preface to his *Fuga Saeculi; or Holy Hatred of the World, containing lives of 17 Holy Confessors of Christ, selected out of Sundry Authours* (1632) to show that Hawkins not only echoes the general structure and intention of Donne's poem but also echoes Donne in specific ideas, images, diction, and even poetic form. Notes that the Jesuit missionary, a contemporary of Donne, obviously responded quite favorably to Donne's poem and associated it with the "contemptus mundi" theme. Points out that, although Hawkins's poem is not remarkable or exciting, it is interesting that in his efforts to provide English Catholics with spiritual reading Hawkins turned to Donne for a model.

⋘ 919. HALL, MICHAEL L. "Searching the Scriptures: Meditation and Discovery in Donne's Sermons," in *New Essays on Donne*, edited by Gary A. Stringer, pp. 211–38. (Salzburg Studies in English Literature, Elizabethan & Renaissance Studies, edited by James Hogg, no. 57.) Salzburg: Institut für Englische Sprache und Literatur, Universität Salzburg.
Suggests that in his sermons, as in the *Devotions upon Emergent Occasions*, Donne "approaches truth gradually, exploring both his own feelings and the words of Scripture, searching for meaning and praying for guidance from the Holy Ghost" and that, since for Donne the Scriptures "hold the key to self-knowledge and to Christian truth," he "feels called upon to act as interpreter of the Scriptures, opening the words for the congregation and unfolding their diverse meanings" (p. 212). Comments on Donne's method of explicating Scripture in the sermons and presents examples of his technique to show that "throughout the sermons Donne's meditative exploration of Scriptural texts is a central rhetorical technique" and that his style "suggests, rather than public oratory, the public re-enactment, or at least re-creation, of a personal meditative journey through the words of a Biblical text—not unlike the records of journeys recounted in the *Essays in Divinity* and in the *Devotions upon Emergent Occasions*" (p. 235).

✒ 920. HARMSEL, HENRIETTA TEN. "The Metaphysical Poets of Holland's Golden Age." *RNL* 8: 70–96.

Shows how four Dutch Protestant poets—Jacobus Revius, Constantijn Huygens, Jeremias De Decker, and Heiman Dullaert—are both similar and different from the English metaphysical poets, especially Donne. Notes that "the strong Calvinist-Biblical stream in the solidifying Dutch identity of their century gives their Metaphysical poetry its characteristic Dutchness" (p. 92).

✒ 921. HAYES, THOMAS W. "Alchemical Imagery in John Donne's 'A Nocturnall upon S. Lucies Day.'" *Ambix* 23, pt. 1: 55–62.

Argues that in "A nocturnall upon S. Lucies day" Donne uses alchemical imagery as a controlling metaphor for the creative process and suggests that the alchemical symbolism in the poem "may be connected to Donne's psychic vision of his sick wife [as reported by Walton]" and thus perhaps "forms an integral part of the poem's inspirational background" (p. 56). Presents a stanza-by-stanza analysis of the alchemical imagery and symbolism in the poem and shows that, just as the alchemist must reduce his materials to their lowest form before he can obtain the magical elixir and must expurge from his life all extraneous matter, "so too must the poet destroy his physical being and reach the nadir of sorrow before he is able to attain lasting peace" (p. 58). For the poet, "the act of writing is a means to this end; like the alchemical process, it too is, in a special sense, a eucharistic celebration—the outward and visible sign of an inward and spiritual grace" (pp. 58–59). Shows how in the poem Donne not only deals with the immediate occasion but also examines his own and the world's possible death and regeneration through the use of alchemical symbolism and demonstrates that "working within the hermetical macrocosm-microcosm trope, the poem moves through a welter of dialectical oppositions—light and darkness, dryness and wetness, sorrow and joy, life and death, sacred and profane love, psychical and physical reality, empirical and imaginative understanding, medieval and Renaissance cosmology—which, at the poem's end, are projected, unresolved, into the future" (p. 61).

✒ 922. HESTER, M. THOMAS. "The '*Bona Carmina*' of Donne and Horace." *RenP* (for 1976), pp. 21–30.

Comments on Donne's specific borrowings in *Satyre II* from Horace's second book of *Satires* to show how Donne modified and adapted his Latin model for his own satiric purposes. Points out that Donne "borrows central satiric techniques from Horace, then, in his own *apologia* for satire, but he modifies the degree of irony with which the satirist is equipped, focuses more fully and seriously on the personal condition of the speaker, and adds a psychological complexity, religious dimension, and verbal ambiguity not present in his Latin model" (p. 28). Suggests that, "while recalling Horace's authoritative conclusion that satire which is good poetry is legal as poetry and as social criticism, the satirist's final admission of his own ineffectiveness serves to reinforce what he has been arguing throughout *Satyre II*—that the abuse of language and law is so widespread that the civilizing force of the words of poetry and law have become largely ineffective" (p. 28). Points out that Donne's acrimonious and somber tone "might be attributable to the poet's actual situation; his own experience as a recusant and the recent death of his brother for harboring a Jesuit priest are implicit throughout the poem and explicit perhaps in his reference (in line 10) to the specific statute from which Henry Donne suffered and died" (p. 28). Maintains that the Horatian echoes and parallels expand Donne's satire beyond mere autobiographical perspective, "add ancient authority and wisdom to his suggestion that the response of the nation to satiric language is a significant barometer of its moral health" (p. 29), "direct attention to the similarity of the condition which the two satirists expose" (p. 30), and force the reader to see not only the likenesses but especially the differences between the two satirists and the two lawyers that they present.

923. ———. "Henry Donne, John Donne and the Date of 'Satyre II.'" *N&Q* n.s. 24: 524–27.

Argues that the main impetus behind *Satyre II*, which is primarily an attack on parasitic lawyers and the corrupt operation of the law and only incidentally on bad poets, was the arrest, mistreatment, and death in 1593 of Donne's younger brother, Henry, for harboring a Jesuit priest, William Harrington. Discusses the recusancy statute under which Henry was arrested and imprisoned; comments on the mysterious transfer of Henry from the Clink to Newgate Prison, where he died; and surveys Donne's Catholic background and connections. Agrees with Grierson and Milgate that *Satyre II* was written in early 1594. Suggests that the legal jargon of the love sonnets of *Zepheria* may have contributed to Donne's description of the corrupt lawyer, Coscus, as a bad poet but that the real impetus behind the poem was the death of his brother at the hands of the state.

924. ———. "'Zeal' as Satire: The Decorum of Donne's *Satyres*." *Genre* 10: 173–94.

Argues that, although his *Satyres* are indebted to Roman models, Donne viewed himself primarily "as a Christian 'rebuker' whose earliest precedents were the Old Testament Prophets" and that his five satires provide a dramatic integration of the rhetorical principle of *laus et vituperatio* "through their portrait of the satirist's gradual realization of the *ethos* which his age identified as that of the Prophets" (p. 174). Presents an analysis of the five satires to show that "to this view of the satirist as a 'zealous' prophet Donne's poems seem mostly indebted, then, especially when they are viewed in the particular climate of opinion in which they were written" (p. 174). Notes that in the English Renaissance the aim and efforts of the classical satirists and the biblical prophets were seen as complementary and points out that, from the time of St. Augustine the Church Fathers agreed that anger, "if initiated by a just cause, used out of love of goodness and hatred of sin, directed at sins rather than sinners, and aimed at moral reformation rather than personal vengeance, was 'righteous' and 'necessary'" (pp. 183–84). Shows how Donne's speaker in the *Satyres* reflects this Christian concept of satirical decorum and finally, after much effort, achieves a balance between his hate and love and exemplifies what the age called Christian "zeal."

📚 925. HILLER, GEOFFREY G. *Poems of the Elizabethan Age: An Anthology.* London: Methuen & Co. xx, 332p.

In the introduction briefly contrasts Donne with the Elizabethan lyricists, noting that his poems give the impression of talk rather than song, that characteristically Donne takes an uncourtly stance and writes with masculine vigor and forthrightness, and that his poems are marked with a strong personal consciousness. Points out Donne's debt to his predecessors in both subject matter and style but notes that "his wit and irony are sharper and more sustained, his imagery and comparisons more ingenious, his departure from convention more defiant than any other writer before him" (pp. 12–13). Likewise, contrasts Donne's satires with those of Wyatt and notes Donne's vigorous and forceful thought, his arresting images, and his rugged and irregular verse. Comments on the personal and dramatic elements in the *Satyres* and suggests that Donne's Juvenalian anger is often tempered by his compassion for human weakness. Reproduces, with notes, "Song: Goe, and catche a falling starre," "Breake of day," "Womans constancy," "The Apparition," "The broken heart," "The good-morrow," *Satyre I, Satyre II,* and "The Baite." Selected bibliography (p. 315).

📚 926. HOGAN, PATRICK G., JR. "The Iconographic Background of the First Verse of Donne's 'A Valediction Forbidding Mourning,'" in *New Essays on Donne,* edited by Gary A. Stringer, pp. 26–44. (Salzburg Studies in English Literature, Elizabethan & Renaissance Studies, edited by James Hogg, no. 57.) Salzburg: Institut für Englische Sprache und Literatur, Universität Salzburg.

Argues that, although Donne's poetry is not characterized by sustained description, "a given passage in Donne, perhaps even a single image, may rely upon what may be called self-contained description, and the graphic apprehension by the reader may depend, in part, upon the iconographic suggestiveness of the image or passage" (pp. 27–28). Discusses Donne's interest in art and artists and "the skill with which he weaves iconographic concepts into the word-fabric of his poetry" and incorporates "various iconographic implications into his poetic images" (p. 38). Suggests that the first four lines of "A Valediction: forbidding mourning" may be partly informed by "graphic representations—ranging from elaborate initial letters in manuscripts or early printed books to illustrations, whether by illumination, woodcut, or engraving—in Renaissance works" (p. 28). Points out that the compass image may have been suggested by pictorial representations of compasses in emblem books, woodcuts, and engravings, such as the well-known compass emblem used by Christopher Plantin, the Belgian printer. Offers examples of paintings, engravings, frescoes, and so on that may "have provided ample stimulus for verbal images suggestive in their compression rather than descriptive through expanded detail" (p. 33). Notes that in "The Storme" (line 4) Donne specifically refers to Nicholas Hilliard, the miniaturist painter, and in *Satyre IV* (line 204) to Albrecht Dürer, and suggests that in "Witchcraft by a picture" Donne "manipulates the concepts implicit in the term 'picture' for humorous purposes" (p. 36). Notes also that the faces of figures in *The Last Judgment* by van Eyck, several of the panels of *The Garden of Worldly Delights* by Hieronymous Bosch, certain paintings by Bruegel, woodcuts in Sebastian Brant's *The Ship of Fools*, and perhaps even Luca Signorelli's frescoes in *The Damned Cast into Hell* and Michelangelo's *The Last Judgment* may be, as it were, analogues to lines 37–44 of "The Autumnall." Discusses briefly external evidence to support Donne's interest in art, such as his will, in which he mentions several portraits and paintings, specifically mentioning Padre Paola (Paola Sarpi) and Fulgentio (Fulgenzio Micanzio) and describing a picture of the Virgin and St. John attributed to Titian.

⌐ ◀§ 927. HOLLOWAY, JOHN. "The Self and Its Regeneration," in *The Proud Knowledge: Poetry, Insight and the Self, 1620–1920*, pp. 158–207. London: Henley; Boston: Routledge & Kegan Paul.
Briefly discusses "A nocturnall upon S. Lucies day" and suggests that "the kind of poetry which invites us to a delighted participation in brilliantly witty verse may in the end begin to reach, as it were, a natural limit" and that thus "beyond a certain point, it cannot hope altogether to satisfy the interests which it encourages readers to cultivate and sharpen" (p. 159). Suggests that, for all its seemingly personal qualities, "A nocturnall upon S. Lucies day" is a private poem made up of ideas that are "dazzlingly interwoven into the contemplation of the personal experience" and stresses that the ideas "are constituents of a common cultural heritage; and it is this, not any personal response or discovery, which provides the poet with what enables him to see his disastrous experience as temporary, and so to resolve and terminate his poem" (p. 160). Compares and contrasts Donne's poem with Cowper's "Castaway" and Arnold's "To Marguerite—Continued" to show how each of the poems deals differently with the problem of the failure of the spirit and isolation.

◀§ 928. HUNTINGTON, JOHN. "Philosophical Seduction in Chapman, Davies, and Donne." *ELH* 44: 40–59.
Notes that modern critics offer apparently discrepant and often contradictory interpretations of "The Extasie," George Chapman's "Ovids Banquet of Sence," and Sir John Davies's *Orchestra* and points out that all

three of these poems focus on the conflicting and ambiguous possibilities inherent in Marsilio Ficino's Platonic theory of *furor amoris*. Suggests that Chapman's and Davies's poems teach two important lessons about reading Platonic poems: "first, that the ambiguity inherent in the dramatic situation is commonly central to the poem's theme and is therefore not to be ignored or denounced but to be accepted and probed; and second, that this ambiguity can be treated from a Platonic point of view as a complementary doubleness that is essential to the depiction of transcendent states of mind" (pp. 54–55). Concludes that, seen in this light, "the doubleness of 'The Extasie' is, not a 'problem' to be solved by selecting one interpretation and rejecting the other, but a conscious rhetorical device that renders the Platonic theory of love's intellectual promise and at the same time acknowledges the threat of moral duplicity" (p. 55).

♨ 929. JOHNSON, H. A. T. "'Despite Time's Derision': Donne, Hardy, and the 1913 Poems." *THY* 7: 7–20.

Suggests a number of similarities and dissimilarities between Donne's love poetry and Hardy's 1913 Poems and argues that both poets "range far more widely than other English poets in pursuit of what one might call notes towards a definition of love" (p. 12). Maintains, however, that "there are affinities, which when the 1913 Poems are in question, become of salient importance, and assist us in forming a true judgement of Hardy's achievement" (p. 12). Notes many similarities in style and language but suggests that more important is their similar way of feeling, their "shared mode of apprehension" (p. 14), especially in their treatment of the theme of time and love. Notes several echoes from Donne in Hardy's 1913 Poems; points out Hardy's admiration for Donne; and observes that at the time of his death Hardy had two copies of Donne's poems in his possession, one of which (Chambers's 1896 edition) was given to him by Edmund Gosse and contains marked passages. Notes also that Hardy acknowledges Donne's influence in the marginal notes in his copy of Samuel Chew's monograph on his poetry.

♨ 930. JORGENS, ELISE. "'Sweetest stay awhile': Six Musical Interpretations." *Centerpoint* 2, iii: 1–10.

Compares and contrasts "Sweetest stay awhile" with Donne's "Breake of day" to show that they are not parts of the same work, as some early songbook sources suggest; that they are, in fact, quite different in tone, language, theme, and uses of the persona, and that "Sweetest stay awhile" was clearly not written by Donne. Discusses six musical interpretations of "Sweetest stay awhile" to show that different musical styles reflect "changing tastes in textual interpretation, which, in turn, are conditioned by changes in the predominant poetic styles" (p. 3).

♨ 931. KEYNES, GEOFFREY. "More Books from the Library of John Donne." *BC* 26: 29–35.

Adds ten (perhaps eleven) titles to his previously published list (entry 566) of books that were either in Donne's possession (213 titles) or that at least passed through his hands (5 titles). Notes that "the majority of books already listed were connected with Donne's work on the Roman Catholic recusants, published in his book *Pseudo-Martyr* 1610" and that "more than half of the books now added seem to have been acquired with the same view" (p. 29). Discusses in some detail two additions of special interest: (1) a school text of Ovid (1584) that contains Donne's signature on the title page and that is now in St. John's College, Cambridge, and (2) a copy of Kepler's *De stella nova* (1606) that contains not only Donne's signature but also many pencil markings in the margins and that is now in the John Rylands Library (see entry 801). Reproduces the title pages of these two works.

932. LATT, DAVID J. "Praising Virtuous Ladies: The Literary Images and Historical Reality of Women in Seventeenth-Century England," in *What Manner of Woman: Essays on English and American Life and Literature*, edited by Marlene Springer, pp. 39–64. New York: New York University Press.

Examines the social position of women in England during the seventeenth century and comments on the representations of them in literature of the period, especially in the poetry of Donne, Jonson, Carew, Suckling, Milton, and Marvell. Stresses that in poetry women were most often presented either as passive models of virtue (usually as upholders of the virtues of restraint) or as examples of the accepted feminine roles of daughter, wife, and mother. Notes that, like Jonson, Donne in his verse epistles praises women primarily as models of virtue that have the power to spiritualize men and thus lead them to virtue and to God. Notes also that for Donne, as for most of his contemporaries, "women were expected to correct the world's immorality by being static *exempla*" (p. 43) and thus their value is directly related to their willingness to withdraw from public life. Points out, however, that in his love poetry Donne does not, for the most part, present women as inaccessible and unattainable figures of pious virtue but rather stresses the pleasure and humanly fulfilling aspects of sexuality. Claims that Donne alone among the secular poets of the time successfully integrated sexual desire with genuine emotional intimacy.

933. LE COMTE, EDWARD. "Donne's 'The Canonization,' line 13." *SCN* 35: 6.

Points out that "forward spring" in line 13 of "The Canonization" ("When did my colds a forward spring remove") is an idiom, found, for example, in *Richard III* (III.i.94), and that in the poem the line most likely means that the speaker's "chills do not hold back the spring" (p. 6).

934. LEWALSKI, BARBARA KIEFER. "Typological Symbolism and the 'Progress of the Soul' in Seventeenth-Century Literature," in *Liter-*

ary Uses of Typology from the Late Middle Ages to the Present, edited by Earl Miner, pp. 79–114. Princeton: Princeton University Press. Examines historically and critically how typological symbolism informs several major English seventeenth-century literary works that deal with the progress of the soul, including Donne's sermons, "Hymne to God my God, in my sicknesse," *Devotions upon Emergent Occasions*, and the *Anniversaries*. Argues that "typological symbolism became in the earlier seventeenth century an important literary means to explore the personal spiritual life with profundity and psychological complexity, and that certain characteristic Protestant alterations in the traditional typological formulae facilitated this exploration" and shows that "these alterations, together with the prominence of the theme of the progress of the soul, arise from the same cause—the new Protestant emphasis upon the application of Scripture to the self, that is, the discovery of scriptural paradigms and of the workings of Divine Providence, in one's own life" (p. 81). Demonstrates how in his sermons Donne often "focuses his typological allusions directly upon the Christian individuals who constitute his auditory—us" (pp. 82–83) and shows how typological symbolism "serves as a means of self-definition and analysis in the *Devotions upon Emergent Occasions* and in the 'Hymne to God my God, in my sicknesse,' and as a vehicle of praise in the *Anniversary* poems" (p. 85). Argues that in the *Anniversaries* Elizabeth Drury becomes for Donne a type of the "regenerate Christian in whom the image of God has been restored through Christ's justifying grace" and thus he presents her "as both recapitulating and foreshadowing other conditions of human goodness past and to come" (p. 87). Maintains that in the course of the two poems, "by extension of the typological patterns enacted by Elizabeth Drury, the speaker relates himself and his audience to Elizabeth's progress" (p. 89).

◄§ 935. LEWIS, MARJORIE D. "The *Adversarius* Talks Back: 'The Canonization' and *Satire I*," in *New Essays on Donne*, edited by Gary A. Stringer, pp. 1–25. (Salzburg Studies in English Literature, Elizabethan & Renaissance Studies, edited by James Hogg, no. 57.) Salzburg: Institut für Englische Sprache und Literatur, Universität Salzburg.

Maintains that the speaker of "The Canonization" is the *adversarius* of *Satyre I*, now older and more advanced in self-discovery through the aid of his virtuous lover, who is "talking back to his friend the satirist of *Satire I* and triumphantly announcing at the end that the situation has completely changed and that their former positions in relation to each other have altered in a way that the critic and adviser could hardly have anticipated" (p. 1). Suggests a possible connection between "The Canonization" and Juvenal's *Satire III*, compares the two, and shows Donne's dramatic improvements on the classical model. Challenges the notion that *Satyre I* is a body-soul debate but rather sees the speaker and adversary as simply two men who are temporarily dominated by two aspects of human nature, the spiritual-intellectual and the physical-sensual. Presents a stanza-by-stanza analysis of "The Canonization" to show that the *adversarius* of *Satyre I* and his virtuous lover become the pattern of constancy and that the speaker of the poem "now has everything the satirist formerly urged him to renounce his love to gain, but has it not in the corrupted form of the world, but in the ideal form of those 'Townes, Countries, Courts' and all they contain" (p. 21).

᠊ᢒᢒ᠍ 936. McFARLAND, RONALD E. "Figures of Repetition in John Donne's Poetry." *Style* 11: 391–406.

Discusses Donne's knowledge of and uses of formal rhetoric in his poetry and focuses primarily on his skillful and varied uses of figures of repetition to show that "much of the effect of his poems comes from a tension between the apparently free-wheeling colloquial phrasing and the apparently conventional figures" and that his manipulation of rhetorical figures is "no less inventive than his variations on the Petrarchan mode" (p. 392). Argues, therefore, that "it is at the level of particular rhetorical devices used in specific contexts that we can best appreciate the workings of both convention and invention" (p. 403). Stresses that, although figures of repetition are only one element of Donne's complex style, his careful and elaborate uses of them show that his use of rhetoric "is neither haphazard nor mechanical" (p. 403). Surveys briefly the theory of repetition in classical and Renaissance rhetorical guides and comments in detail on Donne's uses of six figures of repetition in specific poems: *epizeuxis*, *antanaclosis*, *andiplosis*, *epanalepsis*, *anaphora*, and *polyptoton*. Suggests that occasionally Donne transgresses against the decorum of recurrence, as, for example, in "The Crosse," in which he uses the word *cross* thirty-two times in sixty-four lines. Maintains that Donne's uses of repetition are not necessarily more frequent or more effective than Herbert's or Spenser's but notes that what distinguishes Donne's use is "the intensity he gains through contiguous repetition which he can achieve in various ways and various figures" (p. 402). Discusses in some detail *Satyre IV* to illustrate the point.

᠊ᢒᢒ᠍ 937. MACNIVEN, IAN S. "An Examination of the Love Poetry of Donne and Lorca." *Káñina* (San Jose, Costa Rica) 1: 61–72.

Compares and contrasts Federico García Lorca and Donne as love poets and claims that, in spite of many differences, they share certain important attitudes on love and often treat love in a similar manner. Notes, for instance, that both poets had a certain libertine, yet almost religious reverence for women; were preoccupied with death and its relationship to love; evidenced a strain of sadomasochism; and used colloquial and often earthy language to express their love. Compares and contrasts specifically "The good-morrow" and Lorca's "Gacela del amor imprevisto" and shows how both poems progress from ignorance through discovery to knowledge. Notes, however, that while Donne envisions immortality made possible by love, Lorca recognizes that love "may not be able to stand between man and mortality" (p. 69). Reproduces both poems with an English translation of Lorca's poem by W. S. Merwin (pp. 70–71).

◆§ 938. MAUCH, KATHERINE. "Angel Imagery and Neoplatonic Love in ✓ Donne's 'Aire and Angels.'" *SCN* 35: 106–11.

Presents a detailed critical reading of "Aire and Angels" and suggests three important keys to understanding the poem: (1) the theme of Neoplatonic love, which moves from sense to reason to spiritual understanding; (2) the pun on "angel" as both the heavenly messenger (body of air and essence) and the coin, each corresponding to the three stages of Neoplatonic love—coin (sense, with even the association of prostitution), body of air (reason), and essence (spiritual understanding); and (3) the dialectic pattern of movement from thesis to antithesis to synthesis, "not between the highest and lowest kinds of love but between the highest kind [the male speaker] and a lower kind [the mistress]" (p. 107). Argues that "the speaker's change in tone at the end of the poem does not arise so much from his reflecting upon the baser quality of woman's love as from his considering the fact that while he now knows what is required for an enduring love relationship, he must also accept the fact that a lasting love cannot be the completely mutual kind of love he had sought and had even found—at moments—on levels one and three," since "the bond of total union exists not on earth but in heaven (between angels)" (p. 107). Suggests that the often perplexing change of tone at the end of the poem "might therefore not be insulting, mocking, or even teasing, but rather wistful, or perhaps bittersweet"—an appropriate term "since it suggests a synthesis of feelings" (p. 107). Notes that until line 23 the changing nature of the speaker's love determines the nature of the imagery and that "nothing about her or the duality of her response to his love is described except at the poem's conclusion when her love is first mentioned and is seen to be analogous to the body of a heavenly angel and therefore to be of the type belonging to the second level of the Neoplatonic ladder" (p. 107). Suggests that Donne may be concerned primarily with saying something important about the nature of human love, not with distinguishing between men's love and women's love. Concludes, therefore, that the poem is "about the experience of finally, after much search for an escape from oneself in total union with another, accepting the confines of the self and the peculiarly human love that they make possible" (p. 111).

◆§ 939. MISHRA, J[AYAKANTA] K. "The Fame of the Metaphysical Style of Donne" and "The Name and Nature of the Metaphysical Style," in *The Complex Style in English Poetry—Studies in Donne, Browning and Hopkins*, pp. 11–55. Allahabad: Mitab Mahal.

Notes that parts of this tripartite study of the complex style in English poetry have been published in the *Allahabad University Studies* and in *Pages of English Poetry*; here revised. Only chapters 2 and 3 are devoted to Donne and metaphysical style. Outlines briefly in "The Fame of the

Metaphysical Style of Donne" (pp. 11–23) shifting critical attitudes toward metaphysical poetry, especially Donne's poetry, from the seventeenth century to our own time and concludes that "in spite of much valuable and constructive criticism a certain apologetic tone, a certain patronising strain is the order of the day in discussing the role of the Metaphysical Style of the Seventeenth Century" and that, therefore, "the subject still needs an honest and revised discussion in standard histories of English literature" (p. 23). Argues in "The Name and Nature of the Metaphysical Style" (pp. 24–55) that neither the term *metaphysical*, as it has been traditionally applied, nor more recent designations of the style are satisfactory in describing Donne's style. Suggests that it may be more properly defined simply as "a new style which emerged at the end of the sixteenth century and at the beginning of the seventeenth century at once as a revolt against the prevailing sweet idealized Spenser-[P]etrarchan Platonic, Arcadian—in a word 'romantic' or Spenserian style, and as a bold experiment of a complex, analytical, intellectual, psychological, and powerful kind intended to express fully and powerfully the complex, full-blooded life of the Renaissance times" (p. 32). Examines three features that have been wrongly emphasized as the differentia of metaphysical style—wit, metaphysical shudder, and felt thought—and outlines those features that "really distinguish it from other styles" (p. 40): its intellectuality, realism or truthfulness to life, dramatic quality, and uses of a new language and rhythm. Presents a brief critical analysis of "The Expiration" as an example of metaphysical style.

⊰§ 940. MIZEJEWSKI, LINDA. "Darkness and Disproportion: A Study of Donne's 'Storme' and 'Calme.'" *JEGP* 76: 217–30.

Argues that "The Storme" and "The Calme" as companion poems dramatize Donne's concern and pessimism over the collapse of the medieval and Renaissance view of a man-centered, finite, hierarchical universe and maintains that considered together the poems "show a dialectic of faith and reason, a frustration with disharmony, and a hope for order that mark the later religious poems" (p. 218). Presents a detailed critical analysis of the two verse epistles to show that they are complementary parts of one argument: "The Storme" presents the conflict emotionally, and "The Calme" "broadens the experience and articulates the problem in different terms" (p. 230). Points out that the imagery and paradoxes in the poems reflect Donne's acute awareness of instability, permutability, and flux in the universe and the difficulty of finding permanence and order in this world. Demonstrates that, unlike the *Songs and Sonets*, the two verse epistles "show no attempt to reconstruct a tiny, private world for security" (p. 230) but rather foreshadow Donne's attitude in *The first Anniversary*.

⊰§ 941. NORFORD, DON PARRY. "Microcosm and Macrocosm in Seventeenth-Century Literature." *JHI* 38: 409–28.

Finds alienation a key to much seventeenth-century literature, especially to metaphysical poetry, and comments on "the intensified awareness of self, the cultivation of the private personality, which was generated in the Renaissance by the growing revulsion from orthodox public roles and services" (p. 418). Shows that "the characteristic metaphysical poetic strategy is to use the correspondence between the microcosm and macrocosm to transcend the world by finding that the private world of the lovers or of the worshipper contains the larger universe" (p. 420). Discusses how in his love poetry Donne uses the microcosm-macrocosm correspondence as "a means of expression for himself and his love—his private world" and how he typically "contracts or assimilates the whole world into his microcosm" (p. 420), as evidenced, for example, in "The Canonization" and "The good-morrow." Suggests that Donne "even surpasses Cusanus in his affirmation of the greatness of the contracted world" (p. 422) and that he reflects the fundamental Renaissance polarity between all or nothing, as, for instance, in "A Lecture upon the Shadow" and "A nocturnall upon S. Lucies day." Notes that only in "A Valediction: forbidding mourning" is Donne fully successful in overcoming the world, since in it "the lovers become the circle whose center is everywhere and circumference nowhere" (p. 425).

◄§ 942. OUSBY, HEATHER DUBROW. "A Senecan Analogue to Donne's 'Huge Hill.'" *N&Q* n.s. 24: 144–45.
Points out that a passage from Seneca's letter to Lucilius (Letter 84) may be yet another analogue to Donne's image of the "huge hill" in *Satyre III* (line 79).

◄§ 943. OWENS, ROBERT R. "Donne's South-West Discoverie." *N&Q* n.s. 24: 142–43.
Points out that the discovery of the Straits of Magellan (1519) "provided the English imagination with a new image that would soon be invested with imaginative and symbolic importance" (p. 142) and that the European conception of straits is central to an understanding of "Hymne to God my God, in my sicknesse." Suggests that descriptions of the Straits by Antonio Pigafetta, Maximilianus Transylvanus, Lopez Vas, and Thomas Cavendish provide information on how Donne and his audience would have understood his description of a passage that links the East to the West, the known to the unknown, and, symbolically, life through death to immortality.

◄§ 944. PARINI, JAY. "The Progress of the Soul: Donne and Hopkins in Meditation." *FMLS* 13: 303–12.
Examines Donne's *Holy Sonnets* and Gerard Manley Hopkins's "Terrible Sonnets" as highly dramatic sonnet sequences in the Ignatian tradition. Shows how "each poet transformed his own experience into art as an act of devotion and self-examination" and discusses the relationship between poetry and meditation so that the modern reader can avoid "mis-

reading these great poems through ignorance of their relation to a specific tradition" (p. 303). Compares Donne and Hopkins and finds many similarities between their styles and religious sensibilities. Notes that both found their inspiration in Ignatian spirituality, both project themselves through a consciously created persona, and both "recreate the interior drama of a soul in spiritual progress from desolation to consolation" (p. 311).

✓ ✑ 945. PARRISH, PAUL A. "Poet, Audience, and the Word: An Approach to the *Anniversaries*," in *New Essays on Donne*, edited by Gary A. Stringer, pp. 110–39. (Salzburg Studies in English Literature, Elizabethan & Renaissance Studies, edited by James Hogg, no. 57.) Salzburg: Institut für Englische Sprache und Literatur, Universität Salzburg.

✓ Discusses St. Augustine's view on poetry, especially his notion of an analogy between the Christian poet and the inspired prophet and/or preacher, noting that to him "all worthwhile writing, whether divinely inspired or not, must reveal an intention beneath the superficial and literal in order to promote the truth which is its basis and justification" (p. 111). Calls Donne "one of Augustine's notable disciples" and suggests that Augustinianism is implicit in all of his religious poetry but "has its fullest and most emphatic declaration in Donne's two *Anniversary* poems" (p. 111), in which he functions as both poet and prophet. Shows how the two poems are essentially celebrations of faith, grace, and virtue as these are figured forth by Elizabeth Drury and suggests that, although written before the sermons, the *Anniversaries* "provide us with Donne's fullest and most explicit discussion of the roles of the preacher and the elect body of believers, the metaphorical roles previously assumed by the poet and his audience" (p. 117). Maintains that in the poems Donne shows his audience the way to salvation through recollection; "the recollection is of sin and a sinful world and of perfection and an eternal heaven; specifically, the recollection is of the virtuous figure of a young girl, both her potential to have healed this world and her participation in the perfection of the next" (p. 119). Demonstrates that in all three of Donne's funeral sermons, as in the *Anniversaries*, an individual is remembered and celebrated and in each Donne reveals "the preacher's considerable concern for his audience and its expected and crucial response" (p. 119). Maintains, therefore, that the funeral sermons, as antitypes of the *Anniversaries*, provide important commentary on the poems and "make prominent what Donne treats less directly in his poetic commemoration: the preacher's emphasis on the necessary response of a virtuous audience and the crucial relationship between speaker, audience, and message" (p. 127). Argues that Donne's intended audience "shares with him a commitment to virtue and goodness" and that the poet asks his audience "to accept at the same time a full celebration of the girl's soul as part of its poetic faith and as part of the Word which he preaches," knowing that his audience "will respond in faith to the poet's efforts, for it recognizes the nature of the equation he makes" (p. 135).

946. PAULIN, BERNARD. *Du Couteau à la plume: Le Suicide dans la littérature anglaise de la Renaissance (1580–1625)*. (Les Hommes et Les Lettres: collection dirigée par Jacques Goudet.) Publication de l'Université de Saint-Étienne. Lyons: Éditions L'Hermès. 622p.

Discusses theories about and the practice of suicide in the life and literature of England and the Continent from 1580 to 1625. Mentions Donne throughout, especially *Biathanatos* (pp. 106–23). Calls the work bizarre and unique. Examines its arguments, structure, sources, and casuistical methodology: "Sa doctrine relativiste l'entraîne à faire une critique historique très moderne" (p. 115). Discusses the influence of *Biathanatos* on later thinkers and especially confronts the issue of Donne's sincerity. Shows the importance of death in many of Donne's works, both poetry and prose, and concludes that he "met en évidence le vice fondamental de la méthode des casuistes: ils ont oublié tout simplement la charité" (p. 122).

947. PERRINE, LAURENCE. "Donne's 'Love's Diet.'" *Expl* 35, iii: 20–21.

Rejects Judah Stampfer's suggestions (entry 267) that in "Loves diet" the speaker of the first four stanzas is a woman and the speaker of the fifth is a man. Argues that "the figurative strategy of the poem splits the person of the speaker into two parts" (p. 21): (1) the "I," the rational part of the speaker's psyche, and (2) the "it" or "him," the irrational, emotional part. Maintains that the poem describes "how the 'I' puts the 'it' on a diet and cures it of overweight" and allows "it" "only a low-calorie diet of sighs, tears, and letters" (p. 21).

948. PETRICK, STANLEY R. "Understanding Understanding Poetry." *CHum* 11: 217–21.

Considers some of the complexities of the fourth stanza of "A Valediction: forbidding mourning" to discuss difficulties in producing a satisfactory computer program for understanding poetry. Notes that "a computer model for the understanding of poetry is nowhere in sight" (p. 219).

949. PETTI, ANTHONY J. "John Donne (1572–1631)," in *English literary hands from Chaucer to Dryden*, pp. 96–97. Cambridge, Mass.: Harvard University Press.

Describes characteristics of Donne's handwriting and comments on his uses of punctuation and abbreviations. Reproduces a facsimile of part of a holograph letter to Sir Robert Cotton (1602) now in the British Library (Cotton Cleo., F. viii, f. 293, lower portion). Notes that Donne's holographs are mainly letters, two Latin epigrams on the flyleaves of books, a receipt, and the newly found "A Letter to the Lady Carey, and Mrs Essex

Rich, From Amyens," the latter being the only holograph poem known to exist.

≈§ 950. POLLOCK, JOHN J., ed. *We Lie Down in Hope: Selections from John Donne's Meditations on Sickness.* Elgin, Ill.; Weston, Ontario; Fullerton, Calif.: David C. Cook Publishing Co. 93p.

Reproduces short selection from *Devotions upon Emergent Occasions,* with forty-three accompanying contemporary photographs. Suggests in the brief introduction that Donne wrote the *Devotions* "entirely during the period when he was most ill" (p. 7).

≈§ 951. REICHERT, JOHN. "Understanding and Misunderstanding," in *Making Sense of Literature,* pp. 96–126. Chicago and London: The University of Chicago Press.

Agrees with Wimsatt and Beardsley that line 9 of "A Valediction: forbidding mourning" ("Moving of th'earth") refers to earthquakes and not to the movement of the earth around the sun, as Charles Coffin suggests, but disagrees with their reasoning: "Wimsatt and Beardsley's reading makes good sense of the passage because it is simpler, more complete, and more consistent than Coffin's" (p. 102).

≈§ 952. REISNER, THOMAS ANDREW. "The Rope in Donne's 'Elegie XIV.'" *N&Q* n.s. 24: 527–28.

Argues that the allusion to gold being transformed into rope in "A Tale of a Citizen and his Wife" (lines 64–65) is not based on a free rendering or mistranslation of Plautus's *Autularia,* as conjectured by Grierson, but on an epigram attributed to Plato by Diogenes Laertius and found in Dübner's edition of *Anthologia Palatina* (1872). Notes that a somewhat similar interchange occurs in an epigram variously attributed to Plato, Antipater, or Statyllius Flaccus. Points out that one of the most famous subsequent versions of the epigram can be found in the first collected edition of Shelley's *The Poetical Works* (1839).

√ **≈§ 953. RIEMER, A. P.** "A Pattern for Love—The Structure of Donne's 'The Canonization.'" *SSEng* 3 (1977–1978): 19–31.

Analyzes "The Canonization" to show that, although it "gives the appearance of a sustained argument," it is, in fact, "a tissue of unsubstantiated and insubstantial assertions, false trials, deductions drawn from a play on words, abuse instead of demonstration—in short, a species of *suggestio falsi* and *suppressio veri*" (p. 19). Argues, however, that the serious intention of the poem and its coherence can be found in its complex, symmetrical, and numerological structure. Notes, for example, that the five stanzas of the poem (the number five symbolizing marriage and chaste love in the Renaissance) suggest that the poem is "a celebration of married love" and that "its structural framework may be seen in terms of Platonic transcendence" (p. 28). Points out several possible uses of numerological

symbolism in the poem: the ten key uses and positionings of the word *love* ⟡
(ten equals perfection); the nine-line stanzas (nine equals heavenly perfection and immortality); the use of *love* for the eleventh time in line 39
(eleven equals transgression and symbolizes overweening pride and death);
and the forty-five lines of the poem (suggesting that perhaps it is intended
"as a fantastical gift commemorating the feast-day of the saint of love" (p.
30), St. Valentine, whose feast is 14 February, forty-five days into the new
year. Concludes that "The Canonization" is "simultaneously 'serious' and
flippant, dedicated and jesting, and entirely free of that essentially Romantic conviction that a work of art cannot (and should not) embrace
both polarities at the same time" (p. 31).

◆§ 954. SADLER, LYNN VEACH. "Relations Between Alchemy and Poet-   ✓
ics in the Renaissance and Seventeenth Century, with Special Glances
at Donne and Milton." *Ambix* 24, pt. 2: 69–76.
Discusses the insinuation of alchemy into poetic theory and into poetic
technique during the Renaissance and the seventeenth century and demonstrates this merging "by drawing parallels between poetry and alchemy,
citing the use of alchemical analogies and doctrine in treatises on poetry,
and surveying alchemical techniques in Donne's 'The triple Foole' and
Milton's *Samson Agonistes*" (p. 69). Suggests that in "The triple Foole"
Donne employs the Paracelsian doctrine of "overplus," that is, the curing
of one sorrow (or poison) by using a lesser sorrow (or poison). Says that
the Petrarchan lover in the poem is indeed a triple fool "in his failure to
interpret rightly love, verse, and the purgative process (the Paracelsian
overplus in this case)" (p. 74). Notes that "to the responsive audience,
however, the 'cure' is already in evidence, as the distance between the
complaining speech patterns and the metrical structure of Stanza 1 seems
to lessen" and that even the persona, "as he begins in Stanza 2 to speak of
music, starts also to react to the harmonies of the verse" and thus, in time,
"will become the 'best' fool when he can laugh at his own folly and no
longer resent others learning from his mistakes" (p. 74).

◆§ 955. SANTISTEBAN OLMEDO, FRANCISCO. "John Donne y la idea del
amor." *Estudios de filología inglesa* 3: 99–118.
Comments on Donne's philosophy of love and notes that, since he presents his ideas of love in so many different ways, it is difficult to study his
ideal of love. Points out, for instance, that often a trivial situation leads
Donne to a profound spiritual meditation, as, for example, in "The good-
morrow" and in "Aire and Angels," whereas in other poems he limits
himself to a simple clinical description of sex, as in "Going to Bed." Concludes that Donne's ideas about love move gradually toward the abstract
and the spiritual and that his development in matters of love may result
from his unreciprocated early love affairs.

◆§ 956. SENNHENN, CARL BRAUN. "John Donne, Poet in the Pulpit," in
New Essays on Donne, edited by Gary A. Stringer, pp. 239–60.

(Salzburg Studies in English Literature, Elizabethan & Renaissance Studies, edited by James Hogg, no. 57). Salzburg: Institut für Englische Sprache und Literatur, Universität Salzburg.

Reviews the tradition of the poet-priest in order to understand better Donne's performance as a poet who became a priest and discusses the importance of the sermons as a literary genre in Renaissance England. Points out that, "with a sound theological background and the skills of the poet for his Christian armor, Donne approaches many theological matters poetically" and that for him "the techniques of poetry provide a means to show forth the divine in terms of the human, the spiritual in terms of the physical, and inner spiritual mysteries in terms of concrete, physical realities" (p. 245). Notes that one can observe in the sermons Donne's increasing confidence in his role as a preacher who is also a poet; a great use of metaphor in his sermons; more allusions to aesthetics, rhetoric, and poetry itself; and even an increase in the use of metaphysical wit. Maintains that Donne's public oratory is, in fact, "remarkable to the extent that it depends greatly upon a metaphorical interpretation of the Bible and upon an exegesis of biblical texts by means of metaphor" (p. 258).

৵§ 957. SINHA, V[INODE] N[ARAIN]. *John Donne: A Study of His Dramatic Imagination.* New Delhi: K. K. Bhargawa at The Caxton Press. 187p.

Analyzes the *Satyres, Elegies,* and *Songs and Sonets* to show that Donne's dramatic imagination is an essential feature of his poetry and explains his creative mode. Chapter 1, "Critical Trends and Perspective" (pp. 1–30), surveys major critical estimates of Donne in the twentieth century and concludes that, in spite of the vast amount of Donne criticism, further investigation into his dramatic imagination and method is needed. Chapter 2, "The Dramatic Imagination" (pp. 31–54), examines theories of creative imagination and the dramatic mode and relates these to Donne. Chapter 3, "Satires" (pp. 55–79), attempts to show that Donne went beyond his Renaissance contemporaries in his *Satyres:* "The sheer joy he manifests in the creation of character and the portrayal of human relationships, though only occasionally in the satires, goes beyond the limited end of the satirical form and is a sign of the presence of dramatic imagination" (p. 78). Concludes that, "whenever Donne's poetry succeeds, it is for him not merely a question of literary devices but of an irresistible interest in human character and in the totality of human experience" and "when the dramatic vision fails, there is a descent to the mere intellectual or bathetic as in *Satire V*" (p. 79). Chapter 4, "Elegies" (pp. 81–134), surveys the *Elegies,* comments on dramatic elements in them, and concludes that "it is the dramatic sense which makes all the difference in Donne's poetry; where it is potent his poems are aesthetically effective, but where it is absent or weak his poetry fails and becomes just a *tour de force*" (p. 128). Chapter 5, "Songs and Sonnets" (pp. 135–84), examines the mature love poetry to show the importance of the dramatic mode and analyzes individual poems to illustrate how they reveal Donne's dramatic imagination. Selected bibliography (pp. 185–87).

958. SMALLING, MICHAEL. "Donne's Medieval Aesthetics and His Use of Morally Distant *Personae*: Two Questions, One Answer," in *New Essays on Donne*, edited by Gary A. Stringer, pp. 74–109. (Salzburg Studies in English Literature, Elizabethan & Renaissance Studies, edited by James Hogg, no. 57.) Salzburg: Institut für Englische Sprache und Literatur, Universität Salzburg.

Argues that in his poems and sermons Donne's aesthetic values are almost identical with those of St. Augustine and with the medieval view of poetics. Maintains that Donne firmly believed in the principle of universal analogy and in the notion that efficacy, unity (orderliness and completeness), and truth are the supreme criteria of beauty and that these convictions are demonstrated in nearly everything he wrote. Notes Donne's admiration for the Psalms, which embodied for him the very qualities that he sought in his own poetry. Suggests that Donne's acceptance of the principle of universal analogy "reflects an ardent effort to preserve the medieval Christian belief in the unity of all things" and shows "the extremes to which the poet was prepared to follow the principle of universal analogy" (p. 85) by commenting on "Goodfriday, 1613. Riding Westward," a poem that reflects clearly "a mode of thought which saw all things as in some way related to all others" (p. 89). Points out, therefore, that as a result of his medieval perspective Donne was able to look "everywhere and to everything, uniting East and West, fool and wise men, compasses and lovers, integrating them in a poetic reflection of divine order" (p. 97). Points out that to Donne and to his readers it would be as ridiculous to equate God to man as to equate the speakers of a poem with the poet. Concludes that, "for all his mercurial interests, his fundamental Augustinianism remained steadfast" and notes that, although his speakers may range from fool to saint, "we can distinguish one from the other because the creative mind behind them remains the same, in style and content" (p. 101).

959. SOBOSAN, JEFFREY G. "Call and Response—The Vision of God in John Donne and George Herbert." *Religious Studies* 13: 395–407.

Argues that Herbert in *The Temple* reflects a more personal and intimate relationship with God than does Donne in his *Divine Poems* and observes that "his God speaks to Herbert whereas the Divine in Donne does not speak" (p. 395). Notes that in his religious poetry Donne "reflects most often a dialectic within himself rather than a dialogue with divinity" and thus remains "at a distance from the divine presence" (p. 396). Points out that Donne's imagery is predominantly visual, while Herbert's is more auditory. Examines Donne's concept of God in the *Divine Poems* and concludes that "the dominant idea of God is that of the Transcendence of the Infinite, conceived of as altogether external to and even alien from this present life" (p. 398). Comments on Donne's Christology as it is reflected in his poems and observes that he shows little interest in the humanity and personality of Jesus and that when he infrequently addresses Christ, he seems formal. Stresses that "there is very little of the mystic's understanding of God in Donne" (p. 399) and suggests that Donne's stress on the legalistic aspects of redemption and on the unconditional demands of faith, his preoccupations with his own guilt, and his fear of damnation create barriers between him and his God. Concludes that "Herbert's religious poetry, enriched by the presence and voice of God, speaks of a more significant relationship than does Donne's more objective poetry" but notes that "this would not be to say, though, that Donne's struggle with a silent God touches us less profoundly: for to maintain one's trust in a silent God, a God whom one can no longer see face to face yet with whom one is obsessed, is perhaps the greatest suffering of all for the man of faith" (p. 407).

⋙ 960. STORHOFF, GARY P. "Social Mode and Poetic Strategies: Donne's Verse Letters to His Friends." *ELWIU* 4: 11–18.

Notes that a typical Donnean verse epistle to his friends "involves the creation of an *exemplum*, with the recipient himself usually serving as the model of conduct" and that, since Donne also addresses himself to real problems, "his letters of praise often become paraenetic, praise which ultimately becomes counsel" (p. 11). Shows how in the following four epistles Donne manipulates fiction, tone, and imagery in order to satisfy the requirements both of his immediate recipient and of a more general audience and to avoid breaches in social decorum: "To Mr Rowland Woodward: Like one who," "To Sir H. W. at his going Ambassador to Venice," "To Sr Henry Wotton: Sir, more then kisses," and "To Sr Henry Goodyere: Who makes the Past." Points out that Donne "combines graceful complimentary verse with Christian principles of social responsibility" (pp. 11–12) and that these verse epistles "reveal talents very different from Donne's love lyrics and religious poems" (p. 17). Comments on Donne's public voice, his didacticism, and his "Jonsonian" qualities.

⋙ 961. STRINGER, GARY A., ed. *New Essays on Donne*. (Salzburg Studies in English Literature, Elizabethan & Renaissance Studies, edited by James Hogg, no. 57.) Salzburg: Institut für Englische Sprache und Literatur, Universität Salzburg. i, 262p.

Contains eleven original essays on Donne's poetry and prose, each of which has been separately entered in this bibliography: (1) Marjorie D. Lewis, "The *Adversarius* Talks Back: 'The Canonization' and *Satire I*" (pp. 1–25); (2) Patrick G. Hogan, Jr., "The Iconographic Background of the First Verse of Donne's 'A Valediction Forbidding Mourning'" (pp. 26–44); (3) Leonard D. Tourney, "Donne, the Countess of Bedford, and the Petrarchan Manner" (pp. 45–59); (4) Robert J. Bauer, "Donne's Letter to

Herbert Re-Examined" (pp. 60–73); (5) Michael Smalling, "Donne's Medieval Aesthetics and His Use of Morally Distant *Personae*: Two Questions, One Answer" (pp. 74–109); (6) Paul A. Parrish, "Poet, Audience, and the Word: An Approach to the *Anniversaries*" (pp. 110–39); (7) A. B. Chambers, "*La Corona*: Philosophic, Sacred, and Poetic Uses of Time" (pp. 140–72); (8) Stanley Archer, "The Archetypal Journey Motif in Donne's *Divine Poems* (pp. 173–91); (9) Robert M. Cooper, "The Political Implications of Donne's *Devotions* (pp. 192–210); (10) Michael L. Hall, "Searching the Scriptures: Meditation and Discovery in Donne's Sermons" (pp. 211–38); and (11) Carl Braun Sennhenn, "John Donne, Poet in the Pulpit" (pp. 239–60). Biographical sketches of the contributors (pp. 261–62).

⚜ 962. SULLIVAN, ERNEST W., II. "Dating the Bodleian Manuscript of John Donne's *Biathanatos*." *AEB* 1: 26–29.

Discusses the dating of the only extant manuscript of *Biathanatos*. Notes that the transcription was originally presented by Donne to Lord Herbert of Cherbury, who, in turn, gave it to the Bodleian Library in 1642, and that it contains a presentation letter, hundreds of marginal annotations, and a sixteen-word correction of the text in Donne's hand. Shows that letters of Donne to Sir Robert Ker and to Lord Herbert convincingly indicate that the manuscript was transcribed sometime between 9 March 1619 and 7 May 1629. Suggests that since the manuscript is written on the same paper as are two dated letters found in a Magdalen College manuscript, it is reasonable "to speculate that the transcription took place near the end of the possible dates" (p. 27). Notes that this later date would suggest that Donne maintained an interest in his defense of suicide even after he was appointed Dean of St. Paul's.

⚜ 963. ⸻. "Marginal Rules as Evidence." *SB* 30: 171–80.

Uses the quarto first edition of *Biathanatos* (1647) to discuss "some kinds of problems (initial point of composition, priority of different settings of the same sheet, partial-sheet imposition, and order of imposition of preliminaries) which may require analysis of marginal-rule evidence to obtain a valid solution" (pp. 171–72) and from these considerations develops some general guidelines for the application of marginal-rule evidence. Presents detailed bibliographical information on the composition and printing of the 1647 quarto first edition of *Biathanatos*.

⚜ 964. THOMSON, PATRICIA. "A Precedent for Donne's 'The Comparison.'" *N&Q* n.s. 24: 523–24.

Suggests that Donne's comparison of drops of sweat on his mistress's breast in "The Comparison" (lines 1–6) may be borrowed from Tasso's voluptuous description of Armida in *Gerusalemme Liberata* (XVI. 18) or from Spenser's description of Acrasia in *The Faerie Queene* (II, xii, 78) and therefore may not be part of the supposed anti-Petrarchism of the poem.

965. TOURNEY, LEONARD D. "Donne, the Countess of Bedford, and the Petrarchan Manner," in *New Essays on Donne*, edited by Gary A. Stringer, pp. 45–59. (Salzburg Studies in English Literature, Elizabethan & Renaissance Studies, edited by James Hogg, no. 57.) Salzburg: Institut für Englische Sprache und Literatur, Universität Salzburg.

Stresses the importance of Donne's verse epistles, especially those addressed to Lucy, Countess of Bedford, for a full understanding of his serious uses of Petrarchism. Notes that the epistles as poems "are grounded in Petrarchan conceptions" and "as documents in the history of social relations they mirror the extent to which Jacobean court society accepted the values and the expression of one of the strongest impulses of Italian culture" (p. 46). Explores briefly the literary tradition of Petrarchism, its conceits, attitudes and postures, and love philosophy, and notes that, although Donne occasionally parodies the Petrarchan mode, Petrarchan elements "are as important in Donne's verse epistles as they are in his love lyrics in providing a substratum for serious thought and emotion" (p. 47). Recounts Donne's relationship with the Countess of Bedford and suggests that his verse letters addressed to her "reflect a *conception* of a relationship rather than a history of one, their whole concern being to show Donne's admiration for the Countess and to dilate that admiration with the greatest ingenuity and logical rigor" (p. 48). Argues that Donne's verse epistles to the Countess are more than merely fashionable poses, "for beneath Donne's abject posture is the same insight that provoked Petrarch's own melancholy reflections—an Augustinian sense of the ultimate hollowness of worldly things, the imminence of decay and death, the frailty of all human endeavors" (p. 54). Maintains that the epistles become vehicles for Donne's serious contemplation and philosophical speculation on the nature of virtue and show "the ways literary traditions may shape life as well as literature, how they can mold conceptions of human relationships and become an expressive idiom of social intercourse" (p. 57).

966. ———. "Joseph Hall and the *Anniversaries*." *PLL* 13: 25–34.

Discusses Joseph Hall's "Praise of the Dead, and the Anatomy" and "Harbinger to the Progress" as "the fullest and most perceptive contemporary response to the *Anniversaries*" (p. 25). Comments on Hall's association with the Drury family and with Donne and shows that he was a highly qualified literary critic. Suggests that Hall is a better critic of the poems than Jonson and shows that he found Donne's praise of Elizabeth Drury "neither absurd nor disrespectful," that he "viewed the premises of Donne's poems as reasonable, even traditional," and that he "clearly understood the intention of the *Anniversaries*" (p. 34).

967. WERTENBAKER, THOMAS J., JR. "Donne's 'A Jeat Ring Sent.'" *Expl* 35, iv: 27–28.

Disagrees with the readings of Ray L. Armstrong (entry 387) and Myrtle

Pihlman Pope (entry 861). Suggests that all three stanzas of "A Jeat Ring sent" are addressed to the jeat out of which the ring is made and are about a jeat ring sent back. Argues that the speaker throughout "wonders if the jeat ring has a tale to tell beyond his mistress's message" and in stanza three "reproves the ring for its self-deprecation" (p. 28). Maintains that at the end of the poem the speaker decides to cherish the ring and to flaunt it "as the gesture of one not disposed to treat rings or relationships casually, whatever their form or substance, as was his late inconstant mistress" (p. 28).

⋙§ 968. WILLIAMS, AUBREY L. "What Pope Did to Donne," in *A Provision of Human Nature: Essays on Fielding and Others in Honor of Miriam Austin Locke*, edited by Donald Kay, pp. 111–19. University, Ala.: The University of Alabama Press.
Disagrees with those who maintain that Pope followed Donne's subject matter in his imitation of *Satyre II* and changed only the form and style of the original. Compares Pope's two versions of the satire (1713 and 1735) and Donne's *Satyre II* and shows that by contracting his satire and focusing it on the one evil of venality, as well as by numerous other alterations, Pope in fact changed the subject matter of Donne's poem and "provided his altered subject matter with a dominant, but totally appropriate, pattern of imagery" (p. 111). Notes that one of the major alterations Pope made in his 1735 version was the creation of a new character, Peter, to replace Donne's Coscus and identifies Peter as Peter Walter, a notorious money scrivener of Pope's time.

⋙§ 969. YAMADA, YUTAKA. "John Donne against the Sunne: His Dawn Songs and the Continental Alba." *SES* 2: 29–41.
Suggests that in his dawn songs, "Breake of day," "The Sunne Rising," and "The good-morrow," Donne was obliged to diverge from established Continental models and to modify poetic conventions because of the breakdown of traditional cosmology in his day. Outlines the development of the alba and dawn song and compares and contrasts Donne to various Continental examples. Suggests that "Breake of day" is a parody of the Provençal dawn song and that "The Sunne Rising" is a paradoxical play on the conventional metaphor of lovers as the center of the universe. Comments on how Donne's knowledge of the new science shaped his poetic vision and choices.

1978

⋙§ 970. ABAD, GÉMINO H. "The Verbal Medium: The Means of Imitation," in *A Formal Approach to Lyric Poetry*, pp. 311–66. Quezon City: University of Philippines Press.
Discusses the nature and function of poetic language and comments on

the range and varieties of poetic diction. Points out that poetic language is, by its very nature, "an *artificial* language, since even when it is most like natural speech, it serves a particular artistic end or purpose rather than the natural end of discourse or ordinary conversation" and, therefore, agrees with Elder Olson that at its simplest and most natural level poetic diction can best be described as "language heightened, developed, made more expressive and vivid, made more concise and more strictly relevant, more characteristic of the speaker and his emotion, than ordinary language" (p. 322). Analyzes in some detail the uses of language in Leigh Hunt's "Jenny Kiss'd Me," Tennyson's "Break, Break, Break," Donne's "A Valediction: forbidding mourning," and T. S. Eliot's "Sunday Morning Service" to show that complexity and sophistication in the uses of diction, syntax, metrical structure, and rhetorical and linguistic devices do not determine poetic language. Argues that the language of Donne's poem is successful, not because it is more complex than Hunt's or Tennyson's and not because it is less complex than Eliot's, but rather because it effectively reveals the speaker's character and situation and adequately mirrors the intellectual adroitness and wit that the speaker wishes to convey.

◆§ 971. AERS, DAVID, AND GUNTHER KRESS. "'Darke Texts Need Notes': Versions of Self in Donne's Verse Epistles." *L&H* 8: 138–58.

Analyzes the argument, language, and images in several of the verse epistles, especially "To the Countesse of Bedford: Madame, You have re-fin'd," "To Sr Henry Wotton: Sir, more then kisses," "To Mr Rowland Woodward: Like one Who," and "To Sr Edward Herbert. at Julyers: Man is a lumpe." Argues that the verse epistles reflect the central tensions and preoccupations of Donne's middle life and teach a great deal about the poetic and intellectual strategies he employed in confronting them. Maintains that most of the verse epistles are exercises in self-exploration and are, in fact, Donne's attempts to work out his own self-identity. Comments on Donne's sense of being an alienated intellectual excluded from the society of which he sought to be a part and discusses the complicated metaphysics that he constructed in the verse epistles, "in which a platonic model of eternal value was set off against a market model of use" (p. 148). Notes that Donne's cynical and critical view of the world that had excluded him as well as his self-estimation "were bound up with the former model; yet he clearly wanted a place in the market and so had to assert his use as a secular servant" (pp. 148–49). Suggests that in the verse letters his efforts, therefore, are primarily directed toward finding acceptance in the established, traditional order about him and that "in his quest for incorporation he reluctantly accepts the necessity of turning himself, his abilities, and certain of his poems which are absolutely overt tokens of exchange . . . into commodities" (p. 149). Suggests that the approach used in the essay could be profitably applied to other of Donne's works.

✍ 972. AIZAWA, YOSHIHISA. "John Donne no 'Shūnen tsutō shi' kō" [A Study of John Donne's *Anniversaries*]. Pt. 2. *Bunkei Ronsō* (Hiromae Daigaku Bungakubu) 13, no. 6 (March): 13–25.
Part 2 of a three-part series. Translates into Japanese *The second Anniversarie*. For part 1, see entry 894. Part 3 is a critical study of the *Anniversaries* and appears in *Bunkei Ronsō* (Hiromae Daigaku Bungakubu) 14, no. 3 (March 1979): 1–14.

✍ 973. ASALS, HEATHER. "Magdalene Herbert: Towards a *Topos* for the Anglican Church." *GHJ* 1, no. 2: 1–16.
Discusses how in his sermon of 1627 commemorating the death of Magdalen Herbert, Donne "paints for us the portrait of a lady as the Anglican Church, defining the path of the 'middle way'" (p. 1), and how in Herbert's mother Donne "finds a 'place' where Church and Scripture meet and are reconciled" (p. 2). Comments on Donne's discursive analysis of the Church through his use of Mrs. Herbert as a topos of the Church and suggests that her primary importance for him "is that her life presents a proper Image of God" (p. 8), not to be worshiped but to be followed as an example.

✍ 974. BENITO CARDENAL, LUIS CARLOS. *El Manierismo inglés. John Donne.* (Coleccíon Monográfica, 62.) Granada: Universidad de Granada. 327p.
Chapter 1, "Manierismo y Barroco: Cuestiones Terminologicas Previas" (pp. 13–47), surveys past scholarship on the use of the terms *mannerism* and *baroque*, distinguishes between the two styles, and finds the mannerist style more controlled, intellectually self-conscious, and organic than the baroque. Chapter 2, "Renacimiento, Manierismo y Barroco" (pp. 49–143), distinguishes between Renaissance and mannerist art, comments on mannerism as a "style of crisis," discusses the relationship of mannerism to Petrarchism and to Counter-Reformation seventeenth-century Spanish art, and comments on the interrelationships between culture, society, and mannerist art. Chapter 3, "John Donne, Poeta Manierista" (pp. 145–274), discusses Donne as a mannerist, pointing out his anti-naturalism, his exploration of the theme of deceit, and his specific uses of the conceit. Discusses Johnson's criticism of Donne and compares and contrasts Donne to Crashaw, Marino, Petrarch, Jonson, and Quevedo, noting that there is perhaps a brotherhood between Donne and Quevedo but nothing more. Finds Donne's poetry more than simply witty Petrarchism. Appendix, "La teoria poetica de Thomas Stearns Eliot y la practica poetica de John Donne" (pp. 275–98), comments on Eliot's criticism of Donne and argues that, although Eliot's specific attitudes cannot be strictly applied to Donne's poetry, the terms that Eliot used must be taken into account and can serve as effective approaches to Donne's poetry. Bibliography (pp. 299–317); index of names (pp. 319–25); and general index (p. 327).

◄§ 975. BLOOMER, PEGGY ANN. "A Re-examination of Donne's 'La Corona.'" *EAS* 7: 37–44.

Discusses how in *La Corona* Donne successfully adapts the traditional seven-part rosary and the Continental sonnet stanza (called la corona) to his own purposes: "To the repeating stanza form he added additional repetitions to suggest the circular form of his subject, the rosary, while he enlarged the rosary to become the crown of thorns and a cycle of prayer" (p. 39). Notes that Donne reinforced his metaphor of twining by a repetitive rhyme scheme that "gives the poem a cyclic motion" (p. 39) as well as by the uses of paradoxes and caesuras. Compares briefly Milton's "On the Morning of Christ's Nativity" and Crashaw's "The Holy Nativity of our Lord God" as representatives of seventeenth-century Protestant and Catholic attitudes toward the Nativity and suggests that Donne's emphasis in *La Corona* on the sinfulness of man and his redemption through Christ reflects his distinctly Protestant attitude. Suggests that readers often fail to appreciate the poem because they do not recognize Donne's use of a public voice and his celebratory stance but argues that the poem clearly reflects Donne's skillful craftsmanship and his knowledge of and ability to adapt both Protestant and Catholic literary conventions to his own ends.

◄§ 976. BRITTING, GEORG, ed. "John Donne," in *Lyrik des Abendlandes*, pp. 244–46, 695–96. Gemeinsam mit Hans Hennecke, Curt Hohoff und Karl Vossler; ausgewählt von Georg Britting. Munich: Hanser.

Brief biographical sketch of Donne with a short introduction to his poetry (pp. 695–96) and translations into German of four poems: "Twicknam garden" (by Hans Hennecke), "The Funerall" and "To Christ" (by Curt Hohoff), and "Death be not proud" (by Richard Flatter).

◄§ 977. BROCK, D. HEYWOOD. "Jonson and Donne: Structural Fingerprinting and the Attribution of Elegies XXXVIII–XLI." *PBSA* 72: 519–27.

Reviews the scholarly debate about the authorship of four elegies (numbers XXXVIII–XLI in the Herford and Simpson edition of Jonson). Notes that some scholars have attributed all four poems to Jonson, others have attributed them to Donne, and yet others, especially Evelyn Simpson, have suggested that three are Jonson's and only the second, "The Expostulation," is Donne's. Uses a tagmemic clause-analysis technique to demonstrate that, although all four elegies are remarkably similar, there is sufficient internal evidence to suggest that Jonson wrote three of the poems and that "The Expostulation" "could have been written by either one of the poets but probably should be assigned to Donne on the basis of compelling external evidence" (p. 520). Presents four analytical tables. Suggests that the analysis further demonstrates "that if Donne inspired Jonson to emulative effort in these elegies, as Evelyn Simpson has suggested, his effort was even more *imitative* than *emulative* and that although Jonson may have masterfully imitated Donne's poetic style he could not disguise certain telltale features of his own distinctive structural fingerprint" (p. 527).

◄§ 978. CHING, MARVIN K. L. "The Relationship Among the Diverse Senses of a Pun." *SECOLB* 2, no. 3: 1–8.
Presents a detailed linguistic analysis of the pun on *ravish* in "Batter my heart" to demonstrate "how the seemingly unrelated readings of this verb ('to plunder,' 'to rape,' and 'to charm') are connected" and to delineate "the points of semantic commonality and the departure from these points which all three readings of the verb hold in common" (p. 1). Argues that, although Donne "achieves a dramatic tension through the diverse polysemous and contradictory senses of the pun, he produces an organic whole" (p. 1). Analyzes also the multileveled meanings of the puns *enthrall* and *break that knot* and shows the interrelations between these two puns and the pun on *ravish*. Presents detailed charts of semantic relationships of the various readings of the puns.

◄§ 979. COGNARD, ROGER A. "The Complex Moment: Donne's Imagery in the Verse Epistles." *English Studies Collections* (Special Series), January, pp. 1–29.
Argues for the literary merits of Donne's verse epistles and denies the charges that they reveal "a fawning, insecure, or mercenary poet sacrificing artistry and sincerity alike in the pursuit of friendship and patronage" (p. 1). Shows that, although the earliest verse epistles are mostly commendations on the writings of his friends, such as Rowland Woodward, Everard Guilpin, and others, often commenting on poetry or on proper uses of one's talents, the later epistles fall into definable categories: "self-examination and control, beauty, grace, and honor—all of which are components of virtue" (p. 4) and argues that some, in terms of their logic and wit, are "equal in quality to much of Donne's other poetry, especially in the imagery used to display that wit" (p. 1), a wit that is both sensuous and intellectual. Points out that the imagery of the verse epistles is often "innovative, provocative, occasionally even blasphemous" but displays "a unity, a harmony that is in itself startling because it is realized out of apparent discord," a kind of "unity in multeity" (p. 5). Divides the study into five major sections: (1) The Brooke letters—unity in association and apprehension of thought, (2) the Woodward letters—the beginnings of imagistic themes and techniques in the verse epistles, (3) transitional elements in the imagery of the Wotton letters, (4) the letters to Lady Bedford—imagistic techniques in the poetry of high compliment, and (5) the significance of the imagery in the letters to Lady Huntingdon. Suggests that a detailed study of the imagery in the two epistles to the Countess of Huntingdon strengthens the case for Donne's authorship of the earlier one, strengthens arguments for the dating of both letters, and shows clearly the development of Donne's imagistic technique.

✎§ 980. ———. "Donne's 'The Dampe.'" *Expl* 36, ii: 19–20.

Maintains that the complexity of "The Dampe" arises from puns on two key words, *die* (meaning both death and the sexual act) and primarily *dampe* (which has three obvious and one highly figurative meaning). Notes that, in addition to a check or discouragement; a state of despair or depression; and a noxious exhalation, vapor, or gas, *dampe* can refer to gas in a mine "which snuffed out both the lamps and the lives of the miners" (p. 20). Suggests that the fourth meaning gives thematic unity to the whole poem and that Donne is saying that, "like the '*dampe*' of a mine which stifles the miners, so the lady's *dampe* of love has stifled the persona's enjoyment of her physical mine" (p. 20). Notes also that *mine* was a common Elizabethan image for the womb.

✎§ 981. CROOKS, FIONA. "John Donne—Petrarchan Idealist or Anti-petrarchan Cynic?" *Opus* (University of Rhodesia, Salisbury) 3, 2d series: 24–27.

Surveys Donne's attitude toward love in "Loves growth," "The Extasie," "Loves Alchymie," "The triple Foole," "Confined Love," "Song: Goe, and catche a falling starre," "Womans constancy," "Song: Sweetest love, I do not goe," and "The Sunne Rising" to show that "in his more extreme (and often agonised moments) Donne veers towards cynicism and sometimes idealism" (p. 27) but that the essential difference between him and the traditions of Petrarchism and anti-Petrarchism lies in tone. Notes that Donne is a dramatic poet, not a rhetorical poet, and argues that his greatest love poems "reconcile two apparent opposites and encapsulate them in shared situations" and that, "above all, then, John Donne is the poet of relationships—the poet of 'us'" (p. 27).

✎§ 982. DANIELS, EDGAR F. "Donne's 'Pyramus and Thisbe.'" *Expl* 36, ii: 31.

Suggests that the "cruel friends" who separated the lovers in life and joined them in death does not refer to the parents of Pyramus and Thisbe, as usually thought, but to the lovers themselves. Maintains that the unity and paradox in the epigram are reinforced if the lovers "may be said to have joined themselves as well as separated themselves, meriting the oxymoron of 'cruel friends.'" Paraphrases the epigram: "Two lovers (cruel friends)—slain by themselves, by each other, and by love and fear—have in their parting come together here."

✎§ 983. DENIS, YVES. "'Adieu à l'amour' by John Donne." *CahiersE* 13: 35–39.

Presents a French translation of "Farewell to love" followed by a discussion of three major problems in the poem: (1) the reference to "His highnesse" in line 12; (2) the difficulties in lines 21–30, especially lines 28–30: "Because that other curse of being short, / And onely for a minute made to be, / Eagers desire to raise posterity"; and (3) the problem of interpreting the last line of the poem: "'Tis but applying worme-seed to the Taile." Generally disagrees with Pierre Legouis's reading of the poem as "un acte de renonciation sincère à l'amour et au commerce des femmes" and prefers to see the poem as "une plaisanterie, ailleurs excellente, destinée à divertir les amis à l'auteur le lisait ou le donnait à lire" and as "un discours ironique de bout en bout, le serment de comédie d'un libertin qui, à la suite de quelque deboire physiologique ou sentimental, jure que 'dès demain il se fera couper'" (p. 36).

984. DE SILVA, D. M. "John Donne: an un-metaphysical perspective." *English Bulletin* 2: 1–11.
Cited in *Modern Humanities Research Association Bibliography*, 1978, item # 4737. Unavailable.

985. DONNE, JOHN. *The Divine Poems*. Edited with introduction and commentary by Helen Gardner. (Oxford English Texts.) 2d ed. Oxford: The Clarendon Press. xcviii, 158p.
First edition published in 1952. Preface to the first edition (p. v), preface to the second edition (pp. vi–x), contents (pp. xi–xii), and references and abbreviations (pp. xiii–xiv). General introduction to Donne's religious poetry, divided into two parts: (1) a discussion of the general characteristics of the religious poetry and of the sensibility that informs it (pp. xv–xxxvii) and (2) an extensive discussion of the dating, ordering, and interpretation of the *Holy Sonnets* (pp. xxxvii–lv). The textual introduction (pp. lvi–xcvi) gives a full account of the text of the poems in manuscripts and in the first two editions. List of sigla (pp. xcvi–xcviii). The text (pp. 1–53) is followed by a detailed commentary on the poems (pp. 54–113), prefaced by a discussion of problems of prosody (pp. 54–57). Seven appendices: (1) "Donne's View on the State of the Soul after Death" (pp. 114–17); (2) "Verbal Alterations in the *Divine Poems* in the edition of 1635" (pp. 118–20); (3) "The Interpretation of Donne's Sonnet on the Church" (pp. 121–27); (4) "Donne and Tilman: Their Reluctance to take Holy Orders" (pp. 127–32); (5) "The Date of 'Hymn to God my God, in my sickness'" (pp. 132–35); (6) "'Paradise and Calvarie'" (pp. 135–37); and (7) "Donne's Latin Poem to Herbert and Herbert's Reply" (pp. 138–47). "Supplementary Notes" (pp. 148–58) describe changes made in the second edition and are divided into four parts: (1) "Introduction" (p. 148) comments on new material and information that has come to light since 1952, especially new major editions, the California edition of the sermons, R. C. Bald's *John Donne: A Life* (entry 179), the discovery of new manuscripts, the discovery that the Westmoreland manuscript is in the hand of Rowland Woodward, and the discovery of a verse-letter to Lady Carey in Donne's own hand; (2) "Textual Introduction" (pp. 149–51) discusses revisions made in the textual introduction to the first edition and notes changes necessitated by the discovery of new materials; (3) "The Text" (pp. 150–51) notes alterations in substantive readings, changes in the setting of "A Hymne to Christ," and

the supplying of contracted forms and elisions whenever they are metrically necessary; and (4) "Commentary" (pp. 151–58) contains revisions of notes and points out that headnotes to each poem have been revised to include manuscripts discovered since 1952 (but miscellanies containing only fragments have not been included).

⋙ 986. ———. *The Epithalamions, Anniversaries, and Epicedes.* Edited with introduction and commentary by W[esley] Milgate. (Oxford English Texts.) Oxford: The Clarendon Press. lxvii, 237p.
   Preface (pp. v–viii) notes that epitaphs and inscriptions composed by Donne and early elegies on him are also included. Contents and descriptions of two plates (pp. ix–x), and references and abbreviations (pp. xi–xiii). Discusses in the general introduction (pp. xv–xlv) the major characteristics of and attitudes expressed in Donne's epithalamia, the two *Anniversaries*, and the epicedes. The textual introduction (pp. xlvii–lxiv) discusses the manuscripts and the early editions of the epithalamia, epicedes, "Elegy upon the untimely death of the incomparable Prince Henry," and the two *Anniversaries*. List of sigla (pp. lxv–lxvii). The text (pp. 3–107) is followed by a detailed commentary on the poems (pp. 108–231), including notes on the epitaphs and inscriptions (with translations into English) and on the elegies on Donne, prefaced by a discussion of versification (pp. 108–9). Appendix 1, "Verbal Alterations in the *Epithalamions* and *Epicedes* in the edition of 1635" (pp. 232–34), and Appendix 2, "The Elegy 'Death be not Proud'" (pp. 235–37), a poem possibly by Lucy, Countess of Bedford, which may be a reply to Donne's "Elegy on Mrs. Bulstrode." Index of first lines (pp. 239–40).

⋙ 987. ———. *The John Donne Treasury.* Edited by Erwin P. Rudolph. (Great Christian Classics Series.) Wheaton, Ill.: Victor Books. 94p.
   Anthology of Donne's religious poetry and prose intended for personal meditation or group study. "John Donne, the Man" (pp. 4–10) presents a very general and brief introduction to Donne's life and works and stresses in particular his place in the tradition of devotional literature; Part I, "Devotions upon Emergent Occasions" (pp. 11–46), contains selections from the *Devotions*; Part II, "The Divine Poems" (pp. 47–56), contains ten of the *Holy Sonnets* as well as "Hymne to God my God, in my sicknesse" and "A Hymne to God the Father"; and Part III, "Selections from the Sermons" (pp. 57–92), contains twenty excerpts from the sermons. Each part is introduced by a brief note. All selections are arranged by religious theme. Selected bibliography (pp. 93–94). Jennifer Greene has prepared *Leader's Guide for the Study of The John Donne Treasury* (Wheaton, Ill.: Victor Books), 32p. Contains general remarks on preparing lessons and six lesson plans plus notes for a review session.

⋙ 988. ELLRODT, ROBERT. "La Fonction de l'image scientifique dans la poésie métaphysique anglaise," in *Hommage à Emile Gasquet*

(1920–1977), pp. 43–55. (Annales de la Faculté des Lettres et Sciences Humaines de Nice, 34.) (Études anglo-americaines, vol. 3.) Paris: Belles Lettres.

Compares the use of scientific imagery in the poetry of Donne and selected other metaphysical poets. Maintains that Donne's use of such images is distinctive and original and focuses attention primarily on his images of the circle. Notes that for Donne, unlike Traherne and Marvell, the image is never simply an object of contemplation but is rather a tool of active thought and points out that Donne did not need to be convinced of the truth of images in order to find them poetically useful. Observes that for Donne "seule importe l'exactitude du rapport entre l'idée et l'image" (p. 51). Notes that often Donne uses the unpassively accepted character of his attitude toward the validity of a given image to communicate a tone of mockery and/or intellectual confusion.

᳜ 989. EPSTEIN, E. L. "Playing the Literature Game: A Public and Collective Norm," in *Language and Style*, pp. 22–63. (New Accents, gen. ed. Terrence Hawkes.) London: Methuen & Co.

Presents a linguistic analysis of line 6 of "The Relique": "A bracelet of bright haire about the bone." Points out that "the actual or potential movement of the lips in the physical or mental articulation of a poetic line frequently provides significant dramatic reinforcement of the effect of the line's meaning" (p. 31). Notes that the pronunciation of *bright* and *bracelet*, both front vowels, causes the reader to "smile," whereas *bone*, "a mid-central vowel gliding to the velum (with a pursing of the lips) switches off the light" (p. 31), thus "the 'movement' is essentially metaphorical, a sudden sinking of the spirit from the smiling notions of 'bracelet' and 'bright hair' to the grimness of 'bone'" (p. 33). Diagram (p. 33).

᳜ 990. EVANS, GILLIAN. *The Age of the Metaphysicals*. (Authors in Their Age, gen. eds. Anthony Adams and Esmor Jones.) Glasgow and London: Blackie & Sons. 140p.

Introduces metaphysical poets and their time to students. Chapter 1, "Why Metaphysical?" (pp. 1–19), attempts to define metaphysical poetry and comments on such terms as *metaphysical, wit, satire, conceit, baroque,* and *paradox* and stresses that definitions of these terms "can only provide a starting-point for discussion" since "it is one of the fundamental problems of studying metaphysical poetry that an exception can usually be found to every rule" (p. 19). Chapter 2, "The Poets" (pp. 20–47), sketches briefly the religious, educational, and political backgrounds that the metaphysical poets shared to varying degrees and presents biographical sketches of Donne (pp. 28–35), Thomas Carew, George Herbert, and Andrew Marvell. Chapter 3, "The Poets' World" (pp. 48–70), comments on the society that the poets lived in and wrote for, discusses the influence of the Court, and surveys the history of the period, stressing in particular the importance of religion in society. Chapter 4, "The Poets' View of the

World" (pp. 71–92), discusses the shifting world view in the early seven-teenth century and changing social structures. Chapter 5, "The Shaping of the Poems" (pp. 93–105), comments briefly on the metaphysical poets' experimentation with stanzaic form and rhyme; discusses the major genres—sonnets, elegies, hymns, songs, epistles, dialogues, epitaphs; comments briefly on stylistic devices, rhetorical figures of speech, spelling, and punctuation; and discusses the metaphysical poets' shared views on the nature and function of poetry. Chapter 6, "The Matter of the Poems" (pp. 106–23), comments on the major subject matter of metaphysical poetry—divine and human love; sin, sickness, and death; time and eternity—and stresses how the poets bring together disparate ideas and have shared habits of thought. Chapter 7, "Poetry for Pleasure" (pp. 124–31), surveys briefly the history and development of criticism of metaphysical poetry and sug-gests that "twentieth-century readers, perhaps for the first time since the age of the metaphysical poets themselves, are in a position to appreciate their work on two levels at least: that of the pleasure of problem-solving, and that of the more familiar pleasure of poetry, the sharing of someone else's experience, the recognition of common sensations and shared re-sponses to the happenings of life" (p. 131). Selected bibliography (pp. 132–35), list of metaphysical poets (p. 136), and index (pp. 137–40).

⋙ 991. FLINKER, NOAM. "Donne's 'The Undertaking.'" *Expl* 36, iii: 16–18.

Argues that the speaker of "The undertaking" is not a straightforward spokesman for Donne, as usually thought, but is "a sententious, Polonius-like character" that Donne sets up "as a target for the laughter and mock-ery of the knowing sophisticate" (p. 17). Shows that Donne achieves ironic distance by a "combination of conventional uses of theme and language, along with various kinds of inner contradictions in the logical develop-ment of the speaker's argument" and suggests that "the logical subtleties and the conventional banalities can be seen as the failings of [a] dramatic character invented by Donne more as an object of scorn than as a serious spokesman for spiritual or Platonic love" (p. 18).

⋙ 992. FORREST-THOMSON, VERONICA. "The poet and his tribe: tradi-tion and the disconnected image-complex," in *Poetic artifice: A theory of twentieth-century poetry*, pp. 81–111. New York: St. Martin's Press; Liverpool: Elliott Brothers & Yeoman.

Discusses the influence of Donne on twentieth-century poets. Notes that "in Donne they found a blend of discursive imagery and empirical imagery, or rather discursive imagery disguised as empirical imagery, which seemed to them of quite exemplary value" (p. 81) and that they found in Donne "a poet who found ways simultaneously to innovate and to keep in touch with his readers in poems that use argument plus the presenta-tion of empirical situations" (p. 82). Discusses attempts, especially by Wil-liam Empson and T. S. Eliot, to relate Donne's techniques to the needs of the twentieth-century poet. Comments on Empson's reading of "The Crosse" and compares Empson's "Letter V" with "A Valediction: forbidding mourning" to show "to what extent Empson does copy Donne and then how Empson's interpretation fails to account either for Donne's manoeuvres or his own" (p. 90). Compares also passages from the *Anniversaries* to parts of Eliot's *The Waste Land* to show that what Eliot learned from Donne was that "the conventional and formal features of poetry can be used simultaneously to assert and to deny continuity with the past and with the assumptions of contemporary society" (p. 102). Discusses also James Smith's essay "On Metaphysical Poetry" that first appeared in *Scrutiny* 2 (1934): 222–39 and calls it "the most intelligent study of the conceit available" (p. 87).

❧ 993. FOX, MICHAEL V. "Donne's 'A Nocturnall Upon S. Lucies Day.'" *Expl* 36, ii: 25.
Paraphrases the argument of "A nocturnall upon S. Lucies day" to show that the poem is not formally a lament on the poet's dismal condition but is rather "an ironic expression of a sense of contentment and fulfillment at the speaker's having regained his true condition." Notes that the speaker describes death as a festival and that "he is not bewailing his state, but, as it were, exulting in it." Concludes that "the irony is of course bitter and sharply intensifies the sense of total desolation."

❧ 994. FOXELL, NIGEL. *A Sermon in Stone: John Donne and His Monument in St. Paul's Cathedral*. London: The Menard Press. 22p.
Presents a detailed iconographical and theological explanation of Donne's monument, executed by Nicholas Stone, in St. Paul's to show that by its design, original location in the cathedral, and epitaph the monument is meant to be a sermon on the theme of death and resurrection, especially the resurrection from the death of sin and the resurrection of the body on the Last Day. Suggests that the monument "does not merely, or even principally, represent Donne; but *Ecclesia*: the Church Militant, not yet able to see *Oriens* face to face, but dimly in the mirror provided by the pulpit and the altar at the East End of the church, hearing the word of God and tasting Him in the sacrament" (pp. 17–18). Sees the monument not only as a complex summary of Donne's faith but also as "the last, the best— and least known—example of his wit" (p. 22).

❧ 995. FRIEDERICH, REINHARD H. "Expanding and Contracting Space in Donne's Devotions." *ELH* 45: 18–32.
Suggests that "vivid immediacy and a closely circumscribed sense of place characterize Donne's *Devotions upon Emergent Occasions* and set them apart from other meditations on the art of dying" (p. 18). Notes that in the *Devotions* "all shifts and disorders occur within man's most intimate and yet most unknown space, his own body" and that "the body is constantly scrutinized in its real and imagined relations to the self-reflecting

consciousness as well as to the surrounding space" (p. 19). Discusses how the speaker of the *Devotions*, lying recumbent on his bed, perceives himself and the world about him in unusual and different ways and how he views time and eternity, infinity and space, and stability and motion in ways that shape his treatment of recurrent topics in the *Devotions*. Comments especially on images of space that shape the *Devotions*, such as the body as a house, prison, ruined garden, or temple of the Holy Spirit; the surrounding space and the world as a grave; and heaven as a "place which spells out total security and where contracting and expanding impulses meet in intimate infinity" (p. 29).

❧ 996. ———. "Strategies of Persuasion in Donne's Devotions." *ArielE*
    9, no. 1: 51–70.
    Calls *Devotions upon Emergent Occasions* "an atypical hybrid" (p. 51) among devotional literature and discusses what it is that attracts even modern readers to the work. Discusses how Donne uses formal devices, narrative skill, and complex rhetorical organization to bring the reader to greater spiritual awareness. Shows that by the highly dramatic and searching quality of the *Devotions* Donne not only attempts to involve the reader in the immediate crisis that he experiences but also allows the reader to discover those spiritual crises, of which Donne's sickness is only a literal manifestation, that are common to all men as they search and wrestle with ultimate questions.

❧ 997. GILMAN, ERNEST B. "The Pauline Perspective in Donne, Herbert, and Greville," in *The Curious Perspective: Literary and Pictorial Wit in the Seventeenth Century*, pp. 167–203. New York and London: Yale University Press.
    Discusses how manipulation of perspective in late Renaissance art parallels in many respects the uses of metaphysical wit in poetry. Points out that the Pauline metaphor of the mirror appears frequently in devotional literature "as an image of our imperfect understanding" and that "wherever it appears it carries a concern with the limits of language and a dynamics of the mind striving for illumination against its own darkness" (p. 172). Notes also that "in the Renaissance the Pauline mirror assumes richer metaphoric possibilities by association with the curious perspective: conical or cylindrical 'glasses' could deform images or clarify others distorted anamorphically, while the range of the word *glass* now extended to the marvels of the new optics, refracting lenses, prisms, and telescopes ('perspective glasses')" (pp. 175–76). Comments on how Donne, Herbert, and Greville concern themselves with the difficulties posed by St. Paul's observation that fallen man can perceive ultimate realities only through a glass darkly and how they use wit as a vehicle to achieve sudden illumination and insight into the hidden mysteries that ordinarily lie covered with imperfect language. Discusses in particular Donne's uses of the magnifying glass and mirror in "Obsequies to the Lord Harrington," his uses

of mirrors and spy glasses in "The Canonization," and especially his Pauline vision and his search for a language of "transparent perception" in the *Anniversaries*.

⊷§ 998. GREEN, PAUL D. "Unraveling the True Thread in Donne's *Biathanatos.*" *SPWVSRA* 2, no. 3: 67–77.

Analyzes the argument of Donne's defense of suicide and argues that "one of the single most important factors in *Biathanatos* is its emphasis on the motive of the individual" (p. 67). Suggests that Donne holds "that evil is not absolute but relative to the circumstances and to the motive of the agent" and points out that one of Donne's central aims is "to show that suicide is sometimes the more pressing of two conflicting moral or religious duties—and that at such times it is not only allowable but even obligatory" (p. 68). Concludes, therefore, that "charity, which is at the heart of Christianity, is also at the core of *Biathanatos*" (p. 74).

⊷§ 999. GREENBLATT, DANIEL L. "The Effect of Genre on Metrical Style." *Lang&S* 11: 18–29.

Uses statistical profiles based on the Halle-Keyser theory of iambic pentameter "to demonstrate that the genre of a poem has an appreciable effect on its metrical style, at least for several important seventeenth-century poets, and that the effect of certain genres on metrical style is to some extent predictable" (p. 18). Presents a statistical profiles of selected poems by Donne, Jonson, Crashaw, Herbert, Carew, and Marvell and shows that, "for all the poets tested except Marvell, the data suggest strongly that genre can exert a powerful influence on the metrical stylistic feature of complexity" and that, "in some cases, not only do these poets adapt their styles to different genres, they deal with their common genres in approximately the same way" (p. 23). Notes that "a closer look at the generic means of Donne and Jonson, for example, shows that each genre has nearly the same relation to the poet's overall mean complexity score for both poets" and that Donne and Jonson "have similar notions about what kind of alterations in metrical style are required by each of these genres" (pp. 23–24).

⊷§ 1000. HÄUBLEIN, ERNST. *The Stanza.* (The Critical Idiom, no. 38, edited by John J. Jump.) London: Methuen & Co. viii, 125p.

Mentions Donne throughout this study of the relationships between the stanza and poetic structure. Comments on the stanzaic inventiveness of Donne's poems and briefly discusses his uses of stanzaic closure and framing as well as his development of stanzaic progression. Comments in some detail on the poetic structure of "A Feaver" (pp. 105–9).

⊷§ 1001. HESTER, M. THOMAS. "'All our Soules Devotion': Satire as Religion in Donne's *Satyre III.*" *SEL* 18: 35–55.

Discusses the structure and satirical strategies of *Satyre III* and analyzes the satirical portraits and the Christian psychology of the poem. Argues that satire becomes religion when viewed as the application of the soul's faculties (memory, understanding, and will) to meditation on the nature of true religion. Notes how by "offering the correct use of his own mental faculties as an exemplary alternative to the failures which the satirist ridicules, 'Satyre III' intimates that Donne had more confidence in the ability of satire to effect moral reformation than recent critics have allowed" (p. 36). Points out that the poem is divided into three major parts, each of which deals with the use and misuse of one of the faculties of the soul: (1) the explorers and adventurers of the first section reflect a misuse of memory; (2) the unreflecting and uncritical lovers of the second section show a deficiency in their use of reason and understanding and stand in contrast to the speaker who uses his rational powers to scale the huge Hill of Truth; and (3) the corrupt suitors and officers of the court in the third section reflect the misuse of will as they attempt to manipulate others or allow their wills to be manipulated. Maintains that the speaker both dramatizes and explains how, by properly using the faculties of memory, understanding, and will, man can cure the sickness of his soul and that "the poem dramatizes the internal process on which man's active life must be based" (p. 54).

◄§ 1002. ————. "The Satirist as Exegete: John Donne's *Satyre V.*" *TSLL* 20: 347–66.

Shows how Donne's speaker in *Satyre V* adopts the role of an exegete and attempts to bring the suitor to a realization that, in spite of the corruption of the present legal system in England, justice still remains in the world. Presents a detailed analysis of the poem, notes that it closely follows the prescribed rhetorical principles for a judicial oration, and comments on its complex organization and structure. Argues that Donne's intention in the poem is primarily instruction based on the precepts of Christian charity and observes that "the care with which the satirist presents his explications of the condition of justice in England evinces his faith in the ability of man's reason to begin the recovery of values even in the midst of a confused moral atmosphere" (p. 361). Concludes that the speaker of *Satyre V*, "by relying on biblical texts and accommodating them to the situation of the suitor, emerges as a model of reformation of all 'gamsters' lacking in self-knowledge" and that "the satirist's own homiletic-devotional procedures dramatize for the suitor and the reader the method and means of regeneration" (p. 362).

◄§ 1003. HOOVER, L. ELAINE. *John Donne and Francisco de Quevedo: Poets of Love and Death.* Chapel Hill: The University of North Carolina Press. xxix, 226p.

Compares Donne and Quevedo as "men of their times and of shared traditions" (p. xv) and shows how in their love poetry both manifest a particular baroque sensibility. Introduction (pp. xi–xxix) outlines the major similarities between the two poets and defines the intention and scope of the study. Chapter 1, "European Love Poetry: The Troubadours and Petrarchism" (pp. 3–31), discusses the history and development of the *amour courtois* tradition from the French troubadours through Petrarch and his followers to the love poets of the sixteenth and seventeenth centuries and explains how Donne and Quevedo fit into the Petrarchan tradition and, at the same time, often rebel against it. Chapter 2, "Love's Relationship to Time, Mutability, and Old Age" (pp. 32–51), analyzes three sonnets by Quevedo and Donne's "The Blossome" and "The Autumnall" and comments on how in the love poems of both poets "the preoccupation with time's effects on the lover, the beloved, or love itself bestows a poignant tone, at times nostalgic, at times sinister" and notes that both poets "often employ similar metaphors and images in their varied emotional reactions to these seemingly disparate themes" (p. 34). Chapter 3, "Love's Transcendence of Death" (pp. 52–88), discusses how both poets "expressed the reality of supreme commitment, exaltation, and the transcendence of death" in their poems and expressed "their most glorious affirmations of love's omnipotence in terms of death" (pp. 55–56). Compares Quevedo's sonnets with "The Canonization," "The good-morrow," "The Anniversarie," and "The Relique" to illustrate how both poets were concerned "with the relationship between love and its adversaries—time, mutability, and death" and to show how each "asserts in his own way love's transcendence of these limitations" (p. 86). Chapter 4, "Absence, Love, and Death" (pp. 89–121), comments on how in the love poetry of both poets "the metaphorical association of death with parting, physical separation, and nonrequital in love reflects an acute sense of loss, an awareness and consequent fear of its unavoidable absoluteness" and how "the absence of love or the absence of the beloved correspondingly leads to the absence of life" (p. 90), a corollary that strengthens the union of love with death. Discusses "The Legacie," "The Computation," "A Valediction: forbidding mourning," "The Expiration," "A Valediction: of my name, in the window," and "A Valediction: of weeping," along with Quevedo's sonnets, to show the prevalence of the theme of absence in love. Chapter 5, "The Omnipotence of Death" (pp. 122–51), discusses how Donne and Quevedo "shared a primordial fear of death's imminence, its omnipresence, and its omnipotence" (p. 123). Discusses Quevedo's sonnets and "The Paradox," "A nocturnall upon S. Lucies day," "The Dissolution," and "A Feaver" to show that "in their poetic expression of the metaphysical correspondence between existence and non-existence, between presence and absence, between life and death, and between possession and loss, they reveal the intellectual and emotional attitudes that characterize the Baroque *Weltanschauung*" (p. 151). Chapter 6, "Love, Murder, and Death: Dreams and Shadows" (pp. 152–201), comments on the prevalence of the motifs of the death of love, the beloved-as-murderer, love as violence, and man's inability to distinguish reality from illusion, dreams, and fantasy. Discusses "The Will," "Loves exchange," "The Dampe," "Elegie X: The

Dreame," "The Funerall," "The Apparition," "Farewell to love," and "A Lecture upon the Shadow" as examples of disenchantment with love and of nihilism. Conclusion (pp. 202–10) summarizes the preceding arguments, shows in microcosmic fashion the similarities between Donne and Quevedo as baroque poets, and suggests that the originality and authenticity of both poets resides not so much in their choice of themes as in their ability to perceive the paradoxes of life and to portray intense feeling and complex thought. Notes (pp. 211–15), selected bibliography (pp. 217–23), and index (pp. 223–26).

✎§ 1004. HURLEY, C. HAROLD. "'Covering' in Donne's 'Elegy XIX.'" *CP* 11, no. 2: 67–69.
Points out that the word *covering* in the final couplet of "Going to Bed" is a sexual pun and has a treble significance: "It suggests the conventional clothing imagery that comprises a large part of the poem; it unifies the latter portion of the poem by playing-off against the words 'discovering' and 'coverings'; but most importantly, the common subaudition of 'covering,' meaning 'the stallion copulating with the mare,' vividly dramatizes, in a summary point of wit, the narrator's triumphant sense of power in the sexual mastering of his mistress" (p. 68).

✎§ 1005. IZUBUCHI, HIROSHI. "Yeats no Donne 'Hakken'" [Yeats's Discovery of Donne]. *EigoS* 124: 365–68.
Briefly comments on Donne's influence on Yeats. Notes that from Donne, Yeats learned to add terseness to his more extravagant and romantic lyricism and maintains that Donne also influenced the structure of some of Yeats's poems, especially his dialogues, as well as his expository techniques. Suggests that Donne's poetry was not completely antithetical to romantic sensibilities but showed how the supernatural and the natural world could interpenetrate and coexist.

✎§ 1006. JAHN, J. D. "The Eschatological Scene in Donne's 'A Valediction: Forbidding Mourning.'" *CollL* 5: 34–47.
Argues that the deathbed scene set up in the first two stanzas of "A Valediction: forbidding mourning" is the controlling metaphor of the entire poem and "correlates Donne's erotic consolation with an underlying pattern of death and resurrection, of dissolution and reunion to illustrate Donne's creative procedure" (p. 34). Discusses the eschatological logic of the poem, shows how "last events such as the dissolution and transmutation of the body, the restoration of heaven and earth, and heavenly marriage provide a deep structure for Donne's erotic wit" and explains how "even metaphors drawn from astronomy and alchemy, as well as the poem's striking analogy of lovers to a compass, ultimately stem from eschatological discussions" in which they function "as similitudes to explain supernatural mysteries" (p. 43). Maintains that the poem remains primarily a

secular love poem but shows that "the correspondence between eschatology and passionate love at least intimates a time when those lovers will no longer be bound by the limits of earthly time and space, when physical separation will be as impossible for them as spiritual separation is now" (p. 44). Points out a similar pattern of eschatological consolation in the *Devotions upon Emergent Occasions* and notes that Donne uses eschatological material in a number of his other love poems.

✥ 1007. JONES, R. T. "John Donne's 'Songs and Sonets': The Poetic Value of Argument." *Theoria* 51: 33–42.

Argues that one of the most engaging features of Donne's poetry is his ability to achieve "direct colloquial expression of a felt experience momentarily, against some strong internal resistance that gives it a special force, even a violence; that he has to fight to hold on to the reality that he has grasped" (pp. 34–35). Suggests that a tension between sensibility and intellect can be detected in almost all the *Songs and Sonets* and that there is frequently the "pressing problem of how to justify the felt apprehension, to procure the mind's connivance, even perhaps to bludgeon the poor intellect into a worried acquiescence" (p. 37). Comments on "The Sunne Rising" to show that the primary tension in the poem is between Donne's "conviction of the transcendent supremacy of love and the unreality of the ordinary world" (p. 36). Notes that Donne's arguments in such poems as "Death be not proud" or "The Flea" are often bad arguments or, at least, provisional ones, but that the reader, nonetheless, "admires in Donne his refusal to be intimidated by reason: his uncompromising affirmation of felt conviction, followed by the 'wrastle' of the intellect to catch up and to deal with the implications of the felt truth" (p. 39). Discusses sincerity in Donne's poems and warns against oversimplification: "There is an element of performance in the poems" (p. 40). Shows that the argument of "The Flea" is used "as a form of love-play" (p. 41) and reveals a very complex relationship between thought and feeling. Quotes Raquel Welch, who said that "The brain is an erogenous zone," and suggests that "Donne, by this account, knew more than Dryden about the hardnesses, if not the softnesses, of love" (p. 42).

✥ 1008. KAUL, R. K. "Donne and Webster: The Air of Reality." *RUS Eng* 11: 27–30.

Discusses how the satiric passages in Webster and Donne contain numerous references to contemporary economic conditions and current political events and "give us a feel of the streets of Jacobean London rather like Ben Jonson's comedies" (p. 27). Points out specific references in "Loves growth," "Jealosie," "The Anagram," "The Comparison," "The Bracelet," "A Tale of a Citizen and his Wife," "The Storme," and "The Will." Contrasts Donne and Webster to Shakespeare and concludes that Shakespeare's plays lack the topicality found in Donne and Webster.

⟜§ 1009. KAWASAKI, SHIIGEHIKO. "Image no Okuyuki: 'Me ga haramu koto ni suite'" [The Depth of Imagery: Propagation through the Eye]. *EigoS* 124: 320–24.

Comments on the sexual implications of some of the images in "The Extasie." Discusses the meaning of the allusion to "looking-babies" in lines 9–12 of the poem and explains the importance of this image of propagation for an understanding of the poem as a whole.

⟜§ 1010. KAWASAKI, TOSHIHIKO. "Donne to Mannerism no Kagami" [Donne and Mannerism of the Mirror], in *Kagami no Mannerism: Renaissance Sōzōryoku no Sokumen* [Mannerism of the Mirror: An Aspect of Imagination] (Kenkyūsha Sensho 1), pp. 55–150. Tokyo: Kenkyūsha.

Discusses how mannerist poets and artists employed the metaphor of the mirror and used images of reflection in their work. Examines in some detail Donne's uses of such metaphors and images in his poetry and thus sees Donne as a mannerist poet.

⟜§ 1011. KRESS, G. K. "Poetry as Anti-Language: A Reconsideration of Donne's 'Nocturnall upon S. Lucies Day.'" *PTL: A Journal for Descriptive Poetics and Theory of Literature* 3: 327–44.

Presents a detailed linguistic analysis of "A nocturnall upon S. Lucies day" to show that the process of negation "permeates every facet of the grammer of the poem" (p. 330). Discusses aspects of Donne's "anti-language" and shows how this language faithfully reflects his state of mind in the poem. Suggests that only in this poem is Donne able to give total expression to his sense of despair and that "in doing so he creates a language for this previously not fully articulated anti-world," which, strangely enough, is itself "a major act of creation" (p. 342).

⟜§ 1012. LEIGH, DAVID J., S.J. "Donne's 'A Hymne to God the Father': New Dimensions." *SP* 75: 84–92.

Argues that in each of the last lines of the three stanzas of "A Hymne to God the Father" Donne puns on the name of Ann More and maintains that "this play on words not only adds a fuller dimension to the line itself but also enriches the poem as a final expression of Donne's fascination with the paradox of divine and human love" (p. 84). Comments on Donne's use of puns, especially on his wife's maiden name, and on his life-long fascination with the traditional paradox between divine and human love. Suggests that in stanza 1 of "A Hymne to God the Father" Donne may be expressing some guilt over the inordinancy of his love for Ann More, over his contribution to her difficult life, or even some despair over her death, all of which are "variations on the fundamental theme of the *via negativa*—an excessive attachment to a creature that must be moderated before one can be prepared for union with God the Father" (p. 91). Notes that in the second stanza Donne may be asking forgiveness for his failures toward his wife and for his infidelities and suggests that in the final stanza he comes to recognize that he has completed the negative way and "now he can leap to the transcendent union whereby not having anything he will have All" (p. 92). Points out that the Sun/Son imagery reinforces the notion that Donne and his wife will be reunited in heaven as a result of Christ's resurrection.

◄§ 1013. LINGUANTI, ELSA. "Una crisi di identità: Il 19° degli «Holy Sonnets» di John Donne," in *Critical Dimensions: English, German and Comparative Literature. Essays in Honour of Aurelio Zanco*, edited by Mario Curreli and Alberto Martino, pp. 201–19. Cuneo: SASTE.

Combines structuralist analysis and traditional rhetorical classification in examining the language, structure, and theme of "Oh, to vex me, contraryes meet in one." Finds in Donne's use of antithesis and paradox a binary describing soul and body, its equilibrium interrupted by the intrusion of triadic forms symbolizing God. Maintains that the thematic content, as revealed through semantic patterns, shows that infidelity to God, the beloved, or self is a form of destiny, not chosen behavior, and that ecstasy, whether erotic or mystical, is a disease. Concludes that the alienation and conflict revealed by the poetic "I" express doubts that characterize seventeenth-century thought.

◄§ 1014. LINVILLE, SUSAN. "Donne's 'Holy Sonnets IX.'" *Expl* 36, iv: 21–22.

In part a reply to Stanley L. Archer (entry 291). Argues that "If poysonous mineralls" "moves from prideful disputation, in which reason attempts to exempt itself and man from the special position it places him in, to a humility which recognizes both the rational claim that man's culpability should not be forgotten, and the supra-rational process through which Christ's sacrifice and the speaker's contrition can cancel out that debt" (p. 22). Suggests that such a reading "restores the poem's moral and thematic integrity by showing how its conclusion is related to all its parts, and does so with the need of emendation [Gardner] or reaching too far outside the text [Archer]" (p. 22).

◄§ 1015. LOW, ANTHONY. *Love's Architecture: Devotional Modes in Seventeenth-Century English Poetry*. (The Gotham Library.) New York: New York University Press. xix, 307p. PR 545 D47 L6

Discusses four major modes of devotion that shaped English seventeenth-century religious poetry: (1) vocal prayer (including hymns and songs), (2) meditation, (3) sensible affection, and (4) contemplation. Chapter 1, "Poetry and Devotion" (pp. 1–9), discusses the importance of devo-

tional techniques to an understanding of seventeenth-century poetry, outlines briefly the four modes of devotion, and defines devotion and devotional poetry. Chapter 2, "Divine Song" (pp. 12–35), comments on the
development and use of metrical psalms, literary psalms, hymns, and musical texts in English devotional life of the period, briefly comments on
the influence of devotional music on Donne's poetry and his belief in its
power to move men's hearts, and discusses the importance of sacred song
to the development of stanzaic forms and structures. Chapter 3, "John
Donne: Liturgy, Meditation, and Song" (pp. 36–81), discusses the importance of discursive meditation for Donne's poetry, calling him "the most
purely meditative of English poets" (p. 40), and comments on Donne's
background, training, and natural disposition that formed his religious
sensibility. Analyzes *La Corona* to show that it is a mixture of devotional
modes—partly vocal prayer and hymn and partly meditation. Points out
its impersonality and suggests that the language, method, and tone of the
poem are, in part, liturgical and hymnlike. Notes that "A Litanie" is also
semi-liturgical and, agreeing with Gardner, calls it Donne's "most characteristically Anglican poem" (p. 52). Shows that in the *Holy Sonnets*
Donne "turns to Ignatian meditation for the structure and texture of his
poetry and the primary method of his devotion" (p. 57) and discusses the
first twelve sonnets (according to Gardner's ordering) to show the pervading influence of discursive meditation on individual sonnets and on the
sequence as a whole. Analyzes the devotional mode of "Goodfriday, 1613.
Riding Westward" and calls it "the best of his verse meditations" (p. 71)
and suggests that "Upon the Translation of the Psalms" "is an extraordinary praise of sung devotion, which itself mimics the psalms of praise and
becomes a vocal prayer" (p. 76). Maintains that Donne's hymns are all
direct prayers to God and notes that "they make no attempt to build coherent scenes or achieve more than fleeting compositions of place" (p.
76). Calls "Hymne to God my God, in my sicknesse" "the most continually conceited of Donne's devotional poems" (p. 77); sees "A Hymne to
God the Father" as a penitential hymn; and suggests that "A Hymne to
Christ, at the Authors last going into Germany," an emblematic hymn, is
"the closest Donne came to the somber but confident style of the great
Protestant hymns" (p. 78). Concludes that Donne's religious poetry, therefore, "moves from liturgical to meditative back to liturgical forms, from
confidence to doubt and back to confidence, from vocal praise to intro-
spection back to vocal praise" (p. 80). Mentions Donne in the remaining
chapters: Chapter 4, "George Herbert: Varieties of Devotion" (pp. 82–
115); Chapter 5, "Richard Crashaw: Sensible Affection" (pp. 116–59);
Chapter 6, "Henry Vaughan: Journey to Light" (pp. 160–207); Chapter 7,
"Robert Herrick: The Religion of Pleasure" (pp. 208–34); Chapter 8, "Andrew Marvell: The Soul's Retreat" (pp. 235–58); Chapter 9, "Thomas
Traherne: Mystical Hedonist" (pp. 259–93); and Chapter 10, "Conclusion" (pp. 294–97). Texts of the poetry (p. 299) followed by an index (pp.
300–307).

◄§ 1016. MABBOTT, THOMAS O. "Observations on Poets and Poetry." *BI* 29: 14–35.

Presents excerpts from the notes and letters of Thomas O. Mabbott to Maureen Cobb, later Mrs. Mabbott, mostly written during 1923 and 1924, that contain his observations on various poets and on poetry, selected by Mrs. Mabbott. Comments briefly on Donne's poetry (pp. 17–18), noting that "the conceits, subtleties, and indeed everything characteristic of what Dr. Johnson called the metaphysical school is, I think, rather at war with true poetry—and with Donne, remember that he is a very *uneven* poet" (p. 18). Suggests that "treating Donne as a thinker might prove easier than anything else" (p. 18) and recommends "Song: Sweetest love, I do not goe."

◄§ 1017. MANLOVE C. N. "Donne and Marvell," in *Literature and Reality, 1600–1800*, pp. 3–15. London and Basingstoke: The Macmillan Press.

Argues that in much of Donne's poetry he "is in flight from uncouth fact, to the extent that the point of his poetry is often how far we can give credence to his 'fancy'" and suggests that as a "one-sided poet" he "rarely builds a poem out of the dialectic of opposed views, but argues extreme positions" (p. 3). Notes that Donne's arguments are usually "convincing arguments" rather than arguments that convince and that if an opposing fact is introduced, "he does not incorporate the contradiction and let it modify his approach, but simply denies that it is a contradiction at all" (p. 3). Maintains that for Donne "the extremism and the narrowness are often the point" and that "the creative urge behind most of his poems is a delight in constructing ingenious witty universes and giving credibility to diverse moods and points of view," and, in this respect, "he is more a fantasist than a realist" (p. 4). Disagrees with the readings of both Wilbur Sanders and Murray Roston of "A Valediction: forbidding mourning" and suggests that the argument of the poem is uncertain. Points out that Donne's use of two images in the conclusion of the poem (gold and compasses) to define the lovers' union-in-dissolution "is some index to the fact that he, and the poem hitherto, would prefer to use neither" (p. 5). Suggests also that in the religious poems Donne "shows a one-sided approach to the central issues of sin and spiritual regeneration, shuffling off personal responsibility and seeing the whole process in terms of determinism and of administered grace from God rather than as the partial product of voluntary acts on his own part" (p. 8). Discusses "Goodfriday, 1613. Riding Westward," "Death be not proud," and *The first Anniversary* to show how Donne is prepared "even to make assertions about the world which are demonstrably false, and to try to deny by mere intelligence the hardest fact of all—death" (p. 10). Contrasts Donne's poetry with Marvell's, which achieves a persuasive power "by its incorporation of opposites, by its marriage of idealism to fact, and by its substantiation of the one by the other" (p. 15).

1018. MANN, LINDSAY A. "'The Extasie' and 'A Valediction: Forbidding Mourning': Body and Soul in Donne," in *Familiar Colloquy: Essays Presented to Arthur Edward Barker*, edited by Patricia Bruckmann, pp. 68–80. Ontario: Oberon Press.

Discusses Donne's view of the relation of body and soul, particularly as it is reflected in "The Extasie," "A Valediction: forbidding mourning," and the later prose, to show that his primary concern was "with the process that brings body and soul, natural and spiritual, into relation" (p. 68). Argues that for Donne the relationship between true lovers "reproduces the ideal relation of body and soul" (p. 68) and is a means of harmonizing the two. Shows that both "The Extasie" and "A Valediction: forbidding mourning," in spite of some differences in emotional effect, imagery, language, and tone, "assert and depend upon the same attitudes, and they are attitudes that Donne develops explicitly in his later prose" (pp. 69–70). Maintains that the poems "do not rest upon any mystical idea of love, but upon the active interrelationship of the lovers, on the 'spirits' that vitalize every human act," and argues that, although both poems make use of religious concepts, they work primarily "because they give us the means to reconstruct the experiences they only adumbrate" (p. 77). Argues that for Donne "body and soul, human relations, human love, can participate in the divine mysteries" and that, although usually imperfectly realized in this world, "in making the effort to live up to the ideal pattern, lovers participate immediately in the eternal life promised by faith" (p. 78).

1019. MARCUS, LEAH SINANOGLOU. *Childhood and Cultural Despair: A Theme and Variations in Seventeenth-Century Literature.* Pittsburgh: University of Pittsburgh Press. xii, 305p.

Comments briefly on Donne's attitudes toward original sin and observes that he hedged on the question of salvation for unbaptized infants (p. 49). Discusses also Donne's view of word play, noting that for him "the play of language serves the same harmonizing function as the play of the liturgy" and that "sacred word games are a mimetic recapitulation and validation of the divine plan which overarches the apparent formlessness of everyday human life" (p. 109). Notes briefly also that Donne distrusted "monkish" self-abnegation (p. 141).

1020. MEAD, DAVID G. "'Arms and the Man'—A Note on 'Prufrock.'" *YER* 5, no. 1: 21.

Suggests that Eliot's use of "arms" in "The Love Song of J. Alfred Prufrock" as a symbol of female sexual attractiveness "permits a suggestive allusion to Donne's 'The Relique.'"

1021. MILLER, R. H. "Ernest Hemingway: Textual Critic." *FHA*, pp. 345–47.

Discusses Hemingway's old-spelling text of the epitaph of *For Whom the Bell Tolls* from *Devotions upon Emergent Occasions*. Notes that Hemingway took the passage from Sir Arthur Quiller-Couch's *The Oxford Book of English Prose* (1925) and that he made fifteen alterations (two incorrect) in the galley. Points out that apparently the galley was also carefully checked against the *Oxford Book* text, for the two incorrect alterations do not appear in the first printing of 1940. Notes that a recent resetting of the text by Scribner's introduces a new error. Collates the galley proof, Hemingway's autograph revisions in the galley proof, the 1624 edition of the *Devotions* (STC 7033), and the first printing of the novel. Concludes that Hemingway obviously "wanted Donne's prose in its seventeenth-century purity, and he did a good job of getting it" (p. 346).

1022. MILWARD, PETER, S. J. *Religious Controversies of the Jacobean Age: A Survey of Printed Sources*. Lincoln and London: University of Nebraska Press; Ilkley, Eng.: The Scolar Press. xi, 264p.

Lists *Pseudo-Martyr* (1610) and places it within the historical context of the controversy waged over the Oath of Allegiance commanded by James I. Lists other works involved in the controversy. Notes that Thomas Fitzherbert attacked Donne's defense of the Oath in *A Supplement to the Discussion of M. D. Barlowes Answere To the Iudgment of a Catholike Englishman . . .* (1616). Lists both the Latin and English versions of *Ignatius his Conclave* (1611) and places the work within the context of anti-Jesuit literature that appeared in England during the early seventeenth century. Suggests that Donne wrote *Ignatius* "in a light, satirical vein after his more serious labours spent in defense of the Oath of Allegiance in *Pseudo-Martyr* (1610)" (p. 127).

1023. MORILLO, MARVIN. "The Date of Donne's 'The Canonization.'" *N&Q* n.s. 25: 505–6.

A reply to Susan Burchmore (entry 902). Challenges Burchmore's evidence for dating "The Canonization" after 1606 and possibly as late as 1608/1609. Argues that, "although none of the internal evidence compels a date around 1603, all of it, in conjunction with the apparent disharmonies of poem and life after 1606, make the earlier date a good deal more 'solid' conjecture" (p. 506).

1024. NANIA, JOHN, AND P. J. KLEMP. "John Donne's *La Corona*: A Second Structure." *Ren&R* n.s. 2: 49–54.

Notes that Donne's inclusion of a seventh sonnet in *La Corona* "creates a situation in which one sonnet is placed in a central or axial position" which "allows the remaining sonnets to balance or answer one another" (p. 50). Shows how "the number seven in the numerological tradition carries meanings that complement the circle imagery and the content of the poem" and points out how Donne's use of time imagery "shows how the symmetrical structure of the sequence functions" (p. 50). Points out, in addition, two other general patterns: (1) a movement from God the

Father (Sonnet 1) to God the Son (Sonnets 2–6) to God the Holy Spirit (Sonnet 7) and (2) a movement from night to day, from darkness to light. Comments especially on "Temple," the fourth and central sonnet, as a microcosm of the whole sequence and shows how it "is important because the story carries with it the idea of centrality, foreshadows the resurrection, and concerns itself with the theme of education through the revelation of the Word of God" (p. 52). Shows how the remaining six sonnets, balanced around "Temple," answer each other and also discusses how the highly elaborate uses of rhyme reinforce the meaning of the whole sequence.

✓ ❧§ 1025. PARTRIDGE, A. C. *John Donne: Language and Style.* (The Language Library, edited by Eric Partridge and David Crystal.) London: André Deutsch. 259p.

Presents a linguistic and stylistic analysis of Donne's poetry and prose primarily through a discussion of and notes on selected works from various genres and periods of Donne's life. Comments on selected biographical, historical, and textual information as it relates to the various explications of individual works. Notes Donne's "delight in squeezing the utmost meaning from words" and suggests that in his poetry "dramatic presentation of ideas, originality of phrasing and disregard of formal syntax overshadow other considerations of style" (p. 10). Discusses such matters as Donne's uses of diction, imagery, and conceits; metrical and stanzaic forms; rhyme schemes, pauses, speech rhythms; orthography, punctuation, contractions, elisions, capitalization, and italics; tone and voice; grammar and syntax; analogy, argument, and wit; and numerous rhetorical devices. Divided into ten main chapters: (1) "Donne's Use of Language: The *Elegies* and *Paradoxes*" (pp. 15–35); (2) "The *Satyres, Metempsychosis* [*The Progresse of the Soule*], and Verse Letters" (pp. 36–65); (3) "The *Songs and Sonets*" (pp. 66–97); (4) "*Anniversaries*, Epicedes, Obsequies and Epithalamia" (pp. 98–126); (5) "The *Divine Poems*" (pp. 127–54); (6) "Miscellaneous Prose: *Biathanatos, Pseudo-Martyr, Ignatius his Conclave,* and *The True Character of a Dunce*" (pp. 155–73); (7) "The Prose Letters" (pp. 174–90); (8) "*Essayes in Divinity* and *Devotions upon Emergent Occasions*" (pp. 191–209); (9) "The *Sermons*" (pp. 209–32); and (10) "Conclusions" (pp. 233–43). Each of the chapters contains individual explications of and notes on representative poems or prose selections. Bibliography (pp. 244–49) and index (pp. 251–59).

❧§ 1026. POLLOCK, JOHN J. "Another Donne Pun." *AN&Q* 16: 83.

Points out that "dimme eyes" in line 5 of "Thou hast made me" can be read as "demise," a legal term meaning "the 'conveyance or transfer of an estate by will or lease,' an action which usually occurs at the time of one's death." Notes that the pun "equates Donne's failing eyesight directly with his approaching death and thus emphasizes his spiritual dilemma as he 'runne[s] to death' [line 3] at the same time he dreads it."

❧ 1027. ———. "The 'Everlasting Night' in Donne's 'Hymne to Christ.'" *ES* 59: 119–20.

Disagrees with Helen Gardner, who in the commentary of her edition of *The Divine Poems* (1952) suggests that "Everlasting night" (line 32) in "A Hymne to Christ, at the Authors last going into Germany" refers to death and that in the conclusion of the poem Donne is praying for a literal death because of his unhappiness over the death of his wife. Agrees with Wilbur Sanders's interpretation in *John Donne's Poetry* (entry 366) that "'Everlasting night' represents not death, but 'awe carried to the supreme pitch which is darkness, stillness, nothingness'" (p. 119). Shows that in letters to his friends in the spring of 1619 and in his "Sermon of Valediction at my going into Germany," written at the same time as the poem, Donne does not indicate despair nor a wish for death. Suggests that "to read the poem with Donne's supposed death wish in mind is to risk confusing a most mature and profoundly spiritual utterance with that 'sickely inclination' to suicide which Donne both regretted and renounced in his youth" (p. 120).

❧ 1028. ———. "The 'Harmonious Soule' in Donne's 'Hymne to Christ." *AN&Q* 17: 2–3.

Suggests that "The amorousnesse of an harmonious Soule" in "A Hymne to Christ, at the Authors last going into Germany" (line 18) may refer "to the condition of one's living in peaceful, loving accord with one's neighbor" (p. 3). Points to Donne's "Sermon of Valediction at my going into Germany," written for the same occasion that the poem celebrates, and notes that "Donne's concept of harmony as presented in his sermon serves to emphasize the idea that 'amorousnesse of an harmonious Soule' is a love which is offered to a large extent directly to one's fellow man and not specifically to God" (p. 3).

❧ 1029. PRESCOTT, ANNE LAKE. *French Poets and the English Renaissance: Studies in Fame and Transformation.* New Haven and London: Yale University Press. xiv, 290p.

Notes that Donne had probably read some of Ronsard's love poems and suggests that, in spite of many differences between the two poets, "several passages in Donne strikingly resemble similar moments in Ronsard's poetry" (p. 113). Points out specifically certain resemblances between "The Flea" and Ronsard's sonnet "Cusin monstre à double ailes," "Batter my heart" and "Foudroyes moi le cors," and "The Canonization" and Ronsard's elegy to Marie that begins "Marie, à celle fin." Recognizes that many possible parallels can be accounted for by the common heritage that the two poets shared but suggests that "Donne might have recognized in Ronsard a writer particularly fascinating, like himself, for a carefully modulated voice and sense of self, an often dramatic relationship to the hearer within the poems, varying rhetorical poses, and radical inconsistencies"

(p. 115). Notes that Donne may have parodied Du Bartas's *Weeks* in *The Progresse of the Soule*.

❧ 1030. ROTHSCHILD, HERBERT, JR. "The 'higher hand' in Walton's 'Life of John Donne.'" *N&Q* n.s. 25: 506–8.

Notes that in the 1658 edition of his *Life of Donne* Walton expanded the narrative account of Donne's decision to enter Holy Orders and added a covertly polemical passage to show that King James had been an indispensable vehicle of God's grace in bringing Donne to his decision. Suggests that, although the overt compliment is attributed to Donne himself, it was, in fact, Walton's way of linking James and God "in a manner so typical of Stuart divine-right theory and Cavalier compliment" (p. 508).

❧ 1031. SELDEN, RAMAN. "The Elizabethan Satyr-Satirist," in *English Verse Satire 1590–1765*, pp. 45–72. London: George Allen & Unwin.

Discusses the development of English formal satire during the 1590s and suggests that Donne's satires "combine the 'mixed style' of Complaint, a searing post-Reformation individualistic vision, and the sophisticated dramatic compression of classical satire" (p. 65). Praises the wit and imagery of Donne's style and compares him to Persius and Horace. Explicates briefly *Satyre I* and *Satyre IV*, calling the latter Donne's "nearest approach to a classical model" (p. 63).

❧ 1032. SELLIN, PAUL. "The Date of John Donne's 'Satyre III.'" *SCN* 36: 15.

John W. Moore, Jr., reports on Sellin's paper delivered at the MLA meeting in 1977. Notes that Sellin pointed out an allusion to a polar expedition in the poem that Donne could not have known about before 1598–1602 and argues that, on the basis of similarities between a Dutch medallion and a famous conceit in the poem, *Satyre III* could not have been written until after 1620.

❧ 1033. SHAFER, AILEEN. "Eliot Re-Donne: The Prufrockian Spheres." *YER* 5, no. 2: 39–43.

Suggests that Eliot had in mind line 12 of "A Valediction: forbidding mourning" when he wrote the lines "Do I dare / Disturb the universe?" in "The Love Song of J. Alfred Prufrock" and calls the lines "a telescoped allusion to Donne's conceit that compares idealized love to a disturbance in the universe" (p. 39). Points out other imagistic parallels between the two poems, such as the illness-death conceit, the uses of "let us" at the beginning of each, and the references later on to eyes, hands/arms. Suggests that the allusion to mermaids singing in Eliot's poem may be a borrowing from "Song: Goe, and catche a falling starre" (line 5). Comments also on Eliot's intense interest in Donne during his "Prufrock" period and suggests that Eliot's attempts to amalgamate disparate experiences, to manipulate thought and imagery, and to present highly complex moods and emotions were influenced by his intimate acquaintance with Donne's poetry.

◄§ 1034. SKELTON, ROBIN. "Poetry and Relativity," in *Poetic Truth*, pp. 56–75. London: Heinemann; New York: Barnes & Noble; Agincourt: The Book Society of Canada.

Briefly comments on "At the round earths imagin'd corners" (pp. 67–68), noting that "in order fully to comprehend the poem, we are under no necessity to *believe* the story, for the poetic force lies in the passionate anguish of the speaker, and in his sense of his own guilt" and that "that anguish and guilt are universal; they do not depend for their existence upon any particular dogma" (pp. 67–68).

◄§ 1035. STANWOOD, P. G. "John Donne's Sermon Notes." *RES* 29: 313–20.

Describes in detail notes made by a contemporary, John Burley (or Burleigh), of two of Donne's sermons that he had either heard or perhaps seen in a rough copy of Donne's notes in late 1625 and compares Burley's notes, now in a manuscript volume in Trinity College, Dublin, MS. 419, with the corresponding passages in the published sermons. Points out that the notes "let us view more clearly Donne's activities at this time, plausibly date a previously undated sermon, suggest the likely time and occasion of a series of sermons, and additionally provide the earliest manuscript notice we have so far of Donne's prose" (p. 313). Notes that no autograph notes survive and comments on Donne's usual practice of preaching from memorized notes and on his practice of writing down sermons only if he thought them later worthy of publication. Notes that, "while we cannot know exactly what Donne said as opposed to what he wrote, Burley's notes do bring us nearer than we have ever been to Donne's actual preaching, to his first thoughts as contrasted with the eloquent contrivances of his later study" (p. 317).

◄§ 1036. SULLIVAN, ERNEST W., II. "Bibliography and Facsimile Editions." *PBSA* 72: 327–29.

Points out minor errors in the Arno Press 1977 reprint of J. William Hebel's *John Donne: Biathanatos* (New York: The Facsimile Text Society, 1930), and further notes that, since Hebel's original facsimile reproduced the quarto first edition of *Biathanatos* rather than the more reliable text of the manuscript in the Bodleian Library, the reprint "has only limited usefulness" (p. 327). Notes also that Hebel used a suspect copy of *Biathanatos* for his original facsimile and that "someone extensively doctored the photographs used in its production" (p. 327). Concludes, therefore, that Arno Press's "failure to apply bibliographical principles and information has resulted in an edition of no use to scholars or students" (p. 329).

🍴 1037. ———. "Fine Paper Copies of Donne's *Biathanatos* [1646?]." *BC* 27: 258.

Asks for information about three possible fine-paper copies of *Biathanatos* and about any other copies containing fine paper or presentation materials. Notes that all five located fine-paper copies contain presentation letters by Donne the younger.

🍴 1038. ———. "Manuscript Materials in the First Edition of Donne's *Biathanatos.*" *SB* 31: 210–21.

Describes first-edition copies of *Biathanatos* printed on fine paper and/or containing manuscript corrections, inscriptions, and presentation letters and suggests that they prove that "(1) the undated first issue was published in late September or early October of 1647, (2) some copies were especially printed for presentation, although others were also presented to potential patrons, and (3) the younger Donne, who edited *Biathanatos*, certainly authored some of the corrections and very probably made them all" (p. 211). Notes also that the previously unnoted letter in the presentation copy to the Marquis of Newcastle "proves that *Biathanatos* circulated in manuscript, identifies and graces the genesis of the manuscript which became the printer's copy, and suggests that the younger Donne participated in that genesis" (p. 211).

🍴 1039. SZENCZI, MIKLÓS. "Questions de périodisation de la renaissance anglaise," in *Littérature de la Renaissance: à la lumière des recherches sovietiques et hongroises*, edited by N. I. Balachov, T. Klaniczay, and A. D. Mikhaïlov, pp. 295–326. (Publications du Centre de Recherches de le Renaissance, 3.) Budapest: Akadémiai Kiadó.

Presents a general biographical sketch of Donne and discusses his poetry in relation to earlier traditions, especially Petrarchism. Reviews the history of the critical reaction to Donne. Argues that periodization of literature must be made on the basis of social evolution rather than on stylistic considerations or political and historical events.

🍴 1040. TAKAHASHI, YASUNARI. "Kyūtai Gensō: Donne Renaishi Kanken" [The Illusion of the Sphere: A Viewpoint on Donne's Love Poetry]. *EigoS* 124: 306–9.

Discusses the conceit of the sphere in the *Songs and Sonets*, using "The good-morrow" as an example. Analyzes also related images, such as breasts, dens, wombs, world, and eyes.

🍴 1041. THOMPSON, SISTER M. GERALDINE. "'Writs Canonicall': The High Word and the Humble in the Sermons of John Donne," in *Familiar Colloquy: Essays Presented to Arthur Edward Barker*, edited by Patricia Bruckmann, pp. 55–67. Ontario: Oberon Press.

Discusses Donne's concept of the decorum of language in sermons.

Notes that throughout his life Donne recognized the redemptive power of words and that in his later life he was "acutely conscious of the bond between poetry and sermon" and "pondered well the intricacies of homiletic decorum" (p. 56). Shows that Donne did not always reject high eloquence in favor of the *sermo humilis* but developed a sermon style that was "flexible enough to include the highest and plainest within the compass of every sermon" (p. 59) and that a striking feature of his style is "the frequency of the simplicities among the majesties" (p. 58). Discusses the four abilities that Donne regarded as essential for the effective preacher: "He must strive to be a trumpet to awaken the hearer to a fear of God; he must then be one who sings of the mercies of God . . . ; he must be in manner reverent yet diligent and 'thereby' delightful; and finally he must show by example and conversation that his own life is consonant with his preaching" (p. 68).

◄§ 1042. WELSH, ANDREW. *Roots of Lyric: Primitive Poetry and Modern Poetics.* Princeton: Princeton University Press. ix, 276p.

Discusses briefly the relationship between riddles and metaphysical poetry (pp. 39–44) and points out that both riddles and metaphysical images evidence "a seeing into something in a manner that leads to a valid way of knowing" (p. 40). Comments on Donne's uses of riddles in "Lovers infinitenesse," "The Sunne Rising," "The good-morrow," and "Hymne to God my God, in my sicknesse." Briefly compares Donne to Robert Creeley and Dylan Thomas. Also comments on Donne's use of puns, especially in "Goodfriday, 1613. Riding Westward."

◄§ 1043. WENNERSTROM, MARY H. "Sonnets and Sound: Benjamin Britten's Settings of Shakespeare, Donne, and Keats." *YCGL* 27: 59–61.

Reports on a workshop on Britten's musical settings of poems by Donne, Keats, and Shakespeare at the Lilly Conference on Literature and the Other Arts held 2–4 March 1978 on the Bloomington campus of Indiana University. Notes that Britten's setting of Donne's "At the round earths imagin'd corners" (1945) was played and then analyzed "in terms of the union of poetic and musical elements" (p. 60). Points out that the session focused on the problems that a composer encounters when he attempts to transpose from one artistic medium to another or when he tries to combine media.

Addendum

❧ 1044. WONG, YOON-WAH. *Yüan Kuei yii shui ching* [A Comparative
Study of Two Metaphysical Conceits in the Poetry of Chia Tao and
John Donne]. (Institute of Humanities and Social Sciences. College
of Graduate Studies. Nanyang University. Occasional Paper Series,
No. 76). Singapore, 1977. 18p.

Text in Korean; abstract in English (p. 18). Discusses the nature and
function of the metaphysical conceit, distinguishing it from the Petrarchan conceit. Notes that Chia Tao, a ninth-century Chinese poet, in his
poem "To a Friend" compares the process of writing a poem to that of
drawing water from a well and finds many striking parallels between this
conceit and Donne's compass conceit in "A Valediction: forbidding
mourning." Argues, therefore, that, although Donne and Chia Tao come
from totally different literary traditions, the metaphysical conceit "is an
international literary device" (p. 18).

Index of Authors, Editors, and Translators

Subject Index

(The following is an index of subjects mentioned in the annotations in this bibliography. The reader is advised to check all general studies related to a specific topic.)

Index of Donne's Works
Mentioned in Annotations

(The following is an index of Donne's works mentioned in the annotations.)